BUSINESS POLICY
CASES,
INCIDENTS,
AND
READINGS

BUSINESS POLICY

CASES,
INCIDENTS,
AND
READINGS

Francis J. Bridges

Georgia State College

Kenneth W. Olm

University of Texas

ALLYN AND BACON, INC.
BOSTON
1966

PREFACE

IT HAS BEEN ESTIMATED THAT some 400 colleges and universities in the United States provide course work for business students in the field of business policy formulation and administration. The title of the course is not nearly as important as the fact that colleges are aware that business firms in the nation are demanding and expect new management employees to bring with them some conceptual knowledge and skill in management. This skill can be obtained only through careful study and discussion of real business problems and cases usually taught in a business policy course. Developing conceptual skill in management requires that a student be able to identify overall company problems, analyze the important management issues in functional areas of an organization, and recommend sound courses of action after a careful study and analysis of the facts and relevant data. Having conceptual management skill implies that a manager be able to plan for the growth of the entire organization and not just a part, that the manager make decisions for the benefit of the firm and not for the person, and that the manager become aware of fundamental problems and not just surface issues.

Problems confronting managers are largely unstructured. Generally, no simple solutions to these problems are available; still, responsibility for providing guidance to the firm and making decisions rests on the shoulders of managers. This requires an understanding of the importance of plans, policies, objectives, and procedures which when formally adopted give direction to the efforts of all employees.

This book is dedicated to the educational process of developing managers. Its features are for the benefit of professors and students who strive for more expertness and competency in the management of business firms.

Part I of the book is designed to acquaint students with real administrative policy situations. Using twenty-seven cases as a basis of study, the student finds a variety of business policy questions in cases developed from companies in diversified industries. The cases are relatively short but with sufficient data for complete analysis. Many of them concern the managerial responsibility of lower and middle level managers as well as senior executives. A majority concern business firms *not* classed as "big business." This is realistic in light of the fact that the preponderance of American companies are classed as small- or medium-size firms.

Through case discussions and written analyses of cases, it is anticipated that the student will expose himself to many of the same administrative situations faced by managers in real companies. The development of analytical ability to conscientiously analyze a business policy case and to willingly appraise the merits of this analysis creates an added value in the student which is desired by firms employing our college graduates.

Part II of the book presents a variety of policy incidents in management which requires the student to employ the scientific method of analysis leading to conclusions and decisions. The incidents are true situations taken from organizations which remain anonymous. The expectation is that students will justify their conclusions and decisions derived from a study of the incidents by supporting their views with valid concepts of management and findings of researchers who have published their studies.

Perhaps no pedagogical technique is available to business policy professors today which creates more student interest, stimulation, and response than the incident method. Twenty-five business policy incidents are included in Part II. Some relate directly to the more fully developed cases in Part I and can be used to stress particular management concepts or principles. Others stress a variety of business policy questions not included in the cases. Many of the incidents are so written that they can become the basis of role-playing situations in the classroom.

Part III features a variety of outstanding readings on selected policy subjects. It is the experience and observation of the authors that most courses in business policy require the student to do extensive library research and reading on business policy subjects. By studying many of the best readings on policy subjects in the book, students will have every opportunity and reason for developing a thorough familiarity with literature and new concepts in the field and will also develop a broad background of knowledge to support their premises in many of the cases and incidents.

It should be noted that the cases and incidents listed in the Table of Contents have been annotated so that the professor and student will have some insight to the nature of the case or incident prior to studying it.

Many individuals have made this book possible. Special thanks goes to our colleagues in the teaching profession who provided guidance and tested cases for publication in this book. Numerous business executives have been generous with their time and energy in the preparation of cases. Many graduate students and research assistants have given time and talent in this project. Specifically, Messrs. Omer C. Jenkins, Fred Ingerson, Gary Raffaele and Frank B. Slomchinski of the University of Texas and Mr. William H. Franklin of Georgia State College deserve recognition for their contributions. Additionally, we are indebted to the Southern Case Writers' Association, the Bureau of Business and Economic Research of Georgia State College, and the Bureau of Business Research of the University of Texas for releasing cases for publication which were written under their jurisdiction.

Many of the cases have been provided by companies and outside sources for use as bases for group discussion and are not intended to indicate either correct or incorrect handling of administrative situations. Names of companies and persons involved are disguised.

FRANCIS J. BRIDGES

KENNETH W. OLM

CONTENTS

PART II: INCIDENTS IN BUSINESS POLICY

PART 1

CASES

IN

BUSINESS

POLICY

THE THEORY OF THE CASE METHOD*

J. Philip Wernette

The Importance of Knowing the Theory

THE CASE METHOD, PROPERLY HANDLED, is an excellent way of teaching business administration. The usefulness of the method is increased if both teacher and students understand the basic theory of the method—what it aims to do for both teacher and students, and how it goes about doing it.

If the *teacher* does not grasp this basic theory, he is unlikely to get maximum results from use of the case method.

If the *students* do not understand this basic theory, they are likely to become bewildered and discouraged, and their progress will be delayed.

If, contrariwise, both teacher and students understand the method, the teaching-learning process is speeded and improved.

The purpose of this article, therefore, is to assist in understanding the fundamentals of the system by (a) explaining the basic theory of the case method, (b) indicating the respective roles of instructor and students in the classroom, and (c) suggesting how to study and recite.

Those who understand the use of the case method in *law* courses should be informed that the case method as used in *business* courses is quite different, although it appears similar. No business experiences and no written cases based on them have the authority of a law case decided by a high court. Moreover, since many of the business experiences are written in the form of problems without solutions, rather than complete statements which carry a business story through to its end, the method might more accurately be called "the *problem* method" than "the *case* method."

Understanding the Method

The first step in understanding this method of teaching is to realize that there really are two completely different methods of teaching by the

---

* Reprinted by permission from the January, 1965, issue of the *Michigan Business Review*, published by the Graduate School of Business Administration, The University of Michigan.

use of business cases or problems. One may be called the *lecture method of case instruction*. In this method, the teacher assigns problems for study. He may or may not open the class by asking some student a question. Even if he does so, he does not permit the student recitation to last long; then or at the very opening of the class, he starts to lecture, basing his lecture on the assigned problem or problems. This method of instruction is not without its merits; but they are not those of the second method; they are those of the lecture method.

The second method is the *class recitation case method*. In this method, the instructor talks very little. He evokes discussion from the members of the class and they do most of the talking. He may pit members of the class against one another with respect to their opinions, or he may question the students himself. Key questions in this method of instruction are likely to include these: What do you consider to be the real problem in this case? What do you consider to be the important questions to answer in this problem? What would you do if you were the business executive responsible for making a decision or preparing a plan in this situation? Why would you make this decision, or select this plan instead of doing something else? In this kind of questioning, if there are any relevant accounting, statistical, or mathematical calculations, the teacher expects the student to have made them, and to be prepared to state clearly the nature and content of his calculations.

The significant characteristic is that the students are required to analyze the problem, and be prepared to present and defend their analysis in the classroom. They know this in advance and, therefore, they understand that the method of preparing for the class is to analyze the assigned problems thoroughly.

It is clear, of course, that students cannot reason effectively about business problems unless they have a satisfactory background of understanding in connection with the problem. The statement of the problem may include background information, or it may be obtained from a standard declaratory textbook.

Benefits to Students

The pedagogical theory of the case method of instruction can be described as *acquiring vicarious experience*. Since it is not possible for the students to work in all of the various business firms involved in dozens of cases, this teaching method figuratively brings the firms into the classroom, and lets the students, in imagination, occupy the chairs of business executives. An adage says that experience is the best teacher, if it does not cost too dear. The case method is one way of providing the experience at modest cost. If, for example, a student makes a poor decision, which in real life would have cost millions of dollars, he will learn about his error in the classroom without the massive loss.

The significance of experience, of course, is that few problems are absolutely unique, and skill in handling them can be acquired by experience. There are certain common characteristics of problems and of the ways of going about solving them. If this were not true, it would make no difference to a patient whether he was operated on by a surgeon performing his first operation, or by a doctor performing his thousandth operation. So it is with business and other forms of human activity that involve action by a person. Experience enhances applicable skills.

Another way of describing the pedagogical theory is to say that it is a kind of daily practice in wrestling with problems. A man cannot learn to wrestle physically merely by reading an excellent book on the subject. The book may help; but there is no substitute for practice. The members of the wrestling team practice daily so as to improve their performance in team contests.

The problem method of studying business administration provides this daily wrestle with problems. This daily exercise supplies not only information and understanding about specific types of business problems but also provides practice in the technique of solving problems.

It's the Exercise That Counts

If students understand that this daily wrestle with problems is the purpose of this method of instruction they are likely to cease to be bothered by something that puzzles and bewilders many serious students, accustomed as they have been to declaratory textbooks and definite lecture statements. In a case course, the students find that often the discussion and analysis of the business problem do not produce any "answer." The problem is discussed pro and con. Various considerations and relevant aspects of the situation are analyzed. In the end, a good argument can be made for one decision or the other, or one program or another. When the class discussion concludes at this point, the student may feel confused and perhaps even cheated.

The fact is that for this kind of teaching-learning process, the type of problem just described is frequently ideal. The reason is that a business problem whose analysis leads to a clear-cut, definite, and positive solution is likely to be so simple and, therefore, so easy to analyze as not to present much of a challenge to keen students. Just as a hopelessly one-sided question does not provide a suitable subject for interscholastic debates, so a business problem to which the solution is really clear is unlikely to provide much mental exercise in reaching the solution. The important thing for the student to understand is that it is *the hard exercise that counts rather than reaching a "right answer."*

All this applies, of course, to the classroom. In actual business life, business executives have to bat higher than professional baseball players. An average substantially above .500 is necessary for business success. In legal circles, it is said that hard cases make bad law. They probably do. But in the study of business administration, hard problems—those without plain and clear solutions—provide the toughest exercise, and raise the later business batting average.

Varieties of Cases

Lest the impression be given that there is but one standard pattern of cases—in terms of their nature, objectives, and use—let it be emphasized that this is not true. Some cases are short—perhaps a page or less. Other cases are longer and some of them are very long, running to scores of pages. Some are simple, some are complex; and the short ones are not necessarily the simple ones nor the long ones the complex. In some cases the issue or problem in the business situation is clearly defined. In other cases—ordinarily the longer ones—the point of the case is to discover what the problem is and then to proceed to discuss solutions. In such a case the description of the situation is likely to be lengthy and to contain much information that is irrelevant.

Recording the "Lessons of Experience"

The effectiveness of the case method can be enhanced considerably by engaging in a type of exercise which seems to be rather rare. This exercise is that of drawing from each case some *principles* in the form of currently useful generalizations or rules of action, or ways of thinking. In order to do this, it is necessary simply that at the end of the discussion, class members be invited to suggest the principles that can be learned from the problem that has been analyzed. Each principle that is suggested should be subjected immediately to scrutiny by other class members in order to determine whether they agree that the principle is, in fact, sound. This discussion itself is illuminating. Moreover, it is likely to be surprising how many useful generalizations the members of a class can derive from a problem, and can agree on as being valid. To the ones suggested by class members, the teacher may wish to add some of his own. In any event, if at the conclusion of the discussion, members of the class write down the generalizations thus agreed upon as the "lessons of experience" they increase the definiteness of what they have learned from this kind of study.

The Teacher's Role

Since the class recitation case method involves very little talking by the teacher, it might be supposed that this type of teaching is easy, and requires little preparation. Not so. It is a very different kind of activity from lecturing. For one thing, it requires intense concentration on the part of the instructor on what the student is saying. Inasmuch as it is important to permit—perhaps even to require—the student to go ahead with a suitably lengthy statement discussing the question that he has been asked, the teacher may even find it necessary to take notes on what the student is saying so that he will not have forgotten points on which he wishes to comment, or wishes to secure comment from some other student, by the time the student has finished his statement. Successful teaching by this method requires that the teacher study the case thoroughly in advance, work through the analysis completely, plan the questions to be asked, and the reactions to be sought, depending on the type of responses obtained from the students. If the instructor is undertaking to record grades on oral recitations, he may find that notes taken on the various student comments will help him to determine the grades to be assigned as he ponders the discussion in his office, after class.

The case method of instruction is valuable in helping the teacher to avoid a gradual retreat into an academic ivory tower. First, teaching actual business cases keeps his thinking practical. Second, if he, himself, gathers and writes cases, this activity brings him into contact with businessmen and business firms, and provides firsthand acquaintance with their problems. Third, preparing cases for classroom use sharpens the teacher's concept of the use of cases as a pedagogical method, and helps him to clarify the objectives of his instruction and the aims of his course.

1. AZTEC AWNING AND VENETIAN BLIND COMPANY

Background:

MR. ROGER GRISSOM AND MR. MIKE BERRY were close friends socially as well as at work. Both held high-ranking management positions with a large national firm headquartered in Los Angeles, California.

For the past nine months the two men had spent many hours discussing the possibility of resigning their positions with the company and going into business for themselves. They not only had discussed these ideas, but they had even investigated several small businesses for sale which had been brought to their attention by different business brokers located in the Southern California area.

While several of the businesses brought to their attention had been promising, none of them in the past had met one specific requirement set forth by Grissom and Berry. The requirement stipulated that the business firm be located in southern Texas and have a sales price of not more than $100,000.

Six weeks ago, Harvey Dodish of Dodish Associates, business brokers, visited Grissom and Berry in Berry's home and told them about the Aztec Awning and Venetian Blind Company located in San Diego, California. The firm was for sale at a price of $90,000 and was located in a section of the state which appealed to Grissom and Berry. Furthermore, the Aztec Company was a small manufacturing and sales company which tied in with the managerial talents of the two men.

The more Mr. Dodish described the Aztec Company, the more he interested Grissom and Berry to investigate the company in detail. One week later Roger Grissom visited the Aztec Awning and Venetian Blind Company in San Diego. While Grissom saw nothing to discourage his enthusiasm about the company, he nevertheless felt that a very thorough and analytical study of the company should be made before serious negotiations started.

A week later Roger Grissom and Mike Berry met for dinner and reviewed several additional reports given to them about the Aztec Company by Mr. Dodish. After several hours of discussion, they agreed that with

9

so much at stake, they would have to be doubly careful and completely objective about the possible purchase of the Aztec Company. If the Aztec Company were purchased, it would take all of their available cash; it would mean relocating; it would mean sacrificing their successful career positions; and it would be a calculated risk at best. However, both men had agreed that even though starting their own business would be risky and probably reduce their standard of living for a few years, there were other positive features which they felt would offset the risks.[1]

Grissom and Berry concluded their meeting by agreeing that a third party should investigate the company and advise them.

THE USE OF CONSULTANTS:

Through Berry's contacts with a nearby university, the men retained two college professors of business administration who agreed to survey the Aztec Awning and Venetian Blind Company and make specific recommendations concerning the functional aspects of the business and sales price.

Ten days later Grissom and Berry met the two professors and received a report entitled: "An Evaluation of the Aztec Awning and Venetian Blind Company."

QUESTIONS

(1) a. Should Mr. Grissom and Mr. Berry purchase the Aztec Awning and Venetian Blind Company?

b. If so, at what price?

(2) Assuming that Mr. Grissom and Mr. Berry purchase the Aztec Awning and Venetian Blind Company at your determined price, outline and justify a one-year program of operation leading to a possible net profit.

An Evaluation of the Aztec Awning and Venetian Blind Company

SELECTED HISTORICAL FACTS

A. Company founded in 1946 by Mr. Jack Smith with capital of approximately $350.00.

B. The company is incorporated but appears to be managed much like a sole proprietorship.

C. The major product lines are: (1) Aluminum Awnings; (2) Venetian Blinds; (3) Draperies; and (4) Shower Partitions.

D. Of the product lines under consideration, the best sales year was 1959 with a total of $322,590.38.

---

[1] Mr. Grissom stated that his company had transferred him eight times over a thirteen year period.

E. Over the years the company has had many product lines but through sales experience and financial analysis, determined the present lines to be the "best" for the company.

F. During the years 1956 to 1960, the company was a profitable operation. 1961 showed a total net loss.

G. The management of the company consists of: Jack Smith, President; John Morris, Assistant General Manager; and Wiley Brown, Shop Foreman. (Total Budgeted Salaries = $36,308.60 for 1962).

H. Total full time employees during the first quarter, 1962—seventeen (17).

I. At the peak period of sales and production during the 1950's, total labor force of company was about thirty-five (35).

J. The Aztec Company is non-union. There appears no likelihood that company will become unionized in the near future.

K. Presently, the employees received no fringe benefits from the company other than social security, workman's compensation, and unemployment compensation.

L. In 1959, Mr. Jack Smith acquired the patent rights to manufacture and sell "Shower Partitions."

M. Approximately eighty percent (80%) of retail sales leads are received on the telephone.

Finance

ACCURACY OF FINANCIAL REPRESENTATIONS

The determination of the accuracy of the financial representations made by the owner and the brokers fell into two general categories: (1) determination of the accuracy and validity of the data presented in audit reports, and (2) determination of the accuracy with which this data had been accurately transcribed and furnished to the prospective buyers.

The audit reports have been prepared by a California Certified Public Accountant. He has made the audit for the company for the past few years, and there is reason to believe that his background is sufficient to make data for various years comparable. He is a member of the American Institute of Certified Public Accountants and is bound by their Rules of Professional Conduct as well as such rules as the State of California may have regulating CPAs. In short, nothing came to our attention which would cause us to question the character of the auditor.

The nature of the reports which he has been rendering does not inspire the same type confidence as did the reputation of the CPA himself. His reports have not been audits at all, but to the contrary have been statements prepared from the books without audit. In his various covering letters to the client he has consistently included a statement to the effect that he had not performed sufficient audit procedures to have arrived at an independent accountant's opinion as to the fairness with which the statements presented the financial position and operating results of the company.

The role of the Certified Public Accountant has apparently been one of a super-bookkeeper and tax consultant. He has not performed the usual audit function of an impartial and objective third party evaluating the fairness of the financial statements.

Nothing came to our attention which would cause us to believe that the CPA in question had in any way misrepresented the financial condition or results of operations of the company insofar as the books would cause us to believe that the books contained material inaccuracies, save the owner's statements that he had been "cutting some corners" for federal income tax purposes.

The transcribing of financial data was, for the most part, accurate. We noted one error of $60, which we feel was an honest copying mistake. In all other instances the data previously furnished to you was in agreement with the reports rendered by the auditor.

FINANCIAL CONDITION OF THE COMPANY

The financial condition of the company, as reflected by its balance sheet for September 30, 1961, is included as Exhibit I. This balance sheet was transcribed from the report of the auditor as of that date.

This balance sheet is presented in abbreviated form below:

AZTEC AWNING AND VENETIAN BLIND COMPANY, INC.
BALANCE SHEET

SEPTEMBER 30, 1961

Current Assets (Including Inventory of $46,614.29)	$ 79,611.45
Long Term Receivables (Including Accounts Receivable from Officers of $9,456.90)	12,126.79
Fixed Assets (Cost of $49,845.84, and Accumulated Depreciation of $33,275.05)	16,570.79
	$108,309.03
Current Liabilities	$ 53,681.06
Long Term Liabilities	1,953.42
Unearned Interest Income	967.17
Stockholders' Equity (Including Common Stock of $20,000.00)	51,707.03
	$108,309.03

Any analysis of a balance sheet which is directed toward the determination of what is often referred to as the "real worth" of a company eventually leads to the question of the degree of accuracy with which any balance sheet, prepared on the basis of historic cost can present "real worth." This problem is somewhat minimized in the analysis of the Aztec's balance sheet, since this difficulty is usually centered on the fixed asset portion of the statement. (There is relatively little doubt that the current asset section and the long-term receivables section present cash values of these assets.) The fixed assets of this company do not contain either land or buildings, the two accounts which are most frequently affected by changing price levels.

The Fixed Assets of Aztec are composed of Automotive Equipment, Shop Equipment, Office Equipment, and Leasehold Improvements.

In order to make a determination of how realistically the depreciation charges reflected actual wear and tear, deterioration, and obsolescence, we asked to inspect a copy of the depreciation schedule as reflected by the corporate income tax return. Mr. Smith was unable to find a copy of this return. (The financial report prepared by the Certified Public Accountant did not contain a copy of this schedule.)

Failing to find a copy of this schedule, the depreciation charges were evaluated from available data. The depreciation charge for all automotive equipment was based on an average life of about five years. The shop equipment is being charged off on the basis of a composite life of eight to ten years. The office equipment is being depreciated on the basis of a life of nine to ten years. These estimates of useful lives appear to be reasonable, and are not heavily influenced by the idea of "loading" the income tax return with extremely high depreciation charges.

While we are not professionally qualified to act as appraisers of the market or replacement value of the equipment, we feel that the book figures are within reason for the making of this determination, tempered with the knowledge that the equipment has been kept in good operating condition and that price levels tend to climb upward.

In making an evaluation of the market value of the equipment, it should be noted that the average age of the automotive equipment is about three and one half years, the average age of the shop equipment is about six years, and the average age of the office equipment is about six and two thirds years.

The liability side of the balance sheet reflects debts, which lend themselves to specific measurement and which, therefore, do not create a valuation problem. In summary, it is our opinion that the balance sheet net worth is an accurate measure of the owners' equity, modified by (1) any difference between the replacement cost and the book value of the machinery, and (2) goodwill.

OPERATIONS OF THE COMPANY

Shower Partitions. Considerable emphasis has been placed on the effect which the development of this operation will have on the total company. Abbreviated income statements for this division for the past two fiscal years are shown below:

FOR THE FISCAL YEAR ENDED SEPTEMBER 30, 1961

Net Sales	$50,062.57
Cost of Sales	37,540.90
Gross Profit on Sales	12,521.67
Operating Expenses	23,812.48
Net Loss for the Year	$11,290.81

FOR THE FISCAL YEAR ENDED SEPTEMBER 30, 1960

Net Sales	$46,443.91
Cost of Sales	30,853.95
Gross Profit on Sales	15,579.96
Operating Expenses	20,237.01
Net Loss for the Year	$ 4,657.05

These data are not presented in the sense of being a pure gauge of activity in Shower Partitions for the period under discussion, for it is obvious that a considerable amount of time has had to be spent in developing dealerships and performing other administrative tasks which do not appear in sales data for this period. These data do, however, "tie together" the data for the other three departments which were previously furnished by the brokers.

In analyzing the data presented above, it should be kept in mind that Operating Expenses have been apportioned to the various departments, for the most part, on the basis of departmental sales, and do not represent direct allocations of expense. This could conceivably change the picture somewhat, e.g., a larger portion of travel and entertainment might be applicable to shower partitions in connection with the development of dealerships.

Comparison of 1958 with 1961. We investigated the causes of difference between 1958 (the most profitable year) and 1961 (the least profitable year). Our inquiry was focused in two directions: (1) change in the gross profit ratio; and (2) changes in operating expenses.

The change in the gross profit ratio was explained by Mr. Smith as being due to different levels of shop efficiency. In light of the increase in the gross profit ratio, and considering that general price levels would not explain a decline in costs, this answer seemed to be appropriate.

The question of increases in operating expenses was thoroughly investigated. The general answer to this increase was explained by Mr. Smith as being due to the lack of a firm managerial hand. He purported to have spent so much time on the development of Shower Partition that he did not pay proper attention to the operating costs of the business. He also explained that Mr. Morris, his general manager, has not been doing a good job since his return to the business and that he did not exercise proper control over costs.

Having considered the question of operating expense in general terms, attention was then focused on specific items. A list of specific changes (in rounded dollar amounts) appears below.

CHANGES IN OPERATING EXPENSES FROM 1958 TO 1961

Advertising	UP	$2,500
Accounting and Legal	UP	600
Bad Debts	UP	2,400
Commissions	UP	1,800
Contributions	DOWN	100
Depreciation	DOWN	1,100
Dues and Subscriptions	UP	400
Insurance	UP	1,500
Interest	UP	1,400
Licenses and Taxes	UP	3,000
Miscellaneous	UP	100
Office Expense	UP	1,000
Rent	UP	1,260
Repairs and Maintenance	DOWN	2,100
Salaries—Sales	UP	9,500
Salaries—General	UP	1,500
Telephone and Telegraph	UP	900
Transportation	DOWN	400
Travel and Promotion	DOWN	900
Utilities	UP	200

The increase in operating expenses from 1958 to 1961 amounted to $22,061.67. (The list above does not add to this figure due to rounding.) Of this amount, $16,200, or 73.4%, was caused by increases in four accounts, viz., Advertising, Bad Debts, Commissions, and Sales Salaries. While these four accounts are responsible for the bulk of the increase and are significant for that reason alone, their greater signficance lies in their internal relationship. All are functions of sales effort in a year in which sales decline materially.

A logical inference would be that the increase in advertising was used to stimulate new sales; the increases in Commissions and Sales Salaries were paid for expanding sales; and that the increase in Bad Debts reflected a broadened base of new customers who were more marginal in their financial positions. These inferences do not stand, however, in the light of a better than 30% drop in sales from the preceding year.

The explanation is to be found in loose management control, lessened sales effort by top management, and a general recession in the San Diego area. Smith and Morris were more withdrawn from sales in 1961 than in preceding years, which accounted for a larger portion of the sales being made by persons who were paid commissions and salaries in proportion to sales made. The increase in advertising reflects loose administrative control over operating expenses, and the bad debt increase is tied to the decline in economic conditions in San Diego over the period.

These conditions are apparently capable of being corrected for the most part by either the present management or a new management. They are a reflection of a lack of managerial control, which is discussed more fully in a later section.

RESULTS OF THE CURRENT FISCAL YEAR

Exhibit VII contains a summary of monthly sales by departments for 1957 through the present, and a list of expenses paid for in cash in the first three months of the current fiscal year.

Sales for the month of December are disappointingly low against any standard; sales of venetian blinds in December 1961 are the lowest of any December contained in the summary; sales of awnings in December 1961 are the lowest of any December under study; and sales of draperies are the lowest they have been in any December since the company began to market fabrics.

Mr. Smith stated that the economy of San Diego is on the upswing, and that the sales picture is looking better. He purports to have $25,000.00 of orders on hand. This, however, does not alter the fact that the new fiscal year has started slow in comparison with earlier years.

The owner states that he is more conscious of operating expenses than he has been in the past, and that he will reduce these expenses to $122,000 in the current fiscal year. As previously mentioned, a list of the *cash* expenses paid in each month of the first quarter of the new fiscal year is included in Exhibit VII. When questioned as to how he intended to cut operating expenses so radically, he stated that he had already reduced the number of vehicles from 17 to 9, and that, furthermore, he would fire Morris if he (Mr. Smith) does not sell the business. He did not elaborate on how the functions now being performed by Morris would be carried out.

In summary, there is some reason to believe that sales will be up somewhat in fiscal 1962, though sales data so far do not reflect the upswing. (Smith had predicted sales at $325,000 for the current fiscal year.) Overhead will undoubtedly be lower, though there is reason to believe that Smith will have a difficult time reaching the operating expense target he has set for himself.

BREAK-EVEN ANALYSIS

Present.   Smith stated that his break-even point for the current fiscal year for all departments (including Shower Partitions) is $375,000. Through independent evaluation of the fixed and variable costs, a break even formula for the present operation was developed. The formula is:

$$S = .78S + \$81,760$$

(The computations of the break-even formulae are not incorporated in this report. They are, however, available upon request.)

This formula shows a breakeven point of $371,636.36, which tends to substantiate the analysis of break even made by the owner.

Conservative Jackson-Houston Break-Even Analysis.   Two break-even formulae were developed for the proposed owners. The first of these, labeled "conservative," reflects only such changes in operations as would definitely occur in the transition, e.g., an increase in annual rent. The second, labeled "favorable," incorporates *all* possible economics which Mr. Smith feels could be effected by the new management. These two formulae are intended to establish a range for the new management's operations.

The "conservative" break-even formula for the new management is:

$$S = .75S + \$73,760$$

This formula is based on several fundamental assumptions. First, it assumes the three departments under consideration without adding to or deleting any line currently marketed. It assumes that advertising would be reduced from about 8% of sales to about 3% of sales. It further assumes that rent would increase by $1,000 per year (to $6,000), that officers' salaries would decrease by $8,000, and that travel would be reduced by $1,000 per year. All other items have been held constant to 1961 conditions.

Operations under this assumption are scheduled below.

PROJECTION USING "CONSERVATIVE" BREAK EVEN

SALES	INCREASE OVER 1961 SALES	NET INCOME BEFORE INCOME TAX	POST-TAX PROFIT	RETURN ON $90,000 INVESTMENT
$300,000	29.0%	$ 1,240	$ 868	1.0%
325,000	39.7%	7,590	5,243	5.3%
350,000	50.5%	13,740	9,618	10.7%
375,000	61.2%	19,990	13,993	15.5%
400,000	72.0%	26,240	18,095	20.1%

The following facts, while not a part of this table, relate to the appraisal of the data presented.

Sales of the three departments under consideration in 1961 were $232,565.67.

The best previous year for these three departments in terms of sales has been $332,589.

Taking the best year of each department independently and combining these figures gives a sales figure of $392,915.

Favorable Jackson-Houston Break-Even Analysis. Assuming that the same three departments are to be operated without addition of product lines or deletion of any existing departments, and assuming all economics suggested by Mr. Smith, the break-even formula is:

$$S = .665s + \$83,500$$

Operations under this assumption are scheduled below.

PROJECTION USING "FAVORABLE" BREAK EVEN

SALES	INCREASE OVER 1961 SALES	NET INCOME BEFORE INCOME TAX	POST-TAX PROFIT	RETURN ON $90,000 INVESTMENT
$300,000	29.0%	$17,000	$11,900	13.2%
325,000	39.7%	25,375	17,680	19.6%
350,000	50.5%	33,750	21,700	24.1%
375,000	61.2%	42,125	25,720	28.6%
400,000	72.0%	50,500	29,740	33.0%

The sales data presented at the conclusion of the "Conservative" projection table are applicable to the interpretation of this table.

CONTROLS

The area of financial and administrative controls represents one of the weakest parts of the company.

Like many small companies which have been begun with a minimal amount of capital and have then grown rapidly, this company is an extension of the personality of its owner, Jack Smith. And, also like many other rapidly growing small companies, it has had the degree of control which would be afforded by the top manager through his direct personal attention and understanding of the operation. In short, it is appropriate to say that the company has been run "from the seat of the pants."

The rising operating overhead is testimony to the loose control of the corporation. Smith has in many instances expected the company to "run itself," which it simply is not geared to do. He has also relied heavily on Morris, who has proved to be a lackadaisical manager. (This seems to be attributable to the fact that he went in business for himself in competition with Smith and was not able to keep his business profitable. He subsequently returned to the Aztec Company.)

Control over salesmen has not been good. Smith has expected that the sales people would be, in his term, "self-starters," and has not pushed the sales effort. Instead of aggressively seeking sales, the salesmen have been content to get leads from incoming telephone requests. Smith maintains that about 80% of the leads come from telephone inquires, and that about 80% of these, in turn, are converted into sales.

Internal control over the possibilities of theft and error has not been successfully incorporated into the business. Only in the recent past has the company begun to use a multi-copy invoice for sales to provide control over shipping and billing. Smith does not have monthly financial statements drawn, but receives them semi-annually from his CPA. While he does personally sign checks, he does not have a proper segregation of duties in the office to prevent major theft, particularly in the area of cash sales. To further illustrate the weakness in internal control, he reported that he had not received unqualified opinion audits from the Certified Public Accountant since the CPA had told him that the cost would be prohibitive in light of the weak internal control system.

The company has not been using a budget. Smith expressed an interest in budgeting, however. He expressed himself as follows: "I know I need a budget, but I don't know how to prepare one." He did appear quite proud, however, of his 1962 budget. It developed that his "budget" was nothing more than sales forecasts at break even for the year, and did not concern itself with any items except sales and advertising.

In summary, Smith is a hard working and imaginative owner-manager without formal education in administration who has badly neglected the area of control. This lack is not through contempt of its value but because of lack of recognition of the importance of the area and a lack of understanding as to how controls might be implemented. This area needs the immediate attention of management.

SPECIFIC QUESTIONS

There are some specific finance questions which were researched in your behalf which have not previously been discussed in this section. They are discussed below.

Operating Expense Data for 1959 and 1961. These figures are in Exhibits IV and VI.

Explanation of Commission Expense. A question arose as to why sales, salaries, and commissions were 6.8% of sales in 1958 and 10.2% of sales in 1960, with the company paying a 15% commission to salespeople. This is caused by not paying commissions for sales made by Morris and Roberts, and is a measure of the amount of sales activity on the part of the management.

Rent Expense. Rent expenses for 1958–1961 are detailed below.

1958	—	$3,900
1959	—	4,800
1960	—	4,800
1961	—	5,160

Monthly Sales Data. These are detailed in Exhibit VII.

Production

PRODUCTION PLANNING AND SCHEDULING

The Aztec Company can be classed as an intermittent manufacturer with most production planning and scheduling built around individual orders received by the company. Very little production is to stock and practically no attention is given to forecasting sales scientifically and then scheduling manufacturing accordingly. Some recent attention has been given to the subject of sales budgets and sales quotas by Mr. Smith but it has not yet become part of the organization. Production workers are paid on an hourly basis and must be trained to perform several different jobs. However, since there are no jobs classed as "skilled" jobs, it is not impossible for an employee to work in several different production areas during the day. Orders received over the phone or turned in by the salesmen are written up in triplicate and a copy is sent to the production foreman who becomes responsible for producing the order. When the order is complete the specifications and quantity can be checked against the original order prior to shipment or installation.

QUALITY CONTROL

Due to the relatively simple and few production operations involved in manufacturing a finished product and due to the few specialized pieces of machinery used in manufacturing, the Aztec Company relies mainly on the major supplier of materials and parts and an operator-inspection to provide the necessary control of the quality of goods being manufactured. While operator-inspection is not preventive in nature, the simplicity of manufacturing operations allows good control of quality. There is support evidence in the financial records which indicates that there is little scrap or defection material from the manufacturing process.

INVENTORY AND PROCUREMENT PRACTICES

Approximately $20,000.00 of raw material inventory is in stock. This estimated figure fluctuates according to demand for the products. The shop foreman does all procurement of materials, parts, and supplies needed in the production area. There appears to be *no* centralized purchasing activity nor clear inventory policy which controls production purchases. Purchases for the draperies division occur after sales have been made since only samples are kept on hand for show purposes. Any features or advantages possible through economic lot-size buying of parts or materials for aluminum products are not taken advantage of except when large orders are in hand. The question of how much money can be or should be tied up in inventory to bring about cost savings has not been carefully explored. In the last year, purchasing activities have been on the cautious side since sales volume has declined.

EQUIPMENT AND PRODUCTION LAYOUT

One of the better features of the Aztec Company pertains to the production area layout and condition of the manufacturing equipment being used. While always there is room for improvement, this area shows the result of some careful thought and applied scientific management principles. Work operations tend to flow in a straight line; jigs, fixtures, etc. are located to improve production output and maintain quality performance.

Since full-scale production operations were not observed, it is difficult to state flatly that costs cannot be reduced significantly. However, this area is impressive.

The major defect in production operations is that presently there is a very large excess in capacity of equipment and employees. The point of optimum operation will not be reached until production operations are steady eight hours a day so that full utilization of equipment and employees can be obtained. The estimated output for the three production divisions operating at a point near capacity is as follows:

	OUTPUT PER YEAR	PRODUCTION EMPLOYEES REQUIRED
Draperies	$250,000	10 (1 Supervisor, 2 Installers, 7 Employees)
Venetian Blinds	390,000	9
Awnings	300,000	7 (1 Foreman, 4 Employees, 2 Installers)
Total	$850,000	26 Employees

SOURCE: (1) Projected production figures based on value of sales.
(2) Mr. Jack Smith

JOB DESCRIPTIONS, WORK STANDARDS, AND
EMPLOYEE INCENTIVES

Briefly stated, there are no written job descriptions or developed work standards in the Aztec Company. At one time Mr. Smith introduced an employee profit-sharing plan that was maintained for two years. He stated that there was so much misunderstanding about the plan that it did more harm than good. He dropped the plan.

In the future, written job descriptions and specifications should be developed for all positions in the Aztec Company. Their usefulness is apparent when aiding in the selecting and hiring of employees, training employees, and promoting employees. Scientifically determined work standards also would be of significant value if sales increased and production activities were at full capacity. The work standard would not only tell you how much work to expect from an employee doing a given task in a given period of time but it would allow management to forecast production (units) and production costs once orders were received.

Marketing

SALES MANAGEMENT AND CONTROL

Without any question the function of sales is the life blood of an organization. While profit margins can be increased by reducing costs, the foremost activity which precedes all others is making sales.

During 1960–61, the Aztec Company showed a severe decline in sales in all product divisions. Many reasons were given for this decline: (1) Smith concentrated his abilities and time so much on developing "Shower Partitions" that he neglected the other product lines; (2) the San Diego sales area suffered an economic recession brought on by a temporary decline in governmental activity in the area, an overbuilding situation in housing, and a general decline in business activity which was characteristic of the entire economy of the United States; (3) other management people in the Aztec Company failed to assume the responsibility for sales when Mr. Smith was engaged in promoting "Shower Partitions." The probable answer to the problem involves all of these reasons plus the fact that the sales organization of the Aztec Company appears totally lacking. When eighty percent of sales are an indirect result of advertising and twenty percent are from personal contact, then you either have a tremendously effective advertising program and/or a tremendously ineffective sales force. If, through careful development of a sales program, you could maintain the present response to advertising and at the same time increase sales through personal contact so that it equaled fifty percent of total sales, the Aztec Company could quickly gross $500,000 annually.

MARKET POTENTIAL

There is one school of thought to the effect that you can never saturate the market if you have a good product.

Based on the San Diego Chamber of Commerce bulletin listing monthly economic indicators of the city and county, it appears that during 1958–59, the area was riding an economic peak which was followed by a sharp but relatively short economic decline. The indicators for the last few months show a slight upswing in business activity for the area. Several of these indicators probably correlate reasonably well with sales of the Aztec Company. Examples might be: (1) new home construction; (2) total wages; and/or (3) savings and loan association mortgages.

The more important consideration affecting sales of the Aztec Company would be the long-term growth situation of Southern California. Every statistic predicts that the states of California, Florida, and Texas will show the greatest net increases during the decade of the '60's.

COMPETITION

Aside from a few small one and two room competitors, the Aztec Company does not have extreme competition in San Diego in the field of aluminum awnings and venetian blinds. However, there is more intense competition in draperies since private shops and department stores both provide this service.

The philosophy of the company regarding sales is that every home in Southern California needs venetian blinds, drapes, and awnings. The present owner, Mr. Smith, also believes that the company should consider selling carpets since no inventory would be required and there exists a strong demand for this service. Thus, the company could provide blinds, awnings, drapes, and carpets for home owners, apartments, motels and hotels, and office buildings.

SHOWER PARTITIONS

While the Shower Partition division is not for sale, the purchased Aztec Company would (or could) become the authorized dealer of Shower Partitions in San Diego and the surrounding counties. The addition of this line plus the miscellaneous items sold could become significant in the future.

METHODS OF SELLING

Presently it appears that the company operates the sales program on the principle that the more you advertise the more you sell. Obviously, the media used in advertising affects sales. Also, the timing of the advertising, the training of the sales force, the make-up of sales materials, etc. affects sales.

The Aztec Company's sales program is uncoordinated, uncontrolled, and overadvertised (in dollars). Little attention is paid to developing and creating potential customers. No visit is paid to new families moving into the area. Little has been done toward expanding the sales area toward the South coast. This is not to imply that Mr. Jack Smith is not sales oriented. He stated that he is aware of all of these things but since being a one-man operation primarily, little time is available for developing these programs—especially with his intense interest in Shower Partitions.

Conclusions and Recommendations

Sales—The entire sales program needs review and reorganization.

Production—Considered very satisfactory as to layout and equipment. Eventually recommend the development of job specifications, work standards, and full utilization of equipment and employees.

Finance—Very inadequate administrative controls. Recommend the development of a budget system. The total function stands in need of review and analysis.

Procurement—Consideration should be given to more centralized purchasing. There is the possibility of economic savings as well as providing a tighter control system on dollars invested in inventory. (Lack of inventory control policies.)

Product Lines—Consideration should be given to the addition of a carpet line plus becoming the authorized dealer for Shower Partitions in the San Diego area.

Labor Force—If the Aztec Company is purchased, certain members of the work force should be retained for a while at least. Primarily, Mr.

Wiley Brown, Production Foreman. Also, someone familiar with the administrative details.

Profit Possibilities—It is beyond the scope of this report to answer this question precisely; however, reasonable limits have been established in break-even analysis. These are incorporated in the exhibits.

Sales Price of the Company

1. Inventory—The cost of inventory will be based on the actual cost of the actual inventory at the date of sale.

2. Fixed Assets—While machinery appraisers would be required to determine the exact value of the fixed properties, we feel that they could be secured for not less than $25,000 nor more than $37,500.

3. Goodwill—Based on the foregoing observations regarding inventory and fixed assets, and assuming a $90,000 sales price, the asking price of goodwill is in the range of $32,500 to $45,000. The value of goodwill is contingent upon the company's ability to earn profits, which, in turn, hinges upon the ability of management to increase sales, institute better controls, reduce operating costs, and a willingness to adapt to changes in demand.

4. General—We do not feel that the asking price is exorbitant, but it is our opinion that a negotiated price of between $80,000 to $90,000 is more realistic. (Mr. Smith and brokers emphasized that $90,000 was a firm price.)

EXHIBIT I

AZTEC AWNING AND VENETIAN BLIND COMPANY, INC.
BALANCE SHEET
SEPTEMBER 30, 1961

LIABILITIES AND STOCKHOLDERS' EQUITY

Current Liabilities
Accounts Payable		$ 28,766.60
Customer Credit Balances		1,260.59
Accrued Wages Payable		384.15
Taxes Payable-		
Payroll Taxes	$ 2,102.65	
Property Taxes Accrued	1,507.60	
Sales Tax	498.12	4,108.37
Notes Payable—Citizens National Bank		
(Accounts Receivable Pledged as Collateral)		15,000.00
Installment Notes Payable—Current Maturities		4,161.35
Total Current Liabilities		$ 53,681.06

Long-Term Liabilities
Installment Notes Payable-		
Citizens National Bank of California	$ 5,953.13	
Colonial Bank of San Diego	161.64	
	$ 6,114.77	
Less Amount Due In One Year (See Above)	4,161.35	
Total Long Term Liabilities		1,953.42
Total Liabilities		$ 55,634.48

Unearned Interest Income | | | 967.17 |

Stockholders' Equity
Common Stock	$20,000.00	
Retained Earnings	31,707.38	
Total Stockholders' Equity		51,707.38
Total Liabilities and Stockholders' Equity		$108,309.03

EXHIBIT II
AZTEC AWNING AND VENETIAN BLIND COMPANY, INC.
BALANCE SHEET
SEPTEMBER 30, 1961

ASSETS

Current Assets

Cash—Unrestricted			$ 1,441.20
Cash—Restricted			389.87
Accounts Receivable—			
Customers		$20,459.28	
Employers		153.35	
		$20,612.63	
Allowance for Doubtful Accounts		1,281.16	19,331.47
Installment Contracts Receivable			2,721.60
Federal Income Tax Refund Receivable			8,338.31
Inventories—At Lowering FICO Cost or Market—			
Finished Goods		$ 5,573.99	
Work in Process		606.40	
Raw Materials		40,433.90	46,614.29
Prepaid Expenses			774.71
Total Current Assets			$ 79,611.45

Long Term Receivables

Installment Contracts Receivable		$ 2,669.89	
Loans Due From Officers		9,456.90	
Total Long Term			$ 12,126.79

Equipment

	Cost	Accumulated Depreciation	Depreciated Cost	
Automotive				
Equipment	$20,059.19	$15,826.57	$ 4,222.62	
Shop Equipment	14,419.12	8,120.91	6,298.21	
Office Equipment	12,720.41	7,929.88	4,790.53	
Leasehold				
Improvements	2,657.12	1,397.69	1,259.43	
	$49,845.84	$33,275.05		16,570.79
Total Assets				$108,309.03

EXHIBIT III

1961

EXPENSES (CASH DISBURSEMENTS BOOK)

ACCT.#		OCT.	NOV.	DEC.	TOTAL
600	Advertising	$1,718.82	$1,130.10	$1,130.54	$ 3,979.46
601	Accounting	100.00	100.00	—	200.00
606	Commissions Paid	171.97	324.50	157.99	654.46
610	Credit and Collection	7.50	57.50	44.50	109.50
620	Insurance	226.26	45.27	26.00	297.53
623	Interest	61.00	15.50	197.00	273.50
629	Miscellaneous	7.70	41.93	3.50	53.13
630	Off. Sup. and Exp.	165.38	207.06	112.18	484.62
640	Rent	417.50	417.50	417.50	1,252.50
641	Rental-Awning Equip.	231.75	—	—	231.75
645	Rep. and Maintenance	114.87	220.30	54.95	390.12
651	Samples	152.10	349.54	4.33	505.97
655	Shop Expense	117.00	212.51	103.26	432.77
670	Tel and Tel	265.84	—	291.71	556.55
680	Gas, Oil, and Tires	164.01	374.45	4.85	543.31
681	Transportation-Repairs	143.12	195.58	107.12	445.82
685	Travel & Entertainment	90.95	420.84	7.21	519.00
688	Utilities	115.08	398.22	76.15	589.45
612	Dues and Sub	—	60.00	25.00	85.00
625	Legal	—	100.00	—	100.00
626	Licenses	—	3.00	5.00	8.00
607	Contributions	—	—	100.00	100.00
					$11,813.44

EXHIBIT IV

AZTEC AWNING AND VENETIAN BLIND COMPANY, INC.
OPERATING EXPENSE
1961

	TOTAL	DIRECT LABOR	MFG. EXP.	SELLING	GENERAL
Advertising	$ 20367.65	$	$	$20367.65	$
Accounting	2091.65				2091.65
Bad Debts	3278.99				3278.99
Commissions and Sub-Contract	2058.53			2058.53	
Charitable Contributions	10.00				10.00
Credit and Collection Expense	311.43				311.43
Repair—Office Equipment	1459.86		1644.23		1459.86
Repair—Shop Equipment	1644.23				
Repair—Autos and Trucks	3597.91			3597.91	
Dues and Subscriptions	416.09				416.09
Insurance—Employees	2219.35				2219.35
Insurance—General	1799.19				1799.19
Interest	1626.17				1626.17
Legal	428.70				428.70
Licenses	549.09				545.09
Miscellaneous Expense	170.89				170.89
Office Supplies and Expense	3434.06				3434.06
Rent	5160.00				5160.00
Rentals—Awning Equipment	927.00		927.00		
Repairs and Maintenance	1074.26				1074.26
Salaries and Commissions	101504.57	21020.27		39149.12	41335.18
Samples and Displays	971.99			971.99	
Shop Supplies and Expense	3307.20		3307.20		
Taxes	5893.18				5893.18
Telephone and Telegraph	2937.60				2937.60
Gas, Oil, & Tires	4301.65			4301.65	
Repairs—Auto & Trucks	2475.85			2475.85	
Travel & Entertainment	3650.02			3650.02	
Utilities	1233.81				1233.81
	$178896.92	$21020.27	$5873.43	$76572.72	$75425.50

EXHIBIT V

EMPLOYEE ROSTER OF THE AZTEC COMPANY

FIRST QUARTER, FISCAL YEAR 1962

NAME	JOB TITLE	WEEKS WORKED	TOTAL WAGES PAID THIS QUARTER
* 1	Awning Installer	6	$ 371.00
2	Sales (Drapery)	7	1,108.63
3	Shop Foreman	13	2,077.15
4	————	13	4,500.00
5	Office Secretary	13	819.58
6	Ven. Blind (Straw Boss)	13	691.45
* 7	Awning Installer	9	376.89
* 8	Drapery Sales	1	45.33
9	Shop Foreman (Drapery)	13	1,250.65
10	Seamstress (Drapery)	13	609.53
11	Part-time Office Help	9	147.48
12	Salesman (Retail)	2	150.00
* 13	Part-time Awning	4	151.81
14	V. B. & Drapery Inst.	13	1,171.38
15	Seamstress	13	543.98
16	Awning Installer	8	465.77
* 17	Salesman	3	100.77
18	Drapery Sales (free-lance)	2	43.83
19	Shower Partition	13	698.35
* 20	(Temporary)	1	19.83
21	Awning and V. B. Production	13	638.83
22	Drapery Dept. (slipcovers)	10	464.10
23	Salesman	13	1,382.10
24	Sales Mgr. & Asst. Gen. Mgr.	13	2,250.00
* 25	Awning and V. B. Prod.	2	17.75
26	Salesman	13	1,063.22
* 27	(Bookkeeper)	13	773.05

* No longer employed with company.

EXHIBIT VI
AZTEC AWNING AND VENETIAN BLIND COMPANY, INC.
OPERATING EXPENSES
1959

	TOTAL	BLINDS	AWNINGS	FOLDING DOORS	MISC.	FABRICS
Selling	$ 79042.88	$26187.39	$19769.11	$12887.33	$ 7541.60	$12657.45
Gen'l & Admin.	77051.73	24769.43	19174.37	10721.60	11390.95	10995.38
Total	$156094.61	$50956.82	$38943.48	$23608.93	$18932.55	$23652.83

SELLING

	TOTAL	BLINDS	AWNINGS	FOLDING DOORS	MISC.	FABRICS
Sales Salaries	$ 35120.77	$12320.10	$ 8825.57	$ 6905.95	$ 2109.89	$ 4959.26
Advertising	21271.28	5707.36	6009.94	2278.84	2218.84	5056.47
Transportation	8476.16	3123.46	1888.49	1223.11	1229.89	1011.21
Rep.—Autos & Trucks	7301.92	2690.76	1626.87	1053.67	1059.51	871.11
Travel & Prom.	5750.95	2119.23	1281.31	829.86	834.46	686.09
Short-Wave Radio	614.59	226.48	136.93	88.69	89.18	73.31
Commissions Paid	507.21	—	—	507.21	—	—
	$ 79042.88	$26187.39	$19769.11	$12887.33	$ 7541.60	$12657.45

GEN'L & ADMIN.

	TOTAL	BLINDS	AWNINGS	FOLDING DOORS	MISC.	FABRICS
Gen'l Salaries	$ 46909.61	$14601.90	$12531.76	$ 5978.12	$ 6628.14	$ 7169.69
Rent	4800.00	1010.50	1010.50	1010.50	1010.50	758.00
Rep. & Maintenance	4406.00	1623.61	981.66	635.79	639.31	525.63
Licenses & Taxes	4111.41	1515.05	916.02	593.28	596.57	490.49
Insurance	3718.78	1370.37	828.54	536.62	539.59	443.66
Office Sup. & Exp.	3157.92	1163.69	703.58	455.69	458.21	376.75
Telephone	2564.46	945.00	571.36	370.05	372.10	305.95
Legal & Acctg.	1972.19	726.75	439.40	284.59	286.16	235.29
Utilities	1149.02	241.90	241.90	241.90	241.90	181.42
Rep.—Off. Equip.	1030.51	379.74	229.60	148.70	149.53	122.94
Interest	1012.93	373.26	225.68	146.17	146.98	120.84
Bad Debts	849.31	312.97	189.23	189.23	123.23	101.32
Charitable Contrib.	393.55	145.02	87.68	56.79	57.10	46.96
Sales Discounts	371.51	136.90	82.77	53.61	53.91	44.32
Dues & Subscript.	349.98	128.97	77.98	50.50	50.78	41.75
Credit & Collection	254.55	56.71	56.71	36.73	36.94	30.37
	$ 77051.73	$24769.43	$19174.37	$10721.60	$11390.95	$10995.38

EXHIBIT VII

MONTHLY SALES BY PRODUCT DIVISIONS

1957–1961

		JAN.	FEB.	MAR.	APRIL	MAY	JUNE	JULY	AUG.	SEPT.	OCT.	NOV.	DEC.
1957	(VB)	11,801.34	15,158.40	12,250.36	13,479.83	15,895.20	12,985.56	15,346.90	19,731.19	16,515.52	18,701.37	13,427.14	14,359.16
	(AWN)	4,876.14	4,813.47	5,481.01	11,397.50	12,518.34	14,478.18	8,730.61	8,323.40	6,105.58	10,762.74	6,594.73	3,550.58
	(D)												
1958	(VB)	15,401.64	11,016.10	13,049.89	14,450.01	21,078.19	14,390.52	14,527.67	16,345.54	10,295.35	21,328.76	11,184.52	13,166.63
	(AWN)	3,486.52	7,467.07	12,495.48	14,921.04	17,257.29	13,021.92	14,927.95	8,243.28	8,519.70	8,138.02	5,461.93	3,655.31
	(D)												
1959	(VB)	13,916.46	13,286.90	18,258.12	12,547.13	11,470.62	13,925.20	16,021.86	11,444.00	8,638.34	12,083.13	14,689.76	12,528.88
	(AWN)	5,233.94	6,369.70	14,029.04	7,439.33	13,102.42	9,506.78	12,426.24	11,458.77	2,305.12	14,078.48	6,198.00	5,357.44
	(D)	2,586.84	6,565.41	6,663.67	8,598.56	9,863.49	6,544.02	6,767.15	8,510.65	(1,844.38)	8,460.67	7,681.44	8,186.52
1960	(VB)	12,962.17	8,799.75	11,138.40	8,839.35	10,326.67	7,678.44	6,698.92	7,786.76	4,117.60	5,051.21	5,730.00	10,120.49
	(AWN)	3,087.31	3,484.49	2,838.55	7,326.85	14,518.23	10,583.79	9,048.62	9,959.81	8,542.14	15,321.45	11,802.20	9,998.20
	(D)	8,398.47	8,271.38	9,152.95	8,960.84	7,171.39	5,420.68	5,058.35	5,321.52	4,511.10	7,144.39	5,397.92	9,764.47
1961	(VB)	5,302.46	4,325.51	7,683.45	7,268.26	7,982.12	7,380.48	4,584.41	6,824.63	8,076.35	N.A.	N.A.	5,252.89
	(AWN)	5,916.47	2,841.55	7,652.70	4,796.19	5,689.48	7,572.44	3,671.38	8,869.45	8,273.97			3,359.62
	(D)	2,235.56	3,596.00	2,380.82	4,457.54	2,150.77	6,160.54	3,831.60	4,766.72	3,435.04			6,285.89

VB = Venetian Blinds
AWN = Awnings
D = Draperies

2. BURSON ELECTRONIC MANUFACTURING COMPANY

"CHALLENGING A PROBLEM HAS ALWAYS interested me," commented Ben Burson, Jr., owner of Burson Electronics Manufacturing Company. Mr. Burson had formed his company in April 1963 to manufacture and sell the Blink-Off, an automatic electronic turn signal canceller for motor vehicles, which he had invented and to which he owned patent rights.

General Background

Ben Burson, Jr., had engaged in various phases of the electronics field since the late 1930's. During World War II, he had served in the Army Air Force, attending several special schools at the University of Wisconsin, Yale, and Massachusetts Institute of Technology. He graduated from the program for communications cadets at Yale with experience in weather data equipment and radar. He was highly skilled in radio engineering and after the war helped build several radio stations. He also worked as a research scientist at the local University Electrical Engineering Research Lab and during the late 1950's worked for the Federal Aviation Agency.

It was while working for the F.A.A. that he became interested in the Blink-Off. Mechanical turn signals, which were standard on all American automobiles at that time, required a rather short radius turn to be executed before the mechanical canceller turned off the signal. If the required radius was not transcribed, the operator of the vehicle had to remember to turn the signal off manually. When the driver forgot to turn off the signal, it often resulted in confusion to other drivers. In many instances, this confusion was the cause of a serious accident such as one Mr. Burson witnessed in the fall of 1959. Upon investigation, Mr. Burson found that no automatic device existed to stop the blinks.

Within a year, Mr. Burson developed the Blink-Off. The Blink-Off when wired to the signal indicator circuit of the vehicle circumvented the possibility of failure of the indicator to turn off. The device contained a counter which noted the number of blinks put out by the flasher. After a predetermined number of blinks, the circuit to the signal lamps was automatically broken.

Mr. Burson filed a patent petition in September 1960 and later left the F.A.A. to become chief engineer for a local radio station. The new job provided more personal time for devotion to further development of the Blink-Off and other experiments.

In June 1962, Mr. Robert Waggener, President of Nucleonics Research and Development Corporation, persuaded Mr. Burson to aid him in developing a civil defense device in his spare time. Nucleonics was a small, local corporation formed by Mr. Waggener. Mr. Burson later offered Mr. Waggener an exclusive manufacturing and sales license in the United States on the patent pending for his electronic device to cancel turn signal indicators on motor vehicles.

Nucleonics lacked sufficient capital for automation of the production process of the device, so they began assembling the units by hand. Work continued on other projects, but major concentration was devoted to the canceller which was given the trade name, Blink-Off. When sufficient sales failed to materialize, the controlling stockholder, owner of a local construction materials company, became very dissatisfied with company management. The stockholders voted for dissolution in January 1963, and the corporation was formally dissolved in April 1963. Mr. Waggener left the firm before dissolution, but Mr. Burson was retained to liquidate the remaining inventory of component parts.

All of Nucleonics assets were transferred to the local investor's corporation, subject to all liabilities and obligations. After all obligations were met, Mr. Burson was given the remaining inventory worth an estimated $1,500 in exchange for services rendered and unpaid royalties. He also acquired ownership of the trade name "Blink-Off." The pending patent was finally granted on November 5, 1963.

Burson Electronics Manufacturing Company

Ben Burson was not discouraged by the failure of Nucleonics. "In my opinion," he said, "Nucleonics could have succeeded given a few additional months and more capital to promote sales of the Blink-Off."

Mr. Burson decided to devote his full personal attention to the development of a market for the Blink-Off. He organized his company as a sole proprietorship and commenced production of the units in a small garage. Inquiries and tests were continued with the various state governments for approval. (See Exhibit I for status of approval by each state as of May 1, 1964.) He contacted several automotive manufacturers. All expressed interest in the device and each ordered several units for testing by their own staffs. The top-of-the-line division of one major producer indicated a possibility of specifying the unit as original equipment on a forthcoming model year. These major automobile manufacturing divisions agreed to conduct tests on the unit.

Production was limited each week to the orders on hand because of very limited capital funds. The company was financed solely out of personal funds and the inventory of parts and assembled units received in the liquidation of Nucleonics. No attempt was made initially to raise additional capital until a market had been established for the Blink-Off.

While Mr. Burson had a very modest amount of capital with which to operate his new firm, he was able to earn fees locally by providing technical services when called upon by local radio stations and other users familiar with his abilities. From such fees he was able to support himself without drawing a salary from the firm.

His immediate goal was to develop sales sufficient to generate funds needed to maintain his materials inventory and to support promotional expenses.

With sales averaging only 100 units a month, sufficient funds were not available for an extensive advertising program. As a result, main reliance was placed upon free advertising in the new products section of publications like *Popular Science, Popular Electronics, Traffic Safety, Fleet Magazine News,* and so forth.

An example of one mention of this type was the following published in the March, 1964 edition of *Popular Science:*

> *DO TURN SIGNALS THAT WON'T BLINK OFF* because you didn't turn your wheels far enough make your blood pressure rise? And what about the signals of the man ahead who drives along blissfully ignorant that one of his is on? Well, take heart. The Burson Electronic Manufacturing Co., Omaha, Neb., is marketing a device appropriately named "Blink-Off" that does the trick. It counts the number of flashes and automatically cancels the signal. Your lights won't blink again until you flip the wand to "off" and then back to the direction in which you want to turn. The manufacturer says there are no parts to wear out, no heating elements, no mechanical or clock mechanism, no maintenance. It's about time—European cars for years have had signals that cancel without dependence on the degree of wheel turn.

Mention of the "Blink-Off" in nationally circulated magazines resulted in the receipt of over 700 inquiries for further information in a three-month time span. An attractive explanatory brochure was mailed in answer to all requests for information.

Arrangements were made for two local automotive stores to display and sell the Blink-Off.

All promotional activity was conducted personally by Mr. Burson. No other person was employed by the firm except on a part-time basis when needed.

Marketing

Mr. Burson commented as follows on his marketing strategy:

If we can interest the automobile manufacturers in the Blink-Off, we will have it made. We could then pick up the after-market, but to interest the auto-manufacturers we must backtrack to the consumer public.

Our plan is to interest the state and local governments first. We have approached the Department of Public Safety and the Highway Departments in our own state in the hope that we can interest them. So far we have filled two state orders for units.

The other route we are taking is to interest the individual car owner through advertising in magazines and brochures. Advertising requires substantial funds, however. We are bypassing the trucking and bus fleet owners because many of them are not willing to purchase any safety device unless they receive an insurance credit or reduction in driving costs.

Two mail order companies located in Chicago agreed to put the Blink-Off in their catalogs, and Burson was confident that sales from these two sources would be significant within six months.

Agreements were made with four manufacturers' representatives to sell the unit throughout the United States. The company retained the right to sell without commission directly to the federal government, national chain stores and mail order houses, and to automobile manufacturers.

The suggested retail price for the Blink-Off was set at $14.98 by Mr. Burson because he recognized that a substantial margin was necessary for promotional expenses. Prices quoted to manufacturers' representatives and distributors were $6.95. Manufacturers' representatives were allowed an additional ten percent on all sales by them to distributors. The distributors were expected to price the device at $9.00 to retail outlets. Quantity discounts in the form of freight allowances on shipments of 50 or more were allowed. Special prices were offered to fleet owners and to government agencies on direct sales by bid.

Production

The Blink-Off was assembled by hand operations on a workbench by Mr. Burson and his son. Tools used to assemble the device included a pair of needlenosed pliers, a wire cutter, a one-quarter inch hand drill, and a soldering gun. The components were purchased from various manufacturers in 1,000-lot quantities and consisted of a masonite baseboard, several electronic parts, several lengths of wire, and plastic tubing. For a complete list of parts and costs, see Exhibit II.

A template was used to locate the seventeen holes in the baseboard, which was predrilled for mounting holes and soldering terminals. After the baseboard was drilled with a portable hand drill, the nine soldering lugs were pressed into the designated holes. The electronic parts were then mounted as follows: a relay was fastened via a single self-tapping metal screw; a transformer was attached by means of two small flanges along the edges; a 2N 204 transistor was pressed into its force-fit hole drilled in the baseboard; and the leads for the two capacitors were soldered to the lugs.

The smaller electronic parts were then soldered in place and connected by wires to their respective points. Three terminal wires were attached to brass contact posts in the plastic box, and the baseboard assembly was cemented to the plastic box with epoxy glue. The Blink-Off was then packaged in a cardboard box, complete with mounting screws, connecting wire, and an instruction sheet.

No detailed studies had been made to determine the actual time required to perform each operation, but both Mr. Burson and his son could each hand assemble five units in one hour. Cost estimates prepared by Mr. Burson assumed a total cost, including allocated overhead, of $5.35 per unit in 1,000-lot quantities. Additional cost savings could be made by greater quantity purchases of components should sales warrant large volume purchases. Also, if ordered in sufficient quantities, the baseboard could be obtained pre-drilled ready for immediate assembly.

Product Improvement

Certain improvements were made in the Blink-Off which increased its durability and service. A series of wires attached to the brake prevented the device from cancelling the signal when the driver's foot was placed on the brake.

Another improvement was in the design and durability of the plastic box which housed the components. The original plastic box designed by Nucleonics had proved to be subject to cracking after short periods of service. Mr. Burson purchased a new die for a plastic box which resulted in greater durability and in a considerable reduction in the purchase price of the box.

New Product Development

Mr. Burson had developed a number of other products, two of which were in the patent pending stage and eight more for which patent applications were being prepared. He felt that "most engineers in the electronics field today are shooting for the moon and are thus bypassing the mass market for practical things which would aid the consumer in his everyday living." Thus he was devoting his creative energy to developing consumer oriented products for mass sale.

One invention was a frost detection device for use in commercial refrigerators. This device had a limited market in that Mr. Burson felt it was too expensive an item for home refrigerators.

Another product was an electronic dip stick which would monitor the viscosity condition and level of oil in automobile engines. Mr. Burson was optimistic about the commercial prospects of both products provided they could be marketed aggressively.

Finance

Mr. Burson had invested most of his personal savings and four years of effort in the development of the Blink-Off. Total cash outlays had reached $9,000 on research and development. Several local persons, interested in investing in the Blink-Off, had approached Mr. Burson, but he had refrained from incorporating his firm because he feared that he would lose financial control. He said that he was trying to "prevent making the mistake that Nucleonics had made."

By careful husbanding of cash resources, Mr. Burson estimated that he could continue operations for an indefinite period until large orders for the Blink-Off were assured. Over 1,000 units had been sold by May, 1964, and sales were averaging approximately 100 per month. With the part-time help of his son, he was able to produce up to 150 units a month with ease.

In anticipation of possible large orders, Mr. Burson had designed on paper a production system which would assemble 3,500 units a week with the help of 12 assemblers, one stockman and one test man. Initially Burson would provide all the supervision of production. By using the planned production system and volume purchases, and shipping in bulk containers, he was confident that he could get unit costs below $5.00.

It was estimated that $60,000 would be needed to get an assembly operation underway at the 3,500 unit per week level. If certain parts were to be produced, such as relays, an additional capital investment of $60,000 would be needed.

Only very general inquiries had been made regarding possible financing for the company. Mr. Burson had an oral promise that most of his working capital needs would be provided by a local bank after confirmed orders had been received from reliable customers. No capital would be provided prior to receipt of firm orders, however. In casual conversations with friends, a total of twenty-six persons expressed an interest in investing in his enterprise provided promising orders were received from large companies. He estimated that he could probably sell up to $50,000 in capital stock locally, but he would do so only if absolutely necessary and if he could retain majority control.

Future Plans

Although Mr. Burson had only very limited success in marketing Blink-Offs, he was optimistic that he would eventually succeed in persuading at least one automobile manufacturer to add the Blink-Off as a standard accessory to their new automobiles.

He stated that he was waiting for one of two things to happen. "One, someone will offer to buy out the patent rights at some reasonable figure, paying me so much in cash plus royalties for the goodwill and development of the Blink-Off. Two, the possibility of orders obtained from mail order concerns and manufacturers' representatives might reach the point soon where I could meet virtually all the payroll for an assembly line operation. I would then incorporate, using the money from local investors and from sales of the Blink-Off to develop and exploit my other product ideas."

Two well-established manufacturing firms were contacted in hopes that they would be interested in investing in the Blink-Off. One firm from Chicago was interested in diversifying their product line to include the rapidly growing electronics field. They had tested the Blink-Off and were very interested but felt that payback on such an investment was insufficient to justify the allocation of funds for a new plant. The Board of Directors of the firm appointed a committee to reconsider the proposal. No decision had been made by the end of May.

EXHIBIT I

STATE APPROVAL ON BLINK-OFF*

STATE	NEED TEST	BEING TESTED	NO APPROVAL NECESSARY	SALES PERMITTED
Alabama				X
Alaska		X		
Arizona				X
Arkansas		X		
California		X		
Colorado				X
Connecticut			X	
Delaware			X	
Florida				X
Georgia			X	
Hawaii				X
Idaho				X
Illinois				X
Indiana			X	
Iowa				X
Kansas		X		
Kentucky			X	
Louisiana				X
Maine			X	
Maryland				X
Massachusetts				X
Michigan			X	
Minnesota				X
Mississippi		X		
Missouri				X
Montana			X	
Nebraska			X	
Nevada				X
New Hampshire				X
New Jersey				X
New Mexico				X
New York		X		X
North Carolina			X	
North Dakota			X	
Ohio				X
Oklahoma				X
Oregon				X
Pennsylvania				X
Rhode Island	X			
South Carolina				X
South Dakota			X	
Tennessee				X
Texas				X
Utah			X	
Vermont		X		
Virginia				X
Washington				X
Washington, D.C.				X
West Virginia			X	
Wisconsin			X	
Wyoming			X	

* As of May 1, 1964.

SOURCE: Company records.

EXHIBIT II

ESTIMATED COST OF MANUFACTURING BLINK-OFF*

PARTS	PRICE
Plastic cover	$ .10
Relay	1.50
50 MFD 150 V. condenser	.20
500 MFD 12 volt condenser	.32
Transformer	.50
5000 ohm adjustable resistor	.28
2.2 meg resistor	.017
27 K ohm resistor	.017
1.5 K ohm resistor	.017
1N3755 diode	.24
35274 transistor	.28
Terminals	.072
NE 2 neon bulbs	.058
Terminal board	.036
3 brass screws	.029
6 brass nuts	.058
	$3.724

LABOR AND OVERHEAD:

Labor	.30
Freight	.05
Wastage	.05
Employees tax insurance	.09
Advertising	.02
Package box	.06
	$ .57
Burden = 100%	.57
Plus 12% profit	.15
	$5.01

INSTALLATION KIT:

Wire	.27
Terminals	.074
	.34
Total COST Per Unit	$5.35

* Cost per unit in thousand unit quantities.

NOTE: A Federal excise tax of 8% had been set by the government on the Blink-Off. Mr. Burson paid this out of the $6.95 selling price.

---

3. BOBBY RIVERS SPORTSWEAR, INCORPORATED

"MANY PEOPLE, EVEN SOME OF my competitors, have asked me why I ever located this company in Maryhill. The answer is quite simple. When the agitators struck the plant run by Axel Smith up in Dallas, he decided that the best solution to his problem was to close down and sell his assets and retire. Since I was sales manager for him, he offered me the opportunity to buy, so I formed this company ten years ago with two associates and purchased all the assets from Smith. Since I grew up in Maryhill and knew the people that lived there, I decided to locate my business there. After all, it's only a two hour drive to Dallas, where an active ladies-wear market is well established. Frankly, I like the isolation of a small town, and I am happy with the kind of labor I can find here to work in my plant."

"I believe," continued H. H. Fancher, the president and general manager of Bobby Rivers Sportswear, "that being located in a small town has fewer disadvantages than advantages, at least as far as we are concerned. The only real disadvantage I know of is the need to plan our requirements carefully so that we have all the supplies and so forth that we need. In effect, it takes at least a full day to get what we need from Dallas if it's available there, and it usually is. If not, we may be in trouble."

Company Background

Bobby Rivers Sportswear had prospered from its first year of operation. First year (1953) sales of $275,000 were followed by a steady growth to a peak of $1,300,000 in 1960. Thereafter, sales fluctuated around the $1,000,000 level.

Because of Mr. Fancher's long background in sales and close working relationships with the ladies wear buyers of a large dry goods chain operation, Bobby Rivers Sportswear found its first markets with the chain, and continued to sell close to 80 percent of its output to the chain for distribution to its many outlets throughout the United States.

All capital stock in the company was owned by the three founders. Mr. Fancher, owner of 65 percent of the stock, assumed responsibility as the general manager, and supervised all activities related to design, production, sales, finance and personnel. Mr. Dunning, with a 25 percent ownership, was responsible for miscellaneous activities in the plant, such as shipping, receiving, and maintenance. Mr. Archer, a brother-in-law of Mr. Fancher, and a son of the former owner, held 10 percent of the stock but took no part in the management of the company.

Each partner drew a salary as their main source of income. Dividends were distributed on a conservative basis.

At an output level of approximately $1 million, employment varied from 90 to 100 employees, with a direct labor payroll of between $200,000 and $220,000 annually. At least 90 percent of the employees resided within a 5-mile radius of the factory. The remaining 10 percent lived in rural settlements within 15 miles of the factory. One other garment manufacturer and a toy manufacturer comprised the only significant employers in the community. Mr. Fancher estimated that in 1963 there were less than 25 persons available for employment in the immediate area who were capable of being trained if needed for employment in the sewing departments of any one of the three major employers in Maryhill.

Profitability

Financial and operating results were considered highly confidential. Bobby Rivers Sportswear was admittedly operating profitably, and the rate of profit was generally comparable to that of other garment firms in the state. Whenever sales were in the 8300 dozen garment range annually, profits were comparable to the industry average of approximately 3.5 percent margin on sales, after taxes.

Fancher was troubled by the impending increase in hourly wage rates and payroll taxes in 1963. "It is," he declared, "a lot harder to make a profit in this business today than it was 10 years ago when we started in Maryhill. Then we paid $0.75 per hour to production workers, and piece goods costing $0.80 were made up into a dress wholesaling at $8.75. Today, the same $8.75 sales comes from $1.15 piece goods and $1.15 per hour labor, plus higher social security taxes, postal and freight rates."

Production Process

The designer made the style and drew up the original pattern. Then a pattern girl graded the pattern up or down for different sizes and made different size patterns. The marker girls fitted the pattern to cloth to obtain the least yardage per garment. Fancher stressed the fact that, "That's what makes your money." Fancher made out "cut sheets" which were used to order the correct number of cuts to fill the size and color requirements for a particular style. These "cut sheets" were given to a cutter who stacked piece goods in alternate colors (to prevent shading), stapled markers to piece goods to prevent shifting, and cut out pieces with an electric cutting knife. A stack of piece goods could be cut out for 100 to 500 dresses at once.

Goods were bundled by size and color (all 8's, all 10's, etc. of one color together), and the correct cuts of interlining for that number of dresses were included. Each bundle was numbered, and these bundles were issued to sewing operators. The supervisor had a master book in which she recorded the bundles as they were given to sewers. The employee number, bundle number, part number, amount, style number and color were recorded in the master book which also logged each bundle through each operation. Each girl maintained record cards of what work she had done, and these cards were checked with the master book. All operations had part numbers (i.e., sleeves #6, blouses #7, etc.). The master book provided a record of who did what work, and what rate they were supposed to get per garment or per dozen garments. Operations were highly specialized in that one operator performed one operation only, such as pinking, hemming, making button holes, etc. It was believed that only by rigid specialization could maximum efficiency in production be realized in the minimum of training or "breaking-in" time.

Because of the considerable degree to which tasks had been simplified under the line production system used, most of the jobs in the plant could be performed by relatively unskilled female workers. However, to perform the various tasks at allowed times required a fairly high level of motor skill, which was developed only from training and repetition. Almost all of the employees hired were inexperienced, even though willing to work. Mr. Fancher estimated that in excess of one month of training time was required to get the average inexperienced operator up to standard output and standard quality, and to a point where she was able to function with a minimum of direct supervision.

Standard output was not determined from formal time studies. Based upon his own long experience, plus the fact that the basic operations performed changed very little from one year to the next, Mr. Fancher was confident that he could estimate standards to a satisfactory degree of accuracy. Any discrepancies would presumably be noticed by the one experienced sewing line supervisor.

Bottlenecks in the flow of work tended to occur on occasion because of the absence of a key worker for whom there was no fully trained substitute, or because of the breakdown of a critical machine. Mr. Fancher felt that they were not large enough to support a fully-trained specialist mechanic, so when complicated machines like the button-holer required servicing, either the machine was rushed to Dallas for service or a specially trained mechanic was called from Dallas. Simple jobs could be handled by their own general maintenance man.

Inspection was performed at four points in the production process.

The bolts of material were inspected visually at the time they were laid out in layers on the cutting tables preliminary to the cutting operation. After sewing, seams were inspected when trimmed and threads were clipped. Later, the pressers were expected to check for spots or stains or other flaws which might be present. A final inspection was performed by the packer when he prepared garments for shipping.

Flawed garments were seldom reworked; instead, in conformity with industry practice, they were sold as "seconds" or "rejects" at cut prices.

Judging from the very few returned garments and the relatively small percentage of rejects, Mr. Fancher considered his quality control and inspection procedures quite satisfactory. Less than one percent of units produced were faulty.

Scheduling of Production

The problems encountered in scheduling of production could be divided into three types. Fancher alone handled all scheduling, basing his decisions upon his personal experience and feel for the problem.

The master production schedule was decided by Fancher twice a year for each "season." Based upon an intuitive feel of the market developed from 22 years of selling experience plus 10 years of general management, he was confident that he could guess the probable total sales demand for the garments, if not for individual colors and sizes. Because their key customer was primarily interested in a fixed quality level at a fixed, minimum price, and ordered fairly large quantities at one time, Fancher was able to set his production schedule with considerable assurance as far as basic styles were concerned. Changes, of course, had to be made as reports of sales established which were the better sellers and which were not. Detailed schedules were then altered to reflect specific demand patterns for styles, colors and sizes.

Frequently changed schedules, combined with layout and cutting mistakes, sometimes resulted in fabric shortages. Difficulty was encountered in reordering specific patterns or weaves from suppliers since most fabrics were produced on a one-run basis. To compensate for the possible fabric shortage, Fancher formerly had ordered more of each type of fabric than was expected to be needed. The costs of such overpurchases became prohibitive and, although Fancher took pride in the company's reputation of meeting all promised orders, a policy was adopted to fall short on certain orders and refuse some reorders rather than to continue the extra costs of buying possible excess fabrics.

In setting weekly schedules for particular styles, care had to be exercised to maintain a balance because certain styles required more time on particular operations than others. For example, a shirtwaist required many more buttonholes than most other dresses. Fancher attempted to balance the scheduling of particular styles in any one day so as to keep all of the girls working at approximately the same pace. Rescheduling also was necessary occasionally to avoid disruptions from the absence of a key worker or a key machine, or because of materials or supplies delayed in transit to Maryhill.

On at least one occasion, when Fancher was on an out-of-state sales trip, the company was unable to accept a large reorder because of the lack of authority of the minority stockholders to make decisions concerning large purchases of fabrics. In this case, the supplier had the desired fabric in stock.

The third type of scheduling problem faced by Fancher occurred only when current sales exceeded an annual rate of 8300 dozen dresses, which was the normal capacity of the plant on a one-shift basis. Translated into dollars, an annual sales volume of $1,000,000 was the capacity of the plant. Because Fancher was disinclined to expand the facilities or add a second shift, he chose to sub-contract sewing of garments to two nearby independent contract shops. The company delivered the necessary piece goods and patterns, and received the garments in a finished condition. All sub-contract work was inspected, invoiced, and shipped from Maryhill to customers.

Inspection of contract work often showed a much lower quality of workmanship than that considered acceptable at the Bobby Rivers plant. For this reason, Fancher tried to keep orders within the capacity of the Maryhill factory. The lack of suitable facilities to produce over $1 million worth of garments caused Fancher to reject feelers for a large contract business with a second dry goods chain rather than chance sacrificing the quality image of his line of goods.

Marketing

The company attempted to serve only a limited segment of the ladies ready-to-wear market. Their goal was to produce dresses and suits, using basic, popular fabrics, designed to sell in the medium low-price range. No high-style garments were included in the line, hence the styles produced tended to have more permanency, which in turn resulted in greater emphasis on cost and quality.

Styles authorized for production by Fancher tended toward the more simple and basic, with emphasis on the casual effect. Higher styled garments were frequently proposed by the designer, but not accepted by Fancher.

Fancher felt that much of his success was due to his ability to supply quality goods within specified time deadlines. Many manufacturers in the industry were lax in meeting contractural agreements which sometimes resulted in costly delays or gaps in the product lines of retailers. Fancher made many sales because of his reputation for high integrity.

Dresses and suits tended to have customary retail price levels for given levels of styles, quality of material, quality of workmanship, and so forth. The retail price range aimed for by the company was from $8.95 to $29.95, which resulted in a wholesale price range of $5.75 to $16.75 per garment.

The designing process began with the selection of a retail price for the garment. The selected retail price thus determined the wholesale price and the target cost of the garment. The designer then selected materials, style details, zippers, buttons, and other features to conform to the cost limitation previously established.

Mr. Fancher often wondered about the future course the company was going to take. While he was not disappointed in the progress which had been made to date, the fact that his sales had stabilized at a $1 million annual volume disturbed him a little whenever he found time to reflect on the situation.

The most disturbing change as far as his future was concerned was the rapid expansion of a few large firms into a size he had thought impossible only a few years ago. While his company did not directly compete against these giant firms in the ladies garment market, he recognized that the day might soon come when he had to compete directly with them. If so, he was well aware that he would have to expand considerably and build an effective management team, rather than rely on a one-man controlled operation, which was essentially the case at present.

Suitable sources of capital were a major consideration for expansion, in addition to finding or developing qualified management to assist him. The local bank was able to meet his working capital needs only by calling on a larger correspondent bank in Dallas. The line of credit given to the company was judged to be adequate to support a maximum annual sales volume of about $2 million. If sales were to exceed $2 million within the next two or three years, additional equity capital would have to be raised. Mr. Fancher was presently not inclined to reduce his ownership below 50 percent, and he did not want to liquidate the small investments he had outside the company in order to raise the $100,000 in equity capital he estimated was necessary to permit rapid expansion to a $2–$3 million annual sales level, and still maintain at least 51 percent ownership for himself.

Mr. Fancher expressed confidence that if he chose to take the risk, he could increase his sales volume to $10 million annually within 10 years.

The expansion, although no real plans had ever been made, would be accomplished, in his opinion, largely by the acquisition of existing companies, several of which he knew were for sale. Mr. Fancher further expressed the belief that with the proper lines, he could get over $5 million in annual sales to one buyer alone, without trying to sell to more than one chain or even to other regional buyers for the same chain store which was his best customer.

He estimated that the entire group of stores in the chain purchased between $50–$60 million worth of the type of garments which his company manufactured.

4. CAPITOL CASKET COMPANY

VIGOROUS COMPETITION IN THE CASKET market was one of the many concerns of Robert Shoop, President and General Manager of Capitol Casket Company of Austin, Texas, in late 1963. The Company had experienced steady growth since its founding in 1952, but intense competition made it difficult to generate sufficient capital to support expanded operations. Major competitors were substantially larger than Capitol, and many in the Middle West reportedly had made significant progress in automating their operations. Shoop believed that his production costs were close to those of his competitors, and he was certain that his labor costs were as low or lower. In spite of competition, Shoop was determined to increase Capitol's share of the expanding market in the Southwest.

Background

Capitol Casket Company was organized by Mr. Shoop in 1952. Prior to that time he had been a supervisory employee of a large casket manufacturer in the southeast United States. At a bankruptcy sale he purchased the physical assets of a former casket manufacturer in Austin. With a minimum of capital, two operating companies were formed. One of these, the Southwest Casket Shell Company, produced unfinished wooden casket shells. The other, Capitol Casket Company, purchased shells, finished them into completed caskets, and marketed them throughout the Southwest.

When the demand for metal caskets became apparent, Capitol began to purchase metal shells from a distant supplier. By 1955, the decision was made to switch to metal caskets (except for special order wood models). As a result, Southwest Casket Shell was absorbed into Capitol and surplus wood-working equipment was sold. Tools needed to cut, weld, and finish sheet metal were purchased; and shells were fabricated by Capitol. Casket tops which required special forming operations were purchased from outside suppliers, as were all metal fittings. Equipment to form casket tops was purchased in November 1963. Thereafter, tops were formed by Capitol.

Marketing

A broad line of caskets was produced and sold directly to mortuaries throughout the Southwest. The market was considered to be highly competitive, and all merchandise was sold on a delivered basis. Because of low profit margins, delivery costs tended to limit Capitol's primary market to a three-hundred mile radius. Sales were made as far as four hundred miles north of Austin and fifteen hundred miles west of Austin. Major emphasis was on the area to the west because the most active competition was to the north and east of Austin.

Market potential was estimated by Mr. Shoop from mortality data for Texas and the four neighboring states. Based upon such estimates, Capitol's share of the overall market averaged between 4½ to 5 percent in 1962 and approached 7 percent in 1963. Sales were forecast for a year in advance, by quarters, based upon Mr. Shoop's estimate of probable mortality rates and expected market penetration. He considered his estimates of sales volume to be sufficiently accurate for purposes of general planning, but he was unable to predict demand for particular styles with sufficient accuracy to permit production for stock except for a very limited number of caskets.

The line of caskets to be marketed was established once each year. Styles and design features were retained so long as they sold well. As styles c⁻ design features were dropped, others were added to take their place. Basic styles were obtained from a professional design source; and other ideas were obtained from a trade association, from Mr. Shoop's attendance at conventions, and from his wide contacts in the industry.

Sales were made primarily by direct representation of commission sales persons and Mr. Shoop. No mail or telephone solicitation was used. A limited amount of wholesaling was carried on with small competitors.

The product line was concentrated largely in the middle and lower price ranges. Little attempt was made to compete in the very low and the very high price ranges for finished caskets. Capitol's line of caskets consisted of fourteen basic steel shell styles in the adult size and a more limited variety in non-adult sizes.

Additional variations in completed caskets were possible in respect to exterior colors (15), handle and exterior hardware design (50 varieties in three different finishes), and in interior fittings (more than ten different styles, which could be made from several different materials, and in a limited variety of colors).

An analysis of orders indicated that approximately 50 percent of all orders were for a very limited variety of caskets. As a result, the most popular styles were classified as production models which were produced on a regularly scheduled basis. When orders were received for "production models," they were normally filled out of inventory, or partially completed caskets were assigned to specific orders; and these were generally completed and shipped within 24 hours.

Other orders were classified as custom orders; and these could be filled in from three to five days, depending upon the availability of needed models of shells and the number of orders ahead in painting and finishing. Ordinarily, customizing usually began with the painting operation, followed by the selection of special hardware and a special design and color for the interior fittings.

Production Process

Welded steel caskets make up over 90 percent of Capitol Casket's production. Twenty-gauge zinc-plated steel sheets were purchased at rail carload prices from a steel supply company which warehoused the steel in a nearby city and delivered it to Capitol in truck-load quantities as needed. Approximately ten percent of the sheet steel purchased had been preformed by a stamping plant into the shape necessary for the casket tops, prior to November 1963 when the Company purchased metal-forming equipment to form casket tops in its own plant. Purchase of necessary equipment had been scheduled as soon as increased sales volume justified the additional investment. The Company believed that they could form casket tops with their new equipment at an annual cost saving of about eight percent. Because of low gross profit margins, the probable saving, while small, was considered sufficient to justify the investment commitment. No formal rate of return computations were made, however.

Steel sheets were sheared to shape and tack welded to form the basic shell, and the seams were then completely welded to seal the casket. To attach the tops, hinges were spot welded to both the shell and the top. Wooden strips were bolted to the inside walls of the casket so that the fabric interior could be stapled in place.

To prepare the casket for painting, the welded seams were sanded smooth; and the surface was cleaned and primed, hand sanded, reprimed and sanded again. The exposed surfaces were sprayed with a metalescent (aluminum base) finish; then a coat of clear lacquer was applied and allowed to dry overnight before a final buffing operation was performed.

To complete the exterior, the handles and other decorative hardware were bolted on the shell. Approximately fifty different sets of hardware styles and colors were purchased and kept in stock. Some of the hardware sets were "exclusive" with Capitol Casket in the Southwest because of their participation in a nation-wide trade group (composed of non-competitors) which had developed dies and molds of exclusive design for the manufacture of hardware by subcontractors. Hardware from these dies was made available only to members of the trade group.

Fabric interiors of specified designs were prepared in a sewing room. The material for the interiors (fabric, padding, etc.) was purchased from a textile converter specializing in "casket" textiles. The fabric was first cut to a pattern by one of the workers and passed on to others who basted and sewed the materials on standard commercial sewing machines into the specified shape and design. The interior "package" was hung on a wire hanger, along with an identifying ticket, in the finishing department until it was ready to be installed by a skilled fitter. Completed caskets were made ready for shipment by packing either (1) in a wooden or fiber board carton if sent by common carrier, or (2) in a paper cover if shipped by company truck.

A breakdown of the labor cost as a percentage of total labor cost of the various production steps and the approximate time required to perform each department's operations are shown in Tables I and II, respectively. Figures shown were abstracted from company records by Mr. Shoop.

TABLE I

DISTRIBUTION OF DIRECT LABOR COST

OPERATION	PERCENT OF TOTAL
Press (metal cutting and forming)	10.97
Assembly	28.57
Prime & Sand	7.38
Paint	16.78
Sew	18.43
Trim	9.35
Box and Ship (includes company-employed truck driver)	8.48
Total direct labor	100.00

All manufacturing, storage, and office activities were conducted in a single-story modern plant. The manufacturing area was laid out on a straight-line basis to eliminate back hauling. The existing plant was judged

TABLE II
LABOR TIME REQUIRED TO PRODUCE A STANDARD CASKET

PROCESSES	TIME (MAN-HOURS)
Weld, assemble and sand	4
Clean, wood, prime, sand and paint[1]	2
Rub out, and apply hardware	2
Trim	2
Sew interior[2]	3
Box and ship	1
Total	14

[1] Painted units were always allowed to dry overnight (a minimum of eight hours), hence the production cycle was somewhat longer than the man-hours total.

[2] Sewing was done concurrently with other processes and was therefore not a limiting time factor.

adequate to permit an expansion of about 50 percent before any major adjustment in facilities would be necessary.

Order Scheduling

In order to maintain a reasonably even work load for his production employees and to maintain what he believed to be a desirable inventory of finished and semi-finished goods, Capitol Casket typically scheduled 100 caskets into production each week in 1963. Regular production of that number of units provided for a small stock build-up during slack sales periods sufficient to provide for the several seasonal peak sales periods with no substantial increase in the production rate. Overtime for production workers was scheduled only in periods of unusual sales demand or in the case of large special rush orders.

In the absence of a special-order production model, caskets were finished according to a standard schedule and kept in inventory until needed to fill orders. Typically, nearly 50 percent of the orders were filled directly from finished or almost-finished inventory. The remaining 50 percent were special or custom orders which required special features not usually available in inventory.

Sales orders were relayed to the office by commissioned salesmen in the territory, by orders received directly from mortuaries, or from one of Mr. Shoop's frequent sales trips. Upon receipt of the order a five-part order form was typed. The order form specified the casket number and size, finish or covering, interior color and material, interior design, hardware and shipping carton.

Use of the order form conformed to the following procedure:

Copy 1 (white) of the order form would accompany the casket to the mortuary and serve as a re-order form.

Copy 2 (yellow) was used as a production order for the sewing and fitting departments and, subsequently, as a shipping label for the packaged casket.

Copy 3 (pink) went to the shop to initiate production of the particular casket ordered. If the order specified a standard shell size, the shell would already have been assembled according to standing production orders; and "customizing" would begin with the painting operation.

Copy 4 (gold) served as a delivery receipt if the casket was shipped by company truck. If it was shipped by commercial carrier, the standard bill of lading was used as a shipping receipt; and the gold copy notified the office that the order had been shipped.

Copy 5 (green) was retained in the office as a record that the casket was in process.

Production Costs

Provided they kept costs under tight control, their only real problem was a marketing problem, according to Mr. Shoop. The manufacturing process could be handled quite adequately by reasonably skilled personnel and did not require a great deal of personal attention by him once the procedure was well established. He commented on his control over labor costs without piece rates as follows:

> When Capitol Casket went off the piece-rate, wage-payment system, a simple system of time control was inaugurated. Although a worker was paid on an hourly basis, he was required to record on a time card his beginning and ending time for each casket. We found that the psychological effect of actually accounting for what is accomplished each hour of the day keeps an employee on his toes. We review these cards periodically; and when we see that there are problem areas, we can come back and see what has been happening (and then see what is happening in the current week). The only jobs which were on piece rates were welding, soldering, and assembling. The reason for that situation is that we started the piece rates with an associated company, Southwest Casket Shell. We changed over to complete production of metal caskets when we absorbed Southwest (formerly we had produced only complete wood caskets; and we kept the welding, soldering, and assembly jobs on piece rates because the time studies were already available; but we didn't have time studies for the new jobs and had to put them temporarily on straight time. Our piece rates then were competitive with the high-production plants in the Middle West). This opinion is from factual information I gained from conversation with the people that operated those big plants.
>
> You may wonder why we went off piece rates when our rates were

competitive. The answer is fairly simple; and I do not regret my decision because when we went off the piece-rate system and returned to an hourly wage-payment system a couple of years ago, I would estimate that our productivity increased by 20 percent. We were definitely having trouble with the former system. A lot of people don't recognize the fact that while a piece-rate system establishes a maximum labor cost, it also establishes a minimum cost. In addition, we were forced with a reoccurring problem because as you increase the efficiency of the methods you are using in an operation, it becomes necessary to reduce the piece rate accordingly. Also, since we were engaged in interstate commerce and the wage-and-hour officials ruled that employees working on a straight piece rate must be paid time and a half for "overtime" work, this had the effect of requiring one and a half times the piece rate we had set for all pieces produced in any overtime period. Trying to determine what pieces were produced during the hours worked in any one week in excess of forty hours was a complicated situation for a small manufacturer like us with an absolute minimum of staff. We simply discontinued the piece-rate system; and as I mentioned previously, our labor cost has decreased about 20 percent since then. Possibly one of the reasons was because the employees were much happier without piece rates, especially since all of them were not under piece rates anyway.

Direct supervision over production in the plant was provided by four working supervisors. General production was supervised by Mr. Shoop when he was in the plant. He estimated that about twenty-five percent of his time was spent in supervision of production, twenty-five percent in other administration duties, and fifty percent in sales and promotion. Mr. Shoop considered the costs of the three office persons (including all of his own salary) as administrative costs, and the wages of the production workers as direct factory costs. In order to keep company cost records as simple as possible, the cost of the time spent by Mr. Shoop in supervising production, and the small differential in supervisors' pay, and the two to three percent of labor time spent on maintenance and clean-up were not recorded as factory indirect labor cost. Mr. Shoop felt that since he was aware of the small difference involved, it was not necessary to complicate the cost records with allocations for factory indirect labor. A Production Labor Cost Report was prepared weekly which summarized direct labor costs incurred. A copy of the report form is shown in Exhibit I.

Inventory

Control over inventories was considered by Mr. Shoop to be of major importance to the continued success of his enterprise. Due to relatively limited capital, a close watch was maintained over the total investment in inventories. Based largely upon an intuitive feel for the casket market, plus his forecasts of total demand based upon mortality rates, Shoop periodically determined what his inventories of finished caskets, semi-finished caskets and casket shells, along with the necessary fabrics, hardware, and miscellaneous supplies should be. The total investment was, of course, limited by the company's line of credit with a local bank.

In spite of the wide variety possible in finished caskets, it was necessary to attempt to forecast models, styles, and colors which would sell best in order to have the minimum possible finished goods inventory, yet be able to meet rush demands by customers. Competitive pressures generally required the filling of rush orders within twenty-four hours.

Mr. Shoop recognized that it was impossible to forecast the market, especially in regard to styles and colors, without a considerable degree of error. On an overall basis, inventory was turned five times a year in dollar value. On individual items, inventory turnover varied from fourteen days to over six months. In general the more expensive items turned much slower than the less expensive items.

Basic shells were produced on a relatively fixed schedule; and the inventory of completed basic shells (less hardware and less paint) was normally maintained at 100 units, or the equivalent of one week's production. Painted shells were also held in inventory with a bank equal to one week's production.

Hardware and fabrics were typically purchased in the smallest quantities which would permit quantity discounts. Inventories were limited to approximately thirty days' supply, although a constant watch was necessary to prevent unbalanced stocking of individual styles or fabrics, especially of the more expensive lines. Because of the flexible arrangement with their steel sheet supplier, inventories of sheet steel typically averaged about thirty days' supply. Miscellaneous supplies, such as bolts, screws, paint, lumber, staples, packaging materials, and so forth were typically maintained at levels equal to one month's production requirements.

Objectives

When asked about the objectives for the company, Mr. Shoop replied that his objectives might be stated as follows: "to provide a means of livelihood for my family and myself, to provide an expression of an outlet for my abilities and efforts, and to be a credit to the employees, customers, and community." In a more specific vein, he stated that his goal was to capture 20 percent of the available market in his primary trade territory. At the present, Capitol held about 7 percent; and it ranked about fifth in size among more than twenty manufacturers in Texas. A collateral goal was to become the most integrated producer of caskets in the trade territory. The acquisition of metal-forming equipment in November 1963 was a major step toward realization of this goal. Further steps toward integration would conceivably lead into a wholesaling supply activity, and into hardware manufacturing.

EXHIBIT I

PRODUCTION LABOR COST REPORT

Week Ending _____ 1963

	CURRENT WEEK			MONTH TO DATE	
	# UNITS PRODUCED	LABOR COST	AVERAGE LABOR COST	# UNITS PRODUCED	LABOR COST
PRODUCTION					
Press Room					
Assembly					
Prime					
Paint					
Sew					
Metals Trimmed					
Wood Trimmed					
Shipping Labor					
TOTAL LABOR					
SALES TO DATE					

5. COUSINS PROPERTIES (A)*

1. Nature of the Operations

MR. THOMAS G. COUSINS IS engaged in the business of residential real estate development. Through the various corporations which serve as the basis of his operations, Mr. Cousins purchases tracts of raw land which he improves and subdivides into residential home lots. In these tracts of land appropriate areas are set aside for shopping centers, schools, churches, and apartments. After the land has been improved and subdivided, Mr.

---

* This case was prepared by Professor Albert H. Clark of Georgia State College.

Cousins then either builds and sells single family homes in the $10,000 to $35,000 range on the improved lots, or sells the lots to other builders or individual purchasers. The commercial property is likewise either built upon by Mr. Cousins or sold to other builders and developers. Mr. Cousins, with only minor exceptions, does not engage in speculative building of homes for sale, but generally starts construction only after an individual home buyer has purchased the lot, obtained permanent mortgage financing, and has entered into a construction agreement with one of Mr. Cousins' companies. In the construction of homes, prefabricated house packages are used extensively. In addition to the above operations, one of Mr. Cousins' corporations consists of an insurance agency. Insurance sales of this corporation consist primarily of the sales of "Homeowners" insurance policies to purchasers of the homes which Mr. Cousins sells.

The main operations of the company are comprised of the acquisition, development, and sale of land, and the construction and sale of homes. The company acquires raw land, subdivides it into lots, and makes improvements such as paved roads, curbs, sewers, and facilities for water and other utilities. The land acquired by the company is usually purchased for small initial payments with specified annual payments with terms of from one to ten years, and with interest on unpaid balances at rates ranging from 5% to 8% per annum. The unpaid balances are secured by purchase money mortgages which are general obligations of the company and which normally allow prepayment without penalty. Upon payment of a stipulated amount per acre or per lot, the company is entitled to have the acreage or lots covered by the payment released from the encumbrance of the mortgage.

The company uses its own employees in its development operations as well as consulting engineers and professional land planners for designing and planning its subdivisions and the improvements. The improvements are sometimes financed by borrowed funds covered by encumbrances on the improved land, and are made by independent contractors pursuant to bids. In the case of larger contracts, labor and material payment and performance bonds are furnished.

In addition to selling lots in connection with its sale of homes, the company also sells developed and undeveloped tracts of land to other builders and developers. A portion of land in some of the tracts which the company holds is reserved for possible future commercial development or possible sites for apartments, and the company holds this land for investment. Later this land will be sold or developed by the company. Sales of such land have not produced any material gross revenue in the past.

The company's building activities to date have been exclusively in the Atlanta metropolitan area. Until the spring of 1961 the company contracted with independent contractors to build the homes it sold. Since that time the company has taken over the functions formerly handled by independent contractors except for such functions as land grading, foundations, concrete work, plumbing, electricity, heating, roofing, painting, sheet rock, flooring, and landscaping. The company generally employs its own supervision personnel. The prices of homes sold by the company range from $10,000 to $35,000. The homes contain from 915 to 2,200 square feet of living area, three to four bedrooms, one to three baths, and various built-in kitchen appliances, and they are entirely completed and ready for occupancy before delivery to the homeowner.

The company's method of operation in selling homes is to make land improvements in a portion of a subdivision and then to build two to six model homes for display to the public. The model homes are landscaped and with the assistance of interior decorators are attractively furnished. The company begins its sales promotion program based primarily on radio and newspaper advertising, and the company's sales force of six persons conducts its selling operations from the model homes. This sales force is augmented by additional part-time personnel during special promotions such as openings of model homes. The purchaser is offered the choice of several models and variations with respect to each model. The prospective buyer selects his lot and home style and makes a nominal deposit pending closing of the purchase.

In the case of approximately 75% of the company's sales of homes, the ultimate purchaser simultaneously purchases an improved lot from the company, executes an agreement with the company for the construction of the home, and obtains a permanent mortgage loan disbursable to the company during construction, thus eliminating the necessity for a separate construction loan. In this manner the company reduces the risk generally incurred by speculative builders. In a few instances in the past, the company has constructed homes which it has contracted to sell to purchasers who had commitments for permanent mortgage loans from lending institutions, financing the costs of construction with construction loans. Since 1959 less than 15% of the homes constructed by the company (including model homes) have been built speculatively. Most of such speculative homes (other than model homes) have been built on lots which are difficult to sell. The company has found that such lots become more attractive when homes have been built on them and all grading and landscaping have been completed. The model homes generally have been sold to the public after 6 to 12 months of use.

The company facilitates sales by making arrangements prior to selling for Federal Housing Administration ("FHA") insured mortgage loans, Veterans Administration ("VA") guaranteed mortgage loans, or "conventional" mortgage loans to be made to ultimate purchasers by savings and loan associations and other financial institutions in the business of making residential mortgage loans. Approximately 80% of the homes sold by the company have been financed by FHA or VA mortgages and the balance have been financed by "conventional" mortgages which are not supported by FHA insurance or VA guaranty.

FHA and VA commitments for insuring or guaranteeing mortgage loans may be secured only after meeting certain requirements, specifications and inspection standards established by such Government agencies. Similar but different requirements and specifications must be met in order to obtain conventional mortgage loans. The company processes substantially all customers' applications for mortgage loans. The company's sale of homes depends in large part on its continued ability to arrange for permanent financing for its customers.

The company warrants for one year the sound construction of each home it builds and assigns personnel to provide customer services under these warranties.

2. Nature of the Problem

Early in the operations of Mr. Cousins' business ventures, an accounting firm which he employed convinced him that as far as possible he should arrange his ventures on the basis of establishing a separate corporation for each operation. The idea here, argued the accountants, was to have several small corporations in order to save on federal income tax. They pointed out that the first $25,000 of the earnings of a corporation is taxed at a rate of only 30%. This idea seemed to work fine until the number of ventures began to grow very rapidly. By early 1961 there were eleven small corporations in existence, and in the words of Mr. Cousins, "it was just about at the point of driving everybody crazy keeping track of the money. One corporation had the money and the other one didn't. They were swapping money back and forth and everybody was confused, especially the bookkeepers involved in the operations."

3. Background of the Operations

The first corporation was formed by Mr. Cousins in April 1958 with an initial investment of $3,000. This business was originally a part-time activity of Mr. Cousins, who had been employed since January 1955 by Knox Homes Corporation as a salesman of prefabricated house packages to builders in the Atlanta area. Mr. Cousins, who has always possessed a burning desire to be in business for himself, graduated from the University of Georgia in 1952, receiving the degree of Bachelor of Business Administration. His grades in college reflected those of an average student, but he accounts for this by the fact that he was probably more interested in social activities than in books. He did find time, however, to make the varsity swimming team and earn an athletic letter in this sport. After college graduation, he was obliged to serve two years in the Air Force, as he had received a lieutenant's commission through R.O.T.C. while in college. The major portion of his time in the Air Force was spent as a squadron administrative officer at an air base near Tokyo, Japan. However, while stationed at an air base near Lincoln, Nebraska, during the last few months of his tour of duty, Mr. Cousins had an opportunity to test his ability to sell and apply his initiative in the business world. Through an acquaintance, he met a general agent of a medium-sized life insurance company. In the course of conversation the general agent recognized Mr. Cousins' inborn free enterprising spirit and invited him to try his hand at selling life insurance. Almost immediately he became a successful part-time life insurance salesman by using the technique of approaching prospects during his off-duty hours at night and on weekends.

This brief experience in life insurance selling only whetted Mr. Cousins' appetite to plunge into the business world and try his enterprising talents on a full-time basis. When he was relieved from active duty with the Air Force in September 1954 Mr. Cousins felt that he needed time to think and carefully plan his future course of action. However, he did not want to waste his time during this planning and exploring stage, so he returned to the University of Georgia and enrolled in the graduate business program, partly to take some specific courses he had missed during undergraduate school, but mainly so that he would have time to explore various approaches of getting into a phase of the business world that would give him maximum opportunities.

One of the first problems which he had to face up to was the fact that he had little or no accumulated savings. During his Air Force days he had saved very little money. He found that the G. I. bill and his remuneration from his short venture in the life insurance business was enough to tide him over during this exploration period. However, it became evident that by the first of the year (1955) he must have definite plans made. Not only would his money be exhausted by then, but his burning desire to get into the business world was mounting daily.

During the fall of 1954 while in graduate school Mr. Cousins made frequent trips to Atlanta, which is 65 miles from Athens where the state university is located, talking to various top-level people of several different fields in business. Although he had had successful experience in the life insurance field, he felt that this field would not afford him the unlimited opportunity he was seeking. He seriously considered the investment banking and securities field; however, here again his desire to become the head of his own business as soon as possible steered him away from this business.

Finally, Mr. Cousins settled upon the idea that real estate developing was probably best suited to his ambitions and goals. The next question was what is the best approach to getting started. He considered simply going with one of the large real estate brokerage firms in Atlanta as a salesman. Most of these concerns were also involved in various phases of residential and commercial development work. He felt, however, that he should get into a phase of real estate that would bring him closer to the mechanics of development and financing.

Prior to Christmas holidays at the university Mr. Cousins ran into a friend he had known in his undergraduate days who had taken a job with Knox Homes Corporation, which is located in a small town in middle Georgia, for a few years and was a sales manager. The Knox company was looking for a few new salesmen to call on builders. Mr. Cousins struck upon the idea that this might be a good approach to learn the real estate development business. Early in January 1955 Mr. Cousins visited the Knox home office and after some negotiations he decided to join the firm on the terms that they would give him the Atlanta metropolitan area territory, automobile expenses, a monthly salary of $300, and a sliding scale commission of ¼% to 2% on all of his sales. The prefabricated house packages were priced to the builders in a general range from $2,500 to $4,000.

Mr. Cousins soon found that there were obstacles which he had to overcome in selling prefabricated house packages. Mainly it was a matter of educating the builders to the new idea in home production and pointing out all of the cost advantages thereof. He found his work very discouraging at first, to say the least. Although he did not sell one house package during the first six months he learned a great deal about all phases of real estate development and financing, and he gradually educated many builders in his area to the advantages of using the prefabricated approach to building. Both of the above phases of education were to pay off handsomely almost immediately.

By the latter part of 1955, mostly due to Mr. Cousins' persistent efforts, the prefabricated house package idea began to catch on among the builders in the Atlanta area. Sales, however, did not start to increase rapidly until mid-1956. But by mid-1957, Mr. Cousins was proving himself as the top salesman of the Knox Homes Corporation. In September of 1957 because of his apparent selling success, Knox made Mr. Cousins sales manager for the State of Georgia territory, and in February of 1959 he was made Vice-President of Knox Homes Corporation in charge of all sales. Later in 1959 Knox Homes Corporation became a wholly-owned subsidiary of National Homes Corporation, the largest prefabricated home manufacturer in the country. Mr. Cousins remained as vice-president of Knox until March 1, 1960, when he resigned to devote full time to his own operations.

By early 1958, Mr. Cousins felt that the time had come for him to launch out into his own real estate development operations, at least on a small scale. He decided he should remain as Sales Manager for Knox Corporation and begin his venture only on a part-time basis. He felt that he had acquired enough knowledge of the business to start his own operation, and because of the commissions he was receiving from the territory's sales, he had managed to accumulate a few thousand dollars for the venture. Also, Mr. Cousins wanted to acquaint his father with the real estate business. The latter, who was in his late fifties, had retired from the automobile business a few years previous, and was willing to devote full time to his son's operations. The first corporation, formed in April 1958, was known as Brand-Name Homes, Inc. The young Mr. Cousins provided the capital, about $3,000, and the overall guidance, and his father was to be the administrative head of the organization. The stock of the corporation was divided between the two on a 50-50 basis. The company engaged in buying developed lots and building Knox homes, and employed outside real estate brokers to sell its houses. The company almost immediately turned into a successful venture by building and selling over fifty homes during 1959.

PINELAND FOREST SUBDIVISION

In September 1959, Mr. Cousins became attracted to a piece of property known as Mountain View Plaza in Forest Park which is a south-side suburb of Atlanta. The property was put on the market by a bank which had acquired it in foreclosure proceedings against a bankrupt developer. Being still employed by Knox Homes Corporation, Mr. Cousins felt that he should inform Peter Knox, the President of Knox Homes Corporation, of the venture and invite him to come in on the venture. The result was that in October 1959, Mountain View Plaza, Inc. was formed with 50% of the stock going each to Mr. Cousins and Mr. Knox in exchange for $5,000 capital from each party. In order to increase the working capital, extensive borrowing was incurred from James Talcot Co., a finance company, at a rate of 15% per annum. Since both Mr. Cousins and Mr. Knox were extremely busy with other activities, it was decided to bring Mr. Cousins' father into the corporation. The latter, who had about wound up the Brand-Name Homes operations by this time, was put on a salary basis and, in addition, Mr. Cousins sold his father one-half of his 50% stock interest in Mountain View Plaza at his cost. Consequently, the ownership of Mountain View Plaza was 50% Mr. Knox, 25% Mr. Cousins, and 25% Mr. Cousins' father.

It was at this point that Mr. Cousins' accountants advised the use of a multiple-corporate setup for carrying out the development, building, and sales operations that would be involved in the Mountain View Plaza venture. In order to carry out this approach, Pineland Builders, Inc. was formed in January of 1960 to perform the building operations. It was decided to use Brand-Name Homes, Inc., which was then about finished with its original project, as the selling organization. Mountain View Plaza, Inc. was to be the land owner and developer. Therefore, Mountain View developed the lots and sold them to Pineland Builders, who in turn built the houses and turned them over to Brand-Name Homes to sell on a commission basis. Since the development had about 20 acres of potential commercial property, a company was formed to hold this property for a long-term investment or possibly future commercial development. This property seemed ideally suited for a 200 apartment project site as well as three service stations. Consequently, in July 1960 Metropolitan Commercial Corporation was incorporated and, in turn, bought the 20 acres of land from Mountain View on a long-term note basis. This total operation became known as Pineland Forest Subdivision.

Pineland Forest turned out to be very successful and by early 1961 all but a very few of the lots had been built upon and sold to home-owners. In the meantime, Mr. Knox had sold three-fourths of his 50% interest in the above three corporations to his two sons Peter III and Boon Knox and a friend, W. A. Young, Controller of Knox Homes Corporation.

OAKCLIFF ESTATES SUBDIVISION

In mid-1959 Mr. Cousins spotted another attractive tract of land containing some 260 acres located on the northeast side of Atlanta. It was known as Oakcliff Estates. Although the land looked very appropriate for subdividing and was priced reasonably, Mr. Cousins felt that probably the best move would be to get one of his customers, a builder of Knox homes, to buy and develop the tract. Mr. Cousins approached W. L. Moore, a medium-sized builder who seemed to run his affairs well, with the idea. Mr. Moore was reluctant to take it on because of its large size. He said he would consider the venture if Mr. Cousins would go into it with him. Still employed by Knox Corporation, Mr. Cousins felt that he rightfully should inform Peter Knox, Knox Homes Corporation president, of the deal and invite him to participate. Mr. Knox agreed to enter into the deal, and the result was the formation of Oakcliff Estates, Inc. in February 1960, with Messrs. Cousins, Moore, and Knox each owning one-third of the stock. In addition, in July 1960, Real Estate Sales, Inc. was formed by Mr. Moore and Mr. Cousins to handle the sales of Oakcliff Estate homes.

BRIARWOOD HILLS SUBDIVISION

By late 1959 Mr. Cousins had decided the time had come for him to devote his full time energies to his own investments. Therefore, he decided to leave the employment of Knox Homes Corporation as of December 31, 1959. Knox, however, asked him to officially stay on until March 1 while they sought a replacement for him. In January 1960, Mr. Cousins felt that although he was still with Knox Corporation he should make a concerted effort to expand into new ventures. Consequently he formed Briarwood Hills, Inc. and signed a contract to buy 100 lots in a small subdivision which had previously begun to be developed. Shortly thereafter he decided to sell Mr. Moore, the co-owner of Oakcliff, one-half of the stock in Briarwood Hills. In order to break this operation down into a smaller unit operation for tax purposes, a corporation known as Cosmo Investments, Inc. was formed to handle part of this venture. Because of the slow work of the developer, which resulted from inadequate financing and slow sales, these ventures proved to be somewhat of a headache although moderately profitable.

LARCHWOOD

Late in 1958 while Mr. Cousins was still with Knox Homes Corporation, he convinced Pete Knox that more Knox Homes packages could be sold if a corporation was set up to perform the function of buying raw tracts of land and having the engineering and subdivision planning done so the land would be ready for immediate development. Mr. Cousins reasoned that the problem of the typical small builder to whom they were selling house packages was the capital requirement to hold raw land for the six to eight months period which was necessary to develop the land for homebuilding. Mr. Cousins further reasoned that besides facilitating the sale of house packages, a profit could be realized from such an operation. Subsequently, in December of 1958 Larchwood, Inc. was formed for the above purpose. Mr. Cousins and Mr. Knox felt that they needed an administrative person in the organization to run it so they invited one of their builder-developer friends, Dean Spratlin, to come in with them on the basis of one-third ownership each. Initially, they each put up $20,000 of capital and, in addition, Mr. Knox provided $200,000 of traded stock to the corporation to be used as collateral by Larchwood to obtain bank credit. With the $60,000 from the stockholders and approximately $140,-000 short-term bank credit, the corporation began the purchase of raw land. Mainly through the efforts of Mr. Spratlin, Larchwood acquired four tracts of land within a short period of time. One tract, however, was sold almost immediately at a substantial profit. Two of the tracts retained were located in Atlanta and the third was located in the township of Donelson which is a suburb of Nashville, Tennessee.

By 1960 Larchwood had run out of money and credit, and in the meantime National Homes had acquired Knox Corporation, and National discouraged the idea of using Larchwood as a means of increasing house package sales. So late in 1960, after Mr. Cousins had left Knox Corporation, the stockholders of Larchwood decided that steps should be taken to proceed with development of the tracts so that lots could be sold. By this time, however, between $250,000 and $300,000 had already been spent on the Nashville property, and it was estimated that another half million dollars was needed to develop the property to the point of selling developed lots. A complete sewage disposal system had to be built in order to develop the land for its best use. The next question was where to find a half million dollars.

Because Mr. Cousins had, with the assistance of some friends, formed a Small Business Investment Corporation (First American Investment Corporation), he had become familiar with a rather large SBIC located in Palm Beach, Florida, known as the Florida Capital Corporation. Mr. Cousins contacted this SBIC about making Larchwood a $500,000 loan. Florida Capital Corporation agreed to make the loan but as one of the stipulations they required Larchwood to dispose of all its land except the Nashville tract and to obtain a capital investment of $215,335 in cash from its stockholders to permit repayment of indebtedness in that amount incurred in acquiring and developing the Nashville tract. In order to carry out this requirement, a syndicate made up of Mr. Cousins, Mr. Knox, and several members of Mr. Knox's family was formed to purchase the Atlanta properties from Larchwood.

The ultimate plan for the Nashville property calls for a subdivision containing 1,378 home sites, not including approximately 93 acres reserved for apartments and commercial use. In addition approximately 35 acres are set aside for schools and parks.

CRESCENDO VALLEY

While Larchwood was experiencing the extreme shortage of working capital due to the development cost of its Nashville property, Mr. Cousins decided to help relieve this situation by forming a new corporation, Crescendo Valley, Inc., to buy a tract of land which Larchwood owned in west Atlanta. This tract, which was later subdivided into 118 lots, was located in the Negro district of Atlanta. Crescendo Valley, Inc., whose stock was shared on a 50–50 basis by Mr. Cousins and Mr. Moore, paid Larchwood $113,000 for the tract, $50,000 of which was cash borrowed from a local development company and a New York finance house. This subdivision seemed to be on the way to being a successful venture with well over one half of the homes sold by the early part of 1961.

4. Mr. Cousins' Appraisal of the Situation

As indicated above, Mr. Cousins had become convinced by early 1961 that an overall simplification of his organization was a must. He indicated that his ". . . intentions as far as the future is concerned are winding up all of the companies as soon as they can finish what work they have got to do in all of these developments, and to either liquidate the corporations or take my interest out and put it into only one company. In that company I intend to continue buying and developing land and building houses in that company only. Unless there are some strong arguments to the contrary, I don't ever want any more corporations than that one, and I intend for my future activities to be devoted to that company." Although Mr. Cousins said that he would like to, at least initially, own 100% of the stock in the one corporation he envisioned, he knew that he could not swing this because of the capital that would be needed to buy out all of the outside interest held in these corporations. However, certain personality differences seemed to indicate that Mr. Cousins and Mr. Moore would both be better off if they severed their relationship. Mr. Cousins approached Mr. Moore about a buy-out or sell-out proposition. Neither gentleman felt that individually they would be able to buy all of the interest of the other in every corporation in which they held joint interest. There was also the big problem of placing a value on the interest of each.

EXHIBIT I

COUSINS PROPERTIES
CORPORATE OWNERSHIP INTERESTS
AS OF JUNE 30, 1961

	OWNERSHIP INTEREST				
CORPORATION	T. G. COUSINS	PETER KNOX	W. L. MOORE	I. W. COUSINS	OTHERS
Pineland Forest Subdivision:					
Mountain View Plaza, Inc.	25%	12½%		25%	37½%
Pineland Builders, Inc.	25%	12½%		25%	37½%
Brand Name Homes, Inc.	50%			50%	
Metropolitan Commercial Corp.	25%	12½%		25%	37½%
Briarwood Hills Subdivision:					
Briarwood Hills, Inc.	50%		50%		
Cosmo Investments, Inc.	50%		50%		
Oakcliff Estates Subdivision:					
Oakcliff Estates, Inc.	33⅓%	33⅓%	33⅓%		
Real Estate Sales, Inc.	50%		50%		
Other Corporations:					
Crescendo Valley, Inc.	50%		50%		
Cousins-Moore Insurance Agency, Inc.	50%		50%		
Larchwood, Inc.	25%	24%			51%

EXHIBIT II

STATEMENT OF FINANCIAL POSITION—PINELAND FOREST SUBDIVISION
AS OF DECEMBER 31, 1960

(In Thousands of Dollars)

	MOUNTAIN VIEW PLAZA, INC.	PINELAND BUILDERS, INC.	BRAND NAME HOMES, INC.	METROPOLITAN COMMERCIAL CORP.	COMBINED
ASSETS:					
Current Assets (Including land)	74.1	445.0	21.6	35.3	576.0
Intercompany Accounts	64.9	—	—	—	64.9
Capital Assets	1.4	8.2	5.4	—	15.0
Advances to Officers	—	1.0	3.1	—	4.1
Organization Expense	0.2	0.2	0.1	0.1	0.6
Total Assets	140.6	454.4	30.2	35.4	660.6
LIABILITIES AND CAPITAL:					
Current Liabilities	104.9	391.0	8.2	—	504.1
Intercompany Accounts	—	29.5	1.0	33.4	63.9
Capital:					
Common Capital Stock	9.0	1.0	3.0	2.0	15.0
Earned Surplus	26.7	32.9	18.0	—	77.6
Total Liabilities and Capital	140.6	454.4	30.2	35.4	660.6

EXHIBIT III

STATEMENT OF FINANCIAL POSITION—
BRIARWOOD HILLS SUBDIVISION
AS OF DECEMBER 31, 1960
(In Thousands of Dollars)

	BRIARWOOD HILLS, INC.	COSMO INVESTMENTS INC.	COMBINED
ASSETS:			
Current Assets	88.5	28.6	117.1
Intercompany Accounts	17.6	—	17.6
Capital Assets	4.3	—	4.3
Advances to Officers	22.6	7.0	29.6
Organization Expenses	0.2	—	0.2
Total Assets	133.2	35.6	168.8
LIABILITIES AND CAPITAL:			
Current Liabilities	122.9	9.2	132.1
Intercompany Accounts	—	6.6	6.6
Capital:			
Common Capital Stock . . .	3.0	1.0	4.0
Earned Surplus	7.3	18.8	26.1
Total Liabilities and Capital	133.2	35.6	168.8

EXHIBIT IV

STATEMENT OF FINANCIAL POSITION—
OAKCLIFF ESTATES SUBDIVISION
AS OF DECEMBER 31, 1960
(In Thousands of Dollars)

	OAKCLIFF ESTATES, INC.	REAL ESTATE SALES, INC.	COMBINED
ASSETS:			
Current Assets	1085.0	32.0	1117.0
Intercompany Accounts	5.9	—	5.9
Capital Assets	3.0	5.0	8.0
Advances to Officers	1.0	0.5	1.5
Organization Expense	0.1	0.1	0.2
Total Assets	1095.0	37.6	1132.6
LIABILITIES AND CAPITAL:			
Current Liabilities	1072.2	18.7	1090.9
Advances from Officers	—	0.5	0.5
Intercompany Accounts	—	17.8	17.8
Capital:			
Common Capital Stock	6.0	1.0	7.0
Earned Surplus	16.8	(0.4)	16.4
Total Liabilities and Capital	1095.0	37.6	1132.6

EXHIBIT V

STATEMENT OF FINANCIAL POSITION—
OTHER CORPORATIONS
AS OF DECEMBER 31, 1960
(In Thousands of Dollars)

	CRESCENDO VALLEY, INC.	COUSINS-MOORE INSURANCE AGENCY, INC.	LARCHWOOD, INC.	COMBINED
ASSETS:				
Current Assets	138.7	3.8	1043.7	1186.2
Organization Expense	—	0.2	—	0.2
Total Assets	138.7	4.0	1043.7	1186.4
LIABILITIES AND CAPITAL:				
Current Liabilities . .	141.4	1.8	995.6	1138.8
Capital:				
Common Capital Stock	1.0	1.0	30.0	32.0
Paid in Surplus . .	—	—	2.0	2.0
Earned Surplus . .	(3.7)	1.2	16.1	13.6
Total Liabilities and Capital	138.7	4.0	1043.7	1186.4

EXHIBIT VI

COUSINS PROPERTIES

NET INCOME AFTER TAXES

1/1/60 to 12/31/60

Pineland Forest Subdivision:

Mountain View Plaza, Inc.	$ 8,994
Pineland Builders, Inc.	15,962
Brand Name Homes, Inc.	8,924
Metropolitan Commercial Corp.	(6)
Total	$33,874

Briarwood Hills Subdivision:

Briarwood Hills, Inc.	$ 7,350
Cosmo Investments, Inc.	18,802
Total	$26,152

Oakcliff Estates Subdivision:

Oakcliff Estates, Inc.	$16,781
Real Estate Sales, Inc.	(443)
Total	$16,338

Other Corporations:

Crescendo Valley, Inc.	$(3,709)
Cousins-Moore Insurance Agency, Inc.	1,153
Larchwood, Inc.	24,444
Total	$21,888
Grand Total	$98,252

6. COUSINS PROPERTIES (B)*

AS INDICATED IN THE COUSINS Properties A case, Mr. Thomas G. Cousins had come to the conclusion that a simplification of the corporate structure of his real estate development operations was in order. Also, he felt that it would be best for all concerned if he and Mr. W. L. Moore, one of the principal stockholders in several of the corporations, would sever their relationship. Accordingly, on September 22, 1961, Mr. Moore and Mr. Cousins sat down and agreed upon a settlement of their interest in the various corporations. The result was that Mr. Cousins bought all of Mr. Moore's stock in Oakcliff, Inc., Real Estate Sales, Inc., and Crescendo

* This case was prepared by Professor Albert H. Clark of Georgia State College.

Valley, Inc. In turn, Mr. Cousins sold to Mr. Moore all of his stock in the other corporations of which there was joint interest.

The next logical step seemed to be that of forming the one corporation which Mr. Cousins intended to become the central corporate structure of his business. Although Mr. Cousins had expressed a desire to own 100% of the stock of this corporation initially, he could see that the capital structure of the business would require more equity than he was able to contribute at that time. So as a compromise he decided to include his friend Peter Knox in the organization as well as his father, I. W. Cousins.

On November 22, 1961, the above three persons organized Cousins Properties, Incorporated and acquired all of its common stock in exchange for all or a portion of the stock of the corporations which became its subsidiaries. The corporations and the percent ownership by Cousins Properties, Inc. after this initial transaction was as follows:

COMPANY	% ACQUIRED
Oakcliff Estates, Inc.	71.25%
Real Estate Sales, Inc.	100.00%
Pineland Builders, Inc.	62.50%
Brand Name Homes, Inc.	97.14%
Mountain View Plaza, Inc.	62.50%
Metropolitan Commercial Corporation	62.50%
Crescendo Valley, Inc.	100.00%
Larchwood, Inc.	48.05%
Cousins Insurance Agency, Inc.*	100.00%

* Cousins Insurance Agency, Inc. was established shortly after Mr. Cousins settled with Mr. Moore. Mr. Moore had bought out Mr. Cousins' interest in Cousins-Moore Insurance Agency, Inc.

In December, 1961, Cousins Properties, Inc. purchased the remaining minority interests in the above subsidiaries for an aggregate price of $355,342. This amount was paid by Cousins Properties, Inc. with its notes amounting to $331,770 and its assumption of indebtedness aggregating $31,642. The stock ownership of Cousins Properties Incorporated as of December 31, 1961, was as follows:

STOCKHOLDER	NUMBER OF SHARES	% OF OWNERSHIP
Thomas G. Cousins	67,875	75.0%
Peter S. Knox	15,083	16.7%
I. W. Cousins	7,542	8.3%
Total	90,500	100.0%

Nature of the Problem

Normally, a business operation which is primarily involved in buying and improving raw land and either selling such improved raw land or erecting and selling houses, produces the financial results of generating long-term receivables and short-term payables. This, in turn, usually produces the continual need for additional working capital. The operations of Cousins Properties was no exception to this general rule. And, because of the rapid growth it had experienced, the company found itself in somewhat of a critical position by the end of 1961. At this time the working capital position of the company was extremely poor. The situation had been aggravated by the fact that the company, in an effort to cope with its working capital needs, found it necessary to borrow substantial amounts at high interest rates, and oftentimes it was necessary to offer generous inducements to lenders to make these loans to the company. This excessive use of rather short maturity credit when coupled with the company's thin equity base resulted in a capital structure with extremely high leverage.

It soon became evident to Mr. Cousins that steps must be taken to bring more long-term funds into the corporation. However, he was quick to point out that he wanted to find a way to bring funds into the company without relinquishing his absolute control of the corporation. He had felt for some time that someday it would be necessary to have a public offering of stock. By December of 1961, Mr. Cousins sensed that the time had come to explore the possibility of a public offering.

Original Negotiations with the Underwriters

Mr. Cousins had often mentioned to Ed Albright, a stockbroker friend of his, that he might be interested at some future date in having his corporation "go public." Mr. Albright was with the firm of Wyatt, Neal, and Waggoner, a small local investment banking house in Atlanta. At lunch one day early in December 1961, Mr. Cousins explained to Mr. Albright the current status of his operations and indicated the following reasons why he felt he would like to have a public issue of securities.

1. He would like to have a public market for the stock of the corporation.
2. It would permit elimination of the top-heavy debt structure and would save interest expenses.
3. It would permit him to devote more time to active management of

the business. He indicated that he spent approximately one third of his time negotiating loans, etc.

4. It would place the corporation in a position to make more advantageous purchases of building supplies.
5. It would place the corporation in a position to make more advantageous purchases of land.
6. One profitable aspect of his business was brokering and servicing mortgage loans. With proceeds of the public issue the corporation would establish a mortgage company to place and serve these loans.
7. It would permit the corporation to expand its operations and would generally provide flexibility.

Mr. Albright agreed to take the matter before the partners of his firm. He immediately gathered together the latest financial reports of Cousins Properties and set up a conference with the partners of his firm. Mr. Waggoner, the managing partner, was impressed with the phenomenal growth of the company and indicated that since the company had exceeded the one-quarter million dollar earnings mark, he was in favor of further investigation for possible underwriting. However, Mr. Waggoner indicated that he felt that they should contact one of the New York investment banking houses with which they had done business in the past concerning the possibility of a joint underwriting arrangement. Waggoner had dealt with several New York houses on previous underwritings; however, after careful consideration it was felt McDonnell and Co. should be contacted first since Cousins Properties seemed to be more in line with previous underwritings that McDonnell had handled.

Consequently, McDonnell was contacted and upon their suggestion Mr. Cousins and a member of the Wyatt firm went to New York in late December to present the situation to the New York firm. Mr. Charles Yarborough, of the accounting firm Arthur Anderson Co., and Baxter Jones, Mr. Cousins' attorney, accompanied him to New York. McDonnell and Co. seemed to be favorably impressed with Mr. Cousins' operations and the possibility of a public sale of his stock. However, they wanted to give the matter further study and indicated to Mr. Cousins that he would hear from them within thirty days. Before terminating the conference with the McDonnell people, Mr. Cousins stressed two points: (1) he felt that he would need at least $1.5 to $2.0 million from a public issue, and (2) after such an issue he wanted to be left in a position of absolute control so far as the voting stock was concerned.

Initial Underwriting Proposal

In late January 1962, the head of the syndicate department of McDonnell and Co. came to Atlanta to visit Wyatt, Neal, and Waggoner for the purpose of putting the finishing touches on a joint underwriting proposal between the two firms for Cousins Properties, Inc. After an extensive conference between the two investment banking firms and Mr. Cousins, a letter of intent was issued to Mr. Cousins outlining the details of the proposed public offering and the tentative terms of the underwriting arrangement.

The underwriters proposed that the public offering involve the sale of 10,000 units. Each unit of the offering was to consist of (a) $100 principal amount of debentures, (b) six shares of common stock, and (c) warrants to purchase two shares of common stock. The debentures were to have a ten-year maturity date and a coupon rate of 6½% per annum. They were to be callable at the option of the company during the first year at 106% of face and declining 1% each year until 1968 when redemption would be at face amount. The terms of the debentures provided for a sinking fund to be set up and payments made by the company in the amount of $125,000 each year beginning in 1968. The debentures were to be subordinated in right of payment to the prior full payment of all other creditors of the company. The common stock to be issued would have full voting rights. In order to facilitate the retention of control by Mr. Cousins, the underwriter suggested that before the offering Cousins Properties, Inc. should execute a two for one stock split. The warrants proposed were to be exercisable for a period of five years on the basis of a ten dollar a share purchase price.

The underwriters suggested that the price of the units be offered to the public at $135. Of this unit price, $65 would be allotted to the debentures of the unit, $60 to the six shares of common stock, and $10 to the two purchase warrants. The underwriters indicated that their fee for a full underwriting contract to handle the issue would be approximately 10% of the gross offering price. In addition to this 10% spread, the underwriters required that the company issue them for their individual investment accounts warrants to purchase 10,000 shares of common stock. The underwriters would pay one cent each for these warrants which would be exercisable at a price of $10 per share for a period of five years.

There were several features of the underwriting proposal which concerned Mr. Cousins. One of these features was the 30,000 warrants which would be outstanding. The underwriters pointed out that for the 20,000 warrants issued to the public, Cousins Properties was receiving a gross amount of $100,000 to offset future possible dilution. When Mr. Cousins questioned the 10,000 warrants to be issued to the underwriters at one cent each, they indicated that the underwriting of such an issue was a risky proposition for them and, in effect, they were using this method of compensation as a compromise. Without the warrants, they indicated that their spread would have to be considerably more than 10%. The feature that really disturbed Mr. Cousins was the discounted value ($65 per $100 amount) at which the 6½% debentures were to be sold. He reasoned that this made the effective cost of this portion of the funds in excess of 9%. This feature of high fixed cost of funds was the very thing he was trying to eliminate from his operations. The underwriters stressed that since the debentures were subordinated to all other creditors, it would take a discount of at least 30% on the basis of a 6½% coupon rate to market the issue.

After considerable thought Mr. Cousins decided to proceed on the basis of the underwriters' proposal. After all, he reasoned, Cousins Properties would net approximately $1.2 million from the issue and even if all of the purchase warrants were exercised he would still remain in an absolute control position since he would, even then, hold in excess of 50% of the voting stock of the corporation.

Preparation for the Public Offering

The underwriters had indicated that the public offering should be made as soon as possible. They pointed out, however, that the filing with the Securities and Exchange Commission would probably require considerable time and much work for Cousins Properties, Inc. Mr. Cousins immediately instructed his legal advisers and accountants to begin work on the S.E.C. filing.

Mr. Cousins had felt for some time that he needed to strengthen his organization from a personnel standpoint. The underwriters seemed to think this was a prerequisite for the offering. First there was the need for strengthening his finance and accounting departments. Accordingly, he filled the position of Treasurer of Cousins Properties, Inc. by hiring Mr. A. D. Cannon, Jr. Mr. Cannon, who joined the company on March 1, 1962, had received his MBA degree from the Harvard Business School in 1959 and had served since that time as Assistant Manager of the Atlanta, Georgia, branch of National Homes Acceptance Corporation, the mortgage loan subsidiary of National Homes Corporation. It was Mr. Cousins' idea to develop a full-fledged mortgage loan operation within his company as soon as possible.

Mr. John D. Arndt joined the company in March 1962 as Comptroller. Mr. Arndt, a certified public accountant who holds the BBA and LLB degrees, was an associate attorney with the firm of Sutherland, Asbill, & Brennan, counsel for Cousins. In addition, Mr. William R. Patterson became the Corporate Secretary and a Director of the Corporation in March 1962. Mr. Patterson was the attorney with Sutherland, Asbill, & Brennan who was in charge of handling the legal aspects of the public offering.

According to the suggestion of the underwriters, the corporation executed a two for one stock split on March 20, 1962. After the split the stock ownership of the corporation's outstanding stock was as follows:

T. G. Cousins	135,750
Peter S. Knox	30,167
I. W. Cousins	15,083
Total	181,000

By April 1962, Cousins Properties began to feel the pressure of its deteriorating working capital position. Also, the burden of the 15% interest on the money borrowed from Talcot & Co. was weighing heavily on the company's position. Mr. Cousins decided to try to temporarily remedy the situation by negotiating a new large bank loan. Accordingly, Mr. Cousins called upon the bank with which he usually did business but was turned down on a request for additional funds. He then visited one of the large commercial banks with which he had not previously done business and, on the strength of his pending public offering, requested and received a 6%, $600,000 loan. The terms of the loan were that one-half of the loan became due in 6 months and the balance was payable quarterly thereafter on an installment basis of $37,500 per quarter. Cousins Properties, in turn, used $277,000 of the proceeds of this loan to pay off one of its outstanding loans that was bearing a rate of 15%. The balance of the proceeds was used to reduce other current liabilities and strengthen the liquidity of the company.

The Market Drop

During the spring of 1962, Cousins Properties encountered various delays in the S.E.C. filing for its public offering. There was a vast amount of administrative work involved in putting the company affairs in order for filing the S.E.C. registration statement. In addition, the S.E.C. was functioning behind normal schedule because of the increased number of filings that were accompanied by the bull stock market that had begun in the summer of 1960. By early May it looked as if the public offering could possibly be made by late June. However, the drastic break in prices which occurred on the New York Stock Exchange market in late May had far reaching implications on the general over-the-counter market and especially on public offerings of small, new corporations. In early June, McDonnell and Co. notified Wyatt, Neal, and Waggoner that it felt that because of market conditions, it could not go along with the underwriting of Cousins Properties, Inc. Although Wyatt felt confident about the prospects of Cousins Properties' public offering even in light of current conditions, they indicated that they were reluctant to handle the underwriting alone. By this time Mr. Cousins knew that he must go through with the public offering some way or seriously interrupt the company's plans of expansion.

Long-Term Loan Proposition

In the spring when Mr. Cousins was especially concerned about the discount terms of the debentures included in the underwriters' proposal, he had given serious consideration to the possibility of obtaining a direct long-term loan from some source. He thought that he might be able to get better terms than those represented by the debentures. He had gone as far as discussing with Mr. Knox the possibility of establishing a syndicate to provide a long-term loan to the corporation. However, nothing became of this idea at that time.

Later in the spring Mr. Cannon, the new treasurer of Cousins Properties, Inc., mentioned to a friend of his, a vice-president of a medium sized life insurance company, that Cousins would probably consider negotiating a long-term loan if he could get better terms than those presented by the proposed debenture. The insurance company executive indicated that his company would probably be interested in discussing the matter further. When McDonnell and Co. indicated that they wanted to withdraw from the offering, Mr. Cousins decided to make a concerted effort to negotiate a long-term loan from the insurance company. After lengthy negotiations the insurance company tentatively agreed to commit themselves to lend Cousins Properties $1,000,000 under the conditions that Mr. Cousins could persuade the underwriters to go along with a public offering of common stock which would net the company approximately one-half million dollars.

New Negotiations with the Underwriters

With the tentative commitment from the insurance company, Mr. Cousins proceeded with further negotiations with McDonnell and Co. and Wyatt, Neal, and Waggoner. At first McDonnell and Co. was not interested at all in further negotiations. Wyatt, Neal, and Waggoner, however, was very much encouraged by the tentative commitment from the insurance company and soon persuaded McDonnell to make a new proposal to Cousins Properties in light of the insurance company commitment.

New Underwriting Proposal

By the middle of July, McDonnell & Co. and Wyatt, Neal, and Waggoner came forth with a new public offering proposal which consisted of the sale of 70,000 shares of common stock. It was proposed that the shares be offered to the public at $8.50 per share providing gross proceeds of $595,000 from the offering. The underwriting fee was to consist of gross spread of 10% or $.85 per share. The net proceeds to the company would be $7.65 per share or a total of $535,500. In addition, Cousins Properties would agree to sell to McDonnell and Co. and Wyatt, Neal, and Waggoner, for their respective investment accounts, at one cent per warrant, non-transferable warrants to purchase 1,500 shares of common stock each, or a total of 3,000 shares. These warrants were to be exercisable at any time within five years at $10.20 per share.

The underwriters suggested that Cousins Properties be re-incorporated in the state of Delaware and that the new capitalization consist of two classes of common stock. The 70,000 shares of the proposed offering would be common stock whereas the then outstanding 181,000 shares would become Class B common stock. Both classes of stock would have equal voting rights. The only difference between the two classes of stock was that cash dividends could be paid on the common stock with no dividends or a lesser or equal amount of dividends being paid on the Class B common stock. No dividends could be paid on the Class B stock without an equal amount being paid on the common stock. The Class B stock was convertible at any time into an equal number of common shares. After the public offering, Mr. Cousins with his 135,750 shares of Class B common stock would own 54.08% of the voting shares.

In addition, the underwriters requested that Cousins Properties declare a 12½ cents per share dividend on its common stock before the public offering to be paid to stockholders of record some two months after the public offering date. And further to indicate in the prospectus that this initial dividend declaration was intended to inaugurate a quarterly cash dividend policy.

The Insurance Company Loan Proposal

The one million dollar loan commitment from the life insurance company was contingent upon the successful public offering of Cousins Properties common stock. The net proceeds to the company from this public offering must be at least $475,000. The terms of the commitment were: $600,000 would be advanced to the company promptly after receipt by the company of the proceeds from the public offering of common stock. The remaining $400,000 would be advanced between March 15, 1963 and September 15, 1963, on a date fixed by the lender, provided that: (1) the consolidated net earnings of the company before income taxes for 1962 are at least $600,000 and at least four times the sum of $65,000 plus the annualized interest on any unsecured bank debt of the company outstanding on December 31, 1962, and (2) the company's current assets exceed 150% of current liabilities, as defined.

The loan would bear interest at the rate of 6½% per year on the unpaid principal balance, payable quarterly beginning December 1962. Principal would be payable in quarterly installments of $12,500 each beginning December 1965 through September 1967, and quarterly installments of $35,000 each beginning December 1967 through June 1972, and the remaining balance of $235,000 would be payable in September 1972. The company would have the non-cumulative right to prepay $100,000 in any year without penalty, and in addition would have the right to prepay the loan in full during the fourth year upon the payment of a 6% penalty; the right to prepay the loan in full during the fifth year upon the payment of a 3% penalty; and the right to unlimited prepayment without penalty after September 1967.

The insurance company would have the right to designate one member of the company's board of directors and of its executive committee. Cousins Properties, Inc. would carry insurance on the life of Thomas G. Cousins in the aggregate amount of one million dollars, and such insurance would be assigned to the lender as security for repayment of the loan. The loan would not be otherwise secured by mortgages or by any other specific assets of the company. The company would not be permitted to pay cash dividends in any one year in an amount which exceeds 33⅓% of the consolidated annual net earnings of the company after taxes for the preceding year.

Cousins Properties, Inc. would issue to the lender warrants to purchase 12,000 shares of the common stock of the company upon receipt of the $600,000 advance, and warrants to purchase 8,000 shares of the common stock of the company if and when the additional $400,000 was advanced. The warrants would be exercisable at a purchase price of $8.50 per share at any time within ten years from the date of the $600,000 advance. The warrants would be transferable and would be protected against dilution.

The Point of Decision

By the latter part of August Mr. Cousins was at the point where he had to make a decision. He had some reservations as to the terms of the proposals of the underwriters and the insurance company. So far as the underwriters' proposal was concerned, he felt that the offering price was somewhat lower than that which he had hoped. In addition he was somewhat reluctant to go along with the declaration of common stock dividends as insisted upon by the underwriters. He reasoned that the company could not afford this added commitment of cash drain that soon. And, in addition, he felt that most of the people who would be interested in buying the stock would not be particularly interested in cash dividends. Mr. Cousins also indicated that in his opinion the uncertain stock market would become bullish by the year's end, and that he felt that it may be wise to hold off with the public offering until then in hopes of getting a higher price for his stock. Although the interest rate and maturity features of the insurance company loan seemed acceptable to Mr. Cousins, he was concerned about the 20,000 ten-year purchase warrants that were to be issued to the insurance company. This seemed to be a rather large premium to be paying the lender for making the loan.

EXHIBIT I

COUSINS PROPERTIES

STATEMENTS OF CONSOLIDATED INCOME

The following statements of consolidated income reflect the results of operations of the Company and its wholly-owned subsidiaries since the inception of each.

| | Year Ended December 31 | | | | Six Months Ended June 30 | |
| | | | | | (Unaudited) (Note E) | |
	1958	1959	1960	1961	1961	1962
SALES:						
Houses and related lots	$11,000	$319,139	$1,641,585	$4,327,190	$2,457,688	$1,819,979
Developed lots	—	—	10,800	153,150	—	1,134,750
Undeveloped land	—	99,923	—	—	—	156,800
	$11,000	$419,062	$1,652,385	$4,480,340	$2,457,688	$3,111,529
COSTS AND EXPENSES:						
Cost of sales—						
Houses and related lots	$ 9,789	$271,256	$1,387,424	$3,719,305	$2,089,602	$1,635,732
Developed lots	—	—	6,923	98,300	—	767,440
Undeveloped land	—	61,886	—	—	—	109,933
	$ 9,789	$333,142	$1,394,347	$3,817,605	$2,089,602	$2,513,105
General and administrative	5,160	18,917	68,646	116,062	65,640	94,748
Selling	—	9,924	75,136	128,790	80,195	103,198
Other, net	(70)	(997)	13,082	11,850	(131)	6,380
	$14,879	$360,986	$1,551,211	$4,074,307	$2,235,306	$2,717,431

Income (loss) before provision for income taxes	$(3,879)	$ 58,076	$ 101,174	$ 406,033	$ 222,382	$ 394,098
PROVISION FOR INCOME TAXES (Note D):						
Current	$ —	$ 22,300	$ 34,000	$ 118,000	$ 56,000	$ 188,000
Deferred	—	—	—	47,000	34,000	24,000
	$ —	$ 22,300	$ 34,000	$ 165,000	$ 90,000	$ 212,000
NET INCOME (LOSS) — (Note A):						
Before minority interest	$(3,879)	$ 35,776	$ 67,174	$ 241,033	$ 132,382	$ 182,098
Applicable to minority interests purchased in December, 1961 (Note F)	—	12,101	34,846	57,279	37,438	—
Applicable to continuing interests	$(3,879)	$ 23,675	$ 32,328	$ 183,754	$ 94,944	$ 182,098
NET INCOME (LOSS) PER SHARE OF COMMON STOCK (Note B)	$ (.02)	$ .13	$ .18	$ 1.02	$ .52	$ 1.01

NOTES:

A. See Note 1 to financial statements included elsewhere in this Case for a descripiton of the acquisition by Cousins Properties Incorporated of subsidiaries' shares.

B. Net income (loss) per share of common stock has been computed for each year based on earnings applicable to continuing interests and on 181,000 shares, representing shares owned by the continuing interests.

C. No cash dividends have been paid by any of the companies whose results of operations are reflected in the foregoing statements.

D. See Note 5 to financial statements included elsewhere in this Case.

E. Because of the seasonal nature of the Company's business, the earnings for the six months ended June 30, 1962, are not necessarily indicative of the earnings for the entire year ending December 31, 1962.

F. As explained in Note 1 to financial statements, the excess ($117,239) of the purchase price of the shares acquired from minority interests over the underlying book value applicable to such shares has been included in the balance sheet in the cost of land in process of development and will be charged to income in future periods as the related land is sold.

EXHIBIT II

COUSINS PROPERTIES INCORPORATED AND SUBSIDIARIES
CONSOLIDATED BALANCE SHEETS
DECEMBER 31, 1961 AND JUNE 30, 1962

ASSETS

	December 31, 1961	June 30, 1962 (Unaudited)
CASH, including $27,274 in restricted escrow deposits at June 30, 1962	$ 120,321	$ 253,536
RECEIVABLES:		
First mortgage notes receivable, arising from sales of land and developed lots, $313,740 due within one year and $53,100 pledged at June 30, 1962	$ 134,850	$ 759,690
Second mortgage notes receivable, approximately $18,000, including interest, due annually in equal monthly installments through 1985	220,733	219,126
Stockholders	26,942	26,323
Refundable deposits, pledged as collateral on note payable	25,042	17,346
Other	76,520	200,671
	$ 484,087	$1,223,156
PREPAID EXPENSES, ETC.	$ 47,704	$ 49,105
PROPERTIES HELD FOR SALE, at cost, pledged as collateral on loans:		
Land in process of development (Note 1)	$2,492,377	$2,304,952
Houses under construction, less advance payments by purchasers of $207,011 at December 31, 1961, and $124,779 at June 30, 1962	189,762	552,443
Completed houses	174,359	165,558
Other	63,424	76,350
	$2,919,922	$3,099,303
RENTAL PROPERTIES:		
Apartment buildings under construction	$ —	$ 17,990
Leased properties	—	40,588
	$ —	$ 58,578
FURNITURE AND FIXTURES, ETC., at cost, less reserves for depreciation of $13,496 at December 31, 1961 and $18,246 at June 30, 1962 (Note 7)	$ 46,955	$ 33,675
DEFERRED UNDERWRITING EXPENSES	$ —	$ 12,561
	$3,618,989	$4,729,914

The accompanying notes are an integral part of these balance sheets.

EXHIBIT II (*continued*)

COUSINS PROPERTIES INCORPORATED AND SUBSIDIARIES
CONSOLIDATED BALANCE SHEETS
DECEMBER 31, 1961 AND JUNE 30, 1962

LIABILITIES

	December 31, 1961	June 30, 1962 (Unaudited)
CURRENT LIABILITIES:		
Notes payable—		
Current maturities of long-term debt (Note 4)	$ 801,031	$ 591,516
Construction loans (certain houses pledged as collateral)	360,975	693,691
Bank, 6%, unsecured, due November 1, 1962	—	300,000
Issued in acquisition of minority interests (Notes 1 and 4)	331,770	13,270
Unsecured, payable to contractors, etc.	319,792	171,449
Other notes payable (refundable deposits and $53,100 note receivable pledged as collateral at June 30, 1962)	71,800	64,181
Accounts payable, etc.	298,684	740,563
Accrued income taxes	125,839	268,732
Total current liabilities	$2,309,891	$2,843,402
DEFERRED INCOME TAXES (Note 5)	$ 47,000	$ 64,500
LONG-TERM DEBT, less current maturities (Note 4)	$ 891,461	$1,269,277
CONTINGENT LIABILITIES (Note 2)		
COMMON STOCK AND SURPLUS:		
Common stock (Notes 3, 6 and 8) —		
Common stock, par value $1.00 per share, authorized 300,000 shares, none outstanding	$ —	$ —
Class B common stock, par value $1.00 per share, authorized 200,000 shares, issued and outstanding 181,000 shares	181,000	181,000
Earned surplus, restricted as indicated in Note 3	189,637	371,735
	$ 370,637	$ 552,735
	$3,618,989	$4,729,914

The accompanying notes are an integral part of these balance sheets.

EXHIBIT II (*continued*)

COUSINS PROPERTIES INCORPORATED AND SUBSIDIARIES
NOTES TO FINANCIAL STATEMENTS
DECEMBER 31, 1961 AND JUNE 30, 1962

1. ACQUISITION OF SUBSIDIARIES AND PRINCIPLES OF CONSOLIDATION:

As of November 22, 1961, the Company issued 90,500 shares of its common stock in exchange for the outstanding capital stock held by certain stockholders (representing the indicated percentages of total outstanding capital stock of the individual companies) in the following corporations —

Company	Date of Inception	Percent Acquired
Oakcliff Estates, Inc.	February, 1960	71.25%
Real Estate Sales, Inc.	July, 1960	100.00
Pineland Builders, Inc.	January, 1960	62.50
Brand-Name Homes, Inc.	April, 1958	97.14
Mountain View Plaza, Inc.	October, 1959	62.50
Metropolitan Commercial Corp.	July, 1960	62.50
Crescendo Valley, Inc.	October, 1960	100.00
Larchwood, Inc.	December, 1958	48.05
Cousins Insurance Agency, Inc.	October, 1961	100.00

As of December 1, 1961, the remaining outstanding capital stock of the companies listed above was purchased from minority interests for $355,342, paid primarily by issuance of notes payable, whose price was $117,239 in excess of the underlying book value applicable to these shares. This excess over underlying book value has been included in the accompanying consolidated balance sheet in the cost of land in process of development and will be charged to income in the future as the related land is sold.

The exchange of shares in November 1961 described above was treated as a "pooling of interests" for accounting purposes and, accordingly, the accompanying consolidated financial statements include the accounts of all of the listed companies since their respective dates of inception, after elimination of intercompany investments, balances, transactions, and income and after deduction of the portion of income and surplus applicable to the minority interests purchased.

In addition to the subsidiaries listed above, there were two dormant wholly owned subsidiaries included in the Consolidated Financial Statements.

2. CONTINGENT LIABILITIES:

Certain of the Company's subsidiaries are contingently liable as makers on notes assumed by others as follows:

EXHIBIT II (*continued*)

	December 31, 1961	June 30, 1962
Oakcliff Estates, Inc.	$726,000	$692,000
Pineland Builders, Inc.	302,000	297,000
Larchwood, Inc.	122,000	96,000

3. OUTSTANDING WARRANTS AND RESTRICTION OF EARNED SURPLUS:

In connection with the loan payable to Florida Capital Corporation, described in Note 4, Larchwood, Inc. granted to that corporation warrants to purchase 2,500 shares of Larchwood's common stock at $60 per share, exercisable at any time to July 1, 1971. The book value per share of the 5,000 Larchwood shares then outstanding was $57.37 at December 31, 1961, and $77.01 at June 30, 1962. All outstanding shares of Larchwood are pledged by the Company as collateral on this loan.

Under the terms of the related loan agreement, the earned surplus of Larchwood, Inc. ($41,526 at December 31, 1961, and $139,726 at June 30, 1962, of which $21,573 and $32,733 respectively has been eliminated in consolidation by reason of the acquisition by Cousins Properties Incorporated of certain Larchwood shares as described in Note 1) is restricted against the payment of dividends other than stock dividends.

4. LONG-TERM DEBT:

	Consolidated		Company	
	December 31, 1961	June 30, 1962	December 31, 1961	June 30, 1962
Land mortgage notes — 9% land mortgage note payable to Florida Capital Corporation in quarterly installments of $24,000 each from September, 1962, through March, 1966, with the balance payable in quarterly installments of $8,375, subject to earlier payments for release of individual lots, $550,000 loan authorized by related loan agreement (Note 3) ...	$ 466,480	$ 550,000	$ —	$ —

Other land mortgage notes payable, bearing interest rates from 5% to 8%, June 30, 1962, balance payable $192,140 in 1962, $231,607 in 1963, $153,301 in 1964 and

EXHIBIT II (*continued*)

$118,245 in diminishing annual amounts through 1969, all subject to earlier payments for release of individual lots ..	1,226,012	695,293	210,720	97,540
Bank loan, 6%, unsecured, due in quarterly installments of $37,500 beginning December 31, 1962	–	300,000	–	300,000
Notes issued in acquisition of minority interest (Note 1)— Notes payable, 6%, due—				
December 31, 1964	–	217,000	–	217,000
December 31, 1963	–	98,500	–	98,500
	$1,692,492	$1,860,793	$210,720	$713,040
Less – Current maturities ..	801,031	591,516	113,180	161,270
	$ 891,461	$1,269,277	$ 97,540	$551,770

5. PROVISION FOR INCOME TAXES:

The Company and each of its subsidiaries file their Federal and state income tax returns on an individual basis. Accordingly, the aggregate surtax exemption available for the Company and its subsidiaries has been reflected in the computation of the consolidated provision for income taxes.

The gross profit on certain of the Company's sales is deferred for income tax purposes until such profit is collected in cash. The estimated income tax which will be payable upon such collection has been provided for in the accompanying financial statements.

6. STOCK SPLIT AND SUBSEQUENT RECAPITALIZATION:

In March 1962, the Company's charter was amended to increase the authorized common stock to 500,000 shares and 90,500 shares were issued to stockholders of record as of that date in a 2-for-1 stock split. In connection with this stock split, transfers of $48,059 from capital surplus and $42,441 from earned surplus were made to the common stock account.

In August 1962, the Company changed its domicile to the State of Delaware and effected a recapitalization, authorizing the issuance of 300,000 shares of common stock and 200,000 shares of Class B common stock. The 181,000 shares of common stock outstanding prior to the recapitalization were changed to Class B common stock.

The accompanying financial statements have been retroactively adjusted to give effect to the foregoing.

7. DEPRECIATION, MAINTENANCE AND PROPERTY RETIREMENT POLICIES:

The Company and its subsidiaries use the straight-line method of providing for depreciation of furniture and fixtures, etc. at annual rates of 10% to 25% applied to the cost of the assets.

EXHIBIT II (*continued*)

Expenditures for maintenance and repair of furniture, fixtures, etc. are charged to expense as incurred. Costs of renewals and betterments are capitalized in the property accounts. When properties are replaced, retired, or otherwise disposed of, the cost of such properties and the accumulated depreciation are deducted respectively from the asset and accumulated depreciation accounts. The related profit or loss, if any, is recorded in the income account.

8. STOCK OPTIONS:

In August 1962, the Company adopted a restricted Stock Option Plan under which 15,000 shares of common stock are reserved.

---

7. DELAWARE COMPANY

IN THE SPRING OF 1961, the Delaware Company held its annual meeting of shareholders. A quorum was present, and shareholders holding approximately 85.82 percent of the stock were represented.

Prior to the meeting, several resolutions which proposed amending the bylaws had been submitted to the company. One of those resolutions, submitted by Mrs. Aline Bordon, previously set forth in the proxy statement, was declared in order, moved, and seconded. The resolution proposed amending the bylaws to provide that no corporate funds of the corporation should be given to any charitable, educational, or similar organization except for purposes in direct furtherance of the business interests of the corporation.

Discussion of the Motion follows.

MR. WILLIAM WASHINGTON—I represent Mrs. Aline Bordon. Her grandfather was associated with a founder of Delaware Company in the early days of its existence and has always taken great interest in the welfare and progress of the company. She is very regretful that she can't be here today because of illness, and has asked me to represent her.

The reasons for this resolution, given in the proxy statement are as follows: Your directors are giving millions of dollars of your corporation's money to charity. This seems wrong. Your company is supposedly run solely for the stockholders' benefit. It is not an eleemosynary institution. Many stockholders undoubtedly feel that charity begins at home. Others who can afford donations are certainly entitled to choose their own beneficiaries. The current practice is especially reprehensible when as here nearly $10,000,000 have been given since 1955 to educational institutions, many of which now teach socialism and ridicule businessmen, savers, and investors, as recently explained in the well-documented best-seller, *Keynes at Harvard.*

Expanding a little on that argument, undoubtedly the directors are tremendously busy running the affairs of this gigantic enterprise we're all interested in. They apparently don't have enough time—and I'm very glad of it for the sake of the profits of the company—to spend their energies investigating hundreds of charities to see whether they are charities to which you stockholders would want to have your money given, assuming that the directors should give your money away to anyone over the objection of even a single stockholder.

Actually your company has made unrestricted grants to 429 different educational institutions in this country in the last five years. By merely inspecting the list one could say that some of them were not the kind of college where they encourage companies like ours and stockholders like ours. For example, among the men's colleges Harvard, Yale, and Princeton have been the beneficiaries of the company's donations; and among the women's colleges, Smith, Vassar, and Sarah Lawrence. Those are just examples of places where, on the whole, left-wing doctrines are taught in the economics department.

(To support his point about economic doctrines, Mr. Washington then read from and commented critically on the writings of Stuart Chase, with specific reference to an article by Mr. Chase which appeared in the Spring 1961 issue of the Delaware Company house organ.)

THE PRESIDENT—We in the Delaware Company believe in being good corporate citizens. We think the principle of corporate living is well established. It is encouraged by our tax laws; it has been upheld in our courts; and the public has come to expect it of corporations. Perhaps this was not so, say, some twenty-five years ago, but it is today. In our judgment these contributions are extremely important if the Delaware Company is to merit the good will of the public, which is essential to the prosperity of your company.

When you're a good corporate citizen, it is often necessary to give support to private institutions from which you expect no direct dollar-and-cents benefit—hospitals, community service organizations, the Red Cross, colleges, universities, and so on. If good citizens, corporate and individual alike, did not support these institutions, they would have to turn to the government for support—and that, certainly, is not the way to advance the cause of free enterprise.

As to the merits of giving to one institution, or one type of institution, over another, the possibilities for discussion are infinite. As we normally do in such a situation, we call upon a competent staff to gather information, to study the various facets of the problem, to appraise and analyze the facts, to evaluate the direct and indirect benefit to the company and its shareholders, and to make recommendations to the board. Your directors are then in a position to make a sound decision, and I assure you that in every instance the shareholders' interests are paramount.

We believe that the amount of corporate contribution by this company is reasonable by any standard. In each of the last five years, the total after-tax cost to the company and all of its affiliates for support to educational and philanthropic objectives amounted to 1½ cents per share. In our opinion the benefits, although not necessarily "direct," fully justify this expenditure. It is for these reasons that we oppose this bylaw amendment which would unduly restrict the management in the normal discharge of one of its important responsibilities.

Certainly I take no exception with Mr. Washington or his principal, Mrs. Bordon, with respect to the undesirability of supporting anything unsound and improper. We try not to do that. We know that the group of our people studying these matters is capable, competent, and objective. I would be the first to agree that there is hardly a college or a university in the United States in which some of the faculty do not hold and express views which are contrary to what we, sitting as your board, might think was right and proper.

And yet this goes to the heart of the Bill of Rights. We have freedoms in this country which few other countries have to the same extent, and these freedoms must be protected. If we reserve judgment to any small group of people as to what's right and what's wrong, without the ability of expression, we have lost something we can't afford to lose. In effect, we have to take a bit of the bitter with the sweet.

A SHAREHOLDER—I represent a group of independent investors, the American Shareholders League. Our president, Mr. Barry Jones, had intended being here today but has asked me to come in his stead. Before I read his statement on this resolution, may I make my own personal observation?

Is it preferable to have government interfere in this matter of endowments to universities and colleges? We feel that, as an organization, we certainly don't want any more government interference because we are dedicated to the free enterprise system which has served us so well in this country.

(The shareholder then read a statement from Mr. Jones, opposing the resolution and supporting management's position, in which he stressed the need for industrial leadership, and not just political leadership, in the achievement of social and educational objectives under democratic capitalism.)

THE PRESIDENT—Thank you.

A SHAREHOLDER—I'm the executive director of the Associated Colleges Fund. This association—twenty-five independent liberal arts colleges in New England—is not supported by the Delaware Company. My remarks are not made to protect its interests. While the Delaware Company plays no part in the growth or success of the fund I represent, it does make a substantial and a meaningful contribution to our colleges, and this is what counts.

In her resolution Mrs. Bordon says that many of the colleges the Delaware Company has given to teach socialism, ridicule businessmen, savers, and investors. The fact is that students who have been to college have a much better appreciation of the economic fundamentals of free enterprise. Education means the development of free minds—minds equipped to examine the strange ideas loose in today's world. Mrs. Bordon would protect today's youth from the very things that they must comprehend if our civilization is to deal effectively with the various threats to our existence.

The United States enjoys the luxury of the only truly independent system of higher education in the world. These institutions stand together with free enterprise as one of the principal bulwarks of our free society. Corporations such as the Delaware Company are offered a rare opportunity to help in determining whether this important segment of our society, one whose aims and ideals are not different from those of business itself, will remain independent or become state controlled.

THE PRESIDENT—Thank you.

A SHAREHOLDER—I am speaking in behalf of Mrs. Bordon's resolution. I believe that the Delaware Company and the shareholders should help in religious, charitable, and educational fields, but I think it is a question of the emphasis.

ANOTHER SHAREHOLDER—I'm a vice-president of Central University. I think that most of us take it for granted now that strong colleges and a strong America are more or less synonymous. American philanthropy has done much to assure strong colleges. We are particularly grateful for the role corporate philanthropy has played—has played, I might mention, without any interference with the unfettered pursuit of truth.

A THIRD SHAREHOLDER—I am fully in favor of contributions to charity and education. Our best weapon against communism is education. However, why can we not give scholarships to the gifted sons and daughters of our employees? Did you ever consider this?

THE PRESIDENT—Yes, we have considered that, but we have felt that with a family as large as ours it was difficult to engage in the scholarship business for sons and daughters of employees throughout the organization. Many of them can and do acquire scholarships, but they acquire them because they qualify on other grounds than simply being a son or daughter of an employee.

THE SHAREHOLDER—I know that our company is very much interested in the welfare of its employees. Please consider again direct scholarships to their gifted sons and daughters.

THE PRESIDENT—We shall. May I just say this, that I hope you shareholders will agree with me when I say that we are receptive to your suggestions. We may appear a little obdurate once in a while, but if the suggestions are sound and keep coming up, sometimes we find that they impress us eventually.

A SHAREHOLDER—As the owner with my wife of eight shares, which I managed to purchase after being subjected to some of the economics of these colleges which have been referred to today, I am pleased to be deprived of 1½ cents a share. In fact, I'd be glad to have you deprive me of twice 1½ cents a share.

ANOTHER SHAREHOLDER—I am supporting the management position. I certainly think that management has an obligation in regard to social duty; and in giving wise contributions over the years, we are benefited and so is the entire system. But I do think that the holders should be told in the Annual Report if we give exceptionally large contributions to any one charity or cause in one year.

THE PRESIDENT—Thank you. We'll take that suggestion into consideration.

A SHAREHOLDER—I am in favor of corporate giving, but I do feel it should be done wisely. Many of us do question giving to schools that are heavily endowed and have many wealthy alumni who can adequately care for them. Why not put the money into medical fields or colleges that really need it?

THE PRESIDENT—There are, I believe, about 700 privately supported, regionally accredited, four-year colleges and universities in the United States, and out of that list we have given in the five years in which our Education Foundation has been in being to something like 450. The others are under constant consideration, and unquestionably some of them will receive contributions before many more years have passed. We concur completely in the general thought that you have expressed. What we want to do with our educational giving is to spread it as widely as we can through worthwhile educational organizations in this country.

MR. WASHINGTON—If I don't reply to all the statements made, you mustn't think it was because I couldn't do so.

There's a very serious difference, naturally, among the stockholders of the Delaware Company as to what should be taught. It's quite proper that there should be a difference of opinion. Mrs. Bordon doesn't think that even one penny of hers should be given to causes she doesn't approve of and which she thinks are dangerous to the welfare of this country, and I think many of you will sympathize with that view.

(The Chairman declared voting on the resolution in order. Ballots were distributed, voting proceeded and was completed.)

The vote on the resolution proposed by a shareholder regarding company contributions to philanthropies and education was 3.05 percent in favor and 96.95 percent against. The resolution was thereby rejected. (Approximately 91 percent of the shareholders present voted against the resolution.)

CASE QUESTIONS:

1. What is the nature of the responsibility that profit-seeking business corporations have to higher education?

2. How does one determine that the shareholder's interests have been paramount when contributions to education are made by the Board of Directors?

3. Is it any of the public's business how much or to which educational institution a corporation makes donations?

---

8. ELECTRO-MECHANICS COMPANY

THE ELECTRO-MECHANICS COMPANY was organized in 1951 and operations were begun in 1953 when the company received its first research contract. EMCO entered the field of scientific research specializing almost exclusively in the analysis and control of radio-frequency interference (RFI). The research on RFI measurement and control techniques, and the related equipment which EMCO developed, have as their goal improving the performance of electronic systems (radio transmitters and receivers, radar systems, and missile guidance systems) by eliminating unwanted signals. While continuing its efforts in RFI research and development, EMCO has applied its capabilities to other aspects of the electromagnetic environment and to the area of magnetics. As an outgrowth of its research activities, the company manufactures and markets a line of highly-specialized, precision instruments ranging in application from radio-frequency and magnetic measurements to pressure-volume-temperature controls.

Dr. Morris, the founder, received his Ph.D. in physics, and he was an instructor in physics at a major state university from 1946 to 1951. From 1944 to 1946 he was a technical observer in the U.S. Naval Air Force. Dr. Morris also served as a consultant on the Department of Defense Research and Engineering Program. He holds memberships in honorary and professional scientific societies and is the author of numerous scientific papers and articles in the field of radio-frequency interference.

Physical Facilities

EMCO's operations began in a small laboratory owned by Dr. Morris. As the scale of operations increased in the 1950's, the physical facilities of the company were expanded by means of lease arrangements. As of 1960 the company leased three separate facilities, each of which served a separate function. The main laboratory, which contained 2,500 square feet of floor space, provided engineering facilities, a model shop, and office space for the technical staff. A 300 acre test site, located in the hill country about 20 miles from the main laboratory, provided a range for making various electromagnetic and geomagnetic measurements, and for the testing of radio transmitting and receiving gear. The test site was well suited to these purposes, as it was almost completely free from electrical and magnetic interference caused by electrical machinery and high-voltage power lines. The third facility was an office building which provided the executive and administrative offices for EMCO.

The test site and the office building were leased from Dr. Morris for annual rentals of $2,000 and $3,000, respectively, payable monthly. The laboratory was leased from a person having no connection with the company, and the terms of the lease provided for a monthly rental of $275. All three of these leases were for one-year periods and were renewable at the option of EMCO.

Operations

Operations in the period from 1953 to 1962 were limited to Air Force contracts. These contracts provided for engineering studies whose goal was to determine the feasibility of various techniques to be applied in the analysis and control of radio-frequency interference, and in the area of magnetic measurements. Frequently, the contracts included the development of a prototype unit of the related equipment.

One of several contracts emanating out of the Rome Air Development

Center (New York) consisted of an engineering study leading to a comparative evaluation of various techniques to measure the three-dimensional radiation patterns of electromagnetic emitters.

Illustrative of contracts received from the Air Research and Development Command was a 1956 contract to study the feasibility of an instrument capable of measuring detailed changes in the vertical component of the earth's magnetic field. As a result of this research the company designed and developed a variable-mu magnetometer which had a variety of applications. A three-component version of the magnetometer was later designed to be placed in the nose cone of a rocket.

Several contracts concerned with interference reduction techniques were also obtained from the Wright Air Development Division during this same period.

Data on revenue and net income resulting from these operations are given in Exhibit I. Balance sheets and income statements from 1960 to 1964 are presented in Exhibits II and III (see Exhibit IV for notes to these statements).

EXHIBIT I

REVENUE AND NET INCOME, 1953–1959

YEAR	REVENUE	NET INCOME
1959	$195,591	$6,261
1958	144,348	3,112
1957	113,109	3,355
1956	49,281	1,682
1955	55,965	1,758
1954	47,234	1,484
1953	35,676	1,091

Government Contracts

The largest percentage of EMCO's revenue has been from "cost-plus-fixed-fee" contracts. These contracts set forth an estimated cost of performance and add a fixed fee which represents profit and is a certain percentage of the estimated cost (usually in the range of 5 to 7%). Allowability of costs is determined by reasonableness, the application of generally accepted accounting principles, and any specific limitation on costs included in the regulations or in the contract terms (for example, interest costs are not allowable). All accounts are subject to rigorous audit by government auditors.

After EMCO received a contract, it invoiced the Government monthly for most of the costs incurred and the fee earned during the preceding month. An advantageous feature of this type of contract is the relatively rapid rate at which the company is reimbursed for its costs, thus reducing working capital requirements to a minimum.

The major portion of EMCO's government research contracts have resulted from "unsolicited proposals." In effect, that means that the responsibility for finding areas in which the company can perform R&D work for government agencies rests with EMCO. On these unsolicited proposals the government does not take the incentive in securing Electro-Mechanics' help on a research problem.

Dr. Morris has been EMCO's chief source of success in obtaining these contracts. He frequently visited various government agencies in order to keep attuned to the type of research work which was being done. Dr. Morris sought to relate the governmental agency research problems to the technical capabilities of EMCO; and, if it appeared that EMCO could make a contribution to the research effort, he would assign one or more engineers to begin work on a technical proposal. In the course of the development of the proposal, Dr. Morris would act as technical advisor; and, when the proposal was completed, he would edit it. He would then serve as a liaison between EMCO and the government agency in a series of negotiations directed toward obtaining a contract.

A second proposal would then be written which contained the nature of the technical work agreed upon and cost estimates for the work. A work order would then be co-prepared by EMCO and the agency. This work order, which specified the sequence or phases in which the work was to be done, contained the formal authorization to begin work on the contract. This order was prepared on a standard government form which specified in detail the personnel to be used, material cost, direct labor cost, overhead allocation, and EMCO's fee.

The contract or work order was often referred to as "blue sky" because neither party to the contract could be absolutely sure what the result of the research would be. For that reason the work order was usually prepared in phases which were to be completed in sequential order at specified time intervals. This type of contract was sometimes cancelled after the early phases because the results of the research failed to develop as expected. On the other hand, if at any time during the work it appeared that additional research might prove beneficial, EMCO could apply for an extension or modification of the contract. Modifications and extensions were frequently awarded, when justified by results.

Growth of EMCO

Until 1960, EMCO operated almost entirely under the direction of Dr. Morris, who served as Chairman of the Board, President, General Manager, Technical Advisor, and the company's chief solicitor for new or modified government contracts. During that time his wife, Vera Morris, served as Secretary and Treasurer. However, as operations expanded, he realized the need for several policy changes in order to continue EMCO's record of growth and success. As a result several major policy decisions were made in order to adjust to the changing needs of the firm.

Administration

In order to relieve himself of the growing administrative burden, Dr. Morris had been searching for a capable person to hire as general manager for administration and financial control. Mr. William H. Luedecke, owner of a local engineering company, was hired as Secretary and given a seat on the Board of Directors. He was to assume the position of General Manager as soon as he became familiar with the operations of Electro-Mechanics and had decided to remain permanently as an officer of the company. Mr. Luedecke was appointed Vice-President and General Manager in mid-1960. At that time he continued as owner of his engineering firm; however, a member of his organization assumed the operating management. In his new position with EMCO, Mr. Luedecke was placed in charge of formulating operating procedures, performing administrative work on new proposals or existing contracts, daily plant administration, correspondence, and daily financial data.

Board of Directors

During 1960 the Board of Directors consisted of Dr. Morris; Mr. Luedecke; Robert C. Sneed, a partner in a local law firm, and Vice-President in charge of EMCO's legal work; Vera W. Morris, Assistant Secretary-Assistant Treasurer and a full-time employee in the company; Theo N. Hatfield, Chairman of the Department of Physics at a nearby university; Arthur E. Lockenvitz, a Director of the Military Physics Research Laboratory at the state university and a Professor of Physics; and Albert J. Maloney, a registered representative for a local stock broker, and a director of a local bank.

Capitalization

A second basic policy decision made by the EMCO Board of Directors in 1960 was to increase capital through a public offering of common stock. Previously stock had been held only by Dr. Morris, Vera Morris, and Robert Sneed.

The authorized capitalization of the Company was originally forty shares of common stock of the par value of $25 per share. By a charter amendment in January 1959, the number of authorized shares was increased to 2000 shares of common stock of the par value of $25 per share, of which 570 shares were issued and outstanding as of September 1960. At this time an additional charter amendment paved the way for the public offering by providing for an authorized capitalization of 2,000,000 shares of common stock of the par value of $.10 per share and 100,000 shares of Class B Convertible Stock of the par value of $.20 per share. The 570 shares of outstanding stock were exchanged for the Class B stock prior to the offering, so that at the time of the offering the total outstanding stock of the company consisted of 57,000 shares of Class B stock of which Dr. Morris held 43,000 shares; Vera Morris, 10,000; and Robert Sneed, 4,000. The distinctions between the Class B stock and the 100,000 shares of common to be sold publicly were that the Class B had no rights in case of liquidation, was not transferable before the elapse of 13 months from the date of the offering, and would receive no dividends of any character. After December 1, 1963, all shares of the Class B stock could, at the election of the holder, be converted into common stock on a share-for-share basis.

As of June 30, 1960, the total assets of Electro-Mechanics were $102,000. The net worth of the company consisted of common stock in the amount of $14,250 and retained earnings of $11,833. When the common stock was exchanged for Class B stock in September 1960, the $2,850 difference between the $14,250 stated for common stock at June 30, 1960 and the amount stated for the Class B stock in Exhibit II subsequent to the exchange of shares was credited to Capital Surplus.

James C. Tucker & Co., Inc., Stocks, were retained as underwriters on a "best efforts" basis, and the 100,000 shares were sold at $3.00 per share. James C. Tucker & Co. received $.35 per share as an underwriting fee, and EMCO received $2.65 per share. Of the $265,000 proceeds from the sale, approximately $15,000 was needed to cover other expenses of the offering. According to the prospectus the net proceeds of $250,000 were tentatively intended to be used as follows:

1. $25,000 to obtain additional items of equipment and machine tools needed to conduct research and development.
2. $50,000 to mature short-term debt which the company had been using to finance working capital.
3. $100,000 to increase working capital for existing and future contracts.
4. $5,000 to survey commercial possibilities for systems, devices, and techniques already developed under previous research and development contracts.

5. $50,000 to engage in the final stages of product development for the more promising products.
6. $5,000 to apply for and receive letters of patent on products considered to be of sufficient value to justify patent protection.
7. $15,000 to find and utilize proper sales and distribution systems for company products.

Expansion Plans

In connection with the 1960 public stock offering, EMCO announced plans to increase the amount of research and development work which it had been performing, both in fields in which it had been working and in new areas. In addition, EMCO hoped to utilize the experience it had gained in the performance of its research and development contracts by offering consultant services in its fields of specialization.

Electro-Mechanics was also planning to begin commercial exploitation of devices and techniques which it had previously developed under its research and development contracts. During 1960 prospective purchasers of EMCO's consulting services and planned commercial products were believed to include:

1. All military agencies concerned with electronic compatibility in communications, radar, aircraft, missile, or other weapon systems; space exploration; and detection techniques.
2. Companies producing electronic equipment that must meet F.C.C. or military specifications.
3. Companies concerned with geophysical exploration.
4. Companies performing radio frequency interference services.
5. Companies or agencies engaged in medical electronics.
6. Educational institutions performing research in related areas.

All products developed by EMCO as a result of research performed under contract for government agencies were considered to be legally owned and patentable by EMCO. Dr. Morris felt that an excellent potential existed for commercial sales of EMCO-developed products.

Expansion and Diversification

Electro-Mechanics' first move toward expansion and diversification came in March of 1961. At that time the Luedecke Engineering Company owned by William H. Luedecke was acquired by EMCO. The Board of Directors reportedly felt that this move would help to level off the fluctuating income which resulted from a sole reliance upon government contracts.

Luedecke Engineering was a wholesale jobber of industrial heating, air conditioning, and ventilation equipment. The company had no manufacturing capacity and no technically trained engineers with the exception of Mr. Luedecke. Luedecke Engineering was merged into the EMCO organization as a separate division, with Mr. Luedecke in charge of the division.

Luedecke Engineering had been a profitable organization for several years, and, as a division of EMCO, it continued to generate profits. However, in June of 1963 Luedecke Engineering was resold to Mr. Luedecke, and Mr. Luedecke departed from EMCO. This development came about as a result of several reasons, basic of which was Mr. Luedecke's opinion that EMCO was too dependent upon government contracts.

Entry into Commercial Products

Prior to 1961, EMCO had engaged exclusively in research and development work for the United States Air Force. In 1961 the decision was made to begin development of products suitable for commercial sale.

In order to implement this decision, Dr. Morris induced an acquaintance, Mr. Walter Ruska, to join the company as a commercial products designer and manufacturing consultant. Mr. Ruska was recognized as an authority in the area of pressure-volume-temperature (PVT) equipment. Mr. Luedecke described Walter Ruska as "a master craftsman—a perfectionist." His duties at EMCO were to design PVT equipment and to help develop EMCO's commercial manufacturing capability.

Mr. Ruska left EMCO in the early part of 1963 to take a position with a technical research branch of Rice University. However, during his association with EMCO Walter Ruska developed several PVT products for commercial sales. Two of these products were a series of volumetric pumps and a magnetic circulating pump. Mr. Ruska's reputation was felt to be an asset to Electro-Mechanics, and his name was used extensively in advertising and promotional brochures for EMCO PVT commercial products which he had designed and developed. Also, many of EMCO's manufacturing and assembly procedures were developed and installed by Walter Ruska.

EMCO had maintained a machine shop for construction of parts and the assembly of prototype units for the government. However, with plans made to enter commercial sales, the operations within the shop were revised. It was felt that a larger number of parts could be subcontracted, thus relieving the burden of manufacturing parts from the shop. The primary purpose of the machine shop was to be that of assembling products from premachined parts.

Some differences would still exist, however, in the techniques of assembling commercial and government products. For instance, most finished products delivered to the government were in the form of a prototype. This means that the technical and mechanical aspects of the product were complete, but that little effort or cost has been expended in attempting to refine the appearance of the product. The government was generally only concerned with the research and development of technical aspects of the product.

In contrast, commercial products must not only be technically complete, but they must also be attractive in appearance and ready for use. The introduction of commercial products to the line thus had two ramifications. First, more refined exterior work was required on commercial products. Secondly, the shop procedures were revised to allow for "production runs" of several units as opposed to only one prototype.

EMCO began manufacturing rejection networks and magnetometers. The rejection network, a device developed in connection with a previous Air Force contract, eliminates the fundamental frequency of a transmitter, thus permitting analysis of the spurious radiation emitted by the transmitter. The applications of the variable-mu magnetometer, which measures changes in the magnetic field of the earth, are found in oil and ore prospecting, submarine detection, and space exploration.

Commercial sales were under the supervision of Mr. Luedecke. The main sales personnel were Mr. Luedecke, Dr. Morris, and several other staff engineers. Brochures describing the technical properties of each of EMCO's products were prepared and mailed periodically to manufacturing firms, governmental research agencies, educational institutions, and other possible prospects in the local area. When inquiries were received, someone familiar with the product, usually Dr. Morris, would answer the inquiry by mail or visit the prospective buyer. No advertising other than the brochures was attempted, although Dr. Morris had several scientific articles published in professional magazines.

Occasionally Dr. Morris, Mr. Luedecke, or another engineer would make a road trip, calling on prospective buyers of EMCO products. Frequently these trips were successful in stimulating sales to individuals or organizations who were not familiar with the existence or the applications of EMCO products.

New Physical Facilities

Realized growth and prospects for future growth led EMCO in late 1961 to purchase a 7-acre tract in the country in anticipation of providing for enlarged physical facilities. In late 1962 two acres of this land were sold to an investor, who constructed a building and leased the facilities to

EMCO in June of 1963. All of EMCO's operations, with the exception of the country test site, were then consolidated at this location. The new structure originally provided 9,200 square feet of floor space, but increases in the volume of work in the latter half of 1963 resulted in the addition of a new wing to the building and the construction of a warehouse. As of July 1965 the main building contained 12,500 square feet of floor space, of which 4,000 sq. ft. were devoted to research laboratories; 4,000 sq. ft. to the design engineering and production shop; and 4,500 sq. ft. to general administrative and accounting activities, a coffee shop, and a technical library. The company-owned, 1800 sq. ft. warehouse located close to the main building contained a wood-working shop, additional laboratory facilities, and a storage area. The terms of the lease on the main building provided for monthly rentals of $1,473 for a period of ten years.

The production shop was equipped with various items of general-purpose equipment such as 4 lathes, 3 milling machines, 5 drill presses, and other tools. Major technical research equipment consisted of 16 signal generators, 7 oscilloscopes, 8 receivers, 6 tape recorders, 3 instrumented test vans and trailers, and an assortment of signal measurement equipment.

The Navy Contract

During the first quarter of 1962, EMCO received a $915,000 contract from the U.S. Navy Department, Bureau of Ships. The contract was for the measurement of the radiation pattern of radar installations. EMCO was to develop an automated system which would reduce the total measurement time from six months to less than a month.

In conjunction with research and development on the Navy contract, EMCO announced a new "team effort" policy which consisted of increasing the amount of work subcontracted to smaller companies. Approximately one-third of the work on the naval contract was subcontracted to Sprague Electric Company of North Adams, Massachusetts. Prior to the naval contract, government R&D contracts had ranged from $25,000 to $100,000. Thus, the Navy contract was approximately ten times as large as previous contracts.

This contract consisted of six "tasks," or phases, with a specified portion of the total $915,000 allocated to each of the six tasks. The sixth task, which constituted the largest dollar amount of the total contract, was the development of an instrument package and a 200-foot portable, collapsible tower. The instrument package was to be operated on top of the tower.

The first five tasks were completed or virtually completed in 1963. Of

EMCO's 1963 revenue from government contracts ($621,279), approximately $400,000 came from the Navy contract. This contract provided for a fee of 7¾% of cost.

There was some misunderstanding concerning the nature of the contract, EMCO apparently being unaware that a specific amount of the total contract was allocated to each of the six tasks. This resulted in a cost overrun on four of the first five tasks for a total overrun of approximately $10,000. In the first quarter of 1964 the Navy terminated the contract as a result of a de-emphasis placed on the program of measurement and analysis of the radiation patterns of radar installations. Also, because of the cost overruns, the Navy refused to make any further reimbursements under the contract. EMCO filed a $77,000 claim against the Navy. This claim consisted of $33,000 unreimbursed costs and fees from 1963 operations, the $10,000 cost overrun on the first five tasks, and $34,000 of unreimbursed costs and fees from 1964 operations. When the burden rates were audited at the end of 1964, an additional claim of $6,000 resulted. In the first quarter of 1965 the $77,000 claim was approved by a Navy review board and paid. Of this $77,000, $41,300 went to pay subcontractor costs, thus providing EMCO with $35,000 in net proceeds.

The cancellation of the Navy contract created a financial crisis for EMCO. The delayed recovery of the contract cost and fees was a severe financial setback to the company. Also, the large contract had resulted in a de-emphasis of commercial products in 1963 and early 1964, since a major portion of the production facilities had been occupied in the construction of the tower. Furthermore, the company had become so engrossed in the large contract that efforts to secure other new contracts had fallen off. A lead time of approximately 6 months to a year was usually required to find a new area where EMCO could do research, develop a proposal, and negotiate a contract. This time lag made it extremely difficult for the company to fill the gap in government research work created by the cancellation of the Navy contract. This was compounded by the cutback in government defense spending in the 1964 election year.

Immediately following the contract cancellation, EMCO took several measures to combat the crisis. A major measure was a cutback in the number of personnel employed. In 1960 the company had employed approximately 45 persons, and by 1963 the number of employees had increased to approximately 75. By the end of 1964 this number was reduced to approximately 30. The criterion used in the cutback was, in the words of one company official, "to keep the people whom we had work for." A second major measure was a substantial reduction in the salaries of the officers. Other minor cost reductions were:

1. Monthly rentals of $166 on the test site were waived until such time as financial conditions permitted retroactive restoration.

2. Supplies and materials were ordered in 3-month quantities as opposed to the previous practice of ordering in 6-month quantities.
3. Subscriptions to numerous technical publications were cancelled.
4. Two-color quarterly reports to the stockholders were eliminated. The annual report was replaced by a letter from the President and copies of audited financial statement.

Finance

In 1961, when EMCO purchased the Luedecke Engineering Company, the purchase was financed in part by the issuance of an unsecured note payable to Mr. Luedecke. The balance of this note at the end of 1961 was $46,336, payable in three equal annual installments of $15,412 plus interest at 5 percent. This debt was retired in 1963 in connection with the resale of Luedecke Engineering Company to Mr. Luedecke.

In 1961, the purchase of the 7-acre tract was financed in part by the issuance of a note payable to the land owner. This note, in the amount of $18,550, was secured by a deed of trust on the land, and it was payable in annual installments of $2,000 plus interest at 6 percent. This debt was prematurely reduced in 1962, when 2 acres of the tract were sold to the investor who constructed the company facilities and leased them to EMCO.

In 1964 the note secured by the deed of trust was refinanced by means of a note payable to a local bank. This note was secured by a deed of trust on the warehouse and the 5 acres of land owned by EMCO.

Up until 1964 the company had utilized short-term borrowing from a local bank on an unsecured basis. The notes were personally endorsed by Dr. Morris. Due to the financial difficulties of the company, the short-term note payable at December 31, 1964 was secured by a chattel mortgage on various equipment. In addition, the company agreed to apply $1,000 from the proceeds of the sale of each rejection network and $1,250 from the sale of each pump to this indebtedness. As of July, 1965 the short-term bank loan had been completely liquidated, primarily by means of the proceeds from the settlement of the Navy claim.

Personnel and Organization

When it became clear that Mr. Luedecke was leaving EMCO in 1963, Dr. Morris began to search for a replacement. He also felt that he should increase his administrative staff, which had previously consisted of only himself, Mr. Luedecke, and Mrs. Morris. Accordingly, Dr. Morris obtained the services of W. A. Wood, R. L. Feik, and W. F. Johnson in mid-1963.

Mr. Wood had worked as a Certified Public Accountant from 1946 to 1956. He served as controller of a small photogrammetic engineering company from 1956–1962, and as Executive Vice-President of Geotechnics, Inc., from 1962 to mid-1963. Mr. Wood came to EMCO as Vice-President and Administrative Director, and he relieved Dr. Morris of nearly all administrative duties.

Mr. Feik was hired as the Technical Director in charge of all technical operations at EMCO. He had considerable experience in the supervision of operations similar to those at Electro-Mechanics.

The accounting and financial control of operations was strengthened by the hiring of Mr. Johnson, a CPA, as Chief Accountant. Mr. Johnson was placed in charge of preparing cost estimates, cost control, and all matters relating to daily accounting for operations and the preparation of periodic financial statements. He reported to Mr. Wood.

Both Wood and Feik initially reported directly to Dr. Morris, who continued as President. Later, in mid-1964, the Board of Directors appointed Mr. Wood as President, and Mr. Feik became Vice-President in charge of government contract work. Mr. Wood was in charge of commercial product sales. Both Mr. Wood and Mr. Feik became members of the Board. Other officers and members of the Board included Mrs. Vera Morris, Secretary-Treasurer, and Mr. R. C. Sneed, Vice-President in charge of EMCO's legal work.

Mr. Feik left EMCO in April of 1965. As of July 1965 the organizational structure of Electro-Mechanics appeared approximately as shown in Exhibit V.

Mr. Wood, President, was the general administrative officer of EMCO. He executed all company contracts and supervised the flow of paper work involved in government contracts. The development of cost data which is an integral part of government research proposals is prepared under his supervision. Once a research contract is obtained, Mr. Wood exercises control over contract performance by comparing progress reports and cost reports with the project budgets. When work on a contract was not progressing on time or within the cost requirements, Mr. Wood reviewed these deviations with Dr. Morris. Other major duties of Mr. Wood included supervision of company finances and stockholder relations. In addition, Mr. Wood authorized the production of EMCO's commercial products, and he was in charge of obtaining manufacturer's sales representatives for EMCO's products.

Dr. Morris, Director of Research, remained as EMCO's chief scientist. He continued to be the chief source of EMCO's success in finding potential areas for government research, advising in the preparation of technical proposals, and negotiating the contracts. In addition, he served as technical advisor on the contracts which were obtained. Each government contract was assigned to a group leader who supervised the staff allocated to that contract. Dr. Morris worked closely with the group leaders and their staffs, helping to coordinate the work and advising on technical problems encountered by anyone in the groups.

Although the greatest part of EMCO's government research work came as a result of unsolicited proposals, EMCO also received requests for proposals (RFP's) as a result of having their technical capabilities and areas of interest registered with governmental agencies. When an agency had a specific work requirement, it would send RFP's to a number of firms which had capabilities suited to the research requirements. The RFP's sent to EMCO were directed to Dr. Morris, who evaluated them and decided whether or not to submit a proposal.

Dr. Morris also headed the effort to secure research and product development work in the industrial area. This effort consisted of conferring with industry representatives about particular problems faced by the industry, and attempting to develop a theoretical solution. For example, EMCO's sales representative in the Houston area recently brought a technical problem faced by the natural gas industry to the attention of EMCO. Dr. Morris developed a solution, and then conferred with representatives of that industry in order to determine the exact technical requirements and the extent of the market for the associated product. Mr. Wood stated, "If he gets the right answers, chances are that we will develop it." Although the majority of Dr. Morris's efforts have been directed towards government research in the past, it is expected that industrial research and development will occupy an equal portion of his time in the future.

As of July 1965 EMCO employed approximately 35 persons, consisting of 4 administrative personnel, 2 accountants, 12 engineers, 14 technicians, and 3 machinists. The operations of the mechanical engineering department consisted primarily of commercial product design and production. This department also provided supporting work related to the mechanical aspects of government contract work. The electronic engineering department operated primarily in the area of government contract work. The mechanical engineering department's personnel consisted of 2 mechanical engineers, a shop foreman, and 3 machinists. The majority of the company's operating personnel are in the electronic engineering department.

Recent Operations

In June of 1963, EMCO had a backlog of government contract work totaling approximately $500,000. The backlog stood at approximately $170,000 in June of 1964, and it consisted mostly of contracts which had a short period left to run (3 to 4 months). In December of 1964 the backlog had declined to $100,000; however, by June of 1965 EMCO had begun to fill the gap left by the cancellation of the large Navy contract, and the backlog stood at $180,000. This backlog consisted of contracts whose duration ranged from 6 months to a year. Revenue from government contracts in the first half of 1965 was estimated at $165,000.

For the first half of 1965 revenue from commercial product sales was estimated at $50,000. Net income for this period, from both government work and commercial sales, was estimated at $20,000 before the special credit of $35,700 arising from the recovery on the Navy contract.

The company's best selling commercial product during 1962–63 was the rejection network. This item, which was priced at $1,500 had a market limited to government agencies and research organizations doing radio frequency interference work for the government. EMCO sold approximately 75 of these networks in 1963, 10 in 1964, and 20 in the first half of 1965. The market for this particular network has virtually been saturated; however, EMCO is currently working on a modified version of the network under two contracts (one government contract and one industrial contract). The company felt that there will be increased demand for this modified network.

A recent addition to EMCO's commercial product line is the log-spiral antenna. This specialized antenna, which is priced at $420, is also an outgrowth of a government research contract. This antenna has a broader market than that of the current rejection network. Fifty of these antennas were sold in the first half of 1965, and purchasers included such firms as RCA, Pan American World Airways, and Univac, as well as government research agencies.

The first sales of EMCO's PVT equipment occurred in 1964 when two of the volumetric pumps, priced around $10,000 each, were sold. Two of the magnetic circulating pumps, priced at $450 each, were also sold in 1964. The combined cost of the two volumetric pumps was approximately $30,000, and the combined cost of the two circulating pumps was approximately $1,200. These costs were in excess of the revenue because the company elected to charge off the research and development costs of these products against the first sales. No PVT equipment was sold in the first half of 1965.

EMCO foresees a bright sales picture for both the antenna and the modified rejection network, and Mr. Wood was working actively to develop EMCO's marketing capabilities. As of July 1965 the company had one manufacturer's agent in Houston. This agent, who also handled a line of products compatible with those of EMCO, sold EMCO's products on a commission basis. Mr. Wood reported that prospects were good for obtaining a second agent in the New Jersey area fairly soon, as well as the possibility of a third agent on the West Coast.

In addition to securing manufacturer's agents, EMCO was also negotiating with a large manufacturer of receivers and related electronic equipment. Prospects are fairly good that the manufacturer, who has a nationwide distribution system, might agree to market EMCO's log-spiral antennas as a supplement to their equipment line. If this arrangement could be consummated, it would mean that EMCO would produce these antennas in lots of 100, as opposed to current production in lots of 10. Current production required a week's work by a machinist and about one week for an electronic technician to make the necessary calibrations. The new arrangement would require placing several people on full-time production of antennas.

Future Strategy

In outlining EMCO's plans, Mr. Wood stated: "While government contracts are erratic, they will continue to be an important part of our work in the long run. We currently have the capacity to produce approximately $400,000 to $500,000 in revenue per year from government contracts; however, we expect to maintain total revenue from such contracts at approximately the current level. Future revenue increases will come through placing increasing emphasis upon commercial products. Probably within a year our operations will be comprised of 75% government work and 25% commercial products. Within two years, if all goes well, these percentages will have changed to 50–50." Major reliance would be placed on two products, the log-spiral antenna and the rejection network. Additional research effort, to the extent resources permitted, was scheduled for two new commercial products which the management believed to have considerable promise. Each of these proposed products would represent a substantial departure from their established product lines.

It is this strategy with which EMCO hopes to achieve the goal stated in a March 1965 letter from the President to stockholders, which stated that they hoped "to accelerate the recovery begun and to continue the progress delayed."

EXHIBIT II

THE ELECTRO-MECHANICS COMPANY

Comparative Balance Sheets as of December 31, 1960–64

	1960	1961	1962	1963	1964
CURRENT ASSETS					
Cash	$212,903	$156,127	$123,526	$ 18,220	$ 890
Receivables:					
Government contracts – Note A	58,572	90,764	111,471	151,776	70,464
Trade accounts		18,171	53,628	39,131	18,191
Accrued interest		3,400	2,595	275	228
Recoverable income taxes on carry-back of 1964 loss					3,305
Inventories:					
Raw materials		2,195	3,450	2,959	6,416
Work in process			2,335	36,634	36,083
Finished goods			20,314	1,200	17,308
Prepaid expenses	588		3,743	5,260	3,313
Total Current Assets	$272,063	$270,657	$321,062	$255,455	$156,198
OTHER ASSETS					
Note receivable from stockholder				$ 9,430	$ 6,930
Note receivable on building construction					8,078
Deposits	$ 560	$ 795	$ 3,629	2,532	4,995
Total Other Assets	$ 560	$ 795	$ 3,629	$ 11,962	$ 20,003
PROPERTY, PLANT, AND EQUIPMENT					
Land-mortgaged		$ 26,435	$ 26,435	$ 19,531	$ 19,531
Building				13,243	13,822
Equipment and leasehold improvements	$ 54,683	90,733	120,621	176,964	174,609
Less depreciation and amortization	(35,555)	(48,057)	(61,632)	(80,511)	(96,865)
Total Property and Equipment	$ 19,128	$ 69,111	$ 85,424	$129,227	$111,097

DEFERRED CHARGES					
Research and development costs – Note B		$ 16,097	$ 40,426		
Deferred contract costs – Note C		22,805			
Other	$ 89	903	1,969	$ 4,980	$ 2,930
Total Deferred Charges	$ 89	$ 39,805	$ 42,395	$ 4,980	$ 2,930
TOTAL ASSETS	$291,840	$380,368	$452,510	$401,624	$290,228
CURRENT LIABILITIES					
Notes payable to bank	$ 8,305	$ 5,465	$ 47,500	$ 50,000	$ 53,113
Notes payable to officers					20,000
Accounts payable	1,408	22,653	39,477	34,804	12,476
Accrued wages		7,148	24,351	9,709	10,909
Payroll taxes		1,938	11,596	8,725	3,366
Accrued interest		445	2,198	388	616
Estimated federal income tax	5,233		1,753	676	
Current maturities of long-term debt		17,412	17,412	2,228	2,254
TOTAL CURRENT LIABILITIES	$ 14,946	$ 55,061	$144,287	$106,530	$102,734
LONG-TERM DEBT					
5% note to individual, unsecured		$ 46,236	$ 30,824	$ 10,550	$ 19,440
6% note to individual, secured		18,550	12,550	913	684
6% note to bank, secured					
Insurance premium note					
		$ 64,786	$ 43,374	$ 11,463	$ 20,124
Less current maturities		17,412	17,412	2,228	2,254
TOTAL LONG-TERM DEBT		$ 47,374	$ 25,962	$ 9,235	$ 17,870
STOCKHOLDERS' EQUITY					
Common stock	$ 10,000	$ 10,000	$ 10,000	$ 10,000	$ 10,000
Class B stock	11,400	11,400	11,400	11,400	11,400
Capital surplus	242,884	242,884	242,884	242,884	242,884
Retained Earnings	12,610	13,649	17,977	21,575	(94,660)
TOTAL STOCKHOLDERS' EQUITY	$276,894	$277,933	$282,261	$285,859	$169,624
TOTAL LIABILITIES AND NET WORTH	$291,840	$380,368	$452,510	$401,624	$290,228

EXHIBIT III

THE ELECTRO-MECHANICS COMPANY

Comparative Income Statements

Periods Ending December 31, 1960–64

	1960	1961	1962	1963	1964
Revenue:					
Government contracts – Note A	$203,591	$266,250	$375,387	$621,279	$262,090
Commercial products		79,691	265,873	200,194	55,514
	$203,591	$345,941	$641,260	$821,473	$317,604
Expenses:					
Government contract costs:					
Direct contract costs:					
Salaries	$ 77,810	$109,467	$100,525	$153,017	$103,552
Materials, expenses, and sub-contract costs	30,562	22,141	111,859	196,643	149,988
Indirect contract costs:					
Salaries		23,482	51,177	75,543	63,236
Materials, expenses, and sub-contract costs		16,205	28,193	83,966	41,043
	$108,372	$171,295	$291,754	$509,169	$357,819
Cost of commercial products sold		52,311	210,593	150,122	45,751
	$108,372	$223,606	$502,347	$659,291	$403,570
Administrative salaries and expenses	85,155	105,279	109,448	115,826	5,909
Interest expense–(income)	2,904	(1,926)	579	839	4,653
Uncollectible accounts					
Research and development expense				4,758	23,012
TOTAL EXPENSES	$196,431	$326,959	$612,374	$780,714	$437,144
OPERATING INCOME (LOSS)	$ 7,160	$ 18,982	$ 28,886	$ 40,759	($119,540)
Special charges (credits):					
Special charge – Note C				$ 59,801	
Special charge – Note B		$ 17,498	$ 22,805		
Special credit – Note D				(24,842)	
Federal taxes on income-estimated	2,311	445	1,753	2,203	
Recoverable income taxes on carry-back of 1964 loss					(3,305)
	$ 2,311	$ 17,943	$ 24,558	$ 37,162	$ (3,305)
NET INCOME (LOSS)	$ 4,849	$ 1,039	$ 4,328	$ 3,597	($116,235)

EXHIBIT IV

THE ELECTRO-MECHANICS COMPANY
Notes to Financial Statements

Note A — Receivables on government contracts represent unreimbursed costs and fees under cost reimbursement type contracts. Income from government research and development contracts is reported on the percentage of completion method of accounting. Reimbursement of costs included in income is made by the government subject to subsequent audit. Costs reimbursed through 1964 have been audited and approved.

Note B — Prior to 1963 it was the policy of the Company to defer research and development costs on certain projects, and to subsequently amortize these costs based upon subsequent product sales. The Company decided in 1963 to temporarily discontinue these projects and to charge off all research costs incurred in that year and those previously deferred.

Note C — On March 1, 1961, the Company acquired Luedecke Engineering Company. In connection with the purchase the Company paid $40,303 for work which Luedecke Engineering Company had in process at that time. The Company amortized this cost over the contracts as they were completed.

Note D — This credit represents a gain on the sale of Luedecke Engineering Company.

EXHIBIT V

THE ELECTRO-MECHANICS COMPANY

Company Organization Chart, July, 1965

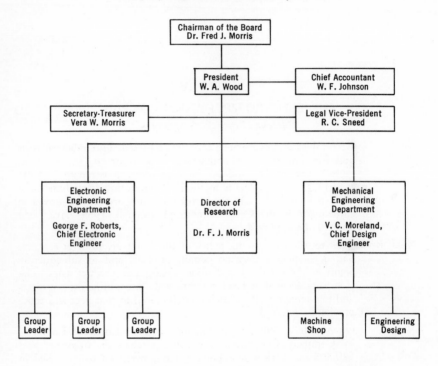

9. GLASTRON BOAT COMPANY

GLASTRON BOAT COMPANY WAS ORGANIZED in October, 1956, to manufacture and sell fiberglass pleasure boats. Production facilities and the company's executive officers were originally housed in a rented warehouse building of 63,000 square feet of floor space. A new plant, containing specially designed facilities, with 41,280 square feet was constructed on a 5-acre site in 1960. Facilities at the new plant included enclosed spray booths, special storage tanks, pumping equipment and piping to handle resin and solvents in large quantities, a repair shop for maintaining company equipment, and a design research laboratory. The plant was designed for a one shift normal capacity of 20 units per day of boats ranging in lengths from fourteen to eighteen feet.

The manufacturing process and the fiberglass materials used in the manufacture of boats were described in a company publication as follows:

> Fiberglass reinforced plastic generally consists, so far as boats are concerned, of three basic glass compositions and a liquid binder called polyester resin. The three types of fiberglas used in the Company's boats are known as fiberglass mat, woven roving, and cloth. All start out as a basic fiber filament produced by extruding molten glass through a minute bushing and gathering it in strands. The strands are processed into (a) yarn from which fiberglass cloth is woven; (b) woven roving which, in effect, is a form of extremely heavy cloth; or (c) fiberglass mat, which in appearance is much the same as felt. In constructing its boats the company utilizes a composition of all three types of fiberglass. The cloth, woven roving, and mat are saturated with polyester resin, which binds the fibers into a dense lightweight laminate, the cloth forming the outer skin.
>
> The manufacturing process used in building the Company's boats was essentially as follows:
>
> Female molds, which are an exact counterpart of the outside surface of the finished boat, are fabricated from fiberglass, usually in two parts consisting of deck and hull molds. The inside surface of the molds are highly polished and treated with a wax or release agent. A coat of polyester resin, pigmented to the desired color of the finished product, is then sprayed onto the mold surfaces and allowed to cure. Layers of fiberglass cloth, mat, and/or woven roving are then tailored to the general contours of the molds and are saturated with resin. Air voids are removed by rollers, squeegees, and brushes, and the resulting laminate is allowed to cure. Various ribs which are designed to provide additional rigidity in the boat and which may be made of wood or premolded fiberglass forms are then attached by means of mat strips saturated with resin and are allowed to cure. The hull and deck are then joined by conventional fastenings. A narrow strip of saturated mat is normally used to further bond the deck to the hull on the inside, although such a procedure is not essential. After the parts of the boat have been joined, hardware, seats, windshield, and other accessories are installed.

Control of Production Operations

Over the past six years since Glastron Boat Company was organized, a relatively simple system of controlling production of fiberglass boats was evolved. The system was considered by the production manager to be as simple as possible for their operations and still maintain the degree of control considered desirable.

After a new boat had been designed and cleared for production, a complete bill of materials was prepared. Each bill was subdivided into sections listing materials to be used at each of the thirty molding, trimming, and assembly stations. Standard times for performing each process were estimated and entered on the form. From the information embodied in the bill of materials the total direct cost of production was estimated.

Materials lists for a particular model boat were prepared for each of three supply shops: (1) Pre-cut raw materials (fiberglass mats, ribs, etc.), (2) aluminum extrusions; and (3) upholstery supplies. These lists were kept on file in the respective supply shops to be used when needed in the preparation of material packages for individual boats.

Production Schedules

Production schedules were set by the production manager on a weekly basis, three weeks prior to the week being scheduled. The three week lead time was considered adequate to enable all materials to be ready and available when needed. Copies of the production schedules were sent to the purchasing agent and all others who needed this information, including the major suppliers.

Schedules were developed with the cooperation of the sales manager after reviewing inventories on hand and current sales trends, plus a consideration of how far along they were in the season. Boat sales were highly seasonal, reaching a peak in the second quarter of the year, and manufacturing schedules necessarily varied from a low of two units per day to a high of twenty units per day. Fiberglass outboard boats had become an annual style item, making any attempt to carry over stock into the next season a high risk venture. Extra care had to be exercised after June 1 to avoid producing items which might be difficult to sell before new models were introduced in August.

Exhibit I shows a portion of a typical schedule. Each model which

EXHIBIT I

EXAMPLE OF PRODUCTION SCHEDULE
FOR FEBRUARY 4 & 5, 1963

Date Model No.	142	143	144	152	155	163
2/4/63	R203064	R203066	T203068	R203070	R203071	G203074
	R 065	T 067	T 069		R 072	G 075
					R 073	G 076
						G 077
2/5/63	R203078	R203080	T203082	R203084	R203085	G203088
	R 079	T 081	T 083		R 086	G 089
					R 087	G 090
						G 091

was to be produced on a particular date was assigned a serial number prefixed by a letter color code. The serial number was listed on the Production Schedule in the block reserved for that particular date and boat model. For example, on February 4, 1963, there were two red, model 142 boats, serial numbers 203064 and 203065, scheduled. From the production schedule the production manager made out the production order cards.

Production Order Cards

A production order card (Exhibit II) was made out for each boat to be produced and dated according to the day production was to begin on that boat. The serial number for the boat was printed on each section of the production order card. The card was pre-perforated into 24 sections, each section authorizing either work to be done, materials to be issued, materials to be prepared for issue, or to serve as identification cards. One week prior to the scheduled production of a particular boat the three cards marked Mat, Upholstery, and Extrusion were detached and distributed to the respective supply shops in order that the materials could be prepared and placed in the area where they would be used. The materials lists were used to determine the exact materials needed for the particular boat. See the Flow Chart in Exhibit III for a schematic model of the production and order control process.

Each morning the production manager separated the production order cards for the boats that were to be started that day into the Deck, Hull, and Assembly portions, and fitted them on the production schedule rack in the factory in the numerical order that production was to be carried out. When the deck and hull molding crews were ready to begin molding a new boat, the corresponding tickets were taken from the schedule rack and the crew was thus notified to perform the operation indicated by the performance ticket. The specific operation ticket was removed from the card and the remainder of the card, along with the partially completed hull or deck, was passed on to the next work station. In each case, the appropriate ticket served as a work authorization for the crew.

For example, boat number R203064—a red, model 142 boat was scheduled for February 4, 1963. When the deck molding crew was ready to begin, they obtained the fiberglass matting, the female mold, and other materials provided for their use at their work station. After the molding operation was completed, one worker removed the ticket D 9 (the ticket directly below D 9—marked Glastron Boat Company, Serial No. R203065 —was stuck face up in the wet resin impregnated fiberglass to serve as permanent identification of the boat) and passed the remaining tickets along with the deck to the deck detail and inspection station. Each subsequent operation was performed as scheduled and the corresponding ticket was torn off the card and retained by the operation performing crew. Ticket D 6A (Deck Storeroom Kit) was presented to the storeroom by the deck assembly crew to authorize the issuance of the deck assembly materials. Ticket D 6A was sent by the storeroom to the Accounting Department for entry on the Payroll and Production Report.

The deck assembly operation was then performed and the remaining ticket (D 5) was left with the deck for further identification.

While the deck was in the process of fabrication, the hull was being similarly molded and assembled. When both the hull and the deck were completed, the joining crew obtained the assembly operation card, presented ticket D 4A to the storeroom and received a joining materials kit. The deck and hull were then joined. The third and final assembly operations were then performed by the appropriate assembly crews. After the boat had been given a final inspection, the release ticket was dated, and any missing parts were noted. The cost information requested on the release ticket was not filled out because it was not considered necessary by the Production Manager.

At the end of each work day, the tickets that had been accumulated at each work station were sent to the Production Manager. From these tickets, indicating work completed, or materials issued, the Production Manager made up a bar graph for each crew indicating the crew's daily performance. The performance tickets were then forwarded to the Accounting Department where they were used to deplete the stock records. The tickets which had been retained by the stockrooms were sent to the Accounting Department for correction of stock depletion records. The system described was used for all boat models. The manufacturing time for all outboard models was considered to be approximately equal.

Production Report

As each boat was completed and taken to the warehouse, the serial number and model number were entered on the Production Report. Also recorded was the time of completion and a list of any missing parts or accessories. At the end of each day, the Product Reports were sent to the Production Manager's office, and the boats completed were checked off the production schedule. The Accounting Department also received a copy of this report to maintain the serial number book and the Payroll and Production Report.

Daily Payroll and Production Report

The Payroll and Production Report was a daily summary of manufacturing operations performed by each crew. A copy of this report is shown in Exhibit IV. The number of all performance tickets used were noted in the units column and the number of employees performing the operation was noted in the adjacent column. From the employee's time cards, the total hours worked were computed and divided into regular time and overtime pay amounts. The standard number of hours for the number of units produced was also noted in the last column for comparison with the actual hours taken. All other labor (indicated as indirect) was similarly summarized for each crew. A weekly Payroll and Production Report, for comparison of total cost versus total product value for each crew was also made up. The comparison was charted on several different bases, and these charts constituted the basis of the reports to management by the Production Manager.

Trends in Manufacturing

A definite development in small pleasure boat manufacturing, beginning about 1960 according to the production manager, was the improved design and construction of boats. Small pleasure boats had changed, he stated, from relatively simple shells to complicated, engineered devices, with sophisticated details to satisfy the demands of boat buyers. Because of the vigorous competition, boat prices tended to remain relatively stable for the same length boat. With the improved construction, the more costly design and engineering effort, and the multiplicity of models to contend with, the manufacturer was faced with a cost squeeze which resulted in decreased profits for most, and the demise of a substantial number of the estimated 200 manufacturers in the four years preceeding 1963.

The demand for small pleasure boats was believed to be very responsive to general economic conditions because of their status as a luxury item whose purchase could be easily deferred for a year or two. Sales were also highly seasonal in nature. Retail purchasers tended to concentrate their buying in the late spring and early summer, and dealers as a rule tended to anticipate demand only by a month or two except for demonstration models.

As a result, more than 70 percent of sales were typically concentrated in the first six months of the year. Boats produced in anticipation of demand but not sold to distributors during the season were offered at special discounts to dealers, resulting in marginal profit. Also, boats produced in the late summer for the next season were often offered with special "pre-season" discounts to encourage dealers to stock boats in anticipation of sale the following spring.

Two major design trends became evident in the small pleasure boat market in 1963. The first was the popularity of the deep vee-type hull, referred to as "Aqua-Lift" by Glastron, which featured a full-length monogedron planing surface to significantly improve performance of larger-sized boats. The second was the inboard-outboard or stern-drive power system, which became highly competitive with inboard boats under 20 feet in length. Stern drive models were sold as "blanks" or with installed power system, as requested by dealers. Production scheduling, as well as fabrication, were more complex for stern drive units. Inventory control became more vital because the more complicated units represented an increased investment of approximately $1400 per unit.

Cost Control

The production manager stated that the major problem which he faced and which he hoped to resolve satisfactorily as soon as possible was that he didn't know with sufficient accuracy what each boat cost to make.

Under their present system of accounting for costs, he had some reasonably dependable averages for all boats made. Some fairly dependable averages could be obtained from the raw data collected on the daily payroll and production report when it was summarized weekly for each crew, but it still required too much clerical time, in his opinion, to find the average cost for every model built during the week.

When the current season's models had been in production for some time and everything seemed to be running well, the production manager considered his cost data to be satisfactory for the degree of control he wanted. But when new models were being introduced to the line, costs often tended to vary from estimates upon which the price list for the whole year's output was based, and it was often difficult to find and correct the trouble quickly.

He felt that it was impossible to determine accurately the cost of particular operations without using stop-watch time studies, and he was not ready to undertake that step. Several years ago the company had used job cards and time clocks to control labor operations, but they soon decided that the system was unworkable and unnecessarily detailed, and abandoned it within six months.

Cost estimates were prepared for all models each season in June and retail price schedules were announced to the trade at a major boat show held in August. Traditionally, prices were fixed for the entire model year. Cost estimates were prepared by the production manager for direct labor, while the purchasing agent prepared estimates of material costs from the bill of materials developed by the designer. A cost breakdown for a typical 15 foot outboard boat indicated approximately 13 percent direct labor, 55 percent direct materials, and 32 percent burden and profit margin. Because certain price ranges were traditional in the industry, each model was generally designed to sell at a particular price. Probable sales volume for each model was estimated and the burden charge to be borne by each model was determined, and the direct labor and materials cost goals were set. Whether or not a particular model was profitable in any season was to a large part dependent upon how closely actual sales matched planning sales, as well as how close actual labor and materials costs were to planned costs.

EXHIBIT II

COST EXHIBIT FORM

DECK STORAGE — D 5	RELEASE DATE ___ MODEL ___ $ MISSING PARTS ___ STANDARD COST $ ___ INITIALS ___	HULL ASSEMBLY — H 5
DATE ___ INITIALS ___		COST ___
DECK ASSEMBLY — D 6	FINAL DETAIL & INSPECTION — A 1	DATE ___ INITIALS ___
		MATERIAL FOR KIT — H 5A
COST ___	COST ___	COST ___
DATE ___ INITIALS ___	DATE ___ INITIALS ___	DATE ___ INITIALS ___
DECK STOREROOM KIT — D 6A	FINAL ASSEMBLY — A 2	HULL SPECKLE — H 6
		$ ___ MATERIAL
COST ___		COST ___
DATE ___ INITIALS ___	DATE ___ INITIALS ___	DATE ___ INITIALS ___
DECK SANDING — D 6	MAT'L FOR KIT — A 2A	HULL SANDING — H 7
COST ___	COST ___	COST ___
DATE ___ INITIALS ___	DATE ___ INITIALS ___	DATE ___ INITIALS ___
DECK DETAIL & INSPECTION — D 8	TRIM — A 3	HULL DETAIL & INSPECTION — H 8

122

EXHIBIT II (*continued*)

GLASTRON BOAT COMPANY
Austin, Texas

Serial No.

COST		INITIALS	COST		INITIALS	COST		INITIALS
DATE	DECK MOLDING	D 9	DATE	MATERIAL FOR KIT	A 3A	DATE	HULL MOLDING	H 9
COST		INITIALS	COST		INITIALS	COST		INITIALS
DATE	EXTRUSION	S 12	DATE	MATERIAL FOR KIT	A 4A	DATE	UPHOLSTERY	S 10

JOINING A 4 MAT S 11

123

EXHIBIT III

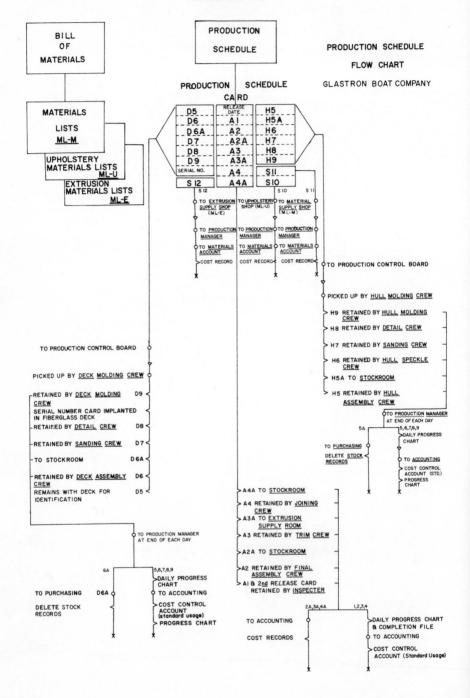

EXHIBIT IV

PAYROLL AND PRODUCTION REPORT

	UNITS-EMP	TOTAL HRS	REG. AMTS	O.T. AMTS	TOT. AMTS	STD
HULL MOLDING						
H 10						
H 9 — 100						
200						
300						
500						
H 8						
S 13 — Wood						
TOTAL						
DECK MOLDING						
D 10						
D 9 — 100						
200						
300						
D 8						
S 11 — Mat						
TOTAL						
ASSEMBLY						
H7 & D7 — Sanding						
H 6 — Speckle						
D 6 — Deck Asbly						
H 5 — Hull Asbly						
A 4 — Joining						
A 2 — Trim & Fin. ASBLY.						
A 1 — Fin. Det. & INSP.						
S 10 — Upholstery						
S 12 — Extrusion Hard Tops						
TOTAL						
INDIRECT						
S 9 — Inspectors						
S 8 — Warehouse						
S 6 — Plant General						
S 5 — Stockroom						
S 4 — Warranty Reruns						
S 3 — Tooling Customer Service						
TOTAL						
SUMMARY						
HULL MLDG.						
DECK MLDG.						
ASSEMBLY						
TOTAL DIRECT						
TOTAL INDIRECT						
TOTAL						

125

EXHIBIT V

GLASTRON BOAT COMPANY

COMPARATIVE BALANCE SHEETS AND INCOME
STATEMENTS EIGHT MONTHS ENDING
APRIL 30, 1963 AND APRIL 30, 1962

ASSETS:	1963 (Cents omitted)	1962 (Cents omitted)
Cash	$ 26,853	$ 56,021
Receivables	488,978	321,046
Inventories	378,113	398,196
Prepaid Expenses	20,937	17,958
Total Current Assets	$ 914,881	$ 793,221
Fixed Assets Less Reserves	337,265	298,304
Investments	7,555	30,881
Deferred Charges & Costs	140,558	217,584
Total Assets	$1,400,259	$1,339,990
LIABILITIES:		
Accounts Payable	$ 300,122	$ 331,166
Notes Payable	144,399	136,615
Current Portion Long Term Debt	7,500	5,120
Total Current Liabilities	$ 452,021	$ 472,901
Long Term Notes Payable	85,027	84,247
Debenture Bonds Payable	438,700	478,200
Other Reserves	7,500	36,834
Total Liabilities	$ 983,248	$1,072,182
Stockholders Equity	$ 417,011	$ 267,808
Total Liabilities and Capital	$1,400,259	$1,339,990
Stockholder's Equity Per Share	1.1915	.7652
Net Sales	$1,979,901	$1,495,223
Cost of Sales	1,507,106	1,201,604
Gross Profit	$ 472,795	$ 293,619
Operating Expenses	280,013	252,821
Operating Profit (Loss)	$ 192,782	$ 40,798
Other Expenses	70,205	56,453
Net Profit (Loss)	$ 122,577	$ (15,655)
Net Profit (Loss) Per Share	.35	(.04)

EXHIBIT VI

ESTIMATED ANNUAL MODEL-YEAR SALES
AND AVERAGE FACTORY PRICES
GLASTRON BOAT COMPANY

MODEL YEAR	UNITS SOLD[1]	AVERAGE FACTORY PRICE[1]
1957	1,050	450
1958	4,600	450
1959	5,900	440
1960	4,600	565
1961	3,400	610
1962	3,000	670
1963	3,100	780[2]

[1] All data estimated by case writer from various sources.

[2] In 1963, five series of boats in lengths from fourteen to eighteen feet were manufactured and sold: These included 14 outboard models with dealer list prices from $599 to $2,499; four inboard-outboard (stern drive) models with dealer list prices from $3,299 to $4,799 (including a 110 horsepower motor); and one inboard seventeen foot model with a dealer list price of $3,999. Factory prices were normally based on a 40 percent dealer discount and a 10 percent distributor discount. Certain extra cost accessories were sold by the factory, such as tops, covers, extra fuel tanks and seats. Skin dive units were sold with motors installed or less motors, at the dealer's option.

10. HARVARD COOPERATIVE SOCIETY*

THE HARVARD COOPERATIVE SOCIETY (known as the Coop) was founded in March 1882 and petitioned the State of Massachusetts for incorporation and received it in January 1903. The Coop was begun with the objective of reducing the cost of living for students at Harvard and at its inception it was specified that goods should be sold at a markup not to exceed 5%, that all sales would be for cash, and that any profits should be added to capital.

Since that time there had been many changes in the guiding philosophy of the Coop and by 1959 its operations were quite similar to those of any other profit-seeking, multi-line department store. For example, the

* This case was prepared by Professor James E. Chapman of Georgia State College.

following practices usually associated with cooperatives had been completely abandoned:

1. Democratic control—rather than control by the members, control was vested in the hands of the 10 persons who held title to the corporate stock as trustees (500 shares authorized and issued, par value $100.00 per share).
2. Sales exclusively for cash—the Coop automatically extended credit to members and upon application and approval to nonmembers.
3. Use of a portion of the profits for education in cooperative ventures—there was no indication that this activity has ever been pursued.
4. Cooperation with cooperatives—there was no formal program for cooperating though it was true that the Coop, as the oldest such college venture in America, has freely given information about its operations to persons in other colleges interested in promoting such a venture.

The Coop in 1959 was an institution characterized by service, competitive prices (it met the prices of both the large Boston department stores and discount houses), patronage refunds to members (averaging 10% on cash sales and, for the past several years, 8% on promptly-paid charge sales), and growth coupled with stability.

Its physical plant consisted of three retail stores: the Harvard Square Store (also known as the Main Store), the Technology Store located on the campus of the Massachusetts Institute of Technology, and the Business School Store located in the basement of Gallatin Hall on the campus of the Harvard Business School. The Technology Store was completely owned by the Coop, the Main Store was owned in part and rented in part, and the Business School Store was rented. In addition, the accounting office, main shipping room, and garage were housed in a separate building owned by the Coop and located at the corner of Massachusetts Avenue and Bow Street.

Membership in the Coop was available at a cost of $1 per year to students, faculty members, alumni, and employees of Harvard, MIT, Radcliffe, and the Episcopal Theological School. Both professional and nonprofessional employees of several teaching hospitals were also entitled to membership (see Exhibit I). Sales were not confined to members; in fact, much effort was directed to attracting nonmember clientele who purchased in excess of net sales in 1958.

Sales increased steadily over the years, and the period 1950–1958 saw such a rapid rate of growth that the Coop made two significant expansions (see Exhibit II). One was the acquisition of the property at the corner of Massachusetts Avenue and Bow Street in 1954 at a cost of $105,000;

the other was the enlargement of the Main Store in 1957 and 1958. This latter was accomplished by leasing (from the Harvard Trust Company) and remodeling the building immediately adjacent to and north of the Main Store.[1] The remodeling expense was quite heavy due to the fact that the load-bearing walls separating the two buildings were largely removed and the buildings made to have the appearance (inside) of a single building. There was also an addition to the rear of the property leased from the Harvard Trust Company, and new fixtures were installed throughout the store. The cost of these improvements was $93,184 during the fiscal year ending June 30, 1957, and $539,759 for the year ending June 30, 1958; total cost of $632,943.

The expanded volume of business in 1958, coupled with the addition of new items plus increased stocks of previously carried items placed quite a strain on the Coop's net working capital and materially lowered the amount of available cash. This had become a matter of much concern to the management of the Coop and particularly to Mr. John G. (Jack) Morrill, General Manager, and Mr. Arthur W. West, Assistant General Manager, for it necessitated the borrowing of several hundred thousand dollars in order to keep the sales and service of the Coop up to par and to allow it to "grow with the community." In the early summer of 1959, alterations were being made on the building at Bow Street and Massachusetts Avenue to accommodate the installation of additional IBM equipment and more accounting personnel. Mr. West estimated the cost of these alterations at $40,000 and everything possible was being done to expedite the job so that the changeover would be accomplished prior to the fall registration. This expenditure, urgently requested by Mr. William Tansey, the Controller, was expected to lower the liquid assets of the Coop still further.

This relative shortage of working capital was not considered critical, nor was it expected to be of long duration; however, all indications were that 1959 would be the biggest year in the history of the Coop (estimated sales $6,707,000) and expectations were that this trend would extend on through the 1960 year (anticipated sales $7,250,000), thus additional cash with which to expand inventories, accounts receivable, and services was highly desirable. Accordingly, in June 1959 the directors and managers of the Coop were investigating ways to increase cash resources.

Officials of MIT had indicated that in the near future (perhaps

---

[1] Under the terms of an indenture with the Harvard Trust Company, the Society (Coop) had agreed to pay an annual rental and a portion of the real estate taxes, through August 1976. In addition, the Society had agreed to pay an annual rental not less than the current amount for the 10 years beginning September 1976 and had the option to extend the lease through August 1996.

within five years) a new Student Union Building would be built and that plans had been made for the Technology Store (MIT Coop branch store) to occupy the first floor of the Union Building which would provide much needed additional floor space. Also, in an effort to beautify the campus and to make it safer for students, plans had been made to construct an underground tunnel for that part of Massachusetts Avenue which bisected the campus. At that time, MIT was expected to purchase the Technology Store because Massachusetts Avenue would run directly beneath it, but more to the point, long-range MIT plans called for razing the store and converting the site into a grassy plot in order to beautify and "balance off" the campus. It had been proposed by some members of the Coop management that the Coop attempt to sell the Technology Store to MIT and rent it on a lease-back arrangement. The Coop believed that $450,000 was a reasonable market value for the land and building and that a fair rental on a lease-back deal would be 1½% of sales (see Exhibit IV). Another possibility was that the property at Bow Street and Massachusetts Avenue be sold and leased back. There was no "ready-made" purchaser for this property, but it was felt that a purchaser could be found without too much difficulty, for the property was located in a highly desirable commercial area. This property had been acquired in 1954 at a cost of $105,000 and had had quite a bit of improvement. Moreover, it was felt that the property had enhanced in value though no estimate of the market value had been made (see Exhibit V). Some of the managers and directors of the Coop felt that it would be undesirable to sell either piece of property and expressed the view that under anything but the most extreme circumstances they felt it better to own than to rent property. At the end of the 1959 fiscal year the Coop owed $150,000, but additional bank credit (of over $300,000) was readily available. In fact, during fiscal 1959, bank loans outstanding had averaged $400,000 at a rate of 4% interest. Fifteen thousand dollars had been paid out in interest.

EXHIBIT I

HARVARD COOPERATIVE SOCIETY
MEMBERSHIP 1950–1958*

	1950	1951	1952	1953	1954	1955	1956	1957	1958
Harvard**	15,397	15,379	15,160	15,398	16,062	17,088	18,279	19,826	21,790
MIT	7,862	7,753	7,532	7,822	7,935	8,199	8,707	9,186	9,504
Business School	1,934	1,989	2,044	2,075	2,256	2,289	2,339	2,660	2,557
Total	25,193	25,121	24,736	25,295	26,253	27,576	29,775	31,672	33,851

* As of June 30 of the indicated year.
** Includes all members except those from MIT and the Harvard Business School.

EXHIBIT II

HARVARD COOPERATIVE SOCIETY
SALES, AFTER PATRONAGE REFUNDS, 1950–1958

1950	$3,082,683.28
1951	3,210,919.88
1952	3,159,295.61
1953	3,287,118.44
1954	3,546,318.80
1955	3,836,016.14
1956	4,346,037.15
1957	4,819,602.69
1958	5,442,064.38
1959 (est.)	6,607,000.00 (before refunds)

EXHIBIT III-A

HARVARD COOPERATIVE SOCIETY

COMPARATIVE BALANCE SHEETS; ASSETS*

(To nearest thousand dollars)

	1954		1955		1956		1957		1958	
CURRENT ASSETS										
Cash in banks	$566		$314		$302		$400		$231	
London funds	—		—		—		—		—	
Accounts receivable	146		178		260		295		363	
U.S. Govt. bonds and other securities	101		176		200		101		—	
Other current assets	2	$815	4	$671	6	$768	6	$802	7	$600
Inventories:										
Harvard Store	$320		$341		$396		$420		$466	
Technology Store	93		113		122		134		151	
Business School Store	15	428	17	471	28	545	31	586	32	650
Total current assets		$1,243		$1,141		$1,313		$1,388		$1,250
FIXED ASSETS (at book value)										
Land		111		135		135		135		135
Buildings	$531		$631		$632		$634		$718	
Less—Res. for depreciation	243	288	258	373	276	356	294	339	312	407
Building equipment	$199		$245		$254		$254		$316	
Less—Res. for depreciation	107	92	115	130	127	126	140	114	150	166
Fixtures	$276		$302		$331		$355		$494	
Less—Res. for depreciation	152	124	167	135	184	147	186	169	195	299

132

EXHIBIT III-A (*continued*)

Automobiles	$ 9		$ 12		$ 12		$ 16		$ 16	
Less—Res. for depreciation	7	2	5	7	7	5	6	10	8	8
Tech building addition										
Construction in progress	4						42			
Leasehold									$221	
Less—Leasehold amortization									8	212
Total fixed assets		$ 621		$ 780		$ 770		$ 810		$1,227
DEFERRED CHARGES										
Unexpired insurance	$ 9		$ 12		$ 16		$ 16		$ 17	
Prepaid rent project X										
Prepaid rent Harvard Trust	6		6		6					
Int. prepaid on notes payable		$ 15		18		22	3	19	1	18
TOTAL ASSETS		$1,874		$1,943		$2,101		$2,217		$2,495

* As of June 30, indicated year. Totals may be slightly incorrect due to rounding to nearest thousand.

EXHIBIT III-A (continued)

HARVARD COOPERATIVE SOCIETY
COMPARATIVE BALANCE SHEETS, LIABILITIES*
(To nearest thousand dollars)

	1954	1955	1956	1957	1958
CURRENT LIABILITIES					
Notes payable	$ 81	$ 92	$123	$126	$200
Accounts payable	4	7	8	10	164
Payroll accrued					14
Ticket sales — payable					
Taxes pay. — City of Cambridge	29	34	38	42	47
Soc. Sec. taxes accrued	4	4	5	5	5
Mass. corp. excise taxes accrued	9	10	13	15	13
Employees' taxes withheld	6	7	8	11	10
Retail dealers' excise tax	1	1	1	1	2
Members' patronage refund	270	290	322	350	372
Membership fees in advance	1	2	1	2	2
Federal taxes on income	28	39	64	67	42
Customers' deposits	5	5	4	3	1
Total current liabilities	$ 439	$ 491	$ 588	$ 631	$ 872
RESERVES					
Employees' pension fund	$ 77				
Depreciation of merchandise	58	70	64	57	50
	135				
CAPITAL STOCK					
Authorized & issued 500 shares					
Par value $100/share	50	50	50	50	50
CAPITAL DERIVED FROM MEMBER FEES	594	621	651	683	717
SURPLUS & UNDIVIDED PROFITS	656	710	749	797	806
TOTAL LIABILITIES & CAPITAL	$1,874	$1,943	$2,101	$2,217	$2,495

* As of June 30, indicated year. Totals may be slightly incorrect due to rounding.

EXHIBIT IV

HARVARD COOPERATIVE SOCIETY
COST AND EXPENSE DATA FOR THE
TECHNOLOGY STORE

		LEDGER	ASSESSED VALUE
Land		$27,233	$28,200
Building	$114,996		
Less res. depn.	44,800	70,196	70,000
Building eqpt.	$ 56,680		
Less res. depn.	32,036	24,644	
Taxes—City of Cambridge		6,363	
Utilities:			
Heat		1,360	
Light		3,500	
Water		200	
Insurance:			
Building		300	
Boiler		300	

Building and building equipment are insured for $236,200

EXHIBIT V

HARVARD COOPERATIVE SOCIETY
COST AND EXPENSE DATA FOR THE
BOW STREET BUILDING

		LEDGER	ASSESSED VALUE
Land		$23,651	$46,700
Building	$94,788		
Less res. dpn.	17,946	76,842	43,300
Building eqpt.	$36,483		
Less res. dpn.	17,946	18,537	
Taxes —			
City of Cambridge		5,832	
Utilities:			
Heat		2,800	
Light		2,500	
Water		200	
Insurance:			
Building*		200	

* Other risks not prorated for this location.

11. JACKSON, NATHAN AND COMPANY*

FOR A NUMBER OF YEARS, Paul Nathan, the president of Jackson, Nathan and Company had been complaining about the lack of efficiency in the firm's accounting department. While he had no training in accounting himself, he felt that the firm was lacking in the type of information necessary to aid in the making of prudent management decisions. He also felt that the systems being used were outmoded and that there was probably a lot of waste in expense since there was no cost control system being implemented.

After much discussion with William Jackson, the chairman of the board, and with two management consultants that had been working with the firm, it was decided to hire a professional accountant to run the accounting department. Mr. Nathan emphasized that the man chosen should have managerial experience and ability in addition to accounting background. There was general agreement on this point although one of the management consultants mentioned that such a combination of managerial skill and accounting efficiency may be difficult to find in one man.

Background of the Company and Its Management

Jackson, Nathan and Company was founded in 1945 by Paul Nathan. He had worked for a number of advertising agencies in various positions of responsibility, reaching the position of vice president and account executive. At the urging of many friends and business associates, he decided to start his own agency. He acquired a number of small accounts and the company started to grow. In 1949, William Jackson joined the company as a vice president. He was an attorney who decided that he wanted to try another type of work. Nathan had known Jackson since they were both children and they had much in common. Nathan also felt that an attorney would lend stability and prestige to the agency and that he could be of definite assistance in the many contractual agreements encountered in the advertising agency business. Mr. Jackson also had a number of contacts in the business world and they both believed that some of these could become clients of the agency.

At present the company is a privately held corporation with Mr.

---

* This case was prepared by Professor William M. Berliner of New York University.

Nathan owning seventy-five percent of the outstanding stock and Mr. Jackson owning twenty-five percent. Mr. Jackson became chairman of the board in 1961 but Mr. Nathan has been and still is the chief executive officer of the corporation.

The firm has grown steadily since its inception and it now has many client firms of varying size. The annual billing ranges between ten and twelve million dollars and the firm would be classified as medium size in its industry. It employs approximately ninety people, with the majority engaged in the creative and client service aspects of the advertising business.

The company is a typical advertising agency with a fairly complete range of services including direct mail, art work, copy, media selection, market research, and some radio and television. The radio and television aspects of the business largely involve the preparation of spot commercials for clients. Larger projects in this area are usually turned over to various firms specializing in radio and television production.

The agency is located in a large eastern city and most of its clients are located here also. The principal selling effort over the years has been performed by Paul Nathan and he still services a number of the firm's important clients. In fact a good portion of his time is spent away from the agency and the active administration of the firm is left to William Jackson. Mr. Jackson had very little administrative experience prior to his affiliation with the agency and he frequently becomes enmeshed in detail, ignoring the broader administrative problems. As a result, there have been many crises and the company retained the services of a management consultant a few years ago to aid in the establishment of more effective management. One of the suggestions made by the management consultant was the development of sound accounting procedures along with various reports which were felt to be necessary for the effective management of the business.

The Accounting Department

At the time the decision was made to seek an outside man to head the accounting department, it was a relatively simple operation. The main functions performed involved accounts receivable, accounts payable, and bank statement reconciliation. They also prepared the payroll for the firm's employees and a separate executive payroll as well. The general ledger was maintained by an outside accounting firm which also prepared a monthly trial balance and profit and loss statement for the management. In a number of instances these statements were late and were of little use except as history. In fact, the partners of the independent accounting firm concurred wholeheartedly in the decision to obtain a qualified accounting manager since they wished to turn over the general ledger to Jackson, Nathan so that it could be maintained internally.

There were fourteen employees in the department, including the supervisor. The supervisor was an employee who had been with the company for about nine years. He had come to Jackson, Nathan from a large food processing company where he was a cost accounting clerk. His formal education ended with high school and most of the accounting knowledge he had acquired was from on the job experience. Although Mr. Nathan had offered to pay for courses in accounting and management for him, he never availed himself of this opportunity. He was an excellent worker, however, doing far more than anyone on his staff, but he was a poor supervisor and he experienced many difficulties with the people working for him. Since he was very fast and accurate, he expected everyone to be this way and unfortunately they all could not live up to his expectations. An added difficulty was the fact that the majority of the employees in the accounting department were women and Mr. Lawrence did not know how to cope with many of their problems. He was fifty-seven years old and had no supervisory experience before he was made head of the accounting department at Jackson, Nathan. He was placed in this position by Mr. Nathan who admired his diligence, loyalty, and hard work. Even though there had been frequent difficulty in the department, Mr. Nathan always excused Mr. Lawrence until the problem became too great.

Much time was spent trying to find a suitable position in the firm for Mr. Lawrence so that he would not be disappointed or lose respect in the eyes of other employees in the company. It was mentioned that since he was a long time employee, a poor example would be established if a responsible position was not found for Mr. Lawrence. After considerable discussion it was decided to make him an assistant to the market research vice president who was responsible for the preparation of a variety of statistical information as well as market research. It was felt that Mr. Lawrence's aptitude for figures and clerical work would make him a valuable assistant.

With the problem of Mr. Lawrence apparently solved, the search for a new accounting supervisor began. It was decided to offer a salary in the low five figure range and seek a college graduate who had studied accounting but who also had considerable supervisory experience. The salary range being offered was three to four thousand dollars higher than that paid to Mr. Lawrence. Everyone agreed that it would not be necessary for the candidate to be a certified public accountant, but that experience in a public accounting firm would be useful. Because of the relative simplicity of the accounting function at Jackson, Nathan and the small size of the department, everyone decided that more challenges would have to be included in the job to attract the type of man desired. The growth possibilities mentioned included vice president for finance, administrative vice president, and controller. With all of these decisions made, advertisements were placed in a large business daily and in the business section of the Sunday edition of one of the city's outstanding newspapers. In addition, two employment agencies that had been used before were contacted and given the job description and asked to send possible candidates for interviews. A procedure for handling candidates was established. This was the procedure:

1. The written resumes received would all be screened by the management consultant to determine the qualifications of the applicant for the position.
2. Each qualified applicant would receive a screening interview by either the management consultant, Mr. Jackson, or Mr. Nathan.
3. An applicant who passed the screening interview would then be interviewed by both of the other men.
4. If the applicant successfully survived the multiple interviewing, he would then be given a battery of psychological tests prepared by the management consulting firm.
5. The final decision would be made by both Mr. Jackson and Mr. Nathan, either of whom reserved the right to reject a candidate. They also decided to call on the independent accounting firm to help determine the applicant's accounting knowledge.

Numerous resumes were received and both employment agencies sent a number of applicants for the position. Approximately thirty-five screening interviews took place. Each one was carried out by one of the three men mentioned above. Approximately ten men passed the screening interview and were subsequently interviewed by the two other men. Five men passed this stage of the interviewing and each was given the battery of psychological tests. Three of these were interviewed by the public accounting firm and all three were judged qualified for the position. The final decision was made by Mr. Jackson and the management consultant since Mr. Nathan was out of town at the time.

The man chosen was Otto Herbert, thirty-six years of age and a graduate of a small eastern college well known for its accounting curriculum. He had varied experience in large companies, most of it in accounting departments where he had supervised small sections of the overall accounting function. The position he left to come with Jackson, Nathan was with a public accounting firm where he performed various special jobs such as setting up and establishing new systems and procedures in client companies. He had never tried to pass the Certified Public Accounting examination in the state and he expressed no interest in doing so. He mentioned that corporate accounting was of greater interest to him and he believed that a small company would give him the greatest opportunity to demonstrate his ability.

When he reported for work, he was told by both Mr. Jackson and Mr. Nathan that he had complete freedom to make any changes in the accounting department that he thought necessary to increase efficiency. It was mentioned that he would get complete cooperation and that he could call on both of them for guidance. In addition, he was also told that he could avail himself of the knowledge of Mr. Lawrence, the now deposed department head who had already started his duties as assistant to the vice president for market research. It is of some interest to note that Mr. Lawrence accepted his transfer with considerable bitterness, believing that he was being kicked upstairs even though Mr. Nathan told him that this was a growth opportunity and that his abilities and aptitudes would be used effectively.

Otto Herbert received no training of a formal variety. He was installed as department head, given the title of accounting manager, and introduced to all of his employees. He was also introduced to various other executives and employees in the company. His orientation was accomplished by a few casual and informal discussions with Jackson and Nathan and what he could find out by talking to his employees and others in the company. No particular attempt was made to channel his thinking and all in all his introduction to both his position and the company was quite superficial. Both Jackson and Nathan felt that a man in this salary range should be able to take charge immediately and become productive. The management consultant did not agree, stating that a certain amount of formal training and orientation was necessary for anyone when taking over a new position. The two owners agreed in principle but they wanted to get the accounting department operating at peak efficiency as rapidly as possible and they did not want to take the time to accomplish any formal training. They added the statement that no one had the time to do the job anyway.

From the beginning, Mr. Herbert found fault with much of his department. He started by changing the office layout and purchasing new desks and file cabinets. He fired three of the newer employees and replaced them with people of his own choice. Feeling that he needed an assistant, he requested and obtained permission to recruit a college graduate with an accounting degree and experience for the job. A young man was found who had graduated from the same school as did Mr. Herbert. This man had no supervisory experience but he had filled two accounting positions, one of which was with a public accounting firm. He had completed part of the requirements for the C. P. A. He and Mr. Herbert got along very well, with the younger man showing great admiration for his superior.

The payroll supervisor was a woman who had been with the company for eleven years. She was a widow with young children to support and she had done payroll work for the company for her entire tenure, rising to the position of payroll supervisor some years ago. Mr. Herbert did not find her to his satisfaction and fired her. She went over his head to Mr. Nathan who reinstated her in her job. He mentioned her long time service to Mr. Herbert and the position of trust she held. He also mentioned that she was a loyal, honest employee and that she would find it difficult to obtain another position because of her age which was fifty-one. Mr. Herbert countered with the opinion that she was inefficient but that he would take her back. Needless to say, the relationship was quite strained. After this incident, Mr. Herbert did not attempt to fire any other employees but he did attempt to change the existing system by calling in his brother who was a salesman for a large accounting machine company. His brother recommended a changeover to the system and equipment sold by his company and Mr. Herbert concurred with this opinion. Both Mr. Nathan and Mr. Jackson turned down his request by stating that a more thorough search and evaluation should take place before deciding on a basic change in the accounting system. Mr. Herbert emphasized that his brother's company was one of the best and his opinion was that their equipment was ideal for Jackson, Nathan. The two principals reiterated their desire for a more thorough evaluation and no other action was taken at the time. Mr. Herbert did not do any further research on a new accounting system.

Frequent arguments took place between Mr. Herbert and the payroll supervisor and most of these were reported by her to either Jackson or Nathan. She was usually pacified and told to do her best. Mr. Herbert was never consulted on his opinions as to the cause of the argument. During this period, the general ledger was turned over to the company by the public accounting firm and Mr. Herbert welcomed this as a display of confidence in him by the management. He mentioned that he would take care of it personally but it was later discovered that he turned it over to his young assistant who had complained about the amount of overtime he was incurring to keep up with entries in the general ledger as well as his other duties.

Three months after Mr. Herbert was hired, Mr. Nathan had the occasion to look over some expense accounts and petty cash requests prepared by various people in the company. As was mentioned earlier, he felt that there was a lot of unnecessary expense incurred. He thought that many of the requests he had looked at were too high or for unnecessary items. He called Mr. Herbert to his office and asked him what he had done about introducing more expense control and how he was handling petty cash disbursements. Mr. Herbert was somewhat nonplussed by the question since he had never been informed of this matter before. He merely mentioned that he was continuing the system in effect when he took the job. Mr. Nathan told him there was no system and he mentioned that one of the reasons he was hired was to introduce efficiency and tighter cost control. Mr. Herbert replied that he would get to work on it immediately. Two weeks later Mr. Nathan asked Mr. Herbert's assistant about the status of the expense control program. The assistant replied that he knew nothing about any program for expense control. Mr. Nathan left and he made no attempt to question Herbert about his efforts in this direction again.

At about this same period, Mr. Herbert approached Mr. Jackson for a loan. He wanted to borrow two hundred dollars from the company loan fund to buy his son a pedigreed puppy. Mr. Jackson told him his request would be considered and terminated the meeting. Since this request aroused his curiosity about Herbert, he asked some of the other executives for their opinions of the accounting manager. Most of them were either noncommittal or negative in their replies. Some mentioned that Herbert had borrowed money from them and had not as yet repaid the loans. When asked the amounts, they mentioned loans ranging from one dollar to twenty-five dollars.

Mr. Jackson went to Mr. Nathan with this information and the request for the two hundred dollar loan and told him about it. Mr. Nathan then informed Mr. Jackson about the petty cash and expense control situation. They called the management consultant and asked for his opinion after bringing him up to date on the circumstances. He suggested that Mr. Herbert should be given the opportunity to explain his side of the various stories and the reasons for his shortcomings. Neither Nathan nor Jackson agreed with this opinion, feeling that Herbert had been given sufficient opportunity in the three month period to prove his worth to the company. The management consultant then stated that since neither principal had any confidence in Herbert's ability and since he was in a position of trust and he could not act effectively without the complete confidence of top management, he should be asked for his resignation. Jackson and Nathan both agreed and the next day Mr. Herbert was called in by Mr. Nathan, given two weeks severance pay and asked to resign and leave the premises immediately.

------

12. KARGL INSTRUMENTS, INCORPORATED*

ON JULY 15, 1963, MR. D. W. HUBBARD, vice-president and general manager of Kargl Instruments, Incorporated made the following

* This case was prepared by Professors C. R. Klasson and K. W. Olm of the University of Texas.

comments regarding the main problems that had confronted him since assuming his present position with the company in October 1961.

> Up until today, I believe that getting our sales effort organized was my main problem. It certainly absorbed most of my time. Now that we have developed a good sales organization, our main problem has shifted to the production area. To support an increased level of sales activity, we need to make some personnel changes in the shop; we need to organize a production control section; and we need to double shop capacity. Since we diversified our product line, our sales prospects have increased to the point where we may have some difficulty producing what has been sold. We are under pressure to finance an expanded level of production and at the same time have increased product development expenditures. Undoubtedly, the most important project during the next few months will be to establish plans to increase our capitalization to support planned growth which we are certain will come.

Company History

Kargl Company of San Antonio, Texas, the predecessor of Kargl Instruments, Incorporated, was founded by Mr. Gilard Kargl in the early 1940's to perform aerial surveys and to design and fabricate needed equipment for photogrammetry. Mr. Kargl, a civil engineer by training, became one of the pioneers in the photogrammetry field when he began mapping with the use of aerial photographs in the middle 1920's. He became interested in determining the best route for a proposed railroad in the hill country of west central Texas. The railroad was never constructed, but his interest in improving aerial surveys resulted in a life-long association in the new industry.

Prior to establishing his own firm, Mr. Kargl had been active in organizing many of the aerial photographic firms in Texas, including Edgar Tobin Aerial Surveys, Jack Ammann Photogrammetric Engineers, and Muldrow Aerial Surveys, to mention a few. For each of these firms Mr. Kargl designed and built a wide variety of photographic and photogrammetric equipment including in 1929 the first autofocusing rectifier ever built in the United States.

Kargl Company was organized in 1949 as a corporation for the purpose of designing and manufacturing precision photo-optical instrumentation. The majority of business done from 1949 to 1959 was prototype design and fabrication of aerial cameras, viewers, projectors, rectifiers, and other aerial film handling equipment. The firm sold its services and products to various agencies of the federal and state governments, major oil companies and other private industrial firms, and to foreign companies and government agencies in Mexico and various Central American countries.

Company Operations Through 1961

Over the years, Kargl Company had come to enjoy an excellent reputation for making high quality precision photogrammetric instruments. This success reflected the untiring and creative efforts of Gilard Kargl, whose primary interest focused upon designing new equipment which could solve new and challenging problems in the photogrammetric field. Being a designer and engineer, Mr. Kargl had little interest in the administrative aspects of his company from the start. No administrative staff was maintained other than a secretary and one clerk. The accounting and financial records were maintained by a part-time bookkeeper at his personal residence. In 1955, Mr. Ray Kelsey, a graduate engineer trained in the photo-optics field, joined the organization and for five years assisted Mr. Kargl in evaluating new designs, supervising the manufacture of all equipment, and assisting in the general management of the company.

During the initial years of operation the company had never employed over twenty employees and had operated on a very informal basis. Manufacturing and office operations were conducted in a building which was located on a five acre tract of land owned by Mr. Kargl. With primary emphasis on the design and fabrication of precision instruments, a minimum of attention was devoted to sales efforts since no sales organization of any kind had been established nor were any full-time salesmen employed prior to 1961. Sales were largely the result of personal contacts of Mr. Kargl and his small technical staff and by the fine reputation of Kargl in the photo-instruments field.

Sales volume and profitability of the company varied considerably from year to year. Gross sales reached a peak of approximately $200,000 in 1956, and a low of approximately $100,000 in 1960. Net profits on sales were considered to be good in the years 1956–58. Sales volume during the 1949–1960 period did not increase significantly because Kargl Company had concentrated primarily upon research and development activities while minimizing production activities. During this period the company primarily fabricated prototype instruments for their customers. Also, inasmuch as Mr. Kargl had assumed the major responsibility for design and engineering work, the amount of inhouse contracts was necessarily limited by the small technical staff.

Recognizing the growth potential for Kargl Products and his lack of interest in the managerial aspects of the business, Mr. Kargl from time to time attempted to interest qualified persons to buy into the company. Early in 1961 he succeeded in finding an investor who was willing to take over the management of his company. In May, 1961, Mr. Kargl sold eighty percent of the outstanding stock of Kargl Company to a small group of investors headed by Mr. Harry Evons. Mr. Evons held substantial interests in several local enterprises and had been actively engaged in business for approximately twenty years. The sale was consummated with the understanding that the three new stockholders would assume major responsibilities for the management of the company, allowing Mr. Kargl to devote his full attention and efforts to designing new photogrammetric equipment.

Reorganization of the Company, 1961

Mr. Harry Evons, as the major stockholder, immediately began a reorganization of the company. He was installed as chairman of the Board of Directors and President, and he began looking for a qualified general manager to handle the day-by-day operations of the company. Of the other two major stockholders, one was elected corporation secretary and the other was elected corporate treasurer. Mr. Gilard Kargl retained twenty percent of the stock and membership on the Board. He assumed the position of executive vice-president, with complete freedom to devote his time and talent to improve the design of existing photogrammetric products and to design new products for the company.

Mr. D. W. Hubbard, with an extensive background in military and civilian aviation and aircraft sales administration, joined the company in October 1961, as vice-president and general manager. Mr. Ray Kelsey who had left the company in 1960, rejoined the company in July 1962, as chief engineer and director of research and development. Kelsey's initial responsibilities also included manufacturing, purchasing, and production control activities.

During the first several months after reorganization, the Board of Directors served as a management committee meeting every week for purposes of making operating decisions and hiring additional personnel as required. Only a few changes were made while the new management group gradually formulated its products and market strategy and established appropriate operational procedures and policies to guide overall company operations. After Mr. Hubbard was hired in October 1961, the Board began to meet only once a month, and members anticipated meeting only on an annual basis beginning in 1964. Harry Evons, the president, moved his personal office to the company on March 1, 1963 and began to take an active part in the company. At that time the name was changed from Kargl Company to Kargl Instruments, Inc. in order to provide the public with a more correct description of the major interests of the company. The other stockholders anticipated taking no active part in company operations other than making major policy decisions from time to time.

The general manager and the chief engineer were usually invited to meet with the Board, and a representative of the company's auditing firm also attended meetings occasionally.

Operating Philosophy of New Management

The new Board of Directors adopted an operating philosophy designed to promote growth as rapidly as possible with the available technical, manufacturing, and financial resources of the company. Long-term gains in the form of capital appreciation of their investment was desired in place of immediate payment of earnings in the form of dividends.

Growth was to be accomplished primarily by a process of (1) product diversification, (2) concentration of research talent on projects and products which promised significant returns, and (3) solicitation of ideas and products from outsiders in need of technical assistance in design, development, and fabrication of prototype products.

No specific guidelines were established for the proposed product diversification program. The new owners were determined to add more products to the present line of photogrammetric equipment which was considered to be very limited. They also wished to add other non-related product lines to level out seasonal and cyclical variations in sales commonly experienced when selling large budget items primarily to the federal and state governments and a few major industrial firms. Since the salaried engineering staff had talents largely restricted to the photogrammetric industry, internal expansion was restricted to those fields until additional engineering talent could be acquired.

Widespread product diversification was encouraged by soliciting from any interested party new and unique designs and ideas needing further research and development provided that the idea promised some reasonably long-term profitable relationship. Exhibit I illustrates the policy established to handle new product ideas submitted by persons outside the company.

While the company was determined to emphasize its research and development orientation, it was also determined to develop its manufacturing capability. New product ideas which were likely to develop ultimately into products manufactured by Kargl were favored over ideas where no manufacturing business was likely to develop. Management recognized that many ideas might not get beyond the prototype stage, but all proposals not specifying at least the fabrication of one prototype were rejected. Usually, the company sought to obtain a research and development contract that included provisions for the fabrication of up to 100 units of the item. They did not refuse to consider contracts calling only for a single prototype where it was felt there was a good possibility of additional orders as well as commercial marketing potential.

Operational Activities as of 1961

At the time of the reorganization, Kargl Instruments was firmly entrenched in the photo-optical instrumentation field with a limited line of well-established commercial products along with a highly qualified, if small, research and development staff available for consultation on special problems in the photo-optical field. The research and development capabilities of the company were gradually expanding under the leadership of Mr. Kargl and Mr. Kelsey until they utilized a staff of fifteen persons in the Engineering Department by October 1963.

The 1961 line of photogrammetric products included three models of aerial cameras.with prices ranging up to $3,500 (the 1963 line of aerial cameras ranged up to $10,000 in price); a line of camera mounts; a patented tilt recording aerial camera; an autofocusing rectifier designed to remove range displacement present in aerial negatives; several models of copy cameras ranging from a small vertical model priced at $8,500 to a large horizontal model priced at $25,000; and a reflecting projector. Because of the high value and custom nature of each of these items, they were usually manufactured only to customer order. On rare occasions, items were manufactured for inventory when sales prospects appeared promising and if costs of producing an additional unit were very favorable. Through the years the company had maintained a camera and instruments repair service until this activity was discontinued in early 1963 because Evons was interested in directing activities to more productive areas in line with new policies. A local camera repair service was available for use by customers.

Technical proposals (bids) were submitted to various U.S. government and military agencies to obtain research and development contracts. Of some thirty proposals submitted during a two-year period, two contracts were awarded to Kargl Instruments. Industry average for contract awards was reported to be approximately one out of 20 submissions. One contract awarded by the United States Air Force Aeronautical Chart and Information Center called for the design of a special combination camera and projector while the other contract awarded by the United States Geodesy Intelligence Mapping Research and Development Agency (GIMRADA) contracted for a micromap camera to produce seventy milemeter photographs of military maps.

New Product Development Program

New product development was the joint responsibility of Messrs. Hubbard, Kelsey, and Dick Evons. This group met periodically to evaluate new product ideas. On occasion Mr. Kargl was informally consulted. After preliminary screening, potentially new product ideas were presented to the President and to the Board of Directors for further consideration and action. Mr. Hubbard, the general manager, stated, "We are interested in almost any product which requires design, development, and fabrication work to produce, even though we are primarily in the photogrammetric equipment business." Mr. Kelsey, the chief engineer and head of research and development, felt that the company's current line of photogrammetric equipment was very small and therefore tended to place the company in a position where it was adversely affected by cyclical fluctuations in the market demand for these products. He was concerned with broadening the product line to reach a diversified market that could help to minimize sudden drops in demand for the company's products. Mr. Dick Evons was very interested in developing non-related products which would not be tied in any way to the photo-optical instrument business.

New Precision Instruments

During the eighteen-month period after the reorganization of the company, a number of new photo-optical instruments were added to the company line including an aerial film viewer; a roll film dispenser; and an image motion compensation camera mount attachment. Along with these new products, the company had received a number of contracts for design improvement and manufacture of a number of photographic instruments. Micro-Film Systems Incorporated contracted with Kargl to redesign and manufacture 100 units of a card-roll-card microfilm duplicator (desk type). These units had an approximate retail price of $1,200. Many microfilm products were still in the idea stage, and the company felt that this would be a worthwhile field to exploit. Special research attention was being devoted to a small company information retrieval system and a micro-printed-circuit camera designed to reduce electronic circuit drawings and subsequently micro print functioning circuits directly on a glass plate. The product development committee felt that successful solution of technical problems encountered in these two projects would likely open up a dynamic and profitable market for the company.

New Non-Optical Products

An unusual product area which the company entered came about when an inventor of a complex mechanical nutcracker brought his product to the company and requested them to manufacture and market it for him on a royalty payment basis. This product had been manufactured and sold with moderate success almost five years previously. After being examined in detail by the product planning group, they decided the product had definite possibilities as a profitable sideline item, provided that the design could be improved by using some of the existing design talent available within the firm. After several months of consideration, the decision was made by the Board of Directors to proceed with the development and marketing of the product. The decision was felt to be in keeping with the broad company policy that proposals will be accepted if they provide for a continuing arrangement whereby the company can design, develop the prototype, arrange for production, and market the product at a profit.

Since the nutcracker was not related to the company line, and Mr. Kargl was mildly apprehensive about his long-established reputation for quality scientific equipment, a decision was made to organize a new products division to be called Krak-All Products, to serve as a coordinating and marketing unit for household and related institutional products. With the exception of overhead allocations, a separate set of accounts was to be established and maintained for the Krak-All Products Division.

The Krak-All line was expanded quickly by the addition of an ice cube cracker, which was identical to the nutcracker except for different cracking surfaces, and by the addition of a portable folding steel outdoor cooking grill.

Other products in the housewares and miscellaneous line under consideration and in various stages of development by October 1, 1963 were a powered can opener, a portable insecticide spray gun, and a small tank gauging mechanism. The development of the spray gun had been completed but the device was not in production. The tank gauge had been patented by the inventors, but production was delayed until a market potential could be established.

Following an informal market survey, an industrial products design consultant was retained to improve the appearance of the nutcracker while company engineers improved the mechanical features of the product and constructed a prototype model suitable for high-speed diecasting operations. Pre-production models were market tested with results judged very favorably by management. Kargl Instruments, Inc. arranged for a booth to introduce the product to a group of manufacturers' representatives attending the semi-annual National Housewares Show at the McCormick Place in Chicago in July 1963. Based upon the advice of several merchandising experts at the show, the proposed retail price of $5.95 was raised to $7.95 in order to provide a better product image and to cover more intensive advertising and promotion expense. Initially the company had not intended to give advertising allowances, but this was changed to provide for a 25 percent allowance. Based upon the favorable market reaction, a decision was made to distribute Krak-All products on a national basis. The uniqueness of the product resulted in the company being given editorial recognition and publicity in such magazines as *Family Circle, Modern Metals*

(September 1963), and on the nationally televised program "The Price Is Right."

The original display box was designed by an industrial designer. Soon thereafter it was redesigned to provide a more suitable visual display for the nutcracker and ice cracker. The new box featured a transparent insert through which the device could be viewed. A contract was entered into with a firm that had suitable diecasting capacity to manufacture the product, and the capability to package, inventory, and ship to customer accounts according to orders received from the Krak-All Division. An initial order of 5,000 units was placed with the sub-contractor. The contract provided for a schedule of price concessions on orders ranging from 5,000 to 100,000. By October 1963 an additional order for 25,000 was placed, and by that date the products were being marketed through nearly one hundred specialty stores, gift shops, and major chains. The company had established a channel of distribution through a group of 20 manufacturer's representatives. Krak-All retained the rights to sell certain key accounts in major cities around the country on a direct basis.

The promising developments in the Krak-All line resulted in the hiring of an experienced distribution executive to assume control of the Krak-All division. Mr. Jules Sterling was appointed vice-president of Krak-All Products in September 1963.

Sales

Kargl Company had no sales organization of any kind and no full-time salesmen until October 1961 when Mr. Hubbard was hired as executive vice-president and general manager. Sales prior to this time were by word of mouth, limited efforts of the technical people, mainly Mr. Kargl, and as a result of selective direct mailings. Mr. D. W. Hubbard sold copy cameras to the oil industry on a part-time basis for Kargl while he was associated with a large local aerial mapping firm in 1958 and 1959. During his initial months in his new capacity with Kargl Company, Mr. Hubbard spent a considerable amount of his time developing new house accounts and soliciting business from existing customers, several of whom were known to him from previous contacts.

In September 1962, Mr. Hubbard prepared a sales projection for all photogrammetric products based upon their past performance, known prospects, and future potential. State highway departments that were currently installing their own departments or divisions for photogrammetry included fifty prospects with a potential sales ranging from $500,000 to $2,000,000 over a period of several years. Large consulting engineering firms currently organizing internal photogrammetric departments in attempts to avoid subcontracting represented a maximum of 1,000 potential customers with sales ranging from $250,000 to $1,500,000 over a period of several years. Aerial surveying and mapping firms that bid on government contracts or performed work for selected clients represented an additional 200 firms with a potential sales volume ranging from $400,000 to over $1,000,000 over a several-year period. Government agencies having internal photogrammetric divisions and departments represented an almost unlimited potential for Kargl Instruments sales. Foreign government agencies currently forming or expanding internal departments also represented a great potential especially in Central and South America where photogrammetry was beginning a rapid growth period. One of the largest and as yet untapped sources of sales was industrial firms which were adding photogrammetric capabilities to solve internal research problems. Typical prospects for this group included the American Can Company, Goodyear Tire and Rubber Company, Aeroflex Corporation, and Northern Pacific Railroad. Because of the potential sales to new customers and because the company was faced with only a few major competitors, Mr. Hubbard projected a significant increase in the photogrammetric end of the business for the next three to five years.

Early in 1963 Keuffel and Esser's new Photogrammetric Systems Division had contacted Kargl Instruments, Inc. requesting them to consider an agreement whereby they would market Kargl's products on a worldwide basis with specific orders being placed by K. & E. f.o.b. San Antonio, Texas. In March 1963, a decision was made by the Board of Directors of Kargl Instruments to accept the marketing arrangement extended by Keuffel and Esser. The marketing agreement called for the distribution of major Kargl photogrammetric products under the K. & E. label throughout the world. Kargl Instruments, however, retained exclusive selling rights in the three state area of Texas, Oklahoma, and Louisiana because it did not want to lose its long-established key accounts in the oil industry, several of which were on the verge of placing orders for equipment. The K. & E. association provided Kargl with a world-wide marketing organization for its photogrammetric equipment. Mr. Hubbard and the Board of Directors considered the arrangement very desirable since they realized the benefits to be derived from the world-wide marketing efforts of a company with K. & E.'s excellent reputation and still continue to establish major sales policies. Along with the sales contract, several products sold by K. & E. were offered to Kargl Instruments for design improvement and manufacture if it was interested and capable of improving them. One of the most promising of these products was a 35 mm microfilm camera, with an approximate retail price of $6,500. Kargl received an initial order for twenty-five redesigned units, with more orders to follow if the product sold well. In commenting about the overall sales potential of the business, Mr. Hubbard stated that the company was definitely attempting to develop a balance between the various types of products produced. Mr. Hubbard felt that graphic arts products represented a very large product potential in that all major oil companies and industrial firms with large drafting rooms and internal photo service departments were potential customers. In the area of research and development he also felt that the potential with government agencies was unlimited since the company had recently obtained a security clearance. For the non-photogrammetric products, it was projected that the company could sell between 50,000 and 100,000 Krak-All products priced at $7.95 during the first season (1963–64). They also estimated that a maximum of 1,000 scale engraving machines could be used in precision machine shops, and these would sell for approximately $850. No estimate of actual sales of these machines for the current year was made, however. Aerial camera sales of sixty units were made between 1949 and 1955. Camera sales in subsequent years fell to a minimum of six in 1961. A substantial recovery of aerial camera sales was noticed in 1962 when fifteen were sold, and higher dollar volume sales were predicted for 1963 and subsequent years.

The following table shows projected, received, and delivered sales for Kargl Instruments for fiscal years 1962, 1963, and 1964.

SALES PROJECTED, RECEIVED, AND DELIVERED
FISCAL YEARS 1962, 1963, AND 1964

FISCAL YEARS		SALES ORDERS	
(APRIL 1 — MARCH 31)	PROJECTED	RECEIVED	DELIVERED
1962	$140,000	$170,000	$150,000
1963	435,000	290,000	235,000
1964	844,000	470,000[1]	175,000[1]

[1] For first five months of fiscal year only.
SOURCE: Interview with company management.

Facilities

Kargl Instruments, Inc. housed all of its operations in a modern, air-conditioned masonry building which included over 13,000 square feet of floor space. Floor space was allocated on the following basis:

	SQUARE FEET
Engineering	3,505
Production	5,436
Light Assembly	495
Administration	1,524
Warehouse	2,654
Total	13,614

Along with all engineering design and drafting work which was conducted on the second floor, photographic and optical laboratory facilities were also maintained. The photographic lab was capable of processing aerial roll film, performing contact and projection printing, and maintaining an inplant photographic facility. While the company did not manufacture lenses, it did maintain optical facilities for testing lenses.

The well equipped production facilities enabled the company to build prototype models of most products it designed or contemplated manufacturing. Identical facilities were used for model building and basic production operations. Production facilities included a sheet metal fabrication shop, an electric and acetylene welding shop, a wood shop, a wiring shop, a painting shop including bake ovens, and associated machining equipment such as lathes, drill presses, milling machines, presses, and grinders.

These facilities were designed and laid out for intermittent production, and were considered unsuitable for other than very small scale production.

Production Operations

Prior to July 1963, Kargl Instruments actively contracted for research work where the company would design a product for a client on a fixed fee basis. Normally such contracts called for the delivery of product specifications and a prototype model. Because of the desire of company management to expand its manufacturing operations concurrently with contract design work, a policy was established whereby the company was no longer interested in simply procuring design work. After July 1963, the company restricted contract design work in that it required minimum production runs of designed products. Because of the unique nature of photogrammetric equipment, such orders were normally limited to between five to twenty-five units of a given item. The highly specialized nature of the product and the generally limited market tended to restrict order quantities. Consequently, Kargl Instruments' manufacturing operations were best described as "job shop" operation. Because of the nature of Kargl's market for most of their products, production facilities were essentially a model shop designed to develop prototypes rather than to produce in any quantity. Once a product was released by the engineering department, three successive models were developed. First, a developmental model, which was used to prove the design concept, was made. Second, a prototype model was made to prove the actual design of the product. And finally a pre-production model was made to check the production tooling.

The engineering and manufacturing departments worked together very closely and in harmony. Upon receipt of a new contract a project number was assigned, a budget was established, and an engineer was assigned to supervise the project. The design engineer worked very closely with the production shop when fabricating the developmental, prototype, and preproduction models. Because of the smallness and informality, the engineer, especially if it was Mr. Kargl, often performed some of the machining operations of the first model.

As a direct result of the new management's attempt to increase the sales volume and profitability of the company, the production requirements had continued to increase noticeably since the beginning of 1962. As of August 1963, the company had a number of orders in house which called for the manufacture of production models. Production jobs in process included a card-roll-card microfilm duplicator of which 100 units were required; the fabrication of twenty-five microfilm cameras; a forthcoming order for twenty 105 mm microfilm cameras; and a possible order for five other products for 100 units each. Mr. Ray Kelsey, the chief engineer, who also supervised the production operations indicated that he expected the current shop force of fifteen people to more than double at the end of 1963. He also estimated that $40,000 worth of new production equipment would be required to handle the increased manufacturing activities. One shortcoming was the lack of space for line assembly operations. However, plans were in process to provide space for assembly in the proposed expansion of the physical facilities scheduled for late 1963. An additional 9,000 square feet of floor space was planned to house expanded production operations which would include additional machining capacity and line assembly operations. The additional building at the rear of the present building was estimated to cost approximately $65,000. Erection started in October 1963, and was scheduled to be completed by December 1, 1963.

Prior to the expansion of the production facilities of Kargl Instruments, the company had maintained informal control over production. With more manufacturing orders coming into the house, increased scheduling problems began to develop. Conflicting demands for available equipment and manpower, and problems of coordinating current projects began to emerge by mid-1963. Recognizing the need to formalize production control, a department was established. A shop superintendent who had formerly been with Kargl and who recently was shop supervisor at a local air base was employed to relieve Mr. Ray Kelsey of that responsibility.

As of 1963, the engineering department had a backlog of orders in house which would keep the department busy until the end of 1963. Mr. Kelsey directed twelve people in the engineering department, three of whom were engineers and the remaining nine were draftsmen and designers. Lead time for new products through the engineering department ranged anywhere from a minimum of three months to a maximum of six months depending upon the complexity of the product involved. More basic research was assumed by Mr. Kargl, with the total development time of some projects requiring as much as a year or more.

Organization and Personnel

Mr. Hubbard, general manager of Kargl Instruments, made the following comments about organizational and personnel changes since he had been with the company:

During the past several months we have been making a number of key organizational changes that we felt were necessary to facilitate the planned growth of the company. Since I came with the company in October of 1961, we have added the following positions to the organization—director of sales, chief of engineering, office manager, and purchasing agent. These were all considered to be necessary functions and positions which had to be established in order to carry out the increased volume of business acquired. The people who assumed these positions, however, each performed a variety of functions above and beyond those designated by their official titles. You can understand that in any small organization this is a typical situation especially when you cannot afford to hire help for all the work that needs to be done.

At the present time we are employing forty-five people. Of this number seven are classified as administrative personnel, thirteen as engineering personnel, and the remaining twenty-five as production personnel. At our present rate of planned growth, we anticipate doubling our engineering and production personnel by the end of 1963. Just recently, a man was hired to fill our last key slot in the production organization. The new shop superintendent will start to work within the next month. With this addition we feel that we have all the key positions well manned with qualified personnel, all of whom take a personal interest in the product and its performance characteristics. We are well aware of the fact that we have a very high overhead payroll cost at present, but we felt it was necessary to hire key department heads in order to facilitate the planned increase not only in engineering but as well in production operations. Our overhead per hour will decrease as production increases.

We have a very unique organization of people here at Kargl Instruments. First, you have probably noticed that we have a relatively young organization of highly qualified personnel each in their own fields and with extensive experience in all phases of the photo optical industry. Second, there is not a man in this organization who has not worked with someone else in the organization in the same field somewhere and sometime in the past. It is impossible to assess the value of such past working relationships and friendships of the people in this shop. Third, I feel we have one of the best balanced boards of directors I have ever seen. Each board member has a unique background, extensive business experience in his own specialty, and readily avails himself to the operating management of this company.

Administratively, we have not attempted to formalize all operations to any great degree. However, we have gradually begun to establish standard operating procedures in the area of sales, engineering, accounting, and manufacturing. We still feel that we are essentially a small and informal operation even though some of these changes gradually have been made. This is one of the definite advantages of the small business firm, and we hope we can keep it that way as we grow.

See Exhibit II for organizational chart of Kargl Instruments, Inc.

Accounting and Finance

Detailed sales forecasts for each product line were not made more than one year in advance. Some members of management believed that things changed so rapidly that they did not have time to do required planning in any great detail. Mr. Evons did not agree with this viewpoint. He felt quite strongly that long range and intermediate range planning had to be done by the top management group, even at the sacrifice of certain other activities. He insisted that planning was too vital to postpone because of daily detail work.

The president decided that better planning could be obtained with the formation of an executive committee. Effective October 17, 1963, the executive committee, composed of the president, the three vice presidents, and the head of engineering and sales were to meet weekly for the purpose of developing operating plans on a short-term, intermediate-term, and a long-term basis. In the words of the president, once the plans were formulated, they were then going to evaluate how they were doing in relation to those plans and forecasts. By this process they would be able to decide where they were and where they were going, and thereby overcome the tendency to get fuzzy about their objectives. He intended, he stated, to keep those areas vital to success sharply in focus.

While he anticipated a detailed plan for the ensuing year, he recognized that they did not have the staff to develop anything but a general plan for a five-year period.

During the summer months, for example, operating management spent approximately ninety-five percent of their time on problems which were projected six months in advance and only about five percent of their time on problems which extended beyond a year in advance. These ideas were to change with the active participation of Mr. Evons and the imposition of his policies.

Each department head submitted a budget for the following fiscal year based on sales projection provided by the director of sales. Personnel, material, administration, and shop overhead budgets were used to prepare a cost of sales budget. Capital expenditures were also included in departmental budgets. Departmental budgets were consolidated into an overall company budget which became the basis for next year's operations. However, Mr. Hubbard indicated that these budgets were merely guidelines for each department head and were not formally approved by the Board of Directors. From time to time changes were required in original estimates because of variations in product orders. Each month the company accountant prepared for Mr. Hubbard a report in which the month's activities were summarized financially and accumulated on a monthly basis. The report included selling price, total sales revenue, cost of sales, and gross profit for each product sold by the company. The report also included a breakdown of administrative overhead, net profit before taxes on total sales, increase or decrease of sales to date over last fiscal year, a cash flow statement, a cash position statement, and end of month bank balance.

The company was in the process of developing a cost accounting system for their inhouse research and development work as well as the production work. Cost standards on completed production were available for reference. The company recognized the value of keeping cost accounting records and it was determined to have as simple a system as was possible to generate needed records.

Kargl Instruments, Inc. was a private corporation, and as of September 1963, had not made a public offering of stock and had not anticipated making such an offer in the near future. While it was a closed corporation, management offered stock to all company employees on a special purchase plan. The key officials were granted a stock option plan as a special incentive.

With the expanding level of sales, the initial capitalization of the business had proved inadequate to finance overall company operations. Working capital was tight since the company sought to finance current operations primarily by short-term bank loans. It was indicated that once a sales contract was received from a reliable purchaser, it was relatively easy to obtain funds from a local bank to finance the project. The company had established excellent working relationships with a large local bank in San Antonio. With careful cash planning, it had developed an excellent credit rating. In view of the planned expansion of the business the company had established a policy whereby no cash dividends would be paid out of earnings until the desired expansion had been realized. The Board of Directors assumed primary responsibility for financing the expanded operations of the company. When the rapid growth made substantial additional funds necessary late in 1962, the Board of Directors sought to obtain long-term capital for the business without resorting to a stock sale. The best available source appeared to be through a Small Business Department Corporation, but after checking into the possibilities of this particular source, it was decided that it would be unadvisable to pursue this avenue. The Board of Directors next considered a public sale of stock, but after further examination felt that it was not practical to attempt to place a public stock issue then since the company had not had sufficient time to establish a good earnings record and an issue at that time would adversely affect the market price of the stock. Consequently, serious consideration was given to accepting offers from several local investors who had expressed an interest in investing in Kargl Instruments, Inc. Kargl had already gained a national reputation for the high quality instruments it produced and was also beginning to establish a regional reputation as a growing company with good prospects for capital appreciation. Because of the apparent growth potential of the company and possibilities for appreciation of its stock, several local investors had expressed interest in getting in on the "ground floor."

As of November 1963, $60,000 of additional stock had been sold. The Board of Directors plan to make available a limited amount of additional stock to interested local investors and then arrange for long-term financing to further the continuing need for expansion indicated by the increased demand for products from "Kargls" customers.

EXHIBIT I

KARGL INSTRUMENTS, INC.
8123 BROADWAY
SAN ANTONIO 9, TEXAS

Kargl Instruments, Inc. is happy to consider ideas submitted by people outside of our company, but it has become necessary to establish a policy to mutually protect both the company and persons who submit ideas for our consideration.

We cannot receive or evaluate any disclosures from persons outside the company except on the understanding that our evaluation of disclosure entails no obligation on our part. It must be expressly understood that no confidential relationship is to exist concerning any information or material submitted to us. The submitter's rights are to be defined solely by patent protection he has or hereafter may acquire.

Large numbers of disclosures are sent to us for our consideration. So many are submitted, in fact, that we cannot undertake to return all material; therefore, you are advised to retain a duplicate of all documents and material in your disclosure. In the event we decide that we have no interest in your disclosure, no reasons for our decisions will be given because to do so may require the release of information we do not wish known outside of our company.

If you wish to make a disclosure in accordance with the above conditions, please sign and date one copy of this agreement and return it to us with suitable material describing or illustrating your idea, and retain the other copy for your files.

Very truly yours,

D. Wm. Hubbard
Vice Pres. — Gen. Mgr.

I have read and understand the terms outlined above and agree to the conditions set forth.

Subject: _____

Date: _____   Submitter: _____

EXHIBIT II

KARGL INSTRUMENTS, INC.

SEPTEMBER, 1963

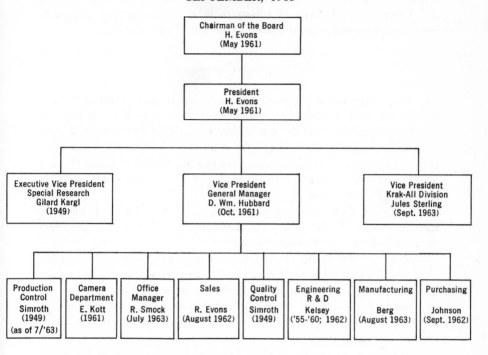

SOURCE: Company officials.

13. MANGOLD TOY COMPANY

MANGOLD TOY COMPANY WAS DETERMINED to perfect a new production process to apply three color designs on one color vinyl used in the production of their biggest selling item, a stick horse. Substantial improvements had been made in most of the production processes used prior to the time James Mangold assumed control of the company in 1956. Many of the new processes were originated by James Mangold and he believed they were unique in the industry until they were successfully imitated by competitors. The company under Mangold was constantly alert to any change which would make its manufacturing more automatic or the product more attractive and colorful so that it could continue to lead all competition in its speciality.

Production averaged over 50,000 dozen units of the stick horse annually for the past six years with an output of approximately 80,000 dozen units in peak years. A variety of other toy items were produced, but the stick horse produced almost 90 percent of total sales.

History of Company

James Mangold was trained as an accountant and practiced successfully in the field of accounting systems before he returned to his home to care for his parents in 1956. At that time he invested $2,800 cash to avert a legal claim against his mother's toy company. Gross assets of the company, consisting of $4,000 in sewing equipment, $2,000 in materials, and $8,000 in facilities, were turned over to James Mangold and his mother retired from the business.

Mangold Toy Company Incorporated, of Granbury, Texas, was incorporated in October 1956, with 1,000 shares of $10 par value capital stock authorized, and 500 shares issued.

When James Mangold started to operate the business in October 1956, the Mangold Toy Company had 12 employees; four worked in the factory and the other eight sewed in their homes. The horses were sold to a wholesaler for $7.20 per dozen and had a suggested retail price of $0.98 each. The gross profit margin was slim due to production inefficiency and very competitive pricing.

After scouting the toy market, Mangold felt that there was a strong potential for substantial growth for a company making toy items. He considered the hand methods then in use by his own company to be extremely inefficient and he concluded that a high level of efficiency was the key to profitable operation. He was confident that by restyling his main product and by lowering the price he would be able to compete successfully in the market.

Changes in Production Processes and Design Since 1956

The basic product design was comparatively drab, with only a string bridle for ornamentation and no paint. The initial change Mangold made in the product was to improve the appearance by using vinyl plastic for the horse heads instead of oilcloth, and adding a fringe cotton mane. Mangold wanted to paint features and decoration on the head but he knew of no paint that would permanently adhere to vinyl. Since the company purchased relatively little paint at that time, the technical assistance of paint salesmen and manufacturers' agents was not made available to Mangold. He proceeded to experiment independently with different types of paint and after 400 to 500 trials succeeded in blending a mixture that would adhere to vinyl and not chip or flake off when the material was flexed. The next problem Mangold solved was how to use a silk-screen process to apply paint on the heads quickly which allowed inexpensive variations on the basic design. When the silk-screening operation was perfected, Mangold started ordering large volumes of paint and paint suppliers then began to offer technical assistance.

By making his horses more colorful and realistic appearing, Mangold was able to ride an unprecedented wave of popularity in children's toys that was sweeping the nation. The magic words "Ride 'em Davy Crockett" on each horse created a demand that caused production to lag severely behind orders for over one year.

As a starting point for speeding production, Mangold redesigned the sheet-plastic horse head and devised a method of cutting double heads at one time, which in turn provided more work than could be handled with the initial work force. When the payroll had risen to 90 employees, 20 of whom sewed in their own homes, it became apparent that productivity had to be increased to reduce rapidly increasing labor costs.

After investigating the Southwest U.S. area without success for machines that would speed production, Mangold found a small company that produced a stuffing machine equipped with an auger attachment that would inject stuffing material automatically. The machine, made by the Ormont Machine Company of New York, would not handle cotton linters, scrap wool, and other non-uniform stuffing material used in the hand method. A source of uniform stuffing was found at the Charles Comider Company of Utica, New York. Felt, cotton, and nylon scrap from the garment industry was chopped to uniform size compatible with Ormont machines. Mangold purchased two Ormont machines (at $800 each), and a carload of Comider scrap for immediate delivery.

Mangold then began to build his production processes around the automatic stuffers. Over four months were required to set up the machines and adapt them to the stuffing of horse heads and to train operators. With the machines integrated into the assembly process, the company was able to achieve a stuffing rate of 4,800 heads per day with only six employees on the operation. Previously, with hand methods, 24 people were needed to stuff 4,800 heads per day.

The high speed stuffing operation required more heads than could be supplied through the painting and drying operation. Several new types and colors of paints were suggested by paint salesmen until a new paint reduced the drying time from 12 hours to 12 minutes. After painting, heads were placed on wire racks to dry. As Mangold pointed out, "When

4,000 to 6,000 heads, each about 12 inches long by 8 inches wide, are placed on racks to dry, they take up too much space in the factory, besides creating a bottleneck in production. It requires additional employees to place the wet heads on racks and stack up the dry ones. As a result, I had to shorten drying time even more."

An expert on conveyor belts and Mangold designed a 50 foot long conveyor with 30 infra-red heat lamps suspended over the belt. The painted heads came off the silk screening machine and were placed on the moving belt where they were dried completely on a two-minute ride and then stacked up automatically at the end of the belt.

Since the capacity of the new fast-drying setup exceeded the old painting operation output, a silk-screening machine that would paint eight heads at once, instead of two as with the previous method, was purchased for $180. The efficiency of the new painting-drying setup reduced the needed work force from ten to three people to paint and dry 4,000–6,000 heads per day. As a further refinement, equipment was purchased to make new silk-screens in the factory by a photographic process. Besides the advantage of not having to wait for purchased silk screens, the cost to the factory was only one-tenth that of hand made units formerly purchased from outside suppliers.

Another step toward increasing productivity was taken when a machine was procured that would paint the wooden dowels used for the "body" of the horse. After the machine was purchased from its inventor, alteration was required to adapt it to the factory's needs. The time, effort, and $1,500 invested paid dividends, however, because the new machine with one operator could paint 20,000 sticks in one day. Stick painting had previously required six employees to take time off from their other duties to turn out 25,000 units per day.

Current Production Process

The production of stick horses started with vinyl sheeting (usually .011 inches thick) stacked 14 sheets high. The sheets, 80 to 90 inches long, were cut with an electric slitter into widths for the particular style of heads to be produced.

The stacks of strips were then run under a press where "blanks" were cut out by a die under 7½ tons of pressure. Each blank yielded two head sides. Since the vinyl sheeting did not have the same finish on both sides, "mirror image" dies were used to cut blanks for the right and left sides of the heads.

The die-cut blanks were then taken to Thermatron three-kilowatt sealing machines where right and left blanks were positioned one above the other and then sealed together around the front half of each head. The sealing machine also seared "tear lines" into the double heads so they could be quickly torn apart. The sealing operation was considered critical as the sealing dies had to coincide closely with the cutting dies to provide a good seal yet not leave double flaps on the outside of the head.

Sealed heads were taken to the silk-screen machines where four pairs of heads were painted at once on one side. The heads then traveled along the conveyor belt where the paint was dried by the heat lamps. The heads were then manually carried back to the silk-screen machine, painted on the other side, dried, and then separated along the tear lines. The heads were then passed to women sewers who attached the cotton fringe mane. The next operation fastened the bridle and bells to the head with a grommet using an automatic Stimson machine. The heads were next stuffed on the Ormont machine and passed to the person who fastened the sticks in the heads with a Senco pneumatic riveting gun.

Completed stick horses were then packed by hand one dozen to a cardboard box. Boxes were stapled, closed, and stored for shipment.

Scheduling and Control of Production

Production was scheduled on a weekly basis by Mr. Mangold. Daily run sheets specified models and colors to be produced. Only rarely was production scheduled in excess of orders on hand. Normal inventory of finished goods did not exceed the equivalent of one week's production, except immediately before the busiest season of the year.

Employees were laid off as orders declined and rehired again when needed. No attempt was made to balance production to avoid employee layoffs.

Sales were forecasted by months for the following year, primarily to plan for purchases of raw materials. In order to obtain quantity discounts and freight savings, scrap filler was purchased in car load lots sufficient for several months' needs. Sheet vinyl and cotton fringe were obtained from nearby suppliers in quantities sufficient only for two to four weeks of production.

Marketing and Costs

The first full year of operation under James Mangold produced sales of 8,000 dozen units. Manufacturers' representatives were utilized in 1958 to obtain better distribution on a national basis, and the price was lowered to $5.40 and $5.70 per dozen from the former price of $7.20 per dozen, in an attempt to increase sales. Faster production methods and greater efficiency in all operations permitted price reductions while maintaining profit margins. The lower price, better distribution, and more attractive product helped to increase sales to 70,000 dozen in 1958. Sales rose to 80,000 dozen units in both 1959 and 1960, with relatively little competition.

In 1961 four different companies started producing stick horses with molded plastic heads. The competing products sold well, and Mangold considered producing similar items. When he ran a cost analysis on the new type of horse heads, his figures showed a wholesale price of $5.70 per dozen was needed to show an acceptable profit. Instead of producing the molded plastic heads, Mangold made the decision to reduce the wholesale price from $5.40 to $4.80 per dozen on his conventional line. The constant stream of improvements he had added to his production process made such a move entirely practical. The added margin made available to manufacturer's representatives and retailers reversed the decline in sales and resulted in final sales of 50,000 dozen units for 1961, when at midyear it appeared that sales might fall as low as 40,000 dozen. All four of the competing new companies ceased producing stick horses entirely in 1962. One major competitor still produced units similar to Mangold's.

Sales slipped again in 1962 but only slightly compared with the 1960–1961 drop. Mangold attributed the 1962 sales drop to 45,000 dozen to the fact that he was physically incapacitated much of the year and unable to give proper direction to sales and production. He had no assistant, and temporary substitutes proved to be unequal to the job.

Mangold was reasonably confidant about the long run market for his main product because he believed that the stick horse qualified as a basic child's toy which would be purchased for small children in much the same manner as blocks and toy guns. As such, he estimated that the U.S. market should absorb 100,000 dozen units a year. He thought that sales should be relatively stable from year to year except for the occasional favorable influence of such developments as the Davy Crockett fad. He was also confident that he could retain close to 50 percent of the market.

Mangold believed that the only certain way to increase industry sales would be to increase the attractiveness of the product. Substantial sales gains had always followed improvements in the product appearance, especially when the product was made more colorful.

Late in 1963 Mangold's attention turned to what he considered to be his major current problem: How to improve the attractiveness of his product by applying a three-color design on heads where he was currently using only one color. He was severely curtailed in working to solve this problem both because of the small amount of time he could spare from his managerial duties and because expenditures on product developments were necessarily limited. Marketing benefits from product improvements were considered to be relatively short-lived due to the fact that such improvements were subject to rapid adoption by his major competitor.

New Production Process Under Consideration

Silk screening reproduction of more than one color would have required an additional painting and drying operation for each additional color. Besides the delay caused by painting the heads two or three times, problems of registry (correspondence in position of the paint designs) made multicolored silk-screening impractical with the equipment available.

Mangold investigated the possibility of applying three-color designs to vinyl using "electro-cals." These were pre-printed designs, made to order by the Electro-Cal Company in Boston, which required heat and pressure to transfer the image from its sheet-paper backing to the vinyl.

An improved appearance was imparted to the horse heads, and the use of electro-cal designs offered promise of speeding the decorating process. All four heads in the sealed blanks could be colored at once, possibly at the same time the heads were sealed and seared in the sealing operation. Mangold was not concerned about the problems of heat and pressure necessary to apply the electro-cals because the dies of the sealing machine could be altered to perform that part of the operation.

He was, however, unable to develop a quick and efficient method to position the four electro-cals in precisely the correct places so that the images would be transferred correctly on the heads. Normal application of the electro-cals consisted of placing two of the transfers face up on a metal surface; then the blank was laid over them and two more electro-cals were placed by hand face down on their corresponding heads. Heat and pressure were then applied and the designs imprinted on the vinyl. The major problem was keeping the bottom electro-cals in position when the blank was positioned. No raised guides could be used as they would cut into the vinyl when heated. Painted guides could serve to initially position the electro-cals, but they would not hold the sheets in position when the blanks were placed on them.

Whether he used the sealing machines or a specially designed machine to apply the electro-cals, Mangold wanted to apply all four designs at once. In addition to speeding the decorating of the heads, applying all the electro-cals at once would eliminate adverse effects to the vinyl caused by repeated applications of heat.

Mangold predicted that when the new color process was perfected the company's sale of stick horses would definitely maintain an annual sales volume of 50,000 dozen units for several years. He had satisfied himself that his company was ahead of its competition in manufacturing processes and distribution and that the anticipated color innovation would give the Mangold Toy Company a strong lead in product design for at least a year.

---

14. MILBANK MUTUAL INSURANCE COMPANY*

FOUNDED AS A MUTUAL AID society in 1892, the Milbank Mutual Insurance Company has grown to be the largest casualty insurance company with home offices in South Dakota. Headquartered in Milbank, it writes casualty and liability insurance on farms, residences, commercial buildings, and autos in South Dakota and the six contiguous states. In recent years, rapid growth has brought a number of benefits to the organization, but also many new problems. The board of directors, finding its present home office inadequate, is faced with the necessity of deciding how it might best locate itself to relieve its present problems and prepare itself for anticipated growth.

History of the Company

The Milbank Mutual Insurance Company, although it has borne that name only since 1951, has been identified with the Milbank community since its founding. On January 26, 1892, a group of young farmers founded a mutual aid society to insure farm buildings and goods. Originally the company was closely identified with the Evangelical Church; during the first year of operation membership was limited to church members and "those in sympathy with the Church." Although the formal identification with the church was dropped after one year, some of the founders and their descendants remained active in the company until the mid 1950's and the name, Evangelical Mutual Insurance Company, was retained until 1951.

In 1897 the aid society was chartered as a mutual insurance company issuing assessment policies. This practice continued until 1949. Only two assessments were ever made; one in the second year of the company's history, the other in the "farm depression" of 1920–21.

Soon after its founding the company extended its coverage to North Dakota and began writing fire insurance on urban dwellings. In 1909 the

---

* This case was prepared by Professor Robert Mittelstaedt of the State University of South Dakota.

company's first offices were opened in Milbank; prior to this all records had been stored and business conducted at the farm home of the company's secretary, John Roth. In 1912, at the request of the South Dakota Insurance Commissioner, the company began to issue policies and keep its records in English; until that time German had been used exclusively.

The company continued to grow; assets in 1900 were about $5,000, in 1945 they were about $625,000. The end of World War II found Milbank a rather typical, small, assessment mutual insurance company.

Beginning with Minnesota in 1949, the company began to add states to its field of operation by extending itself to Nebraska in 1952, Montana in 1953, Wyoming in 1954, and Iowa in 1955.

New types of coverage were also added: commercial buildings in 1949, autos in 1954, farm and city liability in 1956, homeowner's policies in 1958, storekeeper's policies in 1961, and farmowner's policies in 1962.

Recent Growth

By any standard, the Milbank Mutual has evidenced a rapid rate of growth, particularly since World War II. Gross premiums written increased at an average rate of 30.9% per year between 1954 and 1962. During the same period net earned premiums for fire policies have increased 17.3% per year, compared with 15.1% for all U.S. companies and 13.3% for premium volume on fire insurance in the seven state area served by Milbank Mutual.

Between 1959 and 1962 (to give a larger base for comparison) the gross earned premiums on auto policies have increased at an average annual rate of 7.5%, compared with 7.8% for the nation and 5.8% for the seven state area. This short period includes a decrease in Milbank Mutual's premium volume on auto policies in 1961, a year in which the company found it necessary to tighten considerably its underwriting standards on auto policies.

Exhibit I presents the net earned premiums for selected years from 1952 to 1963 by state. Exhibit II presents the net earned premiums by type of coverage from 1960 to 1963. For the first six months of 1964, premium volume was up about 16% over the same period in 1963.

During the same period, management has always tried to maintain financial strength and the "policyholders' surplus" has shown a constant increase. Exhibit III presents comparative balance sheets for selected years from 1952 through 1963.

The board of directors sets their long term goal at an annual growth in premium volume of 10–15%. Any insurance company can always grow by relaxing its underwriting standards; however, Milbank Mutual hopes to maintain its present standards and expand its volume by adding new coverages, new states and intensifying its efforts in present lines and states. No definite and formal plans for expansion to other states have been made, but the company has become licensed in Wisconsin and Arizona.

Method of Operation

As the volume of business has increased, the company's method of doing business has also changed. Milbank Mutual writes insurance through about 1000 agents in seven states. These agents fill out policy applications, which bind the company, and send them to the home office. Here they are processed and, if approved, the agent is billed at the end of the month for the first premium payment, less the agent's commission.

When the number of agents was smaller the company wrote insurance in fewer states; most of the agents attended the annual policyholders' meeting. In recent years contact with the agents has been accomplished through eight field men and annual regional agents' meetings which keep the agents informed of company policies and the company in touch with the agents' views. In 1963, twenty-two such meetings were held throughout the seven states with three or four people from the home office at each meeting.

The handling of claims is an important home office function. When a claim is submitted, a reserve equal to the estimated loss is established and the loss is adjusted. The company has always used adjusting bureaus, but in the past two years has added several adjusters to its staff. Presently it has a company adjuster in Omaha, Nebraska, one in St. Cloud, Minnesota, and four in Minneapolis. Plans are to add to this adjusting staff. In addition, the company hires two repair crews that repair wind-damaged farm buildings in areas where policy holders have difficulty finding skilled help on short notice.

Underwriting is another home office function. About one-fourth of the home office staff is engaged in accepting or rejecting risks from policy applications. Little actuarial work is done by the company. Rates are set mostly by deviating from "bureau rates" in accordance with experience and competition. For new coverages, the company has found that the insurance commissions of most states will let them submit "judgment rates" because they have been found to be financially secure and able to withstand possible losses.

In recent years, the company has had an increasingly large amount of funds to invest. The board has maintained a conservative investment policy with about 80–90% of its investments in municipal bonds and the rest in U.S. Government Securities, corporate stocks, and a very few mortgages. It does very little buying and selling on a day-to-day basis, preferring to hold long term investments. The company deals through Minneapolis and Chicago brokers; in addition it receives many calls from bond salesmen all over the country every day.

Record keeping, policy processing and the issuing of premium notices are important home office functions. This aspect of Milbank Mutual's operation has been highly automated. In 1950 the company installed its first punched-card record keeping system which was modified and expanded several times until an IBM 305 RAMAC was added in 1958. This was replaced by an IBM 1401 installation in 1962.

Although a small company, Milbank Mutual is recognized as a leader in the application of electronic data processing to the insurance field. At present the computer processes all policies, prints premium notices and endorsements, and gives management monthly reports on premiums and losses by types of policy, area and agency, in addition to performing the payroll, agency billing, and other accounting functions. The 1401 is being used close to its 40-hour week capacity and the board is considering adding additional equipment rather than go to a two-shift operation.

Problem

As the premium volume has increased, the size of the home office staff has grown steadily. The present home office building was constructed in 1952 when the staff numbered 25. The full-time staff is now about three times that large and the space problem in the two story, 14,000 square foot building has become critical.

In June 1963 the board of directors decided that the time had come to take steps relative to the building and related problems. At the board meeting four general conclusions were reached.

First, in light of its past growth and future growth goals, the company must evaluate all problems and proposed solutions in terms of its long-run effects. Plans must now be made to allow the company to meet its growth goals and the long-term (15–20 year) consequences of all actions must be of primary consideration.

Second, there were three problems associated with the company's present home office. One was that office space was very short. A related problem was that of parking space. Finally, there was some feeling that because the home office was located in a town of 3,500 people, some difficulty had been experienced in securing and keeping personnel, particularly those with special skills.

Third, the board decided that the two previous conditions made it desirable to consider a number of alternatives including that of moving the company's home office to another city. Legal requirements would make it almost impossible to leave the state, so attention was drawn to Sioux Falls, South Dakota's largest city, as a possible location.

Finally, plans were made for a later board meeting at which there would be a full discussion of all the previously mentioned problems and an attempt to generate and evaluate a number of alternative solutions.

Board Meeting of December, 1963

In December 1963, the board of directors met again to discuss the location problem. The first area of discussion was the present building situation. Figures were studied showing that as of September 1963, there were 59 full- and part-time employees in the general office area, meaning an average floor space of 47 square feet per person. The National Office Managers' Association minimum standard for clerical personnel is 80 square feet. Exhibit IV presents the present allocation of floor space in the home office building, with N.O.M.A. standards for comparison.

An architect's report was examined which showed that the present building could be added to in a number of ways. Additions could be put on the present two floors 20 feet to the west and 20 feet to the north adding a total of 3,800 square feet or another floor could be added to the building, including the west and north additions, which would add a total of 14,600 square feet, or many possibilities in between. However, the architect was under the opinion that a third floor would require interior supporting columns somewhat reducing the available floor space on the first two floors. The architect also reported on his investigation of a building of 13,500 square feet across the street. (See map.) This building, which is for sale but not for lease or rent, was built for and is presently occupied by an automobile dealer. The architect estimated that the cost of the building plus the cost of remodeling it for the company's purposes would be as much as and probably greater than the cost of constructing an entirely new building of the same size elsewhere in Milbank.

Another phase of the discussion had to do with parking. The company presently has off-street parking for about 60 cars and any expansion of the present building would mean that the 15 parking spaces behind the building would be lost. At the present location there appears to be little possibility of increasing this parking space and the nature of the surrounding area makes it undesirable to rely on street parking.

Another phase of the discussion concerned the matter of securing and keeping personnel. The Treasurer and Personnel Director, Mr. Lynn Culver, discussed some of the firm's problems in this regard. He pointed out that the company was still small and had to rely on hiring experienced insurance people, particularly in skilled jobs such as claims work and underwriting. On the other hand, he felt that it was reaching a point in some departments, such as auto claims, where it could begin to hire and train inexperienced personnel.

He also stated that he had experienced some difficulty in getting people trained in the operation of the various aspects of data processing used by the firm. He had used advertisements in large daily newspapers in the region and several employment agencies with little success and had relied mostly on the IBM company for help in this regard.

The problem appeared to be that the firm, in looking for experienced people, had to go to Minneapolis, Omaha, Des Moines or some other large city in the region. Oftentimes the people contacted in these cities were natives or long-time residents of large cities and they (or more often than not, their wives) would not consider moving to a small town in South Dakota. Even when they found one that was willing, further investigation often showed that the prospective employee regarded the idea of moving to Milbank as a short-term affair to get experience so that he could move to a higher paying job in a big city. While the company had always been able to fill its positions, Mr. Culver reported that the number of good applicants was substantially reduced by the fact that the company was located in a town of 3,500 people.

Exhibit V presents a breakdown of the current employees of Milbank Mutual by length of service and Exhibit VI by home town.

Next there was a discussion of the relative merits of Milbank and Sioux Falls. Milbank is a county seat of 3,500 people located in an agricultural area of northeastern South Dakota. It is the only town of consequence in its county and some distance from any larger towns. Watertown, South Dakota (13,000) is 50 miles away, Aberdeen, South Dakota (28,000) is 100 miles. Sioux Falls (65,000) is 140 miles and Minneapolis is 180 miles. The city is served by north-south and east-west bus service, by passenger train service to Aberdeen and Minneapolis but has no air service and little likelihood of it in the near future.

Although the community relies heavily on its position as a trading center for the surrounding rural area, it has more industry than is typical of South Dakota county seat towns. Milbank Mutual is one of five Milbank firms employing over 50; there are two granite quarrying firms, each of which normally employ from 50–100 people, a cheese factory, and a sausage factory.

Milbank has a good school system, many churches, a golf course and a large lake nearby. Many of Milbank's residents make the 3–4 hour trip to Minneapolis several times a year for shopping, big-league baseball, symphony concerts, plays, and other activities which are not available in Milbank or any other closer city.

Sioux Falls, with a 1960 population of about 65,000, is the largest city in North and South Dakota. Because of its size and position, it is a center of wholesale trade in the area. Many national firms (including most of the office machine firms with which the company does business) maintain branches, offices, or some sort of representation in Sioux Falls. In addition, Sioux Falls has a substantial number of manufacturing firms, the largest being John Morrell and Company, a meat packing firm employing several thousand. There are three insurance companies with home offices in the city, although Milbank Mutual probably employs more people than any one of them.

Two small, church-affiliated colleges are located in Sioux Falls along with a commercial college. It has three golf courses, a zoo, several parks, a part-time symphony, little theatre groups, and the usual facilities available in a city of its size. It has bus and airline service but no passenger train service. There is a daily newspaper and several employment agencies. There were, at the time of the board meeting, several office facilities of 8,000–15,000 square feet available.

Sioux Falls has been experiencing quite rapid growth; its population and that of Milbank for 1940–1960 are presented below:

	1940	1950	1960
Sioux Falls	40,832	52,696	65,466
Milbank	2,745	2,982	3,500

Another factor discussed by the Board was the labor market in both communities. The State Employment Service office in Sioux Falls estimated that it had about 100 female applicants for office work on file at any one point of time. Wage rates between the two communities appeared to be about the same.

Exhibit VII shows the wage rates for Sioux Falls and the Milbank Mutual. The lower minimum figures for Sioux Falls result from the inclusion of small offices that do not pay minimum wages in the State's figures. Milbank Mutual is in interstate commerce and must pay a minimum wage of $1.25 per hour ($220/mo.).

The Board also discussed the attitudes of the present employees toward the possibility of a move. The women employees of the firm tend to fall into two groups (just as they do in any large office); young, single girls working until they get married and begin raising a family, and older women whose children are grown. About 40% of the company's female employees are married. An opinion poll showed that about 20% would prefer Sioux Falls and most of the rest would prefer to stay in Milbank but would move to Sioux Falls if necessary.

Most of the male employees, with a few exceptions, were opposed to any move. Several of the men had pointed out that they had family ties or property interests in Milbank; others had wives that worked elsewhere in town and were reluctant to leave. Most of the men owned their own homes and were fearful of a loss they might take if 10–12 homes were suddenly put on the market in a community where 10–20 houses is the customary number for sale at any given time.

Finally, the Board discussed the consequences of any possible action on the city of Milbank. As one of the community's major employees, a move away from Milbank would certainly be a major depressing force on the community's economy. Milbank's civic leaders had contacted most of the members of the Board, one way or another, urging them to stay in Milbank. In addition, many of the company's officers were active in community affairs and many local organizations would miss their presence.

After a discussion of the above problems and situations the Board decided to meet again to discuss the following alternative courses of action.

1. Build an 8,300 square foot addition to the present building by adding a 3 story, 27 by 103 foot structure to the rear of the home office.
2. Build a second building at the edge of Milbank to house the auto division. The office manager and others engaged in day to day operations thought that this would be possible with a minimum of duplication; it would involve hiring a second office manager and renting additional data processing equipment.
3. Build an entirely new structure in Milbank to house the total home office.
4. Move the whole operation to Sioux Falls.
5. Move the auto division to Sioux Falls and retain the fire division in Milbank.

EXHIBIT I

NET EARNED PREMIUMS, BY STATE

SELECTED YEARS, 1952–1963

State	1952	1955	1958	1961	1963
South Dakota	$ 382,576	$ 554,776	$ 846,829	$1,066,043	$1,256,123
North Dakota	654,593	811,168	1,236,710	1,487,216	1,568,103
Minnesota	388,010	875,375	1,894,412	2,557,003	3,413,658
Nebraska		96,195	413,796	507,097	580,539
Montana		10,167	20,048	146,662	281,861
Wyoming		510	3,723	8,587	10,559
Iowa		1,935	60,076	131,674	328,317
Total	$1,425,179	$2,350,126	$4,457,594	$5,904,277	$7,439,160

EXHIBIT II

NET EARNED PREMIUMS, BY

TYPE OF POLICY, 1960–1963

	1960	1961	1962	1963
Farm (Fire & Extended Coverage)	$1,289,157	$1,206,500	$1,201,046	$1,200,046
City (Fire & Extended Coverage)	835,804	835,702	938,678	984,948
Auto	3,423,974	3,384,986	3,873,463	4,415,289
Farm Liability	49,695	65,166	85,171	100,752
City Liability	8,490	8,886	9,423	10,446
Homeowners	232,800	343,037	496,089	642,447
Farmowners	—	—	26,353	83,742
Storekeepers	—	—	400	816
Total	$5,839,920	$5,904,277	$6,630,623	$7,439,160

EXHIBIT III

BALANCE SHEETS, SELECTED YEARS
1952–1963

	12/31 1952	12/31 1955	12/31 1958	12/31 1961	12/31 1963
Assets:					
Cash	$ 118,004	$ 160,383	$ 126,682	$ 218,908	$ 60,526
Stocks & Bonds	1,606,940	1,917,845	3,852,222	6,844,752	8,319,451
Accrued Interest	16,419	21,140	50,416	89,965	109,317
Mortgages	168,974	146,622	216,364	242,773	262,381
Real Estate	181,764	158,022	150,095	141,619	131,619
Others	51,994	91,353	154,479	237,810	303,899
Total	$2,144,095	$2,495,365	$4,550,258	$7,775,827	$9,190,193
Liabilities & Surplus:					
Loss & Loss Adjustment Res.	$ 37,704	$ 222,374	$ 838,240	$1,953,909	$2,387,341
Tax Reserve	47,893	78,330	139,013	195,010	185,766
Unearned Premiums	797,785	1,249,620	2,030,466	2,591,007	3,151,244
Others	4,501	—	6,144	173,640	11,830
Policyholders' Surplus	1,256,212	945,041	1,536,395	2,862,261	3,454,012
Total	$2,144,095	$2,495,365	$4,550,258	$7,775,827	$9,190,193

EXHIBIT IV

MILBANK MUTUAL ACTUAL BUILDING SPACE ALLOCATIONS AT SEPTEMBER 1963 COMPARED WITH NATIONAL OFFICE MANAGEMENT ASSOCIATION STANDARDS

FUNCTION	NO. OF PEOPLE	SQ. FT. FLOOR SPACE	SQ. FT. PER EMPLOYEE	SQ. FT. REQUIREMENTS BASED ON NOMA STANDARDS	
				Low	High
EMPLOYEE-OCCUPIED SPACE					
Fire Division					
Underwriting	6	313	52	440	820
Claims	4	288	72	320	510
Auto Division					
Underwriting	11	785	71	740	1,070
Claims Supervisor	1	123	123	100	250
Claims	3	−261	87	220	410
General					
Treasurer's off.	3	231	77	320	410
Clerical pool	31**	772	25	1,900	2,500
General Office space					
Total	59**	2,773	47	4,040	5,970

176

EXHIBIT IV (*continued*)

Files and access area	–	1,338
Printing	2**	425
Mailing and Supplies	5	463
Machine accounting		
Key Punch	6	426
1401 computer	2	367
Tabulation	2	407
Other IBM	6	559
Total Employee-Occupied space	82*	6,758
OTHER SPACE		
Conference Rooms		519
Inactive Files & Storage		1,679
Rest Rooms		219
Kitchen & Coffee room		523
Heating & Cooling Equip.		577
Aisles, Stairs, reception, etc.		3,725
Total other space		7,242
Total Floor Space		14,000

* Total excludes 15 employees not occupying space in home office: President, 7 fieldmen, 5 repairmen, 2 adjusters.
** Includes 7 part-time employees: 6 file clerks, 1 printing clerk.

177

EXHIBIT V

MILBANK MUTUAL EMPLOYEES BY LENGTH
OF SERVICE, AS OF
JULY 1, 1964

YEAR HIRED	NUMBER OF PRESENT EMPLOYEES BEGINNING WORK		TOTAL HOME OFFICE EMPLOYEES
	FEMALE	MALE	
1940	1		
1949		1	11
1950			
1951	1	1	
1952	1	1	25
1953			
1954		1	
1955			
1956	4		45
1957	3	1	
1958	3	1	
1959	1	2	
1960	5	2	
1961	4	1	69
1962	9	1	
1963	13		
1964	13	1	71
	58	13	

EXHIBIT VI

PRESENT MILBANK MUTUAL EMPLOYEES
BY HOMETOWN
JULY 1, 1964

	FROM MILBANK OR NEARBY	OTHER TOWNS IN S.D.	OTHER STATES
Females	53	2	3
Males	4	5	4

EXHIBIT VII

COMPARISON OF CURRENT WAGE RATES
SIOUX FALLS VS. MILBANK MUTUAL

JOB CLASSIFICATION	MONTHLY WAGE RATES	
	SIOUX FALLS[1]	MILBANK[2]
Receptionist	$190–250	$220–240
Stenographer	185–350	220–260
Clerk-intermediate	200–360	220–265
Clerk-senior (Supervisor)	210–400	250–300
Clerk-Accounting	195–360	260–300
Key Punch Operator	200–250	220–255
Calculating Machine Operator	185–225	220–265
Coder	210–260	220–265
IBM Card Sorter	200–250	220–265
Programmer (Male)	500–900	N. A.
(Female)	N. A.	250–450

N. A. = Not Available.

[1] South Dakota Employment Security Office and Sioux Falls business firms.

[2] Lynn Culver, Treasurer.

MAP I

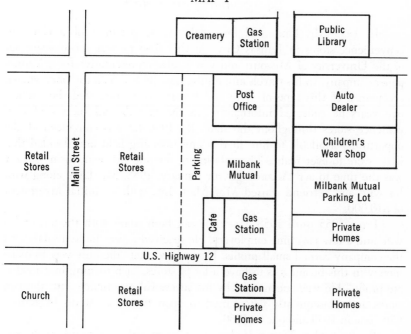

15. MINI-MART, INCORPORATED

MR. RICHARD LANE WAS THE president and major stockholder of Mini-Mart, Inc., which operated a chain of convenience stores that were located in Kansas City, Missouri. In early 1962 Mr. Lane felt that the company had reached an important milestone in its history. Due to several external factors, Mr. Lane knew that he must re-evaluate some of his long range plans and objectives if the company was to continue expanding and prospering.

Mr. Lane's original objectives had been to develop a prosperous family business which would not only earn a good living for himself and his family, but which also would provide a thriving business opportunity that might be passed along to his heirs. He knew that after assessing the company's development to date, he must decide on a future course of action in light of current and expected business and economic conditions. At this time he was not sure just what his decision should be.

Background of Mini-Mart

In 1953 Mr. Lane had first realized the potential of a chain of convenience stores in Kansas City. At this time he was seven years out of the University of Missouri and was a sales representative for a leading paper company. In his travels around the state he had seen the phenomenal acceptance of this type of store and became very interested. For almost two years he collected information on the growth and success of convenience stores throughout the state. By 1956 he was convinced of the opportunity available to him in this mushrooming field and decided that if he were to ever realize his ambition of owning his own business, now was the time to act! Accordingly, in January, 1956, Mr. Lane along with his wife and a friend started Mini-Mart, Inc. with an initial investment of $10,000.

From 1955 until 1958 Mr. Lane ran both stores with the aid of his wife and a few part-time employees. He received a very limited salary and the company earned small profits. He realized that "the only way to make money in this business is to have a lot of stores, each turning in a moderate profit." He was encouraged by his successful experience with the two stores and consequently determined to open two more stores in Kansas City, one in 1959 and one in 1960.

By 1961 Mini-Mart was showing a reasonable profit and an impressive growth in sales. With these statistics, Mr. Lane was able to arrange additional borrowing to finance three more stores, one of which would be located in a nearby community, Port Aransas. The company was paying an effective rate of interest for this debt capital ranging from 11 to 15 percent. Since the company's interest cost was becoming so large and the capital structure was becoming overladen with debt, Mr. Lane felt that it would be unwise to finance further expansion with borrowed money. However, he did not know whether the company was strong enough financially to support an equity issue. Up to this point he had gotten funds for growth wherever they could be found and in any form. Realizing that he could not continue to finance expansion in such a manner, Mr. Lane began searching for the best way to finance further growth of Mini-Mart. He also knew that there would be other problems involved with additional growth and was planning to anticipate them as best as possible and solve them when they appeared.

Concept of Convenience Stores

Drive-in grocery stores or convenience stores developed as a combined result of the post-World War II population shift and the invention of the refrigerator some years previous. Many of the present stores were at one time substations of ice companies who, when their product became obsolete, shifted into the grocery business. With the rapid expansion of urban population and the accompanied growth of the suburb, large supermarkets gradually replaced the old "Mom and Dad" corner grocery stores. It was soon discovered, however, that these converted ice houses were a more convenient spot to stop and buy a few necessary items than trying to go to the supermarket. Thus was born the convenience store concept.

The theory behind the concept of this type of store was that the suburban consumer would be willing to pay a small premium to purchase certain necessary food items due to the store's location, accessibility, and long operating hours. As Mr. Lane described it, "Mini-Mart is not competing for the consumer's regular shopping dollar, only for the convenience dollar."

Mr. Lane had utilized this theory in locating, designing, and stocking the Mini-Mart chain. All of the stores had been uniformly designed and constructed according to Mr. Lane's specifications. A typical Mini-Mart store was open-front with a distinctive decor and arrangement. The store was divided into two sections: the drug section which stocked health and beauty aids, magazines, ice cream, notions, and toiletries; and the grocery section, which contained all the numerous grocery items. Most of the stores had a refrigerated vault of about 220 square feet, five freezers, and parking space in front for about eighteen cars. Because of limited display space only popular brands were carried and usually only one size of an item was stocked.

Organization and Personnel

In 1962 there were four major stockholders of Mini-Mart's 119,728 outstanding shares. Mr. Lane, his mother, and two local businessmen owned approximately 54 percent of the company. The remaining shares were held by approximately 400 other stockholders.

Mr. Lane was Chairman of the Board of Directors, President, and General Manager of the corporation. Other members of the Board included Mrs. Joy Irwin, Mr. Frank Fisher who was one of the four major stockholders, Mr. Lane's mother, an investment banker, the company's legal counsel, and three other businessmen. Mrs. Irwin, who was Mr. Lane's sister, and Mr. Fisher were also both full-time employees of the company.

Mr. Lane, Mr. Fisher, Mrs. Irwin, and a personnel manager were the principal managers of the company from the administrative end. Mr. Fisher was the merchandising manager, Mrs. Irwin, the secretary and bookkeeper, and Mr. Lane handled most of the other functions.

Each individual store had a manager who was responsible to higher management for his store's efficient use of personnel, the receipt of inventory, cash turn-in, and the store's appearance and operation. Mr. Lane felt that each store manager and assistant manager should be well trained in convenience store operations. The personnel manager conducted training sessions periodically to instruct employees in company policy, customer relations, and the completing of company reports. The new men gained practical experience in store operations and became familiar with store items by working in established Mini-Mart stores.

Competition

Mr. Lane realized that the company organization and possibly the overall goals would have to change if it were to grow successfully. His original intention had been to operate a chain of ten stores, but Mr. Lane was now of the opinion that this might be too small. "You can't stand still," he said. "Expansion is defensive as well as offensive. The opening of additional stores keeps new competition from coming in and increases the size of Mini-Mart operations. Morale is high in an expanding organization because there is room for advancement. Stop growing, and personnel become dissatisfied."

There were about thirty-eight stores in Kansas City that were in direct competition with Mini-Mart. Twenty of these were Seven-Eleven Stores, which were part of a large chain that operated about 700 stores throughout the South. In addition there was a Houston chain which had the same number of stores in Corpus Christi as did Mini-Mart. The rest of the competition was provided by several independently-owned drive-in stores spread through the city.

The competition for Mini-Mart was growing, and Mr. Lane felt that if he wanted to maintain his share of the business, he must expand soon to ensure his being able to obtain the best strategic locations in the city for his new stores. (See Exhibit I.)

As a revised goal Mr. Lane hoped to open fifty new stores within the next five to six years. He knew that this was a very optimistic aim, but felt that due to the favorable economy of Kansas City, its proximity to other sizeable midwestern cities, and the rapid population growth in this area due to industrialization, this goal certainly was attainable. He knew that this expansion would require a great deal more managerial talent to handle the multiple problems, but he felt that he was familiar enough with the operation and industry to oversee a business of this size. As far as he was concerned, financing would be the principal hurdle.

Financing

In early 1962 Mr. Lane began negotiations with a local brokerage house to underwrite a stock issue for Mini-Mart. He had decided that since the company's debt position was relatively high, perhaps a stock issue would be preferable. In reaching this decision, Mr. Lane had consulted with his Board of Directors and with the brokerage firm and they had both approved of his idea.

The brokerage firm agreed to underwrite an issue of 80,000 shares of stock on a best efforts basis. Under the agreement, the offering price was $2.50 per share and the underwriter's commission was $0.40 per share.

On the assurance from the underwriters that the entire issue would be marketed, Mini-Mart launched the expansion program. The company preferred to lease the building and land for a ten-year period with a renewal option. However, in the opening of two of the new stores in a nearby town, it was necessary for the company to commit $45,000 in cash for the construction of the two stores in order to get the desired locations.

The stock issue was not as successful as had been anticipated though. Many people cancelled subscriptions when the State Securities Commissioner decided to do some extra investigating into some of the company's past history dealing with previous issues of stock dividends. The offering resulted in the sale of only 38,000 shares, leaving the company in need of more capital in the immediate future. As Mr. Lane said, "We needed $125,000 real bad to pay some outstanding obligations and to open the other stores."

He was determined to continue with the expansion on schedule, however, and immediately began looking for sources of new capital. Mr. Lane felt that the future of his company depended on his finding the best possible source of capital. He had a limited time to search, but wanted to find a company or investor who might be able to furnish not only the needed money, but also could supply some financial management for the company. Mr. Lane realized that much of his present problem was derived from poor financial advice that he had received and was determined to find an investor that could furnish him with some help in addition to the funds.

On the other hand, Mr. Lane did not want to relinquish control of his company, nor did he want to get involved in a very restrictive agreement. He stated, "Much of this company's success to date can be attributed to several unique policies we have formulated in the financing of working capital. I feel that perhaps many investors would not understand the importance or use of such things as 'float' from the sale of money orders to provide working capital, and they might restrict our use of such funds, causing us to obtain the necessary funds from other sources which would probably be more costly."

The first company Mr. Lane approached was Midwestern Investments Inc., a Small Business Investment Corporation (SBIC). The loan proposal made to him by Midwestern Investments' management contained the following major provisions:

1. An immediate loan of $125,000 to finance expansion and to be paid back in monthly installments of $1,562 plus 7 percent simple interest annually.
2. A loan of $100,000 to be made when Mini-Mart exceeded an agreed upon performance: net profit before taxes of 2 percent on gross sales.
3. Midwestern Investments, Inc. was to have an option on 23 percent of the common stock of Mini-Mart. The option price to Mid-W. Investments would vary depending upon the profit performance of Mini-Mart. If the net profit before taxes was maintained at 2.9 percent or greater of net sales for all years after August 31, 1962, the option price would be $2.00 per share at the time of exercise. If the company did not meet this requirement then the option price would drop to $1.50 per share.
4. Two members of the Midwestern Investments' staff were to be elected to positions on the Board of Directors of Mini-Mart. In

addition it was required that Mini-Mart hire a comptroller and that he be approved by Midwestern Investments.

5. Chattel mortgages on all equipment and other properties owned by the company would be required to secure the loan.

6. A pledge of all of the stock of Mini-Mart now owned by Mr. Lane, his mother, and his sister, or acquired by them while the loan continued, was required. In addition the company would be required to take out a life insurance policy on Mr. Lane's life for the amount of the unpaid balance, with Midwestern Investments named as the beneficiary.

7. The company would be required to maintain a current ratio of 1.5 to 1.0 and to have a minimum of $150,000, including surplus, as the capital account.

8. The company could not borrow or incur any indebtedness, could not make any expenditure exceeding $7,000, and could not pay or declare any dividends without the specific consent of Mid-W. Investments.

9. The maximum limits for the compensation of officers and directors of the company for any fiscal year were specified for the period of indebtedness.

Having finished negotiations with Midwestern Investments, Mr. Lane was very tempted to accept their proposal. He realized that he had not had an opportunity to talk with other potential lenders, but was very impressed with Midwestern Investments, and needed the capital as soon as possible.

During the final interview he stated, "I realize that this SBIC deal has several strings attached to it, but I feel that it will be of most benefit to Mini-Mart in the long run. These people are interested in my success, and I know that I will not have to worry about getting good financial advice if I get tied up with them. They wrote the book. I know that I have made some mistakes in the past, but we're still growing and expanding. I feel that accepting Midwestern Investments' proposal will certainly be a favorable step toward a successful future for Mini-Mart."

EXHIBIT I

INDUSTRY REPORT

Surveys by *Progressive Grocer* revealed convenience stores increased 45 percent of 1,100 units in a 30-month period.[1] The first survey published in January of 1960 reported 2,400 drive-in units as of August, 1959. A recent survey published reveals 3,500 drive-in units were in operation at the end of 1961.

Convenience stores are very popular in the South, accounting for 83.5 percent of the nation's bantams. The West claims 10.5 percent, the North Central states 4.1 percent, and the Northeast 1.9 percent of the stores. Many food store operators believe their style of operation requires all-year-round warm weather, but in case histories it has been proven that stores can be successful in states not benefitting from mild weather.

The rapid development of convenience stores is continuing. Reports from wholesalers, company headquarters, and drive-in retailers indicate another 40 percent to 50 percent growth in stores by 1965. The greatest growth potential is predicted for the West and certain trading areas in the North Central and Northeast, with predictions that 300 to 400 new units will be opened each year and that eventually drive-in bantams will do 10 percent of total grocery sales.

Convenience stores are popular because they satisfy a want in the changing mode of living. Shoppers want more convenience and are willing to spend a few extra cents for a limited number of items to avoid long supermarket checkout lines. Another reason for their popularity is that shoppers can purchase many fill-in requirements on Sunday, holidays, and in the evenings. Persons appear impressed with the modern facilities, cleanliness, and perhaps most important in many cases, the neighborly way in which they are being treated.

Operators know the convenience store mode of retailing is highly successful, requiring small capital investment and yielding a good return on investment. Wholesalers note a small rate of failures in comparison to the successful stores they have added to their accounts. Advancements in refrigerated equipment of the multi-deck and air curtain types have permitted the stores to merchandise a wide variety of perishables in limited space. However, it is generally agreed upon by convenience store management that location is of prime importance in the opening of a successful store. For this reason, managers contemplating new units are becoming more cautious.

---

[1] Industry report is condensed from "Convenience Stores," *Progressive Grocer*, New York, October, 1962.

EXHIBIT II

MINI-MART, INC.

COMPARATIVE BALANCE SHEETS

	FISCAL YEARS ENDED 8/31				NINE MOS. ENDED 5/31/62
	1958	1959	1960	1961	
ASSETS					
Cash	$ 4,619	$20,498	$ 9,915	$ 18,953	$ 25,518
Receivables	–	530	584	1,118	10,804
Inventories	24,121	30,138	41,854	61,295	89,915
Prepaid expenses	605	3,473	2,555	6,434	16,261
Net Fixtures and Equip.	18,172	16,668	36,296	74,246	89,454
Other Fixed Assets	320	320	520	875	16,182
Leaseholds	–	6,000	22,000	20,576	69,829
Total Assets	$47,837	$77,627	$113,724	$183,497	$317,963
LIABILITIES AND NET WORTH					
Accounts Payable	$25,530	$25,632	$ 30,238	$ 56,945	$ 82,425
Current Notes Payable	800	1,092	452	4,298	37,885
Accrued Taxes	487	794	791	1,700	5,258
Notes Payable	3,000	21,833	43,314	68,416	42,297
Common Stock	16,000	33,414	50,146	58,946	59,639
Paid-in Surplus	17,414	16,732	4,321	–	71,301
Retained Earnings	(15,394)	(21,870)	(15,538)	(6,808)	19,158
Total Liabilities	$47,837	$77,627	$113,724	$183,497	$317,963

EXHIBIT III
MINI-MART, INC.
STATEMENT OF INCOME AND RETAINED EARNINGS

	FISCAL YEARS ENDED 8/31				NINE MOS. ENDED 5/31/62
	1958	1959	1960	1961	
SALES	$273,271	$301,668	$514,115	$824,956	$919,777
Cost of Sales	222,477	248,482	419,794	672,713	731,432
GROSS PROFIT	50,794	53,186	94,321	152,243	188,345
OPERATING EXPENSES:					
Advertising	251	1,084	2,227	4,325	5,732
Depreciation	1,434	1,524	2,408	4,142	9,717
Insurance	786	910	1,516	2,494	2,193
Interest	493	303	2,410	2,719	3,463
Legal and Auditing	723	935	825	1,814	4,699
Maintenance, repairs, etc.	4,669	4,278	10,549	20,929	12,620
Rent	7,438	7,339	12,515	17,950	20,846
Salaries	24,298	28,012	44,710	71,246	89,168
Taxes	3,490	2,957	5,453	8,323	8,335
Telephone and Utilities	2,673	2,588	5,376	9,572	12,414
Total Operating Expenses	46,255	49,930	87,989	143,514	169,187
NET INCOME	4,539	3,256	6,332	8,729	19,158
Add: Retained Earnings—9/1	(5,299)	(15,394)	(21,870)	(15,538)	(6,809)
	(760)	(12,138)	(15,538)	(6,809)	12,349
Less: Stock Dividend	(14,634)	(9,732)	—	—	(22,332)
Deficit Transferred to paid-in capital per quasi-reorganization on February 16, 1962	—	—	—	—	29,141
RETAINED EARNINGS—8/31	(15,394)	(21,870)	(15,538)	(6,809)	19,158

16. MOONEY AIRCRAFT, INCORPORATED

THE PRESIDENT AND CHAIRMAN OF the Board of Mooney Aircraft, Hal Rachal, had called a special meeting of the Mooney Aircraft Company Executive Committee to consider the problem of deciding upon the future location of Mooney's expanded facilities. Mr. Rachal stated the alternatives available to Mooney as follows:

1. Accept the offer of the Kerrville Industrial Foundation of 22 acres of land, located adjacent to their present site adjoining the airport;
2. Construct the proposed expansion at another location; or
3. Move their entire operations to a new location in another city.

History

Mooney Aircraft Company was organized on June 18, 1948, by Arthur Mooney with the financial support of two associates. Mooney was an aircraft designer and engineer. His associates provided most of the capital, having previously given financial and administrative assistance to two prominent light plane manufacturing companies. The original plant was located in Wichita, Kansas, but was moved to Kerrville, Texas, in February 1953 because of several factors: an adequate labor supply, expected lower cost of production, lower taxes, and an excellent climate for flying. Production began in the corner of a hangar at Louis Schreiner Municipal Airport in Kerrville. In the latter part of 1953, the main financial backer died and the company found itself with practically no operating capital, even though some $400,000 had been invested in research and development of two aircraft, one of which was in production.

Hal Rachal and Norman Hoffman were partners in a successful fixed-base flying service located at Midland, Texas. In 1954, they were visited by the publisher of *Flight Magazine* in connection with the solicitation of advertising. The publisher thought that the partners were prospects to take over the Mooney operations and he persuaded them to look into the potentials of the company. After considering the proposition in some detail, the two men agreed to take over operation of the company if two conditions were met: (1) all stockholders would return their stock to the company, and (2) if a satisfactory settlement could be reached with the creditors of Mooney. When these two conditions were met in July, 1954, the doors of Mooney Aircraft opened again. The business grew steadily after the new

Model 20 was introduced, and another expansion in sales occurred after the Model 20 was converted to an all-metal plane in 1961.

In 1962, Mooney management saw the need for a large expansion of production facilities to meet the growing needs of the company. The company had expanded its physical plant by building frequent additions as sales increased. By mid-1962, a need for a much larger expansion was recognized—one that would more than double its present facilities.

Mooney had expanded as far as possible on the land covered by its city/county lease at the airport. Local resistance to Mooney had developed to the point that company expansion proposals met with opposition from local groups.

Mooney investigated several alternatives with no success. Federal regulations would not permit construction any closer to the present landing strip. The space occupied by a local flying service would have provided the needed area, but the owner refused to be moved to a proposed new hangar.

With the increasing urgency of the situation, Mr. Rachal went to the City and County fathers to learn whether they were willing to provide additional land for the proposed physical expansion. After little response, Mr. Rachal approached the Kerrville Chamber of Commerce with a specific proposal to accomplish the land purchase. He suggested a bond issue of $750,000 to be repaid by Mooney in the form of rent over 30 to 40 years. The bond would be a "full faith and credit" bond and would be used as needed to develop expansion. The proposal caused a furor among certain powerful influences in the local community and met with such comments as, "We're throwing money down a rathole."

By late 1962, no concrete proposals had yet been made by the local townspeople. A press conference was held in Kerrville a day in advance of the annual showing of new models to dealers and distributors. Representatives of all the leading aviation magazines were present. Among those in attendance was Max Karant of *AOPA Pilot Magazine* who was a close acquaintance of Mooney management. During the session, Mr. Karant asked Mr. Rachal, "Hal, what are you doing in Kerrville?" Mr. Rachal answered in length, citing such reasons as labor, climate, and weather, but not mentioning the present problem in Kerrville. To this reply, Mr. Karant again asked, "What are you doing in Kerrville?" *Flight Magazine* publisher George Haddaway, one of the individuals largely responsible for Mr. Rachal's original contact with Mooney, was also present at the press conference. Mr. Haddaway knew of the local problem and began asking leading questions. After a long series of questions, Mr. Rachal finally stated that "Mooney *might* be forced to go elsewhere for its projected plant expansion." As a result of this statement, two publications mentioned that Mooney was interested in another location for its proposed physical expansion. Mention of this appeared in *Business and Commercial Aviation* and the *AOPA Newsletter* which had a circulation of nearly 90,000 (Exhibit I).

The results of this publicity were greater than any expectations. In connection with this situation, Mooney received over 1500 written inquiries from every state in the union and more than 2100 phone calls. One offer went as far as to propose to move the entire plant intact, move any employees who wished to remain with the company, buy any unissued stock, finance all the proposed buildings and equipment, and give every executive a membership in a local club. Another community offered to give Mooney hundreds of acres of land adjoining an abandoned government airport for the nominal price of one dollar. See example in Exhibit II.

Organization

Mr. Rachal and Mr. Hoffman have been the primary promoters of Mooney and both reside in Midland, Texas. Mr. Rachal conducts a law practice, in addition to his partnership with Mr. Hoffman in West Texas Flying Service at Midland. He serves Mooney as both president and chairman of the board and flies to Kerrville several days each week to attend to company business. Mr. Hoffman manages West Texas Flying Service and serves as vice president in charge of sales and advertising at Mooney.

Al Mooney resigned in 1959 to join Lockheed. In February 1960, Mr. Ralph Harmon was hired as vice president in charge of manufacturing and engineering, heading the Kerrville operations. Mr. Harmon had gained prominence for his design work for Cessna, Beech, and McDonald and was well-known for his ability to model parts with production in mind, which is a prime reason for the low initial cost of Mooney's aircraft.

The Executive Committee of the company includes Mr. Rachal, Mr. Hoffman, Mr. Harmon, Richard S. Martin (sales manager), and E. B. Hunnicutt, secretary-treasurer.

The Industry

The utility aircraft industry has a relatively stable product design, since the private plane, unlike the automobile, has infrequent changes in design. For example, the original plans for Mooney's Model 20 were drawn in 1948, and still have an estimated ten to twelve years of production life remaining.

The number of private planes in use has been increasing because of the advantages of faster travel for both business and pleasure. Many World War II pilots have reactivated their licenses for this reason.

The Product

Originally Mooney manufactured only a one-place, wooden wing plane, the "Mooney Mite." In September 1955, production began on the combination wood and metal "Mart 20," a four-place plane. After joining the firm, Mr. Harmon redesigned the plane and by October 1960, the production of a completely metal aircraft, the Mark 21, was underway.

In comparable models, Mooney has been able to pass such established firms as Beech, Cessna, and Piper in unit sales. Sales of the Mark 21 were 387 units in 1962, which led the industry in four-place retractable-gear planes. (Exhibit III)

Management mainly has stressed four advantages of the aircraft: low initial cost, low operating cost, low maintenance cost, and low depreciation. Exhibit IV shows many of the claimed advantages of the "Mooney Master," a fixed-gear version of the "Mark 21," over other makes of aircraft. The cost differentials among the "Mooney Master" and other fixed gear planes are shown in Exhibit V.

Company Location

Kerrville is a small city of 10,000 population, known best for many guest ranches, children's camps, and health resorts. The community enjoys a fine climate, interesting hills, and quiet atmosphere. It relies extensively on sheep, goat, and cattle raising industries, and serves as a regional market for wool and mohair.

Mooney was the only manufacturing industry of any size located near the community. Its payroll was exceeded only by that of a U.S. Veteran's Hospital located on the outskirts of the city. The company took active interest in the welfare of the community. Mooney provided direct employment to many local residents. According to a May 1963 publication of the Kerrville Industrial Foundation, there were 11 unemployed males out of a working force of 3,273 and 32 unemployed females out of 1,965.

As evidenced by the reaction of the city to Mooney's expansion proposal, some local antagonism toward Mooney existed. Some of the reasons for this situation were believed by management to be as follows:

1. A few local people had apparently lost small investments as a result of the reorganization of the company.
2. Some local businessmen possessed an unprogressive attitude, with their orientation primarily toward agriculture.
3. A prejudice existed against operation by management who were not natives of Kerrville.

4. The higher wages paid by Mooney tended to "upset the local labor market."
5. Aviation was a bit removed from the quiet atmosphere of Kerrville. Some local townspeople failed to realize the significance of the acceptance of private planes.

Local banks were also antagonistic. As late as January 1963, one bank had advised outside inquirers that "Mooney will go broke anytime." A local store went so far in 1961 as to send the company a notice that it would no longer cash company payroll checks. As a consequence of this relationship, Mooney maintained its banking connections in Fredricksburg, a community 24 miles away. The Fredricksburg bank reported Mooney's financial condition as "sound, with an excellent growth record."

Labor Situation

Mooney employed 460 people in 1963. By the end of 1965, employment was expected to be 850, and was projected to 2,200 after the proposed plant expansion had been completed in 1970. (Exhibit VI) The local labor market had been almost fully utilized. For expansion, the company was forced to recruit in surrounding towns in order to secure an adequate number of employees. Almost all managers and technical personnel were recruited from other cities, many from out-of-state locations.

Aircraft production operation required about 60 percent skilled laborers and 25 percent semi-skilled. The remaining 15 percent were engineers, administrative and clerical personnel. All new production employees were trained on the job and many positions required Federal Aviation Agency certification. In this connection, management felt that less time could be spent training employees if Mooney were located in a more industrialized community. Mooney paid generally higher salaries than other Kerrville employers, but its wages were estimated to run 10 percent to 20 percent under those paid to comparative classes of workers by other aircraft manufacturers in other locales.

In 1959, a representation election was held and the International Association of Machinists was named to represent the employees. Actually Mooney never signed a contract with the union and its membership included only around 15 to 20 employees.* Mr. Rachal utilized much of his time in Kerrville to personally conduct labor negotiations with the business agent about various union grievances. Lately, the management had become concerned with much of the union propaganda and was attempting to combat it through a series of speeches by Mr. Rachal and articles in the *Mooney Mirror*. (Exhibit VII)

---

* Later, a labor agreement was signed in February 1964.

Finance

The sales of Mooney Aircraft increased steadily after 1955 (Exhibit VIII. According to Mooney management, the company had an excellent record of earnings and had shown remarkable growth. Capital improvements, including buildings and equipment, have added to the increasing asset value of the company. But because of its growth, the company was faced with a shortage of working capital and consequently relied on immediate sale of all production to remain in a liquid financial position. No financial data were released by the company.

Other Factors Affecting Decision

All sales of aircraft were handled through 51 distributors, 101 dealers, and 16 foreign outlets. All aircraft were picked up by the dealers and flown to the new owners. Because of this arrangement, management felt that it would be impossible to find a central location because of the international scope of the market. The delivery schedules of vendor parts and supplies to Kerrville were satisfactory. Mooney provided its own tooling. The only large distant purchases were the engines from Pennsylvania and propellers from Ohio.

The community of Kerrville provided Mooney with excellent fuel, water, and electric service. Other advantages of the location were the Texas right-to-work law and the ad valorem taxes. The local climatic conditions were very favorable to the necessary daily testing of the finished aircraft.

Criteria for Expansion

As a consequence of the situation in Kerrville, the company was forced to formulate definite criteria for its expansion in case of relocation elsewhere. After long deliberation by management, it was decided to state the following minimum requirements necessary for any specific location:

1. Large local labor pool
2. Location in a state with a right-to-work law
3. 50 to 80 acres of land available on suitable terms
4. Building of 100,000 square feet under one roof expandable to 500,000 square feet in 5 years
5. Parking area for 700 to 1000 employees' cars
6. Minimum airplane parking for 200 aircraft

Kerrville Offer

Becoming concerned over the possible loss of Mooney, two local businessmen began to stir up interest in keeping Mooney. They talked to members of the Industrial Foundation, in which were some local banking antagonists. Mooney's campaign was assisted when the friendly editor of the *Kerrville Times* wrote several editorials and articles explaining the benefits of having Mooney in Kerrville.

As a result of an intensive campaign, the Industrial Foundation, a division of the Kerrville Chamber of Commerce, offered to lease a tract of 22 acres adjoining the present Mooney plant for a nominal sum. A promise of additional land near the airport, when needed, was also made.

Executive Committee Meeting

Because of the urgency of the situation, Mr. Rachal decided that a definite decision was needed in respect to the future company expansion and that the decision should be made immediately. Thus, the Executive Committee members of Mooney Aircraft were assembled for a special meeting on Saturday, February 24, 1963.

Mr. Rachal called the meeting to order, and after a brief resume of the situation, proceeded to summarize the problem. He stated the alternatives available to Mooney as follows:

1. Accept the offer of the Kerrville Industrial Foundation of 22 acres of land,
2. Construct only the proposed expansion at another location, or
3. Move the entire operation to a new location.

All members of the Executive Committee were aware of the need to arrive at a prompt decision. They were also aware of the important effect the decision would have on the future of the firm.

Underlying issues awaiting consideration as soon as the location of their expansion was decided were the following:

1. Major new additions to their product line were under consideration.
2. Significant new improvements in their present product line were nearly ready to be moved from research and development into production, with substantial sales increases expected as a result.

After a period of discussion Mr. Rachal called for a vote by the Committee.

EXHIBIT I

Newsletter — November 1962

MOONEY "MASTER," new addition to company's 1963 line, is stripped-down fixed-gear version of Mark 21, is priced ($13,995) to compete with Cherokee, Musketeer. At later date owner can convert ship to retractable gear with $1,600 kit. "Master" identical to Mark 21 in dimensions, weight, is produced on same assembly line, has own paint scheme. Performance compared with Mark 21 makes interesting comparison:

	Mark 21	Master
Top speed	185	147
Cruise (75%)	180	141
Climb (f.p.m.)	1,010	780
Service ceiling	17,200	12,000

Meanwhile, company planning five-fold expansion is actively seeking offers to build new plant at another interested community, admits frankly that Kerrville is disinterested in building up local industry. Interested communities contact H. F. Rachel, Mooney president, Kerrville, Tex.

BUSINESS/COMMERCIAL AVIATION — December 1962

AVIATION INTELLIGENCE

BIG FUTURE for company is predicted by Mooney management. Projected dollar volume for '62 is around $5½ million with 380 to 400 aircraft sold. Hal Rachel, company president, told B/CA that he anticipates $10 to $20 million within ten years "if a project we are now studying develops."

KEY PROJECT is probably development of more sophisticated single engine airplane in 250 hp class, disclosed to B/CA by Ralph Harmon, Mooney v-p of engineering. Harmon said that designing and building tooling for bigger airplane are under way as engineering progresses, is coordinated with design of high performance twin.

BURGEONING FIRM is feeling need for more room to grow. Lack of adequate local skilled labor, poor weather conditions, unsympathetic attitude of Kerrville town fathers are making Mooneymen look elsewhere for new facilities. Original plant will probably remain active in Kerrville for some years but larger city, preferably in Texas, is being sought for new site, will eventually house entire operation.

EXHIBIT II

COPY OF TYPICAL LETTER RECEIVED BY MOONEY

December 11, 1962

Mr. E. E. Carman
Mooney Aircraft, Inc.
P. O. Box 72
Kerrville, Texas

Dear Mr. Carman:

It was a pleasure to visit with you by telephone yesterday about the expansion plans for Mooney Aircraft. As a result of our conversation, we are much better informed about what you have in mind for future expansion, and what kind of information that you would like from us.

We are sending, in a separate envelope, one of our latest Industrial Brochures, a picture of the hangar at our airport, a map showing the layout of the runways and the location of the property, a sketch of the hangar area, a copy of a labor report for Hempstead County prepared for us by the Arkansas Employment Service dated March 29, 1962, and some testimonials from local industries that we have assisted in recent months. In addition to the enclosed labor information, we have a number of local people who make their homes in Hope and work at the Red River Ordnance Depot and the Lone Star Ordnance Plant in Texarkana. A good number of these people are rated as skilled personnel that would very likely prefer to work at home rather than drive 35 to 40 miles, each way, every day. Located within a 25 mile radius of Hope, we have four other communities with a combined population of more than 10,000 that would have some skilled people that would be prospects for a plant such as yours.

We sincerely believe that we have everything that your Company would need for a plant at our local Airport. We also are confident that we can come up with the financing that you might require for this project, and we are definitely sure that your people would find a sense of friendly and cooperative spirit among the citizens of our town.

We extend to you, and other Company Officials, a most cordial invitation to visit us and see first hand just what we have to offer. In the event that you would desire some additional information, we would be happy to supply it.

Sincerely yours

(signature)

B. N. Holt, Secretary
Hempstead County Industrial
Foundation, Incorporated

By H:jc

EXHIBIT III

COMPARATIVE SALES OF LEADING PRODUCERS
OF UTILITY AIRCRAFT

YEAR	BEECH Bonanza/ Debonair	CESSNA 210	PIPER 400/260/ 250/180	MOONEY Super/21/ Master
1962	358	281	380	387
1963	333	156	246	502
1964 (Est.)	535	283	303	650

SOURCE: Company records.

EXHIBIT IV

COMPARATIVE FEATURES ADVERTISING EXHIBIT

YOU GET MORE FOR YOUR MONEY WITH MOONEY			
FEATURE	MOONEY MASTER	BEECH MUSKETEER	PIPER CHEROKEE
Horsepower	180 hp	160 hp	180 hp
Cruise (75% Power)	141 mph	135 mph	141 mph
Climb	780 fpm	710 fpm	720 fpm
Useful Load	1100 lbs.	1000 lbs.	1135 lbs.
Take-off Roll	890 ft.	890 ft.	775 ft.
Landing Roll	550 ft.	595 ft.	600 ft.
Stall Speed	57	62	57
Range (75% Power)	680 miles (48 gal.)	792 miles (60 gal.)	695 miles (50 gal.)
Propeller	Constant Speed Controllable	Fixed Pitch	Fixed Pitch
Cowl Flaps	Standard	None	None
Flaps	Hydraulic (0° to 33°)	3 Position	3 Position
Controls	Dual (Standard)	Dual (Extra)	Dual (Standard)
Cyl. Head Temp. Gauge	Standard	None	None
Brakes	Individual Toe (Standard)	Individual Toe (Standard)	One Hand Brake
Generator	50 Amp	35 Amp	35 Amp Alternator
Super Sound Proofing	Standard	. . . .	. . . .
Manifold Pressure Gauge	Standard	. . . .	. . . .
Retractable Entrance Step	Standard	None	None
Steerable Nose Wheel	Standard	None	Standard
Tinted Glass	Standard	None	None

From Manufacturer's published figures

EXHIBIT V

PRICE COMPARISON ADVERTISING EXHIBIT*

airplane model	base price including same basic equipment	full gyro panel	Narco Mark 10 communication and Omni	ADF (T-12B) & rotating beacon	marker beacon	TOTAL COST
Beech Debonair (62)	$21,975.00	550.00 (re-mfg.)	2575.00	1340.00	290.00	$26,730.00
Cessna 210	$24,625.04	825.00	2495.00	1275.00	260.00	$29,460.00
Cessna 205	$22,295.00	825.00	2495.00	1275.00	260.00	$27,150.00
Cessna Skylane	$18,990.00	295.00 (approx. exchange)	970.00 (approx. exchange)	1275.00	260.00	$21,790.00
Piper 250 Comanche (super custom)	$26,080.00	std.	1565.00 (approx. exchange)	120.00	std.	$27,765.00
Mooney Mark 21	$16,450.00	730.00	2218.00	1300.00	275.00	$20,973.00

* Prices shown are approximate and figured on comparable equipment in each category. You may make your own calculations on any equipment desired.

EXHIBIT VI

EMPLOYMENT IN MOONEY AIRCRAFT, INC.

YEAR END	NO. ON PAYROLL
1955	84
1956	110
1957	128
1958	180
1959	225
1960	300
1961	420
1962	430
1963	460
1964 (Projected)	575
1965	850
1970	2200

SOURCE: Company records.

EXHIBIT VII

MOONEY MIRROR

MARCH 1963

PUBLISHED FOR EMPLOYEES OF MOONEY AIRCRAFT, INC., OF KERRVILLE, TEX.

Hal Rachal Addresses All of Mooney Family

In a Thursday afternoon meeting, voluntarily attended by company employees, Hal Rachal, President of Mooney Aircraft, Inc., paid tribute to the Mooney Family. Stressing the teamwork of each department with another, Rachal pointed with pride to the leadership which the Mark 21 had attained in 1962. "All of us working together made this possible," Rachal declared.

In a surprisingly frank discussion, Rachal traced the financial history of Mooney Aircraft since he and Norman Hoffman, Vice President in charge of Sales, took control of the company on July 1, 1954. With complete candor, he spoke of the loans he had arranged to keep the company going. He declared with no little pride that, "the company has never missed a payroll."

Rachal spoke at length of the profits of the company over the past several years. He stated that labor and materials have absorbed profits as well as several loans which he arranged. The equipment and supplies enabled production to turn out the airplanes that captured first place for the company in 1962 and set the stage for further gains this year.

President Hal pointed to future production possibilities in his statement that he "would like to see you folks produce more airplanes than our three competitors combined!"

In his discussion, Rachal answered firmly, charges from an outside element that the company had mistreated its employees by contributing a thousand trees to the recent Arbor Day activity in the county.

Pointing out that the trees cost only thirty cents apiece and that Mooney was one of many business firms in the county to support the program, Rachal offered to personally pay for the trees if the employees felt that the company had acted unwisely in participating in the beautification plan. A show of hands indicated that only nine of the more than 400 employees at the meeting objected to the company action.

Rachal pointed out that the contribution of the trees was a modest effort when compared to the many thousands of dollars which the city and county has put up to acquire land for Mooney expansion and a water supply system to supply fire protection to Mooney property.

"The same element," Rachal said, "has advised Mooney employees through handbills on their autos, that the company gave salaried employees more vacation time than hourly workers received." Rachal declared that the average salaried employee works 2,652 hours annually, as compared to 2,080 hours for the hourly employee. "For this additional 572 hours," said Rachal, "we give the salaried worker 48 hours more vacation per year." A showing of hands indicated that the vast majority of hourly employees felt that vacation time was fairly administered.

Referring to other charges by Local 725 of the I.A.M., Rachal branded as a

complete misstatement of fact, that the company was holding out for an agreement to limit its employees to their present income for a five-year period.
Reading from a copy of his proposal to the Bargaining Committee, Rachal explained that the company has repeatedly offered, since June of 1962, a plan
for employees based on taxable profits of the company and the cost of living
index established by the Federal Government. Included in the company proposal is the employee bonus plan for production efficiency.
In his closing remarks, Rachal stated that negotiations with the Bargaining
Committee would continue until an agreement had been reached, which
would be completely fair to all Mooney employees.

EXHIBIT VIII

MOONEY AIRCRAFT, INC.

ANNUAL SALES

YEAR	NO. OF PLANES	DOLLAR VALUE
1955	9	$ 300,000.
1956	70	780,000.
1957	100	1,140,000.
1958	162	2,090,000.
1959	181	2,480,000.
1960	172	2,470,000.
1961	286	4,270,000.
1962	387	5,500,000.
1963	502	6,700,000.
1964 (Estimated)	650	9,540,000.

SOURCE: Company records.

17. ESCUELA DE ADMINISTRACION DE NEGOCIOS PARA GRADUADOS ESAN MUEBLES INDUSTRIALES S.A.* (INDUSTRIAL FURNITURE, INC.)

IN OCTOBER OF 1964 Mr. Holger Smitt and Mr. Knud Fabricius
were faced with the problem of expanding production capacity in their
firm, Muebles Industriales S.A., (MINSA). This firm, located in Rimac,
a suburb of Lima, Peru, was producing sewing machine cabinets for the
Singer Sewing Machine Company. Singer had offered to purchase up to
900 cabinets a month, but MINSA's production capacity was only about
300 cabinets per month. Smitt and Fabricius were considering a number

* This case was prepared by Research Associate D. Clay Whybark, Escuela de
Administración de Negocios para Graduados, Lima, Peru.

of possibilities for increasing production both in the Lima area and in Pucallpa, a city on the Ucayali River in the jungles of Peru. Interesting opportunities existed also for expansion into furniture manufacturing, plywood manufacturing, a lumber sawmill, and prefabrication of sewing machine cabinets.

Background

Smitt and Fabricius had varied experiences before coming together in Peru. Mr. Knud Fabricius came to South America with a large Danish construction company, Christiani & Nielsen, in 1937. He started with this company in Venezuela, and in 1942 was transferred to Bolivia as a construction supervisor. After three years in Bolivia, he came to Peru, still with Christiani & Nielsen, to supervise a number of their construction projects. He left the company in 1946 to join the Cerro de Pasco Corporation, a large mining company operating in Peru.

Cerro de Pasco provided opportunities for Mr. Fabricius to broaden his experience. He initially signed up for a 3-year stay, but ended up staying 14. Before leaving Cerro de Pasco, he was directly in charge of all maintenance and construction work for the plant, the supporting facilities, and had completed a major plant expansion. Fabricius also supervised the maintenance of the Cerro de Pasco railroad line and equipment.

The other partner, Mr. Holger Smitt, was a licensed tool and die maker from Denmark. He graduated from the Engineering School at the University of California in 1947 and began his engineering career with General Motors in Pontiac, Michigan. After a short time, he left General Motors to join the Gladding-McBean Corporation as a plant engineer at their Lincoln, California branch, where he was in charge of plant construction and equipment installation in a company expansion program. Later he moved to the Armco Construction Company in Fresno, California, where he supervised construction of slaughterhouse and bulk plant storage facilities.

Building on this experience, Mr. Smitt formed his own construction company and successfully bid on several contracts in California, North Dakota, and Arizona. In Arizona he purchased an airplane parts manufacturing company to which he was attracted as an opportunity to settle down in Phoenix, to manage his own business, and to use his skills as a machinist and tool and die maker. Somewhat later he sold this business and left for Lima, Peru, "just to see what he could find."

Shortly after Mr. Smitt's arrival in Lima, a mutual friend introduced him to Mr. Fabricius. Mr. Smitt recalls, "We met on a Saturday morning and that afternoon we were in business together. Somehow or other we both hit it off from the beginning." Thus in 1961 began Metallic S.A. They purchased a plant in Surquillo, a suburb of Lima, and set up a foundry for casting domestic faucet valves and fittings.

The new valve company had just started to get its production up to a commercial scale when a friend, employed by a Danish machine company, gave them a lead on a contract for the construction of a fishmeal dryer. The partners hastily submitted a bid in the Metallic name and were somewhat surprised to find they had won the contract. They began construction of the dryer in an open space on the Metallic plant site. This first job in the fishmeal industry led to several other requests for bids as the news of the quality of the company's products spread.

A fishmeal boom began in 1963 and Metallic began constructing complete plant installation—cookers, dryers, presses, and baggers, all with matching capacities. They also continued to bid on individual equipment. As the orders came in, Metallic cut back the valve making operation and moved the men out into the equipment construction area. From time to time during this period, the company also bid on and won contracts for structural steel components on various construction jobs. The result of these efforts are summarized in the financial statements of Metallic S.A. shown in Exhibit I.

The partners shared the workload roughly on the basis of their previous experiences, and profits were divided equally. Mr. Smitt says, "I probably spend more time indoors working on design, contacts, and the administrative part of the business than Knud does, because I've had experience running and managing my own business. On the other hand Knud can't be beat when it comes to getting the production job done. With his years of supervising construction and production crews, he seems to be able to come up immediately with the ideas that will get the men to do the work the best possible way. I never will forget the time a truckdriver dumped one of our 25 ton fishmeal dryers in the Huarmey River about 600 meters from the plant to which it was supposed to be delivered. Knud went up there and within two days had the thing out of the river, installed in the plant and operating perfectly. You can see why Knud spends more of his time out working with the boys in the shop than I do."

Initial Contact by Muebles Industriales S.A. (MINSA)

In late 1963, Mr. Gino Rossini, the owner of Muebles Industriales S.A., approached Smitt and Fabricius for funds. Mr. Rossini's company was a small firm located in Rimac, another suburb of Lima about 45 minutes by car from Metallic. They were producing cabinets for the Singer Sewing Machine Company. According to Mr. Rossini, his firm had been operating only one year, but already held orders for 400 sewing machine cabinets per month. He felt the firm could produce this volume which was sufficient to insure good profitability. The present problem, he said, was "short term" financing of the increased production necessary to fill the Singer orders.

Mr. Rossini felt that S/. 300,000 would be sufficient to finance an increase of production to 400 cabinets per month. He initially requested a straight interest-bearing loan but later agreed to give partial ownership in the company, because he said, "prospects look good enough for everyone." He ultimately offered a 25 percent ownership in return for the S/. 300,000 loan.

Smitt and Fabricius felt that it was an appealing proposition. The year 1963 had been quite successful and adequate funds were available. Holger Smitt talked to Rossini and offered him the S/. 300,000, but asked for a 50 percent ownership interest rather than the 25 percent. A period of negotiations followed and Mr. Rossini finally agreed to accept the proposal, and the money was paid to him. As Smitt later reflected, "The proposition was very interesting to us, particularly because of the ownership part. We would get an ownership interest just for making the loan and the loan would be paid back. In addition, it looked like a relatively easy way for us to expand. Perhaps the most convincing part, however, was Mr. Rossini's salesmanship. If he walked in here right now, I think he could talk me out of my life's savings in less than ten minutes."

Early Operations of Muebles Industriales S.A.

Shortly after Smitt and Fabricius loaned the funds to MINSA, Mr. Rossini returned to ask them for money to help him over another crisis. He said that he had underestimated the funds necessary to increase the production and that a little more money would put the company in a sound financial position. Smitt and Fabricius decided they would increase the loan on the condition that they could increase their ownership position at the same time. They finally persuaded Mr. Rossini to accept this condition even though it would leave him with less than 50 percent ownership. The amount of the loan was increased by S/. 100,000 and the Smitt and Fabricius ownership increased to 65 percent.

Before long Rossini was in again requesting additional money, and Smitt and Fabricius, deeply concerned with the management of the company, decided to institute tighter control over the MINSA operations. As a condition to getting an increase in the loan, Mr. Rossini agreed to use a dual signature checking account and to give a more active management role to Smitt and Fabricius. Fabricius made several suggestions to Mr. Rossini for increasing production. This did not bring immediate results, however, and production continued erratic and inefficient. The dual signature control slowed transactions down somewhat but had some effect on costs. Still it became necessary to add further funds from time to time and Smitt and Fabricius became more and more deeply involved in the MINSA operations.

Mr. Smitt recalls, "We were having a terrible time. We were busy trying to keep our own company under control and this guy decides to dump all the effective management of Muebles Industriales on us. We were swamped! By this time we had about S/. 700,000 invested in MINSA, and production still wasn't increasing appreciably. Rossini seemed to believe that he was at his ultimate capacity, but about the most he ever produced in one month was 200 cabinets, still far short of requirements and less than breakeven. His average production was even worse— about 100 per month. We were particularly unhappy with Rossini's spending money like mad every time he received a payment from Singer. He would receive a check for S/. 100,000 from Singer and immediately turn around and write checks for S/. 300,000 and send them all over to us for approval. By this time we had obtained complete ownership of the firm and Rossini was our employee. We just inherited the thing."

Fabricius felt that with some ship improvements and changes in methods, layout, and organization, MINSA would be able to produce 300 cabinets per month quite easily. Anything more would be difficult because of lack of space in the plant. Singer Sewing Machine had kept its offer open to take any cabinets produced up to 400 a month, so there was no sales problem. In the meantime Singer was filling its requirements with cabinets produced in Japan and two local plants, Ostolaza S.A. and Ciurlizza Maurer. The price and quality of the Japanese cabinets were equivalent to those made by MINSA, but Singer wished to develop a local source of supply for those cabinets it was importing. The total Singer requirement was about 2,700 units per month.

The 30 to 40 shop workers of MINSA were supervised by an Italian shop foreman who had considerable experience in woodworking. Fabricius regarded this foreman as a very capable man who had been hindered by continual requests to do special projects for Rossini's friends. He agreed with Fabricius that the company could produce 300 cabinets per month with the present staff and some improvements in methods. They agreed further that even at the higher production the administrative and general costs would be the same and only the cost of goods sold would increase.

No statements of the financial position of MINSA, except those sent to the Government, had been available during this period. In early 1964 Mr. Smitt asked his accountant to try to piece these figures together. The result was an approximation of the December 1963 balance sheet and income statement for that year. These documents are shown in Exhibit II.

One of the problems was what to do about Mr. Rossini who was earning a salary of S/. 15,000 per month. Smitt and Fabricius felt they could readily obtain a better plant manager for this salary and then transfer Mr. Rossini to Sales Manager. They asked a friend in Denmark to find someone who might be interested. He suggested a young, experienced Danish cabinet-maker with a background in furniture design and construction. This experience was attractive to them because they had considered the possibility of an expansion into furniture design and manufacture.

Smitt and Fabricius also considered outright sale of the company. In the early part of 1964 the market value of the assets of the firm was approximately S/. 1,000,000. The company had little "going concern" value other than the Singer contract. Total outstanding debts were approximately S/. 1,600,000, of which S/. 700,000 were owed to Smitt and Fabricius, and S/. 900,000 to others. Smitt states, "It didn't make much sense to us to seriously consider selling the company when we almost surely would have lost S/. 600,000 of our investment. It seemed to us that the only way we could recover any of this would be to keep the firm and operate it ourselves." However, neither Smitt nor Fabricius felt that they had enough time to manage both Metallic and MINSA effectively at the same time.

Smitt and Fabricius decided to fire Mr. Rossini, and brought the young cabinet-maker, Mogen Sorensen, from Denmark to serve as Production Manager. During the months of April, May, and June, while Sorensen was receiving training and orientation, the process changes and equipment moves outlined by Mr. Fabricius were put into effect. Production gradually increased, but the plant was still unable to produce the hoped-for 300 cabinets per month primarily due to space limitations for assembly and finishing. Production figures and income data are shown in Exhibit III.

Smitt and Fabricius reviewed the plant changes with Singer and at the same time proposed a modified cabinet design. Shortly thereafter Singer increased its standing order from 400 cabinets to 900 cabinets per month including a number of the modified cabinets. Fabricius felt that, with the new changes, production could reach, but probably not go above 300 cabinets a month in the present location. Singer stated that they would hold open their increased order to cover Smitt and Fabricius if they wished to expand Muebles Industriales.

In the fall of 1964 there were few local producers of high quality, modern Scandinavian Designed furniture, and Smitt and Fabricius had frequently discussed the opportunities this presented for MINSA. Sorensen had brought furniture designs and manufacturing know-how with him from Denmark and, shortly after his arrival, produced several experimental pieces of modern furniture. However, with production of Singer cabinets restricted by plant capacity, there was no opportunity for production of furniture.

Production Processes

Production of the Singer cabinets is relatively simple. The raw materials are rough-cut lumber, plywood, and special veneers. The lumber and plywood are cut to standard sizes and shapes for assembly and glueing. The plywood pieces are covered with matched slices of veneer to form the outside surfaces of the cabinets. The lumber and veneered plywood are glued together to form panels, which are in turn glued together to form the finished product. Sanding is done both before and after glueing. The cabinets are sprayed, hand-rubbed and re-sprayed to provide a durable high luster finish.

Singer sewing machines are used throughout Peru—from areas of high humidity and mild temperature such as the coast, to the extreme altitudes and temperatures of the mountains, into the hot and humid climate of the jungle. Singer found that conventional plywood and pressed wood cabinets warped under some of these conditions. MINSA solved that problem by using sandwich type panels made up of narrow strips of wood glued between two pieces of veneered plywood.

It is the policy of the company to purchase local materials if possible. Rough-cut lumber comes from Pucallpa. When available, plywood is also purchased in Pucallpa; otherwise imported plywood is used. Select local veneers are used in most of the cabinets. The wood is brought to Lima wet and dried for about one month before use because it cannot be dried sufficiently in Pucallpa without a kiln.

In the early part of 1964 MINSA had some difficulty obtaining rough-cut lumber and Smitt visited Pucallpa to discuss the matter with the company's buying agent. The buyer explained that the lumber is cut along the streams that flow into the Ucayali River, and floated down the Ucayali during the rainy season into Pucallpa, where it is rough-cut. The sawmills buy from independent loggers and resell to the agents after sawing. Every year the loggers go further back into the jungle to fell large trees to cut. Logs were in short supply in Pucallpa because light rains didn't fill the tributaries sufficiently to float out logs cut some distance from the main river. Mr. Smitt also found that the local sawmills were selecting the better grades of lumber for their favorite clients. Other companies purchasing through representatives in Pucallpa were experiencing similar difficulties to those of MINSA.

While in Pucallpa Mr. Smitt was struck with the potential advantages of operating a plant for pre-fabricating cabinets in this jungle area. Pre-fabrication in Pucallpa would enable the Rimac plant to concentrate on assembly and finishing of the parts brought from Pucallpa. This in turn would permit an estimated increase in overall production of about 200 units per month or a total capacity of about 500 units per month. The company would also have direct access to logs during periods of short supply and the opportunity of obtaining the best grades of logs if they were located in Pucallpa. Mr. Smitt gathered further information on these possibilities, and the provisions of an Industrial Promotion Law which gave tax advantages and duty free import privileges to firms operating in the Peruvian jungle, for discussion with Mr. Fabricius. A brief description of the geographical relationship and characteristics of Lima and Pucallpa are found in Exhibit IV.

Possibilities in Pucallpa

There was a readily available labor supply in Pucallpa at slightly lower rates than in Lima. Even if MINSA paid slightly more than the going rate to attract the best workers, it would still enjoy an estimated 10 percent savings in labor costs. The pre-fabrication would result in a savings in transportation costs as well because the present rough cut lumber from Pucallpa is approximately 50 percent waste. Mr. Fabricius felt that the combined effect of these factors would represent a net savings of 7% of the Cost of Goods Sold for the company.

Mr. Fabricius obtained quotations of about S/. 40,000 on plant sites and buildings large enough to produce parts for up to 1,000 cabinets a month. He estimated that it would cost S/. 300,000 to move the equipment not used in assembly and finishing from Rimac to Pucallpa. An additional S/. 750,000 would be required to purchase, transport and install a sawmill facility, and the additional equipment necessary for pre-fabrication and increasing the capacity. A kiln would cost approximately S/. 350,000 installed and would be necessary in Pucallpa.

Smitt and Fabricius also considered construction of a plywood plant in Pucallpa. The only other plywood plant in Peru selling to the Lima market was already located in Pucallpa. Even at theoretical capacity, which this plant had never been able to reach, it could supply no more than 25 percent of the plywood demand. Smitt and Fabricius concluded they would be able to sell all the output of a plant with a capacity of 1,000 sheets per day, or 250,000 per year. MINSA would require about 40 sheets a day to produce 1,000 Singer cabinets per month. Plywood prices, for the grades used by MINSA, delivered in Lima were about S/. 50.00 per sheet. Selling at this price Smitt and Fabricius estimated they could realize a gross margin of S/. 15.00 per sheet. They estimated total administrative and general expenses of approximately S/. 2,500,000 at capacity production. They expected no problems in reaching this level and felt that further expansion could be accomplished by multiple shifts.

Bids were obtained from several manufacturers of plywood equipment. The most attractive was for rebuilt, guaranteed, used German equipment, which was S/. 4,020,000 installed and ready for operation in Pucallpa. Mr. Fabricius had located generating and steam-power equipment which he estimated could be purchased and installed for S/. 1,070,000. With this equipment he felt they would be able to produce plywood, deliver it to Lima and sell it in an average of just over one month from raw material to sale.

Design and cost of the plant for plywood production would be dependent upon the decision as to cabinet pre-fabrication. The plywood plant and land would cost approximately S/. 40,000 if built separately from a pre-fabrication plant. If both were built, the plywood plant could be added to the pre-fabrication plant for approximately S/. 20,000 additional.

Possibilities in the Lima Area

Even with pre-fabrication done in Pucallpa the space limitations of the Rimac plant would allow only about 500 cabinets a month production, so Smitt and Fabricius decided to look for larger assembly and finishing facilities in Lima. Adjoining the Metallic plant in Surquillo was a building which, with some modifications, could readily accommodate production in excess of 1,000 cabinets per month, with or without pre-fabrication in Pucallpa. Open space at the back of the lot would make possible future expansion. The price of this lot and building was S/. 1,250,000. Mr. Smitt estimated that modifications necessary to adapt the site to either complete construction or just assembly and finishing of cabinets could be accomplished for an additional S/. 600,000. If operations were confined to Surquillo it would cost S/. 100,000 to move from Rimac and new equipment costing S/. 750,000 would have to be purchased to bring capacity up to 1,000 per month. If the pre-fabrication was done in Pucallpa these expenditures would not be necessary because the Pucallpa plant investment would include them and little would be moved from Rimac to Surquillo. Exhibit V gives other costs.

The possibility of purchasing the site next to Metallic was appealing to both men. Mr. Smitt stated, "if we take on any of these possible additional projects, we feel that our management capabilities will be stretched enough without the additional complications of having plant locations scattered from Surquillo to Rimac to Pucallpa. Besides that, Metallic also has space for future expansion or for storage of our plywood sheets if we decide to go ahead with the plywood plant in Pucallpa."

Mr. Sorensen urged that the company take advantage of a sub-contract which the company had been offered by Estudio 501, a local furniture manufacturing company, for the construction of 1,000 chairs. Estudio 501 would supply all material, drawings, and instructions, and MINSA would cut, sand, and assemble the chairs. Mr. Sorensen felt that this contract would provide highly desirable furniture manufacturing experience in anticipation of MINSA's entrance into the furniture market on its own. Training would not pose much of a problem because the contract could be stretched out over sufficient time to allow an adequate training. He estimated that additional equipment costing S/. 50,000 would be needed. Mr. Fabricius estimated that even after allowing for start-up costs, a few additional personnel and allocation of some overhead expenses, the company would net about S/. 40,000 on this contract before taxes.

Smitt and Fabricius estimated that if the company decided to design and build its own line of furniture, an addition of approximately S/. 500,-000 in equipment would be needed, over and above the S/. 50,000 worth of equipment necessary for the sub-contract work. This investment would not change even if some of the furniture pre-fabrication were done in Pucallpa, because the costs of transporting and installing the equipment would be the same for either Pucallpa or Surquillo. The furniture operation could be housed on the Surquillo site by investing an additional S/. 800,000 in new buildings. If the operations were split only S/. 600,000 would be needed to construct additional buildings in Surquillo but S/. 50,-000 for land and buildings in Pucallpa would be needed.

With such an installation, a high-quality line of modern furniture could be produced and sold at an estimated rate of S/. 500,000 per month. Furniture cost of goods sold would be an estimated S/. 300,000 per month and, because Singer cabinet manufacture would share them, general and administrative costs would be about S/. 100,000 per month. If the furniture operations were not combined with the Singer cabinets, the Surquillo site would need only S/. 600,000 in additional buildings for a Lima only operation or S/. 500,000 in Lima and S/. 50,000 in Pucallpa for a split operation. The general and administrative costs would increase to about S/. 150,000 per month in this case, because the Singer cabinets would not be sharing these costs.

Mr. Sorensen felt there would be no problem in selling this volume of furniture and that expansion to higher volumes would be easy with the addition of further equipment and manpower. There were a few firms manufacturing modern furniture with Scandinavian designs among which were: Estudio 501, Fimac, and Ciurlizza Maurer. None of these were making pieces with the same designs as Mr. Sorensen brought from Denmark. He felt his pieces would be most similar to the furniture imported directly from Scandinavia.*

1960 — S/. 80,104
1961 — S/. 45,296
1962 — S/. 7,905
1963 — S/. 60,209.

SOURCE: Estadística del Comercio Exterior.

At the same time Smitt and Fabricius were considering an offer of S/. 1,750,000 which had been received for the equipment, patterns, and inventory of the valve and faucet manufacturing portion of the Metallic operation. The net book value of this portion of the assets was slightly more than S/. 2,000,000. Sale of the valve and faucet operation would release enough plant space in Surquillo to permit separating the finishing operations from the cabinet assembly operation. It was felt that this would aid in maintaining the quality of the cabinets. A recent increase in import duties on valves, Mr. Smitt felt, would ensure valve sales of over S/. 2,000,-000 annually approximately peak production capacity in the present foundry space. The duty might make possible a 25 percent increase in prices but there was local competition, so some of the increase in prices would be absorbed by increased selling expenses. Smitt estimated that with valve operations at capacity, they should be able to net 20 percent on sales.

Metallic's contract and fishmeal plant manufacturing activities were fairly self-sustaining and required little management time. The work force was experienced and the foremen were capable. Once a bid had been submitted and a contract let, actual construction proceeded with little top management attention. On the other hand, the valve section had just recently been reactivated again after a prolonged shut-down, and the problems of re-establishing quality, maintaining output, and marketing the product would require considerable management time. These problems would dilute the attention which Smitt and Fabricius could devote to any of the potential new projects in Muebles Industriales.

In summarizing the prospects for these various alternatives, Mr. Smitt stated, "We are intrigued with the possibility of starting an operation in Pucallpa, both from the standpoint of gaining a foothold in that area, with all its tax advantages, and for what it would do for our operation here in Lima. We don't want to spread ourselves too thin or bite off more than we can chew, so we're looking at this offer to purchase our valve manufacturing operation very carefully. We are trying to decide whether we want to be essentially a woodworking business, a metal-work-

---

* Peru imported wooden furniture from Scandinavia in these amounts.

ing business, or both. All of these possibilities sound good, but we want to do only those which are really worthwhile and which we can handle. If we go to Pucallpa I thought I would spend most of my time there getting the plant started and Fabricius would take care of things here. He would come over when I needed his help for something. We think we can raise enough money for any of these alternatives, but it might also pay to sell the valve line and use those funds. This might be good from the management standpoint as well as that of cost. Essentially it boils down to deciding what things to do and in what order to do them.

EXHIBIT I

BALANCE SHEETS

(Sales in thousands)

	DEC. 31 1961	DEC. 31 1962	DEC. 31 1963
ASSETS			
Current Assets			
Cash	2	14	5
Accounts Receivable	73	2,712	7,811
Inventory	131	866	4,946
Prepayments	21	272	223
Total Current Assets	227	3,324	12,985
Fixed Assets			
Building and Fixtures	199	304	409
Machinery and Equipment	1,680	3,467	4,139
Organization Expense	102	102	102
Less Depreciation	143	507	1,135
Net Fixed Assets	1,838	3,365	3,515
Total Assets	2,065	6,690	16,500
LIABILITIES AND CAPITAL			
Accounts Payable	652	1,104	3,920
Notes Payable	864	3,389	5,772
Bank Loan	101	416	3,013
Reserves	47	186	609
Total Liabilities	1,664	5,095	13,314
Capital	500	1,000	1,500
Earned Surplus	(99)	595	1,686
Total Capital	401	1,595	3,186
Total Liabilities and Capital	S/. 2,065	S/. 6,690	S/. 16,500
INCOME STATEMENTS			
Net Sales	814	7,011	10,030
Other Income	2	59	34
Total	816	7,070	10,064
Production Costs	479	3,033	5,195
Gross Margin	337	4,037	4,869
General Expenses	152	1,439	2,172
Other Factory Expenses	61	530	637
Salaries	209	1,307	237
Interest	14	66	137
Total	436	3,342	3,183
Net Profit (loss) before taxes	S/. (99)	S/. 695	S/. 1,686

EXHIBIT II

BALANCE SHEET AS OF DECEMBER 31, 1963

(Sales in thousands)

ASSETS			LIABILITIES AND CAPITAL		
Current Assets			Accounts Payable	S/.	40
Cash	S/.	13	Notes payable[2]		1,432
Accounts Receivable		5	Bank loan		142
Inventories		154	Reserves		77
Prepayments		125	Total Liabilities		1,691
Total current assets		297	Capital		500
			Earned Surplus		(613)
Fixed Assets[1]			Total Capital		1,578
Equipment		962	Total Liabilities		
Organization Expense		319	and Capital		3,269
Total Fixed Assets		1,281			
Total Assets	S/.	1,578			

[1] The building in which Muebles Industriales was located was rented.
[2] Includes S/. 700,000 in Notes payable to Smitt and Fabricius.

INCOME STATEMENT

1963

(Sales in thousands)

Gross Sales	S/. 1,846
Minus Discounts	21
Net Sales	1,825
Production Costs	1,044
General Production	186
Gross Margin	595
Other Expenses	
Wages and Salaries	693
General Expenses	232
Social Laws	95
Interest	21
Total Other Expenses	1,041
Net Profit (loss) before taxes	(449)

EXHIBIT III

PRODUCTION AND SALES BY MONTH

(Income in thousands of sales)

YEAR		JAN.	FEB.	MAR.	APR.	MAY	JUNE	JUL.	AUG.	SEPT.	OCT.	NOV.	DEC.
1962	Total Income[1] S/.												115
	Cabinets S/.												108
	Number of cabinets produced												100
1963	Total Income[1] S/.	54	125	85	49	118	99	168	141	682		243	82
	Cabinets S/.	33	125	85	49	118	99	125	141			216	70
	Doors[2] S/.							42		6			
	Fair[3] S/.									676			
	Number of cabinets produced	35	165	80	45	110	92	116	131			201	65
1964	Total Income[1] S/.	135	76	65	136	116	113	252	246	269			
	Cabinets S/.	135	75	65	135	106	105	252	246	269			
	Number of cabinets produced	135	60	60	127	98	102	248	220	253			

[1] The total income does not always equal the total of cabinets, doors or the fair construction because of miscellaneous income received.

[2] Muebles Industriales made doors for a local firm as a trial product.

[3] Muebles Industriales bid on and won a contract for some special construction for a local fair which was worked on in September and October 1963 although payment was received in September.

215

EXHIBIT IV

MUEBLES INDUSTRIALES S.A.
DEMOGRAPHIC AND GEOGRAPHIC DATA

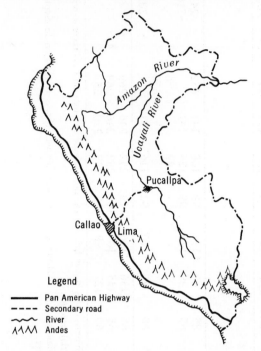

Legend
— Pan American Highway
- - - Secondary road
~~~ River
ΛΛΛΛ Andes

   Lima is the capital of Peru and the Lima-Callao area is the industrial and market center of the country. Roughly 20% of the Peruvian population lives in this area (approximately 10,800,000 population in Peru 1964); the highest average incomes, levels of economical activity, and portion of the population economically active are centered in this area as well; for example, somewhat more than 50% of all Peruvian salary is paid in this region. The weather is mild year round and there is hardly any rainfall at all. All services are available in this cosmopolitan South American capital.
   Pucallpa on the other hand, is located on the banks of the Ucayali River (one of the rivers that flows into the Amazon) in the Peruvian jungle. The city itself has a population of about 26,000 and most businesses use their own generators for power production. The principal activity apart from agriculture is related to production of rough cut lumber. The temperatures are high (mean annual temperature nearly 80°) and there is much rain (nearly 60 inches per year) mostly from November to April, although it rains some throughout the year.
   The road from Lima to Pucallpa is 842 kilometers long. It rises from sea level in Lima to 4,843 meters in the first 150 kilometers. From there it drops to nearly sea level again at Pucallpa. When the weather is good the trip by truck is about three days, but during the rains there can be delays of up to several days while slides are cleared from the road. Improvements now in progress should cut the good weather time to two days, but the danger of slides in the mountains will still persist.

EXHIBIT V
COST AND FINANCIAL DATA
ESTIMATED TOTAL ANNUAL ADMINISTRATIVE AND
GENERAL EXPENSES AT VARIOUS VOLUMES
OF PRODUCTION

VOLUME OF CABINETS	SHOP IN PUCALLPA AND LIMA	SHOP IN LIMA ALONE
300/mo.	S/. 1,520,000	S/. 1,065,000
500/mo.	S/. 1,780,000	S/. 1,350,000
900/mo.	S/. 2,420,000	S/. 1,970,000

INCOME STATEMENT PROJECTION AT 300/mo. LEVEL IN RIMAC SHOP*

Sales	S/. 3,600,000
Cost of Goods Sold	2,400,000
Gross Margin	1,200,000
Administrative and General	1,065,000
Profit before tax	135,000
Taxes	28,000
Profit after taxes	S/. 107,000

* The working capital invested at this level is approximately S/. 366,000. This includes a one month supply of raw material being dried for use. The cost of the raw material is approximately 21% of sales.

18. NUCLEONICS RESEARCH AND DEVELOPMENT CORPORATION

"WITHIN THIRTY DAYS WE COULD be turning out a thousand a day," Robert G. Waggener, president of Nucleonics Research and Development Corporation, said about his company's newest product. The device, an automatic electronic turn signal canceller for motor vehicles, was emerging from the development stage under the name of Blink-Off, and the company was in the throes of transition from a solely research operation to a combined production and research and development operation.

Company Background

Waggener studied mathematics at The University of Texas, graduated in 1954 with a degree in mathematics, and then served as a commissioned officer in the U.S. Army Corps of Engineers. After his military service he immediately returned to Austin and entered the Graduate School of The University of Texas with the aim of earning the degree of Doctor of Philosophy in physics. While doing graduate work, he supported himself by working at odd jobs which included grading and supervising laboratory work in the Physics Department. During this period he met many persons and made many friends whose interest and abilities lay in the scientific field. These contacts stood him in good stead when, in the spring of 1961, Waggener had an opportunity to combine his desire for a business career in Austin with his scientific training. Several of his friends, who knew of his interests and education, agreed to help him set up and finance a small company to engage in the research, development, and manufacture of scientific devices.

By combining and contracting the words nuclear and electronics, Waggener gave the company the distinctive name of nucleonics. Four individuals helped to found the corporation, and two of them agreed to contribute more capital than the others. Within two weeks after the formal incorporation, in the spring of 1961, the stockholders who had been counted on to supply the majority of the money withdrew their promised financial support.

Waggener, in the name of the new corporation, had leased a building near The University of Texas Balcones Research Center on McNeil Road in North Austin. Office equipment, scientific instruments, and tools had been purchased. Although the odds seemed strongly against him, Waggener was determined not to terminate his venture just because capital was lacking. He again turned to odd jobs for sufficient income to allow his company to keep the doors open while he sifted thousands of ideas to find a few suitable products to develop and manufacture for sale.

In the summer of 1961 the world political situation was tense, and as a consequence governmental authorities recommended that various types of companies develop civil defense products. Nucleonics explored the civil defense field and turned out prototypes for several devices, such as radio-actuated early warning devices and detectors of fall-out radiation. Before any of these products had been placed into production, public apathy developed in the civil defense movement, and through the winter of 1961 and the early months of 1962 Nucleonics was unable to produce and sell any of the civil defense products on a profitable basis.

The very limited resources of the company were being used for research and development, and the lag in developing a profitable product placed the company in a severe financial position. Waggener's limited income from other part-time jobs was not sufficient to continue support of the company. Waggener, therefore, searched for a financial source which could offer help of a substantial nature. He finally encouraged a prominent Austin businessman, the general manager of a successful scientific company, to join his board of directors. With the help of this new board member and another business acquaintance, Waggener was able to arrange for the owner of a profitable local construction materials company, who was seeking investment diversification, to finance Nucleonics' efforts in return for 67 percent of the capital stock. Waggener retained 10 percent of the stock and continued as president of the company with the new stockholder serving as treasurer with sole control over cash disbursements. The financial arrangement involved the extension of a $50,000 line of bank credit, with the provision that Nucleonics would, within a "reasonable length of time," repay all borrowed funds plus a similar amount to the company granting the financial aid. Within six months the new major stockholder insisted upon increasing his interest to 80 percent to realize certain tax benefits. The additional 13 percent interest was acquired at nominal cost from the five minority stockholders, including Waggener, by a threat to withhold the previously promised extension of credit.

By March 1962 Waggener had decided to shift emphasis from civil defense products and, by a process of elimination, had compiled a list of potential products which he felt were suited to Nucleonics' capabilities. The new financial backer concurred with Waggener's selection of products and agreed to finance additional development, subject to his item-by-item approval and the line of credit limitation.

Because of his experience with the short-lived civil defense movement, Waggener was determined to pick products that would ensure a long-lived sales potential but were not subject to immediate domination by larger, better established companies.

After the additional financing had been arranged, Waggener added four men whose training was suited to the proposed Nucleonics development program. A part-time secretary was also employed. At that time the staff included a total of 7 employees. A total of some $4,500 of research equipment and electronic parts was also purchased to enable the personnel to pursue research, development, and pilot production along the lines laid out by Waggener.

New Product Development

Early in 1962 special design of a neutron-gamma ray discriminator-detector was developed for use by laboratories engaged in nuclear physics research. The device was designed to provide a simple, yet reliable means for fast neutron detection. The device had a basic price of $600, and Waggener estimated the market for such a product to be about 400 units. While the idea was not considered patentable, he estimated that it would cost a competitor about $50,000 to develop a similar model. The direct cost of manufacture was estimated at $150 per unit; the remainder of the price represented development cost and gross profit. Ten units had been sold by November 1, 1962, and sales inquiries were promising.

The product upon which Nucleonics was concentrating most of its effort and resources was the Blink-Off. The inventor, Ben Burson, Jr., offered Waggener an exclusive manufacturing and sales license in the United States on a patent pending for an electronic device to cancel turn signal indicators on motor vehicles. A patent had been applied for through a Washington, D.C., attorney in 1960.

The Blink-Off met Waggener's criteria for a product that had potential mass application yet was not being produced by larger companies. Basically, the Blink-Off served as a backup or a safeguard against driver forgetfulness. Mechanical turn signals, which were standard on all American automobiles at that time, required a rather short radius turn to be executed before the mechanical canceller turned the signal off. If the required radius was not transcribed, the operator of the vehicle had to remember to turn the signal off manually. When the driver forgot to turn off the signal, it often resulted in confusion to other drivers. In many documented instances, this confusion was the cause of a serious accident. The Blink-Off circumvented this possibility when wired into the signal indicator circuit of the vehicle. The device contained a counter which noted the number of blinks put out by the flasher. After a preset number of blinks, the circuit to the signal lamps was automatically broken. (See Exhibit I for sales release describing the Blink-Off.)

Waggener believed the device was applicable to every vehicle on the road, but he stressed the fact that the idea was of particular value to large trucks because, for the most part, truck turn signals did not incorporate even a mechanical canceller. The driver had to turn such signals off manually in all cases.

Waggener believed the trucking and the passenger bus manufacturers offered the key to widespread acceptance for his company's device. He contacted several large truck and trailer manufacturers, including General Motors, Ford, and Fruehauf. Some definite interest was shown in the Blink-Off, and Waggener anticipated contracts for large orders in the near future.

Although Nucleonics had manufactured a total of some 200 Blink-Off units for testing and display purposes in these months, Waggener stated that Nucleonics was willing and ready to turn out 1,000 units a day within thirty days after obtaining a definite sales contract. Waggener felt he could do this with his present facilities by simply adding more persons to work on the production line. Waggener insisted that hand soldering was the most difficult operation involved in the production of the Blink-Off. All circuitry was hand wired, and the components were mounted by hand on a predrilled baseboard.

Because of the estimated capital investment involved in setting up a partially automated assembly process, the Blink-Off was to be assembled by hand operations on a workbench. The only tools necessary were a pair of needle-nosed pliers, a wire cutter, a soldering gun, and a one-quarter inch electric drill. The components of the Blink-Off consisted of a masonite baseboard, several electronic parts, several lengths of wire, and a plastic cover. Exhibit II presents a list of the required parts, with costs for each item.

A template was used to locate the seventeen holes in the baseboard, which was predrilled for mounting holes and soldering terminals. After the baseboard was drilled with the portable hand drill, the nine soldering lugs were pressed into the designated holes. The electronic parts were then mounted in the following sequence: a relay was fastened via a single self-tapping metal screw; a transformer was attached by means of two small bolts and nuts; a large transistor was pressed into its force-fit hole drilled in the baseboard; and the leads for the two capacitors were soldered to the lugs.

The smaller electronic items were then soldered in place and connected by wires to their proper points. Three terminal wires were attached to brass contact posts in the plastic box, and the baseboard assembly was fastened to the box by means of four small bolts and nuts. The Blink-Off was then ready for packaging in a cardboard box, accompanied by mounting screws, connecting wire, and an instruction sheet.

Preliminary time and motion studies indicated that one employee using the method outlined above could produce an average of 20 units a day. Waggener anticipated the need for a production force of 40 assemblers to provide for an output of 800 to 1,000 Blink-Offs daily to meet anticipated volume sales contracts.

Current manufacturing facilities would serve with little alteration. Two long workbenches would be divided into work areas for each assembler. A full complement of hand tools and parts needed to assemble Blink-Offs would be provided at each work station. A total floor space of 1,250 square feet was available for production operations.

Provided preliminary estimates of standard output of 20 units per assembler per day were realized, direct labor costs at an average labor rate of $1.25 per hour were estimated at approximately $.50 per unit. Total parts cost for an assembled unit was estimated at $4.28 in 1,000-lot quantities. Estimated cost included the cost of a plastic case which was estimated at $.70 in 100-lot quantities and at $.40 in 1,000-lot quantities. Larger quantities had a cost schedule of $.126 per unit plus $1,870 for dies. Faulty units, scrap, and returns were estimated to average $.15 per unit. Royalties were to be paid to the inventor on a sliding schedule, as shown in Exhibit III. In 1,000-unit quantities, estimated direct costs totaled $5.50 per unit plus overhead burden of $1.65.

The basic unit had a list sales price of $19.95. Trade discounts, as shown in Exhibit IV, ranged from 40 percent to a maximum of 60 percent for vehicle manufacturers. No formal market survey had been made to establish the probable market for the Blink-Off. The potential market had been subjectively estimated to include most of the trucks and busses in a commercial operation in the United States and a substantial proportion of the new passenger vehicles produced, especially those used primarily for commercial purposes (taxis, fleets, etc.). While no specific sales target was ever stated, Waggener insisted that the Blink-Off, as a fully developed device, was worth in excess of one million dollars if it were to be sold to another company.

Actual sales of the Blink-Off in the three months during which it was available totaled slightly over 100 units. The slow development in sales could be explained in part by several factors. The serious shortage of working capital prevented the development of the necessary sales organization and of any extensive advertising or promotional activities. Much of the selling was done by Waggener, in addition to his many other responsibilities. Some local radio advertising was obtained on a trade-out basis in return for engineering services. Main reliance was placed on direct mail solicitation and on receiving free advertising by being mentioned in new products announcements in trade journals.

Considerable enthusiasm was displayed by almost every person to whom the Blink-Off was demonstrated. Enthusiasm was seldom translated immediately into sales, however. The main problem, according to Waggener, was to get the approval of state authorities to permit installation on commercial and public vehicles. An estimated expenditure of $2,000 would be needed to have the required tests made and to pay the required fees in each state. In some states the necessary approval was relatively easy to obtain. Other states had failed even to acknowledge Nucleonics' request for approval. The status of approval by each state as of November 30, 1962, is shown in Exhibit V. The state of Texas did not specifically approve the device, stating that "the device can be marketed in the state of Texas without approval as long as it is used as a supplement to the turn signal system." In order to facilitate adoption, Nucleonics petitioned the Society of Automotive Engineers Lighting Committee to hold hearings for the purpose of setting standards for such a device.

Waggener reported that a major nationwide tire chain had expressed a definite willingness to retail the Blink-Off as soon as approval was received from all states. He also reported that he had been informed that the Detroit and Dayton city bus lines had added the Blink-Off to the specifications for all new busses purchased by them.

Most challenging of all was an expression of interest from a major auto manufacturer. Nucleonics was requested to quote a firm price, not to exceed $5.00 per unit, on lots of 100,000 units, without plastic cover, packaged in bulk, and priced F.O.B. Austin. The treasurer reported a strong disinterest in the prospects of selling the Blink-Off at such a low price, even in 100,000-unit lots. While not stating his position precisely, he implied that Nucleonics should produce nothing unless it could get a profitable price. Waggener became convinced that the treasurer was more interested in selling the rights to produce the Blink-Off than he was in producing and selling the final product.

Future Prospects

Nucleonics had yet to show an operating profit, and the final results for 1962 were not likely to be profitable. Even greater losses would have been incurred had not Waggener been drawing only a subsistence salary, and all but one other employee worked only on a part-time basis. Aggressive sales efforts were not undertaken, and new projects and expenditures were indefinitely postponed because of the difficulty in obtaining required item-by-item approval from the treasurer for all new expenditures. In November 1962 Waggener was uncertain about what course of action he should take to keep Nucleonics afloat. At that time the total investment in the company included about $20,000 in stock and $25,000 which had been borrowed under the $50,000 line of credit. (See Exhibits VI and VII for copies of the financial statements.)

Sales prospects for November and December seemed good enough to earn a small profit for the last two months, even if not for the whole year. Waggener was confident that with his new knowledge about how to manage a research and manufacturing firm he could operate at a profit next year if he could stay in operation. To substantiate his confidence, he estimated that his break-even point had been brought down to a sales volume of less than $6,000 a month, based on a variable cost ratio of approximately 60 percent and a current fixed cost of approximately $2,500 monthly. He was anxious to bid for the auto manufacturer's business, in spite of the objection of the treasurer and controlling stockholder.

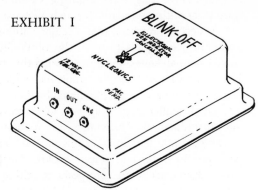

EXHIBIT I

"BLINK-OFF"

Electronic Canceller For
Automotive Turn Indicators

Prevents You From Being A
Flashing Menace On The Road

SPECIFICATIONS

1. Completely electronic (no clock, thermostat, or heavy moving parts).
2. No reset delay (immediately after cancellation, the indicators can be restored by a mere flip of the indicator switch).
3. In attractive sturdy plastic box: Dimensions 6¼ × 2¾₁₆ × 4⅜″.
4. Made of easily replaceable, nationally known, standard, dependable parts.
5. Comes adjusted to effect cancellation after 50 to 70 flashes of the turn indicator.
6. Complete with mounting screws, hook up wire, and adaptors.
7. Easily installed: Beneath instrument panel, seat, or under hood.
8. Causes little or no loss of brilliancy of turn indicator lights before cancellation.
9. There is no noise from clicks or buzzes.
10. Guaranteed for one full year.
11. Two models available: Fixed time at factory, or adjustable time by individual.

MODELS AVAILABLE FOR AUTOMOBILES, TRUCKS, OR BUSES

12v. with negative battery terminal to frame, fixed and variable units.
12v. with positive battery terminal to frame, fixed and variable units.
6v. with positive battery terminal to frame, fixed and variable units.
6v. with negative battery terminal to frame, fixed and variable units.

(Other Models Available On Request)

OUR SUGGESTED RETAIL PRICE: $19.95 FOR FIXED UNIT
$21.61 FOR VARIABLE UNIT.

EXHIBIT II
ESTIMATED COST OF MANUFACTURE OF BLINK-OFF

ITEM	PER UNIT IN 1,000-UNIT LOTS	PER UNIT IN 10,000-UNIT LOTS
2N 404 transistor	$ .25	$ .23
1N3754 diode	.24	.22
Transformer	.44	.38
Relay	1.79	1.45
Capacitor	.304	.304
Capacitor	.35	.35
NE-2 neon bulb	.075	.062
Plastic box	.40	.126*
Terminals	.126	.126
Board (masonite)	.03	.03
Shipping box	.055	.052
Resistors	.12	.08
Miscellaneous	.10	.06
Wastage	.15	.10
Direct labor	.50	.50
Payroll taxes	.03	.03
Freight in	.15	.10
Printing instructions	.02	.02
Royalty payments	.37	.08
Total (subtotal)	$5.50	$4.30
Overhead burden	1.65	1.31
Total cost	$7.15	$5.61

* Add $1,870.00 tooling cost.

EXHIBIT III

BLINK-OFF ROYALTY SCHEDULE

UNITS SOLD PER YEAR	ROYALTY PER UNIT
0 — 999	$ .37
1,000 — 4,999	.22
5,000 — 9,999	.12
10,000 up	.08

EXHIBIT IV

RECOMMENDED PRICES TO DISTRIBUTORS AND ORIGINAL EQUIPMENT MANUFACTURERS

UNITS	NET PRICE (F.O.B. AUSTIN)
1 — 249	$12.00
250 — 499	11.00
500 — 999	10.25
1,000 — 4,999	9.60
5,000 — 9,999	8.84
10,000 up	8.08

EXHIBIT V

STATE APPROVAL ON BLINK-OFF*

STATE	NEED TEST	BEING TESTED	NO APPROVAL NECESSARY	SALES PERMITTED
Alabama	X	X		
Alaska	X			
Arizona	X			
Arkansas	X			
California	X			
Colorado	X			
Connecticut			X	
Delaware			X	
Florida		X		X
Georgia			X	
Hawaii				
Idaho		X		
Illinois				
Indiana			X	
Iowa	X			
Kansas		X		
Kentucky			X	
Louisiana	X			
Maine				
Maryland	X			
Massachusetts		X		X
Michigan			X	
Minnesota				
Mississippi	X			
Missouri	X	X		
Montana			X	
Nebraska			X	
Nevada	X			
New Hampshire	X	X		
New Jersey	X			
New Mexico		X		X
New York	X			
North Carolina			X	
North Dakota			X	
Ohio		X		
Oklahoma	X			
Oregon				
Pennsylvania				
Rhode Island	X			
South Carolina				X
South Dakota			X	
Tennessee		X		X
Texas				X
Utah	X			
Vermont	X			
Virginia				X
Washington	X			
Washington, D.C.		X		X
West Virginia				
Wisconsin			X	
Wyoming			X	

* As of November 30, 1962.

EXHIBIT VI

INCOME AND EXPENSE

NUCLEONICS RESEARCH AND DEVELOPMENT CORPORATION

For the period June 1962 through October 1962

INCOME

Sales and services			$ 3,358.48

EXPENSE

Manufacturing			
Raw materials			
Inventory 6-1-62	$2,375.00		
Purchases	2,783.69		
	$5,158.69		
Less: Inventory 10-31-62	4,097.37		
	$1,061.32		
Direct labor	4,662.60		
Indirect labor	1,356.44		
Other manufacturing expense	956.15	$ 8,036.51	
Finished products			
Inventory 6-1-62	$ 585.00		
Inventory 10-31-62	2,071.92	1,486.92	6,549.59
Gross profit (loss)			$ (3,191.11)
Research and development costs			
Labor	$6,297.57		
Materials and supplies	614.90		
Other research expenses	260.94	$ 7,173.41	
General and administrative expense			
Salaries—administrative	$3,550.01		
Salaries—office	1,415.00		
Other administrative expenses	5,237.26	10,202.27	17,375.68
Net loss			$(20,566.79)

EXHIBIT VII

BALANCE SHEET*

NUCLEONICS RESEARCH AND DEVELOPMENT CORPORATION

OCTOBER 31, 1962

ASSETS

Current
Cash on hand and on deposit		$ 483.14	
Inventories			
Parts and supplies	$ 4,097.37		
Finished products	2,071.92	6,169.29	
Accounts receivable		2,319.30	$ 8,971.73

Fixed assets
Research equipment		$ 812.37	
Office furniture and equipment		2,482.26	
Leasehold improvements		568.46	
		$ 3,863.09	
Less: Allowance for depreciation		568.43	3,294.66

Other
Utility deposits		$ 100.00	
Organization expense		112.35	
Prepaid interest		107.69	
Prepaid insurance		417.29	737.33
			$ 13,003.72

LIABILITIES

Current
Notes payable—Capital National Bank	$ 25,500.00	
Installment notes on office equipment—current portion	506.04	
Accounts payable—for parts and expenses	2,250.95	
Payroll and withholding taxes	1,074.62	
Accrued interest	274.10	$ 29,605.71

Long term
Installment notes on office equipment—noncurrent portion		210.84

Net worth
Capital stock			
Common stock—2,000 shares at $10.00		$ 20,000.00	
Retained earnings (deficit)			
Balance 6-1-62	$(16,246.04)		
Net loss—five-month period ended October 31, 1962	(20,566.79)	(36,812.83)	(16,812.83)
			$ 13,003.72

---

* Without audit.

229

19. O'CONNOR MARINE SERVICE

ON JUNE 1, 1960, MR. JASON KELLEY, manager of the O'Connor Marine Service, and Mr. Patrick Smith, assistant manager for the business, were discussing the past year's operation of the O'Connor Marine Service. The fiscal year of the company had ended May 31, and both Jason Kelley and Patrick Smith realized that O'Connor Marine Service had been anything but a financial success during the 1959–1960 year. The owners of the business, Mr. Rex O'Connor and Mr. Luke O'Connor also were well aware of this fact and had visited the Marine Service operation a few days earlier to discuss this problem with the two managers. In essence, they had told Jason Kelley and Pat Smith that they had a free hand to do whatever was necessary to make the O'Connor Marine Service a profitable operation during the coming years as long as major policy decisions first were cleared with them.

Company Background and Development

The O'Connor Marine Service had been organized June 1, 1958, under a general partnership agreement between Mr. Rex O'Connor and Mr. Luke O'Connor. This business was just one of several business activities which the O'Connor brothers administered under a general partnership agreement. They entered this particular field because of the tremendous surge of interest in boating and yachting by the American public since World War II (see Exhibits I and II), and because of the availability of a desirable piece of waterfront property located in the heart of a tourist area approximately 40 miles north of Boston, Massachusetts.

During the summer, fall, and winter of 1958–1959, Mr. Jason Kelley, manager, and Mr. Patrick Smith, assistant manager, along with a work gang, developed the acquired waterfront property, so that by the spring of 1959, the O'Connor Marine Service was in a position to offer several services similar to those offered by other boating centers, or "marinas" as they were called by yachtsmen. These services included (1) summer dockage, (2) winter boat storage, (3) hull and engine repairs, (4) marine store merchandise, and (5) miscellaneous services such as gasoline, snack bar, showers, laundromat, and storage lockers.

The total investment including land, building, repair equipment, piers, etc., approximated $250,000. One piece of major equipment purchased was a "travellift." The travellift was an adaptation of the travellift used for lifting and hauling lumber in the northwestern section of the

United States. This piece of equipment alone cost $15,000, plus an added cost of $10,000 for constructing a pier which was necessary for the travel-lift to go out over the water and lift a boat (up to 25 gross tons) out of the water for hull and engine repairs. In addition to this equipment, O'Connor Marine Service had a large repair building and storage shed with a rail track extending in the water which allowed boats of up to 100 gross tons to be pulled out of the water for major repair work. This building was used as a storage building during the winter months. Other buildings (see Exhibits III and V) included a small machine shop which had a heating unit so that work could be performed there in the winter months; a marine merchandise store which was stocked with basic marine equipment, parts, and accessories for small boats; and a small building for the snack bar, laundromat, showers, and lockers. At the beginning of the summer season, 1959, inventory in the marine store had been valued at close to $16,000.

Operational Activities, 1959–1960

During the fiscal year, June 1, 1959, to May 31, 1960, the O'Connor Marine Service operated at a net loss of approximately $57,000. The exact amount of the loss is not known to the management at this time because the O'Connor Marine Service is just one of several business activities administered under the general partnership between the O'Connor brothers. Furthermore, the outside accounting firm engaged to audit the financial records has not had time to properly study the records and determine proper expense allocations to the various enterprises of the partnership. However, Jason Kelley and Pat Smith realized the financial loss of the 1959–1960 year's operation was significant. They also realized that during the peak season, July 1 to September 1, the operation was profitable.

After much discussion, Kelley and Smith agreed that the O'Connor Marine Service financial problems were due to many factors but the most obvious were:

1. A lack of more dockage space.
2. Seasonal fluctuations in demand for their business services.
3. The necessity to maintain a nucleus of skilled labor.
4. A limited number of services provided by the firm.

Physical Limitations

The primary service provided by O'Connor Marine Service is that of dockage space for small or large boats wishing to tie up overnight or for a few days. In addition, many customers who live in the vicinity rent dockage space on a seasonal basis so they can maintain their boats at O'Connor's throughout the summer months. During the peak season this is a profitable activity for the business. Of the 63 slips available for renting in the summer of 1959, all 16 foot slips and 30 percent of the remaining slips were rented on a seasonal basis. On an average daily calculation, 80 percent of the slips were occupied during the summer season. Other space is taken up by larger boats which sometimes have an over-all length of up to 100 feet. The pricing of dockage service is based on the length of the slips occupied by the boats if they do not exceed 45 feet in over-all length (see Exhibit III), and by the length of the vessel if they tie up at the main dock and exceed 45 feet in length. The O'Connor Marine Service had as many as nine of the larger boats tied up at the same time during the 1959 season. Mr. Jason Kelley feels that one way to put the O'Connor Marine Service on a more profitable basis is to provide more dockage space as demand increases. In talking with adjoining property owners, he realizes this possibility is out for the present time since neither owner is willing to sell his waterfront property at any reasonable price and since all owned waterfront property is being utilized.

Seasonal Fluctuations in Business Activity

The O'Connor Marine Service business clearly fluctuates with tourist activity in the area. The peak season for tourists runs from July 1 to September 1. Also, if any severe weather conditions arise which cause tourists to stay away from the area or vacationers to leave the area, the O'Connor Marine Service business suffers. Pat Smith vividly recalls the month of August 1959, when the first hurricane warning of the season occurred and practically all of the people in the resort area departed overnight for a safer location.

In attempting to analyze the seasonal activity of their business, the two managers developed a very simple schedule showing the work activities they were most concerned with during the seasons of the year.

FALL	WINTER	SPRING	SUMMER
(slow season)	(very slow season)	(busy season)	(peak season)
Pulling boats for winter storage. Covering some boats for outdoor storage.	Miscellaneous activities.	Overhauling boats, repair work, merchandise store sales to individuals for boat repairs.	Dock rentage, hull & engine repair work, store sales, other services.
Approximate number of employees 8 (Includes 3 administrative employees)	Approximate number of employees 8	Approximate number of employees 10	Approximate number of employees 20

Labor

The number of skilled shop employees which are maintained throughout the year are five. These men are paid on an hourly basis from $1.75 to $2.50 per hour. Mr. Kelley and Mr. Smith feel that even though it is expensive to carry these men on the payroll through the winter months, it is less expensive than trying to replace them each year if they are laid off. Since there are very few jobs the year around for these skilled people in this resort area, Mr. Kelley has had no labor turnover problem. During the peak season, additional skilled labor is added as needed for hull and engine repair work and college students are added to the dock force for pumping gas and doing miscellaneous jobs. A public school teacher is employed in the summer to manage the marine store.

The total wage bill for all labor (skilled, semiskilled, and administrative), in 1959–1960, was $52,500.

While the O'Connor Marine Service is seriously affected by the short summer season, other neighboring businesses also are affected. Several times business groups and civic groups have worked together to try and promote the area so more people would be attracted to the vicinity. They also have attempted to stage and promote special events which would stimulate crowds and lengthen the summer season. In the past two years a major golf tournament was held plus an annual fishing rodeo. In the opinion of Pat Smith, both events were failures.

Service Diversification

While the services provided by the O'Connor Marine Service are several and more than the typical marina offers along the New England shoreline, the idea of broadening the service line has run through the minds of the partners as well as the managers. Several informal discussions have been held to discuss this subject. They all agreed that the manufacture of small boats was out due to the required investment in plant, machines, etc., needed to develop volume production to be competitive. Other considerations involve the purchase of a line of boats which would be sold by the O'Connor Marine Service. Another idea discussed was the possibility of wholesaling marine paints. As yet, no action has been taken regarding any of these or other ideas.

Pricing and Competition

Exhibit IV shows rates for boat dockage, labor rates, haul out rates, and storage rates. Gasoline is priced one cent a gallon above the price of the same gasoline for automobiles. All price charges are considered competitive. According to the manager, Mr. Kelley, the major difficulty in pricing comes from customers who fail to understand the charge for hull or engine repairs. Unlike an automobile mechanic, a boat repair man is unable to quote an estimate on hull or engine repairs until a boat is hauled out of the water, and is in the shop with the engine torn down. Considerable expense and time is involved prior to this point and many times customers are shocked at the price charged even though Mr. Kelley feels that O'Connor's prices are reasonable; in fact the O'Connor Marine Service lost money on this phase of the operation during 1958–1959. For this type of work, the price is determined by adding the haul out charge to the labor charge (depending on labor-skill, see Exhibit V), plus standard list prices for parts needed. Occasionally the charge runs $100 or more. The managers would like to attract and encourage the owners of larger boats to use their dockage and repair services since it is felt that they are not as concerned with the expenditure for service as much as small boat owners. Furthermore, the marine storekeeper believes that an owner of a large boat spends much more for proper upkeep of his boat and accessory equipment than the owner who is a "do it yourself" man and owns the smaller boat.

Advertising

The O'Connor Marine Service does not have an advertising budget as such but the manager, Jason Kelley, believes in advertising and promotes business through advertising as much as he can. Every spring a modest ad is run in the boat section of the *New York Times* for three days a week for several months. The same is done in the Boston newspapers. A one-quarter page ad is displayed in the May, June, and July issues of the magazines, *Yachting* and *Motor Boating*. Also, some direct mail advertising is used plus the distribution of attractive hand-outs listing radio weather report schedules of the major radio stations in the northeastern section of the United States. The hand-outs were distributed to boat owners tied up in marinas from Long Island to Boston in the early summer of 1959. Mr. Kelley believes this was an effective advertising method although he is not exactly sure how much business came to the O'Connor Marine Service because of it.

Approximately $5,150 was spent on advertising the services of the firm in the 1959–1960 years.

Present Status

As of May 31, 1960, gross sales of the O'Connor Marine Service totaled $77,911.00. This is broken down as follows:

1) Customer Sales—Materials (gasoline 20%,
   repair parts 60%, store sales 20%) $39,278.00   (50.1%)
2) Customer Sales—Labor   29,287.00   (37.8%)
3) Customer Sales—Dockage (misc.)   9,346.00   (12.1%)

     Total, Gross Sales $77,911.00

While all cost figures are not available at this time, it is apparent to Jason Kelley and Pat Smith that of the four classes of service offered to the boating public, boat dockage and the marine merchandise store are profitable operations but the boat maintenance and repair activities are operated at a loss.

Jason Kelley concluded the discussion with Pat Smith by suggesting that both of them set forth a two- to three-year program of development for the O'Connor Marine Service. After comparing notes the following week, they would agree on the best features of both programs and present them as one program to Mr. Rex O'Connor and Mr. Luke O'Connor for their consideration. They both desired to see the O'Connor Marine Service operate in the black during the 1960–1961 year, if possible, and certainly during the 1961–1962 year.

QUESTIONS

1. What kind of analyses should be made by Mr. Kelley and Mr. Smith to develop a sound program of operation for the O'Connor Marine Service?
2. What should Mr. Kelley and Mr. Smith do to make the O'Connor Marine Service a profitable operation?

EXHIBIT I

HISTORICAL TRENDS IN THE BOATING INDUSTRY

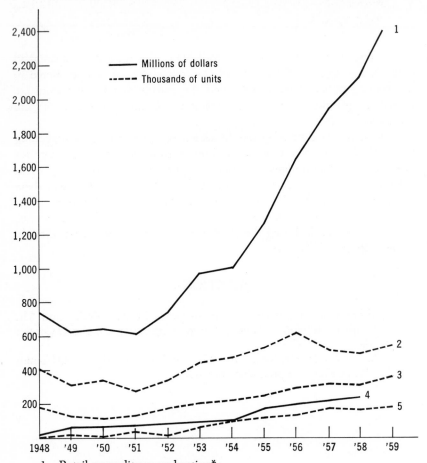

1 Retail expenditures on boating*
2 Outboard motor unit sales*
3 Outboard boat unit sales*
4 Factory shipments**
5 Boat trailer unit sales

SOURCE: National Association of Engine and Boat Manufacturers and Outboard Boating Club of America.

** SOURCE: Bureau of the Census, U.S. Department of Commerce.

EXHIBIT II

AVERAGE ANNUAL RETAIL EXPENDITURES PER
RECREATIONAL BOAT IN USE

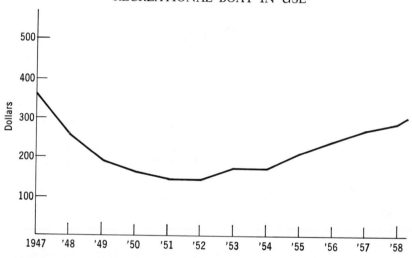

SOURCE: National Association of Engine and Boat Manufacturers and Outboard
Boating Club of America.

EXHIBIT III*

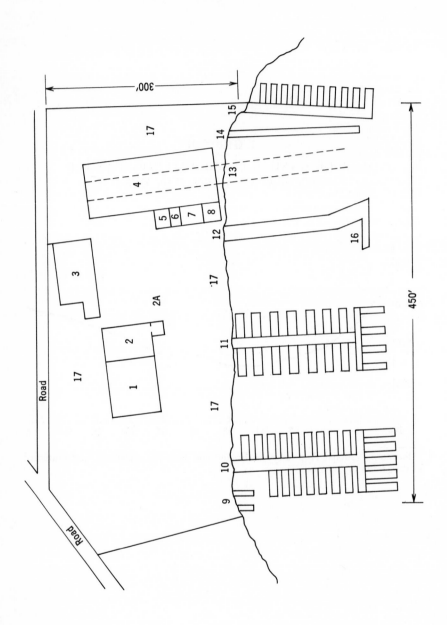

* Not drawn to scale.

EXHIBIT III (*continued*)

1. Woodworking Shop
2. Machine Shop
   2A. Manager's Office
3. Office and Store
4. Storage Shed (can store 16–30 foot boats in winter)
5. Showers and Toilets
6. Laundromat and Ice Storage
7. Snack Bar
8. Lounge
9. Travellift Slip
10. "A" Dock: 4–45' slips, 17–30' slips, 180' long
11. "B" Dock: 3–45' slips, 18–30' slips, 6–25' slips, 180' long
12. "C" Dock: This is the fueling dock 180' long
13. Railway, 100 tons
14. "D" Dock; Used in conjunction with railway, also dockage, 165' long
15. "E" Dock; 15–16' slips, 170' long
16. Gas pumps
17. Parking areas
18. Outdoor Boat Storage area

EXHIBIT IV

O'CONNOR MARINE SERVICE
RATE SCHEDULE

DOCKAGE

16' Boat Slips	$125.00	June 1 to September 30
	40.00	Per month
	10.00	Per week
	1.60	Per day
30' Boat Slips	200.00	June 1 to September 30
	75.00	Per month
	19.00	Per week
	3.00	Per day
45' Boat Slips	275.00	June 1 to September 30
	120.00	Per month
	30.00	Per week
	4.50	Per day
Main Dock	8¢ per foot per day	Seasonal Rate
	9¢ per foot per day	Monthly Rate
	10¢ per foot per day	Transients

Dockage includes water and electricity for lighting and radio. Additional appliances arranged for, based on average consumption.

LABOR RATES

Engine Mechanics	$4.50 per hour
First Class Mechanics, all trades	4.00 per hour
Common Labor	3.00 per hour
Machine tool time (extra)	.50 per hour
Welding, gas, electric, or cutting	5.50 per day

HAUL OUT RATES

$1.00 per foot plus labor

OUTBOARD MOTOR STORAGE RATES

1 to 5 horsepower	$10.00
6 to 9 horsepower	12.00
10 to 15 horsepower	15.00
16 to 25 horsepower	17.00
25 horsepower and up	18.00

This includes draining, flushing, and refilling lower unit with gear oil, draining carburetor, removing plugs, and oiling pistons and rings.

APPENDIX

NEW TYPE BOAT YARDS CATER TO OWNERS, TOO*

Before the automobile could become a practical possession, someone had to invent the service station. The boating industry, ever eager to compare its present boom with the beginning of the automobile age, is busily inventing the seaside version of superservice.

The result is a relatively new breed of boat yard—almost universally called the marina. As the pictures indicate, the scope of these purveyors of seaside service far outdistances their usual highway counterparts—combining, at their most elaborate, the activities of an automobile service station with those of a motel in its most advanced stage of development.

Though not all are so elaborate as this, the marina most often offers not only storage, repair, and fueling facilities, but stores, bar service, baths, and sometimes swimming pools and hotel rooms. This expansion of facilities, of course, brings with it problems of high construction cost, difficult financing, and slow return on investment that few service stations have had to cope with— and this tends to keep marinas from multiplying as fast as demand.

Boost for Boats

What marinas mean to the boat industry is clear, however. With 8-million pleasure boats in backyards and boat basins, the strain on service facilities is acute all over the country. Thousands of boat owners have discovered that having an outboard on a trailer is only the first step toward sport on the bounding main and the scramble to get it into the water on weekends has turned into a major traffic tie-up. Thousands who would like to leave their boats moored at dockside instead of hauling them in and out find themselves tacked on the end of a long waiting list.

Boat manufacturers, so far rather complacent toward the shortage of facilities, are getting more and more worried. For the first time since the boating boom began in earnest, sales of new boats are leveling off.

The talk in the industry is that if sufficient berthing and launching facilities were available, there would be an immediate demand for 2½-million more boats—not only by prospective first-boat customers who have no place to keep one, but by present boat owners who want to trade up to a larger boat, for which dock space is an absolute necessity.

Countrywide Story

Wherever you turn, the story on crowded docks and launching ramps is the same. Chicago's Park District, which manages the city's Lake Michigan waterfront, won't even accept applications for the few hundred slips available— the waiting lists are already too long. Metropolitan New Yorkers have to travel miles to Long Island Sound harbors, up the Hudson River, or down the nearby New Jersey shore, to find a snug harbor. Texans, with their 241,000 boats, complain about lack of good facilities. New Orleans needs 5,000 new slips, according to the *Times-Picayune* boating editor.

Even where new marinas are building, the boat owners' blues don't disappear. A municipal marina in Alamitos Bay at Long Beach, Calif., which now accommodates a respectable 500 boats, has 3,000 applicants for 1,300 new slips. Boat owners who would like to tie up at the new Boston Harbor Marina are put off pending completion of two new piers.

Shoreside Boom

The insatiable demand is sparking a boom in shoreside facilities, but the type of growth that results is not always the best for the boating industry. In many areas, marinas are sprouting like weeds, creating shoreside slums—and running into opposition from local residents and bodies politic.

The big marinas with attractive multiple facilities, which are often a boon to their localities, are still something new, and are few and far between. Though they promise to make boating bigger and better than ever—and though boat owners are big spenders and will pour between $2-billion and $3-billion into the sport this year—the big marinas are too expensive and hard to finance for most investors to handle.

High-Cost Projects

A really good permanent marina can cost several millions, and there's no magic formula that guarantees a fast return on investment. Prices for real estate in areas suitable for marinas have doubled, tripled, sometimes jumped more than 100 times. Construction cost for decent moorings runs from $1,000 to $2,000 per slip when the basic amenities such as dockside electric power, lights, and water are included. Even at the highest rentals, this means a payout time of five to 10 years.

If building a marina is tricky, financing it is even harder. Banks, insurance companies, and most brokers turn a cold shoulder to the risk. There are all too few successful examples to go by.

Fanciest

Terra Mar, at Saybrook, Conn., the fanciest marina on the New England coast, is one of the few private marinas in the million-dollar class, and it has had plenty of trouble making ends meet so far. In two years of operation, it has gone through three reorganizations of management and ownership. This year it's just starting to go into the black.

Its costs show the complications in building shoreside facilities. The backers of Terra Mar invested about $110,000 in its 110 slips, but shoreside construction, including grading and fill, ran up nearly $800,000 more.

The salient feature of Terra Mar is its docks, but the greater part of its revenues come from its "boatel" facilities—a three-story hotel, restaurant, swimming pools, and so on. The marina operations—docks rentals and sales of fuel—

supply less than a third of revenues, according to E. T. Crown, a professional hotel man who now manages the entire operation.

Terra Mar's slip charges are high for New England waters—its 54 permanent tenants pay from $175 to $300 a year for space, and transients are charged a minimum of $5 a day.

So far this year, Terra Mar has been full every weekend. It usually has about 20 transient boats each weekday. A large proportion of the transients take advantage of hotel accommodations—at $18 to $22 per day per person, with dinner and breakfast. Pier 66 in Fort Lauderdale, Fla., another "boatel," also finds that yachting people welcome the chance to sleep on solid ground.

General Pattern

Terra Mar is at one extreme of the broad range of operations known as marinas. It emphasizes the hotel and entertainment services, sends boats in need of repairs or maintenance services to nearby boat yards.

Most marinas go at it the other way round—the great majority are patterned after or are outgrowths of existing boat yards. But they are similar to Terra Mar in not depending solely on slip rentals for revenue.

In a survey of 190 marinas, the National Assn. of Engine & Boat Manufacturers found that nearly a third of their revenues came from sales of boats, accessories, or equipment, another third from repairs, boat rentals, and miscellaneous services such as bars, restaurants, winter storage charges. Another 10% of income came from gasoline and oil sales, 20% from mooring and slip rentals. These proportions vary widely with individual marinas.

In general, the pattern of marina development has been for a small operator to start with a dock, add services gradually as he can afford them and as he sees their profit potential.

Municipal Backing

Because of the difficulty in getting private financing, most of the fanciest and best marinas in the country have had municipal backing; it's almost the only way, in fact, a multimillion-dollar project can get under way.

In Fort Lauderdale, Fla., the city took over the 450-slip Bahia Mar Marina in 1952, four years after private operators built it. With more city money poured in, it has boomed; assets now total $3,289,442, and it will gross about $500,000 this year. Slightly under half its revenue comes from slip rentals, the balance about evenly from concession leases and sales of its marine store. Last year, the city got $67,851 profit from it, besides the business it has brought local merchants.

One good marina seems to help another. Sales of the successful Pier 66 in Fort Lauderdale, built as an experimental marina by Phillips Petroleum Co., with a hotel and shopping center along with its 142 slips, have jumped from $135,000 in 1958 to an estimated $250,000 this year. Lauderdale Marina, a privately operated business nearby, is adding $1-million worth of facilities.

Miami and Dade County also have publicly owned docks for yachts; with 700 slips; but despite these and some 3,600 private and commercial slips in the area, dock space is very tight in the winter season.

244 CASES IN BUSINESS POLICY

West and North

Southern California has been a bit slower than Florida in providing for boating enthusiasts, but is making up for it fast. In the Los Angeles area, several municipally backed marinas are being built or expanding. The $12-million Long Beach marina is now being expanded from 500 slips to 1,800.

At Playa Del Rey, Los Angeles County is going all out to build the largest small craft harbor in the world, accommodating 6,000 boats with land storage for 2,500 more. But even this will hardly make a dent in demand.

Northern communities with a shorter boating season are far behind. Chicago park authorities, reluctant to yield any of the city waterfront to boating facilities, recently turned down a request to build a $12-million private marina. Milwaukee's docks can handle only about 5% of the boats owned by county residents. The city has plans for a $2½-million marina, however.

The New York City area has not had any major new marinas as yet—though several fancy new ones, including Terra Mar at Saybrook, have gone up farther out, in various parts of Long Island Sound. So far, most metropolitan yachting activity has centered at City Island, a tight little island off the Bronx that is completely surrounded by shipyards devoted to yachts and small craft.

Except for yacht clubs, City Island's shoreside facilities tend to be strictly for painting hulls, scraping bottoms, and overhauling engines. But a new boatel is planned for City Island soon, a large marina with motel type facilities is under construction about 20 miles up the Hudson from New York, and a municipal marina has been recommended to New York's Board of Estimate.

---

20. PRESSURE INSTRUMENT CORPORATION

MR. W. M. RANK, PRESIDENT and chairman of the Board of Directors of Pressure Instrument Corporation, was considering, with a local securities broker and underwriter, approval of the final draft of a prospectus offering 60,000 shares of 6% Second Series Cumulative Convertible Preferred Stock to be offered at $10 per share. The activities of the past few weeks in connection with the stock issue caused Mr. Rank to reflect on the development of his company and to consider the factors which had encouraged him to attempt another public offering of stock.

November 30, 1960, climaxed the fifth consecutive year of profitable operations, and in his opinion, the future was bright. All that was needed was adequate financing to enable PIC to become an important factor in the differential pressure investment market.

In the early years following incorporation in 1949, operations were sufficient to pay salaries and earn a modest living for the owners, but profits had been negligible. The recent favorable growth in profits had encouraged Mr. Rank to reconsider his desire for almost complete ownership and to "go public." Most of the outstanding stock, both common and preferred, was held by members of the immediate family, and a close personal friend. A few shares were held by other company officers and directors. The terms of the proposed new stock issue provided for 6% cash dividends payable quarterly. The stock was to be non-voting as long as dividends were current. If four consecutive quarterly payments were passed, however, each holder of the shares was entitled to one vote per share on all matters submitted to the stockholders. Although the company had never paid any cash dividends on the outstanding common shares, in 1960 and January 1961, retained earnings of $31,000 and $32,500, respectively, were transferred to the common stock account in connection with 5% stock dividends on the common shares. Mr. Rank felt sure there would be no problem in meeting the preferred dividends, but Mrs. Rank, his wife and secretary-treasurer of the company, was not in complete agreement with the sale of preferred stock. "We have never paid any dividends, so why should we put ourselves in the position of being required to pay them?" she had stated prior to the sale.

The proceeds from the sale of the preferred issue were to be used to pay off a portion of the outstanding debt amounting to $165,000 to purchase additional machine tools costing about $10,000 and to provide an additional $250,000 in working capital if the entire issue could be sold.

Company Background

In 1945, William M. Rank and his wife left the engineering staff of a major oil company and moved to an oil production center. With an initial investment of $750 they opened an engineering service and repair agency for precision instruments used in the oil, gas, and petrochemicals industry. Most of the work consisted of maintenance and repair on various types of gauges and valves. The repair and service business in the area was sparse, however, so the Ranks began to produce and market new gauges and valves.

In these early years Mr. Rank spent a major portion of his time trying to develop improved instruments and measuring techniques. The profits from the sale of valves and gauges enabled him to expand his research facilities, and in 1948, he succeeded in patenting his first marketable invention—the Rank Non-freezing Instrument Bearing.

In 1949, they incorporated their business as the Pressure Instrument Corporation and began to produce a wide line of differential pressure instruments for the oil, gas, and petrochemicals industries. The president, utilizing the facilities of the Company, carried on research and development work on a series of bellows-type flow meters known as differential pressure responsive devices. These instruments were placed on the market and became the Company's major products thereafter.

By 1955, the Company had developed and perfected the manufacturing processes, assembled much of the necessary machinery and equipment and improved the design of the parts and assemblies required for the production of these instruments. A substantial portion of the tooling for larger-scale production was completed and available for use as the market developed.

The Company outgrew its plant facilities by 1957. Seeking a better labor market and closer proximity to sources of supply, the Company moved into a new, larger plant at Austin, Texas. The president owned the land on which the building was located and the construction was financed on a sale leaseback arrangement with the contractor.

In its new plant, the Company continued its product development attempting to effect a 100% coverage of the measurement field. By 1961, they were producing 96 models of the differential pressure responsive devices and in addition a complete line of pressure and temperature recorders and indicators, transmitters, and liquid level controllers.[1]

Organization

The Company's organization in 1961 appears as Exhibit I. President, chairman of the board, and majority stockholder was Mr. W. M. Rank. Upon graduation from college in the thirties, he went to work for a major petroleum company where he acquired his initial instruction and training in precision instruments. From there he went to another petroleum company in Texas, as head of the instrumentation department, and then to an engineering consulting firm in Ohio. Desiring to return to Texas, he accepted a position in the instrumentation department at the refinery of a major oil company near Houston.

He met Mrs. Rank, a junior engineer employed by the same oil company, and they moved to Odessa where they worked together in setting up the initial repair agency. She held the title of Secretary-Treasurer and has been a member of the Board of Directors from the time of incorporation.

Vice-president in charge of research and development was W. R.

---

[1] By 1961, the president had obtained, and assigned to the company, the following seven patents issued by the United States Patent Office: No. 2,712,968; Nos. 2,762,391–3; No. 2,827,716; No. 2,829,673; and No. 2,890,721.

Wilson, P.E., who had served for over twenty years as Dean of Engineering at a nearby state university prior to his retirement. He had worked on a part-time basis for PIC since that time.

Other members of the board of directors were an attorney, who also served as general counsel to the Company and handled substantially all of the firm's legal work; and Mr. J. H. Evans, vice-president in charge of sales and purchasing. Evans joined the firm in 1956. Prior to coming with PIC, Mr. Evans had been employed in a management capacity by several automotive firms.

Mr. W. M. Rank, Jr. joined the firm in early 1960 after obtaining his B.A. degree. In 1961 he held the title of Assistant Secretary and was learning to manage the business. He had spent several summers in the production department as an apprentice machinist. A consensus of the employees was that young Bill would assume major sales responsibilities in the near future, and that he probably would take his father's place as president within five years.

President's Co-ordinating Committee

The co-ordinating committee met once each month, according to the president, "to discuss operating problems and aid in the dissemination of information to each of my department heads." This committee was made up of each of the departments' heads and other corporate officers. "Of course, either Mrs. Rank or I speak with each of our managers frequently as the need arises. Since she is not only a graduate engineer, but also in charge of accounting, Mrs. Rank is in an excellent position to evaluate alternatives, although she doesn't always have enough patience to develop a full understanding of all aspects of the business."

Mr. Rank felt that these meetings were really in the nature of morale builders for his staff, since most of his real "thinking" was done at night. "I think people work better when they understand the facts."

Products and Markets

The major product of the Pressure Instrument Corporation is a liquid-sealed bellows-type flow meter of which the Company has seven series in 96 different models. While the initial purpose for developing the bellows-type fluid flow meter was to measure gas and liquid flow in the petroleum industry, the applications have multiplied manifold into other diverse fields where precision and reliability of flow measurements are highly important factors. A cross section of the regular commercial factory orders for this type of meter reveals applications in the current missile construction program to control oxygen, nitrogen, and helium proportion-ing flow at high pressures and velocities, for exacting flow proportioning and control in the petro-chemical industry, and for installations in measuring differential pressures in municipal and industrial filtering systems and sewage effluents control. Power stations use the meter extensively in air, water, and steam flow, both for direct pressure indication and for differential pressure recording and indicating. In more unique applications the fluid flow meter can be found in the food industry for measurement of fruit juice flow, in the air purification systems of submarines, and in wind tunnels for determining differential pressures for aeroplane and space flight models. Where fluid flow is to be measured or controlled, there seemed to be new demands arising daily for the bellows-type fluid flow meter. The diversity of the market and the need for such an instrument with great accuracy, outstanding reliability and ruggedness against shock accounted for the growth in sales of Pressure Instrument Corporation.

The seven series of flow meters manufactured by the Company range from the compact and light weight PIC 200 series differential pressure unit to the PIC 1000 and 5000 series which supply the industry with high differential pressure instruments not previously available. These particular series were added to the Company's line of flow meters in 1960 to meet the demands of industry.

During 1960 the Company entered the electronics field, producing the basic sensing devices required for the use of electronic equipment. The markets for these products were essentially the same as for the flow meters.

Sales and Marketing

Three major competitors also engaged in the manufacture of differential pressure flow meters. These were a Division of Minneapolis-Honeywell Company, the Foxboro Company, and the Barton Instrument Company. A number of minor competitors also offered more limited lines of differential pressure instruments. Minneapolis-Honeywell and Foxboro, with many products in addition to flow meters, were estimated to control approximately 30% of the market. Most of the remaining 70% of the market was reported to be between the Pressure Instrument Corporation and Barton Instrument Company, with Barton having a larger share. Barton Instrument Company was the older of the two companies, but PIC was believed to have a wider selection of differential pressure flow meters and indicators for specific applications.

Sales were made to a customer list of nearly 200, including a variety of governmental agencies and defense contractors. About 50% of sales were made to governmental agencies and contractors; about 30% to the oil and chemical industry; and the remaining 20% going to other industrial and municipal users. The largest single contract received to date had been for approximately $100,000.

The Company had twenty-two sales representatives located primarily east of the Mississippi River. The majority of these representatives are engineers who know the problems of the industry in their respective areas. The company does not employ salaried salesmen for field service work. The Company believed that better coverage of the market was obtained with commissioned sales representatives than could be had with a salaried sales force. The use of commissioned sales representatives cost approximately 11% of gross sales ($87,000 on $774,000). In 1960, the sales department operated on a direct budget of $62,800. Expenditures were primarily for: (1) sales exhibits; (2) training conferences in instrumentation; (3) direct mailing of advertising brochures; and (4) cost of the sales manager's office.

The Company's advertising program in trade publications was minimal. The Company considered participation in various exhibits throughout the United States to be the most effective advertising media available. One year, for example, its products were exhibited at three Instrument Society of America Conferences and exhibits. These exhibits were held in Houston, San Francisco, and New York. Educational exhibits were presented at the Southwestern Gas Measurement Short Course, Norman, Oklahoma; at the Symposium of Instrumentation of the Process Industry, A & M College, College Station, Texas; and at the Appalachian Gas Measurement Short Course, Morgantown, West Virginia. Mr. Evans, vice-president in charge of sales, stated that "the company has found that these exhibits are the most effective media for the introduction of new products to industry because large numbers of instrument specialists, including engineers and management personnel, can be reached within a relatively short period of time, and a minimum of expense. They become interested in our products because the user is able to inspect and see the unit in operation." In addition, the Company presented papers and conducted classes in instrumentation at conferences and short courses.

Extensive direct mailing of advertising brochures to prospective customers was utilized. When contact with a prospective customer was established, the sales representative in the area was notified by the Company of the customer's needs. The Company felt that direct mailing was an invaluable aid to the field sales representatives. The direct mailing not only established an initial contact, but also enabled him to know something of his customer.

The Company attempted to hold the percentage of sales to any one customer (mainly governmental) to less than 25%–30% to prevent becoming over-dependent on any one source of income. The company qualified as an eligible vendor on various governmental publications which list procurement sources for government contracts. It regularly received government publications listing the availability of subcontract opportunities, especially those applying to "small businesses."

Sales in Europe were handled through a sales representative in England, South Africa and Australia. License agreements with well-established instrument companies in Canada and Argentina made PIC products available in those countries, unhampered by monetary and tariff restrictions. Negotiations were under way with a large Japanese instrument company to manufacture PIC products for distribution in the Far East. Other negotiations were under way with other large instrument companies abroad where economic conditions were deemed favorable for the manufacture and distribution of the Company's products.

Raw Materials

The Company produced a wide variety of flow meters by using two basic units around which many variations were constructed. Raw materials purchases were guided by two factors, according to Mr. Evans: 1) the anticipated requirements for standard units, and 2) the requirements for parts needed on special or custom orders. Of the basic metal requirements, about 35% were off-the-shelf items for which practically no lead time was necessary. For the other 65%, a lead time of from two weeks to one month was required. Metals were purchased mainly in bar or sheet form, and were received by truck from distributors in Houston and Dallas, on a next-day basis. Transportation costs were not considered a major factor in comparison to the other costs of manufacture.

The production shop was responsible for the raw materials inventory. The stock room, located next to the production department, stocked and maintained the inventory at prescribed levels which were based on experience by the production manager. When a prescribed minimum level was reached, the stock clerk prepared a requisition for the desired raw material and forwarded it to Mr. Evans for processing.

Manufacturing Facilities and Processes

The Pressure Instrument Corporation plant was constructed in 1957 in a new industrial district located at the northern edge of a city of

100,000 population. The plant included a modern one-story brick building with approximately 16,000 square feet of floor space, located on a five-acre plot. The Company manufactured within this one plant 98% of the components used in its products. Late model automatic machines for production of precision parts, specially designed assembly equipment, and the best testing equipment available were used in the production department.

Production runs for parts and assemblies were made in uniform predetermined quantities, based largely on records of previous demand for parts. Although economic order quantities were not computed in any formal sense, the parts room had a pre-established stock level for all parts. The parts stock level was based on past experience as to the number and type of each part that would be needed during a specified period of time. Parts were drawn from the parts room for sub-assembly and assembly on the basis of specific orders. Almost every order received has some peculiarity or special specifications. For example, in a given part one order might specify stainless steel for a particular item, and the next order might specify brass. When any part stock level had fallen to the pre-established minimum stock level, production was alerted and a manufacturing order was scheduled.

Production in 1961 was operating with a basic 8-hour shift. Capacity of the existing plant was approximately 30 standard units per day on a one-shift basis with 40 production workers. When the need arose, a second shift could be added with little difficulty because of the favorable local labor market.

The production department was divided into three sections with each section under the charge of a foreman. These sections were the machinists, the press section, and the production equipment section. Machinists were qualified to do close, special work. Machine operators handled the production equipment, and each operated one particular machine to produce one particular part.

Because of the nature of the work and the tight specifications, quality control and production were closely co-ordinated. Set-up men in the parts production department also served as inspectors. Spot-checks were conducted throughout the parts manufacture. Parts were again spot-checked in the parts room by the quality control supervisor. During assembly, spot checks were regularly conducted. A 100% pressure test was conducted to check the instrument sealing. An "over-range and under-range" was conducted on 100% of the finished assemblies to see if the seal between the two sides was functioning properly. Each instrument was calibrated by an inspector to within ±½% accuracy limits. The assembly was then sent to the shipping department, where a general inspection was conducted by the quality control supervisor before the unit was sealed in a plastic bag and packaged for delivery.

To meet the government's rigid specifications for cleanliness, a separate "clean-room" was required for the cleaning, assembling, and testing under optimum conditions, of instrumentation for liquid oxygen, nitrogen and rocked propulsion fuels services. Because of the exacting requirement of instrument assembly, the entire plant was both air-conditioned and humidity controlled.

Labor

The Company felt that Austin's labor market offered an ample supply of semi-skilled and skilled workers to fill its needs. Job competition in the area created competitive attitudes and high production incentive. The president stated that one of the essentials for successful operations was maintaining a high level of morale, both at the top and bottom levels of the Company. When morale and/or production appeared to be dropping, the president would hold a general meeting of personnel to discuss problems and generally explain factors of the Company's operation. The workers were not organized and no such step was anticipated by the president. The minimum wage at Pressure Instrument Corporation was $1.25 per hour, with a small premium above the minimum wage for skilled workers. Total employment varied between 60–80 with an average of 50 full-time production workers, about ⅔ of whom were semi-skilled.

Research and Development

The research and development program of the Company called for continued efforts to develop and perfect instrumentation for future markets. In addition to this objective, the program called for continued product improvement. The Company was planning the addition of a new research department in which prototypes could be produced. The president performed most of the engineering research work on an individual basis as time permitted. The 1960 operating reports indicated a budget of $6,800 for engineering and research activities. Draftsman wages and supplies accounted for most of the budgeted expense. None of the president's salary was included therein.

Until 1960, each meter was guaranteed for a period of one year to maintain an accuracy of ±½%. In 1961 the guarantee was extended to two years since experience records had shown that no more than one in a hundred had come back within a year. The general feeling towards quality of the products was expressed by the president's son, "Our products are so good they should sell themselves. A contractor shouldn't use another instrument."

General Objectives

The Company planned to continue its program of foreign expansion with the establishment of large instrument companies as licensed manufacturers of PIC products in order to overcome economic and tariff barriers. The Company also planned for further expansion into the electronics field if new products could be developed. Research and development would not only seek out and develop new instrumentation for the future, but it would also seek to improve on present products and to maintain the Company's reputation for high quality, precise, and durable equipment.

The Company's underwriter issued the following statement in respect to the Company:

"The company has been successful in obtaining substantial contracts for defense projects, both directly from the federal government and from contractors. P.I.C. instruments are being used in launching facilities, at Atomic Energy installations, on atomic submarines, in jet tanker planes, and at more than fifty Air Bases. Based on quotations now outstanding and negotiations now underway, P.I.C.'s defense participations over the next two years could double, triple, or quadruple all of 1960's sales. P.I.C. has the plant, the capacity, the supervisory personnel, and the overall ability to increase production 500%. While the defense phase of P.I.C.'s potential has been emphasized because of the massiveness and immediacy of defense contracts, it is not, nor does it expect to be, dependent on defense for its greatest growth. Industrial and utilities market potentials are so vast as to be staggering. Instrumentation is an industrial frontier which can and will bring developments of such importance as to tax the imagination. P.I.C. is not a small regional concern; its products are marketed world-wide."

The paragraph labeled "Opinion" stated the following:

1. The Company's products are second to none.
2. The instrumentation industry is a field susceptible of tremendous growth.
3. Personnel, plant, production methods are all that could be desired, and management believes its costs are as low as or lower than competition.
4. A stepped-up sales program recently started, keyed to an engineering approach, should result in greatly increased sales.

5. Competitive position, both product-wise and price-wise, is entirely satisfactory.
6. Research and development consistently maintained is the goal of management and the key to future growth and success.
7. P.I.C. has everything needed for greatly expanded sales and profits.

EXHIBIT I

PRESSURE INSTRUMENT CORPORATION

PARTIAL ORGANIZATION CHART

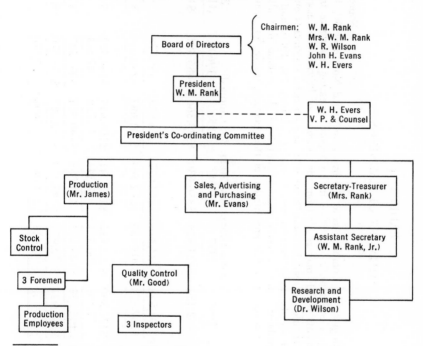

SOURCE: Interpretation of Case Writer.

EXHIBIT II

SUMMARY OF EARNINGS

Source: Company Prospectus

The following summary of earnings of the Company as to the five years ended November 30, 1960, has been examined by an Independent Certified Public Accountant, as set forth in his report appearing elsewhere in this Prospectus, which report is qualified as to any adjustments which may result from the outcome of litigation discussed in Note 1 (a) to the financial statements. The summary should be read in conjunction with the financial statements and related notes included in this Prospectus. The information for the three months periods ended February 29, 1960, and February 28, 1961, has been prepared from the accounts without audit; however, management is of the opinion that all adjustments (consisting solely of normal recurring accruals) necessary to a fair presentation of the operating results for such period have been made.

| | YEARS ENDED NOVEMBER 30, (Audited) | | | | | THREE MONTHS ENDED | |
	1956	1957	1958	1959	1960	2-29-60 (Unaudited)	2-28-61 (Unaudited)
Net Sales	$462,152	$424,828	$356,636	$373,366	$686,391	$176,629(A)	$105,407(A)
Cost of Sales (Direct Material, Parts, Labor, and Patent Amortization)	194,578	223,348	154,072	171,679	395,778	116,938	52,511
Gross Profit	$267,574	$201,480	$202,564	$201,687	$290,613(B)	$ 59,691	$ 52,896
General & Administrative Expense	$126,350	$ 82,131	$125,741	$105,645	$144,403	$ 25,076	$ 27,318
Selling Expenses	72,303	66,371	28,344	43,759	62,834	15,059	11,330
	$198,653	$148,502	$154,085	$149,404	$207,237	$ 40,135	$ 38,648
Operating Income	$ 68,921	$ 52,978	$ 48,479	$ 52,283	$ 83,376	$ 19,556	$ 14,248
Non-Operating Income	—	1,424	1,061	696	2,170	51	240

EXHIBIT II (*continued*)

	$ 68,921	$ 54,402	$ 49,540	$ 52,979	$ 85,546	$ 19,607	$ 14,488
Other Expense							
Interest Expense	$ 8,274	$ 8,005	$ 13,352	$ 17,546	$ 23,362	$ 4,681	$ 3,755
Other Non-Operating Expense	99	231	252	1,435	3,941	89	2,700
Total Other Expense	$ 8,373	$ 8,236	$ 13,604	$ 18,981	$ 27,303	$ 4,770	$ 6,455
Income Before Federal Income Tax	$ 60,548	$ 46,166	$ 35,936	$ 33,998	$ 58,243	$ 14,837	$ 8,033
Provision for Federal Income Tax	1,615	18,506	13,187	12,179	24,666	6,306	2,802
Net Income	$ 58,933	$ 27,660	$ 22,749	$ 21,819	$ 33,577	$ 8,531	$ 5,231
Less, Preferred Dividends	—	1,517	4,145	4,715	4,723	1,181	1,181
	$ 58,933	$ 26,143	$ 18,604	$ 17,104	$ 28,854	$ 7,350	$ 4,050
Earnings per Common Share (C)	.09	.04	.03	.03	.04	.01	.01
Dividends Paid per Common Share	—	—	—	—	(C)	—	(C)

(A) The difference in net sales between the first quarter of the current fiscal year compared to the corresponding quarter of the previous year is accounted for in part from a slight fall-off in orders and in part by the failure to ship an export order of $30,000 upon which production was completed but documentation had not been cleared.

(B) Decrease in percentage of 1960 gross profit is due to extraordinary, nonrecurring expense, including overtime wages and additional labor costs, incurred on missile contract work performed in 1960.

(C) Earnings per share of common stock are based on the number of shares (683,550) presently outstanding after giving effect to the issuance by the Company of 5% stock dividends on its outstanding Common Stock in 1960 and in January, 1961.

(D) Annual dividend requirements on the Preferred Stock of the Company, including the Second Series Preferred Stock, should all of the 60,000 shares be sold, will be $40,723.

EXHIBIT III

PRESSURE INSTRUMENT CORPORATION
BALANCE SHEET
NOVEMBER 30, 1960 AND FEBRUARY 28, 1961

ASSETS

	Nov. 30, 1960 (Audited)	Feb. 28, 1961 (Unaudited)
CURRENT ASSETS		
Cash on Hand and in Bank	$ 24,665	$ 2,664
Accounts Receivable—Trade	195,064	205,352
Notes Receivable	9,096	8,856
Inventory	327,479	345,841
Prepaid Expense	10,519	21,394
Other Cash (Restricted)	25,000	25,000
Total Current Assets	$ 591,823	$ 609,107
FIXED ASSETS		
Shop Machinery and Equipment	$ 270,980	$ 271,316
Dies and Tooling	118,782	120,290
Automobiles	17,348	17,348
Office Furniture	12,096	12,195
Leasehold Improvements	37,088	38,082
Total Fixed Assets	$ 456,294	$ 459,231
Less, Depreciation Sustained . . .	187,472	200,752
Net Fixed Assets	$ 268,822	$ 258,479
INTANGIBLE ASSETS		
Patents	$ 132,905	$ 137,611
Research and Development	49,583	61,499
Trade Mark	100	100
Total Intangible Assets	$ 182,588	$ 199,210
OTHER ASSETS		
Guaranty Deposits	$ 580	$ 435
Investments	2,000	2,000
Cost of Stock Issues	63,486	62,605
Other Receivables	525	70
Total Other Assets	$ 66,591	$ 65,110
Total Assets	$1,109,824	$1,131,906

SOURCE: Company Prospectus.

PRESSURE INSTRUMENT CORPORATION
BALANCE SHEET
NOVEMBER 30, 1960 AND FEBRUARY 28, 1961

LIABILITIES

	Nov. 30, 1960 (Audited)	Feb. 28, 1961 (Unaudited)
CURRENT LIABILITIES		
Accounts Payable—Trade	$ 85,879	$ 72,996
Notes Payable to Banks	180,605	215,605
Notes Payable (Small Business Loan & Others)	86,961	90,277
Accrued Payroll Taxes	14,435	9,344
Accrued Payroll Payable	4,038	1,510
Other Payables	1,852	5,341
Federal Income Tax Payable	8,075	8,075
Accrued Interest	2,249	739
Total Current Liabilities	$ 384,094	$ 403,887
LONG TERM LIABILITIES		
Small Business Loan—with Bank Participation	$ 148,311	$ 144,629
OTHER LIABILITIES		
Federal Income Tax Deferred	$ 54,060	$ 54,060
Reserve for Current Year Federal Income Taxes (1960–1961)	–0–	2,802
Total Other Liabilities	$ 54,060	$ 56,862
CAPITAL		
Convertible Preferred Stock (Authorized 30,000 Shares, $10.00 Par, 6% Cumulative) 7,871 Shares Issued	$ 78,710	$ 78,710
Common Stock (Authorized 700,000 Shares, $1.00 Par) 651,000 Shares Issued at Nov. 30, 1960, and 683,550 Shares Issued at Feb. 28, 1961	651,000	683,550
Less excess of recorded consideration (principally par value of stock issued) for patents and other assets acquired from the predecessor company or the principal stockholder over the ascertainable cost or other proper carrying value in the accounts of the predecessor company or such stockholder	(262,900)	(262,900)
	$ 388,100	$ 420,650
Earned Surplus	$ 56,549	$ 27,168
Total Capital	$ 523,359	$ 526,528
Total Liabilities and Capital	$1,109,824	$1,131,906

EXHIBIT IV

PRESSURE INSTRUMENT CORPORATION
STATEMENT OF SURPLUS
EARNED SURPLUS

	YEARS ENDED NOV. 30, (Audited)					MONTHS ENDED FEB. 28, 1961
	1956	1957	1958	1959	1960	(Unaudited)
Balance at Beginning of Period	$(55,075)	$ 3,858	$30,001	$48,605	$62,217	$56,549
Add, Net Income for Period	58,933	27,660	22,749	21,819	33,577	5,231
	$ 3,858	$31,518	$52,750	$70,424	$95,794	$61,780
Deduct						
Preferred Dividends Paid	$ —	$ 1,517	$ 4,145	$ 4,715	$ 4,723	$ 1,181
Amortization of Stock Issue Expense	$ —	—	—	3,492	3,522	881
Common Stock Dividend	—	—	—	—	31,000	32,550
		$ 1,517	$ 4,145	$ 8,207	$39,245	$34,612
Balance at End of Period	$ 3,858	$30,001	$48,605	$62,217	$56,549	$27,168

SOURCE: Company Prospectus.

EXHIBIT V

SELECTED DATA ON PRESSURE INSTRUMENT CORPORATION
YEARS 1961–1964*

REPORT DATE	SALES	NET INCOME	EARNED PER SHARE	COMMON SHARES	STOCK-HOLDERS	LONG-TERM DEBT	PREF'D.
Nov. 30, 1961	$492,043	$ 7,730	$ .01	683,550	n. a.	$135,840	$201,430
Nov. 30, 1963	331,350	31,552	.04	717,727	1105	133,360	385,210
Nov. 30, 1964	513,168	59,502	.08	717,727	n. a.	n. a.	n. a.

n.a. = not available.
* SOURCE: Moody's Industrials.

_____

21. RAILWAY INDUSTRIAL EQUIPMENT COMPANY

RAILWAY INDUSTRIAL EQUIPMENT COMPANY WAS organized to develop, produce and market a new type of railway container which William E. B. Snead had invented. The new company represented only one of many interrelated business interests of Mr. Snead. With a new product requiring a sizeable investment in time and finances, William Snead was anxious for the Railway Industrial Equipment Company to get the new product on the market and the new company self-supporting as soon as practicable.

Background

Mr. Snead, a leading businessman in the area, was the chairman of the board of one of the largest quarry companies in the state. The quarry operations were a tribute to Mr. Snead's extraordinary abilities as a welder, inventor, and innovator, for almost all of the early operating equipment used in the quarry had been built from scrap materials when capital was very limited.

Mr. Snead was formally trained as an engineer, but most of his time was devoted to numerous business activities. When not engaged in the operations of his various quarry sites, he could be found flying his personal plane to and from various business meetings in the United States. Between business trips and general supervision of his quarry activities, he would spend his time drawing up designs and developing new products with the aid of a crew of men at one of the quarries.

The Product

During the spring of 1963 Mr. Snead and a work crew had developed a new bulk stone container to the point that the containers were ready to be tested in actual use. At that time, the first of several patents connected with this particular product were applied for.

The containers were, in effect, large portable hoppers which could be lined up on any flatbed railroad car so that the typical flatcar could be used to carry as much bulk crushed stone as a "gondola" car. Six containers could be placed on a typical car, and they could be lifted on or off any car or side dumped on a pivot with a crane. The obvious ease in loading, and especially unloading, made the product especially attractive to many handlers of bulk cargo, such as construction companies building roads or dams. It meant that a rail car could be unloaded in minutes where it formerly took hours to unload a gondola by shovel, wherever temporary locations were not specially designed to permit unloading by hopper. The containers also had the further advantage of freeing the flatcar for other use, as they could be nested on top of each other and sent back to the quarry, twenty-four to one car. It was felt that the containers would always remain with the cars, but they did give the cars extra flexibility should they be needed for other purposes.

Initial Problems Encountered During the Development Stages

Initial tests of loaded cars were made, and it was proved that the containers could be transported loaded over long distances without loss of cargo or damage to the cars. However, the tests also established that the supposed loading and unloading advantages of the containers were not as great as initially hoped for. The containers could be gravity-fed, like any gondola, but it required as much as three hours to secure them to the deck of the flatcar with the same required blocking of any trailer or container. This meant that the time saved at the delivery end of the trip was negated, to a great extent, by the loss of time and cost of blocking at the point of shipment. Mr. Snead redesigned the containers to overcome this relative disadvantage and, in the process, added another patent to his credit.

A wrecked flatcar was purchased at a nominal cost and repaired. Twelve steel channels were placed into the deck of the car so that the containers would fit into the channels in such a way that they required no shoring and could be dumped from either side of the car or lifted directly off of the car. It was thought that the requiring of a specially rigged car might be a detriment to getting the product accepted. Fortunately, preliminary estimates showed that the channels would not interfere with the normal use of the car for other purposes.

Marketing

By the fall of 1963 the product had been developed to the point where it was believed to be a unique concept in railroad cargo handling, feasible and adaptable to the economic handling of a wide variety of materials, and speeding up turn-around time of the cars.

It was necessary for the company to decide whether to sell or license the patent idea to a large railroad equipment manufacturer or to attempt to manufacture and market the containers. The former alternative meant that control over the future of the product would be relinquished, and the only financial return would be from royalty payments. To choose the latter alternative meant that more capital and time, both of which were limited, would have to be invested in the product.

The latter alternative was chosen by Snead because he felt that the idea was conceived with the thought of seeing it grow and develop into a profitable company as a result of the developer's own efforts and not that of an outsider. He also felt that other ideas of his would be developed later which could complement Railway Industrial Equipment Company's operations and provide it eventually with an extended line of railway products. Another major factor considered in making his decision was the attractive possibility that the new company could provide financing for the development of new ideas and concepts that he would likely conceive later. The decision to produce and market directly meant investing scarce capital funds in the new company, but it also promised high returns in the long run if the product could be marketed successfully.

Realizing that an intensive marketing effort was needed, a local marketing consultant was called in to develop a marketing program for the product. Mr. Snead needed more time to spend on his other interests, and he found it impossible to devote more than a few hours each week to the new product. The consultant had previously helped develop a marketing program for base materials and agricultural limestone sold by a Snead enterprise. Because of the success of the marketing program, Mr. Snead decided that the consultant's experience and skills would be valuable in the successful marketing of the new inventions.

The Marketing Program and Policies

The first step in the marketing program was to develop a name for the invention that would be descriptive and easy to remember. Thus, the containers became "Skip-Haulers." Immediate steps were taken to have the new name registered.

Next a basic marketing policy was formulated. The idea for a desirable course of action was inspired by an article published in *Printer's Ink*. The subject of the article was the Pullman Company, which had managed to reverse the downward trend in the railroad equipment industry—a result of a general apathy in the railroad industry with respect to specialized services to shippers. As truckers continued to gain more and more of the railroad's customers, the demand for new rail cars and equipment diminished.

Pullman had been able to reverse this trend through a change in their long-standing marketing policy of selling only to the order of the railroads.

Instead, Pullman concentrated on developing and selling their ideas for special service cars to shippers and then expected the shippers to encourage the railroads to provide the new cars.

Although Mr. Snead had already attempted to introduce the idea to representatives of the three railroads serving the area, they had expressed little interest. Roalroad Equipment adopted a policy similar to Pullman's. Contacts with the shippers were closer than with the railroad companies. The consultant believed that the best way to create a demand for "Skip-Haulers" would be to interest shippers rather than to attempt to interest the railroads directly. A brochure which contained pictures and a description of the new concept of cargo handling was developed for use in selling the shippers on the idea. It was expected that shippers would then exert pressure on the railroads to provide "Skip-Haulers" for their use.

The prototype car was demonstrated to one important shipper who was so pleased with its potential that he said he could keep twenty cars busy as soon as they were made available. The problem was that it was not known just how long he would be able to keep the cars busy and that he was not willing to purchase the cars. He wanted them made available either by the quarry or the railroad.

Unfortunately, it was found that it was one thing to have a policy and even have a customer, and entirely another thing to implement that policy, when it meant dealing with the management of railroads and the regulations under which they operate.

It was found that the one car specially equipped for "Skip-Haulers" could not be placed into service until it had been registered and had passed safety inspection. The safety inspection was a minor problem, since the car was as good as new. The next requirement was getting the registration.

The problem was brought up during a meeting with the president of the local short-line railroad which served one of the quarry properties. This meeting was attended by the railroad president, the president of the quarry company, the marketing consultant and his assistant. The railroad president suggested several alternatives as to how to get the car registered.

It was thought that the company could register the car under Railway Equipment's own name, but the railroad president pointed out that the company might not be able to control the car's use once it was placed into service. However, during a later interview he mentioned a shipper that had full control over his cars.

It was then suggested that the short-line road register the car, but the president vetoed this idea by pointing out the fact that a short-line road cannot own any cars or they would be forced to pay higher per diem rates on other railroads' cars and that would remove any operating cost advantages they have.

The most promising alternative seemed to be that of leasing the car to one of the three large railroads in the area, so that car would be under their control and could be used by local shippers. Everyone seemed in agreement on this alternative and at the end of the meeting the railroad president said that if he were the owner of the car and the related ideas and concepts, he would sell everything outright to one of the large railroad equipment companies and let them worry about it. In answer to this, it was pointed out that the idea was developed with the thought of seeing it grow into something as a result of the inventor's own efforts, and therefore this suggestion was an unacceptable solution.

Getting the car accepted by the railroads was seen to be a problem in itself. In spite of the continued demands from their shippers for more gondola cars to handle the present stone traffic on the railroads, there was little or no incentive for the roads to invest in new equipment, especially to handle commodities which called for very low freight rates. In order to get around this problem, it was decided that the only way to get the car registered would be to find out which of the three railroads appeared to be most subject to persuasion. If necessary, the possible loss of business originating from the quarry could be emphasized.

Production Plans

Long-range plans were tentatively made, and estimates were prepared as to how much the special cars would cost to alter. Since the shop where the original car and "Skip-Haulers" were built was unable to produce them on anything but a limited or hand-made process, it was decided to have the work subcontracted until the idea had proven itself wholly acceptable at which time production facilities would be built. The "Skip-Haulers" could be built in any shop which was capable of cutting and assembling the heavy steel sheets used. This could be done in railroad shops, shipyards, or by any railway equipment manufacturer.

One shipyard gave a preliminary estimate of $1,000 per "Skip." It was estimated that it would cost an additional $400 to add the channels to redeck a flatcar. A new flatcar could be built for approximately $14,000.

Financing

Before any construction contracts were let, Railway Industrial Equipment Company had to get the financing necessary to pay the builder. The company would also have to find shippers and railroads willing to lease the cars and the "Skip-Haulers."

Only enough capital was available to provide for one modified flatcar and six "Skips" for test purposes. Consultations with various bankers revealed that financial aid would be forthcoming if the company could obtain firm contracts from shippers and the railroad. This meant that the railroad which registered the prototype car would have to be cooperative in allowing many shippers to see and use it. It also meant that Railway Equipment had to be extremely careful in selecting its first railroad lessee, for the company was depending on the proper use of the equipment by one railroad to demonstrate feasibility.

Future

The shipper who had promised to keep twenty cars busy had become concerned as to when the promised cars and "Skips" would be made available to him. Another potential customer expressed interest in the idea and he requested that the cars be made available to him for use on a substantial two-year project upon which he had entered a bid. In the event Snead's quarry received the materials-supply contract, he estimated that twenty-four cars could be utilized for that job. Another shipper wanted to see the car and "Skips" in action with his particular commodity before he would commit himself for a specific number.

These and other developments only served to indicate that this new concept of bulk cargo handling was feasible and adaptable to the handling of all the commodities flowing from the quarries. With that in mind, Mr. Snead next developed a truck body which would be able to load and unload the Skips from flatcars and also dump them. He was wondering just how long he would be able to continue his development efforts, for he felt that his other interests could not go on subsidizing those efforts much longer. In addition, he felt that if the product were not in use on the rails soon, its chances of success would be lost if the present high interest in new rail innovations were to diminish.

An executive of the railroad which seemed to be the brightest prospective lessee of the car and "Skips" agreed to meet with the marketing consultant to discuss lease terms. A meeting was held between Mr. Snead, the consultant and the president of the local short-line railroad in order to decide on the type of leasing offer to present to the major railroad.

Two types of leasing agreements could be made. Railway Equipment could lease the cars on a mileage basis, but the return would only be large if the cars were used constantly on a fairly long haul. The other choice was a straight time lease for a flat monthly rate. The latter method was chosen because it meant a guaranteed income and possibly a faster return on investment, due to the fact that all of the proposed runs for the cars were for relatively short distances (under 150 miles).

A new problem was also discussed. The railroad which had been chosen owned very few flatcars and it was not known whether these would be made available for conversion to "Skip" carriers. This meant that Railway Equipment would have to have new cars built or scour the countryside for unused flatcars which could be purchased at a reasonable rate. It was decided that this problem would be handled at a later date and in accordance with the wishes of the leasing railroad.

It was also decided that the prototype car would have to get on the rails immediately. Therefore, if necessary, it would be offered to the railroad on terms which would be so favorable that the road would not fail to accept.

The following day the consultant obtained the figures of the expected business the "Skip-Haulers" would generate and also the present amount of railway business from the quarries. The railroad's share of the freight revenue was determined from these figures, and it was decided that, if necessary, they could be used as a selling point. It was also decided that, if necessary, the quarries would give the railroads a guarantee that the cars would be kept busy.

The consultant estimated that the local quarry's trade could use almost 500 cars equipped with the "Skip-Haulers." Projecting this figure to cover the quarries which were in direct competition with the Snead quarry, the estimated number of cars was well into the thousands. National estimates were difficult to make due to the many varied uses to which the "Skips" could be put.

As the consultant prepared an outline of his presentation, he was concerned about a favorable reception by the railroad. While there were alternative prospects, hope for an early financial success for the new venture appeared to be dependent upon the favorable outcome of the forthcoming meeting with the executive of the major railroad.

22. REYNOLDS MACHINERY COMPANY*

ON JUNE 1, 1962, ATTORNEYS for two minority stockholders met with attorneys for the majority stockholder of Reynolds Machinery Company in an attempt to settle out of court an eight-year dispute. The minority stockholders, Lawrence Tipton and Gregory Lancaster, were

* This case was prepared by Professor Richard L. Norgaard of the University of Texas.

suing the president and majority stockholder, Harold Reynolds, for mismanagement and the malicious suppression of dividends. The plaintiffs had asked the court for:

1. Damages in the amount of their losses sustained in the decreased value of their equity resulting from Mr. Reynolds' mismanagement.
2. Dividends in the amount that had been suppressed.
3. Liquidation of the corporation.

As the basis for their action, the two minority stockholders had cited the following interpretation of a state civil statute:

> Courts, under their general equity powers, may in the more extreme cases of abuse of minority stockholders by a majority stockholder, decree liquidation of solvent corporations and accordingly appoint a receiver for that purpose, or the less drastic purpose of rehabilitation.

The background of events which had brought the parties to this bizarre and tragic position had started in 1938 when Mr. Reynolds, then a shipping clerk in Tulsa, Oklahoma, had decided to start his own business. He secured a job as a manufacturer's representative for a line of machine tools. He soon realized that the buyers wanted fast delivery as well as an opportunity to see the goods firsthand. As a result, he started buying machines and machine tools from the manufacturer for his own inventory and then selling to the customer directly from his inventory. Although business developed slowly, each succeeding year showed an increase in profit. By 1946, Reynolds Machinery Company had 15 employees and sales of $280,000.

In 1948, Mr. Reynolds hired two men, both of whom had just completed school, Lawrence Tipton (age 22) and Gregory Lancaster (age 20). Mr. Reynolds, who was 47 years old at the time, spent a great deal of time with his new employees teaching them about the business, about how to sell, and about how to keep the company accounts. Both Messrs. Tipton and Lancaster responded to Mr. Reynolds' encouragement. Mr. Reynolds was so pleased with their work that, in 1950, he made them each 10 percent partners. Although there were never any partnership papers, the accountant for the firm made the necessary entries in the company's capital account. This partnership, along with the increased activity because of the Korean war, gave the firm a tremendous boost. In 1953, Mr. Reynolds gave his partners an even bigger share of the firm, raising each of their partnership interests to 20 percent. He believed this to be a just reward for their diligent efforts.

Throughout this period, the relationship between Mr. Reynolds and Messrs. Tipton and Lancaster was less like partners and more like father and sons. Mr. Reynolds had even suggested that he would like to adopt Mr. Lancaster, who came from a large family. He took a major interest in the social life of Messrs. Tipton and Lancaster, expressing either approval or disapproval of the girls that they escorted.

In 1954, without prior warning, Mr. Reynolds sought to reduce the extent of the partnership arrangement unilaterally. He had sent a note to the partners stating that, from that time on, Mr. Tipton would be a 15 percent partner and Mr. Lancaster, a 12 percent partner. Mr. Reynolds' only explanation had been that the reason for his action was "completely outside his control." During the interim between Mr. Reynolds' increasing the two men's partnership interests and his attempt to rescind the arrangement, several disputes had arisen among the three men as to the best method for conducting the affairs of the business. One example developed as a result of the firm's new building. Mr. Reynolds wanted to have his desk "out on the floor," but Messrs. Tipton and Lancaster both had desks in glass-enclosed offices, with the approval of Mr. Reynolds. One Monday, six months after the company had moved into its new quarters, Messrs. Tipton and Lancaster found that, on the Sunday before, all the partitions of their offices had been ripped out by the employees, at the insistence of Mr. Reynolds. His explanation was that everyone should be "out on the floor." He had seemed to resent any suggestions made by the two younger partners, stating that Reynolds Machinery was "his" company and that he would run it as he saw fit. Animosities then had increased to the point that Mr. Reynolds had informed the two men that, as of that time, they could consider the profit-sharing arrangement "permanently terminated."

The two younger men had resisted this proposal, stating that they were full partners in the firm and, as such, could not have their partnership interests terminated by unilateral action on Mr. Reynolds' part. After prolonged negotiations, a written settlement of the dispute was made in December 1955. This agreement had called for the three parties to divide the $80,000 in government bonds owned by the business, according to their partnership interests. Further, Mr. Reynolds was to receive $30,000 in cash from the firm. A corporation was then to be organized with the remaining assets. Stock ownership was to be allocated on the same basis as the partnership interests, as follows: Harold Reynolds, 60 percent; Lawrence Tipton, 20 percent; and Gregory Lancaster, 20 percent. It was further agreed that:

1. Each of the owners would serve both as an officer and as a director of the corporation, with Mr. Reynolds serving as president and chairman of the board and the two younger men as vice-presidents.

2. The board of directors would be composed of five members.
3. Each of the officers would be appointed for a one-year period, with initial salaries being $12,000 per officer.
4. Directors could be removed without cause upon the vote of a majority of the shares of the outstanding stock.
5. Any party might enter a competing business immediately upon ceasing to be an officer and employee of the corporation.

During this period, when the proposal to alter the structure of the firm to a corporation was being discussed, the antipathy disappeared and Mr. Reynolds was "sweetness and light." However, neither of the younger men believed that this about-face was completely genuine; nevertheless, because they felt a responsibility to Mr. Reynolds and since they had received reassurances from their attorney, they agreed to the formation of a corporation.

Formal organization had hardly been completed when hostilities began anew, with the initial overt acts being those of Mr. Reynolds. He reprimanded both of the younger officers openly before subordinates and indicted them for various omissions on their part, most of which were of a petty nature; and he also promoted an employee over Messrs. Tipton and Lancaster. Mr. Reynolds further told them that they were to keep him constantly advised as to their whereabouts. In addition, long and abusive letters were sent to Mr. Lancaster, informing him that:

1. He was to report to work at 7:00 a.m. and work until 6:00 p.m., with thirty minutes off for lunch. These hours were to continue until further notice.
2. He was not to use company time to care for personal errands, as it had been his custom to have dental work done on frequent occasions.
3. He was not to leave his desk nor converse with fellow workers in the mornings until such time as he had attended to all the mail for which he was responsible.

The two vice-president resented these displays, feeling that such reprisals and restrictions were inappropriate for officers of the company who also served as directors. Nonetheless, the hostilities continued until, in December 1956, both vice-presidents resigned and started a competing business.

As can be seen in Exhibits I and II, Reynolds Machinery Company had enjoyed very prosperous operations up until the time of incorporation, at which time profits began to decline rapidly. For example, the pretax profits during the last nine months of the partnership were $98,000, whereas, during the succeeding year as a corporation, the firm reported only $42,000 in profits before taxes. Sales, however, continued to remain fairly stable, with even a slight expansion occurring until, by the time that legal proceedings were begun in 1961, sales had totaled $1.7 million. Such an expansion was possible, even under these circumstances, because Reynolds Machinery had a group of excellent employees, as well as a well-established market which was generally free from major competition.

Shortly after the two vice-presidents, Messrs. Tipton and Lancaster, had resigned and had begun competing with Reynolds Machinery, Mr. Reynolds wrote a letter to a third party stating that he intended to use his influence as chairman of the board of directors to see that no dividends were paid so long as the two former officers were stockholders. He further indicated that he would not buy the stock from the two men for even a small fraction of its value. In another letter to a supplier, which was considering taking its franchise from Reynolds Machinery and giving it to the firm of Messrs. Tipton and Lancaster, he stated that he had "pulled a fast one" on his partners when he got them to agree to incorporation. Subsequently, Mr. Reynolds' wife and daughter were elected as board members.

Messrs. Tipton and Lancaster were bewildered as they observed the sales of Reynolds Machinery increase slowly, while profits continued to decline drastically, reaching an all-time low of $1,782 in 1959. In addition, the company's board of directors had declared no dividends since the date of incorporation. When, during 1960, earnings rose to only $3,483, Messrs. Tipton and Lancaster concluded that their former employer was deliberately minimizing the reported net income for Reynolds Machinery in order to avoid the payment of a dividend. They noted also that Mr. Reynolds' salary had increased from the original $15,000 in 1956 to $60,000 in 1960. Thus, Messrs. Tipton and Lancaster began searching for evidence that could be presented in court showing mismanagement on Mr. Reynolds' part. Their evidence included the following:

1. Sales had remained fairly stable over the years during which the business was incorporated; yet, net profits declined steadily. The cost of goods sold had remained stable, indicating that the causal factor in the profit decline was a large increase in general and administrative expenses, over which Mr. Reynolds had control.

2. Inventory had been allowed to double over the period from 1956 through 1961. On a constant sales volume, this increase seemed unnecessary. The only reason evident for the increase was to afford an outlet for cash so as to keep the firm's cash balance at a minimum, thereby avoiding the payment of dividends. In view of the extraordinarily large increase in inventory in 1961, the two stockholders had obtained the court's permission to have an inventory check made by an independent certified public accountant. The accountant's report contained the following statements:

The value of the inventory appears to be understated by $131,099, valued on the basis of cost or market, whichever is lower. There is every reason to believe that even this does not sufficiently state the real value of this inventory.

3. Accounts receivable also had doubled over the six-year period, indicating a lack of sound credit and collection policies and procedures.
4. In establishing the net profit, Mr. Reynolds had allowed general and administrative expenses to rise by adding several new employees to the payroll. One of the employees, Mr. Reynolds' brother, stated that several employees had nothing to do but that Mr. Reynolds did not seem to care how much extra he spent.

All of these events culminated in the suit which both partners had brought against Mr. Reynolds in October 1961. During the period from 1957 through 1961, both Messrs. Tipton and Lancaster had tried repeatedly to get Mr. Reynolds either to purchase their stock or to sell his stock to them. The business they had started in 1957 was now beginning to prosper, and they felt that they could weld the two businesses together very successfully. At the same time, they were loath to take such drastic action as a suit. They were particularly opposed to declaring a dividend payment, since that would distribute a substantial part of the earnings to the government because of double taxation: once on net income and again on dividends. On the other hand, a "buy-out" might either mean no taxes or, at worst, a small amount of capital-gains tax. Thus, they realized that, if they did win their case in court—and there was every likelihood of this happening—only the government and the attorneys would be the winners.

Although it might be thought that the younger men would be resentful and want to punish Mr. Reynolds, they did not, in fact, feel this way. They believed that Mr. Reynolds' actions were explainable. They reasoned that Mr. Reynolds feared that, under the partnership, Messrs. Tipton and Lancaster would eventually control the firm because they took only a small "draw" leaving their residual to accumulate in the business, whereas Mr. Reynolds did not. They also reasoned that Mr. Reynolds believed that they had earned a share only in the income of the firm, but not in its assets, and that, once they had left the concern, they did not deserve even that. While Messrs. Tipton and Lancaster felt it their duty to try once more to settle the matter, they realized this would be difficult since Mr. Reynolds had previously stated he would buy them out for $75,000 (which he had stated was his maximum), an offer which the younger men had turned down as ludicrous. However, since they were now sure that Mr. Reynolds would never agree to sell, they knew they would have to state a price for which they would sell their shares.

EXHIBIT I

REYNOLDS MACHINERY COMPANY
INCOME STATEMENTS, PARTNERSHIP
(Year Ending December 31)

	1950	1951	1952	1953	1954	1955*
Net sales	$279,963	$694,883	$1,680,389	$1,952,948	$1,438,422	$1,093,066
Cost of goods sold	224,073	561,256	1,463,831	1,657,762	1,152,500	889,673
Gross profit	55,890	133,627	216,558	295,186	285,922	203,494
General and administrative expenses**	40,141	54,582	84,945	127,694	148,531	105,488
Net profit from operations	15,749	79,045	131,613	167,494	137,391	97,905
Other income (expense)	—	—	—	—	—	
Net income	$ 15,749	$ 79,045	$ 131,613	$ 167,494	$ 137,391	$ 97,905

* Nine months.
** Includes depreciation.

EXHIBIT II

REYNOLDS MACHINERY COMPANY

INCOME STATEMENTS, CORPORATION

(Year Ending December 31)

	1956	1957	1958	1959	1960	1961
Net sales	$963,519	$1,131,740	$1,092,392	$993,295	$1,060,033	$1,672,731
Cost of goods sold	749,508	914,846	849,035	775,298	826,402	1,231,303
Gross profit	214,011	216,894	243,357	217,997	233,631	441,428
General and administrative expenses*	179,847	205,802	205,691	220,794	228,380	296,177
Net profit from operations	34,164	11,092	37,666	(2,797)	5,251	145,251
Other income (expense)	8,077	(1,361)	(8,715)	5,146	(745)	(1,375)
Net income before taxes	42,241	9,731	28,951	2,349	4,506	143,876
Federal income tax	16,743	2,937	11,444	567	1,023	66,561
Net income	$ 25,498	$ 6,794	$ 17,507	$ 1,782	$ 3,483	$ 77,315

* Includes depreciation.

275

EXHIBIT III

REYNOLDS MACHINERY COMPANY

BALANCE SHEETS, PARTNERSHIP

(As of December 31)

	1950	1951	1952	1953	1954	1955
ASSETS						
Current assets						
Cash	$ 561	$ 7,448	$ 11,354	$113,458	$162,114	$ 9,018
Accounts receivable	45,877	111,167	249,711	167,386	129,501	133,416
Inventory	39,877	95,644	110,727	89,151	130,334	140,335
Total current assets	86,315	214,259	371,792	369,995	421,949	282,769
Fixed assets	2,749	3,963	6,097	6,839	8,880	26,567
Other assets	—	—	—	—	—	—
Total assets	$89,064	$218,262	$377,889	$376,834	$430,829	$309,336
LIABILITIES						
Current liabilities	$47,553	$ 70,130	$ 77,457	$ 63,700	$ 29,923	$ 26,954
Fixed liabilities	—	—	—	—	—	—
Other liabilities	—	—	—	—	—	—
Total liabilities	47,553	70,130	77,457	63,700	29,923	26,954
CAPITAL						
Harold Reynolds	41,147	127,992	250,014	241,681	272,384	198,213
Lawrence Tipton	145	9,980	25,069	35,451	63,735	41,915
Gregory Lancaster	219	10,160	25,349	36,002	64,787	42,254
Total capital	41,511	148,132	300,432	313,134	400,906	282,382
Total liabilities and capital	$89,064	$218,262	$377,889	$376,834	$430,829	$309,336

EXHIBIT IV

REYNOLDS MACHINERY COMPANY
BALANCE SHEETS, CORPORATION

(As of December 31)

	1956	1957	1958	1959	1960	1961
ASSETS						
Current assets						
Cash	$ 18,563	$ 26,007	$ 31,204	$ 11,888	$ 13,312	$ 24,618
Accounts receivable	91,016	152,408	118,470	100,904	112,185	188,067
Inventory	217,509	304,845	322,192	280,440	294,814	513,911
Prepayments	—	—	—	27,667	26,915	—
Total current assets	327,088	483,260	471,866	420,899	447,226	726,596
Fixed assets	88,865	92,796	91,916	92,365	101,519	106,273
Other assets	47,735	16,413	19,858	13,954	3,999	7,709
Total assets	$463,688	$592,469	$583,640	$527,218	$552,744	$840,578
LIABILITIES						
Current liabilities	$ 98,231	$205,315	$173,561	$118,372	$142,653	$391,243
Fixed liabilities	50,000	65,600	57,400	49,200	41,200	37,800
Other liabilities	7,309	3,658	8,534	9,672	12,763	1,069
Total liabilities	155,540	274,673	239,495	177,244	196,610	430,112
CAPITAL						
Common stock	280,000	280,000	280,000	280,000	280,000	280,000
Paid-in surplus	1,061	1,061	3,960	1,924	1,924	1,924
Retained earnings	27,087	36,735	60,185	68,050	74,210	128,542
Total capital	308,148	317,796	344,145	349,974	356,134	410,466
Total liabilities and capital	$463,688	$592,469	$583,640	$527,218	$552,744	$840,578

277

―――――――

23. SMOKEY MOUNTAIN IRON WORKS, INCORPORATED*

THE VICE-PRESIDENT AND GENERAL MANAGER of the Smokey Mountain Iron Works, Inc., had recently attended an executive management seminar sponsored by a state university. During the seminar, many management ideas and concepts had been presented by the staff members to the executives who attended the seminar. One particular subject which had been mentioned by several of the staff concerned the responsibility and duty of top management to plan for and develop a program of management succession. Mr. Homer Chase, Jr., Vice-President and General Manager of Smokey Mountain Iron Works, Inc., accepted this responsibility as part of his role in his organization. However, while he knew that a program of management succession was sound, he also knew that it required planning and implementation by all of top management in a company if it were to become workable. Furthermore, as he viewed the subject it meant having competent experienced personnel ready to assume more responsible management positions in the event a higher level manager died, was retired, fired, became disabled, etc. Additionally, a review of the subject of management succession prompted him to re-study the organization structure, the company policies, the wage and salary program, job descriptions, and individuals making up the present management team. Homer Chase, Jr. ended his preliminary review of the question by concluding that the college professors at the seminar had some good ideas, but talking about them was one thing and applying them was another.

Two months later, Homer Chase, Jr. traveled from the Asheville, North Carolina, plant (commonly known as the "Highview" plant) and visited the Richmond, Virginia, plant (commonly known as the "Piedmont" plant). His uncle, Howard Smith, was located there and served as company President and Chairman of the Board. During their lengthy discussions over a two-day period, Mr. Howard Smith listened to his nephew's ideas for upgrading the management personnel, planning for a line of succession for the key management positions, and other studies related to strengthening the organization. While the suggestions sounded pretty good to Mr. Smith, he felt that most of that "stuff" was out of books and typically would excite any young manager with ambition. He told his

―――――――

* Reprinted with permission of the Southern Case Writers' Association.

nephew to go ahead and put down his plans on paper and after the next Board meeting they would go over some of the "specifics." He warned, however, that new ideas and changes would be slow to introduce in Smokey Mountain because:

1. Our first responsibility is to stay solvent as a manufacturer in a declining industry with a diminishing market.
2. Every manager we've got employed has held his present job at least ten or fifteen years and they aren't likely to change their ways overnight.
3. These men (managers) were employed when we needed them to know one thing—either production, sales, purchasing, etc.—and not a "damn" one of them except Steve Stone knows much else.
4. It costs money to train personnel, make these studies and maybe add another man or two. We just can't afford it.
5. Furthermore, unless we can diversify our product line and sell like "hell" for the next year or two, we're not going to have any of these management problems facing us.

Homer Chase, Jr. returned to the Highview plant and immediately became bogged down with union negotiations that lasted a week longer than he anticipated. Shortly after he signed the union-management contract for the coming year his Secretary told him that Mr. Howard Smith was on long distance.

(Essence of telephone conversation)

Howard Smith—Homer, we've got a real problem on our hands now. Bob Pirkle (General Manager, Piedmont Plant) was taken to the hospital yesterday with a heart attack. At his age (62) anything can happen. Even if the docs get everything under control it may be six months or a year before he can get back to the plant on a limited basis.

You'd better get over here pronto and talk about a replacement for Bob. Your ideas of a few days ago begin to make a little more sense.

Homer Chase, Jr.—Howard, I'm sorry to hear about Bob. Please tell him that we're all behind him at the Highview Plant. Say . . . give me a day to scratch out some notes and I'll see you on Wednesday by lunch time. Thanks for the weak vote of confidence.
(End of conversation)

The next day Homer Chase, Jr. reviewed every manager in the organization who could be considered a possible candidate for the position of General Manager at the Piedmont plant and wrote down his thoughts about each. His second review of the personnel narrowed the candidates down to four but as he boarded the plane to Richmond, he still was undecided on which one to recommend to his uncle.

FIGURE I

ORGANIZATION CHART—SMOKEY MOUNTAIN IRON WORKS, INC.—1964

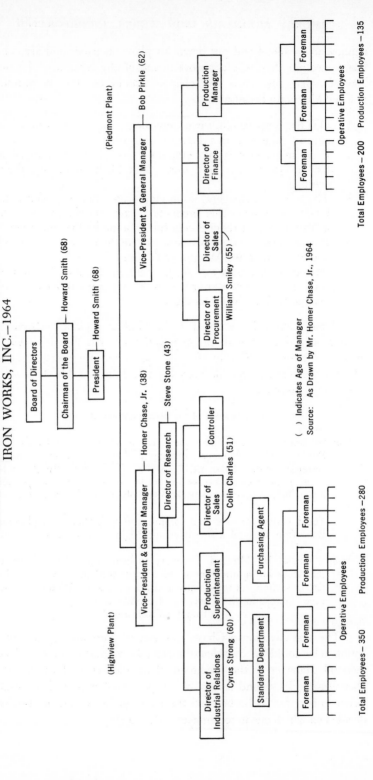

( ) Indicates Age of Manager

Source: As Drawn by Mr. Homer Chase, Jr., 1964

History of the Company

The Smokey Mountain Iron Works, Inc., marked its one hundredth (100th) anniversary in 1964, having originated as the Blue Ridge Iron and Preservative Works in 1864. In 1876 the company was sold to Mr. Howard Smith's grandfather, Clifford Smith, who reorganized the operation and constructed the present plant at Richmond, Virginia, in 1878. The older Mr. Smith had invested $14,000.00 originally in the company. At that time the firm had one major customer, one major product and sales totaling $48,000.00 annually. After losing $3,900.00 in the first year of operation Mr. Clifford Smith raised prices, diversified his product line and borrowed money to expand his marketing territory. The company temporarily lost the one major customer when prices were raised but added many more customers when salesmen created new sales markets. At that time the company was manufacturing agricultural implements.

In 1902 the company expanded manufacturing operations by opening a plant outside of Asheville, North Carolina. This plant became known as the Highview Plant. For tax reasons, the Highview operation was incorporated separately but both the Highview and Piedmont companies were controlled by a holding company headed by Mr. Clifford Smith. A major reason for the Highview plant was to obtain labor at lower wages and get away from organized labor which had unionized the Piedmont plant in Richmond before the turn of the century.

In 1908, Mr. Paul Stone, a brother-in-law of Mr. Clifford Smith, was employed to learn the business. Subsequently, he became a production foreman, shop superintendent, and General Manager of the Highview plant in 1931.

Shortly before America's entry into World War I, Mr. Clifford Smith brought his nephew, Howard Smith, into the business. In 1926, Howard Smith was made President of the Richmond Company at the age of 29. By this time, both companies had enlarged their product lines to include the manufacture of sinks, tubs, and sanitary ware.

In 1931, the Highview plant got into financial difficulty primarily because of over investment in inventories and severe drop in sales. At this point, Mr. Howard Smith started taking an active management role in both companies. To improve the financial condition of the Highview plant, he cut salaries, cut employees, lowered production, reduced inventories, and replaced the general manager with Mr. Paul Stone. Mr. Stone who had been in production operations for 23 years at that time stayed very much "production oriented" until his retirement in 1954. His attitude toward the sales department over the years was reflected in a past statement attributed to him: "We'll produce it—you sell it!"

Because of federal legislation passed in the late 1930's, the holding company controlling the Highview and Piedmont companies had to be dissolved. The two companies now became one corporation with two plants, each operating independently. Both plants continued to enlarge sales up to World War II. In 1938, Mr. William Smiley joined the Piedmont operation. Mr. Smiley worked one of the sales territories of the Piedmont plant and increased sales the first year he took over that territory. However, he left the organization in the war years to go into the army. Also at this time, Mr. Clifford Smith retired as Chairman of the Board and was replaced by Mr. Howard Smith.

Historically the Highview plant is considered to be more production-minded, a lower unit cost producer, than the Piedmont plant which is considered more "sales" oriented. Mr. Homer Chase, Jr., says this was probably true before World War II but since each plant operates independently and since each buys some manufactured products from the other, it is less true in 1964 than at any other time. The Highview plant has managed to remain non-union through the years.

In the post-war years, 1946–1949, Mr. Colin Charles and Mr. Steve Stone were employed by the Highview plant: Mr. Charles as Sales Manager and Mr. Stone (son of the General Manager) as a production trainee. Also in this period, Mr. Homer Chase, Jr., nephew of the President, was employed to work for the Piedmont plant in sales under the direction of Mr. William Smiley, who had rejoined the organization as Sales Manager after the war. The only other significant change in personnel at this time took place when Mr. Bob Pirkle was promoted to General Manager of the Piedmont plant.

From 1946 to 1950, both companies enjoyed prosperous years selling in a market that was "hungry" for consumer products. However, several of the products that had been manufactured for over fifty years began to drop in sales. Demand for cast iron sinks and tubs diminished yearly and according to Howard Smith these products were in demand only because there were enough marginal producers going out of business to allow Smokey Mountain Iron Works to pick up their customers. The management of both plants began to consider seriously the question of widespread product diversification. From 1950–1964 one or both of the plants of Smokey Mountain Iron Works, Inc. added these products to their manufacturing and sales line: commercial cooking equipment and heaters and cooking equipment for mobile homes.

Total sales had increased slightly every year from 1959 to 1964, but the growth was more attributable to enlarging the sales market to include the far western states and Canada, than to an increase in demand in the established sales areas.

One significant personnel change took place in 1954. Mr. Paul Stone,

General Manager of the Highview plant, retired after serving the organization 46 years. Mr. Homer Chase, Jr., nephew of the Company's President, took his place with the title, Vice President and General Manager, Highview plant.

EXHIBIT I
NOTES ON COLIN CHARLES*

Background

Sales Manager, Highview Plant. Age 51. Joined company in 1946; previous training with a shipyard as a student-engineer; employed by large automotive company for two years prior to World War II. Is a graduate electrical engineer. Finished college during the depression (1935). Native southerner—married with two college-age sons.

In World War II was a Major in the Supply Corps; has stayed in the active reserve for 20 years; retired as Lt. Colonel. Big civic worker; active in Y.M.C.A. program; civic clubs; sales executive groups; title in 1946—Sales Manager; same title today but with 16 salesmen under him.

As A Manager

Conservative in outlook (according to Howard Smith). Has inertia and is too easily satisfied (Howard Smith). Has the attitude—"if something is going good, don't rock the boat." (Howard Smith)

His sales philosophy is to go for a good profit margin per unit sold; doesn't like low price policies, volume sales, etc. Good detail and procedures man; reports are turned in on time and are complete. Runs a tight sales department; good control system over salesmen; delegates when necessary; assumes full responsibility for the sales function; not afraid to make decisions but appears to "over simplify" problems; fairly good initiator of ideas although not a great innovator of new products, etc.; rarely bothers me unless necessary. Is technically competent in sales but knows very little about production processes, industrial relations, or administration and finance. Is knowledgeable about company procurement procedures and the research and development program. Is very much "quality" conscious. Can't get along with Cyrus Strong, Plant Superintendent. Strong feels the sales department is a favored department; Charles doesn't feel Strong should make (compensation) as much as the Sales Manager. Charles feels the production department is a favored department also.

* Comments in Exhibits I, II, III and IV are recorded as stated by Mr. Homer Chase, Jr., Vice President and General Manager of the Highview Plant. Some of the opinions about the managers are attributable to the President, Mr. Howard Smith, but incorporated in the notes of Mr. Homer Chase, Jr.

EXHIBIT II
NOTES ON STEVE STONE

Background   Age 43; married; holds a metallurgical engineering degree from
a southern university. When in college, he was a co-op at the
plant in the foundry section. Joined organization in 1946 after
serving four years as an officer in the United States Army Air
Corps. From 1946 to 1950 he worked with R & D, did design
work and product studies; 1950–1953 was purchasing manager
at Highview; 1953–1959 was Assistant to the Production
Superintendent in a staff capacity. In this position he became
familiar with general administration of the plant, financial
policies, and personnel; also studied the possibility and feasibility of adding new product lines; also studied machinery
processes related to manufacturing new products. Since late
1959, has been active in sales research, which is a staff position
created to support the sales department.

As A Manager   Has a good knowledge of the cost control system. Since 1959
has been Director of Research accountable only to the Vice
President and General Manager at Highview. Stone knows the
business as well as any of the managers. He's had exposure to
all of the functional areas. Only problem is habit of "talking
down" to people. Makes enemies easily! (Howard Smith)

Stone is intelligent and knowledgeable about company operations; poor human relationist; is at odds with the Production
Superintendent. Question his ability to "lead" subordinates;
never been in a straight line position with operative people
under him. At one time (1954) when the former General
Manager of the Highview plant retired, Steve Stone thought
he would be made General Manager at Highview. Is considered most effective when on special projects.

EXHIBIT III

NOTES ON CYRUS STRONG

Background

Started to work in 1920 at age 16. Been with company 44 years. Was first employed as a maintenance helper. Worked up through the ranks in production to present position of Production Superintendent, Highview plant. Has high school education and good basic intelligence. Married with four children; all children are college graduates with outstanding records.

As A Manager

Strong is an essential man in the organization; his integrity, motivation and knowledge of production operations places him far above anyone else, in value to the company. (Howard Smith)

He's a living institution to other employees. They consider him a "tough" boss but fair. He works himself much harder than the men; quite often he will work on the weekends. Never mentions overtime or pay increases; rarely takes as much as half of his vacation time each year. Strong knows the product, production processes and factory personnel—has been on company negotiating committee with union for years; has a good appreciation of production costs and production statistics. Has tried to work through others via delegation in last few years but has some difficulty communicating effectively. Has the habit of "doing a job himself" if others can't do it. Knowledge of administrative finance, purchasing, and sales is limited.

EXHIBIT IV

NOTES ON WILLIAM SMILEY

Background   Age 55—high school education; native of Virginia. Started to work with the company in 1938 as a territory salesman with the Piedmont plant in Richmond, Virginia. Smiley left the company in World War II to go into service. After the war he re-joined the firm, this time as Director of Sales.

As A Manager   In his first year with the company, his territory sales increased over those of previous veteran salesmen. Without question he is the finest salesman in the company; he loves to sell. (Howard Smith)

Smiley is very energetic and confident. As a manager he is poor; doesn't control activities or personnel effectively; is not a "detail" man. Very weak on training subordinates; never wants to fire anyone; rarely disciplines anyone. The President handles some of the management problems in Sales.

Smiley married his former secretary. Has 26 years seniority with the Piedmont plant. Limited knowledge of production and assembly operations, purchasing, personnel and finance. Good knowledge of credits and sales; very likeable and personable; gets along with everyone.

EXHIBIT V

TABLE OF COMPENSATION AND YEARS OF SERVICE FOR SELECTED MANAGER OF THE SMOKEY MOUNTAIN IRON WORKS, INC.*

		YEARS OF SERVICE	ANNUAL SALARY
Howard Smith	President and Chairman of the Board	47	NA
Homer Chase, Jr.	Vice President and General Manager, Highview Plant	17	NA
Bob Pirkle	Vice President and General Manager, Piedmont Plant	34	$19,000
Steve Stone	Director of Research, Highview Plant	18	14,000
William Smiley	Director of Marketing, Piedmont Plant	26	16,500
Colin Charles	Director of Sales, Highview Plant	18	16,000
Cyrus Strong	Production Superintendent, Highview Plant	44	15,700

* Information on a management financial incentive program which may add dollar income to the listed annual salary figure is not available.

24. STEELEX CORPORATION

THE STEELEX CORPORATION BECAME a separate entity in the late nineteen-thirties when the original firm, Metals Supply Company, Incorporated, went into bankruptcy. At that time several managers of the original company joined together to form the Steelex Corporation.

The Steelex Corporation, now in its twenty-third year of continuous operation, has survived several crises brought on by the years of World War II and the Korean War. Today it is considered to be one of the leading companies in the metal supply industry. Because it was primarily a distributor instead of a metals producer, Steelex found it extremely difficult to maintain satisfactory inventory levels during war years. In the early 1940's and 1950's, the stock levels of the company were practically zero. However, during the nonwar years the company has followed a policy of diversifying its stock and competing vigorously. In 1960, sales of all items totaled approximately ten million dollars.

Present Operations and Facilities

During the last few years the Steelex Corporation has followed a policy of stocking any and all items that its customers might demand. This means that thousands of items are stocked, carried in inventory, and made available to customers upon receipt of an order. The top management of Steelex realizes that this is a costly practice but, upon an analysis of sales lost in prior years because of failure to have certain items on hand, it is considered to be a sound policy.

The most important division of Steelex Corporation is the Warehouse Division. This division administratively is headed by Mr. Ronson Holcomb. Over the past five years Mr. Holcomb has expanded his division so that there are fifteen major distribution centers located in the Midwest and in the south central part of the United States. At each of these distribution centers, all items sold are carried in inventory. Each distribution center maintains warehouse facilities ranging in size from 35,000 to 100,000 square feet. In order to have proper control of the thousands of items in inventory, Mr. Holcomb and his staff have separated all items into fifty-seven classes of products. The product classes range from steel mill products to plywood and building materials.

Competition

Competition in this industry has been very keen in the last few years. Since numerous standard specifications are used by customers when ordering materials, the method of competing with other metal distributing firms is on the basis of price, service dependability, and assurance of supply.

During the recession years beginning in 1958, the management of the Steelex Corporation has held numerous meetings to discuss (1) how to reduce costs and (2) how to increase sales. It was pointed out to Mr. Holcomb that the future existence of the Steelex Corporation depended on the successful management of the Warehouse Division.

Organization of the Warehouse Division

The Warehouse Division maintains a central office in New Orleans, Louisiana. Mr. Holcomb and his staff coordinate many of the activities of the distribution centers from this office. However, at each of the fifteen distribution centers there exists a branch manager, an assistant branch manager, two or three branch product managers, and a clerical and warehouse staff. Figure I shows the typical organization of a warehouse division distribution center.

Altogether, at the fifteen distribution centers there are forty product managers. A product manager quite often is as much a salesman as he is an industrial materials buyer. Many orders and requests for information are received at the distribution centers via the telephone. The product manager has the responsibility to follow up on all such requests for information and attempt to consummate a sale if possible. However, his primary responsibility is that of an industrial materials' purchaser and inventory control manager.

Reorganization of the Warehouse Division Staff

Three months ago Mr. Holcomb carefully surveyed the growth picture of the Warehouse Division of Steelex Corporation. He concluded that with the tightening competitive situation, slowdown in sales due to the slackening of general business activity, and large inventories on hand, some management changes were in order. To free himself from burdensome control activities and administrative details, he requested the transfer of Mr. Balkom Jones from the controller's office to the Warehouse Division. Mr. Jones accepted the transfer to become manager of procurement and inventory control under Mr. Holcomb.

During his first three months in the newly created job Mr. Jones took time to survey all activities at each of the distribution centers. He discussed every functional activity of each center with the branch managers and their staffs. He then studied all reports, records, and statistical summaries of the Warehouse Division for the past year at the home office. With his own background knowledge of Warehouse Division operations plus what he learned from his three-month study of current operations, Mr. Jones narrowed his attention to the subjects he considered most strategic and, in instances, the most critical to the immediate success of the Warehouse Division.

FIGURE I

ORGANIZATION OF DISTRIBUTION CENTER,
WAREHOUSE DIVISION

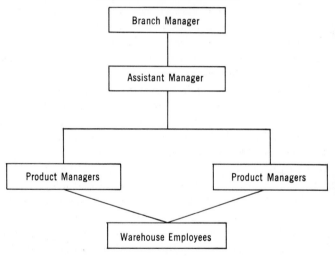

Explanation of Duties:

(1) Branch Manager —Primarily concerned with sales; responsible for all activities of the distribution center; works closely with warehouse division manager and his staff.

(2) Assistant Manager—Primarily responsible for the administration of the distribution center office; responsible for distribution center records, accounts, and reports.

(3) Product Managers—Primarily responsible for buying of materials carried in inventory for sale; act as an inside salesman; responsible for controlling inventory and assisting in the forecast of sales.

Inventory Control

In analyzing the current inventory control practices and policies, Mr. Jones realized that the product managers play a major role in the success or failure of the Warehouse Division.

The product managers procure all of the materials stocked in inventory and have the responsibility for controlling the inventory within prescribed policy limits. Their inventory objective is to have all product items on hand when demanded by sales orders but, at the same time, to keep inventory figures low enough so that turnover will be satisfactory with a minimum of capital invested in the inventory.

Under the present incentive plan, all management personnel in each distribution center share in a profit-distribution plan if inventory turns over at least four times a year. The plan provides for one percent of the dollar value of average inventory on hand to be distributed among the management personnel of a distribution center at the end of each fiscal year.

In determining what to procure for stock the product managers receive assistance from the branch manager and, on occasion, assistance from the Warehouse Division staff. However, for the most part, they make their own decisions in regard to ordering and reordering items for stock. In an effort to standardize this procedure, the Warehouse Division manager developed a guide for product managers to follow when planning industrial materials purchases. This guide suggests that product managers purchase items on the basis of the past 90-day sales record of that item but in no event to be less than the 90-day projected sales of that item.

As of now, Mr. Jones feels that the product managers pay only slight attention to the purchasing aids developed by the home office and in reality procure materials on the basis of (1) the current demand for items, (2) their "feel" of the market, and (3) inventory depletion or approaching depletion.

The Sales Forecast

One of the first questions raised by Mr. Jones when he accepted his new position concerned the sales forecast of the Warehouse Division. He discussed with Mr. Holcomb the method of forecasting, the use of the results, and the real value of the sales forecast. Mr. Jones concluded that the sales forecast was determined by four factors:

1. The sales record of each distribution center during the past year by class of product. This record includes total items sold by product

classes, in units and in dollars; the balance of inventory of each product class; and the profit derived on sales by product classes.

2. The statements by distribution center managers regarding the expectation of sales for the coming year. (This statement is based upon their experience to merchandise products effectively and their "feel" of the market.)

3. New additions to the line which theoretically would help stimulate sales of items in all product classes.

4. General business conditions in each distribution center sales territory.

Upon the accumulation of the above data from all distribution centers, Mr. Holcomb analyzes the data, adds whatever information he has on the subject, and determines a final total sales figure which becomes the forecast for the coming year. The total sales forecast figure and the sales forecast for each distribution center is then sent to the distribution center managers. Normally the forecasted sales are high, due to the belief of Mr. Holcomb that it is a good psychological factor for stimulating more intensive sales efforts on the part of the distribution center managers and salesmen in the field.

Overinvestment in Inventory

The most serious problem of the Warehouse Division as explained to Mr. Jones by Mr. Holcomb, and known to Mr. Jones from work in his previous job, concerns the large sums of money tied up in inventory. When expected sales fail to materialize, when the sales forecast is abnormally out of line, and when product managers fail to control inventory properly, the Steelex Corporation ends the fiscal year with a shortage of working capital and unusually high variable costs because of unusually large inventories. This directly affects the profit position of the firm and its competitive position in the industry.

In 1961 the top management of Steelex Corporation still considered the company to be in a dangerous inventory position due to the very heavy procurement of materials prior to the steel strike and shortly thereafter in 1960. With general business conditions getting worse instead of better, the expected sales for the year failed to materialize, and Mr. Holcomb was under pressure to revise inventory policy, increase sales, and reduce costs pertaining to warehousing and distribution.

Personnel Problems

As a result of meeting with Mr. Ralph Carlson, the personnel director, Mr. Jones realized that attention should be given to the job of product manager. Mr. Carlson pointed out that these men are selected and employed by the distribution center managers, they are trained on the job, and they are relatively low paid. The top management of Steelex Corporation feels that there is enough of a built-in incentive in the job of product manager, because of the profit-distribution plan and the opportunity to advance to distribution center manager, to offset the relatively low pay. Furthermore, the wide spread in salary between a distribution center manager and product manager is an incentive in itself to encourage product managers to do a superior job and be promoted to the higher position. Top management believes it is justified in demanding quality performance from the product managers.

In attempting to review the requirements of the branch product manager's job, Mr. Jones noted that, besides being in charge of procuring industrial materials for inventory, the product manager is forced into a clerk's role when maintaining a Kardex system; he also acts as an inside salesman; and he's an administrator in the sense of managing all of his activities and those of employees under his supervision. In summary, the product manager must have (1) product knowledge, (2) customer knowledge, and (3) administrative knowledge.

Mr. Carlson also pointed out to Mr. Jones that in a previous product-manager turnover study, he found that product managers left the company either through dismissal or resignation because of these general reasons: (1) failure to understand the job, (2) lack of initiative, (3) low pay, and (4) lack of opportunity to advance.

Mr. Carlson's comments to Mr. Jones about the product managers' performance supported some comments on the same subject by several distribution center managers. In general, they felt the product managers were doing satisfactorily considering their responsibilities, their experience, and their compensation. While there was a large overinvestment in inventories, the distribution center managers did not feel that all of the blame should be placed on product managers. They complained of a lack of clear-cut inventory policies for guiding decisions of product managers. They also complained of the terrific pressure placed on making sales and the relative lack of attention placed on controlling costs.

Shreveport Distribution Center

At the Shreveport Distribution Center, Mr. Otis Bedeaux, Manager, showed Mr. Jones the summary pages of one class of products kept in stock (see Appendix). This summary gave the following information:

CAPTION	COLUMN NUMBERS	REMARKS
Item number	—	
Description	0–1	
Usage of each item	2–3	For years 1957, 58, 59, 60
Delivery time	4	
MDEI	5	Minimum Desired Ending Inventory
Order quantity	6	This is the minimum quantity Steelex Corp. can buy from suppliers
Maximum	7	
Comments on spread of risk among customers	8–9	
Stock on hand	9–10	
Overstock	11	
Discontinued or obsolete stock	12–13	Efforts usually made to get factory to take back
Decision concerning use, transfer, or sale	14–17	
Other remarks	18–19	

Mr. Bedeaux pointed out the condition of the inventory by item for Class 01 of the product classes. He emphasized that the number of items overstocked and the quantity of the overstocked items (Column 11) were way out of line with what he thought was sound inventory management. While he accepted responsibility for the decisions of the product managers, he stressed again that one of the causes of the overinvestment in inventories was the failure of top management to communicate clear and consistent inventory management policies to the distribution centers. Mr. Bedeaux also pointed out that the inventory condition of Class 01 was typical for all product classes at the Shreveport Center and, as far as he knew, typical of most of the product classes stocked at each of the distribution centers of the company.

ITEM NO.	DESCRIPTION		1957	1958 (USAGE)	1959	1960	DELIVERY TIME	M D E I	ORDER QUAN-TITY	MAXI-MUM	COMMENTS ON SPREAD OF RISK AMONG CUSTOMERS
1	Rus 032 X 36 X 120		.123	679	0	0	?				—
2	Rus 040 X 36 X 96		0	0	0	0	?	0	500	500	—
3	2024-T3 MF	032X48X144	—	0	923	131	90 days	212	500	712	—
4	2024-T3 MF	050X48X144	—	259	550	0	45	105	500	605	—
5	2024-T3 MF	063X48X144	—	2065	1049	913	30	523	500	1023	
6	2024-T3 FS	016X36X144			17	2506	15	1113	500	1613	1 Customer
7	2024-T3 MF	025X48X144	5828	2359	2065	120	45	1128	500	1628	
8	2024-T3 MF	040X48X144	7168	5306	4076	440	30	1848	500	2348	
9	2024-T3	050X48X96	—	—	—	0	30	0	2000	2000	
10	2024-T3	050X48X144	3492	3761	3362	6330	15	1843	500	2343	
11	2024-T3	063X48X144	6131	7706	13135	16780	60	4760	500	5260	
12	2024-T3	090X48X144	1238	1441	615	61	60	354	500	854	
13	2024-T3	125X48X144	3803	4392	3193	5071	15	1790	500	2290	
14	3003-0 MF	125X48X144	1365	171	33	767	?	231	500	731	
15	3003-H14 MF	625X36X120	3843	3696	205	1107	60	962	500	1462	
16	3003-H14 MF	032X36X120	9307	12678	752	2869	15	2785	500	3285	
17	3003-H14 MF	032X48X120	8441	5999	2350	471	15	1877	500	2377	
18	3003-H14 MF	032X48X144	3530	5999	4263	2495	15	1772	500	2272	
19	3003-H14 MF	040X48X96	—	7022	1528	2553	30	1443	500	1943	
20	3003-H14 MF	040X48X120	21698	17236	13488	4615	30	6205	500	6705	
21	3003-H14 MF	040X43X144	33978	5718	6365	2209	45	5251	500	5751	
22	3003-H14 MF	050X36X120	12259	299	770	107	?	128	500	628	
23	3003-H14 MF	051X48X96	7927	3333	8321	69	60	2137	500	2637	2 Customers
24	3003-H14 MF	050X48X120	11702	6532	6048	143	15	2660	500	3160	
25	3003-H14 MF	063X48X96	1839	2264	2264	2988	15	1017	500	1517	
26	3003-H14 MF	063X48X144	14101	14277	14992	937	15	4820	500	5320	
27	3003-H14 MF	081X48X144	2298	3611	383	656	15	755	500	1255	
28	3003-H14 MF	090X48X144	19677	5714	5882	1166	60	3529	500	4029	
29	5005-H14 MF	025X36X96	—	1226	718	1373	45	431	500	931	
30	5005-H14 MF	025X36X120	—	1863	2269	897	60	653	500	1153	
31	5005-H14 MF	032X36X120	—	5177	1039	1013	45	940	500	1440	
32	5005-H14 MF	032X48X120	—	4409	3431	1165	45	1170	500	1670	
33	5005-H14 MF	032X48X144	—	1975	482	710	45	414	500	914	
34	5005-H14 MF	040X36X120	—	1887	9854	2390	30	1837	500	2337	
35	5005-H14 MF	040X48X96	—	—	4227	4488	30	1760	500	2260 ·	
36	5005-H14 MF	040X48X120	—	4909	21293	10784	30	4808	500	5308	
37	5005-H14 MF	040X48X120	No Record			No Record			500		
38	5005-H14 MF	040X48X144	—	3446	7476	4641	30	2023	500	2523	
39	5005-H14 MF	050X48X96	—	—	1378	209	60	320	500	820	
40	5005-H14 MF	050X48X144	—	399	3766	6051	30		500		
41	5005-H14 MF	050X48X144	—	15751	2292	1729	30	2570	500	3070	
42	5005-H14 MF	063X36X96	—	2528	491	44	45	398	500	898	
43	5005-H14 MF	063X36X120	—	—	1187	135	60	267	500	767	
44	5005-H14 MF	063X48X144	—	14321	12098	6395	30	4265	500	4765	
45	5005-H14 MF	080X48X144	—	—	4036	1477	60	1113	500	1613	
46	5005-H14 MF	090X48X120	—	—	3462	1643	60	1031	2000	3031	
47	5005-H14 MF	125X36X96	—	—	1728	176	45	384	500	884	
48	5005-H14 MF	125X36X120	—	159	2280	159	30	337	2000	2337	
49	5005-H14 MF	125X48X120	—	1069	7615	1497	60	1323	500	1823	
50	5005-H14 MF	125X48X144	—	17486	13877	5851	30	4839	500	5339	
51	5005-H14 MF	190X48X144	—	—	9164	3445	30	2547	500	3049	2 Customers
52	5005-H32 MF	190X48X144	—	—	1041	0	30	210	2000	2210	1 Customer
53	5005-H34 MF	190X48X144	—	—	260	0	45	52	500	552	1 Customer
54	5052-H32 MF	032X48X144	6346	393	305	1041	60	868	500	1368	
55	5052-H32 MF	040X48X144	0	602	448	27	45	140	500	640	
56	5052-H32 MF	091X48X144	—	242	2226	3861	15	822	500	1322	
57	5052-H32 MF	125X44X144	—	—	972	4754	60	1156	2000	3156	
58	5052-H34 MF	032X48X144	108	461	307	0	?	95	500	595	
59	5052-H34 MF	050X48X120	28	503	1585	148	?	246	500	746	
60	5052-H34 MF	090X48X144	1814	5562	14726	20606	15	4646	500	5146	2 Customers

10	11	12	13	14	15 16 17	18 19 20 21
STOCK ON HAND	OVER-STOCK	DISCONTINUED OR OBSOLETE STOCK		DECISION CONCERNING USE, RETURN, TRANSFER, OF SALE		OTHER REMARKS
0					To be sold as Building Sheet	
684	184		684		To be sold as Building Sheet	
1072	360		500	500#	Available for Trans.	
547	0		547	547#	Available for Trans.	St. Louis — Space Jet Aircraft
1534	511					
570	0					
731	0					
602	0					
1716	0					
662	0					
2310	0					
1106	252					
512	0					
512	0		512	512#	Available for Trans.	
2917	1455		1500	1500#	Available for Trans.	
696	0					
953	0					
1270	0					
510	0					
1791	0					
584	0					
3771	3143		2500	2500#	Available for Trans.	
978	0					
542	0					
920	0					
517	0					
1204	0					
614	0					
948	17					
673	0					
903	0					
2791	1121		1500	1500#	Available for Trans.	
1029	115					
1454	0					
1524	0					
9332	4024		5000	5000#	Available for Trans.	
570	?					
1536	0					
3947	3127		3000	3000#	Available for Trans.	
1052			1052			
10857	7787		5000	5000#	Available for Trans.	
1148	250					
2909	2142		2000	2000#	Available for Trans.	
1121	0					
766	0					
3332	301		3000	3000#	Available for Trans.	
2307	1423		1000	1000#	Available for Trans.	
2485	148		1500	1500#	Available for Trans.	
2352	529		1000	1000#	Available for Trans.	
1000	0					
1040	0					
1041	1169		1041			Sub for 5005-H14
2201	1649		2201	2201#	Available for Trans.	
1896	528		1000	1000#	Available for Trans.	
437	0					
540	0					
5465	2309		3000	3000#	Available for Trans.	
1729	1134		1729	1729#	Available for Trans.	
1652	906		1652	1652#	Available for Trans.	
792	0					

---

25. THE LOCKHEED JETSTAR

IN 1956, LOCKHEED AIRCRAFT CORPORATION undertook a company-funded program to develop a turbojet aircraft capable of carrying seven to ten passengers and a crew of two. The program was initiated in response to a developing trend of requirements for an executive-style jet in the military and business aircraft markets. Five years of intensive effort preceded the first production model which flew in July, 1960. The following year, after successfully completing final performance tests by the company and the Federal Aeronautics Administration, the plane was certified for production on August 29, 1961. Certification concluded the $138 million program which introduced the first corporate jet, the Lockheed JetStar.

Deliveries commenced the next month, and during the two years following certification, JetStars logged 25,000 flight hours or about 11,000,000 miles. However, neither the business nor the military requirements grew initially as rapidly as was expected. A slight but persistent upturn began in late 1963, and by the spring of 1965, three domestic and four foreign aircraft producers had also introduced corporate jets. Drawn into tight competition for a still limited number of users, the challenge to Lockheed lay in the area of marketing.

The Lockheed JetStar

The JetStar is basically a ten-passenger, medium range turbojet. It will operate under all weather conditions at speeds up to 550 mph and altitudes of 43,000 feet. Its range is about 2,250 miles. Due to the JetStar's short field landing and take-off characteristics, it is estimated that 1,100 airports in the United States and Canada can be used and 2,500 throughout the world. An emergency drag parachute is provided for those situations where adverse landing conditions might result in an overrun.

Four Pratt & Whitney engines are incorporated in dual nacelles mounted on the aft fuselage. The JetStar, however, can operate safely on three engines, while maintaining 30,000 feet of altitude, and it can operate on two engines, maintaining 16,000 feet of altitude at 34,000 pounds gross weight. Furthermore, because the Federal Aeronautics Administration has approved three-engine take-offs, if an engine is inoperative the aircraft can be flown directly to the maintenance base, rather than removing and shipping it with the resultant delays. The JetStar is the only executive-style jet which employs four engines.

Although a basic airframe design is followed in production, many optional features are available to develop the JetStar around individual requirements. For example, a weather avoidance radar system can be supplied and a variety of instruments selected according to the preferences of the operating pilot. Also, the JetStar is not normally delivered with completed interior furnishings. This allows the owners to determine specifically the layout and furnishings desired, within space and weight limitations, and negotiate separately with specialist interior-outfitting companies. One such firm is located in Texas.

Operating costs vary according to usage. The basic airplane with full standard equipment can be purchased for approximately $1,500,000. Interior furnishings and optional electronics typically amount to about $200,000. Under these conditions, the operating costs per flying hour are shown in the table below.

DIRECT OPERATING COSTS—DOLLARS PER FLYING HOUR

ITEM	BASIS	ANNUAL UTILIZATION—HOURS		
		400	600	800
Fixed Costs:				
Crew salary	$32,000 annual total for pilot and co-pilot plus 22.5% for fringe benefits	$ 98.00	$ 65.30	$ 49.00
Insurance	1.75% for hull and public liability based on purchase price, $1,700,000	72.50	48.30	36.25
FIXED COSTS WITHOUT DEPRECIATION		$170.50	$113.60	$ 85.25
Variable Costs:				
Fuel	$0.30/gal, 1200 statute miles	$132.00	$132.00	$132.00
Oil	$12.00/gal, 0.026 gal/hr	0.31	0.31	0.31
Airframe and engine line maintenance	5.0 manhours/flt hr; $4.50/labor hr.	22.50	22.50	22.50
Airframe and engine line maintenance material		21.25	21.25	21.25
Reserve for engine overhaul	$12,400 per engine per overhaul; TBO overhaul 1400 hrs.	35.40	35.40	35.40
TOTAL VARIABLE COSTS		$211.46	$211.46	$211.46
OPERATING COSTS		$381.96	$325.06	$296.71
ACTUAL COST TO CORPORATION (48% TAX BRACKET)		$198.62	$169.03	$154.29

For comparative purposes, the following table shows the operating costs of the JetStar with respect to two-engine turboprop and piston aircraft, assuming about 750 hours annual utilization.

ITEM	JETSTAR	TURBOPROP	PISTON
Crew	$ 51.00	$ 51.00	$ 51.00
Insurance	94.50	65.00	25.00
Fuel and Oil	142.50	65.00	90.00
Maintenance	72.25	60.00	50.00
Depreciation	210.00	175.00	135.00
Total $/hr	$570.25	$416.00	$351.00
Block Speed–mph	495	315	270
Total $/statute mile	1.15	1.32	1.30

The Lockheed-Georgia Company, where the JetStar is produced, operates and maintains a complete customer service program and facility. Lockheed field representatives are available to new owners during the initial period of service to assist in pre-delivery preparations, orient company personnel to the JetStar, and provide technical assistance. The representative also helps in flight-checking and maintains liaison with the Lockheed plant. Company pilots are given ground training at the Lockheed plants after which an instructor pilot and flight engineer are assigned to the owner's base of operation. During this time, the instructor pilot provides as much flight training as desired by the corporate pilot, while the flight engineer helps the ground crew with handling and maintenance. Maintenance training includes a factory course on the JetStar and its systems prior to delivery of the plane. Refresher courses are offered to assure that mechanics remain up-to-date.

As of April 1965 Lockheed had sold approximately 70 JetStars. The Federal Aeronautics Administration registry showed 32 were in domestic private operation; the remainder had been sold to the United States and foreign governments. Deliveries were taking place at a rate of two units per month.

The Business Aircraft Market[1]

The third largest market for aircraft and aeronautical products is general aviation, which includes business, pleasure, agricultural, instructional, and utility flying. By 1965, some 85,000 general aviation aircraft were in operation in the United States, flying approximately three times

---

[1] Information in this section was excerpted from the U.S. Industrial Outlook 1964, U.S. Department of Commerce, Business and Defense Services Administration, Section ER 89, and the U.S. Industrial Outlook 1965, pp. 80–85.

the number of hours flown by commercial airlines. Business aircraft account for about half of all general aviation flying. According to the National Business Aircraft Association, in 1964, 18,538 firms owned or leased 35,739 aircraft, about 20,000 of which were used primarily for business purposes.

Shipments of general aviation aircraft during the past ten years have fluctuated because of their close relationship with capital spending. The long-term trend, however, has been upward, and it is expected that increases in general aviation production and sales will continue. The rate of increase depends on general economic activity, especially in the volume of sales of business aircraft, the fastest growing sector of general aviation.

Shipments of all executive, business, and personal aircraft in 1965 are expected to exceed 9,800 units valued at $300 million. This represents a gain of 17 percent in value over 1964 shipments of slightly less than 9,000 units valued at $260 million. The development of turbine-powered executive aircraft, ranging in price from about $400,000 to more than $1 million, will bring United States and foreign manufacturers into tighter competition for this necessarily limited market. In addition to the four domestic and four foreign executive jet producers, several United States and European manufacturers are beginning to aggressively market high-speed turboprop corporate aircraft. Estimates of the total world market for these aircraft range up to 500 units per year over the next five year period. The United States would be a market for 100 to 150 units annually.

In April, 1965, the Federal Aeronautics Administration registry listed 163 business jets as in domestic operation. Of these, 89 were of civilian manufacture and the remaining 74 were aircraft converted to business usage such as the military T-33. It was estimated that 300 business jets were on order from the industry, and that by 1975, approximately 3,500 business jets would be in operation.

Marketing the JetStar

The JetStar salesman is a professional whose background might typically include civilian or military pilot experience, a degree in aeronautical engineering, or experience in aircraft production, design, and related areas. Inasmuch as demonstration flights are a major factor in the marketing function, an experienced pilot-copilot crew is made available to the salesman as he requires. It is not unusual, for example, to fly a prospective customer on a "whirlwind" business trip to introduce the convenience and speed of the JetStar.

Contacts with potential customers are established in several ways. Requests for descriptive literature about the JetStar are followed up by a call or visit to the requesting party. Through aircraft equipment trade shows and organizations such as the National Business Aircraft Association, contacts and leads are also established. The Federal Aeronautics Administration aircraft registry can be examined for current business aircraft owners who represent potential JetStar customers.

The JetStar marketing program can be considered as directed primarily toward three potential customer groups: those who presently do not utilize any type of business aircraft, relying instead on commercial airline transportation; those who currently employ a non-jet business aircraft or are planning to purchase one; and those who are considering the purchase of an executive jet. In any case, JetStar marketing is a sophisticated task. Not only is there competition from other corporate jet manufacturers, but also a form of competition from commercial airline service and medium-size non-jet aircraft. In meeting this competition, one marketing approach has been developed around the concept of value. The operating cost information given in the earlier tables shows that in general the hourly expense of the JetStar exceeds that of non-jet and commerical airline travel. Value, however, is a broader consideration than cost alone. For example, transportation is even less expensive by train, or bus, or car. It is argued, then, that the decision to purchase a JetStar cannot be based on a direct comparison of alternative costs; it should encompass all considerations related to executive travel. In effect, the executive jet may be viewed as a management tool.

This is but one approach employed in marketing the JetStar. In a sense, Lockheed's introduction of a corporate jet was an innovation, developed after a significant investment and not completely without risk. The fact that other aircraft producers followed this lead indicates at least in part that the concept of the executive jet has been a successful one. How well the JetStar marketing program develops and employs marketing approaches which are likewise innovations will determine if future leadership in the corporate jet market can be maintained.

APPENDIX

JETSTAR CASE

Lockheed Faces $80 Million JetStar Loss[1]

Lockheed Aircraft Corp., which has spent $100 million developing the JetStar, must sell at least 250 more of these utility transports to recapture its investment and probably will halt production if new orders fail to materialize early this year.

---

[1] Reprinted by permission of *Aviation Week* and *Space Technology*. Written by David H. Hoffman.

Despite initial Air Force interest in 300 JetStars—the figure circulated in 1956 when industry was asked to design at its own expense a utility jet transport capable of carrying 8 to 10 passengers—Air Force orders now total only 16. With sales to all sources holding at 43 (AW Jan. 8, p. 67), Lockheed estimates current JetStar losses at about $80 million. Of this, $65 million has been covered by before-tax write-offs and $10 million is in administrative costs not reflected on Lockheed profit and loss statements. The balance, $6 million, may be recovered from future sales.

To break even, the company must sell 300 JetStars. But the odds are heavily against a request for any mission support aircraft, whether Grumman Gulfstreams, Fairchild F-27s or JetStars, in the Fiscal 1963 Air Force budget. Orders for corporate JetStars, moreover, have not kept pace with Lockheed forecasts.

At a current rollout rate of two aircraft per month, it takes Lockheed about nine months plus interior installation time to build a JetStar. Of the 43 JetStars on order, about 17 were to be delivered by Jan. 1. As a result, Lockheed is assured of enough business to keep its JetStar assembly line here active through most of 1962.

But during this first quarter, the company probably must decide whether production in 1963 can continue without additional sales. It is doubtful whether this decision can be postponed, for Lockheed builds the JetStar on a lot basis and tries to gain enough orders during a specified time span before releasing subsequent lots for production.

Air Force JetStars, all of which will be operated by Military Air Transport Service, are of three types: five C-140As for flight-checking navigation aids, five C-140B mission support aircraft with convertible interiors and six VC-140s primarily for carrying ranking diplomats and political personalities within continental U.S. All VC-140s will go to the 1254th Air Transport Wing, Special Air Missions, at Andrews AFB, Md.

JetStar was originally proposed as a twin-jet transport powered by British-built Bristol Orpheus engines rated at 4,850 lb. thrust on takeoff. But Air Force wanted better performance and did not look with favor on the foreign powerplant even though Curtiss-Wright was to build it, under license, as the TJ37A1. Commercial interest in the twin-jet JetStar also was limited to one or two corporations.

Congressional records indicate that Air Force, during Fiscal 1959 through 1962, actually was authorized funds to purchase at least 30 to 35 C-140-series transports. Here is a breakdown of how much Air Force sought, how much Congress appropriated and how much was spent:

• Fiscal 1959. Air Force asked for $21.8 million and Congress appropriated the whole amount. Of this, only $8.8 million was obligated for the five C-140As.

• Fiscal 1960. Congress again appropriated the entire sum requested by Air Force, $23.4 million, for 14 bomb-navigation system trainers, but none of this money was spent.

• Fiscal 1961. Air Force budget did not include a request for C-140 funding. However, Air Force received authority to spend $12 million for the six VC-140s in December, 1960.

• Fiscal 1962. Air Force requested $19.1 million to buy C-140s, but Congress voted only $10 million, which was used to purchase the five C-140B mission-support aircraft.

Going into Fiscal 1963, the balance sheet showed that Air Force had sought a total of $64.3 million for over-all C-140 purchases, Congress had allowed $55.2 million and the service had spent $30.8 million. According to the late Robert Gross (AW Aug. 15, 1960, p. 51), former Lockheed chairman, the continuing emphasis placed upon missiles and space projects by the Eisenhower Administration, and the downgrading of manned aircraft to make more money available, channeled federal funds away from C-140 procurement. Tactical aircraft rather than support aircraft were accorded the highest fiscal priority.

In an effort to keep its JetStar project alive over the long-term, Lockheed is concentrating on convincing Air Force that the plane is an ideal aircraft for shortening supply lines to U.S. missile sites. Critical components could go via JetStars to remote bases not served by commercial carriers, Lockheed contends. It also hopes that Air Force requirements in this area will lead to the purchase of about 100 aircraft.

Concurrently, the company is attempting to link C-140 sales to the foreign manufacture of Lockheed F-104 fighters. West Germany, The Netherlands, Belgium, Italy, Canada and Japan have been licensed to build a total of 1,329 F-104s. Most of these will be equipped with systems similar to the North American Search and Ranging Radar (NASARR) that furnishes air-to-air position, terrain avoidance, contour mapping and slant range-to-target information to their pilots.

Lockheed has proposed the C-140, with four to seven training consoles installed in its cabin, as a flying classroom for foreign F-104 pilots. Such students could devote their whole attention to mastering the weapon system aspects of the airplane, while benefiting from over-the-shoulder instruction, Lockheed maintains. There would be no need to fly the F-104 while learning to use systems such as NASARR, as is now the case in even two-place F-104s, according to Lockheed.

Two JetStars sold to the West German defense force may be used later for this purpose.

In addition, there is a strong probability that negotiations in progress for months will result in West Germany's buying 8 to 10 more C-140s for training aircrews.

Robert I. Mitchell, director of marketing for Lockheed-Georgia Co., and recently assigned to JetStar sales on a full-time basis, believes that Air Force also has a valid requirement for about 300 C-140B mission support transports and for 30 to 40 flying testbed C-140s to check out weapon system components at relatively high airspeeds and altitudes. A need for 100 C-140Bs and 35 testbed JetStars, stated by Air Force during early preparation of its Fiscal 1963 budget, apparently failed to win Defense Department approval (AW Jan. 8, p. 21).

When used for mission support, the C-140's direct operating cost of 42 cents per aircraft nautical mile averages 26% less than that of the Douglas C-47, 29% less than that of the Convair C-131, and 47% less than that of the Douglas C-54, according to the company.

JETSTAR DEVELOPMENT TIMETABLE

August, 1956   Air Force issued requirement for jet utility transport (UCX) with 8–10 passenger capability to be developed at industry's expense.

January, 1957   Building of prototype started at Lockheed's California Division in Burbank.

September, 1957   JetStar, powered by twin Bristol Orpheus turbojets, made 35-min. first flight from Edwards ABF, Calif.

February, 1958   Phase 2 testing completed by Air Force.

November, 1958   Production of standard aircraft started at Lockheed-Georgia Co. in Marietta.

January, 1959   Pratt & Whitney JT12A turbojet selected to power JetStar; decision made to market aircraft only in four-engine configuration.

October, 1959   Air Force named JetStar winner of UCX competition.

June, 1960   Air Force ordered first five JetStars to check navigation aids in ATC system.

April, 1961   First Air Force JetStar delivered by Lockheed.

August, 1961   Federal Aviation Agency issued 4B Transport Category Type Certificate to JetStar and granted Lockheed-Georgia Co. production certificate.

On the civilian side of the sales picture, 25 JetStars have been ordered by U.S. and foreign corporations or heads of state. Of the three JetStars sold to heads of state, one will carry President Sukarno of Indonesia, but Lockheed refuses to disclose nationality of the other two purchasers.

Lockheed admits that early interest in the JetStar, which stemmed from corporations seeking to acquire it largely for prestige purposes, has dwindled. On the other hand, the manufacturer feels that after more commercial deliveries have been made, the close-knit fraternity of corporate pilots will begin discussing the JetStar's capabilities, and at this point, the aircraft will begin selling itself.

Dilemma of the corporate pilots is another factor that seems to favor an upturn in JetStar orders. If the corporate chief pilots who control the fleets of the larger companies vote against buying fast, turbine-powered, new equipment, the companies' top executives can be expected to make greater use of airline jets. This trend will curtail the companies' own flying operation and decrease the need for pilots. As a result, pressure is generated to purchase aircraft such as the JetStar.

The JetStar's initial price, its range and its takeoff runway requirement probably are partially responsible for slow sales to date. Less interior, the aircraft costs commercial or military purchasers $1,366,330, or about one-fifth the cost of a Boeing 720B with turbofan engines. JetStar's maximum range of 2,520 stat. mi., achieved with a payload of 1,640 lb. and Visual Flight Rule fuel reserves, is not quite transcontinental under all weather conditions. And, to satisfy civil air regulations, the fully loaded aircraft requires a 6,425-ft. runway to depart on maximum range missions.

Lockheed emphasizes these points in rebuttal:

• JetStar's speed—One recently flew 2,660 stat. mi. nonstop from Ontario, Calif., to Boston, Mass., in 4 hr. 30 min. at an average ground speed of 590 mph.—this more than compensates for any required refueling stops. Even if fuel is taken on en route, the JetStar can fly coast-to-coast in less time than any competitive transport.

• JetStar's takeoff field length requirement decreases to 3,900 ft., enabling it to operate from at least 1,000 U.S. airports, on typical stage lengths of 1,000 stat. mi. Flying such a mission, the transport would carry eight passengers, a crew of two, full baggage and fuel reserves. Over 2,000-mi. distances. JetStar would need an airport with 4,180 ft. of runway.

• JetStar's price includes full support services, such as pilot transition and both classroom and on-the-job training for mechanics employed by the purchaser, as well as a fully instrumented airplane. Also, Lockheed has formed an international network of factory representatives to aid JetStar customers.

Pilots lacking experience in turbine-powered aircraft may attend an optional three-day course covering the turbojet engine, meteorology, high speed flight, jet aircraft navigation, operation and use of radar and high altitude physiology. Normal two-week ground school follows this introduction, or refresher, and includes 4 hr. on the general airplane, 8 hr. on electrical systems, 12 hr. on hydraulics, 4 hr. on fuel, 12 hr. on the JT12A engine, 4 hr. on pneumatics, 4 hr. on radios and radar, 8 hr. on instruments and the autopilot, 16 hr. on performance and 8 hr. on JetStar operation.

Standard JetStar flight training involves 20 hr. of transition in the aircraft. This may be devoted to one pilot, or split between several. The average corporate pilot dispatched here earns an Airline Transport Rating in the JetStar after about 10 hr. of transition in the aircraft, Lockheed reports.

---

26. THE MICHIANA BAKING COMPANY*

The Industry

THE BAKING INDUSTRY IS COMPOSED of two main segments. The larger consisting of those firms producing bread, cakes, pies and other similar products for immediate consumption, accounts for 80% of the value of the total product. The remaining firms engage in the production of crackers, cookies, pretzels and other specialties. The three largest firms in the cracker and cookie segment are National Biscuit Company, with annual sales of over 400 million, Sunshine Biscuits, Inc., and United Biscuit of America with sales of approximately $100 million and $130 million, respectively.

To compensate for rising costs of labor, ingredients, and packaging materials, leading biscuit and cookie bakers have increased mechanization of equipment for mixing, cutting, baking and packaging. The entire manufacturing process for many types of these products is now completely automated.[1] Yet in spite of this, direct wages are reported to have absorbed one quarter to one third of the sales dollar in recent years.[2]

---

* This case was prepared by Professor Walter Kramer of Portland State College.
[1] Standard and Poor's Current Analysis, June 1960.
[2] Ibid.

The high cost of distribution is perhaps the most serious problem in the industry. While increased mechanization may have curbed the rise of production costs, distribution costs for a variety of reasons have continued to mount. The chain stores with their ability to price their private brands of soda, graham, and other such crackers significantly lower than the national brands, suggests some exception to this.

To expand volume, reduce unit distribution costs, and to increase profits, cracker and cookie bakers produce many varieties of such products. Stable crackers yield only modest profits. The addition of new, higher profit margin varieties has been generally beneficial. Most firms have not diversified beyond this. Sunshine Biscuit, however, has recently added potato chips and other such items to its lines.

The Michiana Baking Company

One of the oldest and most respected firms in the cracker and cookie baking industry, The Michiana Company has been responsible over the years for the introduction of many improvements and innovations in products, and production processes and equipment. The firm's net sales and net income for the past 10 years are shown below.

YEAR	NET SALES	NET INCOME
1950	$10,622,304	$240,870
1951	12,746,817	190,729
1952	13,658,478	226,909
1953	15,116,248	228,468
1954	14,314,042	152,106
1955	14,002,366	201,481
1956	15,109,761	189,876
1957	15,577,909	153,757
1958	16,060,795	17,994*
1959	16,094,296	158,181

* Deficit.

Net income for 1959 represented a significant improvement over the preceding year and in management's opinion was due to greater concentration of sales effort in new and more profitable items, increased efficiency and more stringent controls in production and distribution. To make the most efficient use of productive resources, to avoid idle capacity, and to stimulate demand, Michiana places continuous stress upon the development and introduction of new varieties with generally higher profit margins. The industry is so competitive, however, that successful new products are subject to quick imitation.

The officers of Michiana are keenly aware of the complex problems facing them and believe that the greatest opportunity for future profits is to be found in improved production methods, continued concentration on new products and constant attention to the development and implementation of new methods of distribution and sales.

Distribution of Michiana's Products

While cookies and crackers with the Michiana label may appear at various places throughout the world, the company's distribution is largely confined to that portion of the United States that lies east of the Rockies. For marketing purposes this area is divided into two parts. Zone 1, or the midwest region consists of the city in which the plant or bakery and general offices are located, and in addition the region immediately surrounding it, an area about 150 by 300 miles. Zone 2 consists of the balance of the market area or the rest of the United States in which the products are sold.

Approximately 60% of the sales volume measured in dollars or tonnage is sold and distributed in Zone 1 and the balance in Zone 2. With the exception of a very small number of house sales, the marketing of the products in Zone 2 is through independent distributors. These distributors may handle either cookies and crackers of a competitor along with Michiana products or only those of Michiana. The sales and distribution in Zone 1 are solely through company-owned branches, with one slight modification. In the city where the plant is located, sales are handled out of a city sales office separate from the plant but distribution is direct from the bakery. Exhibit I represents a diagram of the sales and distribution organization for Zone 1, the midwest region.

Each branch is divided into two divisions, one representing sales and one the physical distribution function. The sales force is under the supervision of Mr. George R. Jones, midwest sales manager who reports directly to Mr. E. H. Sperry, vice president in charge of sales. The Portal branch is an exception since it is under the direct supervision of Mr. Sperry.

The warehouse and distribution functions are supervised by Mr. L. L. Wrex who reports to Mr. L. N. White, treasurer. The distribution for the Metro branch is handled directly from the bakery.

Sales to chain stores are an important source of revenue for Michiana and require special handling. In the midwest region 65% of total volume is sold to such accounts. The General Sales staff, including four field supervisors, works with central buyers and store supervisors in this region. The central buyer of the chain decides whether or not one of Michiana's products should be put on or kept off the list of those items the local store manager may purchase. These buyers will limit the list of a particular company's products to those that they feel are most profitable. This ordinarily will be less than 25 of Michiana's 140 varieties. Often the addition of one variety will mean the dropping of another from the list. The chain salesmen working out of the local branches work with the local chain-store managers to sell those Michiana products that the store manager has been authorized to stock.

The division of the sales and physical distribution functions is typical in the cookie and cracker industry. Because these products are subject to deterioration and because of the intense competition in the field, it is important that the stock at all inventory locations be rotated and kept up to date, and that the best shelf position and presentation be attained. Constant attention to this housekeeping function is necessary to avoid excessive returns or what is worse, consumer dissatisfaction with the product because of staleness. Brand loyalty is thought to be insufficient to prevent the consumer from purchasing a competing product if the Michiana variety is not available. The problem of lost sales due to stockout is given considerable attention.

Under the circumstances the salesmen service the rack. All salesmen have assigned routes and call on all accounts with few exceptions at least once a week. When he calls on the store his job is to check the stock on the shelves, rearrange and rotate it if necessary. If the display is short, he gets the necessary additions from the stockroom. He checks the stock to see if it is sufficient, but not excessive to carry the store until he returns. He makes up an order for the necessary additional stock and has it authorized by the store manager or owner. He may arrange with the manager for special promotions for certain varieties. He may set up "end displays" that is, stacks of packages of a certain cookie or cracker at the end of aisles. Depending on the sales program, he may engage in this and other promotional activities as often as permitted by the store owner or manager. These activities are modified and adjusted according to the size and sales potential of the outlet.

At the end of the day the salesmen gather together their orders and give them to the office staff at the branch where the orders are filled from the inventory there. Orders from the sales staff at the Metro branch are filled from the bakery. Metro branch accounts for approximately 50% of the dollar volume of sales in the midwest region. All billing of credit accounts is done from the general office at the main plant.

Deliveries are made to the stores on the second day after the salesmen take the order. Generally the delivery man unloads the goods in the stockroom and gets a receipt. In a few circumstances he may also put goods on the shelf. In the case of cash customers he makes collections. With the exception of chain stores and institutional accounts most customers are on a cash basis. One delivery truck can service the routes of two to three salesmen. All deliveries are made on the first four days of each week because of the refusal of the chain stores to accept delivery on Fridays.

The branch operations manager is responsible for all operations at the branch except selling. This includes supervision of drivers and loading crews, and maintenance of adequate inventory of merchandise. Minimum inventory of each variety is determined by averaging the sales of the item for the previous four weeks and multiplying by 3.5 less the sum of stock on hand and stock on order. The inventory is reviewed each week to maintain the minimum.

Each branch has a minimum of three trucks; none except the Metro branch has more than six. In total the company operates 44 of its own trucks in the local service, including 18 that serve only the Metro area. Movement from the bakery to the branch is via common carrier truck.

Before World War II, Michiana served an area considerably beyond the midwest region through its own branches. During the war, because of gasoline and tire restrictions, as well as other reasons, all branches beyond the midwest region were closed and distribution and sales entrusted to independent distributors. After the war was over, one of these branches was re-established. Two years ago the territory was again assigned to an independent distributor. At the same time, four branches in the midwest region were closed and their territory divided among the remaining branches. This resulted in larger territories for the salesmen, larger quotas, greater volume and lower costs for the remaining branches. Management indicates that they are interested in further possibilities of using independent distributors but that such organizations with adequate financial responsibility, coverage of the market, warehouse facilities, transportation equipment and personnel, are difficult to find. Of primary concern is the proper service of the chain store accounts.

At present the discount arrangement with the independent distributors in Zone 2 is as follows: On carload or truckload shipments, a quantity discount of 25% of list price is allowed. In addition, a scale of quantity discounts permits a distributor to earn as much as 2% more in discounts. The quantity discount on less than carload or less than truckload shipments is 20%. The cash discount is 1%. There is no advertising discount for distributors. Michiana pays full minimum freight charges on all carload or truckload shipments. On less than carload or truckload shipments, freight charges, prorated on the carload or truckload rate, are absorbed by Michiana.

Expansion of the distribution facilities at the bakery faces some serious hurdles. The plant itself is effectively hemmed in on three sides. It has no loading dock at tailgate level. The dock can accommodate only three trucks at a time. There is little area for storage of trucks; nor is there a garage. What driveway facilities there are, are seriously congested. During the peak production periods, January, February and March, storage facilities are inadequate and additional space must be sought nearby.

Experiments were conducted a few years ago in the use of driver-salesmen in outlying areas. According to Mr. Wrex this was discontinued as unsuccessful. The truck salesmen could not get over the route one-third as quickly as the salesmen, nor were they as effective in the promotion function.

Some thought has been given to the possible cost savings of leased trucks as against the operation of company-owned trucks. However, as Mr. Wrex put it, "Certainly the lessor has to make a profit and we save that cost by operating our own trucks and furthermore, our trucks are of various ages and replacement costs are never very large at any one time."

Mr. Wrex is aware that perhaps some deliveries, because of their size, do not cover costs. On the other hand, since marginal costs of delivery vary so widely no minimum order restriction has been established. "As long as we are driving past the account we may as well stop and pick up the extra sales," he commented. It is suspected that it might be useful to know more about the profit contribution of the various products.

Mr. Wrex is aware that inefficiency in the distribution of Michiana's products can have a serious and significant effect upon the firm's profit and he is engaged in a constant search for lower distribution costs. He was particularly concerned about the situation at the Niles branch for which he had just received the operating statement for the last four weeks. This statement is shown as Exhibit II.

The Niles branch serves approximately 2,400 accounts, or 10.6% of the total accounts of Zone 1. Although the territory of this branch is largely rural, chain stores account for 38% of sales volume. The breakdown of accounts by types of outlet is as follows:

Supermarket chains	3.8%
Smaller chain outlets	1.9
Independent supermarkets	3.8
Independent stores	
(Sales of less than $15 list per week)	71.6
Charitable or government	3.8
Restaurant	13.2
Not Classifiable	1.9
Total	100.0%

EXHIBIT I

THE MICHIANA BAKING COMPANY

MIDWEST REGION

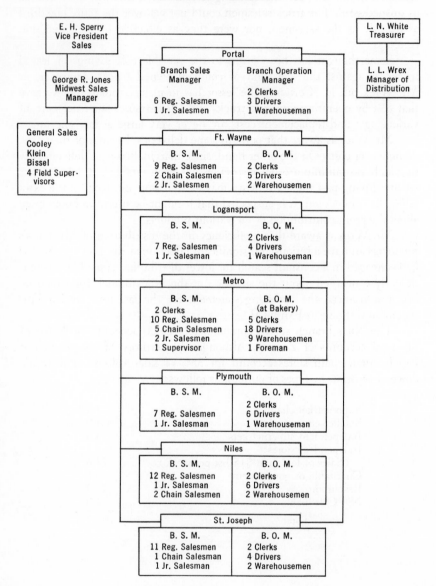

EXHIBIT II
THE MICHIANA BAKING COMPANY
NILES BRANCH

	4 WEEKS	%
Sales at list price	56534	
Returns at list price	1146	
Net sales at list price	55388	100.00%
Cost of goods sold	33150	59.85
Gross margin	22238	40.15
Trade discounts	2594	4.68
Promotional discounts	0	0
All other discounts	92	.17
Total discounts	2686	4.85%
Loss on returned merchandise	1046	1.89
Sales, salaries and commission	5762	10.38
Salesmen's expenses, reimbursed	202	.37
Samples	228	.41
Headquarters sales office	146	.26
Branch office manager's salary	814	1.47
Sales supervisor's salary	684	1.24
Sales supervisor's expense	130	.23
Sales promotion expense	126	.23
Agency advertising expense	3904	7.05
Coop. advertising	942	1.70
Payroll tax	840	.87
Total sales expense	14464	26.10%
Shipping room—finished goods and traffic expense	392	.71
Shipping dock, plant	352	.69
Freight and drayage	434	.78
Agency building expense	812	1.47
Drivers' wages	2382	4.30
Misc. delivery expense	186	.34
Gas and oil	324	.58
Truck repairs	216	.39
Truck depreciation	34	.06
Truck insurance and taxes	116	.21
Payroll taxes and insurance	280	.50
Total warehouse & delivery exp.	7740	13.99%
Total operating expense	24890	44.94%
Operating profit	(2652)*	(4.79)*
Admin. and other costs	1220	2.20
Net before taxes	(3872)*	(6.99)*

* Deficit.

27. U.S. AIRCRAFT CORPORATION

THE AUSTIN COMPONENT PARTS PLANT of the U.S. Aircraft Corporation was constructed in 1941 to provide facilities for the manufacture of reciprocating engine accessories for the military services during World War II.

Through the subsequent Korean conflict fabrication and machining had been keyed to high-volume output of a limited variety of jet engine parts. Accessories were produced for a single model during much of that period. The defense procurement picture changed rapidly after Korea to one which featured low-volume, largely development work on new jet engines of greatly increased thrust. These new engines required the newer high-temperature alloys which tended to be difficult to process efficiently under familiar processing techniques. By the fall of 1956, the plant was converted to primarily a sheet metal shop engaged in fabricating and heat treating such parts as combustion casings, liners, exhaust nozzles, and guide vanes for jet engine power plants.

Prior to 1958, equipment layout and control systems had been developed to deal with a relatively large volume output of similar parts. For example, most manufacturing operations had been subjected to detailed planning, down to individual tasks, in order to promote standard, high-volume production. Processing operations, once largely machining, changed to largely sheet metal forming and welding in nature. Production shifted to more complex parts for more sophisticated power plants, of which there were more models. An inevitable result was more operations and more pieces to each assembly. Tooling became much more complex for the required sheet metal work, primarily because forming dies were essential even for the very short production runs encountered under the new procurement pattern.

Output had decreased about 50% during the period from 1956–57. Direct labor manpower was reduced proportionately during this period, while indirect labor manpower was reduced more slowly. Direct labor payroll averaged about 20% of output value, while manufacturing overhead (including indirect labor) was at a level of 56% of output value in 1957.

Manufacturing overhead expenses failed to fall as rapidly as output until a cost reduction drive was initiated in late 1957. The drive resulted in the removal from the payroll of most of the time-study personnel and production dispatchers. This group of time-study personnel had been used to set piece prices on new jobs along with minor day-to-day methods work. Dispatchers had been used to assign specific jobs to the production workers, both jobs which had been priced as well as unpriced jobs (day-work).

Between 1957 and late 1958, average incentive hourly earnings rose from $2.75 per hour to $3.60 per hour (not including cost-of-living adjustment). Production, measured in terms of percentage of shipping date promises kept to promises made, dropped from about 65% to 35%.

A combination of other factors further contributed to the rise in costs and low-level performance. The greater variety of products and declining volume resulted in lower production runs. New high-temperature resistant materials tended to be brittle which, along with unfamiliar processing requirements and tighter tolerances, led to serious shortcomings in quality performance. More frequent and extensive rework also contributed to the failure to meet original schedules.

A review of the performance of the Austin plant caused consideration of possible closing of the plant if the performance could not be improved in early 1958. The decision was made by the U.S. Aircraft management to continue operation of the plant but under a new manager. Mr. George Holley, the new manager, the seventh since 1942, was told he had one year to prove that the plant could be restored to competitive operation under his management.

Competitive operation refers to the need for the Austin plant to offer its services in competition with outside suppliers for available subcontract business. Price, quality, and delivery were basic factors in determining which suppliers received production contracts. The Austin plant was notably deficient in all three factors by early 1958. Examples of performance deficiencies were:

1. Deliveries averaged eight weeks behind schedule, with delivery dates met about 35% of the time.
2. Manufacturing cycle exceeded planned cycle by five weeks.
3. Rework and extra work totaled 19% of planned labor.
4. The parent company's main assembly plant was re-inspecting 100% of all parts received from Austin.
5. Less than 35% of the available business from the parent company was produced by the Austin plant.
6. Direct labor incentive earnings averaged 61% over expected rates.
7. Actual over-all unit costs exceeded budgeted costs by 22%.
8. Cost of quality (control) approximated 15% of output costs.
9. Total Manufacturing Loss Account (work in excess of planned) exceeded $¾ million.
10. At the labor load then current, overhead appeared to be high by $1 million.
11. A major contract on which costs averaged $5,000 per unit was subsequently lost to a competitor who bid $1,200 per unit, while a second competitor bid $2,000.

The new plant manager, Mr. George Holley, had been engaged in manufacturing staff work for U.S. Aircraft Corporation, although he had held a variety of line positions since working his way up through the ranks from a machine shop apprentice about 25 years before. In his new position as plant manager he became eligible for the company's management incentive compensation plan.

On his first day in his new position, Holley called all top-level staff to a meeting in his office where he introduced himself and announced his immediate plans. At this meeting he repeated the one-year ultimatum to get competitive, and he requested that all his staff think through carefully the major problems with which they were faced and what they were planning to do about those problems. Each was asked to prepare a report to that effect and present it as soon as possible to be reviewed by Holley as a basis for subsequent action. With that they were excused. Upon departing, one of the functional managers remarked, "I don't need to write any report—I already know what is wrong—nobody will cooperate with me in getting out production." Holley found three of his staff lacking, these being replaced shortly thereafter.

As of May 1958, the organization of the plant was in general as shown in Exhibit I. Subsequent changes completed by May, 1959, may be noted by comparing Exhibit II with Exhibit I.

Mr. Holley recognized that the shop employees and the union in particular were waiting to see what action would be taken; so he decided to present his views to them as soon as feasible. Three months later he called a general meeting for each shift for such a purpose. The following are some quotations from that first talk to all employees:

> I've asked your supervisors to invite you here so that I can give you first-hand some information about our problems—and our plans to correct them.
> Most of you have been told by one means or another . . . that we had to make drastic changes—and make them fast—or lose to competition.
> Under war-time conditions, normal competitive practices often need to be pushed aside to gain the objective—namely, to win the war. Obviously, the loose practices prevalent in war-time cannot be allowed under normal competitive conditions.
> Manufacturers who once worked with us in winning a war are now competing against us for the limited available business.
> To obtain this new (job shop) business, our plant must change . . . it must learn to adapt itself to working under continuous product design changes and continuous manufacturing changes. A year ago our situation was precisely that we were trying to perform work under left-over war-time, mass-production conditions.
> It is no secret that we are on trial and that we are fighting to prove that we can be a competitive business. Reasons: poor quality, poor deliveries, and high costs.

To win this struggle for survival we must recognize that quality, delivery, and costs are the fundamentals of competition . . . and that these are the elements which we must learn so well that they influence and control every action that we perform.

Our objective must be to improve our quality, delivery, and manufacturing costs to the point where we are absolutely the best in all these categories.

Our customers who purchase components . . . rate quality as being more important than either delivery or costs. Our quality last year was far from being acceptable in the eyes of all customers. Only in this way can we beat any competition, anywhere, anytime.

I would like to underscore that this is a real tough job.

He concluded his detailed recital of progress made to date with the following:

Our progress charts clearly indicate that our decisions (changes in organization, control procedures, etc.) have been correct so far.

We've turned down the right road. We're a bit late, and the road ahead is rough—this means a lot of cooperation and hard work.

I can understand some people disagreeing with the precise method or details of a particular situation, but I can't understand why some people think that the way to disagree is to interrupt work—especially when interruption does tremendous damage to everybody in the plant.

As your plant manager, it is my task to develop leadership and a team, of which you are all members, that will win. I shall continue to work through this leadership to apply a dynamic, winning plan for the revival of this business. Today I seek your support in carrying it out.

Major Changes Initiated by Holley During His First Two Years as Plant Manager

A. SHOP OPERATIONS

Shop operations was viewed as the area most in need of immediate reorganization. Mr. Holley called for Mr. Walter Kramer, a graduate of a large midwestern engineering school who had worked for U.S. Aircraft Corporation for about 20 years in various line and manufacturing staff assignments, to take on this assignment. Kramer was given an "indefinite assignment" for several months to give him an opportunity to survey operations thoroughly and formulate his plan of action, after which time he replaced the "temporary" production superintendent and proceeded to put his reorganizational plan into effect.

Principal organizational changes may be noted by comparing Exhibit II with Exhibit I. All planning functions, dealing with how work was to be done on the floor, such as process drawings, methods, tools, job rates and materials lists, were taken from Manufacturing Engineering; Production Control, dealing with scheduling, dispatching, expediting and materials requisitioning, was reinstated as a technical staff under the new position of Manager–Shop Operations. These organizational changes were felt to be necessary because, according to Kramer, "If there are any groups of people who should be working together (under a single boss), it is these three. After this change, we began to function as we should."

"The next big problem (after the above changes were made) was one of setting goals and measurements to determine progress toward those goals," stated Kramer. "As I saw it," he continued, "most of our foremen were very capable men—all they needed was leadership, strong support, and the realization that we expected the very best from them thereafter— and furthermore, we were going to get it."

The first goal was to regain control over direct labor performance. A study was undertaken by a management trainee to determine how badly out of kilter the job pricing and incentive payment plan was. The major conclusion of this study was that "there is every indication that the piecework incentive system is out of control." At that time the average pieceworker's earnings were about 61% over ERE (expected rate of earnings). Causes contributing to such a state of affairs were found to be: (1) excessive looseness in "standards," permitting the worker to earn what he chose, and (2) lack of control over work performed, permitting pieceworkers to charge excessive time to daywork operations, while actually working on piecework jobs and building up average earnings.

At the time of the study, it was estimated that pieceworkers were spending their time as follows: (a) 3% on jobs with standard prices (believed to be fairly dependable),[1] (b) 8% on jobs with special prices (believed to be reasonably dependable),[2] (c) 39% on jobs with temporary prices (of doubtful validity),[3] and (d) 50% on jobs with no prices (i.e., daywork).[4] Of the daywork jobs (50%), 28% had estimated times and 22% had no estimates placed on them.

A sample study of jobs performed indicated that on daywork jobs with

---

[1] "Standard" piece prices were those prices set where the manufacturing method had been established. The labor contract provided that there would be no change in a "standard" price except where there was a change in manufacturing method.

[2] "Special" piece prices were those prices set where the work priced usually repeated itself infrequently, or was in small quantities, or had some special feature or purpose.

[3] "Temporary" piece prices were those prices set where the manufacturing method was under development or had been changed, or the average pieceworker on the job had not yet attained normal performance.

[4] For daywork jobs performed by incentive workers, payments were usually based on 85% or 100% of average earnings, depending upon circumstances surrounding the job when work was performed.

estimated times, pieceworkers were only 46% efficient (e.g., jobs priced to require 114.8 hours required 251.2 hours to complete). However, on jobs with temporary prices (standards), a sample study of jobs performed indicated that the pieceworker's efficiencies averaged 158% (e.g., jobs priced to require 905.4 hours only took 571.5 hours to perform). The net effect of this situation was that work which was expected to cost $87 per week for the typical operator was instead costing $130 per week, based on an expected rate of earnings of $2.25 per hour and a daywork rate of 85% of average incentive earnings.

Piecework earnings estimates were predicated on a base rate of $2.25 per hour for the average qualified incentive worker, based on the going rate for comparable work in the metal trades in the community. By working at an "incentive pace" the well-motivated worker was expected to earn an additional 10% to 25%. In late 1958 the average incentive worker was, in fact, earning 61% over his expected rate of earnings.[5] Thus, in fact, the $2.25 per hour worker was expected to earn about $2.76 per hour but actually was earning $3.61 per hour.[6] For non-incentive workers, rates varied from about $1.50 per hour to $3.50 per hour for top skills. During this period, the average dayworker received about $2.45 per hour.

The first corrective step taken was to put piecework prices on all jobs (rework included) as soon as possible. Within two years' time, 95% of all operations were priced (with 25% having standard prices and 70% having temporary prices). Stopwatch time studies were used initially. Later, standard data charts were used exclusively to set standards. For initial temporary prices, main reliance was placed upon the job knowledge of foremen, each of whom was required to reprice all "temporary" piecework prices in their departments—on the basis of what they "knew" the job could be done for.[7] In most cases, the temporary piecework prices were arbitrarily reduced in half, which set up strong objections by the union.

After one year the net effect of the above changes was to reduce direct labor costs by approximately 37%. An estimated 17% decrease in cost resulted from removing the opportunity to work on unpriced jobs, thereby requiring a more sustained "incentive" effort on the part of the workers. Another 20% decrease was attributed to the downward adjustment in temporary prices.

Kramer estimated that, with one more year of intensive effort, another 15% reduction in direct labor cost would be possible by carrying out

---

[5] Various work groups, in fact, earned at different rates in excess of their ERE. The lower their ERE, relatively, the higher their rate exceeded that level. The net effect of this action was to virtually equalize take-home pay of each group.

[6] All wages and salaries were subject to a cost-of-living adjustment of about 8%.

[7] The contract provided that the company would "replace a temporary price with a standard price in six months if reasonably possible under the circumstances."

a systematic program of methods improvements and by setting up accurate standards based on a satisfactory working pace for all jobs. Standard data charts were under development from data obtained from other plants and previous time studies which could be used to expedite establishing all job standards thereafter.

The second corrective step undertaken by Kramer was to develop a workable system for measuring the performance of his production foremen. He established what were referred to as "foremen accountability" meetings monthly. In addition to the foremen, his general foreman, and Kramer, there would be in attendance a representative of planning, quality control, labor relations, time standards, and cost. Accountability charts were prepared for each foreman, detailing his department's performance in regard to the following factors: (1) labor variance as a percent of total planned labor, by total and by key subdivisions such as set-up, day-work, overrun, rework, and wage adjustments; (2) percent of piecework jobs priced; (3) schedule promises kept, by item; (4) percent attained of cost reduction goal as determined by plant manager on an over-all basis, then allocated; (5) total scrapped material, by dollar value; (6) realization of manufacturing loss budgeted, based on planned labor (i.e., labor spent for "rework," "extra cost," and "make-right" over and above labor time required for good output); (7) worker injury record; (8) "housekeeping" rating; (9) direct payroll supervised; and (10) inspection and failure cost as a percent of planned labor. At each monthly meeting the chart for the foreman present was discussed and he was asked to comment on his recorded performance. Any matter affecting areas of interest of the staff men (planning, time study, etc.) present could be discussed directly with that person concerned. Kramer used these meetings to give a brief (5–10 minute) presentation to each foreman on where the plant as a whole stood in regard to cost goals, delivery promises, and quality improvement, so that the foreman was cognizant of the broad picture.

A third corrective step taken during this period was to develop and implement a supervisory cost reduction program. The system was based upon the allocation of a plant-wide bogey (established somewhat arbitrarily by the plant manager) to all unit supervisors, who in turn were required to establish unit cost reduction committees to plan for the achievement of allocated cost reductions bogeys in their units. Each unit committee (over 20 in the plant) had a chairman and a secretary, counseled with the unit supervisor, and reported projects undertaken and dollar savings achieved monthly to the Manager–Shop Operations. Those committees that exceed bogeys received recognition and consideration for promotion and rate increases. In 1960 with a goal of $513,000 in savings, half-year results reported 193% progress.

The fourth major corrective step taken at this time was to reorient the personnel in their approach to the problem of planning and controlling production under job-shop conditions. The former Planning Supervisor was returned to his old position of general foreman, where he had an excellent performance record. He had taken his best foremen with him into Planning, even though they were not experienced in planning. Because these men proved to be trainable, they were retrained in Planning and paper-work procedures and they were retained by the new Supervisor. A new Planning Supervisor capable of planning complex operations under job-shop conditions operations was promoted from within the plant.[8] A new Production Control Supervisor was brought in from outside when the former Production Control Supervisor could not adjust to new requirements and was fired. Component parts for product assemblies were scheduled into and out of a foreman's department on the basis of newly-determined manufacturing cycles for each product. Each foreman was made responsible for getting the parts out within his allotted time cycle, which varied from two to ten weeks in the plant, in addition to the six-week cycle for the contributing parts department. Each general foreman was provided with all needed materials and was thereafter responsible for getting a completed assembly out before the due date.

Temporary relief from schedule pile-up was afforded the new Manager–Shop Operations when the plant manager sought to bid for new contracts only where there was a definite chance to meet the delivery time and cost estimates involved. That policy tended to prevent overloading shop operations with resultant loss of control over costs and delivery schedules. Control was maintained by strongly insisting that shop planners come up with facts upon which intelligent bids could be based.

Obviously, quality control procedures had a decided effect upon shop operations so Kramer was vitally interested in the development of more effective procedures by the new manager of Quality Control. Kramer's major complaint had been the effect of the former manager's attempt to cut costs by failing to provide for effective in-process inspection in the plant. The result of no in-process inspection was a high frequency of faulty parts being introduced into product assemblies. A high incidence of rework and extra cost work, as well as missed delivery promises, resulted.

B. QUALITY CONTROL

Mr. Jim Logan, the new manager for Quality Control, had been associated with U.S. Aircraft in a wide variety of assignments, in addition

---

[8] Under the old planning system, plans once made could be used long after, possibly to produce as many as 10,000 parts. Thus, time and effort could be expended to plan operations in great detail. Untrained labor could also be utilized readily when plans were greatly detailed. By 1958, shop runs had been reduced to an average of 100, with frequent changes in design, making detailed planning too costly and time consuming.

to having worked previously at the Austin plant. Logan was chosen to develop a quality control system in the Austin plant about six months after Holley took charge. Up to the time of Logan's arrival, Quality Control was looked after directly by Holley. Logan believed that the problems encountered trying to control quality at the Austin plant were primarily caused by a failure to adopt a total quality control concept. His plan for improvement in quality began with an attempt to establish control over quality from initial receiving of materials, through fabrication and final assembly, and to the receipt of the product in good condition by the customer.

The former plant organization had a very limited quality control function applied across-the-board for all products. Quality foremen supervised final inspection of products. (See Exhibit I.)

Three product lines were chosen as the basis for the new assignment of quality responsibilities. A Quality Control engineer was put in charge of planning for the quality problem in each product line. Under his supervision in each product group were three subfunctions: (1) process control engineering, charged mainly with responsibility for handling complaints on the production line; (2) quality control planning, charged mainly with planning inspection procedures and equipment; and (3) quality control foremen, charged with responsibility for carrying out a "preventive inspection" procedure at all steps in the production process of his product line. A new position of advanced quality control engineer was set up, with the incumbent responsible for the formulation of advanced plans and any newly acquired across-product line quality responsibilities.[9]

Logan devoted considerable effort to develop internally the qualified staff necessary to operate under his new plan. Frequent staff meetings were held to explain what had been developed and what performance was expected of each man in Quality Control. Numerous night-time off-duty training sessions were held to up-grade skills. As a result of those efforts, Logan believed that a considerable esprit-de-corps had been built up and as a result turnover of quality control personnel was held to a relatively low level, considering the extensive changes brought about, including the substantial up-grading in skills required.

As performance of the quality control personnel improved, and as they were able to inspire and enforce quality improvements on the line, it became evident that 100% inspection could be replaced by sampling as dependability increased. Customers became willing to use sampling at their receiving inspection stations.

In line with the top-level desire for measurement, wherever possible,

---

[9] See Exhibit III for a fuller explanation.

Logan began the development of a plan to measure quality performance of line foremen, viewing this as a function of the performance of his own staff. The basic measure developed was referred to as "quality costs by foremen," which related appraisal cost (cost of inspection) and failure cost (cost of scrap, rework, sorting) as a percent of planned labor expenditure in each foreman's area.[10] Large charts were prepared showing in rank order the position of each foreman relative to other foremen and in respect to appraisal and failure cost percentages. Detail charts indicated the dollar amounts in categories of quality cost for each foreman. These records informed the foreman of all quality costs charged to his record, in addition to showing how he ranked in relation to all other foremen in the plant. In addition, the charts indicated by color coding which Quality Cost man was responsible for which foreman, and therefore how much Quality Cost cost was charged to each Quality Cost engineer.

One indication of progress made in regaining control over quality costs was the record in regard to repair cycles.[11] In 1958 one major product required an average of 18 repair cycles per product unit before final acceptance, each cycle costing an average of $50. By 1960, under the reorganized plan of operation, the average number of repair cycles per product unit had been reduced to four. Another indicator of progress was the decline of quality costs to a level of about 12% of output costs by 1960.

C. MANUFACTURING ENGINEERING

Mr. Hal Stevenson had some 15 years' experience in a variety of line and staff assignments with U.S. Aircraft. At the Austin plant, the manufacturing engineering function had been considerably reduced in extent by the time Stevenson was brought in to supervise this function about six months after Holley became plant manager. Even previous to Holley, a cost-cutting drive had effectively stripped the department of time study personnel. (See Exhibits I and II.)

Stevenson concentrated his corrective efforts in three areas: (1) reorganization of the maintenance function and modernization of equipment to reduce heavy maintenance costs, (2) tightening of control over tooling, planning, and costs, and (3) establishment of a long-range methods improvement program to reduce processing costs.

Maintenance problems arose largely out of past maintenance practices as well as present equipment obsolescence. Approximately 70% of

---

[10] Quality costs included, in addition to the two above costs, "prevention" costs. The cost of quality engineering and planning to prevent discrepant parts being made.

[11] A repair cycle was the time required to "back-up" a product after a defect had been discovered, then to undo or correct that defect, and return the product for further processing.

all machine tools were over 18 years old. Many of these machines had been operated on a high-volume, three-shift basis for most of that period; thus they were well-worn and generally inadequate for tight tolerance work. Maintenance labor standards were largely non-existent. Replacement of old and inadequate machine tools was not planned systematically. Most of the major machine tools were government-owned and replacement generally was restricted to tools from government surplus stocks when contract requirements justified such action.

Stevenson set up a separate maintenance records unit under his direction to handle the problem of government facilities responsibility. All matters pertaining to government facilities (land, plant, and equipment) as required by regulation were the responsibility of this unit (all records, reports, factory layouts, and preparation of proposals to replace machinery and equipment). The government facilities unit undertook to justify substantial requests for new machine tools from government surplus stocks to provide machines capable of holding tighter tolerances, capable of faster rates of output and subject to lower maintenance costs. In addition, new equipment expenditures were requested from company funds, although such equipment addition and replacement requests by the Austin plant were generally subjected to a two-year payout criterion by company management.

Maintenance labor had been under consideration for a work sampling study to develop useful standards of performance, although that program was temporarily shelved when labor misunderstanding developed. Historical maintenance cost records were available only for each machine tool group.

Two manufacturing engineering specialists devoted full time to the investigation of all high-cost elements in each major product. Materials, tooling, and processes were subjected to analysis designed to bring about long-range processing cost reductions.[12] Planning time was also devoted on a minor scale to work-simplification projects.

Goals for cost reduction resulting from methods improvements were set for the department by the plant manager to insure continuing progress in the over-all cost reduction goals for the plant each year.

Stevenson was faced with the necessity of tightening control over tool and die expenses, especially that portion chargeable to indirect labor. All tool and die labor devoted to specific contracts was chargeable to direct labor. Formerly when declining demand for tooling labor resulted in excess manpower, the extra labor time was used for miscellaneous tasks and charged to indirect manufacturing expense. Stevenson's approach to expense control was to develop forecasts of tooling labor required to sup-

---

[12] See Exhibit IV for examples of improvements adopted as a result of work by this group in 1959.

port specific contracts. Work forces were then adjusted quickly by temporary layoffs or hires to compensate for fluctuating demand, with a resultant 23% decrease in the amount of tooling labor charged to overhead in 1959.

D. MATERIALS

Under the pre-Holley organization, Jim Sheehan, Manager–Materials, had been responsible for all day-to-day production control activities and materials, requisitioning, as well as purchasing, receiving, and shipping. According to Holley's appraisal of this unit, Sheehan's organization was "weak, without good procedures, and he was so busy putting out fires that he didn't have time to do his own job."

Many of the difficulties referred to above were attributable to the constantly changing nature of the product mix as the plant shifted to low-volume developmental work utilizing new and unfamiliar materials, some of which, such as Rene '41, required the development of additional sources of supply.

Lacking any marketing organization at the plant level, customer relations suffered and customer liaison was virtually nonexistent on a planned basis. No specific person or unit was assigned solely the responsibility to maintain control over engineering changes or schedule changes coming in from their customers. Lacking delegation of authority in this area, the plant manager was undoubtedly often involved directly in such matters.

Sheehan, with over 30 years of experience in U.S. Aircraft Corporation, was retained by Holley to bring about tighter control over his key function of purchasing and inventory control. Production control was shifted to the Manager–Shop Operations. Added to Sheehan's responsibilities were those of customer liaison—all contacts with customers were thereafter to be coordinated by him to bring about improvement in relations with customers by bringing to their attention services provided by the Austin plant and by serving as a means of processing customers' complaints and suggestions.

After Production Control was shifted to the Manager–Shop Operations, Sheehan's materials group could give greater emphasis to purchasing activities and to controlling inventory levels in relation to output volume and product mix. A desirable ratio of inventory to annual sales volume was considered to be about $1 of inventory to $5–$6 of annual output (depending on the product mix). Previously inventory reduction lagged behind output declines, ranging as high as $1 of inventory to $4 in output. By mid-1960, inventories had been reduced to a $1–$5 ratio.

Inventory control procedure emphasized controlled ordering of materials based on master production schedules and on lead times required to process material in the shop and on purchase lead times for critical materials. Auditing of materials use on the shop floor was also carried on.

Tentative purchasing schedules were developed every six months based upon master production schedules with actual buying based on a three-month period and with deliveries scheduled to provide for minimum stocks of raw materials on hand.

The basic materials procedure was outlined as follows:

1. Planning developed a master materials list from assembly drawings.
2. Materials list was then sent to Production Control who then developed from the master schedule a detailed list of materials necessary for each product by time periods.
3. The Order Group in Production Control combined materials requirements into purchase requisitions which were forwarded to Materials for actual purchase.
4. Purchase order was prepared by Materials and forwarded to qualified vendors, subject to any company-wide commitments.
5. Incoming Quality Inspection reported to Materials when goods were received and they measured up to established specifications, after which they were stored under control of Materials.
6. When needed for production, Production Control would requisition and Materials would physically release to the shop.

Consideration was given to economical quantities in making purchasing commitments by adjusting the three-month purchase period as necessary. Fabrication of standard parts (often referred to as contributing parts—small, commonly used), in the shop was based on economic lot size calculations where press setups were involved.[13] Other processing operations were not considered sufficiently important volume-wise to justify departure from processing order quantities.

E. EMPLOYEE RELATIONS

The employee relations function had been organized with Kirk Woods, as the manager, reporting directly to the Relations manager located at headquarters. Holley requested that the employee relations manager thereafter report directly to him so that he could be fully informed and on top of the touchy labor relations situation he faced in his efforts to tighten control of labor performance at the Austin plant. Closer coordination was made possible between line supervision and union relations staff as a result of the change.

Kirk Woods had almost 20 years of service in employee relations work with U.S. Aircraft Corporation and was well-known in the Austin community. His scope of operations under Holley did not change much except to add salary administration to the typical functions performed in employee relations departments. The company policy, as he viewed it, was to pro-

---

[13] All make-or-buy decisions made by Planning based on available facilities or ability to make.

vide all those services which the Austin plant needed to operate effectively and which it could afford to carry.

The Austin plant had long been organized by an active, aggressive, and strong union. For nonexempt workers, strict seniority prevailed for all job changes. Performance standards were accepted by the workers along with an incentive wage payment system, subject to typical limitations in the labor contract regarding changing of standard times or prices.

According to Mr. Woods, labor relations could be characterized as having been "peaceful" in the past, with a minimum of discipline imposed on the workers.

Mr. Woods said that Mr. Holley had succeeded in developing sufficient integration in management attitudes all down the line so that in all of the problems encountered he (Woods) and his union relations staff had been supported all the way. Viewed in retrospect, Woods believed that Holley had "stiffened the spines" of the people dealing with the workers and the union, so that when discipline was imposed and standards were introduced or tightened up, each supervisor and employee relations man was able to function more effectively than in the past. When the union business manager asked Holley to discuss with him the standards changes, Holley refused to do so, stating that his employee relations manager was at the plant for that purpose.

Tightening of standards met considerable resistance on the part of the workers affected, with 12 formal grievances filed and with several "walkouts" resulting because of the piece pricing program.

When new prices were announced in September, 1958, for one area, the workers requested a meeting on company time to discuss the issue and were refused. As a result, 25 people "walked off" the job without processing a grievance as required in the labor contract.[14] The 25 workers were penalized with a three-day layoff without pay. The union considered the penalty unnecessarily severe and filed a grievance, processing it through all three steps. With an adverse ruling from company management, the union called a strike for a period of three days.

One month later, the 25 people from the punch press department mentioned above started a job "sit down," for which they received a one-day layoff. Ultimately a grievance was processed through arbitration and the penalty was upheld by an "impartial arbiter" as "reasonable."

Several months later, the same operators again filed a grievance over standard prices. Along with 175 other employees, they participated in an

---

[14] "There shall be no strike, sitdown, slowdown, employee demonstration or any other organized or concerted interference with work of any kind in connection with any matter subject to the grievance procedure . . . unless and until all of the respective provisions of the successive steps of the grievance procedure . . . have been complied with, or if the matter is submitted to arbitration. . . ."

"illegal" work stoppage for which a three-day layoff penalty was imposed. The *Union News* reported to their members the following:

> The union will lodge a vigorous protest against the Company's scrapping of an agreement on rates in Austin at a company level grievance meeting next week.
>
> Austin workers are up in arms over this arbitrary action (down-grading of job rates) by the Company. It was the same case that caused the Austin people to walk out several months ago.
>
> Austin workers are determined that they will not yield to any management attempt to introduce charted prices nor to attacks on the present wage structure.

The grievance was then processed through the full procedure with no change in the company position and no further strike or work stoppage by the union on this issue.

A different group of workers became involved in a grievance when the plant dispatchers (hourly rated, nonexempt workers, subject to wages and hours law) complained about the imposition of additional duties without increases in compensation. In this dispute the *Union News* took a strong stand as follows:

> Following notification that their request for a classification upgrade had been turned down by Company management, the dispatchers at Austin Plant have voted unanimously to strike.
>
> Management has heaped more and more responsibility upon the dispatchers without increasing the rate of pay of the group.
>
> Fed up with the increase in responsibility with no increase in pay, the dispatchers filed a grievance demanding the job responsibilities be reviewed and the rate increased.
>
> No progress has been made at steps one and two, despite recommendations from Company supervisors close to the job that the rate be increased (two steps or more).
>
> Disillusioned and disgusted with management's attitude, the Austin dispatchers are determined that they will militantly fight for their rights.

The grievance was processed through all three steps, with management insisting that the dispatchers had not previously been assigned a fair day's work. In March, 1960, 180 people walked out for a meeting for one-half hour, which was contractually legal, then all returned to work except the dispatchers who remained away for several days. No penalty was imposed as it was a "legal" strike.

The last in this series of walkouts occurred when some 70 other operators walked out for two days in March, 1960, to protest adjustments of temporary piece prices on their work. Since all steps in the grievance procedure had not been utilized, the work interruption was "illegal" and a one-day layoff penalty was imposed by management. The union objected bitterly, suggesting new management was in order.

Again, from the *Union News:*

Austin operators unanimously endorse strike by secret ballot.

The dispute, which revolves around slashes in temporary prices has been boiling for some time. In fact, it grew so hot that the operators staged a two-day demonstration for which the company has slapped them with a one-day layoff penalty.

Why is it that when this plant has finally secured plenty of orders and production is flowing smoothly some company "lame-brain" takes it upon himself to agitate the workers and upset the production schedule.

Maybe a shakeup in management should be considered at this plant.

Woods stated that penalties were determined in staff meetings after having considered what was necessary to discourage deliberate interruptions when so much work was behind schedule. He further stated that the employees (if not the local union stewards) had taken much of this penalty action with understanding.

F. ACCOUNTING

The accounting organization remained relatively unaffected since the plant accountant continued to report to company headquarters rather than directly to the plant manager.

Accounting reports were subject to some change in order to take into account the drive to reduce costs and the different basis headquarters used to measure the Austin plant. Additional cost analysis work was performed and there was an increased emphasis on the importance of providing the kind of cost data and counsel to management that would assist them in taking corrective action to reduce costs. The key items of cost and expense were subjected to close scrutiny. Particular emphasis was placed on reporting promptly the ratio of unplanned to planned direct labor. Unplanned labor refers to inspection, rework, extra costs, setup, etc. Planned labor refers to that labor which represents good pieces that will be shipped to customers. Some manufacturing loss was accepted as normal to their operations. However, attempts through mid-1960 were unsuccessful in reducing this amount below $350,000.

An intensive review of manufacturing overhead expenses was made each quarter, and budgets were established for the subsequent quarter.

Some further indication of the progress made in reducing over-all costs may be obtained from the following analysis showing the reduction in cost of the same parts from 1958 to 1960.

	1958	1959	1960
Parts — Group I	$12,917	$ 9,944	$ 8,006
Parts — Group II	16,075	12,355	10,498
Parts — Group III	10,046	7,521	6,047
Total	$39,038	$29,820	$24,551
Percent (1958 base = 100%)	100%	76%	63%

Of the available business for major products the Austin plant produces, it was estimated that in 1960 they were sole producers of one product, and they produced about 50% of the parts for two other major products.

Summary

From an over-all viewpoint, Mr. Holley had recognized that changes in the nature of the market for the Austin plant had to be met by compensating changes in the system of operation. Not only must these changes occur, but they must come quickly and with a minimum disturbance in labor relations.

Holley had recognized that most of the operating people were willing to change to the required new approach. He had believed that they were qualified and therefore didn't need to be replaced. His basic program of action was to take a sharply different approach to the planning of work and to keep up the pressure to change on the part of all employees. He consistently expected more from his people as they became better trained and adapted to new methods of operation.

In mid-1960, Holley viewed the progress of the Austin plant as very heartening, but with much progress yet to be made in reducing costs of operations. Further long-range improvements in the position of the Austin plant would depend in part upon satisfactory progress in advancing mechanization under job shop conditions.

Questions

1. Appraise the general approaches taken by the plant manager regarding:
   a. His efforts to reduce labor costs.
   b. His efforts to improve delivery performance.
   c. The steps he took to improve quality.
   d. His effectiveness in dealing with the line supervisory, personnel and staff (planning) supervisory personnel.
   e. His handling of labor relations.
2. Appraise the approach taken by key subordinates.
3. What problems appear to remain unresolved at this time (mid-1960)?
4. What future can you see for the Austin Plant?

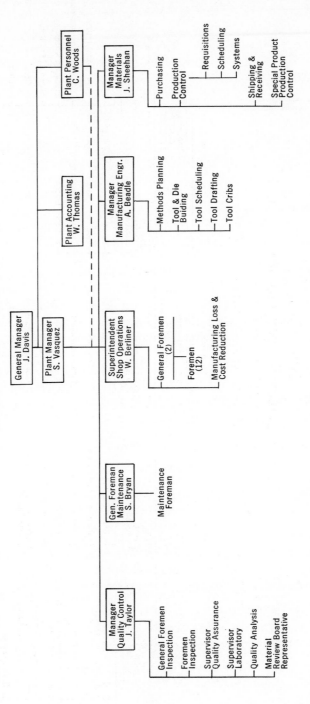

EXHIBIT I

U.S. AIRCRAFT CORPORATION
AUSTIN PLANT
PRE-HOLLEY ORGANIZATION

General Manager
J. Davis

Plant Manager
S. Vasquez

Plant Accounting
W. Thomas

Plant Personnel
C. Woods

Manager
Quality Control
J. Taylor

— General Foremen
Inspection
— Foremen
Inspection
— Supervisor
Quality Assurance
— Supervisor
Laboratory
— Quality Analysis
— Material
Review Board
Representative

Gen. Foreman
Maintenance
S. Bryan

— Maintenance
Foreman

Superintendent
Shop Operations
W. Berliner

— General Foremen
(2)
— Foremen
(12)
— Manufacturing Loss &
Cost Reduction

Manager
Manufacturing Engr.
A. Beadle

— Methods Planning
— Tool & Die
Building
— Tool Scheduling
— Tool Drafting
— Tool Cribs

Manager
Materials
J. Sheehan

— Purchasing
— Production
Control
— Requisitions
— Scheduling
— Systems
— Shipping &
Receiving
— Special Product
Production
Control

EXHIBIT II

U.S. AIRCRAFT CORPORATION
AUSTIN PLANT
HOLLEY ORGANIZATION

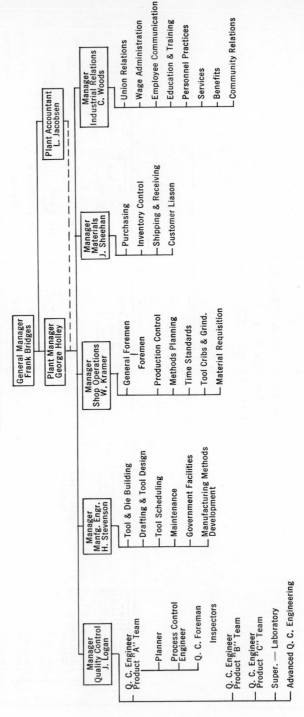

General Manager
Frank Bridges

Plant Accountant
L. Jacobsen

Plant Manager
George Holley

Manager
Quality Control
J. Logan
- Q. C. Engineer Product "A" Team
- Planner
- Process Control Engineer
- Q. C. Foreman
- Inspectors
- Q. C. Engineer Product "B" Team
- Q. C. Engineer Product "C" Team
- Super. — Laboratory
- Advanced Q. C. Engineering

Manager
Manfg. Engr.
H. Stevenson
- Tool & Die Building
- Drafting & Tool Design
- Tool Scheduling
- Maintenance
- Government Facilities
- Manufacturing Methods Development

Manager
Shop Operations
W. Kramer
- General Foremen
- Foremen
- Production Control
- Methods Planning
- Time Standards
- Tool Cribs & Grind.
- Material Requisition

Manager
Materials
J. Sheehan
- Purchasing
- Inventory Control
- Shipping & Receiving
- Customer Liason

Manager
Industrial Relations
C. Woods
- Union Relations
- Wage Administration
- Employee Communication
- Education & Training
- Personnel Practices
- Services
- Benefits
- Community Relations

EXHIBIT III

MAJOR RESPONSIBILITIES OF NEW QUALITY
CONTROL TEAM

A. Quality Control Engineer
   1. Review and obtain changes to Engineering Drawings to minimize Quality Problems prior to manufacture.
   2. Review and approve Process Drawings.
   3. Establish visual standards of quality.
   4. Function as Engineering Representative on M. R. B.
   5. Establish Quality System needed (what, when, where, how much and how to inspect).
   6. Establish and maintain measurements, evaluations and control of quality costs:
      a. Prevention
      b. Assurance
      c. Failure

B. Process Control Engineer
   1. Establish the measurement system for Quality Plan.
   2. Analyze information from measurement system; conduct investigations, pinpoint failure causes, initiate and obtain corrective action.
   3. Review and resolve *all* customer complaints on quality problems.
   4. Initiate and obtain corrective action on vendor defective material.
   5. Conduct process capability studies.
   6. Review preliminary shop operations planning sheets for correctness of process operations. (Heat Treat, Weld Repair, etc.)

C. Quality Control Planner
   1. Accurate measuring tools and equipment in shop.
   2. Prepare procedure sheets detailing the quality system.
   3. Work in conjunction with shop operations planners to assure proper inspection operations at proper time on preliminary planning sheets from which D.O.'s are prepared.
   4. Approve all gage designs.
   5. Utilize shop operations gages and fixtures where practical and specify to S. O. Planner additional gages or fixturing required for quality assurance.

D. Quality Control Foreman
   1. Direct inspectors to follow quality system and obtain quality assurance.
   2. Interview—accept—train—assign inspectors.
   3. Direct product flow through inspection areas to planned schedule.
   4. Measure inspectors—quality & quantity.
   5. Provide information feedback to Process Control Engineer.
   6. Routine foreman responsibilities regarding safety, cleanliness, etc.

EXHIBIT IV

METHODS IMPROVEMENT EXAMPLES

The first example involved the need for a tapered section on sheet stock for a high-volume part.

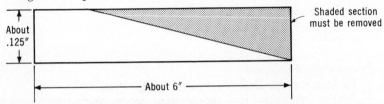

Formerly the material was purchased flat and then machine-rolled. After investigation by Stevenson's group, the material was found to be susceptible to chemical milling, and thereafter was purchased ready for use from the vendor, at an annual saving of about $100,000.

A second example involved the processing of three air bleed holes in the trailing edge of vanes. Because of the small diameter holes involved, and the extreme acute angle of entry, twist drilling was inaccurate and expensive. By use of electrical discharge machining, the required holes could be processed for approximately $3 per piece. Subsequent investigation led to the try-out of a reverse-plating process (electro-chemical effect), which proved satisfactory and resulted in a reduction in cost of $1 per piece for an annual saving in excess of $60,000.

PART II

INCIDENTS
IN
BUSINESS
POLICY

AN INTRODUCTION TO THE INCIDENT METHOD

THE WIDESPREAD USE OF THE incident method in classrooms and in management training programs in recent years is based on the premise that the most characteristic task of the manager is that of making decisions.

The incident method as a pedagogical technique is not standardized. However, generally speaking, it is a presentation of a few facts about a dynamic situation leading to a decision-making responsibility on the part of one or more of the characters in the incident. By studying incidents which involve people in a formal organization structure, one is able to analyze the situation from a management point of view.

Most students and practitioners of management readily agree that, each day, they are confronted with decisions for which there exists no precedent, no formula, no procedural manual, no guiding policies, and few, if any, factual premises. To make decisions of this type calls for a knowledge of managerial principles and concepts as well as a philosophy of thought, a personal system of values, a professional code of ethics, and a view of what constitutes business morality. It is the opinion of many that a manager's ability to handle such situations effectively will determine to a large extent his growth and development in the organization.

From the student's point of view, the incident method involves reading and studying the incident, determining the primary and secondary management issues, viewing the situation in light of what caused the incident, deciding what to do about the incident, and determining how to avoid these or similar problems in the future. It is imperative that a student analyzing an incident draw conclusions and make recommendations based on fact as much as possible and on logically developed conclusions, beyond the point of factual analysis. To provide justification for a recommended decision or course of action in an incident, the student should support his conclusions with sound management concepts or base his recommendations on the findings of competent researchers doing work in the subject area being studied. Every effort should be made to relate conclusions and recommendations to a proven practice or principle of management.

The use of the incident method is valuable as a teaching technique in all areas of management. Incidents may be used as a basis for class discussion, written analysis, as a prelude to role playing, and as a supplemental study to the case method.

Since the incidents are based on true situations, students find them involving and intriguing. Doing reading and research on some subject introduced in an incident becomes purposeful and meaningful. Perhaps no pedagogical technique is available for classroom usage today which creates more student interest, stimulation, and response than the incident method.

Business policy incidents as introduced in Part II of the book stress questions and problem areas concerned with management's responsibility to give guidance and direction to the efforts of employees as all work toward the accomplishment of pre-determined organizational objectives. Some objectives tend to be departmental, functional, or company-wide. Specific questions introduced in the incidents pertain to the role of line and staff managers, members of boards of directors, supervisory managers, middle managers, and executive managers.

The use of the incident method will prove exciting and challenging but it must be stressed that the analysis of incidents demands the same exacting objectivity and scientific analysis as that employed in the case method.

1. A DISMAL FAILURE

AFTER TWO YEARS OF OPERATIONS the small firm owned and managed by Fred Jones and Arthur Riley became inoperable.

Jones and Riley were close friends who formerly worked together as mechanical engineers for a large industrial firm. Their friendship was based partly on their joint interest in creating new and different gadgets which they displayed to their friends and fellow employees. For several years they enjoyed this hobby.

In the spring of 1962, Fred Jones discussed a new idea for making a gadget which Arthur Riley thought was worth considering as a salable manufactured product. The proposed product was an aluminum device which could be fitted to the top of home chimneys and serve as a damper, rain shelter, and insect deterrent. Both men enthusiastically undertook the job of creating a design for the item and a working model. Within a six month period all flaws had been eliminated from the product, and all parts had standard specifications. Furthermore, Jones and Riley had applied for a patent. With these steps accomplished, the two men made the decision to start their own business and manufacture the new product which they called "Chimney Guard." To finance the business initially, each man borrowed $10,000 and received 50 percent of the common stock in exchange for his investment. Jones resigned from his job to devote full time to the business, but Riley retained his job and agreed to work in the business at nights and on the weekends until it could support both men and their families.

Manufacture and sale of "Chimney Guards" totaled 2,000 units in 1963. Each finished unit was priced at $15 and cost about $7.50 to manufacture. They advertised their product in home building journals, hardware dealers' magazines, and at home show exhibitions in New York and Chicago. Most sales orders were received through the mail even though two men were employed on a straight commission basis to call on retail hardware stores. Both Jones and Riley were optimistic that demand for the product would increase during the coming year regardless of the fact that the company showed a net loss of approximately $10,000 at the end of the first year.

To take advantage of unused production capacity and to lower unit cost of production, they decided to manufacture "Chimney Guards" at the highest rate of production possible during the first six months of the coming year and then have Jones concentrate on selling the product himself during the last half of the year at the same time maintaining the advertising and sales program throughout the year.

At the end of the third quarter of the second year, Jones told Riley he was going to have to find a paying job in order to support his family decently. The business had 5,000 "Chimney Guards" in leased inventory space, and orders for the second year of operations had totaled only 1,700 units to this time.

Both Jones and Riley agreed it had been a good experience, but they had borrowed $10,000 each to start the business and the firm's outstanding debts totaled $4,800.

2. ACCEPTING AUTHORITY

PRODUCTION SUPERVISORS AT THE COLONIAL Box Factory were employed with the understanding that they would be expected to do all that was necessary to get production out and meet the demand whether it called for working long hours or not. They were paid on a straight salary basis and received a yearly bonus contingent on over-all plant performance and profit.

During the summer months the Colonial Box Company handled an abnormal number of orders because of seasonal demand, and thereby the employees worked long weekly hours and on Saturdays. During the month of July, the plant superintendent announced to all supervisors that they would be expected to work Sundays until production caught up with demand. He emphasized that they should make this announcement to their employees and should expect to work seven days a week for about four weeks.

On the first Sunday after the announcement eight supervisors of seventeen were absent. Most employees showed up since their hourly wage rates doubled for overtime work.

On Monday, the plant superintendent held another meeting with the supervisors and pointed out the seriousness of the loss of production because of their absence on Sunday. He implied that if this occurred again on the following Sunday, some personnel shifts would likely occur.

On the following Sunday, again only eight supervisors of the seventeen showed up for work. At the end of that day, the plant superintendent estimated that the value of lost production on that day alone amounted to approximately $5,000.

---

3. BOARD OF DIRECTORS

SEVERAL MEMBERS OF THE RESEARCH department of a large manufacturing company pooled their resources and incorporated a small business designed to provide a metal heat-treating service to those firms in the region which at the time sought this service from companies located several hundred miles away. The information concerning the firm was obtained by the incorporators from the State Industrial Development Commission. The Commission encouraged the development of new business in the state and gave whatever aid or advice it could to new or prospective owners.

Six financial contributors to the new company became directors. The directors realized their role would consist primarily of policy-making duties with respect to organization goals and objectives plus specific attention to functional problems with which the managers might want their help.

Dr. Horace Wattham, a director and one of the founders of the company was a highly valued chemical engineer employed in the research department of the large manufacturing company. His technical advice to the new organization already had proved invaluable. Other members of the Board of Directors had made significant technical contributions also. Technically speaking, the company had proved in the first six months of existence that its service was satisfactory and customers were abundant.

With demand for its services increasing, the board employed a new man, William Bentley, upon the recommendation of the president. This brought the total number of employees to four. The new employee was a specialist in heat-treatment of metal and was a friend of the president. He was placed in a staff position so he could be of value to the entire organization. The director had recommended initially the development of a formal organization structure so that there would be clear-cut lines of authority, responsibility, and communication from the very beginning. The organization chart was as follows:

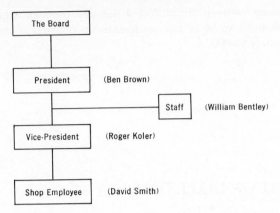

Ben Brown, president of the company, contacted Horace Wattham at his home one evening. He stated he needed advice from the director before the company "fell apart." It seems that he recommended employment of Bill Bentley to provide technical assistance which Roger Koler was not giving. Koler was an original incorporator and financial contributor to the firm; he had resigned from his research job along with Brown to work at the new business full time, but not once had he proved his worth to the company in a technical sense. Brown stated that Koler was extremely jealous of Bentley and both men tended to confuse David Smith by giving him conflicting orders. Bentley did not like Koler because he felt he was afraid to get his hands dirty and really did not know what to do. Brown said he himself worked in the shop nearly as much as Smith, but Koler claimed he was not about to start managing that way. Brown said that Koler claims a manager works through others and does not get involved in non-management activities.

Brown proposes that the directors do something about Koler before he ruins the company.

---

4. BUSINESS RECIPROCITY

BENJAMIN HARRIS, A SENIOR SALES representative of Catus Equipment Company, learned of a job opening in the regional headquarters office of his firm. Upon hearing of this opening, Mr. Harris remembered that the son of the largest buyer in his sales territory was interested in working in the city where the regional headquarters were located. The son had just graduated from college.

After discussing the proposition with Max Freud, Regional Manager, Mr. Harris placed a telephone call to the buyer and suggested that his son come to the home office for an interview. Immediately after the interview, the buyer's son, Waldo Hines, was hired for the job.

Benjamin Harris was impressed by Waldo's progress. He demonstrated enthusiasm for his job and assumed responsibility readily. Mr. Harris communicated this information to Waldo's father and assured him that Waldo was a real asset to the company and a pleasure to work with. Whether this information influenced the industrial buying habits of the senior Mr. Hines is not clear. However, orders from Mr. Hines and his company increased steadily in size over a period of several months.

Approximately six months after Waldo's employment, his work performance began to lag. His interest and enthusiasm disappeared and long periods of absence from his work became routine. Mr. Harris was made aware of Waldo's increasingly poor performance but decided not to inform his father, in hopes that Waldo's work habits would improve.

Both Mr. Harris and the regional manager talked to Waldo about his work performance. Waldo convinced them he would perform more effectively, but pointed out that if this job did not work out, he could always go to work for his father's firm.

Two weeks later Freud called Harris long distance and told him he was firing Waldo. He pointed out that Waldo had missed the last four days of work without giving any excuse and apparently had no regard for his job. Freud stated that he wanted Harris to know first in case he wished to notify Mr. Hines, Waldo's father.

---

5. COMMUNITY CITIZEN

THE PHILOSOPHY OF THE PIEDMONT Shoe Company included being a good community citizen wherever it served. The company's only manufacturing plant was located in a southern town of some 60,000 people. For over thirty years the company had supplied capable managers and other employees to help the community progress in all directions. Employees were active in civic clubs, church work, city government, and education. The company itself made available to approved groups its facilities and grounds for meetings, picnics, and recreational activities. More than once the company had stepped in to help city leaders reach their financial goals when various fund drives fell short of the needed amounts. The company had an excellent image in the eyes of the public and had practically no labor problems. Several times over the thirty-year period union organizers had attempted to sell the employees on union representation, but not once had enough interest been shown to justify a vote on the subject.

While the management of Piedmont Shoe Company enjoyed and appreciated their position in the community, they were becoming concerned that perhaps the "city fathers" were relying too heavily on the company to provide leadership and money for civic purposes. A quick study of the company's financial contributions over the past five-year period for a variety of worthwhile projects substantiated their earlier thoughts.

YEAR	TOTAL CONTRIBUTED
1960	$18,612.00
1961	21,209.00
1962	33,581.00
1963	35,000.00
1964	39,019.00

While about seventy-five percent of all money the company contributed each year was to the local Community Chest, the Piedmont management felt that a stopping point had to be reached before the firm became a recipient of the Community Chest program itself. What concerned management currently, however, was the request by the 1965 Chairman of the Community Chest Drive that he be allowed to budget a contribution of $35,000 from the company for the coming year. As understood by management, this contribution would be over and above any sum contributed by the several hundred employees.

---

6. CREATIVE ARTS, INC.

CREATIVE ARTS, INC., OPERATED A large number of retail stores which specialized in the sale of a wide variety of art supplies. The stores were located in a five-state area and were supplied from a central warehouse located adjacent to the general offices in Atlanta, Georgia.

The president of Creative Arts, Inc., Mr. Grant, had long been a believer in decentralized operations and had given the managers of the stores a relatively free hand in administration. The major criteria used to determine whether the stores were managed competently or not related directly to net profit or loss shown annually and the volume of business of each store.

While there was relatively little centralized authority over the stores, two key functions, accounting and advertising, were administered directly by the home office.

During the past year Creative Arts had experienced a significant loss in sales and profits for the first time in fifteen years. It was believed that the loss was attributable to the increase in competition, especially by some large department stores that had added art supplies to their full line of merchandise.

Mr. Grant believed that one possible solution to the problem was to increase advertising efforts. To finance the increased advertising program, each store was to budget an additional fifty percent to advertising for the coming year.

Two months after the enlarged advertising program had begun, Mr. Grant received several letters and calls from retail store managers. They disagreed with the philosophy and strategy of the new advertising program; they criticized the concentration of advertising effort on promoting Creative Arts, Inc. itself rather than promoting the respective retail stores which collectively made up Creative Arts, Inc. The retail store managers pointed out that customers came to their stores because of the service given rather than because their stores were part of Creative Arts, Inc. Furthermore, since their stores were financing most of the advertising program, they resented the fact that they were not able to plan and develop their own advertising programs on a local basis.

---

7. DEAR ANN

RUFUS JONES SAT IN THE office of the personnel director for the first time. In all of his years of employment with Continental, he had never had an occasion to request such a meeting. Continental was a huge company, and he felt a little guilty about bothering someone as high up in the organization as the personnel director.

After introducing himself to the personnel director, the following conversation took place.

Rufus: Sir, I'm sorry to take up your valuable time but I have a problem that none of my bosses will help me with. They hear my story and then tell me to "work it out"! I don't know what they mean—"work it out"! I need some help!

Personnel Director:	Well, Rufus, tell me your story. This is one of my jobs and I want to help you if I can.
Rufus:	Well, let me start by saying I have been with Continental since the early 50's. I was hired as an electronics technician, Class B, but was later upgraded to a technician and a little later promoted to lead man. A few years after this I became a replacement supervisor and two years later a permanent supervisor. I've held this job for two years. If you'll excuse me, I'll tell you that I know my job as well as anyone because I came up through the ranks. I'm married with two children and recently became a grandfather.

Well, my problem is this. One of my employees is nineteen years old. He is married. His wife's name is Doris and she is sixteen. They are expecting in the next ninety days. I did know the exact date of the expected arrival and the names they had selected if it were to be a "he" or a "she," but I've forgotten. He has been employed by Continental for nine months. May I point out that his production is above average. Any job you assign to him is done immediately and done well. I guess I would have to say he is one of the best young producers I've ever had. Well, anyway, my problem is this boy's own problems. He constantly tells me about his problems and asks for advice.

Personnel Director:	Rufus, what are some of the young man's problems?
Rufus:	Sir, I'm glad you asked. I made a note of a few of them.

Just this week he's told me he can't sleep because his wife is pregnant. Seems she sleeps all day and wants to talk all night. Asked me what I would do? I didn't know what to say.

Then he decided he wanted to buy a car. Make, model, and financing are left up to me. I got out of this one by going to a meeting.

Yesterday, he decided he wanted to start back to school and take some night courses. Wanted me to tell him what subject would be most beneficial to him.

The things he wants to talk about during working hours, during my coffee breaks, and during by lunch hour would fill a notebook. He even came over to my house one night and stayed three hours. My wife fell asleep while he was talking! Sir, how can I overcome this problem of being a Dear Ann to him without being sarcastic or hurting his feelings? He's a good production worker.

8. ECCENTRIC PROGRAMMER

WILFRED NORTZ, COMPUTER PROGRAMMER WITH the Electronics Testing Corporation, walked into Project Manager Fred Wilson's office and announced that he was "through," "finished," and absolutely compelled to resign from the company. With the conclusion of that statement, he headed out the door with the announcement that he would be back in an hour to pick up his final pay check.

Wilson reflected on his problem. Nortz had been sent to his project facility some 200 miles from the home office to run some tests on a new computer which had been installed recently. The outcome of the tests was most significant in that the future work of his project group could not proceed much more until Nortz completed his tests. However, Nortz was accountable to Sid Young who had been sent to Wilson's facility along with Nortz. Sid Young's job was to supervise Nortz and coordinate his work with that of Wilson's project group. On several occasions in the past two weeks, Nortz had told Wilson that Sid Young was demanding too much of him, motivating him through undue pressure and having him work overtime and on weekends. Nortz said that Young hardly knew a computer when he saw one and had little appreciation of the stress and strain he (Nortz) was under. Wilson also reflected that he had talked with Sid Young about this matter just two days before and had been told that Nortz was one of those eccentric, specialized staff people who had been "babied" in their jobs all their working lives. Young had stated that with the deadline to complete the tests less than a week away, Nortz was going to finish these tests on schedule if he had to sleep beside the computer and be spoon-fed.

9. FORCED DEMOTION

BILL SNYDER HAD JUST RESIGNED his position as Special Products Representative with the Mid-Valley Plastics Corporation. His annual salary was $15,000, the same as it had been two months ago, when he was told by the President of the firm that he was being relieved of his duties as Vice-President of Manufacturing and being assigned to the job of Special Products Representative.

For seven years Snyder had been Vice-President of Manufacturing. He helped organize the firm in the early days and pioneered many production changes in the company that allowed it to grow and prosper when many competitors were being forced out of business. Snyder was a self-educated manager who had a real "feel" for tools, equipment, machines, and anything associated with manufacturing. Someone told him once that he had tremendous mechanical aptitude and that he should have gone to college and studied engineering.

When the President of Mid-Valley Products told Snyder of his demotion, he pointed out that Bill should have known the change was coming. He emphasized the fact that the company now employed 400 people as against 50 when Bill first joined the organization and that a manager today had to know more and do more than just manage machines and materials. The President told Snyder that he was too valuable a man to lose but too risky to keep at the vice-president's level. Furthermore, the company had just hired a young man with a graduate engineering degree to take his place. This man would become Bill's boss and help him with his new assignment.

When Snyder met the new vice-president, he realized then that he could not work with a man ten years his junior who apparently had never dirtied his hands repairing or maintaining equipment. He wondered, What could a fellow like this know about manufacturing?

10. GENERAL IN DISGUISE

MR. CHAUNCEY STILLMAN, RECENTLY RETIRED President of Chincey Credit Company, had been a real asset to the organization for over twenty-five years. However, because he had "grown up" in the company with so many of the present management people, some had taken his friendship as an excuse for "retiring on the job." They were non-productive managers who generally looked tired, stayed busy with inconsequential activities, and made few decisions if they could help it.

Members of the Executive Committee in charge of finding a replacement for Mr. Stillman knew of the non-productiveness and managerial apathy that existed in the management ranks. They considered the retirement of Mr. Stillman an opportunity to do something about the situation.

In discussing possible replacements for Mr. Stillman, members of the Executive Committee recognized that several of the vice-presidents were capable of managing the business. However, they were concerned that they too would overlook the performance and apathy displayed by a number of their fellow-managers and carry on much as Mr. Stillman had.

One member of the Executive Committee suggested that they bring in a proven administrator from the outside for a one or two year period and let him clean up the organization and then be relieved of his duties. Accordingly, Lt. General H. L. "Bull" Bronson (retired) was interviewed by members of the Executive Committee and willingly agreed to the two-year assignment. It was pointed out to General Bronson that no one, now or in the future, was to know that his appointment was limited nor know the objectives of his employment as president.

The announcement of the new president came as a real surprise to all employees and the general public. However, President Bronson quickly allayed doubts about his efficiency and capability in handling the job. By the end of his first month in office, few people made any comment about the selection.

By the end of six months President Bronson began making pointed demands of his management personnel. Each manager, on several different occasions, had been requested on short notice to turn in progress reports, one-year recommendations plans, market forecasts, and similar reports, directly to the President. His reaction was usually quick and critical. Many managers began to feel the pressure from above. Several managers had been criticized openly in management meetings by President Bronson and had resigned. Several others indicated they might resign if they found better jobs.

By the end of the first year, six managers had resigned and six had been fired. No vacated management position on any high level had been filled, but instead the President reorganized the entire company and consolidated several of the functional activities. During this time non-management personnel turnover had been normal.

During his second year as President, General H. L. "Bull" Bronson received veiled threats on his life over the phone and in the mail and faced an open rebellion by his remaining managers. Never once did he make any effort to be friends with other operating officers of the company nor with business executives in the community.

Oddly enough, during President Bronson's tenure, profits showed a gain primarily due to the increase in efficiency which reduced operating costs.

At the end of two years, Simon Blake, Chairman of the Board, announced to the employees and stockholders that President Bronson had resigned because of poor health and was retiring from the business world. A new president would be announced at the next meeting of the Board of Directors.

---

11. GEORGIA PEACHES

ZEKE HOLLAND IS OWNER AND MANAGER of a vegetable and peach cannery located in middle Georgia. For years he had processed and canned vegetables and peaches for national grocery chains but always at a small profit margin. At the expiration of his last contract he decided to more wholly integrate his organizational activities not only by processing and canning peaches but also by retailing them through a cooperative grocery chain that included some 500 stores. His brand label showed the picture of a beautiful smiling girl with the words underneath: "Miss Georgia Peaches."

The cooperative grocery chain through which Zeke Holland would retail his canned peaches left advertising practices and price policies to the individual supplier.

In light of not more than $5,000 available for advertising during the first year, Zeke Holland was faced with several questions concerning price policies:

1. Should "Miss Georgia Peaches" be priced competitively with other brands even though it is a new product?
2. Should "Miss Georgia Peaches" be priced lower than other brands to stimulate demand for the new product, even though profit margin would be almost eliminated?
3. Should "Miss Georgia Peaches" be priced one or two cents higher than competing products and appeal to the "quality conscious" buyers?
4. How shall the $5,000 for advertising be best used to support the decision concerning prices?

---

12. GREAT EASTERN POWER COMPANY

GREAT EASTERN POWER COMPANY OPERATED in a densely populated state bordering the Atlantic Ocean. The demand for its product, electric energy, was growing at such an expanding rate that top management of the company foresaw the problems of producing and supplying this energy several years in advance. Thus, it was imperative that the company purchase land, develop plans for constructing electric generating plants, and manage its financial affairs so that it would be in a position to construct power generating plants and satisfactorily meet demand for electric energy as it developed.

As one of the acts in this planning process, the Company purchased a strip of land, about twenty-five acres in size, bordering the Atlantic Ocean, in the town of Oceanville. Oceanville was a resort town of 5,000 people, on the fringe area of part of the state that was highly industrialized. Management of Great Eastern had determined that the greatest need for additional electric energy in the state during the next five years would be in the fifty-mile area surrounding Oceanville. Thus, this site for an electric generating plant was considered ideal because of its nearness to the inland waterways which would serve as an economical means for transporting coal to the proposed electric generating plant and because of its nearness to the market area.

Upon hearing of the proposed construction of an electric power generating plant in Oceanville, a citizens' committee was organized, composed mostly of homeowners in the vicinity of the purchased site. Even though the nearest home to the proposed plant would be more than a quarter of a mile away, the committee appealed to the City Board of Commissioners to turn down a request by the company to rezone the area for industrial use. They pointed out that their property would be devalued, their recreational areas would be ruined, and the sight of the plant would be an eyesore to the tourist. Additionally, many citizens objected to the "smog" that might be created by the plant in operation. Company spokesmen appeared before the city commissioners and pointed out the positive features of locating a power plant in Oceanville. They estimated the annual tax revenue to the city, the number of citizens who would be employed, and the amount of spending in Oceanville from employee pay checks.

Commission members argued the pros and cons of the question and decided that a special referendum should be held the following month so that all citizens of Oceanville could voice their opinions. The question on the referendum ballot was to read:

> Should Oceanville Point (proposed site of the power plant) be developed into a municipal recreation area or be used for industrial or commercial purposes?
>
> ( ) Yes, as a recreational area
> or
> ( ) Yes, for industrial or commercial purposes

The top management of Great Eastern Power Company called a meeting to discuss their best course of action in light of the announced referendum.

13. INDUSTRIAL SURGERY

NORTHPORT TEXTILE MILLS OPERATED NINE mills producing a variety of cotton and synthetic materials. One of these mills located in Freeville, Virginia, had been in operation over sixty years. The entire town of Freeville, population 3,500, existed because of the mill. Formerly Freeville had been an agricultural center as well as a textile town, but its agricultural importance diminished in the 1930's.

The management of Northport Textile Mills had long ago thought of closing down the Freeville mill, but because it still was considered marginal and had an abundance of skilled labor at that time, it remained in operation.

Recently, however, cost analysts and engineers on the staff of Northport Textiles reported to the controller that it would take a two-million-dollar expansion and re-modernization program to operate the Freeville mill economically. With the textile industry as competitive as it was, there appeared no economic justification to support the operation of the mill. Its continued operation would only jeopardize the profitability of the entire organization.

The mayor of Freeville heard of the proposed closing. He immediately met with the President of Northport Textiles and begged him to reconsider his decision. He pointed out that Freeville would be a "ghost town" in six months if the mill closed. He voiced the opinion that two out of three people in Freeville would have to go on government relief or try to relocate if the mill were closed.

The President of Northport Textiles told the mayor he would review the matter and call him in a few days.

14. J AND M AND G

MAGGIE SMITH HAS THE TITLE of Inspector Manager. She has all of the authority and responsibility needed to select and employ her own subordinates when an opening occurs. At the same time, she has all of the authority and responsibility needed to discharge unsatisfactory subordinates. There are no formal hiring or firing policies which she must adhere to.

Three of Maggie Smith's subordinates are female inspectors. For simplicity they will be referred to as J, M and G. J and M are full-time and G is part-time. J's performance is somewhat better than M's and G's, but J does not get along well with the others.

M and G have complained about J, and J has also complained about G. In all cases, it is a clash of personalities, and all have talked about quitting their jobs.

Maggie Smith approached each with the advice that they not let the others get them down but instead accept the challenge to be a leader and strive to work harmoniously with the others. Since Maggie Smith's talk with each of the inspectors, conditions have improved. However, G has continued to work only a few days a week.

Maggie Smith is now faced with hiring another full-time inspector. G would be the logical choice since she is fully trained, but this might result in a flareup with J. J does good work but is the most troublesome employee.

The question facing Maggie Smith is whether she should employ G full time and cope with the risk of losing J or hire a new girl to train with the possibility that the problem will still exist.

---

15. MASS EXODUS

THE SUNDRY PRODUCTS COMPANY IS a multi-million dollar corporation consisting of six major divisions. The general or corporate offices are located in New York City. Of the six divisions, the general offices of Division 3 have been located in Memphis, Tennessee, for over fifty years. Division 3 has had its own organizational structure consisting of a president, operating vice-president, and other officers plus a total of some 250 employees. This division has operated with a considerable degree of independence relative to corporate headquarters in New York City.

In conjunction with a program of expansion, modernization, and automation throughout Division 3, there were, necessarily, many changes in top management. The most recent change was the transfer, six months previously, of a corporate vice-president to Memphis as President of Division 3. Within a month of the new president's arrival, he announced to the divisional personnel that the Memphis general offices would be moved to New York City within two years for purposes of consolidating the administration of the Sundry Products Company.

The morale of the employees, already deteriorated because of the many sudden changes in policies and procedures introduced by the new president, hit an all-time low. Resignations of key personnel became routine. Managers and assistant managers as well as experienced employees sought employment with other firms rather than transfer to New York City.

The Sundry Products Company's executive vice-president, upon hearing of the resignations, called the Division 3 president and asked him how he expected to maintain an effective work force for the next two years.

---

16. OLD FASHION CANDY COMPANY

THE LABOR FORCE OF THE Old Fashion Candy Company was fully integrated with a vast majority of the production employees being Negro.

Over the years, the management of Old Fashion paid their employees comparable wages with competitors and provided many extra benefits on a voluntary basis. These benefits included advances on wages, payment of court fines if the employees had no money, aiding employees with their monthly financial notes if they got behind on payments, and giving all employees a dressed turkey and other food products at Christmas.

During the past five years, the Negro production employees had been approached several times by union organizers. On two occasions enough union support was created to petition for an election to determine if the union would have jurisdiction over employees with respect to bargaining rights. On both occasions the union was defeated but by the narrowest of margins. It was felt that a friend of management, a Negro lawyer, defeated the union in the second election by appearing before the employees and defending management's position.

The unanimous opinion of the owners who managed the company was that if a union ever won an election to represent their employees, they would sell the company outright or close it permanently. This was not a course of action they wished to take, but on the other hand, they did not intend to engage in all of the responsibilities of union negotiation and be bound by a contract which limited a great deal of their managerial authority.

Several of the managers predicted that another election could be expected during the coming year.

17. ONE-WAY MANAGEMENT

A MAJORITY OF THE MEMBERS on the Executive Committee of Consolidated Chemicals Company were lunching in a secluded dining area of a private club. Their real purpose in meeting was to discuss the resignation of John Hargrove, recent president of Consolidated Chemical. It appeared that Hargrove had told several members of the Executive Committee that the reason for his resignation was essentially the same as that of the three previous presidents, all of whom had held the position less than six months. The reason given was that no one with initiative, intelligence, or pride could hold the title of President and still get along with Ellis Clairbourne, Chairman of the Executive Committee.

As all members knew, Ellis Clairbourne had been president of Consolidated Chemical for twenty-nine years. Under his guidance the firm developed from a marginal entity in the industry to one of the giants. Its sales had increased beyond the 200-million mark, and employees totaled nearly 7,000. It was only when Ellis Clairbourne's health began to fail slightly that he volunteered to move up to the position of Chairman of the Executive Committee with the stipulation that he would step down only when he thought he could be of no value to Consolidated Chemical.

Hargrove's comments were very similar to the ones made by previous presidents. It was emphasized that according to Clairbourne's actions, there was only one way to do anything—Clairbourne's way! Hargrove complained he was over-ruled time and time again, he was by-passed often, and in fact, sometimes he was the last person in the organization to know what new policies were being introduced.

Hargrove's final comment was, "If you want a president, hire Clairbourne."

18. OUT ON A LIMB

AFTER TEN YEARS OF MODEST growth in a strongly competitive market, the Aircool Aluminum Awning Company faced a decision as to whether or not it should sell the business to a national supplier of aluminum awnings. The price was "right," but the Smith brothers, who owned the firm, felt they had developed a prosperous and manageable business from an "idea," and they disliked the thought of selling out and learning some other business.

A year later, the same national supplier of aluminum awnings approached them with an offer to enter into a three-year contract to purchase all aluminum awnings the firm could manufacture. Again the price was "right," and the brothers decided to make the contractual agreement.

As time went on, the Smith Brothers quickly lost the demand for their product from the general public which once represented the only market they had. This was to be expected with the firm primarily producing on contract for the national supplier of aluminum awnings and with no advertising or sales program to maintain demand from the general public.

At the end of three very profitable years, the Smith brothers contacted the national supplier of aluminum awnings and requested that the contract for supplying aluminum awnings to them be renewed or renegotiated. By return mail the brothers received this letter:

Gentlemen:

Please be advised that our firm will no longer be interested in negotiating an agreement with you for the purchase of aluminum awnings.

Our business relationship has been most pleasant, and I hope most profitable for you. However, with the forecast that there will be a sharp decline in demand for aluminum awnings across the nation next year, we believe that our needs for aluminum awnings can be met through the operations of our own production facilities.

Thank you for your inquiry.

Sincerely,

Ray Black

Ray Black
Executive Director of Purchase

---

19. PART-TIME MANAGER

ALL OF SAM FULLERS' TWELVE years with the Harvester Corporation had been spent in the accounting department. Having established himself as a diligent worker and popular individual among superiors, peers, and subordinates alike, he was recently given the position of supervisor of the Data Processing Section. Sam had ample experience in this area and seemed to retain his ability to get along with his workers while maintaining efficient operations in the department.

One afternoon, after Sam had completed most of his "desk" work, he began to move casually about the department observing operations. Upon reaching the sorter section he noticed that work was somewhat behind because of the absence of one of the machine operators. The work had to be completed before the night shift arrived at 4:30 p.m., and it was obvious that another man was needed. Sam had spent several years in this section in his earlier days with the company, and when he realized that no man could be spared from any of the other jobs, he took off his coat, grabbed a tray full of invoices and began operating the vacant machine.

Meanwhile, the head of the accounting department was in Sam's office with some important reports that had to be signed and handled by Sam. These unexpected reports were due to be mailed within the next half-hour. The department head waited impatiently for fifteen minutes and then began searching for Sam. Upon finding him working feverishly behind a sorter with the clerks, the head of the accounting department exploded. He shouted that Sam belonged in his office and not out doing the machine operator's work for them. The sorting work was completed on time; the reports were late. The next day Sam received a notice to report to the office of the vice-president.

----

20. PROGRESS ON PURPOSE

CARL BOLLING IS A PARTICIPANT in the company's training program titled, Systems and Procedures Studies. The participants meet once weekly for two hours over an eight-month period. The program is staffed by a local college professor.

As part of the requirements of the program, each participant is required to undertake a work study project of his own choosing with the idea of critically analyzing the work activities observed and suggesting improvement for them through the application of techniques and ideas learned in the program. It was stressed by the professor at the beginning of the program that the "human element" was one of the prime factors to pay attention to when undertaking such a study.

Carl Bolling has the title of Planning Engineer. In this capacity, he engages in coordinating activities between the Operating, Production, and

Engineering Departments. His selected work study project for the training program deals with the purchase and order of heavy equipment for installation in new plants being constructed by the company. It concerns specifically the control of costs associated with purchased equipment which sometimes sits crated on a new plant location for weeks before it is ready for installation. Carl Bolling had analyzed the scheduling procedures of the Construction Department and the purchasing procedures of the Operating Department plus the required specifications and design of equipment by the Engineering Department. It was his opinion that thousands of dollars yearly could be saved by the company if the Construction and Operating Departments would adopt the formal planning and purchasing procedures which he proposed. He felt very convinced that his analysis of the problem was sound and his analysis of potential cost savings was accurate.

Upon submitting his work study project to fellow participants in the training program, he felt pleased that the group and professor endorsed his project as "sound" and "well done." Upon submitting his proposal to his immediate boss, the Vice-President of Engineering, he was gratified to know that the Vice-President planned to propose the introduction of his new procedures at the next meeting of the Executive Management Committee.

Two weeks later the Vice-President of Engineering called Bolling to his office and told him his suggested planning and purchasing procedures had been presented to the Executive Management Committee. The reaction had been violent! They resented a mere planning engineer crossing functional lines and making recommendations in areas other than his own. They disliked the implication that their activities were costing the company thousands of dollars yearly, and they issued a feeling through the Vice-President of Engineering that in the future, he (Bolling) would be considered "persona non grata" in their departments.

The Vice-President of Engineering suggested to Bolling that maybe it would be best if he were transferred to another division in the company. At least he would not run the risk of meeting these executives personally.

---

21. RISK AND UNCERTAINTY

DEXTER STEELS WAS A BUYER and distributor of steel and related metal products. Its sales territory included twelve states with warehouse facilities located in six of them. One warehouse carried inventory to serve the market area of approximately two states.

The profit picture of Dexter Steels, Inc. had been very static. For a five-year period, the profit position of the firm had changed only slightly. This situation was somewhat unexplainable to stockholders who were well aware of the increase in demand by industrial users for products competitive with those inventoried and sold by Dexter.

To satisfy the demands of stockholders, the President of Dexter Steels, Inc., replaced the general manager in charge of sales and inventory with Mr. Harry Cannon.

Mr. Cannon came to Dexter Steels from a position of sales manager with a firm engaged in the manufacture and sale of children's toys. His performance record had been outstanding in his previous job. It was only after a considerable effort and sizeable salary increase that the president of Dexter had been able to convince Mr. Cannon that he was badly needed by the company to take charge of sales and inventory activities.

After he arrived, Mr. Cannon studied the sales records and market predictions in the steel supply industry. He predicted that demand for the hundreds of items carried by Dexter Steels and other competitors would, without question, increase. Cannon made the statement to his salesmen and inventory managers several times in staff meetings that increasing sales was going to be the salvation of Dexter Steels.

After two months on the job, Cannon released printed copies of his policies and objectives to his salesmen and inventory managers:

1. We shall endeavor to purchase and stock in sufficient quantities at each warehouse *all* items that we list in our supply catalogue.
2. Whenever it is deemed economically feasible, we shall procure large quantities of products for inventory on an economic lot size basis.
3. The increased cost of carrying much larger inventories can be offset by increased sales which should be derived from maintaining a full line of steel products.
4. Prices of our products are going to be comparable to the competition.
5. Sales quotas are being increased 50 percent.
6. Advertising efforts in the future will be geared more to Dexter Steel products and service and not to an institutional approach promoting steel products.
7. Year-end bonuses will be awarded to those in sales and inventory who exceed their performance records of last year.

For the next six months, inventory managers reported the largest stock of steel products that had ever been carried; salesmen reported a slight increase in demand with good prospects of much greater demand occurring during the last half of the year.

At this time, the "word" came out that there was a very strong possibility of a prolonged strike occurring in the steel manufacturing industry within thirty days. Negotiations between the union and companies were not progressing very well and a strike appeared forthcoming.

Harry Cannon asked for and received approval from the President of Dexter Steels to immediately purchase a large quantity of available steel products from any source of supply available. With the threat of a six-to-eight-week strike, it would be disastrous to try and operate Dexter Steel without sufficient inventory.

The steel strike occurred as predicted. However, through government pressures, public opinion, and fearful economic consequences, the strike was settled within a week.

At the end of the year, the president announced sadly to the stockholders that due to unexpected costs and overinvestment in inventories, the company had shown a net loss for the first time in five years. He predicted a much better year ahead with sufficient inventory already on hand to match expected sales for the first ninety days.

----

22. SAFETY CONTEST

THE PERSONNEL DIRECTOR AND OTHER management personnel became alarmed at the increasing accident and severity rates among employees. While many of the operative employees worked in dangerous areas and were involved in hazardous jobs, every effort had been made to reduce accidents by installing shields and safety devices, by requiring employees to wear metal helmets and safety shoes, and by having safety posters displayed at prominent places in the plant.

To bring about renewed interest in the safety program, the personnel director received approval from higher management to "kick off" a safety contest between departments. The contest was made competitive on the basis that the department which showed the greatest percent decrease in accident and severity rates over a one-month period compared to their same accident and severity rate for the same month of the previous year, would receive a special prize. Additionally, each employee in the winning department would receive a clock-radio valued at $30. All prizes were to be awarded at the annual company picnic shortly after the conclusion of the contest.

As safety reports were turned in to the personnel director, he was extremely pleased to note the sharp decrease in the number of accidents reported. With the exception of one department, all had shown great improvement in reducing accidents.

When the company picnic was held and prizes awarded to the winning department, all top management personnel expressed their congratulations to the employees for their splendid participation in the safety program.

Only one month later, the Personnel Director reviewed the safety reports from the departments with astonishment. Without exception, every department accident and severity rate was higher than it had been before the contest began.

---

23. THE AIRFLIGHT EQUIPMENT COMPANY

MR. GEORGE SMITH WAS APPOINTED General Manager of the Airflight Equipment Company in March 1964. The Airflight Equipment Company was a wholly-owned subsidiary of the parent company, International Aviation.

Prior to Smith's appointment as General Manager of Airflight Equipment Company, he had had experience with the parent company for twenty years in a diversity of positions. His background included that of a project engineer, a production department head, and recently for several years a top liaison specialist between the controller's office and production department heads. He was considered a seasoned veteran in management in the aircraft industry.

When the president of International Aviation discussed the new appointment with Smith, he told him to look over the operation very carefully for several months and assume his new duties on July 1. The president pointed out that Airflight Equipment Company had been showing losses at an increasing rate for the last three years in spite of an increase in demand for their line of products and services. The president implied to Smith that if the subsidiary could not show a profit during the next fiscal year, it would be sold or closed down.

For three months, George Smith studied all cost information, production records, organizational changes, and miscellaneous data that could be obtained about Airflight Equipment Company, without actually moving his office to the premises. He noted the following facts about the management and the organization during the past year:

1. Net loss had exceeded one million dollars.
2. Number of production staff personnel (standards, production control, quality control, and inspection) had been reduced by ninety percent.

3. During five months of the year, the number of defective products returned to the plant from customers exceeded the number of finished products shipped to customers.
4. Labor turnover averaged thirty-five percent during the past year.
5. Only 25 percent of the production jobs were standardized with permanent rates.
6. Employees in the production area had wide latitude in determining rates of output, working conditions, vacation policy, and other actions affecting them.
7. Management had few problems with the three unions representing three distinct segments of the work force.
8. Wage rates of non-management personnel were equal to or higher than the rates paid for similar skills in the competitive labor market.
9. The recently dismissed general manager had been in the position for four years and was well liked by most of the management personnel and other employees.

On Smith's first day in his office on the new job, he dictated a letter to all department heads and requested that they meet in the conference room the following morning at 9:00 a.m. Additionally, he requested that they be prepared to discuss their specific operations in light of the company's record during the past year.

---

24. THE POLYGRAPH TEST

THE NEWHARDT & BRITT DEPARTMENT STORE employed some 385 employees. While it was a most profitable company, the management was concerned with reports by department heads that pilferage was becoming a major problem. Supervisors of security agents employed to protect the store against outside theft reported no increase in losses from that source.

To insure against continued pilferage, the management of Newhardt & Britt posted an announcement on the employees' bulletin board which read as follows:

TO: Newhardt & Britt Employees

It has come to our attention that a small number of our employees are pilfering merchandise. Because a few bad apples can ruin a barrel, the management desires to protect those honest and faithful employees who have made a career for themselves at Newhardt & Britt. Accordingly, the consulting firm of Hass and Todd will administer a polygraph test to all employees between August 1 and November 1. When your name is posted for the test, please cooperate fully so we may gain information which will make us a better organization. It is the promise of management that no employee will be discharged because of information obtained from this test.

Your understanding will be appreciated.

Lawrence Bailey
Executive Vice-President

While some employees resigned prior to taking the polygraph test, employee turnover was not considered abnormal between August 1 and October 1.

By October 15, the firm of Hass and Todd made a report to management. The report read in part as follows:

"While 319 employees have undergone the polygraph test, results indicate that less than three percent of them have engaged in a program of planned theft. However, 91.2% of the employees responded positively to the question: Have you at any time ever taken merchandise from Newhardt & Britt?"

The management of Newhardt & Britt was considering the recommendation from Hass and Todd that they follow up this test with another required polygraph test of all employees six months from that time. With information on employees from two polygraph tests, management would be in a position to discharge those who had continued to pilfer.

---

25. TITLE VII

SAC'S, INC., A LARGE RETAIL department store employing over 300 people, was confronted with complying with the Equal Employment Opportunity Act. The Act which became effective on July 2, 1965, has broad and sweeping implications for personnel decision making. Title VII of the Act deals with equal employment opportunity and creates an Equal Employment Opportunity Commission, whose duty will be to investigate written charges filed under oath by aggrieved persons. Also inserted into Title VII is the statement that the Act should not be construed to prohibit the use of "ability tests" in selection.

The personnel director of Sac's, Inc. conferred with higher management to discuss the introduction and use of personnel tests when hiring new employees in light of the recently enacted Equal Employment Opportunity Act. After studying the Act carefully, the management of Sac's felt that the personnel director was on safe ground in using "ability tests" as part of the selection procedure. However, they suggested that any test to be used in the future to aid in the selection of qualified employees be given to all present employees so that a norm could be determined to compare test scores of applicants.

The personnel director considered the recommendation of higher management sound and concluded that the test more likely to be given to all future applicants for jobs would be a general intelligence test. Therefore, arrangements were made to give a general intelligence test to all employees. When all tests were scored they were arranged in an array that separated management personnel scores from non-management personnel scores. To the personnel director's surprise, the average general intelligence score of management personnel was only four percent higher than that of non-management personnel. Equally surprising to the personnel director was the observation that many high bracketed managers had lower general intelligence scores than a number of non-management personnel.

The personnel director was somewhat perplexed by how he would use general intelligence tests to aid in the selection of qualified employees.

PART III

READINGS
IN
BUSINESS
POLICY

PREFACE TO READINGS IN BUSINESS POLICY

BUSINESS POLICY IS CONCERNED WITH developing a capacity for the rational determination of corporate objectives and policies. The competitive opportunities of the firm must be analyzed, a corporate strategy developed in light of those opportunities, and an organization and a program of action established to implement the strategy in a dynamic environment.

The serious study of business policy emphasizes the need for long-range planning by the firm. Policy decisions include those decisions which are basic to the continued profitability, and even to the survival, of the firm in a competitive environment.

In selecting this collection of readings, it was our objective to include a number of writings on various aspects of business policy which would be useful to students in their study of that subject. The writings included in this selection have been used by the authors at various times in their own courses in business policy because of the insight each selection offers to a particular aspect of business policy.

These writings were published originally in a wide variety of sources, many of which are not readily available to students.

Many excellent selections could not be used because of their length, or because of their highly specialized treatment of limited aspects of business policy. Other important readings may have been omitted by oversight, and we welcome the reader's suggestions for additions or substitutions to our selections.

For the instructor with his own favorite collection of readings, we invite him to select those readings from our collection which best fit into his pattern of teaching, and to supplement these with his own selections which are made available to his students.

We are grateful to the authors whose works are used and to the publishers whose permission to reprint materials is acknowledged in footnotes to each selection. Their consent has aided us to provide what we hope will be the basis for a better understanding of business policy by students of the subject.

A. MANAGEMENT OF THE CORPORATION

1. THE BOARD OF DIRECTORS AND BUSINESS MANAGEMENT*

Melvin T. Copeland and Andrew R. Towl

An Abstract

THE BOARD OF DIRECTORS IS responsible for directing the management of a corporation. Directors, either individually or as a group, however, cannot participate directly in the multitude of functions required to operate effectively the business of a corporation, although the law typically states that the board of directors shall "manage" the corporation. Rather the board must direct the management of the corporation's affairs, in a practical sense, by delegating operations to the executive organization to which it has given authority and to which instructions have been provided. The corporation's immediate welfare as well as its long-term existence depend on the effectiveness with which the directors perform these important functions.

The board of directors must select the corporation's chief executive. This is a decision of far-reaching significance and is one of a director's most important responsibilities. Succession to the position of chief executive is not in most cases automatic, and the decision warrants a full-scale appraisal of the corporation's requirements for leadership as well as close scrutiny of the abilities of potential candidates.

---

* An abstract of *The Board of Directors and Business Management* (Cambridge: President & Fellows of Harvard College, 1947). Reprinted with permission of the publisher.

Although a board delegates operations to the chief executive and his organization, the final responsibility for success rests with the members of the board of directors. Thus, the directors must provide executives with policies for guiding and directing the corporation's activities. The directors formally determine many of these policies; other policies are established by precedents resulting from administrative decisions of the executive organization. These decisions, however, are subject to review by the board of directors. In either case, effective policy formulation is a joint product, with contributions being made by both the directors and the operating organization. Informal discussions between individual board members and executives contribute significantly to policy formulation in many corporations. In these discussions, however, and indeed in all dealings with the operating organization, directors must exercise discretion lest their actions tend to undermine the established lines of executive responsibility.

A corporation, to enjoy continued success, must be directed and managed with a spirit of enterprise. This spirit of enterprise must be reflected by the company's policies. Moreover, directors must encourage operating executives to exercise initiative, and they must provide the leadership for undertaking new and untried ventures.

Directors must keep themselves adequately informed of what is going on within the corporation. To do this, both overall check-ups and policy check-ups are required. The overall check-up serves to indicate the corporation's general condition and to give clues as to strengths and weaknesses. The policy check-up is a follow-through to ascertain how a particular policy decision is working out in practice. Check-ups do not imply lack of confidence in the management. Rather they are evidence of the teamwork between the directors and the management essential in a corporate undertaking.

A director's primary tool in carrying out his duties is the discerning questions he asks. Discerning questions often open up areas where action or at least a thorough review of policy is called for. They can lead to new policy decisions and provide a stimulus to executive action; they can be used effectively for checking up on results; and they can be educational both to board members and to operating executives.

Individual directors must often face unpleasant tasks in carrying out their mandate to direct the management of a corporation. Major maladjustments or deteriorating situations frequently require action that is both time-consuming and unpleasant. A man assumes the risk of having to face unpleasant tasks when he accepts a directorship. Ability and willingness to face these situations are requirements for the competent director.

In order to perform effectively its many important duties, the board must command real leadership and have the effective support of the many diverse groups having a stake in the corporation's success: the executive staff and the rank and file of employees; the stockholders; the creditors, suppliers, and customers; and the general public. A board of directors' legal authority alone does not provide the real power which it needs for implementing a constructive program. A board has effective authority only when it has won the confidence of the various groups at interest. Earning and maintaining this support are important conditions under which a board must function.

The motives that induce able men to accept directorships vary greatly. Non-financial considerations appear to be primary influences. The challenge inherent in the tasks of a director; opportunities for experience; the opportunity of association with business leaders; and a sense of obligation to the business community appear to be among the significant motives for influencing competent men to accept directorships. Having accepted directorships, able men retain their positions as long as opportunities are afforded for active participation in the corporation's affairs and as long as they can feel a real sense of contribution to the corporation's welfare.

Important qualities that are desirable to have represented in the membership of a board of directors are summarized as follows: honesty and integrity, compatability, interest in the welfare of the corporation as a whole, long-range point of view, ability to evaluate changing conditions, ability to appraise men, courage, ability to ask discerning questions, and a spirit of enterprise. While each director may not possess all these qualities, a well-balanced board will have all these qualities represented. A good board, moreover, will have balance in the age and experience of its members. Selection to secure this balance is to be preferred to a selection to afford representation for special interests.

Most boards of directors tend in practice to be self-perpetuating bodies. Hence directors must assume the responsibility of self-discipline and self-examination. Each director should catechize himself searchingly periodically to determine if he can and is fulfilling his obligations and living up to commendable standards of conduct.

----

2. THE COMPANY PRESIDENT—AND THE IMPOSSIBLE JOB THAT HAS TO BE DONE*

FOR THE PAST YEAR WE have been exposed to a number of discussions of the role of the President. These books, columns, articles and TV analyses have, of course, focused primarily on the task of the man whose office address is 1600 Pennsylvania Avenue, Washington, D.C. But the

----

* From the *Acme Reporter,* 1961 Series, No. 1.

sheer quantity of material has perforce stimulated us to ponder the role of any chief executive, in business or otherwise, and the internal and external stresses and problems that assail him.

The subject is not an easy one because it is the very essence of the office that the man shapes the job. How different was the function of a president in the 1860's, compared with the 1960's! Furthermore, the nature of the organization—be it business, academic, political, or charitable—cannot help but affect the role of its top man. The large, decentralized, diversified established company faces very different problems from those handled by its fast-growing, specialized, technically oriented neighbor. A manufacturing enterprise demands different qualities from an advertising agency.

Nevertheless, there are some generalizations that can be made about the office of president, and it is to these that this article is addressed. Six, in particular, emerge as significant: the aloneness, the power, the dependence on others, the pressures of time, the need to live in the future, and the multi-faceted responsibilities and opportunities.

At the Peak

Almost every man who has held or holds the presidency of a business comments (in his more thoughtful and relaxed moments) about the "loneliness" of his job. He does not mean, of course, that he is physically alone; a constant stream of people flow through his office door. What he does feel is the finality of his task of making the decisions, the hazards of being the scapegoat for things he does as well as things he does not do.

This is true even of men who move up from the highest posts in the hierarchy other than that of the president. One man, who as executive vice-president had been making decisions for years, told friends after he reached the top spot that he had never realized before how much he had relied on the very existence of someone higher up who had the ultimate authority. "All of a sudden," he said, "there's no one here but me. I can check with others, listen to their ideas, bounce my thoughts off them —but there is no one whose approval I can get, who will serve as the front man. It's all on me, now." "The buck stops here," proclaims a sign on one presidential desk.

This aloneness has many results besides a possible inner feeling of anxiety—or of exultation, depending on the individual. For one thing, a president has to struggle to maintain his objectivity. As the man in the corner office, he is the focal point for all those who work immediately around him. He has no one to call him down, at least on a day-to-day basis, and few who will even criticize him, or disagree with his pet proposals.

It may be, of course, that in the handful of truly major decisions he faces in the course of his presidential career, he makes a special effort to "see all sides." This is a difficult feat to pull off for anybody, under any circumstances; for a president, even if he sincerely puts his mind to it, this may be virtually impossible. Even so, the more serious problem comes in the host of seemingly minor yet collectively decisive decisions he makes from day to day. In the major choices, at least he has the benefit of the many interests and individuals who rise up and put forth their point of view. But, in the lesser decisions, few people come in; he is not under pressure from a number of quarters; and he is tempted to decide on the basis of his own instinctive reactions. Gradually the effects of these occasions pile up until suddenly the president finds that his freedom of action on the big decisions is sharply curtailed by the weight of his own minor decisions in the past.

This tendency to subjectivity which is an inevitable companion of the aloneness of the office manifests itself in other ways, too. Since there is no real "job description" for the president, and since the chances are that there would be nobody to enforce the specifications on the chief executive if there were such a document, he can—within reason—do what he feels is important at the moment. The pitfall here is, of course, that unconsciously all of us tend to do what we like to do rather than what needs to be done, so it is not surprising that presidents often tackle those parts of the business which they enjoy and let the rest go, thus running the risk of throwing the organization out of balance or neglecting important areas that need attention. It is interesting to note, incidentally, that directors instinctively recognize this fact when they pick presidents; they say that "old Jones was a great fellow for developing subordinates (or handling customers, or dealing with the unions, or whatever it might be); what we need to succeed him is someone who will tighten things up a bit."

To counteract this human tendency to "do what comes naturally," to close the gap in objectivity, the president needs advice and guidance. But where can it come from? Even with the best will in the world, his associates cannot supply it except in a very general way. True, they can exert a subtle pressure on the boss; he is always somewhat subject to their reactions, and realizes that he must not get himself way out of line or he will no longer have a team under him. But this kind of control is very general indeed, and does little more than set the outside limits on what he can and cannot do. As a matter of fact, because of long relationships, a president may know in advance how his vice-presidents are going to react to any move he proposes; and instinctively overact to begin with so he will come out where he wants to—and thus get his way without effective guidance from his subordinates. Because of the nature of the situation, insiders simply cannot play a productive role in this respect.

There are various sources of "outside" guidance and advice. Some presidents turn to friends—though this has usually not proven to be satisfactory because they cannot know the details of the problem; or they only see it as the president sees it, since he is their only source of information about it. Others have set up special advisory boards—but the success of this arrangement depends purely on the president's receptivity to the advice. He is not obligated to take it, especially since these groups are basically creatures of his own invention.

Others turn to consultants, who confirm or refute the president's judgment, and provide an objective based on experience in a wide range of other, similar situations. Though subject to some of the same difficulties as the advisory board, consultants can be helpful—especially if they also work with other key people in the firm, so that their advice has more chance of being put to work. This approach, of course, differs from the temporary, "help-us-put-out-the-fire" calling in of consultants; it involves using their help on a continuing basis. This way, they get to know the problems and people involved, which is good—so long as the president does not go to the other extreme of leaning too heavily on noncompany personnel.

The board of directors is, of course, the other main source of guidance, or even sometimes active leadership. But, here again, its success depends very much on how it is constituted and how active it is—both of which matters the president himself influences to a considerable degree. Parenthetically, the stronger and more independent a board, the better overall leadership the organization is likely to receive. One president recently argued vigorously with one of his executives who was trying to convince him that he would be better off "without these pesky laymen poking their noses into everything." The chief executive, who scrupulously kept out of the process of selecting the board, took precisely the opposite view, saying that the group might be "pesky" at times, but was absolutely indispensable to balanced leadership of the organization.

The Fountain of Power

The president of one of the nation's largest companies heard one of his assistants talking about the power of his office not long ago, and questioned him about the phrase. "Why," he said, "I don't have any particular power—I just have a job to do here, and some decisions to make."

When one lives with any responsibility long enough, he becomes so absorbed in the details of it and so used to the privileges and accoutrements which may be the superficial marks of power that he loses sight of the tremendous significance of even a lifted eyebrow or a curt dismissal, let alone an actual decision. In a company, people are always trying to guess and interpret the thoughts, wishes, and even inclinations of the president

—and sometimes an organization can get tied up because of a misinterpretation. For example:

> One president, faced with a building program, casually mentioned to an associate one day that "we have to go up in the air." This passing comment was quickly translated into an expensive set of architects' plans for a skyscraper. The arrangements were made for construction, and the final presidential approval sought. Though the president, in fact, did not like the plans, the project was so far down the pike, so many people were committed to it, and he was so conscious that it was his comment that had started the chain reaction, that he felt he could not veto the arrangement.
>
> Another chief executive spent six months trying to clear away the wreckage he caused when he casually mentioned one day that he might be needing an executive vice-president sometime. The rumors went through the company that someone was being brought in from the outside—and scotching the stories was a very real problem.

This power shows itself in many ways of which the president may be only vaguely aware. For example, he serves as a model for his subordinates in countless matters. Does he set some kind of balance between work and relaxation, hobbies and business? If he does, his associates—to varying degrees—will follow suit. Does he maintain rigid standards on expense accounts and fringe use of company facilities, or the opposite? In either case, others will reflect the same standards or lack of standards. Does he take his job seriously, wade into problems with vigor and decisiveness, even enthusiasm? If so, this same attitude will find expression in those who work with him.

It is the nature of man to look for models and that tendency is considerably reinforced if the model also happens to be the man who is hiring and firing, promoting and punishing.

The president's power is expressed in another related fashion; he sets the climate for the organization as a whole just as he offers a model for his associates. When General Eisenhower was considering the possibility of being a candidate for President, he is said to have sounded out a number of political leaders and pointed out to them that he knew little of the technicalities of the job. "All I can bring to the office," he is supposed to have said, "is a tone of high moral standards, tolerance, and prudence." "That is precisely what we need," the politicians replied. "You have outlined the principal function of the presidency—to set the tone for the government and the nation." Similarly, the president of a business sets the tone of his company: dynamic, aggressive, risk-taking, orderly, cautious, rational, ruthless—or whatever it may be. So any president has to be constantly aware of the impact that his attitudes, personality, and approaches to problems have right down through his entire organization.

It hardly needs be said that the ultimate expression of presidential power lies in the scope of the decisions that he makes. By the time a matter reaches his desk, it has far-reaching implications for men and communities beyond his abilities often to foresee and comprehend. If he views these issues merely as questions to be decided without maintaining a sense of the impact of his decisions, he will indeed see himself as simply "doing a job" rather than as wielding tremendous power and, consequently, bearing great responsibility. This is not easy; the results of his acts may be far away in terms of both time and distance. He is isolated from them to a large degree; it is hard for him to reach into the homes and communities and offices which will be affected by his decisions, and, given the complexity of modern business, often hard to trace the results of the aye or nay that he speaks. But they are there nonetheless and he must conduct himself in consciousness of them.

This problem is probably too personal, too individual, for the president to find help from any *group* of people, no matter how knowledgeable or how objective. Some presidents find support—or at least a person to talk to, to think aloud with, a sounding board to try out ideas on without commitment to action—in some individual member of their executive team who serves as a personal confidante or foil. Sometimes this man has the title of "assistant to the president"; sometimes he is the executive vice-president or treasurer or controller or has some other formal position. But, whatever he is called, his can be one of the most delicate and valuable posts in the company. He need not be exactly like the president; indeed, he is more useful if he is just different enough to strike a few sparks. Nor need he agree on everything; it is actually better if he draws the president out sometimes. But the point is that he acts not as another person—he is the president's alter ego, an extension just separated enough to be a conscience or doubting Thomas, as well as a handler of many matters the way the president himself would have done it if he had been called on to do it.

There are, of course, dangers in this kind of role. Employees, colleagues, and stockholders may fear a Rasputin and may resent a kind of hidden influence over which they have little control. Furthermore, if these people become mere ventriloquist's dummies, they lose their effectiveness.

Here, once again, the only true help to the president lies in himself—in understanding that he has a problem, that perfect solution is impossible, and that he must have the wisdom to seek independent advice when he needs it rather than to fear it.

Far Behind the Lines

"The day of the shirtsleeves manager is going fast," says a top insurance executive. "No longer can the president see for himself what the problem is, and make his decision on the basis of first-hand observation and evaluation. More and more he is forced to depend on others, to rely on reports and memoranda."

Many forces have contributed to this separation of the general from the front lines; any practicing business manager can tick them off with ease. Fortunately this development coincides with remarkable strides in the techniques of assembling, presenting, analyzing and utilizing data of all kinds. But all too few top businessmen are facile with these techniques; their training in handling figures has, in all probability, been limited to accounting and statistics taught from the viewpoint of the accountant or statistician rather than the manager. Sampling, probability theory, the use of computers, linear programming, discounted cash flow—all these seem to be matters better left to the bright young staff people who have been highly trained.

This practice presents two difficulties: in the first place, only the president can decide when one particular procedure or another is applicable, whether or not the information gained is worth the cost of securing it, what information should be fed into the analysis, and how it should be weighted. For no matter how refined the techniques may be, there is a large dash of the judgmental that goes into them—and that kind of decision can only come from the president. So a company cannot capitalize on new devices to their fullest without active and continuing top management participation.

Secondly, someone has to check on the experts, on the reasonableness of both their input and output, on the general outlines of their methodology. It may well be that this person could not actually perform the operation himself, but he has to have some "feel" for it so that he can ask the right questions, feel confident in evaluating the results, develop perspective enough to see the strengths and weaknesses of a particular approach in a given situation.

It should be pointed out here that there are substantial developments just over the horizon in the behavioral sciences field as well. As the study of how people act in organizations—and why—moves increasingly from the "common sense" approach to the scientific, a body of knowledge is being assembled. While much of this may not be in quite as usable a form as the material being uncovered in the physical sciences, it soon will be— and its impact on business management will be just as explosive. To this area, too, the president must direct his attention.

Presidents have almost no choice in this matter anymore. Because of the armchair nature of their jobs, because of the multiplicity and complexity of the factors entering into their decisions, because of the availability and accessibility of masses of information with modern techniques, they have to turn to staff experts and modern innovations in data processing. But they are caught in the trap of the weaknesses in their past training. Perhaps in this area more than any other, presidents in particular and top managers in general need to go back to school, or in effect to start schools of their own within their companies through formal training programs.

The Sands of Time

Like dollars, hours can be borrowed, manipulated, used for various purposes, stretched to considerable lengths—but sooner or later you find that there are limits beyond which you cannot go. There is not an endless supply; at some point choices must be made; and one cannot borrow against the future forever.

In the judicious use of time lies one of the great challenges to the president. He has community responsibilities because he stands for his company in the community—some even say that the president's principal duty is the creation of a company image. He has ceremonial responsibilities —greeting meetings, preparing in-company messages, going on inspection tours, giving out the 25-year pins, cutting ribbons. He has to deal with whatever problem anyone cares to bring to him, large or small. He has to study reports, make company appointments, keep communications channels open, settle fights. He has to spot and train his successors—which is no mean task in itself. He has to think, to plan, to generate ideas, to keep up with developments in management, to improve his own skills.

How much time should he assign to each of these functions? How can he select the kinds of in-company issues with which he wants to and should deal, and those which should be delegated? On what basis does he decide which community undertakings he should accept and those which should be turned down?

Clearly, there is no overall answer to these questions, but the danger is that the president, "doing what comes naturally," will make a series of ad hoc decisions on the use of his precious hours instead of consciously budgeting them in terms of the company's needs. A man in this job can come to feel omnipotent, can get the idea that there is no end to his energy, to the amount that he can get done. But there is, and ulcers and heart attacks attest to it. In this sense, advisers are like physicians: they help him to budget his strength and make the best use of his powers.

The Crystal Ball

One president, whose enterprise can afford virtually as many aides as he feels the situation demands, has a man on his staff who is laughingly called "The Great Anticipator" by his colleagues. This man's job is to sit and think—to look ahead at potential problem areas and point them out to the operating executives.

In most companies, the president has to be his own "Great Anticipator." His "thoughts while shaving," his intuitive sense of what lies ahead, his sensitivity to pitfalls and possibilities are the product of long years of experience. One flash of warning, of insight can be of inestimable value to the firm if he sees that it is pushed through to the point of effectiveness. Some observers have even gone so far as to say that such "serendipity" is the real virtue for which the stockholders pay their chief executive.

Over and above these moments of insight, which may or may not come to a given president, it is his task to make sure that someone is taking a systematic, rational look at the road ahead. The details of long-range planning may not be the president's job; the structuring and guidance of it certainly is. Over and over again specialists in this developing management concern have pointed out that the top executives in a company must be closely and enthusiastically involved if the planning is to have any real effect; and, above all the president must show that his heart is in it.

Seeing into the future is not the only problem here. The president must be willing to lay his influence on the line to push the plans—and the people—hard. An energetic chief executive will do this automatically if he is really in charge of the planning.

Furthermore, the president is responsible for the guessing of others. Clearly he cannot or will not be able to inspect every budget request, every proposal made by the long-range planners. But he himself must have some convictions about the company's future direction so that he can provide true leadership, like a ship captain who selects the destination and stands constant watch to make sure that his crew really takes the ship there.

In fact, the planning itself is a discipline by which a president keeps himself from taking the status quo for granted; and at the same time he can use it to train his subordinates to reach out for new ways to meet new challenges. It is not an easy responsibility to be the prime mover in a company, and to have to steer into the uncertain future rather than sail comfortably in the familiar present. The president needs all the help he can get in the form of maps, with the currents and tides carefully charted; he still is the one who must anticipate the danger of storms and the strength of favoring winds—and alert the whole crew.

The Impossible Job

Finally, a president has no way to measure his own effectiveness and the correctness of his decisions and his method of operation—no way, at least, which can bring him a sense of total satisfaction. A salesman's volume increases or it doesn't; a new production machine works or it doesn't; a stock issue is successful or it isn't. For many aspects of business, there are some tangible measures of success. But for the president these yardsticks are very hard to come by. He must proceed through the thicket of his job, guided primarily by faith in his judgment based on his long experience.

In fact, much of the president's function is to establish the ground rules and conditions which will permit his subordinates to chalk up the tangible results. Some presidents claim that the only real measure of their success is in the people who work for them; if they are growing in skill and stature, moving ahead in their professional careers, then, say these chief executives, they can feel satisfied with their presidential performance.

It is true, of course, that over a fairly extended period of years the company's financial position may represent some indication of the chief executive's competence. But so many factors and people enter into the results shown on the balance sheet—and the president knows this better than anyone—that no personal triumph is practicable. Furthermore, there are so many measures of corporate success at any given moment that it is hard to decide just what is success and what is not.

Thus, even a superficial review of some of the characteristics of the presidency brings home one fact: it is literally an impossible job. It is not only unique, complex, demanding, lonely, powerful, and, for many, eminently satisfying—it is the job that can't be done.

So the president has to make himself aware of the full dimensions and potential of his office, analyze just how much of the role he himself is capable of filling, and organize to see that the rest of it is done. Thus we find not just "The President," but "The Office of the President" headed up by the chief executive but filled out with people who, together, can make up the composite that provides the peak leadership any enterprise demands. It is a wise chief who sees his post in terms of "The Office of the President," seeks help in objectively delineating his personal role, and, while continuing to provide the indispensable quality of personal leadership, goes as far as possible to organize for the impossible job.

Of course, it is just here that a president offers his company the competitive leverage to pull ahead of other companies. Because the job *is* impossible, there is a real premium for organizing, for drawing on all the internal and external sources of strength available, so as to come closer to doing it than competitors are. He will be leading his company, and his company will be leading the parade.

3. DIAGNOSIS OF MANAGEMENT PROBLEMS*

Edward T. P. Watson

WHILE EXPERIENCE IS STILL RECKONED as the best teacher of administrative skills, many businessmen are convinced that the knowledge and learning that are gained from management training courses, university programs, and business literature will help an executive develop faster. To be sure, there appears to be no simple, direct relationship between the acquisition of knowledge and the improvement of skill. But we can agree on the more limited proposition: *although skill is basically "an ability to translate knowledge into action," and as such is learned by "doing"; nevertheless certain kinds of knowledge can lead to better ways of thinking, and thinking is itself a skill which can help a businessman to learn more about the situations he faces from day to day.*

How can the executive put business knowledge and theory to work for him? What does the literature have to say that will help him in solving management problems?

Admittedly, scholarly discussions of business do not always produce results that are useful to the practitioner. Writers frequently seem to be preoccupied with the construction of theories at the expense of an adequate demonstration of how their theories can be put to work. However, there is at least one concept which, it seems to me, can be very useful. This concept concerns the "processes of administration"—setting objectives, planning, organizing, and controlling. The approach is not new; it constitutes the framework of analysis in much of the current literature on management problems. But there has been too little concern with the problems of actually applying it.

If any theory is to be really serviceable to administrators, it must enable them to understand the problems of a here-and-now situation and must provide assistance when a course of action is needed. In addition, it must be flexible enough to be employed in the variety of situations that a businessman encounters. It is my purpose to show that the processes of administration provide a framework which satisfies these conditions.

* From the *Harvard Business Review,* January–February, 1958, Vol. 36, No. 1, pp. 69–76. Reprinted with permission of the publisher.

AUTHOR'S NOTE: This article is based on research conducted under a fellowship from The Ford Foundation.

John Doe, Trouble-Shooter

In order to be specific, let us take someone who must view a company's situation from the top-management level and who has not yet developed a high degree of conceptual skill in viewing company problems as a whole. In other words, let us take a straw man; we might call him "John Doe" and assume that his previous service with the company has been limited to one or two major departments.

Although we may be pushing Mr. Doe a bit too fast, in view of his background and preparation, let us suppose that he has just been promoted to a top-level job and is determined to get a good grip on the problems of his company. He has a mass of data on all aspects of the company's operations, including statistical reports and financial statements over a period of years. Classifying the material according to departments, he applies many standard measures of efficiency, and soon begins to unearth various trouble spots scattered throughout the company.

After spending considerable time on analysis, he attempts to draw up a statement of the company's problems. He finds declining sales, a strained financial condition, rising production costs, and related difficulties. His previous thinking has been along departmental lines, and he tends to think about top management's job in the same way—as a collection of sales, production, finance, and other departmental activities. Unfortunately he finds that in dealing with top-level problems he cannot make them fit departmental categories; the problems have a way of cutting across department boundaries in a most disconcerting fashion.

It is difficult for him to decide whether the major problems represent weak selling, inadequate financing, or poor production. Nor is it very helpful to tag these problems with a composite term, "sales-finance-production." Tackling inefficiencies within each department is like stamping out minor fires without quenching the main blaze, but Mr. Doe has trouble viewing management's job in any way other than as a collection of departmental responsibilities. If there are inefficiencies within the departments, how else should the difficulties be eliminated except by tackling them one by one?

METHOD OF ANALYSIS

It is at this point in Mr. Doe's struggle that a conceptual framework ought to provide some perspective. Since departmental activities are inter-related, and since the impact of some force on the company's operation is likely to produce ripples of reaction in other quarters, many of the trouble spots within various departments are probably related to one another. The first step, then, is for Mr. Doe to regard such trouble spots as *symptoms* rather than as problems to be tackled head-on, and to try to get an overall picture. To use an analogy, the doctor does not necessarily treat rash and headache as separate ailments, but attempts a fundamental diagnosis.

Secondly, to get an overall view, Mr. Doe needs some meaningful way of talking about the underlying problems which have produced such diverse symptoms of trouble. At higher levels of management, problems tend to overlap departmental boundaries, and the departmental tags, like sales, production, and so forth, often do not fit. The processes of administration provide a more adequate way of generalizing about these underlying issues. They not only offer a logical system of inquiry but also may suggest some additional analyses that Mr. Doe has overlooked when examining the basic data.

Do the symptoms point to some failure of management in setting objectives? In planning? In organizing or controlling? Examining the symptoms in the light of these processes may be very revealing for Mr. Doe.

Setting Objectives

Although objectives have often been discussed in broad terms, such as profit and responsibilities to stockholders, labor, and the community, a narrower definition may be more helpful here. As Lyndall F. Urwick has pointed out:

> "Profit can be no more the objective of a business than betting is the objective of racing, making a score the objective of cricket, or eating is the objective of living."[1]

Urwick advocated phrasing the primary objective in terms of the exact nature of the products or services which the business exists to make or render. This is a practical approach, although I think we can improve on it slightly by having "objective" refer to the niche or part of the market that the company wishes to acquire by offering some product or service. In thinking about a company's objective, in other words, we can go beyond the product or service itself to the kind of demand involved—for example, the demand for finely tailored men's clothes or specific types of food products.

If management has a fixed idea that its business is to make a specific product such as stiff collars or steam locomotives, it can easily overlook what is happening to consumer demand because of competing products or changes in the public's tastes. There is a big difference between holding on to a particular slice of consumer demand and holding on to a specific product. For example:

> A manufacturer of a mechanical computing machine harnessed all the company's resources to make a better and better machine. The company

---

[1] *The Elements of Administration* (New York, Harper & Brothers, 1943), p. 27.

ignored the challenge of other kinds of office equipment, as well as the more recent development of electronic devices, until the field of competitors had passed by. Only one other company made a similar machine; it had a wide line of office equipment and would have been a tough opponent if this one-product manufacturer had elected to wage a price war over the remaining market.

Suppose the manufacturer had seen his objective as satisfying the demand for calculating equipment of any kind (as long as its manufacture was consistent with his resources). This point of view might very well have led to closer relationships with the market, and these closer ties might have revealed the limitation of the existing product, as well as the opportunities for satisfying the demand with other products.

One thing that makes this matter of objectives so important is that most companies' product lines are undergoing slow but steady change. The fact that sales volume is often rising while such changes are taking place tends to divert management's eye from what is going on. Yet it is just as easy to overlook trends threatening to one's market niche as it is to drift into markets that are inconsistent with resources and goals. Consequently, unless management *regularly* reviews its marketing situation and company objectives, it is likely to be dangerously late in sizing up a new trend.

TRACING FAILURE

To return for a moment to John Doe and his diagnosis of his company's problems, we may find that many of the symptoms he has uncovered can be traced to some failure in the area of objectives: uncertainty about the firm's position in the market, the attempt to enter markets without adequate resources, or a failure to adjust to changes in the external world.

Mr. Doe may have to do a good deal of interviewing and study to turn up such a failure. It is not likely to be readily apparent, especially since executives usually pay lip service to the importance of setting objectives even if they rarely do much soul-searching about them. But if a careful investigation *does* reveal a failure in this area, Mr. Doe can give management every assurance that intelligent efforts to cope with the problem will bring significant results—results that may show up not just in one management function but in many.

Here we come to an important difference between the diagnostic approach and a more superficial attack on symptoms. If one starts with the thought, "Our trouble is lack of sales," or "What we have to do is cut costs," or "We need better managers," the chances are that he will find plenty of evidence to support his case. A failure in setting objectives is likely to show up in all of these ways. Consequently, the investigation will end prematurely, and management's efforts to set things straight, however drastic, will fall short. This is the kind of thing we see happening all the time among companies dominated by functional thinking, and it is no wonder that specialists in sales, industrial engineering, industrial relations, and so on can almost always discover "what is wrong" in an ailing company simply by applying their specialized knowledge.

But even though he takes the diagnostic approach, Mr. Doe may not trace the company's trouble to objectives. This means that he should go on to the other processes of administration.

Planning Strategy

The choice of a particular niche in the market is the starting point for planning a strategy that can give the firm some kind of competitive advantage. Management needs a plan based on the characteristics of the market, the resources of the firm, and the conditions of the economic environment —a plan that promises a profitable advantage. Strategy is, of course, closely related to the choice of market. For example:

> When Cluett, Peabody and Co., Inc., decided to shift from stiff collars to men's shirts many years ago, one of the problems confronting management was the competition from small, low-overhead companies that used cheap labor and inexpensive materials to turn out shirts selling under two dollars. Cluett, Peabody decided to avoid this competition by making a shirt embodying style and quality and selling between $2 and $5. The company thus created a new niche and a new product.
>
> At that time the plan included other considerations that took into account every aspect of the business. The management decided to use the established trade name, *Arrow*, and to make sales through a selected number of exclusive stores, which would help carry the advertising. It trained salesmen to *sell* rather than take orders. It established a merchandising department to keep abreast of fashion trends and come up with new styles, fabrics, and colors.
>
> While manufacturing had to be reorganized, the company's experience in making collars could be utilized in making part of the shirt. Management felt that its finances were adequate for the task, but that executive training and education were necessary. In effect, it examined the entire plan to change course with the company's resources and the characteristics of the market in mind.

Good strategy involves a recognition of those activities which are most essential to success at a particular time; the importance of various company efforts may shift with different stages of growth and development. In one period production may command attention, while in another sales or some other activity may be more important. Unless the administrator can gauge what areas need special attention at particular times, he may find that his neglect of a critical point has resulted in loss of market position.

All of this may seem obvious enough in principle, but it is not so easy to do the right thing in practice. For one thing, strategy becomes embodied in company policy, and a policy can sometimes become a sacred cow, which succeeding managements hesitate to change either because of a feeling that it is difficult to argue with success or a belief that present trends are fads which will soon disappear.

As a result, we hear of such cases as the company in the 5-and-10-cent store business which held on to that price classification long after its competitors had moved into higher-price merchandise—even though the spirit of the old policy was violated to the extent that cups and saucers, and other goods usually bought in combination, were separately priced so the traditional price tag limits would not be exceeded.

SCHEDULING & COORDINATION

Planning of still another kind is also required. What will the company produce during the year, season, quarter, or other period for which it can do advance planning with some certainty? How much will be produced, and when will it be produced? Management must make these decisions in advance of sale. When the production period is long or when there are seasonal peaks, plant and workers need to be employed efficiently in order to avoid excessive inventory, loss of business, or labor problems.

The planning function brings into clear focus problems that arise from viewing top management's job as a collection of departmental activities without relating them to a larger purpose. The sales department may want more varieties of the product available on shorter notice than the production department can supply. The production department, if left to its own devices, may want to standardize on fewer products with longer runs and with a good deal more lead time than the sales department can accept. Furthermore, there may be brisk competition between departments for available resources. All the major departments must take part in planning, but management must resolve conflicting purposes in terms of what will contribute most to attaining the company goal.[2]

DIAGNOSTIC TOOL

For Mr. Doe this means that, regardless of the kind of planning, an appreciation of the sequence as well as the initial timing of a program is important. He must ask himself if any of the symptoms stem from failure to develop strategy or some other aspect of planning.

If there *is* a carefully thought out plan, he may find that some of the departmental troubles have been "budgeted for," so to speak; that is, in balancing the needs of one department against another, management may have purposely taken a calculated risk and decided that, in view of its limited resources, the cost of temporary inefficiency in one area would be

[2] See Bruce Payne, "Steps in Long-Range Planning," HBR March–April 1957, p. 95.

more than offset by the long-run gains in another area. In such a case the question becomes whether the cost is greater than anticipated; and, if so, whether the plan should be revised. The presence of planning may thus be a valuable diagnostic tool which can aid Mr. Doe in his analysis of the company's problems.

But suppose Mr. Doe avoids the usual pitfalls and still does not find that planning is the key. He can go on to the next step in his diagnosis— another of the processes of administration.

Organizational System

As a company grows, its organization presents new problems of adaptation. For instance, new divisions of responsibility may become necessary if certain activities—such as research—are to receive adequate attention, or different relationships among departments may be required to reduce the strain on overloaded executives. Decisions may have to be made at different levels since overcentralization produces a slow-moving enterprise. New and old staff activities need to be fitted into the organization in ways that contribute to the quality of work and decision. Management must also devote attention to the ever-present task of training personnel.

The job of adaptation is complicated by the social characteristics of an organization. Change upsets the existing customs and routines, and vested interests oppose reduction in authority or shrinkage in the scope of activities. Moving too fast, therefore, *can* result in demoralization.

CONCEPTUAL FRAMEWORK

On the foregoing points there is likely to be little disagreement. American executives tend to be "organization conscious," a fact borne out by the seemingly endless series of organizations and reorganizations which go on in so many firms. At first glance, therefore, it might seem that Mr. Doe should have little trouble getting to the root of any failure in this process of administration. In actuality, however, just the opposite is true. Accurate analysis of an organizational problem is one of the most tricky jobs there is; yet this is also an area where snap judgments abound.

Perhaps the most important thing Mr. Doe needs, if he hopes to proceed very far in his analysis, is a systematic way of talking about "organization." There is a tendency to use the dichotomy of "an organizational problem" as against "a human relations problem"—a dichotomy that would be more useful if we were dealing with discrete items like sheep and goats. Unfortunately, a structural difficulty is likely to be accompanied by disturbed personal relationships and other problems, so that, if we focus on only one of them, we will surely get a distorted picture. There are so many dimensions to an organizational situation that it is quite easy to find what one wants to find. If it is "status," it will be present; if it is "bureaucracy," that will likewise be in evidence; or if it is any one of a number of concepts, applicable in part but not exclusively so, that too will be found.

The verbal short cuts we use in discussing organization produce mistaken notions of agreement. In talks between persons who understand the total picture perhaps no confusion will arise, but agreement at a fairly high level of abstraction may conceal fundamental differences in the way the details of a situation are analyzed. Hence, we need to make a greater effort to examine and talk about organizational systems in terms of the many mutually interdependent elements involved, such as structure, social groups, and individuals.

Our task is complicated by the need to focus on the separate elements and also to retain an understanding of "the total situation." By that we mean—in the words of Mary Parker Follet—"not only trying to see every factor that influences the situation, but even more than that, the relation of these factors to one another."[3] We are forced to resort to some kind of analytical framework before proceeding very far. An organization has several dimensions, each of which we can examine separately as long as we keep in mind their mutual interdependence:

The Job Structure. In surveying the job structure for trouble spots, management needs various points of view. The technician can judge the feasibility of methods and procedures while the industrial engineer can analyze tasks from the standpoint of simplification of operations. The administrator, on the other hand, should look at quite different questions: Does the job structure take advantage of specialization and technical know-how? Is it economical? Does it afford adequate control, attention from management, and coordination with related activities? The executive can also examine the levels at which decisions are made to see if further centralization or decentralization at specific points will improve the structure.

The investigation may reveal difficulties that have shown up as frictions between people. Similarly, the inquiry may show that troubles in communications or lines of authority are in part symptoms; that what might be superficially diagnosed as a "communications" failure, for example, may really be a "communications *and job structure*" failure.

The Authority System. The assignment of a job carries with it the assignment of authority to fulfill its responsibilities. In the literature of business there are many proverbs about the definition, allocation, and recognition of authority, all of which are useful as general guides but which are limited in value when the main concern is building cooperative relationships.[4] On the fringes of departmental responsibility, many prob-

---

[3] Henry C. Metcalf and L. Urwick, Editors, *Dynamic Administration: The Collected Papers of Mary Parker Follet* (New York, Harper & Brothers, 1941), p. 187.

[4] See Herbert Simon, *Administrative Behavior* (New York, The Macmillan Company, 1957), Chapter II.

lems crop up where solutions seem to depend more on cooperative intent than on greater precision in defining authority. When authority relationships are disturbed, furthermore, feelings are likely to become so intense that restoration of peace depends more on improvement in personal contacts than on redefining authority.

The traditional literature of business has a great deal more to say about the relationships between a superior and his subordinates than about the job relationships of people who are in *different channels of authority,* but who must nonetheless cooperate to get the work done. In checking to see if symptoms of trouble are due to organizational failures, Mr. Doe will do well to look at both types of interaction. Some writers have assumed, no doubt, that cross relationships between persons in different channels of authority would be properly influenced when necessary by appeal to the superior who was in charge of all the activities in question. In practice, of course, these full-dress hearings often fail to produce cooperative behavior and, to avoid undesirable consequences, may be used only in cases of last resort.

Sometimes the way in which tasks can best be performed does not coincide with the manner in which authority is supposed to be distributed according to traditional beliefs. A study of line and staff relationships has shown that they do not reduce to a simple formula according to which the staff always "advises" or "persuades."[5] As an expert in some matters, the staff man often ends up with the actual power to make certain decisions, regardless of what the organization chart says. The danger—which may or may not materialize but which certainly should be watched—is that, as a result, the line supervisor's role as a manager will be considerably weakened.

The Communications System.   Assignment of jobs and allocation of authority together establish certain *formal* channels of communications, around which can be developed a system of communication that in turn is important to the support of the authority relationships.[6] The *informal* channels elaborate the network through which people interact; here adequacy depends primarily on the individuals' behavior and capacity for communication.

Real skill in communication is so difficult to achieve that Mr. Doe will probably be able to trace some of the trouble to this source. The problem is what to do about it once he has brought the matter to top management's attention. In the long run training may help, but in the short run the gains are likely to be limited to improving communication

---

[5] Charles A. Myers and John C. Turnbull, "Line and Staff in Industrial Relations," HBR July–August 1956, p. 113.

[6] See Chester I. Barnard, *The Function of the Executive* (Cambridge, Harvard University Press, 1938).

on the informational level and to improving other aspects of the organizational system that indirectly affect communication. It is also possible that management will recognize its responsibility—as a distinct function—to create a better environment for communication.

The Social System. The formal relationships within a business constitute a structure around which informal activities develop. The members of the organizational system are also members of many smaller, interlocking groups (informal organizations) which are held together by bonds of common interest. Changes of many kinds can disturb or upset social relations within these groups, with repercussions throughout wide areas of organization.

Social systems are an expression of people's desires to share with others common experiences, attitudes, and beliefs; and as such, social systems give an individual support and security that add meaning to the world of work. On the other hand, group norms are also an effective measure of control over individual behavior. Social custom is, of course, not always amenable to management's purposes, but neither is it always opposed. The members of a group may develop a strong identification with their work and hence with the company goal assigned to them. So, the social system is important.

The Individuals. An administrator is accustomed to judging the adequacy of individuals in performing specific jobs, but he also finds it impossible to ignore their ability or inability to relate themselves to others. He must realize that though people are sensitive to the norms of the group, they also retain many individual feelings. Their behavior is influenced not only by the work environment but also by their off-the-job life. Although there may be some grounds for accusing modern man of being a conformist with respect to dress, food, the movies he sees, and so on, he still remains highly individualistic in his beliefs about himself, his motivations, his hopes, and his goals.

INTERDEPENDENT FUNCTIONS

Since the five dimensions of an organizational system just discussed are mutually interdependent, changes in one area will affect the others. *All* areas are likely to be affected from time to time by planning, control, and operating decisions, as well as by unionism, community norms, economic trends, and other factors outside the company. The sensitivity of the organizational system and the interdependence of its parts can be illustrated in countless ways. Here is one example of the kind of thing that can happen:

The management of a medium-size company decided to add some new products to the line in an effort to stem sagging sales. The new items demanded more technical knowledge than the plant manager possessed, so a new man was hired and given the title of superintendent.

For many years plant organizations had been quite stable with manufacturing routines undergoing little change. Certain groups of the skilled workers had won preferred position with respect to wages and treatment by management. However, the new manager's position and relationship to the organization were never made clear. Instead of functioning as a technical adviser, he assumed more and more operating duties. Changes in layout and equipment broke up customary working habits and shattered groups that previously had been tightly knit. Some of the skilled groups went directly to top management, bypassing the superintendent, and won wage increases, while others with less preferred positions became so concerned over job security that they attempted to keep production on certain jobs from increasing very much.

The new manager became too absorbed in operating details to establish any relationships with the employees or the plant manager, and top management followed company tradition in leaving the plant to be run by plant executives. The downward spiral in performance resulted in a loss on the new products.

If Mr. Doe confines his analysis to two or three aspects of the organizational system, he again may end up attacking symptoms instead of causes. In the above example, for instance, any trouble in communication, status, or lines of authority is bound to reflect, at least in part, the failures of individuals or else the disruption of the social system.

But suppose again that Mr. Doe applies diagnosis and still has not been able to identify his company's trouble. He can carry his investigation further and look at the control process.

Control Process

Even though the administrator may visualize what the objective should be, how it should be reached, and who is to do the job, he still has to put plans into action and establish a form of control as well as follow up to see that plans are carried out. Managers cannot always anticipate events, so at times plans must be modified very quickly. Some scheme is needed to apprise management of what is taking place at the consumer level; otherwise, production and sales get out of kilter.

Control is the function of checking on performance and measuring results against some standard. Depending on what is being controlled, the standard can be in terms of target dates for completion of certain jobs or in terms of efficiency measures of some kind such as unit costs, direct labor costs, return on investment, and so on. At the lower levels of organizational activity, the techniques of the cost accountant and industrial engineer are easily applicable if tasks become crystallized into routines and procedures. But if top management is uncertain about its objectives or has failed to plan ahead, control at lower levels can be undermined, as in the following case:

> A company sold through wholesalers, who for some time had assumed the burden of deciding what the market would take. Then one year the wholesalers shifted this burden to the manufacturer by buying in smaller quantities and reordering when necessary. Since the product had a seasonal pattern, orders did not arrive in a regular fashion throughout the year.
>
> The management spent a lot of time tinkering with a scheme to divide the orders on hand among the various departments to even the work load, but no one had begun work on a sales plan that would permit coordinated action in all departments. Failure to do this planning produced trouble all along the line: no work at some times, overtime at others, a shortage of parts for orders that came in unexpectedly, and lack of direction for the sales force. Moreover, without a clear-cut goal and a plan broken down into manageable steps, and without an organization to fix responsibility for executing the plan, attempts at control were hopelessly ineffective.

Control is not easy under the best of circumstances, as experienced executives know. There are difficulties in knowing what information is critical and how to get it. There is also danger in relying on a single technique, such as formal reports from below.[7] One company president had the habit, if he had confidence in a man, of never going near his department. Sometimes this confidence turned out to be misplaced. When this happened, serious problems easily developed because there was a lag between the outbreak of trouble and the time it showed up in reports. The goal of being completely informed will probably never be attained by many, but the tendency for bad news to be filtered out as information goes upward is a factor with which Mr. Doe should reckon.

Often linked with control is the term "coordination." If an effective job is done in selecting objectives, planning, organizing, and controlling, the net result will be a coordinated effort. To do this, executives at all levels must know what they are to attain, how to attain it, who is to do each job, and when modifications of plans and activities are needed. In other words, coordination is not a separate and distinct function of management but is a composite of other functions that are highly interrelated and that depend for their individual effectiveness on skillful management.

Conclusion

The line of inquiry that Mr. Doe has been following does not guarantee "an accurate diagnosis or your money back." Sometimes important evidence is overlooked or the significance of data is misevaluated,

---

[7] See John G. McLean, "Better Reports for Better Control," HBR May–June 1957, p. 95.

even by executives who have experience, knowledge of techniques, and imaginative powers in isolating significant facts and evaluating them.

If we assume, however, that Mr. Doe has done a careful job of investigation and interpretation, he will emerge with a clearer view of the company's underlying problems than he could have obtained by thinking only in terms of departmental categories. He now has some "handles" to take hold of. If his analysis shows that the symptoms stem largely from failures in certain management processes, he will be able to muster the evidence to show how these failures have produced ripples or even waves of reaction throughout the company, and will be able to avoid such generalities as "The company needs more sales," or "The company's problem is a lack of profit."

The aim of this particular method of analysis is to gain a fuller appreciation of the underlying problems that plague management, rather than to focus too much attention on the "tagging" of a problem as one, let us say, of planning or control. Although there are many such problems common to all business, the manner in which a particular business is affected and the way in which treatment should be administered are never quite the same from case to case.

Once he sees the focus of the symptoms, Mr. Doe may ask himself, "What should I do about it?" Here, once again, he will find the concept of processes of administration useful in formulating a plan of action:

> For what part of the market does the company want to compete in view of its resources and the requirements for the job?
> What kind of planning must management do to provide for growth, an intelligent strategy, and answers to the "what," "how much," and "when" of the product line?
> What kind of organizational structure, personnel, and training are required?
> What kinds of controls should management have if it is to be "fast on its feet" in adjusting to unforeseen and changing circumstances?
> Does management reappraise all these functions from time to time, particularly when control information shows unusual discrepancies?

IDEAS & ACTION

These concepts may not appear to be particularly new, but the way of thinking involved in the use of them is apparently different from much current practice.[8] A point of view can make a big difference in the way an executive looks at and relates the facts of a situation. Much depends on his ability to establish an orderly relationship among factors in the eco-

---

[8] See Charles E. Sumner, Jr., *Factors in Effective Administration* (New York, Columbia University Press, 1956).

nomic and social environment, in the firm's own market, and in the operations of the company. He must be aware of the "totality" of the firm, but this is an abstract ideal unless he can think of company activities in terms of the objective, plans for attaining the objective, the organizational system created to do the job, and the controls required to adjust to an evolving situation.

Profit lies at the end of a long chain of interrelated activities. No single link in the chain seems less important than any other, although a good many theoretical discussions of profit maximization seem to focus primarily on cost control, optimum levels of output, the equating of marginal revenues and marginal costs, and so on. While these factors are certainly important and deserve careful attention, they need to be put in perspective by top executives. Far greater possibilities for profit show up in focusing on the basic design of a business—the direction it is going, its scheme of operations, the interconnection of its parts. The key to success lies in the *processes* of administration.

---

4. THE POLICY FORMATION PROCESS*

Paul M. Dauten, Jr.

The "Rabbit Function" of Policies

FIRST OF ALL, LET US note that the policy complex has many dimensions. For example, policies even have what might be considered to be a "rabbit function": policies beget policies! We might also relate policies to the "chicken-versus-egg" argument: while it is clear that existing policies generate derivative policies and possibly even revisions of existing policies, it is not altogether clear whether the revised policies come as a result of the existing general policies or whether the old general and more specific policies give way because newer ones have conscientiously or unconsciously

* From *Proceedings of the Annual Meeting, 1962, Academy of Management,* pp. 93–102. Reprinted with permission from the publisher. The author gratefully acknowledges his discussions with Mr. Carl W. Muhlenbruch, President of TEC-SEARCH, Inc., Educational and Technical Consultants, Evanston, Illinois and Mr. Richard Oehler, Industrial Engineer, McDowell Aircraft Company, St. Louis, Missouri. He is also indebted to some of his students at the University of Illinois for providing several of the extensions of the basic ideas presented herein.

superseded them or made them obsolete or inappropriate. Thus, policies seem to be self-circular in nature—the new policies in one sense control the old, since they tend to determine whether the old ones will remain; but existing policies, both old and new, control the formation of still newer ones.

Policies Are Action Oriented

Basically, policies are important because they make possible relatively stable expectations regarding the behavior of participants in an organization. This is to say, policies make possible *predictable* results.

But policies have generally been viewed rather statically, rather than dynamically. It is here contended that policies must, for best results, be viewed as action-concepts, such as the action diagrams drawn on the blackboard by the football coach, the hopscotch diagrams that we, as children, drew on the sidewalk, or even more complex action-type diagrams, such as PERT[1] and CPT,[2] that are now being used by business in military circles for planning, programming, and decision-making.

Policies Have Many Attributes

Policies have many facets. They seem to possess the following attributes:

1. Policies are action-oriented.
2. Policies are standards for solving problems.
3. Policies energize and, at the same time, direct, focus, channel, restrict, re-generate, modify, and utilize these energies.
4. Policies include objectives and values as master policies.[3]
5. Policies have as their most conspicuous *distinguishing* characteristic the idea of "relatedness."
6. Policies exist in a hierarchy.
7. Policies are both formal and informal.
8. Policies relate to the present and to the future and are *flexible* blueprints for action; or, more precisely, policies are flexible blueprints for relating purposes and action.
9. Policies relate to every aspect of the (organizational) hierarchy.
10. The motivational or energizing forces of policies are people's needs, wants, goals, and desires. These consist of physical, social, esthetic, intellectual, and moral or spiritual needs and desires.

---

[1] Programmed Evaluation Review Technique.

[2] Critical Path Technique.

[3] Thus, to make a profit and to be friendly are policies and values as well as objectives.

11:   Policies must be flexible, so that the firm will be in a position to cope with the many uncertainties that cannot be accurately predicted.

As a corollary to this last statement, it should be noted that business firms which forecast poorly must have a more flexible policy framework than those which are able to forecast more accurately.

Organizations Have These Same Attributes

So much for policies. Let us now consider the attributes of organizations:

1.   Organizations are action-oriented.
2.   Organizations have standards for solving problems.
3.   Organizations energize, and, at the same time, direct, focus, channel, restrict, re-generate, modify, and utilize these energies.
4.   Organizations include objectives and values as master structuring elements.
5.   Organizations have as their most conspicuous *distinguishing* characteristic the idea of "relatedness."
6.   Organizations exist in a hierarchy.
7.   Organizations are both formal and informal.
8.   Organizations relate to the present and to the future and are *flexible* blueprints for action; or, more precisely, organizations are flexible blueprints for relating purposes and action.
9.   The (organizational) hierarchy is a hierarchy of policies.
10. The motivational or energizing forces of organizations are people's needs, wants, goals, and desires. These consist of physical, social, esthetic, intellectual, and moral or spiritual needs and desires.
11. Organizations must be flexible so that the firm will be in a position to cope with the many uncertainties that cannot be accurately predicted.

As a corollary, business firms which forecast poorly must be more flexibly designed or organized than those which are able to forecast more accurately.

Policy Changes Are Organizational Changes

From this comparison of the attributes of policies and organizations, it seems quite evident that policy matters and organizational matters are identical in meaning. If this is true, policy changes are organizational changes! The purpose of policies—and of organization—is to bind or relate such things as time; place; people; physical, monetary and intangible assets; decision making and decision-making centers; means-ends chains;

organizational knowledge, attitudes, and skills; activities; methods; information; the internal and external environment; and personal, organizational, and social values and goals.

Job Descriptions

A job description is a flexible standard bounding and describing what each job holder is to do under varying circumstances and showing how his role is related to other roles that must be played in an organization. As such, a job description is basically a policy.

Individual Attitudes Versus Organizational Policies

Among other things, attitudes . . .

1. Are standards for solving personal problems.
2. Include personal objectives as master attitudes.
3. Exist in a hierarchy.
4. Relate to the future.
5. Relate to every aspect of one's personal life.
6. Must be flexible.

Similarly, policies . . .

1. Are standards for solving organizational problems.
2. Include organizational objectives as master policies.
3. Exist in hierarchy.
4. Relate to the future.
5. Relate to every aspect of organizational life.
6. Must be flexible.

An organization utilizes the individual attitudes of its managers to develop organizational policies. Although policies are sometimes formulated by one or two individuals, an organization's policy decisions are typically formed by attitude consensus in regard to the best plan of action for reaching the organization's goals. These pooled attitudes become the formal and informal policies of the company. It might correctly be said that they represent the official and unofficial attitudes of the company.

The Corporate Zone of Compliance

But what happens when we conjoin, or bring together, individual attitudes and group policies? Here Chester Barnard's "zone of indifference" (or Herbert Simon's "zone of acceptance") become relevant. Indeed, it seems that a new term, the "zone of compliance" would also be useful in this connection as a means of describing what the organization expects of its participants. This "zone of corporate compliance" in interaction with an individual's zone of acceptance raises the usual questions concerning the "inducements-contributions balance"; or we might speak of the "compliance-acceptance balance." The whole idea seems basically to be a demand-supply relationship.

To extend Barnard's idea, there are both *internal* and *external* zones of acceptance and both internal and external areas of corporate compliance, depending on whether we are considering transactions between a company and its "internal" members, such as employees or managers, or whether we are concerned with the firms' transactions with "external" participants, such as suppliers and customers. In this connection, some authors speak of "role strain." Thus, if management asks an individual to accept or do something which lies at the fringes or boundaries of his zone of acceptance, a certain degree of role strain results. In such a case, management's job is to bring the corporate zone of compliance and the individual's zone of acceptance into an area of (mutual) compatability. Motivation of a positive or negative type is relevant in this connection.

Generally speaking, the policies of the organization and the attitudes of the individuals either represent, or relate closely to, the strengths and weaknesses of the corporation and to the strengths and weaknesses of the individuals. It is for this reason that corporations spend so much time and money on executive-development programs, which tend to enhance or extend the individual executive's area of acceptance and to clarify for the executive the organization's zone of compliance. Thus, executive-development programs tend to bring these two zones into closer correspondence.

The Organizational Frame of Reference

The policy system of the organization is the organization's personality structure, and this structure of organizational values is useful to the organization in assessing the desirability of alternative courses of action. This structure of official and unofficial organizational attitudes consists of a hierarchy of formal and informal policies. It represents the organization's frame of reference and is a master standard for solving organizational problems.

The corporate frame of reference is constantly being modified as the organization encounters and deals with new experiences. Accordingly, succeeding decisions are evaluated in the light of a slightly revised frame of reference. Through this process, the organization gains experience and maturity in its decision making. As in the case of an individual, the organization at times makes unwise decisions, perhaps under stress and strain, and these could be costly decisions, which it will later regret.

Each sub-unit of the enterprise has its own organizational personality consisting of a structure of more localized policies which, in a successful organization, will reflect higher-level policies. Such group personalities, either for the entire organization or for its constituent parts, are sometimes called "syntalites." If the organization as a whole is a healthy one, the individual departmental syntalites are united by means of a larger, grand synthesis of policies into a fully integrated personality structure.

The Role of Organizational Authority

This overall organizational frame of reference in the form of a structure of policies might advantageously be considered to be a master control mechanism in the form of "cognitive-evaluative controls." The role of authority in such a control system is to induce or even enforce change within the organization. Psychologists tell us that personality changes will not occur unless they are accompanied by emotional changes of some kind. In fact, some psychologists contend that a personality change is, by definition, an emotional change. Through the emotional disturbance, the psychophysical mechanism of the body has been altered and the human organism is equipped in a slightly different way to cope with future problems. Stating the matter in another way, the role of authority is to provide either a positive or negative emotional experience, which tends to force individuals to direct their efforts toward the accomplishment of organizational purposes.

If the authority structure reflects the mature judgment of managers, such motivated compliance with the managers' wishes will ordinarily be desirable for all concerned, and may even assist subordinates and others in their personal development and maturation. However, many scholars point out that if compliance with management's wishes is enforced rather than positively motivated, it will not have a desirable influence upon employees. These writers wisely suggest that a preferable form of managerial control is one of "self-control" on the part of each individual. Imposed authority should be considered a temporary expedient, which becomes unnecessary when dealing with more mature individuals.

Policies lose variety at higher levels in the organizational pyramid. But, according to a well-known law of cybernetics, controls, to be successfully applied, must possess the necessary degree of variety to match the variety of the system to be controlled. This apparent contradiction presents some interesting and challenging problems for the executive charged with the responsibility of establishing a comprehensive system of practical controls throughout an enterprise.

The Characteristics of Policies Exist on a Continuum

Policies may be described in terms of boundaries or limits. The characteristics of policies may exist along the following kind of continua: from concrete to abstract; from local to cosmos-wide; from specific needs to general ends; from short-range to long-range; from current to future; from consumption expenditures to investment expenditures; from specific assets to all assets; from complete rigidity to complex flexibility; from completely formal to completely informal; from no freedom to complete freedom; from a highly creative environment to one that inhibits creativity; from no initiative to full initiative; from no value to great value; from no energy to a great store of energy; from completely static to highly dynamic; from fixed to variable; from personal to social; from internal to external; from complete friendliness to complete unfriendliness; from highly esthetic to completely repugnant; from perfect honesty to outright untruthfulness and dishonesty; from justice to injustice; from one objective to a whole range of objectives; from a zero dollar-value to unlimited dollar amounts; from the simple to the highly complex; from complete harmony to a complete lack of harmony; from orderliness to chaos; from great risk to no risk; from a high degree of safety to a great exposure to danger; from taking no action to taking any action; from conscious and deliberate action to action that is unconscious and habitual; and so on.

It is important to note that the zones of acceptance of individuals and the zones of compliance of the company lie somewhere along these attitudinal and policy limits that have just been listed.

Building in Flexibility

Policies should be flexible but not flaccid, both in the organization of one's personal life and in the case of organizing for business. Examples of flexibility include: the use of movable partitions; the skipping of channels of organizational command; the use of interchangeable parts; the development of transferable skills through executive development programs; and the use of money, or cash. The degree to which one is able to build optimum flexibility into an organization depends on one's skill and competence. Since flexibility is frequently achieved only at a cost, the availability of funds sometimes limits the degree of flexibility that can be achieved by an organization. The concept of flexibility is particularly important in attempting to bring the zones of compliance of a company and the zones of acceptance of individuals into an area of mutual compatability. Communication is a vital and necessary ingredient in the relating or linking process that is accomplished by means of various kinds of policies.

But while flexibility as a policy is important, it must not be used indiscriminately or as an excuse or substitute for building the optimum organization structure. As an example, the use of certain types of special-purpose equipment will, as a general rule, add to profit, if the firm can utilize such equipment at or near full-capacity.

Indeed, in this morning's session, Professor Joe Carrabino suggested quite rightly that the real limits to organizational size may be the ability of its managers to structure the increasingly complex organization. It is here suggested that this complex structuring must be accomplished through the development of a system or hierarchy of interrelated policies and that the complexity of developing such a structure grows at some undetermined *geometric* rate as the size of the organization increases.

The Policy Wheel

The use of several illustrations will prove helpful in understanding the nature of policies. The first illustration is a policy wheel, shown in Figure I.

FIGURE I
THE POLICY WHEEL

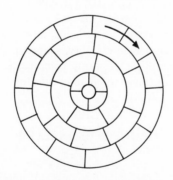

The hub of the policy wheel represents basic motivational policies in the form of principles, objectives, and personal ideals, which act as initiating factors in the organization. Derivative policies and activities in the form of sub-objectives exist in ever-widening concentric circles.

The second illustration refers to the zone of compliance of an organization and the zone of acceptance of an individual. The zone of compliance represents what the organization requires or expects from an individual. The zone of acceptance represents what the individual is able and willing to do as a participant in the organization. As can be seen from the diagram, all of these zones have flexible boundaries or limits.

In Figure II, Diagram A, the individual's zone of acceptance meshes rather nicely with the organization's zone of compliance. In Figure II, Diagram B, we find a possible unstable situation in which the employee must look to other organizations and his other organizational associations to satisfy a large number of his basic wants, needs, and desires. *What an individual wants, needs, and desires appears to be rather closely related to his personal attainment level in terms of knowledge, attitudes, and skills.*

FIGURE II

ZONES OF ACCEPTANCE
AND COMPLIANCE

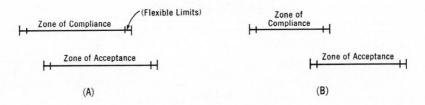

(A)   (B)

The next illustration, Figure III, presents the concept of group personality, or syntality. The dotted enclosure describes in a rough sort of way the portion of each person's knowledge, attitudes, and skills that contribute to the overall corporate syntality, or group personality. The diagram depicts the relationship of zones of compliance and acceptance for a large corporate organization and its board of directors.

FIGURE III

GROUP PERSONALITY

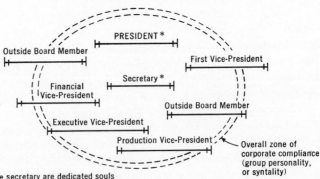

*The president and the secretary are dedicated souls who have fully identified their own personalities with that of the organization

Figure IV shows the familiar organizational pyramid and illustrates the formality and informality of the organization's zone of compliance at various levels in the organizational hierarchy.

FIGURE IV

THE ORGANIZATION PYRAMID

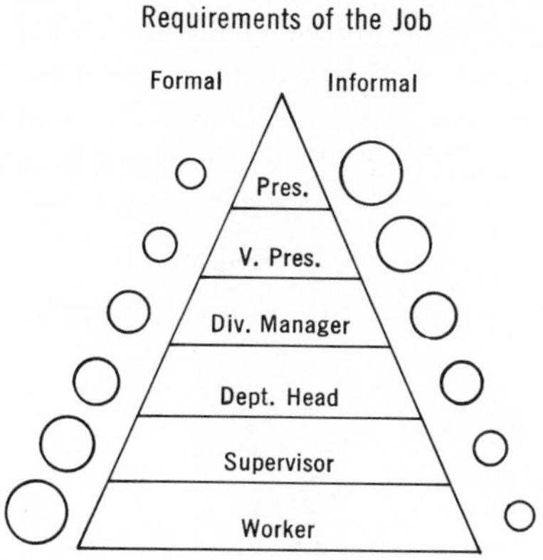

Requirements of the Job

The diagram illustrates that while the *formal* requirements at the top level may consist of nothing more than "making a good profit" and fulfilling certain other abstract goals, the *informal* requirements for the top-level executive may be quite demanding. For example, the company expects the top-level executive to dress neatly, conservatively, and appropriately. He must not swear or curse in public and must deal with other individuals in such a manner as to create a favorable corporate image. In many other ways, too, he is expected to act in certain informally prescribed ways.

But at the worker level, the situation is just reversed. The *informal* demands upon the worker are relatively few in number, whereas the *formal* requirements of his job, such as, for example, punching in on the time clock are many, and are generally clearly and specifically spelled out for him.

The various possible effects of conformity are interesting, but can only be touched upon here. Conformity can be initiated by top executives or at lower levels in the organization. Executives might initiate informal conformity of dress among all office personnel, for example, in an effort to control, through social pressure, the informal requirements of their subordinates as they go about their work. On the other hand, *workers* at lower levels may attempt through the pressures of conformity to strike a better balance between the informal and the formal demands of their jobs. The objective here would be to try to reduce the heavy formal requirements of their jobs, as, for example, by establishing an informal coffee break or by starting to call executives by their first names.

The Policy Nucleus

Figure V indicates that the policy hierarchy may advantageously be likened to a nucleus with various electrons rotating about it. The nucleus consists of the more fundamental and basic policies in the form of primary values and objectives and basic plans of action that act as initiating forces

FIGURE V
THE POLICY NUCLEUS

Nucleus of fundamental policies, objectives, and values

Electrons represent internal and external participants

in the organization. The electrons represent the internal and external participants of various kinds, who are related to, and participate in, the activities of the organization in many ways. If some members are not strongly motivated by the organization's nucleus of policies, or if other nuclei exert a stronger attractive pull, these members will fly off on tangents toward other organizations which attract them more strongly.

The Basic Role of Policies

In formulating policies, a manager is directly attempting to cope with the simultaneous interrelationships of the many relevant variables of organization under changing objectives and changing conditions. These variables in the form of such familiar concepts as the number of levels of authority; the extent of the span of control; the degree of centralization versus the degree of decentralization; the selection of alternative styles of leadership and supervision; the level of investment expenditure; the ratio of equity capital to total capital; the job content of various jobs; and many others, must be properly selected and interrelated so that the firm will best be organized to accomplish its changing objectives in a dynamic environment. Clearly, this policy structure will be at least somewhat different for each organization and substantially different for organizations that are pursuing different objectives.

The Practical Value of Policies

It is hoped that these ideas concerning the nature of business policies will be of direct practical help to businessmen as they go about building their organizations. For example, it is sometimes stated that top-level executives spend as much as 90 percent of their time in formulating and interpreting policies. If these top-level businessmen were to become aware of the nature of policy formulation as an activity, they would realize that what they are attempting to do in formulating and revising policies is to build a better organization in the form of an optimally-designed action-structure that can flexibly and successfully cope with changing business problems over the years.

It thus becomes clear that policies must be reconsidered and probably revised whenever a company's forecasts undergo revision. This would follow from a consideration of the role of policies in linking the activities of the organization to its external environment. Similarly, policies will require modification whenever other elements in the external environment change, such as legal restrictions or governmental regulations and requirements of various types.

Policies should also be changed, it seems, whenever higher-level policies are modified. As a final example among many others that could be cited, policies will change whenever a businessman gains improved insight and understanding into the nature of what he is trying to accomplish.

Concluding Comment

From the foregoing discussion, it becomes evident that organizations and policies are very closely related. Indeed, for all of us who might call ourselves "managementors," organizations and policies are certainly "old-hat" concepts. But have you ever carefully considered whether "the hierarchy of policies" and "organization" are perhaps one and the same concept?

B. LONG-RANGE PLANNING AND STRATEGIC POLICIES

1. DEVELOPMENTAL MODELS AND CORPORATE GROWTH*

Seymour Tilles

MANY MANAGERS HAVE A VIEW of their company's future which is strikingly analogous to the child's view of himself—asked what they want their company to be several years from now, they are likely to say, "bigger." The preoccupation with growth is not something to be lightly dismissed. The feeling that "you have to grow or die" is widespread in the business community. What has rarely been given explicit attention, however, is the question: "What does growth mean for a company?" Is it simply having a greater volume of total sales, with nothing else changing? Or does growth have a greater range of implications than merely bigger numbers on the sales reports?

In order to explore this issue, we ought first to take a look at what the term growth means in several fields where it has been given explicit attention for quite a while: biology, economics and psychology.

Biological analogies to the firm have been a feature of the academically-oriented literature on business administration for quite some time. Consequently, the approach of first seeing what the biologists have to say about the growth process is merely the continuation of an established

---

* From the *California Management Review*, Spring, 1964, Vol. VI, No. 3, pp. 29–36. Reprinted with permission from the publisher.

tradition. Moreover, growth is such a fundamental biological process that it would be a serious omission if we did not take advantage of whatever insights into this process may have been gained by students of life in its more fundamental forms.

As for economics, there is no doubt that the firm may be meaningfully considered to be a "small economy." In fact, economists use the term *micro-economics* when dealing with problems of the individual firm to emphasize the inclusion of the individual company within the realm of relevance of economic theory. One of the issues about which there is a good bit of economic writing is economic growth, and we would therefore be remiss if we did not also see what these ideas had to offer the serious student of business enterprise.

The field of psychology is also relevant to an understanding of corporate development. For just as the sixteen-year-old child is not only bigger than the six-year-old, but also "different," so the company with annual sales of $10 million is not only bigger than the one with annual sales of $1 million, it is also "different." Part of that difference is the way it thinks of itself.

Let us look at each of these developmental models, and see what they tell us about the process of growth. Then, let us look at a case history of a growth company, and see if these models really help us to understand this specific example better.

Ludwig von Bertalonffy

One of the biologists who has contributed greatly to a variety of concepts important to the business world is Ludwig von Bertalonffy. His early formulation of the biological organism as an open system led him to become a major contributor to the field of general systems theory, an area of increasing promise for business administration.

Von Bertalonffy[1] refers to the growth process as follows:

> P. Weiss, in a lucid review of physiology, has distinguished the following component processes of development:
>
> 1. *Tactical Displacement*: Movement of embryonic parts relative to one another, resulting in definite distributions and formations of germinal material. . . .
> 2. *Internal Organization*: The passage from the original unitary conditions of the embryo into a mosaic of partial regions in some degree independent of one another. . . .
> 3. *Histological Differentiation*: The passage of the individual cells from an original state of uniform appearance into the various states of morphological and functional specification. . . .
> 4. *Growth*: The enlargement and multiplication of cells. . . .

---

[1] Ludwig von Bertalonffy, *Modern Theories of Development: an Introduction to Theoretical Biology* (Harper & Row, 1962), p. 138.

Von Bertalonffy refers to these phases as formation, segregation, differentiation, and growth.

Regardless of the names applied, however, the four critical phases through which an organic system (including the firm) appears to grow are: (1) getting started; (2) getting organized; (3) becoming different; and (4) getting larger. These phases are, of course, intimately related, and each has a great influence on the others.

GETTING STARTED

The initial organization of a business firm is the basis from which its history springs. In many cases the development of the firm can only be appreciated by a consideration of the ingredients and circumstances which led to the creation of a particular corporate entity.

This observation has both personal and organizational significance. The "genetics" of business can be meaningfully examined in terms of both people and companies. These two are difficult to separate, for in the early stages of corporate growth the firm and the man are largely indistinguishable. For example, take such companies as McGraw-Hill, Underwood, du Pont, Ford—the names call to mind the colorful people who imparted their own personality to a firm and industry. However, even where the company is a relatively impersonal entity, a careful examination of its origins can help in understanding its subsequent history. It is regrettable that the disciplined methods of genetics have never been applied to an examination of corporate mergers. There is little doubt that a careful appraisal of the attributes of the partners that make for a strong and lasting combination has been too little researched. Certainly, the corporate scene is strewn with hybrids that are the apparent result of acquisitive passion, rather than a prudent mating of complementary strains.

Starting a Company

Companies get started in one of several ways. An individual may start a company himself, or a group of individuals may get together and start one. Alternatively, two or more companies may merge to create a more comprehensive entity, or a company may divest itself of one of its divisions in classical biological style. Each of these beginnings represents a completely different embryonic enterprise. The subsequent pattern of development is likely to be quite different in each case. Firms begun by single individuals face a quite different problem in the phase of internal organization than do firms begun by groups of individuals. They are less likely to suffer from the internal strains which are inherent in firms started by groups. The "squeeze-out" is one malady to which the individual entrepreneur is immune.

INTERNAL ORGANIZATION

The way in which the tasks are divided among the members of the organization has a fundamental influence on the way the organization develops. This has been demonstrated with respect to large organizations,[2] and if it is true for the large, well-established organizations, how much more true must it be for the smaller firm, which must walk a narrow line between excessive overhead costs on the one hand and inadequate attention to some major function on the other.

As far as I know, the division of labor in small organizations has never been seriously studied, and this is most unfortunate. The biological analogy suggests that this is a most important variable in its development, and may well play a decisive role in its subsequent evolution.

Moreover, this issue continues to be a critical one as the company develops. Indeed, one prerequisite for success as the company grows is the ability to reappraise, and to modify, its internal structure. Unless this can be achieved, the strategic capabilities of top management are apt to be hamstrung by organizational arrangements which are no longer appropriate to its new size.

Growth Problems

Listen, for example, to one executive reminisce about the problems encountered by his firm after a period of rapid growth:

> Why was the company not getting better results? We assessed our management team as being more than fully competent to do the job. Our engineers and production people were certainly good enough to handle the operations of that day. We concluded that much of the blame for the development and production tie-ups was due to a lack of management coordination and control, which in turn was largely attributable to the unwieldy organization under which we were operating during a stage when emphasis changed from development of products and markets to production.[3]

DIFFERENTIATION

An important issue in the development of companies is: What makes us different from anyone else in this business? The biological model of growth is of interest with respect to this question of differentiation because it is clear that in biological organisms, differentiation *precedes* growth. That is, the organism first becomes specialized and then it becomes larger.

One very good illustration of this sequence in real life is Bobbie Brooks, Inc., a specialized manufacturer of casual clothes for young

---

[2] See especially, "Strategy and Structure," Chandler, M.I.T. Press, 1962.

[3] *The Solartron Electronics Group, Ltd.* (Lausanne: L'Institut pour L'Etude des Methodes de direction de L'entreprise [IMEDE], 1962), p. 4.

women. When the company started in Cleveland, in 1939, it had a capital of $4,000 and faced competition from forty-six other manufacturers in Cleveland alone. Following its first year in business, during which it had $100,000 in sales, it decided to concentrate on a segment of the market it described as the "new, modern young adult women," and to sell an entire wardrobe of casual clothes designed particularly for the fifteen to twenty-four age group. In addition, it concentrated its sales efforts on the smaller stores rather than the larger ones. The company offered the small store a complete wardrobe for its young adult customers which was fashionable, moderate in price, and high in quality. This was a radical departure from the conventional concept of the manufacturer's mission in the industry and was the basis for the company's spectacular growth.

GROWTH

Firms grow larger in a variety of ways. One is by acquisition and merger. A second is by increasing the number of locations at which a particular activity is carried on. A third is by simply getting bigger at a single location. Each of these has quite different implications for management.

Whenever a firm chooses to grow by acquisition and merger, the major internal changes occur in the jobs of the top management. The acquired firm's middle management and its labor force may frequently be virtually unaffected by the transition. But top management's job will now be quite different, especially if its previous experience has been in a single industry at a single location.

By contrast, when a firm grows by getting larger at a single location, the major impact is likely to be at the middle and lower levels, although the top levels will also be somewhat affected. This is because growth at a single location involves increasing job specialization and additional levels of hierarchy, and both create major organizational problems.

Separate Traffic Function

For example, a candy company which had grown rapidly decided that it required a separate traffic function. The discussion over what sort of a person should be traffic manager, and who he should report to resulted in a fundamental reappraisal of the relationship between the manufacturing and the marketing functions. This came about because the new traffic manager would be taking over part of the responsibility that they had previously been charged with.

Growth by adding locations has its major impact on headquarters groups that must now work with a geographically dispersed group of people. In addition, some jobs may be split apart in order to make the field units viable entities. For example, a department store which had traditionally operated from a single downtown location decided to grow by opening suburban stores. As it opened additional stores, the buyer's job became a critical bottleneck. While the company had operated at a single location, the buyer had maintained complete over-all responsibility for buying and selling a particular line of merchandise. As additional stores were added, however, it proved necessary to split this responsibility into separate buying and selling functions. It took four years to work through the transition. However, once it was accomplished, the number of additional stores that the organization could handle was vastly increased.

As the firm grows, whether at a single location or at many, it undergoes basic changes in internal structure. A serious consideration of size, both current and intended, is essential if structure is to be meaningfully appraised. Moreover, growth is a difficult process, because internal arrangements must be modified to accommodate changing size, and these modifications are painful.

However, growth involves not merely changes in structure. It also involves changes in the way resources are allocated and in the way the company thinks of itself. We will consider these next.

While economists have been concerned with growth for a very long time, the economist's concept of growth and the internal problems of business management remains regrettably distant. And yet, the two are not really so very different. In these days of giant corporations and small countries, there is not even a difference in scale. (General Electric employs 250,000 people, which is about one quarter the size of Israel's labor force.) Moreover, the growth concepts developed by economists have some interesting implications when applied to the individual firm.

A Popular Model

One of the more popular models of economic growth recently expounded is that of Rostow.[4] Rostow is concerned with identifying the major phases of growth and with examining some of the factors that explain the movement of an economy from one phase to the next. He identifies the major phases as pre-take-off, take-off, and maturity. Take-off is the phase during which rapid growth occurs and is therefore of particular relevance to the firm. Indeed, Rostow's discussion of the problems inherent in moving to take-off is also a listing of the major problems faced by every "growth" company once its product begins to be accepted. He identifies these as: (1) the building of an effective national state, (2) financing the take-off, and (3) the problem of social overhead capital.

---

[4] W. W. Rostow, The Stages of Economic Growth, A Non-Communist Manifesto (Cambridge University Press, 1960).

THE BUILDING OF AN EFFECTIVE NATIONAL STATE

While Rostow never says exactly what he means by "an effective national state," I believe it is important to distinguish between two essential elements of an operating state: the leaders as individuals and the administrative machinery. Of the two, I think there is no doubt that the leaders as individuals are the major variable affecting both the growth of corporations and the economic development of nations. Nasser in Egypt, Nkrumah in Ghana, and Ben-Gurion in Israel are key factors in the development of their respective countries.

Indispensable or Not?

In business, as in national states, the energetic and resourceful founder-father always causes considerable speculation about the issue: What will it be without him? The sure answer with respect to the founding fathers, both of countries and of companies, is that it will be very much different. And the more successful he is, the greater the succession problem he leaves. A change in leadership invariably represents a change in direction; the challenge to both nations and companies is to create an administrative framework which will permit a degree of continuity to be obtained through successive changes in top managers.

One point that Rostow mentions explicitly in discussing the prerequisites for economic growth is the broadening of personal affiliation from smaller to larger units. This is true of the emerging nations of Africa and Asia, where an early challenge to new states is the imposition of a national identity upon tribal affiliation. It is also true of Western Europe where the new structure of the Common Market raises some agonizing choices between economic growth and the sovereignty of the sub-unit. Nor is the issue yet completely resolved here in the United States. After almost three centuries of the union, the relationship between the states and the Federal government is still a highly controversial issue.

The question of the affiliation with a broader entity is also important in the business organization. A common method of achieving growth is acquisition and merger; and an essential issue in a company growing this way is precisely this problem of achieving some balance between what may become a division of a broader organization, and the wider entity. The means of accomplishing this are often very similar in both countries and corporations. It consists of a combination of persuasion, coercion, and representation in central decision-making bodies. However, unless this problem can be overcome in one way or another, there is little prospect for accelerating the pace of economic growth. This is because rapid growth requires that the central unit be able to influence the allocation of resources. The process by which the central authority mobilizes the resources to be allocated, and the allocation decisions, is likely to be essentially political. But once the decision has been made, the authority of the central agency must prevail.

FEEDING THE GROWTH PHASE

A fundamental issue related to the growing organization is: Where will we get the resources to support growth? In newly developing economies, this is primarily a question of increasing the surplus available from the basic activities, usually agriculture and extractive industries. In the corporate case, we must distinguish between the new management's taking over the relatively stagnant organization, and the formation of a completely new organization. However, in both cases, the question of the resources which will support growth is a critical one. Consequently, in both phases we would expect to find a set of policies which would result in the generation of relatively large short-run surpluses and their reinvestment in additional volume and supporting functions. This may be accomplished in a variety of ways: by the choice of new products with large profit potential; by cost reduction on conventional product lines; by deferred compensation through stock options and other devices which minimize current expenditures and gain commitment to future expansion.

Another major source of resources is, of course, external agencies; and here, too, there is considerable similarity in a policy amenable to rapid growth used by both countries and companies. This policy is to mobilize the greatest amount of external resources consistent with the retention of control. The attitudes of many governments which restrict foreign investment because they fear the power which thereby accrues to outsiders are quite reminiscent of the owners of small but growing firms who limit the amount of external funds they will use, either because they do not wish to "be in the clutches of the banks," or "do not wish to mess with minority interests."

THE PROBLEM OF SOCIAL OVERHEAD CAPITAL

One of the key prerequisites of rapid economic growth is investment in social overheads—in activities which are nevertheless essential. In fact, without such investment, especially in such fields as education, transportation, and housing, economic development cannot be sustained. This problem of social overhead capital is precisely analogous to the question of overhead in rapidly growing companies, and presents the same sort of issues to the manager of how much to invest, when, and where, in order to make good use of the limited resources available. Nor are the careful calculations based on quantitative criteria likely to be of very much use to the managers of countries or of firms when they are presented with the problem of what to do with their limited funds. In this case, as in so many others, the manager resorts to artistic criteria, such as "balance," rather than scientific criteria, to decide whether his overhead budgets are realistic.

Thought-Provoking Model

One of the most thought-provoking models for the manager interested in understanding corporate growth is that of E. H. Erikson, who has long been interested in how children develop from a psychological point of view. His work, primarily because of the approach he has used, has particular relevance to business administration. His concern has been:

> The unity of the human life cycles and the specific dynamics of each of its stages, as prescribed by the laws of individual development and social organization.[5]

Here, in a single sentence, are the essential things that make his line of inquiry of interest to management: he is concerned with the individual as a whole, he is concerned with the identification and exploration of phases of development, and he is interested in considering both factors related to the individual himself and to the environment in which he grows. These are, clearly, the specifications for a model which would be useful for an understanding of corporate growth: it should be concerned with the company as a whole, it should help in the identification of phases of corporate growth, and it should include factors related both to the organization itself and to the environment in which it operates. Well, then, let's see what Erikson's work specifically offers us:

EXHIBIT I
STAGES IN PERSONAL DEVELOPMENT

PHASE	CRISIS	KEY ISSUES
Infancy	Trust vs. Mistrust (I am what I am given)	Relationship with others who give
Early childhood	Autonomy vs. Shame, Doubt (I am what I will)	Ability to co-ordinate a number of highly conflicting action patterns
Play age	Initiative vs. Guilt (I am what I can imagine)	What kind of a person am I?
School age	Industry vs. Inferiority (I am what I learn)	Learning new skills
Adolescence	Identity vs. Identity diffusion	(Commitment to a specific strategy)*

---

5 "Identity and the Life Cycle," selected papers by Erik H. Erikson, *Psychological Issues* (New York: International Universities Press, 1959), Vol. I, No. 1, Monograph 1.

* Added by author.

First, Erikson offers a way of identifying what is significant about a particular phase of development. He does this in terms of the basic issues which must be resolved at a particular phase of development. Moreover, he suggests that how a basic issue is resolved at one phase of development directly affects the problems that a person will have to resolve at subsequent phases of development.

Corporate Growth

Each of these ideas is particularly appropriate to an understanding of corporate growth. While the particular stages identified by Erikson in the development of the child do not precisely parallel meaningful phases of corporate growth, they are suggestive of significant crises in the company's development. And, as Erikson says, "Each successive step is a potential crisis because of radical *change in perspective.*"[6]

Erikson identifies the stages in personal development, and the basic crisis associated with each, as shown in Exhibit I.

These phases are suggestive of comparable phases in corporate growth. They are not really distinct phases, having sharp boundaries. They overlap greatly. Thus, at any time in a company's growth it will probably have to face all of these problems simultaneously. However, one or another of them is likely to be its major problem at a particular time.

One illustration of the evolution of a major organization through these various phases is the McGraw-Hill Book Company. At its inception, Mr. McGraw established some clear-cut policies concerning the firm's relationship to the two major groups who supported his publications: readers and advertisers. He insisted that the interest of the reader be paramount, and that the publications provide him with authoritative information for use in his profession or business. And toward the advertiser he insisted on honesty in circulation claims. Later, when the firm went public, it had to decide what its relationship to investors would be.

Added Publications

As the firm added additional publications and also entered the field of book publishing, it became increasingly necessary to co-ordinate a number of conflicting action patterns. This was accomplished by exercising close financial control, but leaving the individual units almost completely autonomous with respect to other issues. As the firm has grown, more and more functions are being handled by centralized staff units. However, the concept of editorial autonomy has remained valid.

Within the book part of its business, its initial mission is being re-

---

[6] "The Healthy Personality," *Psychological Issues, op. cit.,* p. 55.

assessed. The revolution that has swept the educational field is still in full swing, and this publisher, like all others who wish to remain in the field, must adapt to it. The emergence of teaching machines, educational TV, and systems concepts in education have made this issue both urgent and important. Thus, the company is still learning new skills.

These three models of growth: the psychological, the biological, and the economic, all share certain common attributes which may permit us to generalize a theory of growth. First, each is concerned with a separation of the total "growth" process into a series of distinct phases. Growth is shown to be not so much a single process which goes on, but rather the ordered sequence of quite different kinds of processes. Second, each phase, by its nature and duration, vitally affects the subsequent phases of the process. In all three models, each growth phase is characterized by a set of characteristic crises or developments whose resolution acts as a major constraint on the further development of the unit. It follows from this that in each model incidents which occur early have greatly magnified repercussions at later stages of development.

These observations have dwelt on what was similar in each of these models. But a true synthesis must put together not only what is common in each of these growth models; but also what is diverse in each of them. Thus, the psychological model suggests that growth involves a change in the way the unit thinks of itself, and in the way others think of it. The biological model suggests that growth is a change in both the *size* and *structure* of the organism. And finally, the economics model suggests that growth is a change in the relative importance of various kinds of activities and in the way in which the unit allocates its resources. All of these appear relevant to the question of growth in the firm. The growing firm must learn to think of itself in new ways, to change its structure, and to allocate resources in quite different ways as it increases in size. These are essential challenges to the management of the growth firm.

Phases of Growth

And finally, each of these models implies that following the phases of growth, there is, inevitably, a period of maturity—during which there will be no growth, but a variety of problems associated with maintaining of position. This is the phase whose existence many entrepreneurs deny but which their successors must face.

Finally, let us take a specific example of a company that has grown substantially, and show how the models described earlier help clarify the various phases in its development. As an illustration, let us take the case of Texas Instruments—partly because its increase in annual sales is a typical economic take-off curve, and partly because so much is known about it from publicly available sources of information.

What is now Texas Instruments was started as Geophysical Service, Inc. (GSI) in March 1930. However, its current phase can be said to date from December 6, 1941, when GSI was sold by its original owners to a group of four employees.[7] This group had a number of important characteristics. It had a clearly established leader, both by virtue of seniority and equity position. Each of the men was both quite capable in a given field, and yet able to take on difficult assignments in other areas. And none of them was related to any other. It is interesting to observe how these characteristics appear in the founding groups of other successful growth companies as well. Indian Head Mills is one case that comes to mind.

Geophysical Exploration

While geophysical exploration remained the core of the business through the war, toward the end of the war two of the company's founders began to think about the postwar future of the firm. In terms of the biological analogy, they decided on an important basis for differentiation. As reported in a recent issue of *Fortune*:

> Haggerty and Johnson liked each other, lunched together a lot, and shared certain opinions. One of these, they now recall, was that the military rivalry between the U.S. and the Soviet Union would begin when the hot war ended. This meant that there would be a need for military electronics. They thought there would be a place for a small, young company, that could successfully blend electrical and mechanical technology, and that they could start out in electronics manufacturing as a career supplier of military equipment.
>
> At the time they began thinking this way, there was no military electronics industry per se, only some special jobs done according to the military's requirements.[8]

In terms of Erikson's model, they were still at the childhood stage co-ordinating a number of conflicting action patterns. Specifically, what they decided to do was to add a Laboratory and Manufacturing Division to complement the existing exploration services. This was a key decision, for it was this division that was subsequently to dwarf the original mission of the business.

At this stage in its evolution, the company was still in the pre-take-off era of its growth. However, it took a number of actions which

---

[7] "Meeting the Problems of Rapid Expansion," *General Management Series*, No. 185 (A.M.A., 1957).

[8] "The Men Who Made T.I.," *Fortune*, November 1961, p. 120.

were significant. In economic terms, it began to invest heavily in social
overhead capital. In 1947–1949, a chief industrial engineer, a personnel
director, and a manager of manufacturing were added to the Laboratory
and Manufacturing Division.[9] And in 1951, in psychological terms, it
drastically revised its concept of the kind of company it was going to be.
To begin with, it decided to become primarily a manufacturing company,
rather than a geophysical service outfit. And, secondly, it decided "not to
be satisfied with being a good small or medium-sized company, but to become a good big company."[10]

Following these decisions came additional heavy investments in overhead—especially in engineering, where a semiconductor products group
was established. In Erikson's terms this would correspond to learning
new skills. These new skills led directly to another steep climb in sales
and the company was, indeed, headed for maturity.

Internal Specialization

During this period of rapid growth, a considerable amount of internal specialization was also occurring. In fact, Texas Instruments has
based its internal organization on subdivisions which have facilitated the
maintenance of control as the part of the central authority. As reported in
Fortune:

> The organization rests, not upon the divisions, but upon subdivisions
> called "Product Customer Centers." A P.C.C. is a small, relatively autono-
> mous chunk of business with all the basic functions included "so far as they
> make sense." There are about fifty of these little businesses in T.I.: for
> example, two for power transistors (one for high power, one for low signal),
> one for entertainment transistors, one for diodes, etc. The P.C.C. has no
> fixed form, but it combines the functions of engineering, manufacturing, and
> marketing of a product or group of products, and centers the responsibility in
> a manager. . . .
> T.I. finds in this structure the flexibility it needs in its very technical,
> fast-moving business. The P.C.C.'s can be expanded and contracted quickly
> as markets change, without harming the whole organization.[11]

Today, Texas Instruments is a mature organization. This is not to
say that it is static; but there is little likelihood that future growth will be
as spectacular as past performance has been. It is a good big company,
and like other good big companies it must now concern itself with remaining vital, so as to preserve its leadership position. Its problem now
is not so much growth as health.

9 *Op. cit.*, A.M.A.
10 *Ibid.*
11 "Where Texas Instruments Goes from Here," *Fortune,* December 1961, p. 236.

2. THE STRATEGY OF PRODUCT POLICY*

Charles H. Kline

THE FIRST CONCERN OF MOST businessmen is the content of their product lines. No other problem of management affects profits more directly. Few problems require more constant attention from management.

Active executives make decisions almost every day that affect the product line in such matters as allocations of manpower, factory space, or sales effort. Frequently they must also decide major product questions— whether to undertake a new development project, to introduce a new product, or to eliminate an old one. Mistakes in any of these are usually costly, and may even be ruinous.

To help get better and faster decisions on problems of product-line content, executives in a number of manufacturing companies have developed formal product policies. These policies summarize the business characteristics which experience has shown successful products must have. In effect, each policy is a statement of long-range strategy that defines the means for a particular company to make the greatest overall profits.

Experience has shown that a product policy serves these three main functions:

(1) A product policy helps to provide the information required for decisions on the product line. It tells lower management and professional staffs of market analysts, research workers, and industrial engineers what top management needs to know. Furthermore, it provides a convenient framework around which this information can be organized.

(2) Also, a product policy gives executives a supplementary check on the usual estimates of profit and loss. Even though modern techniques of market research, sales forecasting, and cost estimating are often surprisingly good, the data they provide are still only approximations.

It is often impossible to make any realistic financial estimates at all—for example, at the start of a long-range research program. At other times available sales and profit data may not be significant. An unsatis-

---

* From the *Harvard Business Review*, July–August, 1955, Vol. 33, No. 4, pp. 91–100. Reprinted with permission from the publisher.

factory record for an existing product may reflect a basic mistake in product policy, but it may also be the result of poor organization, unsuitable sales and promotion, faulty design, or inadequate plant facilities.

An analysis in terms of a basic product policy shows up weak spots in the financial estimates and indicates imponderable factors that cannot easily be reduced to numbers.

(3) Most important of all, a product policy guides and directs the activities of the whole organization toward a single goal. Only rarely are product decisions made solely by top executives. More often such decisions require the specialized knowledge of experts in many fields— research, development, engineering, manufacturing, marketing, law, finance, and even personnel.

The original idea for a new product may occur to an engineer at the laboratory bench, a copy writer in the advertising department, or a salesman in the field. Between the first concept and the final decision by top management to introduce the new product there comes a long series of investigations, analyses, research and development studies, pilot production runs, and marketing tests. This work is expensive and time-consuming, and it involves a great many people in the organization. To complete these indispensable steps as quickly and thoroughly as possible requires good teamwork and a clear idea of management's overall policy.

A sound product policy, well prepared and well taught to all professional and supervisory employees, is thus an important tool for co-ordination and direction. It applies not only to those major decisions which are the ultimate responsibility of presidents and general managers but also to the many day-to-day decisions by which lower-level employees shape the course of a business.

Analyzing Resources

The first step in developing a product policy is to make a careful inventory of a company's resources along the lines suggested in Exhibit I. Every company is unique. As a result of its history, experience, and personnel it has certain strengths and certain weaknesses that distinguish it from other business organizations. The ideal product policy makes the best use of a company's strong points and avoids its weak points.

In this sense every business enterprise is specialized, so that it is best suited to perform only certain services or to produce only certain types of product. The product lines of many large and successful corporations are so extremely varied that this point is often missed. One well-known company makes everything from light bulbs to jet engines, and another has a product line ranging from flashlight batteries to synthetic fibers. Although at first glance it may seem difficult to relate such diverse products to a single product policy, closer analysis shows that they all have in common certain strategic business characteristics which are related to company resources.

Developing the Policy

It is these business characteristics that make up the elements of product policy. Individually they are all well known. Every business executive deals with one or another of them daily. But in developing a product policy he must look at all these strategic points together. Let us see how they fit into an overall policy.

FINANCIAL STRENGTH

In many respects the most important characteristic of any business is the investment required to enter it. This investment includes the land, buildings, and equipment needed for the business; the required inventories of raw material, work in process, and finished stock; and the funds necessary to carry accounts receivable and provide cash for working capital.

EXHIBIT I
INVENTORY OF
COMPANY RESOURCES

Financial strength	Money available or obtainable for financing research and development, plant construction, inventory, receivables, working capital, and operating losses in the early stages of commercial operation.
Raw material reserves	Ownership of, or preferential access to, natural resources such as minerals and ores, brine deposits, natural gas, forests.
Physical plant	Manufacturing plant, research and testing facilities, warehouses, branch offices, trucks, tankers, etc.
Location	Situation of plant or other physical facilities with relation to markets, raw materials, or utilities.
Patents	Ownership or control of a technical monopoly through patents.
Public acceptance	Brand preference, market contracts, and other public support built up by successful performance in the past.
Specialized experience	Unique or uncommon knowledge of manufacturing, distribution, scientific fields, or managerial techniques.
Personnel	Payroll of skilled labor, salesmen, engineers, or other workers with definite specialized abilities.
Management	Professional skill, experience, ambition, and will for growth of the company's leadership.

These components of the total investment are all related to the volume of sales. Investment in inventories, receivables, and cash varies almost directly with sales. Even the investment in such fixed assets as land, buildings, and equipment must be scaled to the volume of product to be sold. Thus a given operation may require a high capital investment merely because the volume of sales will be large. Many merchandising ventures are of this type.

In manufacturing industries, however, capital requirements usually depend on process economics. Some products inherently require manufacture on a larger scale than others. Exhibit II compares the size of plant, as measured by the number of employees, in four types of establishment in the chemical process industries. As the exhibit shows, synthetic rubber

EXHIBIT II

SIZE OF MANUFACTURING ESTABLISHMENTS
FOR VARIOUS PRODUCTS

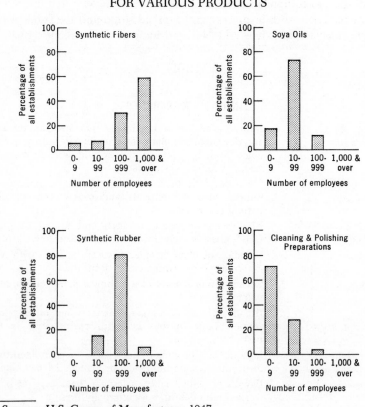

Source: U.S. Census of Manufactures, 1947.

and synthetic fiber plants are always large, soya oil mills are usually of moderate size, and plants producing cleaning and polishing compounds are generally small. The typical synthetic fiber plant has a thousand times more employees than the typical cleaning and polishing compound plant. The difference in fixed plant investment is probably much greater.

Small companies with limited financial resources are restricted to businesses that require a relatively low investment. On the other hand, large and wealthy corporations have the choice of entering either high-investment or low-investment businesses—though experience has shown that such companies are most successful (indeed, sometimes only successful) in high-investment businesses, where large-scale operations do give them a competitive advantage.

In these connections, the observation made by Crawford H. Greenewalt, president of du Pont, is significant:

> "There is much misconception also about the relationship between big and little businesses. . . . No little business could compete with us in nylon for the reason that no such business could bring together the capital and technical resources required for an efficient producing unit. We, on the other hand, have no interest in competing in spheres where we can make no substantial technical contribution, and there are many activities, particularly in the fields of marketing and distribution, that small businesses can do better than we. . . .

EXHIBIT III

BREAKEVEN CHARTS FOR MANUFACTURE OF SPECIALTY SEMIFABRICATED PRODUCT IN LARGE AND SMALL COMPANIES

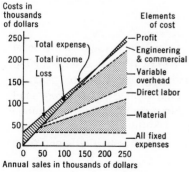

CASE A
Actual Results in Large Corporation

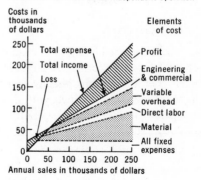

CASE B
Estimated Results in Small Independent Operation

"Let me cite an example. We make nylon yarn and sell it to whoever will buy. Your wife buys, let us say, a nylon blouse. Between the sale of that yarn and that blouse are the throwster who twists the yarn, the weaver who weaves it, the finisher who finishes and dyes it, the cutter who makes the garment, and the retail store that sells it. For the most part these are small businesses."[1]

As a general rule, the smallest economic unit that has the facilities to undertake a given operation performs it most efficiently. That is why, when large companies enter low-investment businesses, they very often run into difficulties. To illustrate:

The breakeven charts shown in Exhibit III summarize the findings of a cost analysis of the manufacture and sale of a specialty product under two sets of conditions: (a) actual operating results in one of the largest corporations in the United States; and (b) the estimated results in a small independent business.

The product in question was a semifabricated material with a small but assured market potential of about $200,000 annually. The investment in plant equipment necessary for this volume of sales was about $25,000.

As the left-hand chart shows, the large corporation needed a sales volume of $216,000 per year to break even on this product. The small company, however, could make money anywhere above the breakeven point of $55,000 in annual sales shown in the right-hand chart. At the breakeven volume of $216,000 for the large company, the small company would net $72,000 before taxes.

Comparison of the two charts shows that the lower costs in the small company would come partly from lower fixed charges, raw material and direct-labor costs, and commercial, administrative, and engineering expenses. An operating manager primarily concerned with this one product could reasonably be expected to make small savings in these items. But the principal advantage of the small company would be its far lower variable overhead costs, estimated at less than half those of the large company.

Actually this analysis was made by the large corporation after several years of poor operating results. When this cost study became available, the product was dropped.

SALES VOLUME

The financial strength of a company also influences the desirable level of sales for its products. A large volume of sales requires a large investment. For the reasons already mentioned, large companies are generally most successful in products with a large annual volume of sales, and small companies in low-volume specialty items. However, the acceptable range in dollars will obviously vary from one type of business to another.

Sales volume depends partly on the number of potential applications

[1] From a speech reported in *Chemical and Engineering News*, October 10, 1949, p. 2896.

of a product, the number of potential customers, and the size of the area in which it will be distributed. These factors also determine the degree of stability in the sales volume. A product with only one application and relatively few customers is liable to sudden obsolescence and violent fluctuations in sales. Therefore most large companies seek products with broad markets and avoid items salable only to one or two customers, the government, or the armed forces. The small company can sometimes afford to take more chances, for it has more flexibility to turn around and adjust to changing circumstances.

DISTRIBUTION CHANNELS

Channels of distribution consist largely of intangibles. There may be some investment in warehouses, trucks, and offices, but these facilities may also be rented. In any case the fixed investment is generally small. Perhaps for this reason business executives sometimes overrate the flexibility of their distribution channels.

Engineers and production men are particularly apt to assume that a salesforce can always handle "just one more" product, regardless of its market. Even sales managers sometimes say that a product will "sell itself" or "take no effort." As a result, one of the commonest problems in business today is that of the single salesforce trying to cover too many markets.

Professor Melvin T. Copeland summarizes the problem this way:

"Early in my research work in the field of marketing, I found that when a company was catering to two different markets, such as the consumer market and the industrial market, for example, better results typically were secured by segregating the salesforce into two groups, one for each type of market. It appeared that ordinarily a salesman could not be continually shifting back and forth between different types of buyers without having his effectiveness materially impaired. The buying habits and the buying motives of the two types of buyers were so different as to involve difficult mental shifts by the salesman. . . ."[2]

Any new product has a great advantage when it can be sold to the same consuming groups as existing products. The new product benefits from the company's accumulated knowledge of the markets, close relationships with customers, and public acceptance which the salesforce has built up over the years.

On the other hand, a new product is at some disadvantage when it must be sold in entirely new markets. In this case the company must build entirely new distribution channels for the product. Sales executives must develop new sales and promotional concepts, hire and train a new sales-

---

[2] Melvin T. Copeland, *The Executive at Work* (Cambridge, Harvard University Press, 1951), p. 85.

force, perhaps select new distributors, and ultimately win new customers. These steps are costly and time-consuming, and they may prove a steady drain on executive effort that could be better spent elsewhere.

Accordingly a product intended for an entirely new market should generally have other advantages strong enough to justify the risks involved in distribution.

EFFECT ON PRESENT PRODUCTS

A going concern cannot forget the products which are already earning assets.

Ideally every addition to the line should improve the profitability of present products. When a company such as Westinghouse develops a new electrical appliance, it increases the overall demand for electricity and thus increases the market for its turbines, generators, transformers, and other power equipment.

Unfortunately, situations of this sort are rather rare. For practical purposes a proposed new product will be satisfactory as long as it does not hurt the sale of present products. Of course, the situation is different when a new product makes an old one obsolete. It is obviously better for a company to replace its own products than to let a competitor do so.

COMPETITION

In entering a new market a company should usually have some advantage over present and potential competitors in the field. At the least it should have no disadvantage.

The number and type of competitors a company will have to face in a new business generally depend on the capital investment required to enter the business. Where the investment is high, the number of competitors is fairly small, but they are usually strong, well entrenched, and difficult to dislodge. On the other hand, where the investment is low, there may be so many small, relatively weak companies in the field that poor pricing practices prevent any one from making a reasonable profit.

Executives in some companies with national distribution make it a policy not to enter any new market unless they believe they have enough advantages over competition to capture at least 20% of the market on a sound pricing basis.

CYCLICAL STABILITY

Steady, nonseasonal demand is nearly always desirable in a product. It is desirable also to have a product that is relatively independent of fluctuations in the business cycle.

Capital goods and some consumer durable goods are particularly vulnerable to periods of depression. Some companies in these fields lay special stress on new products that go into consumer nondurable markets. These products include not only items sold to the ultimate consumer, such as paints, drugs, lubricants, or antifreeze, but also industrial materials sold to fabricators or processors of consumer goods—for example, tetraethyl lead to gasoline refiners or tin cans to food packers.

RESEARCH AND PATENTS

Research brings profitable new products and leads to strong patent positions. It can also be very expensive. Products which offer the opportunity for important technical achievement are generally most attractive to financially strong companies, especially those which already have large research staffs as corporate resources. Smaller companies tend to avoid businesses requiring much development. Many small companies operate in highly technical fields, but these are usually rather specialized.

The attitude toward research and development also varies from one company to another on purely strategic grounds, regardless of size. Some companies specialize in very technical products. They carry on as much research as they can afford, continually seek out new technical fields for development, and even abandon older products that have reached a fairly stable technology and are no longer protected by patents. Joel Dean describes one such company in these terms:

> "It is a fairly conscious policy of one of the large chemical companies to choose only those new products that have been developed by its product research organization and that are distinctive enough in both chemical and manufacturing requirements to be protected for some time to come. The counterpart of this policy is to abandon products when they have degenerated to the status of commonly produced commodities. The company advances to new monopoly positions as fast as economic progress wears down the walls of the old."[3]

In a company like the one just described any product that does not offer much opportunity for technical advances is not very attractive.

On the other hand, some companies concentrate on making old or relatively nontechnical products better and cheaper than any one else. Here the emphasis is usually on expert low-cost production or aggressive merchandising. The company resources are primarily the production or sales staff, and the need for much research is an unfavorable factor.

RAW MATERIALS

In the event a company owns or controls a source of raw material, it has a resource which it should obviously use whenever possible. However,

---

[3] Joel Dean, *Managerial Economics* (New York: Prentice-Hall, Inc., 1951), p. 130.

most companies must buy all or the greater part of their raw materials. These preferably should be basic commodities that are readily available in constant supply from several sources. They should also be free of any restrictive competitive control. Any raw material available from only one source is vulnerable to interruption by strikes, fires, bankruptcy, or other disasters—and even, on occasion, to the supplier's flat refusal to sell.

Distant and unreliable sources are also dangerous. For example:

> One large company is a heavy consumer of Indian mica. Because of unsettled conditions in India and throughout the world, this company always keeps a protective inventory of about one year's supply. Since the total expense of maintaining an inventory for a year (including interest, taxes, insurance, warehousing, and losses) is about 20% to 25% of its cost, this company pays a heavy penalty for its unavoidable dependence on an unreliable source.

Freedom from competitive control is especially important for raw materials used in large quantities. Thus:

> After World War II several chemical companies developed methods for polymerizing styrene to polystyrene. After spending considerable sums on technical developments, the companies all eventually abandoned these projects. Executives realized that they would have to buy styrene from the basic producers, who also made and sold polystyrene. As converters of a material under the control of competitors, they would be at the mercy of more integrated companies both as to supply and in regard to the relative price level of the two materials.

VALUE ADDED

The fate of those styrene projects calls attention to the strategic value of highly integrated businesses. The best measure of integration is the value added by manufacture—that is, the spread between the cost of raw materials and the total cost of making the product, expressed as a percentage of total cost. Where distribution costs are high, the value added by manufacture and distribution is a more appropriate measure.

A high value added means that the product demands a high plant investment or considerable expense in engineering, labor, or supplies. These requirements give producers greater scope for improving efficiency, reducing costs, and developing a superior product. Furthermore, all these factors represent capital requirements. For this reason a high value added by manufacture is usually more desirable for the large company and less important for the small one.

MANUFACTURING LOAD

In many types of manufacturing, executives have some freedom of choice in deciding whether to produce standard products that can be sold from stock or custom products made to the individual customer's order.

Standard products sold in large volume can be made most economically with equipment specially designed for mass production. The heavy capital investment and high volume of sales make such products particularly suitable for large companies.

On the other hand, the smaller company with limited capital may find it more profitable to make custom products or to supply standard products in a larger number of grades, sizes, and finishes. This type of manufacture substitutes labor for expensive and inflexible plant equipment. Operating costs are higher but can sometimes be offset by higher prices. Furthermore, since the investment is smaller, lower margins may still give a satisfactory return.

The job-shop processing of industrial goods—for example, custom molding of plastics—is an example of diversified manufacturing load where the small company has a great advantage over the large. The production of fashion goods is another. Professor Copeland describes this situation:

> "From an administrative standpoint, style merchandising calls for rapid adjustment to continual and frequent changes in demand. Designing, purchasing, production, pricing, and sales have to be adjusted quickly to each change in a volatile market, and the various activities are so closely interdependent that they must all be adjusted almost simultaneously. Under these circumstances the activities of an enterprise manufacturing style merchandise are not sufficiently standardized or stable to permit the delegation of much decision-making to lieutenants. Hence, the small manufacturer who can constantly feel the pulse of the market and who can transmit his instructions directly and immediately to the operating forces is in a strategic competitive position. In such an industry the advantages of quick decision-making and speedy transmittal of decisions to operatives more than offset the economies which might otherwise be gained from large-scale manufacture."[4]

Stating the Policy

Even this brief review shows that different companies may take diametrically opposite positions on each of a dozen or more points of product strategy. The contrast in overall policy between two hypothetical companies is illustrated in Exhibit IV. Both companies are assumed to be manufacturers of synthetic organic chemicals and similar in all respects except one—size. In size they are assumed to differ by a factor of 1,000 as measured by their net worths. As the exhibit shows, this one difference is reflected in almost every aspect of their product policies.

In practice the differences between companies are never so simple

---

[4] Op. cit., p. 149.

and pronounced. Consequently the differences between product policies are often more elusive, though nonetheless real.

EXHIBIT IV

EXAMPLES OF PRODUCT STRATEGY
IN LARGE AND SMALL COMPANIES

PRODUCT REQUIREMENTS	COMPANY A NET WORTH $500,000,000	COMPANY B NET WORTH $500,000
Capital investment	High	Low
Sales volume	Large volume	Small volume
	Mass markets	Specialized markets
	Many applications	Many to few applications
	National distribution	Local or specialized distribution
Similarity to present distribution channels	High to moderate	High
Effect on going products	Good to fair	Good
Competition	Relatively few companies	Few to many companies
	Sound pricing	Sound pricing
	Good possibility of securing a large percentage of the market	Desirable market position variable
Cyclical stability	High	High
Technical opportunity	Great	Moderate to small
Patent protection	Great	Great to none
Raw materials	Basic materials	Intermediate or basic materials
	Many suppliers	Many to few suppliers
Manufacturing load	Standard products	Standard or custom products
	Mass production	Specialized production
	Few grades and sizes	Few to many grades or sizes
Value added	High	High to moderate

Whatever policy is adopted, it must generally be reduced to written form if executives and employees are to use it throughout a company. The statement of policy may be a series of short definitions, as in these excerpts paraphrased from the instructions of a large manufacturer of industrial goods:

1. *Sales volume:* Each product line should have a large potential volume of sales. It should be useful in a number of different applications and salable to a large number of customers.

4. *Patent protection:* Each line should be well protected by patents arising from the company's own discoveries or acquired by purchase or other means.

9. *Effect on present products:* Each line should improve the company's overall sales and profit position. It should preferably help to promote the sale of the company's other products. If, however, it would hinder the sale of other company products, it should have a greater potential long-range profit than the products in conflict with it.

The statement may also be written up as a series of questions arranged as a check list. The following excerpts are paraphrased from such a statement developed by a well-known manufacturer of consumer goods, whose strategy was "to serve the market for nondurable household goods bought by large numbers of families with a fairly high frequency of purchase":

1. *Customer advantage:* Does the proposed product offer the customer an advantage?
   a. Is it superior to competition in a major property?
   b. If equal to competitive products in use properties, can it be sold profitably at a lower price?
2. *Mass market:* Is there a mass market for the product?
6. *Stability:* Will the product be free of undue breakage or deterioration from normal handling in distribution?
8. *Permissibility:* Will the product conform to applicable government regulations?

To summarize the appraisal of actual products against the product policy, one large materials processor supplements the formal statement with a simple check form. Exhibit V shows this company's summary appraisals of two proposed new businesses. In Case A, although the proposed business was quite different from the company's present lines, it did represent a favorable overall pattern. In Case B, on the other hand, the overall pattern was poor even though there were several favorable points, such as a general similarity to the present operations. The company in question developed Case A into a major new business but did not consider Case B further.

Applying the Policy

A product policy is especially helpful as a suplement and check on the usual estimates of profitability in three types of product activity: (a) development of new products; (b) vertical integration in manufacturing; and (c) elimination of old products.

NEW PRODUCTS

Research and development programs usually proceed stepwise, and in a completed project executives must make at least four major decisions:

1. To undertake preliminary exploratory research, either technical or commercial.
2. To launch a full-scale development program.
3. To build a pilot plant and conduct pilot market tests.
4. To build a commercial plant and put the product on the market.

If the development does not satisfactorily meet the requirements of the company's overall product policy at each of these check points, it should be dropped or seriously changed.

EXHIBIT V

EXAMPLES OF SUMMARY PRODUCT APPRAISALS BY A LARGE MATERIALS PROCESSOR

CASE A: A GENERALLY FAVORABLE PATTERN

	RATING				
	Very good	Good	Fair	Poor	Very poor
Sales volume	x				
Type and number of competitors	x				
Technical opportunity	x				
Patent protection		x			
Raw materials		x			
Production load		x			
Value added		x			
Similarity to major business				x	
Effect on present products			x		

CASE B: A GENERALLY UNFAVORABLE PATTERN

	RATING				
	Very good	Good	Fair	Poor	Very poor
Sales volume	x				
Type and number of competitors					x
Technical opportunity				x	
Patent protection					x
Raw materials		x			
Production load			x		
Value added		x			
Similarity to major business	x				
Effect on present products	x				

Of course, at the start of an exploratory research program there will not be enough information for a complete analysis of the project. An important part of the development will be to obtain the needed information through marketing research, product research, and engineering studies. Nevertheless, early analysis of the information that is available can help prevent such wasted projects as those on the conversion of styrene already mentioned.

Executives can ensure proper consideration of product policy in development work by requiring a brief analysis of each project whenever they must authorize major operating expenditures. One company that controls research and development work by formal "development authorizations" has incorporated such an analysis in its standard authorization form. Despite some initial protests from the research department, the system has worked well for several years now.

INTEGRATION

Should a company make or buy a component part or raw material? Captive production gives certainty of supply, control of quality, and the possibility of substantial cost savings. It may also divert capital from more profitable end products and lead a company into unrelated fields in which it cannot operate efficiently. Furthermore a captive production unit lacks the spur of competition. It may produce only at high cost and lag behind in technological development.[5]

Analysis in terms of a company's product policy helps to indicate these dangers. In general, a company should produce its own parts or materials only when all three of these conditions are met:

1. The raw material considered as a product by itself meets the requirements of the company's product strategy.
2. Internal consumption is large relative to the output of a plant of economic size—say, over 50%. (Otherwise the company is adding a new product, not primarily integrating.)
3. Production will give substantial savings—or profits, if the material is to be sold externally as well.

Somewhat similar considerations apply when a company decides whether to sell an intermediate product or to process it further toward the form in which it will finally be used. Each additional step in manufacture eliminates the cost of intermediate distribution, increases the value added by manufacture, and adds to total profits. However, further processing can also lead a company into fields where it cannot function as efficiently as its customers.

Here again an analysis in terms of product policy is useful. As a

[5] See Carter C. Higgins, "Make-or-Buy Re-Examined," HBR March–April 1955, p. 109.—The Editors.

general rule, further processing is justified only when all three of these requirements are satisfied:

1. The new end product resulting from further processing meets the requirements of the company's product strategy.
2. The cost of the present product is large relative to the total cost of the new end product—say, over 50%.
3. The new processing step will improve the profitability of the over-all operation.

OLD PRODUCTS

The analysis of unsatisfactory products already made and sold is a less common but widely needed application of product policy. Some executives periodically review all product lines to eliminate obsolescent items and to prevent the diversion of effort on low-volume, relatively unprofitable products. For example:

> After such a survey one company with annual sales of $40,000,000 eliminated sixteen different products with a total volume of $3,300,000. It also made a number of improvements in methods of handling the products retained.
>
> Over the next three years the company's total sales increased by one-half and its profits by some twenty times. Among the many factors contributing to these spectacular increases, top executives have stated that dropping unsatisfactory products was one of the most important.

Building for the Future

Besides helping the executive himself make better decisions on product questions such as those just discussed, a good product policy helps to build teamwork throughout the organization. If soundly conceived, clearly stated, and thoroughly understood by all supervisory and professional employees, the policy can be an important tool for control and coordination.

Finally, this approach to product strategy can also have a very dynamic effect in shaping the future development of a company. There is no need to take the present weaknesses for granted. If different resources and a different product strategy show greater promise for the future, then the analysis will indicate where the company must change and strengthen itself. On this basis management can take the constructive steps that are needed.

3. STRATEGIES FOR DIVERSIFICATION*

H. Igor Ansoff

The Red Queen said, "Now, *here,* it takes all the running *you* can do to keep in the same place. If you want to get somewhere else, you must run at least twice as fast as that!"[1]

SO IT IS IN THE American economy. Just to retain its relative position, a business firm must go through continuous growth and change. To improve its position, it must grow and change at least "twice as fast as that."

According to a recent survey of the 100 largest United States corporations from 1909 to 1948, few companies that have stuck to their traditional products and methods have grown in stature. The report concludes: "There is no reason to believe that those now at the top will stay there except as they keep abreast in the race of innovation and competition."[2]

There are four basic growth alternatives open to a business. It can grow through increased market penetration, through market development, through product development, or through diversification.

A company which accepts diversification as a part of its planned approach to growth undertakes the task of continually weighing and comparing the advantages of these four alternatives, selecting first one combination and then another, depending on the particular circumstances in long-range development planning.

While they are an integral part of the overall growth pattern, diversification decisions present certain unique problems. Much more than other growth alternatives, they require a break with past patterns and traditions of a company and an entry onto new and uncharted paths.

Accordingly, one of the aims of this article is to relate diversification to the overall growth perspectives of management, establish reasons which may lead a company to prefer diversification to other growth alternatives,

* From the *Harvard Business Review,* September–October, 1957, Vol. 35, No. 5, pp. 113–124. Reprinted with permission from the publisher.

[1] Lewis J. Carroll, *Through the Looking-Glass* (New York, The Heritage Press, 1941), p. 41.

[2] A. D. H. Kaplan, *Big Enterprise in a Competitive System* (Washington, The Brookings Institution, 1954), p. 142.

and trace a relationship between overall growth objectives and special diversification objectives. This will provide us with a partly qualitative, partly quantitative method for selecting diversification strategies which are best suited to long-term growth of a company. We can use qualitative criteria to reduce the total number of possible strategies to the most promising few, and then apply a return on investment measure to narrow the choice of plans still further.

Product-Market Alternatives

The term "diversification" is usually associated with a change in the characteristics of the company's product line and/or market, in contrast to market penetration, market development, and product development, which represent other types of change in product-market structure. Since these terms are frequently used interchangeably, we can avoid later confusion by defining each as a special kind of product-market strategy. To begin with the basic concepts:

> The *product line* of a manufacturing company refers both to (a) the physical characteristics of the individual products (for example, size, weight, materials, tolerances) and to (b) the performance characteristics of the products (for example, an airplane's speed, range, altitude, payload).
> In thinking of the market for a product we can borrow a concept commonly used by the military—the concept of a mission. A *product mission* is a description of the job which the product is intended to perform. For instance, one of the missions of the Lockheed Aircraft Corporation is commercial air transportation of passengers; another is provision of airborne early warning for the Air Defense Command; a third is performance of air-to-air combat.
> For our purposes, the concept of a mission is more useful in describing market alternatives than would be the concept of a "customer," since a customer usually has many different missions, each requiring a different product. The Air Defense Command, for example, needs different kinds of warning systems. Also, the product mission concept helps management to set up the problems in such a way that it can better evaluate the performance of competing products.
> A *product-market strategy,* accordingly, is a joint statement of a product line and the corresponding set of missions which the products are designed to fulfill. In shorthand form (see Exhibit I), if we let π represent the product line and μ the corresponding set of missions, then the pair of π and μ is a product-market strategy.

With these concepts in mind let us turn now to the four different types of product-market strategy shown in Exhibit I:

> *Market penetration* is an effort to increase company sales without departing from an original product-market strategy. The company seeks to improve business performance either by increasing the volume of sales to its present customers or by finding new customers for present products.

EXHIBIT I
PRODUCT-MARKET STRATEGIES FOR
BUSINESS GROWTH ALTERNATIVES

Markets / Product Line	μ_0	μ_1	μ_2 - μ_m		
π_0	MARKET Penetration		MARKET DEVELOPMENT		
π_1	PRODUCT DEVELOPMENT				
π_2			DIVERSIFICATION		
⋮					
π_n					

Market development is a strategy in which the company attempts to adapt its present product line (generally with some modification in the product characteristics) to new missions. An airplane company which adapts and sells its passenger transport for the mission of cargo transportation is an example of this strategy.

A *product development* strategy, on the other hand, retains the present mission and develops products that have new and different characteristics such as will improve the performance of the mission.

Diversification is the final alternative. It calls for a simultaneous departure from the present product line and the present market structure.

Each of the above strategies describes a distinct path which a business can take toward future growth. However, it must be emphasized that in most actual situations a business would follow several of these paths at the same time. As a matter of fact, a simultaneous pursuit of market penetration, market development, and product development is usually a sign of a progressive, well-run business and may be essential to survival in the face of economic competition.

The diversification strategy stands apart from the other three. While the latter are usually followed with the same technical, financial, and merchandising resources which are used for the original product line, diversification generally requires new skills, new techniques, and new facilities. As a result, it almost invariably leads to physical and organizational changes in the structure of the business which represent a distinct break with past business experience.

Forecasting Growth

A study of business literature and of company histories reveals many different reasons for diversification. Companies diversify to compensate for technological obsolescence, to distribute risk, to utilize excess productive capacity, to reinvest earnings, to obtain top management, and so forth. In deciding whether to diversify, management should carefully analyze its future growth prospects. It should think of market penetration, market development, and product development as parts of its overall product strategy and ask whether this strategy should be broadened to include diversification.

LONG-TERM TRENDS

A standard method of analyzing future company growth prospects is to use long-range sales forecasts. Preparation of such forecasts involves simultaneous consideration of a number of major factors:

General economic trends.

Political and international trends.

Trends peculiar to the industry. (For example, forecasts prepared in the airplane industry must take account of such possibilities as a change-over from manned aircraft to missiles, changes in the government "mobilization base" concept with all that would mean for the aircraft industry, and rising expenditures required for research and development.)

Estimates of the firm's competitive strength relative to other members of the industry.

Estimates of improvements in the company performance which can be achieved through market penetration, market development, and product development.

Trends in manufacturing costs.

Such forecasts usually assume that company management will be aggressive and that management policies will take full advantage of the opportunities offered by the different trends. They are, in other words, estimates of the best possible results the business can hope to achieve *short* of diversification.

Different patterns of forecasted growth are shown in Exhibit II, with hypothetical growth curves for the national economy (GNP) and the company's industry added for purposes of comparison. One of the curves illustrates a sales curve which declines with time. This may be the result of an expected contraction of demand, the obsolescence of manufacturing techniques, emergence of new products better suited to the mission to which the company caters, or other changes. Another typical pattern, frequently caused by seasonal variations in demand, is one of cyclic sales activity. Less apparent, but more important, are slower cyclic changes, such as trends in construction or the peace-war variation in demand in the aircraft industry.

If the most optimistic sales estimates which can be attained short of diversification fall in either of the preceding cases, diversification is strongly indicated. However, a company may choose to diversify even if its prospects do, on the whole, appear favorable. This is illustrated by the "slow growth curve." As drawn in Exhibit II, the curve indicates rising sales which, in fact, grow faster than the economy as a whole. Nevertheless, the particular company may belong to one of the so-called "growth industries" which as a whole is surging ahead. Such a company may diversify because it feels that its prospective growth rate is unsatisfactory in comparison to the industry growth rate.

EXHIBIT II

TREND FORECASTS

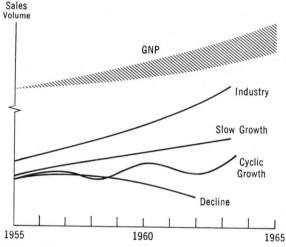

Making trend forecasts is far from a precise science. The characteristics of the basic environmental trends, as well as the effect of these trends on the industry, are always uncertain. Furthermore, the ability of a particular business organization to perform in the new environment is very difficult to assess. Consequently, any realistic company forecast should include several different trend forecasts, each with an explicitly or implicitly assigned probability. As an alternative, the company's growth trend forecast may be represented by a widening spread between two extremes, similar to that shown for GNP in Exhibit II.

CONTINGENCIES

In addition to trends, another class of events may make diversification desirable. These are certain environmental conditions which, if they occur, will have a great effect on sales; however, we cannot predict their occurrence with certainty. To illustrate such "contingent" events, an aircraft company might foresee these possibilities that would upset its trend forecasts:

> A major technological "breakthrough" whose characteristics can be foreseen but whose timing cannot at present be determined, such as the discovery of a new manufacturing process for high-strength, thermally resistant aircraft bodies.
>
> An economic recession which would lead to loss of orders for commercial aircraft and would change the pattern of spending for military aircraft.
>
> A major economic depression.
>
> A limited war which would sharply increase the demand for air industry products.
>
> A sudden cessation of the cold war, a currently popular hope which has waxed and waned with changes in Soviet behavior.

The two types of sales forecast are illustrated in Exhibit III for a hypothetical company. Sales curves S_1 and S_2 represent a spread of trend forecasts; and S_3 and S_4, two contingent forecasts for the same event. The difference between the two types, both in starting time and effect on sales, lies in the degree of uncertainty associated with each.

EXHIBIT III

A HYPOTHETICAL COMPANY FORECAST—
NO DIVERSIFICATION

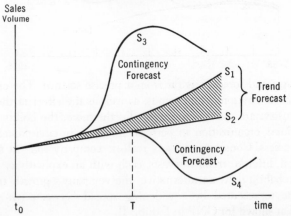

In the case of trend forecasts we can trace a crude time history of sales based on events which we fully expect to happen. Any uncertainty arises from not knowing exactly when they will take place and how they will influence business. In the case of contingency forecasts, we can again trace a crude time history, but our uncertainty is greater. We lack precise knowledge of not only *when* the event will occur but also *whether* it will occur. In going from a trend to a contingency forecast, we advance, so to speak, one notch up the scale of ignorance.

In considering the relative weight we should give to contingent events in diversification planning, we must consider not only the magnitude of their effect on sales, but also the relative probability of their occurrence. For example, if a severe economic depression were to occur, its effect on many industries would be devastating. Many companies feel safe in neglecting it in their planning, however, because they feel that the likelihood of a deep depression is very small, at least for the near future.

It is a common business practice to put primary emphasis on trend forecasts; in fact, in many cases businessmen devote their long-range planning exclusively to these forecasts. They usually view a possible catastrophe as "something one cannot plan for" or as a second-order correction to be applied only after the trends have been taken into account. The emphasis is on planning for growth, and planning for contingencies is viewed as an "insurance policy" against reversals.

People familiar with planning problems in the military establishment will note here an interesting difference between military and business attitudes. While business planning emphasizes trends, military planning emphasizes contingencies. To use a crude analogy, a business planner is concerned with planning for continuous, successful, day-after-day operation of a supermarket. If he is progressive, he also buys an insurance policy against fire, but he spends relatively little time in planning for fires. The military is more like the fire engine company; the fire is the thing. Day-to-day operations are of interest only insofar as they can be utilized to improve readiness and fire-fighting techniques.

UNFORESEEABLE EVENTS

So far we have dealt with diversification forecasts based on what may be called *foreseeable* market conditions—conditions which we can interpret in terms of time-phased sales curves. Planners have a tendency to stop here, to disregard the fact that, in addition to the events for which we can draw time histories, there is a recognizable class of events to which we can assign a probability of occurrence but which we cannot otherwise describe in our present state of knowledge. One must move another notch up the scale of ignorance in order to consider these possibilities.

Many businessmen feel that the effort is not worthwhile. They argue that since no information is available about these unforeseeable circumstances, one might as well devote the available time and energy to planning for the foreseeable circumstances, or that, in a very general sense, planning for the foreseeable also prepares one for the unforeseeable contingencies.

In contrast, more experienced military and business people have a very different attitude. Well aware of the importance and relative probability of unforeseeable events, they ask why one should plan specific steps for the foreseeable events while neglecting the really important possibilities. They may substitute for such planning practical maxims for conducting one's business—"be solvent," "be light on your feet," "be flexible." Unfortunately, it is not always clear (even to the people who preach it) what this flexibility means.

An interesting study by The Brookings Institution[3] provides an example of the importance of the unforeseeable events to business. Exhibit IV shows the changing make-up of the list of the 100 largest corporations

EXHIBIT IV

CHANGES IN LIST OF THE 100
LARGEST INDUSTRIAL CORPORATIONS

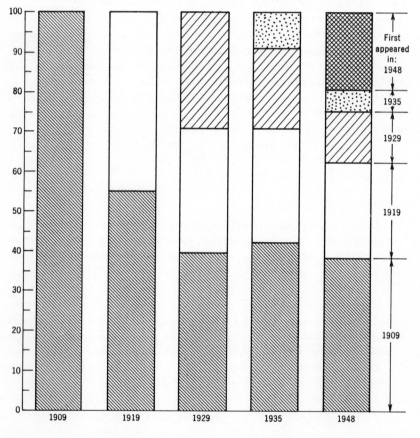

---

[3] A. D. H. Kaplan, op. cit.

over the last 50 years. Of the 100 largest on the 1909 list (represented by the heavy marble texture) only 36 were among the 100 largest in 1948; just about half of the new entries to the list in 1919 (represented by white) were left in 1948; less than half of the new entries in 1929 (represented by the zigzag design) were left in 1948; and so on. Clearly, a majority of the giants of yesteryear have dropped behind in a relatively short span of time.

Many of the events that hurt these corporations could not be specifically foreseen in 1909. If the companies which dropped from the original list had made forecasts of the foreseeable kind at that time—and some of them must have—they would very likely have found the future growth prospects to be excellent. Since then, however, railroads, which loomed as the primary means of transportation, have given way to the automobile and the airplane; the textile industry, which appeared to have a built-in demand in an expanding world population, has been challenged and dominated by synthetics; radio, radar, and television have created means of communication unforeseeable in significance and scope; and many other sweeping changes have occurred.

PLANNING FOR THE UNKNOWN

The lessons of the past 50 years are fully applicable today. The pace of economic and technological change is so rapid that it is virtually certain that major breakthroughs comparable to those of the last 50 years, but not yet foreseeable in scope and character, will profoundly change the structure of the national economy. All of this has important implications for diversification, as suggested by the Brookings study:

> "The majority of the companies included among the 100 largest of our day have attained their positions within the last two decades. They are companies that have started new industries or have transformed old ones to create or meet consumer preferences. The companies that have not only grown in absolute terms but have gained an improved position in their own industry may be identified as companies that are notable for drastic changes made in their product mix and methods, generating or responding to new competition.
> "There are two outstanding cases in which the industry leader of 1909 had by 1948 risen in position relative to its own industry group and also in rank among the 100 largest—one in chemicals and the other in electrical equipment. These two (General Electric and DuPont) are hardly recognizable as the same companies they were in 1909 except for retention of the name; for in each case the product mix of 1948 is vastly different from what it was in the earlier year, and the markets in which the companies meet competition are incomparably broader than those that accounted for their earlier place at the top of their industries. They exemplify the flux in the market positions of the most successful industrial giants during

the past four decades and a general growth rather than a consolidation of supremacy in a circumscribed line."[4]

This suggests that the existence of specific undesirable trends is not the only reason for diversification. A broader product line may be called for even with optimistic forecasts for present products. An examination of the foreseeable alternatives should be accompanied by an analysis of how well the overall company product-market strategy covers the so-called growth areas of technology—areas of many potential discoveries. If such analysis shows that, because of its product lines, a. company's chances of taking advantage of important discoveries are limited, management should broaden its technological and economic base by entering a number of so-called "growth industries." Even if the definable horizons look bright, a need for flexibility, in the widest sense of the word, may provide potent reasons for diversification.

Diversification Objectives

If an analysis of trends and contingencies indicates that a company should diversify, where should it look for diversification opportunities?

Generally speaking, there are three types of opportunities:

1. Each product manufactured by a company is made up of functional components, parts, and basic materials which go into the final assembly. A manufacturing concern usually buys a large fraction of these from outside suppliers. One way to diversify, commonly known as *vertical diversification,* is to branch out into production of components, parts, and materials. Perhaps the most outstanding example of vertical diversification is the Ford empire in the days of Henry Ford, Sr.

    At first glance, vertical diversification seems inconsistent with our definition of a diversification strategy. However, the respective missions which components, parts, and materials are designed to perform are distinct from the mission of the overall product. Furthermore, the technology in fabrication and manufacture of these parts and materials is likely to be very different from the technology of manufacturing the final product. Thus, vertical diversification does imply both catering to new missions and introduction of new products.

2. Another possible way to go is *horizontal diversification.* This can be described as the introduction of new products which, while they do not contribute to the present product line in any way, cater to missions which lie within the company's know-how and experience in technology, finance, and marketing.

---

[4] Ibid., p. 142.

3. It is also possible, by *lateral diversification,* to move beyond the confines of the industry to which a company belongs. This obviously opens a great many possibilities, from operating banana boats to building atomic reactors. While vertical and horizontal diversification are restrictive, in the sense that they delimit the field of interest, lateral diversification is "wide open." It is an announcement of the company's intent to range far afield from its present market structure.

CHOICE OF DIRECTION

How does a company choose among these diversification directions? In part the answer depends on the reasons which prompt diversification. For example, in the light of the trends described for the industry, an aircraft company may make the following moves to meet long-range sales objectives through diversification:

1. A vertical move to contribute to the technological progress of the present product line.
2. A horizontal move to improve the coverage of the military market.
3. A horizontal move to increase the percentage of commercial sales in the overall sales program.
4. A lateral move to stabilize sales in case of a recession.
5. A lateral move to broaden the company's technological base.

Some of these diversification objectives apply to characteristics of the product, some to those of the product missions. Each objective is designed to improve some aspect of the balance between the overall product-market strategy and the expected environment. The specific objectives derived for any given case can be grouped into three general categories: *growth objectives,* such as 1, 2, and 3 above, which are designed to improve the balance under favorable trend conditions; *stability objectives,* such as 3 and 4, designed as protection against unfavorable trends and foreseeable contingencies; and *flexibility objectives,* such as 5, to strengthen the company against unforeseeable contingencies.

A diversification direction which is highly desirable for one of the objectives is likely to be less desirable for others. For example:

If a company is diversifying because its sales trend shows a declining volume of demand, it would be unwise to consider vertical diversification, since this would be at best a temporary device to stave off an eventual decline of business.

If a company's industry shows every sign of healthy growth, then vertical and, in particular, horizontal diversification would be a desirable device for strengthening the position of the company in a field in which its knowledge and experience are concentrated.

If the major concern is stability under a contingent forecast, chances are that both horizontal and vertical diversification could not provide a sufficient stabilizing influence and that lateral action is called for.

If management's concern is with the narrowness of the technological base in the face of what we have called unforeseeable contingencies, then lateral diversification into new areas of technology would be clearly indicated.

MEASURED SALES GOALS

Management can and should state the objectives of growth and stability in quantitative terms as *long-range sales objectives*. This is illustrated in Exhibit V. The solid lines describe a hypothetical company's forecasted performance without diversification under a general trend, represented by the sales curve marked S_1, and in a contingency, represented by S_2. The dashed lines show the improved performance as a result of diversification, with S_3 representing the curve for continuation of normal trends and S_4 representing the curve for a major reverse.

Growth.   Management's first aim in diversifying is to improve the growth pattern of the company. The growth objective can be stated thus:

Under trend conditions the growth rate of sales after diversification should exceed the growth rate of sales of the original product line by a minimum specified margin. Or to illustrate in mathematical shorthand, the objective for the company in Exhibit V would be:

$$S_3 - S_1 \geqslant \rho$$

where the value of the margin ρ is specified for each year after diversification.

EXHIBIT V

DIVERSIFICATION OBJECTIVES

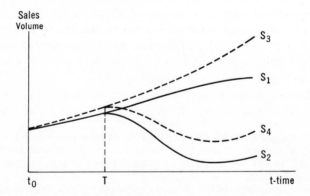

Some companies (particularly in the growth industries) fix an annual rate of growth which they wish to attain. Every year this rate of growth is compared to the actual growth during the past year. A decision on diversification action for the coming year is then based upon the disparity between the objective and the actual rate of growth.

Stability. The second effect desired of diversification is improvement in company stability under contingent conditions. Not only should diversification prevent sales from dropping as low as they might have before diversification, but the precentage drop should also be lower. The second sales objective is thus a stability objective. It can be stated as follows:

> Under contingent conditions the percentage decline in sales which may occur without diversification should exceed the percentage drop in sales with diversification by an adequate margin, or algebraically:

$$\frac{S_1 - S_2}{S_1} - \frac{S_3 - S_4}{S_3} \geqslant \delta$$

Using this equation, it is possible to relate the sales volumes before and after diversification to a rough measure of the resulting stability. Let the ratio of the lowest sales during a slump to the sales which would have occurred in the same year under trend conditions be called the stability factor F. Thus, $F = 0.3$ would mean that the company sales during a contingency amount to 30% of what is expected under trend conditions. In Exhibit VI the stability factor of the company before diversification is the value $F_1 = S_2/S_1$ and the stability factor after diversification is $F_3 = S_4/S_3$, both computed at the point on the curve where S_2 is minimum.

Now let us suppose that management is considering the purchase of a subsidiary. How large does the subsidiary have to be if the parent is to improve the stability of the corporation as a whole by a certain amount? Exhibit VI shows how the question can be answered:

> On the horizontal axis we plot the different possible sales volumes of a smaller firm that might be secured as a proportion of the parent's volume. Obviously, the greater this proportion, the greater the impact of the purchase on the parent's stability.
>
> On the vertical axis we plot different ratios of the parent's stability before and after diversification (F_3/F_1).
>
> The assumed stability factor of the parent is 0.3. Let us say that four prospective subsidiaries have stability factors of 1.0, 0.9, 0.75, and 0.6. If they were not considerably higher than 0.3, of course, there would be no point in acquiring them (at least for our purposes here).
>
> On the graph we correlate these four stability factors of the subsidiary with (1) the ratio F_3/F_1 and (2) different sales volumes of the subsidiary. We find, for example, that if the parent is to double its stability (point 2.0 on the vertical axis), it must obtain a subsidiary with a stability of 1.0 and 75% as much sales volume as the parent, or a subsidiary with a stability of 0.9 and 95% of the sales volume. If the parent seeks an improvement in stability of, say, only 40%, it could buy a company with a stability of 0.9 and 25% as much sales volume as it has.

EXHIBIT VI

IMPROVEMENT IN STABILITY FACTOR AS A RESULT
OF DIVERSIFICATION FOR $F_1 = 0.3$

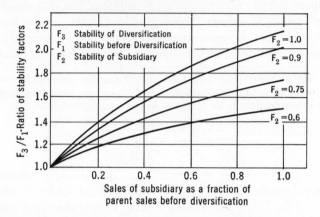

Sales of subsidiary as a fraction of
parent sales before diversification

This particular way of expressing sales objectives has two important advantages: (1) By setting minimum, rather than maximum, limits on growth, it leaves room for the company to take advantage of unusual growth opportunities in order to exceed these goals, and thus provides definite goals without inhibiting initiative and incentive. (2) It takes account of the time-phasing of diversification moves; and since these moves invariably require a transition period, the numerical values of growth objectives can be allowed to vary from year to year so as to allow for a gradual development of operations.

Long-Range Objectives

Diversification objectives specify directions in which a company's product-market should change. Usually there will be several objectives indicating different and sometimes conflicting directions. If a company attempts to follow all of them simultaneously, it is in danger of spreading itself too thin and of becoming a conglomeration of incompatible, although perhaps individually profitable, enterprises.

There are cases of diversification which have followed this path. In a majority of cases, however, there are valid reasons why a company should seek to preserve certain basic unifying characteristics as it goes through a process of growth and change. Consequently, diversification objectives should be supplemented by a statement of long-range product-market objectives. For instance:

One consistent course of action is to adopt a product-market policy which will preserve a kind of technological coherence among the different manufactures with the focus on the products of the parent company. For instance, a company that is mainly distinguished for a type of engineering and production excellence would continue to select product-market entries which would strengthen and maintain this excellence. Perhaps the best known example of such policy is exemplified by the DuPont slogan, "Better things for better living through chemistry."

Another approach is to set long-term growth policy in terms of the breadth of market which the company intends to cover. It may choose to confine its diversifications to the vertical or horizontal direction, or it may select a type of lateral diversification controlled by the characteristics of the missions to which the company intends to cater. For example, a company in the field of air transportation may expand its interest to all forms of transportation of people and cargo. To paraphrase DuPont, some slogan like "Better transportation for better living through advanced engineering," would be descriptive of such a long-range policy.

A greatly different policy is to emphasize primarily the financial characteristics of the corporation. This method of diversification generally places no limits on engineering and manufacturing characteristics of new products, although in practice the competence and interests of management will usually provide some orientation for diversification moves. The company makes the decisions regarding the distribution of new acquisitions exclusively on the basis of financial considerations. Rather than a manufacturing entity, the corporate character is now one of a "holding company." Top management delegates a large share of its product-planning and administrative functions to the divisions and concerns itself largely with coordination, financial problems, and with building up a balanced "portfolio of products" within the corporate structure.

SUCCESSFUL ALTERNATIVES

These alternative long-range policies demonstrate the extremes. No one course is necessarily better than the others; management's choice will rest in large part on its preferences, objectives, skills, and training. The aircraft industry illustrates the fact that there is more than one successful path to diversification:

Among the major successful airframe manufacturers, Douglas Aircraft Company, Inc., and Boeing Airplane Company have to date limited their growth to horizontal diversification into missiles and new markets for new types of aircraft. Lockheed has carried horizontal diversification further to include aircraft maintenance, aircraft service, and production of ground-handling equipment.

North American Aviation, Incorporated, on the other hand, appears to have chosen vertical diversification by establishing its subsidiaries in Atomics International, Autonetics, and Rocketdyne, thus providing a basis for manufacture of complete air vehicles of the future.

Bell Aircraft Corporation has adopted a policy of technological consistency among the items in its product line. It has diversified laterally but

READINGS IN BUSINESS POLICY

primarily into types of products for which it had previous know-how and experience.

General Dynamics Corporation provides a further interesting contrast. It has gone far into lateral diversification. Among the major manufacturers of air vehicles, it comes closest to the "holding company" extreme. Its airplanes and missile manufacturing operations in Convair are paralleled by production of submarines in the Electric Boat Division; military, industrial, and consumer electronic products in the Stromberg-Carlson Division; electric motors in the Electro Dynamic Division.

Selecting a Strategy

In the preceding sections qualitative criteria for diversification have been discussed. How should management apply these criteria to individual opportunities? Two steps should be taken: (1) apply the qualitative standards to narrow the field of diversification opportunities; (2) apply the numerical criteria to select the preferred strategy or strategies.

QUALITATIVE EVALUATION

The long-range product-market policy is used as a criterion for the first rough cut in the qualitative evaluation. It can be used to divide a large field of opportunities into classes of diversification moves consistent with the company's basic character. For example, a company whose policy is to compete on the basis of the technical excellence of its products would eliminate as inconsistent classes of consumer products which are sold on the strength of advertising appeal rather than superior quality.

Next, the company can compare each individual diversification opportunity with the individual diversification objectives. This process tends to eliminate opportunities which, while still consistent with the desired product-market make-up, are nevertheless likely to lead to an imbalance between the company product line and the probable environment. For example, a company which wishes to preserve and expand its technical excellence in design of large, highly stressed machines controlled by feedback techniques may find consistent product opportunities both inside and outside the industry to which it caters, but if one of its major diversification objectives is to correct cyclic variations in demand that are characteristic of the industry, it would choose an opportunity that lies outside.

Each diversification opportunity which has gone through the two screening steps satisfies at least one diversification objective, but probably it will not satisfy all of them. Therefore, before subjecting them to the quantitative evaluation, it is necessary to group them into several alternative overall company product-market strategies, composed of the original strategy and one or more of the remaining diversification strategies. These alternative overall strategies should be roughly equivalent in meeting all of the diversification objectives.

At this stage it is particularly important to allow for the unforeseeable contingencies. Since the techniques of numerical evaluation are applicable only to trends and foreseeable contingencies, it is important to make sure that the different alternatives chosen give the company a broad enough technological base. In practice this process is less formidable than it may appear. For example, a company in the aircraft industry has to consider the areas of technology in which major discoveries are likely to affect the future of the industry. This would include atomic propulsion, certain areas of electronics, automation of complex processes, and so forth. In designing alternative overall strategies the company would then make sure that each contains product entries which will give the firm a desirable and comparable degree of participation in these future growth areas.

QUANTITATIVE EVALUATION

Will the company's product-market strategies make money? Will the profit structure improve as a result of their adoption? The purpose of quantitative evaluation is to compare the profit potential of the alternatives.

Unfortunately, there is no single yardstick among those commonly used in business that gives an accurate measurement of performance. The techniques currently used for measurement of business performance constitute, at best, an imprecise art. It is common to measure different aspects of performance by applying different tests. Thus, tests of income adequacy measure the earning ability of the business; tests of debt coverage and liquidity measure preparedness for contingencies; the shareholders' position measures attractiveness to investors; tests of sales efficiency and personnel productivity measure efficiency in the use of money, physical assets, and personnel. These tests employ a variety of different performance ratios, such as return on sales, return on net worth, return on assets, turnover of net worth, and ratio of assets to liabilities. The total number of ratios may run as high as 20 in a single case.

In the final evaluation, which immediately precedes a diversification decision, management would normally apply all of these tests, tempered with business judgment. However, for the purpose of preliminary elimination of alternatives, a single test is frequently used—return on investment, a ratio between earnings and the capital invested in producing these earnings. While the usefulness of return on investment is commonly accepted, there is considerable room for argument regarding its limitations and its practical application.[5] Fundamentally, the difficulty with the concept is that it fails to provide an absolute measure of business performance

---

[5] See Charles R. Schwartz, *The Return-on-Investment Concept as a Tool for Decision Making*, General Management Series No. 183 (New York, American Management Association, 1956), pp. 42–61; Peter F. Drucker, *The Practice of Management* (New York, Harper & Brothers, 1954); and Edward M. Barnet, "Showdown in the Market Place," HBR July–August 1956, p. 85.

applicable to a range of very different industries; also, the term "investment" is subject to a variety of interpretations.

But, since our aim is to use the concept as a measure of *relative*
performance of different diversification strategies, we need not be concerned with its failure to measure absolute values. And as long as we are
consistent in our definition of investment in alternative courses of action,
the question of terminology is not so troublesome. We cannot define
profit-producing capital in general terms, but we can define it in each case
in the light of particular business characteristics and practices (such as the
extent of government-owned assets, depreciation practices, inflationary
trends).

For the numerator of our return on investment, we can use net earnings after taxes. A going business concern has standard techniques for
estimating its future earnings. These depend on the projected sales volume,
tax structure, trends in material and labor costs, productivity, and so forth.
If the diversification opportunity being considered is itself a going concern,
its profit projections can be used for estimates of combined future earnings. If the opportunity is a new venture, its profit estimates should be
made on the basis of the average performance for the industry.

CHANGES IN INVESTMENT STRUCTURE

A change in the investment structure of the diversifying company ac-
companies a diversification move. The source of investment for the new
venture may be: (1) excess capital, (2) capital borrowed at an attractive
rate, (3) an exchange of the company's equity for an equity in another
company, or (4) capital withdrawn from present business operations.

If we let i_1, i_2, i_3, and i_4, respectively, represent investments made in
the new product in the preceding four categories during the first year of
diversified operations, we can derive a simple expression for the *improvement* in return on investment resulting from diversification:

$$\Delta R = \frac{(p_2 - p_1)(i_2 + i_3 + i_4) + (p_2 - r)\, i_1 - i_2 r + (p_1 - r)(i_2 + i_3)^1\, I/I}{I + i_2 + i_3}$$

where p_1 and p_2 represent the average return on capital invested in the
original product and in the new product, respectively, and quantity I is the
total capital in the business before diversification.

We can easily check this expression by assuming that only one type of
new investment will be made at a time. We can then use the formula to
compute the conditions under which it pays to diversify (that is, conditions
where ΔR is greater than zero):

1. If excess capital is the only source of new investment ($i_2 = i_3 =
   i_4 = 0$), this condition is $p_2 - r > 0$. That is, return on diversified

operations should be more attractive than current rates for capital on the open market.

2. If only borrowed capital is used ($i_1 = i_3 = i_4 = 0$), it pays to diversify if $p_2 - p_1 > r$. That is, the difference between return from diversification and return from the original product should be greater than the interest rate on the money.

3. If the diversified operation is to be acquired through an exchange of equity or through internal reallocation of capital, $p_2 - p_1 > 0$ is the condition under which diversification will pay off.

A COMPREHENSIVE YARDSTICK

The formula for ΔR just stated is not sufficiently general to serve as a measure of profit potential. It gives improvement in return for the first year only and for a particular sales trend. In order to provide a reasonably comprehensive comparison between alternative overall company strategies, the yardstick for profit potential should possess the following properties:

1. Since changes in the investment structure of the business invariably accompany diversification, the yardstick should reflect these changes. It should also take explicit account of new capital brought into the business and changes in the rate of capital formation resulting from diversification, as well as costs of borrowed capital.

2. Usually the combined performance of the new and the old product-market lines is not a simple sum of their separate performances; it should be greater. The profit potential yardstick must take account of this nonlinear characteristic.

3. Each diversification move is characterized by a transition period during which readjustment of the company structure to new operating conditions takes place. The benefits of a diversification move may not be realized fully for some time, so the measurement of profit potential should span a sufficient length of time to allow for effects of the transition.

4. Since both profits and investments will be spread over time, the yardstick should use their present value.

5. Business performance will differ depending on the particular economic-political environment. The profit potential yardstick must somehow average out the probable effect of alternative environments.

6. The statement of sales objectives, as pointed out previously, should specify the general characteristics of growth and stability which are desired. Profit potential functions should be compatible with these characteristics.

We can generalize our formula in a way which will meet most of the preceding requirements. The procedure is to write an expression for the present value of ΔR for an arbitrary year, t, allowing for possible yearly diversification investments up to the year t, interest rates, and the rate of capital formation. Then this present value is averaged over time as well as over the alternative sales forecasts. The procedure is straightforward (although the algebra involved is too cumbersome to be worth reproducing here[6]). The result, which is the "average expected present value of ΔR," takes account of conditions 1 through 5, above. Let us call it $(\Delta R)_e$. It can be computed using data normally found in business and financial forecasts.

FINAL EVALUATION

This brings us to the final step in the evaluation. We have discussed a qualitative method for constructing several overall product-market strategies which meet the diversification and the long-range objectives. We can now compute $(\Delta R)_e$ for each of the overall strategies and, at the same time, make sure that the strategies satisfy the sales objectives previously stated, thus fulfilling condition 6, above.

If product-market characteristics, which we have used to narrow the field of choice and to compute $(\Delta R)_e$, were the sole criteria, then the strategy with the highest $(\Delta R)_e$ would be the "preferred" path to diversification. The advantages of a particular product-market opportunity, however, must be balanced against the chances of business success.

Conclusion

A study of diversification histories shows that a firm usually arrives at a decision to make a particular move through a multistep process. The planners' first step is to determine the preferred areas for search; the second is to select a number of diversification opportunities within these areas and to subject them to a preliminary evaluation. They then make a final evaluation, conducted by the top management, leading to selection of a specific step; finally, they work out details and complete the move.

Throughout this process, the company seeks to answer two basic questions: How well will a particular move, if it is successful, meet the company's objectives? What are the company's chances of making it a success? In the early stages of the program, the major concern is with business strategy. Hence, the first question plays a dominant role. But as the choice narrows, considerations of business ability, of the particular strengths and weaknesses which a company brings to diversification, shift attention to the second question.

This discussion has been devoted primarily to selection of a diversifica-

---

[6] See H. Igor Ansoff, *A Model for Diversification* (Burbank, Lockheed Aircraft Corporation, 1957); and John Burr Williams, *The Theory of Investment Value* (Amsterdam, The North-Holland Publishing Co., 1938).

tion strategy. We have dealt with what may be called *external* aspects of diversification—the relation between a company and its environment. To put it another way, we have derived a method for measuring the profit potential of a diversification strategy, but we have not inquired into the *internal* factors which determine the ability of a diversifying company to make good this potential. A company planning diversification must consider such questions as how the company should organize to conduct the search for and evaluation of diversification opportunities; what method of business expansion it should employ; and how it should mesh its operations with those of a subsidiary. These considerations give rise to a new set of criteria for the *business fit* of the prospective venture. These must be used in conjunction with $(\Delta R)_e$ as computed in the preceding section to determine which of the overall product-market strategies should be selected for implementation.

Thus, the steps outlined in this article are the first, though an important, preliminary to a diversification move. Only through further careful consideration of probable business success can a company develop a long-range strategy that will enable it to "run twice as fast as that" (using the Red Queen's words again) in the ever-changing world of today.

EXHIBIT VII

In a highly diversified company . . . there is a natural tendency to assign a single executive the responsibility for so many diverse businesses that he becomes a jack of all trades and a master of none. . . .

This is serious, because American business competition no longer permits survival of businesses without managers of special intelligence and competence in their individual fields. Therefore, as a continuing process, we attempt to organize our company [W. R. Grace & Co.] so that the manager for any business or group of businesses is as expert in them as his competition. This is sometimes difficult. As one important aid, we have tried to minimize the number of management levels; we have tried to keep the organization "flat." The more management levels you have, we feel, the more friction, inertia and slack you have to overcome, and the greater the distortion of objectives and the misdirection of attention. In this you must always be on your guard, because levels of management, like tree rings, grow with age. As one company president put it, "If all an executive does is agree with his subordinate executive, you don't need both of them."

Ernest C. Arbuckle, "Diversification," *Management for Growth,* edited by
Gayton E. Germane
Stanford University, Graduate School of Business, 1957, pp. 85–86.

4. HOW TO EVALUATE CORPORATE STRATEGY*

Seymour Tilles

NO GOOD MILITARY OFFICER WOULD undertake even a small-scale attack on a limited objective without a clear concept of his strategy. No seasoned politician would undertake a campaign for a major office without an equally clear concept of his strategy. In the field of business management, however, we frequently find men deploying resources on a large scale without any clear notion of what their strategy is. And yet a company's strategy is a vital ingredient in determining its future. A valid strategy will yield growth, profit, or whatever other objectives the managers have established. An inappropriate strategy not only will fail to yield benefits, but also may result in disaster.

In this article I will try to demonstrate the truth of these contentions by examining the experiences of a number of companies. I shall discuss what strategy is, how it can be evaluated, and how, by evaluating its strategy, a management can do much to assure the future of the enterprise.

Decisive Impact

The influence of strategy can be seen in every age and in every area of industry. Here are some examples:

From the time it was started in 1911 as the Computing-Tabulating-Recording Co., International Business Machines Corporation has demonstrated the significance of a soundly conceived strategy. Seeing itself in the data-system business at a time when most manufacturers were still preoccupied with individual pieces of equipment, IBM developed a set of policies which resulted in its dominating the office equipment industry.

By contrast, Packard in the 1930's was to the automobile industry everything that IBM is today to the office machine industry. In 1937, it sold over 109,000 cars, compared with about 11,000 for Cadillac. By 1954 it had disappeared as an independent producer.

Strategy is, of course, not the only factor determining a company's success or failure. The competence of its managerial leadership is signifi-

* From the *Harvard Business Review*, July–August, 1963, Vol. 41, No. 4, pp. 111–121. Reprinted with permission from the publisher.

cant as well. Luck can be a factor, too (although often what people call good luck is really the product of good strategy). But a valid strategy can gain extraordinary results for the company whose general level of competence is only average. And, conversely, the most inspiring leaders who are locked into an inappropriate strategy will have to exert their full competence and energy merely in order to keep from losing ground.

When Hannibal inflicted the humiliating defeat on the Roman army at Cannae in 216 B.C., he led a ragged band against soldiers who were in possession of superior arms, better training, and competent "noncoms." His strategy, however, was so superior that all of those advantages proved to be relatively insignificant. Similarly, when Jacob Borowsky made Lestoil the hottest-selling detergent in New England some years ago, he was performing a similar feat—relying on strategy to battle competition with superior resources.

Strategy is important not only for aspiring Davids who need an offensive device to combat corporate Goliaths. It is significant also for the large organization faced with a wide range of choice in domestic and international operations. For instance, the following corporations are all in the midst of strategic changes, the implications of which are worldwide in scope:

Massey-Ferguson, Ltd., with 26 factories located around the world, and vying for leadership in the farm-equipment industry.

General Electric Company and Westinghouse Electric Corporation, the giant producers of electrical equipment who are recasting their competitive policies.

Singer Sewing Machine Company, trying to make its vast assets yield a greater return.

Dynamic Concept

A strategy is a set of goals and major policies. The definition is as simple as that. But while the notion of a strategy is extremely easy to grasp, working out an agreed-upon statement for a given company can be a fundamental contribution to the organization's future success.

In order to develop such a statement, managers must be able to identify precisely what is meant by a goal and what is meant by a major policy. Otherwise, the process of strategy determination may degenerate into what it so often becomes—the solemn recording of platitudes, useless for either the clarification of direction or the achievement of consensus.

IDENTIFYING GOALS

Corporate goals are an indication of what the company as a whole is trying to *achieve* and to *become*. Both parts—the achieving and the becoming—are important for a full understanding of what a company hopes to attain. For example:

> Under the leadership of Alfred Sloan, General Motors achieved a considerable degree of external success; this was accomplished because Sloan worked out a pattern for the kind of company he wanted it to be internally.
>
> Similarly, the remarkable record of Du Pont in the twentieth century and the growth of Sears, Roebuck under Julius Rosenwald were as much a tribute to their modified structure as to their external strategy.[1]

Achieving. In order to state what a company expects to achieve, it is important to state what it hopes to do with respect to its environment. For instance:

> Ernest Breech, chairman of the board of the Ford Motor Company, said that the strategy formulated by his company in 1946 was based on a desire "to hold our own in what we foresaw would be a rich but hotly competitive market."[2] The view of the environment implicit in this statement is unmistakable: an expanding overall demand, increasing competition, and emphasis on market share as a measure of performance against competitors.

Clearly, a statement of what a company hopes to achieve may be much more varied and complex than can be contained in a single sentence. This will be especially true for those managers who are sophisticated enough to perceive that a company operates in more external "systems" than the market. The firm is part not only of a market but also of an industry, the community, the economy, and other systems. In each case there are unique relationships to observe (e.g., with competitors, municipal leaders, Congress, and so on). A more complete discussion of this point is contained in a previous HBR article.[3]

Becoming. If you ask young men what they want to accomplish by the time they are 40, the answers you get fall into two distinct categories. There are those—the great majority—who will respond in terms of what they want to *have*. This is especially true of graduate students of business administration. There are some men, however, who will answer in terms of the kind of men they hope to *be*. These are the only ones who have a clear idea of where they are going.

The same is true of companies. For far too many companies, what little thinking goes on about the future is done primarily in money terms.

---

[1] For an interesting discussion of this relationship, see A. D. Chandler, Jr., *Strategy and Structure* (Cambridge, Massachusetts Institute of Technology Press, 1962), pp. 1–17.

[2] See Edward C. Bursk and Dan H. Fenn, Jr., *Planning the Future Strategy of Your Business* (New York, McGraw-Hill Book Company, Inc., 1956), p. 8.

[3] Seymour Tilles, "The Manager's Job—A Systems Approach," HBR January–February 1963, p. 73.

There is nothing wrong with financial planning. Most companies should do more of it. But there is a basic fallacy in confusing a financial plan with thinking about the kind of company you want yours to become. It is like saying, "When I'm 40, I'm going to be *rich*." It leaves too many basic questions unanswered. Rich in what way? Rich doing what?

The other major fallacy in stating what you want to become is to say it only in terms of a product. The number of companies who have got themselves into trouble by falling in love with a particular product is distressingly great.[4] Perhaps the saddest examples are those giants of American industry who defined their future in terms of continuing to be the major suppliers of steam locomotives to the nation's railroads. In fact, these companies were so wedded to this concept of their future that they formed a cartel in order to keep General Motors out of the steam locomotive business. When the diesel locomotive proved its superiority to steam, these companies all but disappeared.

The lesson of these experiences is that a key element of setting goals is the ability to see them in terms of more than a single dimension. Both money and product policy are part of a statement of objectives; but it is essential that these be viewed as the concrete expressions of a more abstract set of goals—the satisfaction of the needs of significant groups which cooperate to ensure the company's continued existence.

Who are these groups? There are many—customers, managers, employees, stockholders, to mention just the major ones. The key to corporate success is the company's ability to identify the important needs of each of these groups, to establish some balance among them, and to work out a set of operating policies which permits their satisfaction. This set of policies, as a pattern, identifies what the company is trying to be.

THE GROWTH FAD

Many managers have a view of their company's future which is strikingly analogous to the child's view of himself. When asked what they want their companies to become over the next few years, they reply, "bigger."

There are a great many rationalizations for this preoccupation with growth. Probably the one most frequently voiced is that which says, "You have to grow or die." What must be appreciated, however, is that "bigger" for a company has enormous implications for management. It involves a different way of life, and one which many managers may not be suited for—either in terms of temperament or skills.

Moreover, whether for a large company or a small one, "bigger," by itself, may not make economic sense. Companies which are highly prof-

---

4 See Theodore Levitt, "Marketing Myopia," HBR July–August 1960, p. 45.

itable at their present size may grow into bankruptcy very easily; witness the case of Grayson-Robinson Stores, Inc., a chain of retail stores. Starting out as a small but profitable chain, it grew rapidly into receivership. Conversely, a company which is not now profitable may more successfully seek its survival in cost reduction than in sales growth. Chrysler is a striking example of this approach.

There is, in the United States, a business philosophy which reflects the frontier heritage of the country. It is one which places a high value on growth, in physical terms. The manager whose corporate sales are not increasing, the number of whose subordinates is not growing, whose plants are not expanding, feels that he is not successful. But there is a dangerous trap in this kind of thinking. More of the same is not necessarily progress. In addition, few managers are capable of running units several times larger than the ones they now head. The great danger of wholehearted consumer acceptance or an astute program of corporate acquisition is that it frequently propels managers into situations that are beyond their present competence. Such cases—and they are legion—emphasize that in stating corporate objectives, bigger is not always better. A dramatic example is that of the Ampex Corporation:

> From 1950 to 1960, Ampex's annual sales went from less than $1,000,000 to more than $73,000,000. Its earnings went from $115,000 to nearly $4,000,000. The following year, the company reported a decline in sales to $70,000,000, and a net loss of $3,900,000. The *Wall Street Journal* reported: "As one source close to the company put it, Ampex's former management 'was intelligent and well-educated, but simply lacked the experience necessary to control' the company's rapid development."[5]

ROLE OF POLICY

A policy says something about *how* goals will be attained. It is what statisticians would call a "decision rule," and what systems engineers would call a "standing plan." It tells people what they should and should not do in order to contribute to achievement of corporate goals.

A policy should be more than just a platitude. It should be a helpful guide to making strategy explicit, and providing direction to subordinates. Consequently, the more definite it is, the more helpful it can be. "We will provide our stockholders with a fair return," is a policy no one could possibly disagree with—or be helped by. What *is* a fair return? This is the type of question that must be answered before the company's intentions become clear.

The job of management is not merely the preparation of valid policies for a standard set of activities; it is the much more challenging one of first deciding what activities are so strategically significant that explicit decision-

---

[5] "Ŗ for Ampex: Drastic Changes Help Solve Big Headache of Fast Corporate Growth," *Wall Street Journal*, September 17, 1962, p. 1.

rules in that area are mandatory. No standard set of policies can be considered major for all companies. Each company is a unique situation. It must decide for itself which aspects of corporate life are most relevant to its own aspirations and work out policy statements for them. For example, advertising may be insignificant to a company which provides research services to the Defense Department, but critical to a firm trying to mass-merchandise luxury goods.

It is difficult to generalize about which policies are major, even within a particular industry, because a number of extraordinarily successful companies appear to violate all the rules. To illustrate:

> In the candy industry it would seem safe to generalize that advertising should be a major policy area. However, the Hershey Company, which is so successful that its name is practically the generic term for the product, has persistently followed a policy of no advertising.
>
> Similarly, in the field of high-fidelity components, one would expect that dealer relations would be a critical policy area. But Acoustics Research, Inc., has built an enviable record of sales growth and of profitability by relying entirely on consumer pull.

NEED TO BE EXPLICIT

The first thing to be said about corporate strategy is that having one is a step forward. Any strategy, once made explicit, can quickly be evaluated and improved. But if no attempt is ever made to commit it to paper, there is always the danger that the strategy is either incomplete or misunderstood.

Many successful companies are not aware of the strategy that underlies their success. It is quite possible for a company to achieve initial success without real awareness of its causes. However, it is much more difficult to successfully *branch out into new ventures* without a precise appreciation of their strategic significance. This is why many established companies fail miserably when they attempt a program of corporate acquisition, product diversification, or market expansion. One illustration of this is cited by Myles L. Mace and George G. Montgomery in their recent study of corporate acquisitions:

> "A basic resin company . . . bought a plastic boat manufacturer because this seemed to present a controlled market for a portion of the resin it produced. It soon found that the boat business was considerably different from the manufacture and sale of basic chemicals. After a short but unpleasant experience in manufacturing and trying to market what was essentially a consumer's item, the management concluded that its experience and abilities lay essentially in industrial rather than consumer-type products."[6]

---

[6] *Management Problems of Corporate Acquisitions* (Boston, Division of Research, Harvard Business School, 1962), p. 60.

Another reason for making strategy explicit is the assistance it provides for delegation and for coordination. To an ever-increasing extent, management is a team activity, whereby groups of executives contribute to corporate success. Making strategy explicit makes it far easier for each executive to appreciate what the overall goals are, and what his own contribution to them must be.

Making an Evaluation

Is your strategy right for you? There are six criteria on which to base an answer. These are:

1. Internal consistency.
2. Consistency with the environment.
3. Appropriateness in the light of available resources.
4. Satisfactory degree of risk.
5. Appropriate time horizon.
6. Workability.

If all of these criteria are met, you have a strategy that is right for you. This is as much as can be asked. There is no such thing as a good strategy in any absolute, objective sense. In the remainder of this article I shall discuss the criteria in some detail.

1. IS THE STRATEGY INTERNALLY CONSISTENT?

Internal consistency refers to the cumulative impact of individual policies on corporate goals. In a well-worked-out strategy, each policy fits into an integrated pattern. It should be judged not only in terms of itself, but also in terms of how it relates to other policies which the company has established and to the goals it is pursuing.

In a dynamic company consistency can never be taken for granted. For example:

> Many family-owned organizations pursue a pair of policies which soon become inconsistent: rapid expansion and retention of exclusive family control of the firm. If they are successful in expanding, the need for additional financing soon raises major problems concerning the extent to which exclusive family control can be maintained.
>
> While this pair of policies is especially prevalent among smaller firms, it is by no means limited to them. The Ford Motor Company after World War II and the New York Times today are examples of quite large, family-controlled organizations that have had to reconcile the two conflicting aims.

The criterion of internal consistency is an especially important one for evaluating strategies because it identifies those areas where strategic choices will eventually have to be made. An inconsistent strategy does *not* necessarily mean that the company is currently in difficulty. But it does mean that unless management keeps its eye on a particular area of operation, it may well find itself forced to make a choice without enough time either to search for or to prepare attractive alternatives.

2. IS THE STRATEGY CONSISTENT WITH THE ENVIRONMENT?

A firm which has a certain product policy, price policy, or advertising policy is saying that it has chosen to relate itself to its customers—actual and potential—in a certain way. Similarly, its policies with respect to government contracts, collective bargaining, foreign investment, and so forth are expressions of relationship with other groups and forces. Hence an important test of strategy is whether the chosen policies are consistent with the environment—whether they really make sense with respect to what is going on outside.

Consistency with the environment has both a static and a dynamic aspect. In a static sense, it implies judging the efficacy of policies with respect to the environment as it exists *now*. In a dynamic sense, it means judging the efficacy of policies with respect to the environment *as it appears to be changing*. One purpose of a viable strategy is to ensure the long-run success of an organization. Since the environment of a company is constantly changing, ensuring success over the long run means that management must constantly be assessing the degree to which policies previously established are consistent with the environment as it exists now; and whether current policies take into account the environment as it will be in the future. In one sense, therefore, establishing a strategy is like aiming at a moving target: you have to be concerned not only with present position but also with the speed and direction of movement.

Failure to have a strategy consistent with the environment can be costly to the organization. Ford's sad experience with the Edsel is by now a textbook example of such failure. Certainly, had Ford pushed the Falcon at the time when it was pushing the Edsel, and with the same resources, it would have a far stronger position in the world automobile market today.

Illustrations of strategies that have not been consistent with the environment are easy to find by using hindsight. *But the reason that such examples are plentiful is not that foresight is difficult to apply.* It is because even today few companies are seriously engaged in analyzing environmental trends and using this intelligence as a basis for managing their own futures.

3. IS THE STRATEGY APPROPRIATE IN VIEW OF THE AVAILABLE RESOURCES?

Resources are those things that a company *is* or *has* and that help it to achieve its corporate objectives. Included are money, competence, and facilities; but these by no means complete the list. In companies selling consumer goods, for example, the major resource may be the name of the product. In any case, there are two basic issues which management must decide in relating strategy and resources. These are:

What are our critical resources?
Is the proposed strategy appropriate for available resources?

Let us look now at what is meant by a "critical resource" and at how the criterion of resource utilization can be used as a basis for evaluating strategy.

Critical Resources.   The essential strategic attribute of resources is that they represent action potential. Taken together, a company's resources represent its capacity to respond to threats and opportunities that may be perceived in the environment. In other words, resources are the bundle of chips that the company has to play with in the serious game of business.

From an action-potential point of view, a resource may be critical in two senses: (1) as the factor limiting the achievement of corporate goals; and (2) as that which the company will exploit as the basis for its strategy. Thus, critical resources are both what the company has most of and what it has least of.

The three resources most frequently identified as critical are money, competence, and physical facilities. Let us look at the strategic significance of each.

Money.   Money is a particularly valuable resource because it provides the greatest flexibility of response to events as they arise. It may be considered the "safest" resource, in that safety may be equated with the freedom to choose from among the widest variety of future alternatives. Companies that wish to reduce their short-run risk will therefore attempt to accumulate the greatest reservoir of funds they can.

However, it is important to remember that while the accumulation of funds may offer short-run security, it may place the company at a serious competitive disadvantage with respect to other companies which are following a higher-risk course.

The classical illustration of this kind of outcome is the strategy pursued by Montgomery Ward under the late Sewell Avery. As reported in *Fortune:*

"While Sears confidently bet on a new and expanding America, Avery developed an *idée fixe* that postwar inflation would end in a crash no less serious than that of 1929. Following this idea, he opened no new stores but rather piled up cash to the ceiling in preparation for an economic debacle that never came. In these years, Ward's balance sheet gave a somewhat misleading picture of its prospects. Net earnings remained respectably high, and were generally higher than those of Sears as a percentage of sales. In

1946, earnings after taxes were $52 million. They rose to $74 million in 1950, and then declined to $35 million in 1954. Meanwhile, however, sales remained static, and in Avery's administration profits and liquidity were maintained at the expense of growth. In 1954, Ward had $327 million in cash and securities, $147 million in receivables, and $216 million in inventory, giving it a total current-asset position of $690 million and net worth of $639 million. It was liquid, all right, but it was also the shell of a once great company."[7]

Competence. Organizations survive because they are good at doing those things which are necessary to keep them alive. However, the degree of competence of a given organization is by no means uniform across the broad range of skills necessary to stay in business. Some companies are particularly good at marketing, others especially good at engineering, still others depend primarily on their financial sophistication. Philip Selznick refers to that which a company is particularly good at as its "distinctive competence."[8]

In determining a strategy, management must carefully appraise its own skill profile in order to determine where its strengths and weaknesses lie. It must then adopt a strategy which makes the greatest use of its strengths. To illustrate:

> The competence of *The New York Times* lies primarily in giving extensive and insightful coverage of events—the ability to report "all the news that's fit to print." It is neither highly profitable (earning only 1.5% of revenues in 1960—far less than, say, the *Wall Street Journal*), nor aggressively sold. Its decision to publish a West Coast and an international edition is a gamble that the strength of its "distinctive competence" will make it accepted even outside of New York.
>
> Because of a declining demand for soft coal, many producers of soft coal are diversifying into other fields. All of them, however, are remaining true to some central skill that they have developed over the years. For instance:
>
>> Consolidation Coal is moving from simply the mining of soft coal to the mining *and transportation* of soft coal. It is planning with Texas Eastern Transmission Corporation to build a $100-million pipeline that would carry a mixture of powdered coal and water from West Virginia to the East Coast.
>>
>> North American Coal Company, on the other hand, is moving toward becoming a chemical company. It recently joined with Strategic Materials Corporation to perfect a process for extracting aluminum sulfate from the mine shale that North American produces in its coal-running operations.

[7] "Montgomery Ward: Prosperity Is Still Around the Corner," *Fortune*, November 1960, p. 140.

[8] *Leadership in Administration* (Evanston, Illinois, Row, Peterson & Company, 1957), p. 42.

James L. Hamilton, president of the Island Creek Coal Co., has summed up the concept of distinctive competence in a colorful way:

"We are a career company dedicated to coal, and we have some very definite ideas about growth and expansion within the industry. We're not thinking of buying a cotton mill and starting to make shirts."[9]

Physical Facilities. Physical facilities are the resource whose strategic influence is perhaps most frequently misunderstood. Managers seem to be divided among those, usually technical men, who are enamored of physical facilities as the tangible symbol of the corporate entity; and those, usually financial men, who view physical facilities as an undesirable but necessary freezing of part of the company's funds. The latter group is dominant. In many companies, return on investment has emerged as virtually the sole criterion for deciding whether or not a particular facility should be acquired.

Actually, this is putting the cart before the horse. Physical facilities have significance primarily in relationship to overall corporate strategy. It is, therefore, only in relationship to *other* aspects of corporate strategy that the acquisition or disposition of physical facilities can be determined. The total investment required and the projected return on it have a place in this determination—but only as an indication of the financial implications of a particular strategic decision and not as an exclusive criterion for its own sake.

Any appraisal of a company's physical facilities as a strategic resource must consider the relationship of the company to its environment. Facilities have no intrinsic value for their own sake. Their value to the company is either in their location relative to markets, to sources of labor, or to materials; or in their efficiency relative to existing or impending competitive installations. Thus, the essential considerations in any decision regarding physical facilities are a projection of changes likely to occur in the environment and a prediction about what the company's responses to these are likely to be.

Here are two examples of the necessity for relating an evaluation of facilities to environmental changes:

Following the end of World War II, all domestic producers of typewriters in the United States invested heavily in plant facilities in this country. They hypothesized a rapid increase of sales throughout the world. This indeed took place, but it was short-lived. The rise of vigorous overseas competitors, especially Olivetti and Olympia, went hand in hand with a booming overseas market. At home, IBM's electric typewriter took more and more of the domestic market. Squeezed between these two pressures, the rest of the U.S. typewriter industry found itself with a great deal of excess

---

[9] *Wall Street Journal,* September 11, 1962, p. 30.

capacity following the Korean conflict. Excess capacity is today still a major problem in this field.

The steady decline in the number of farms in the United States and the emergencè of vigorous overseas competition have forced most domestic full-line manufacturers of farm equipment to sharply curtail total plant area. For example, in less than four years, International Harvester eliminated more than a third of its capacity (as measured in square feet of plant space) for the production of farm machinery.

The close relationship between physical facilities and environmental trends emphasizes one of the most significant attributes of fixed assets—their temporal utility. Accounting practice recognizes this in its treatment of depreciation allowances. But even when the tax laws permit generous write-offs, they should not be used as the sole basis for setting the time period over which the investment must be justified. Environmental considerations may reveal that a different time horizon is more relevant for strategy determination. To illustrate again:

> As Armstrong Cork Company moved away from natural cork to synthetic materials during the early 1950's, management considered buying facilities for the production of its raw materials—particularly polyvinyl chloride. However, before doing so, it surveyed the chemical industry and concluded that producers were overbuilding. It therefore decided not to invest in facilities for the manufacture of this material. The projections were valid; since 1956 polyvinyl chloride has dropped 50% in price.

A strategic approach to facilities may not only change the time horizon; it may also change the whole basis of asset valuation:

> Recently a substantial portion of Loew's theaters was acquired by the Tisch brothers, owners and operators of a number of successful hotels, including the Americana in Florida.[10] As long as the assets of Loew's theaters were viewed only as places for the projection of films, its theaters, however conservatively valued, seemed to be not much of a bargain. But to a keen appraiser of hotel properties the theater sites, on rather expensive real estate in downtown city areas, had considerable appeal. Whether this appraisal will be borne out is as yet unknown. At any rate, the stock, which was originally purchased at $14 (with a book value of $22), was selling at $23 in October 1962.

Achieving the Right Balance. One of the most difficult issues in strategy determination is that of achieving a balance between strategic goals and available resources. This requires a set of necessarily empirical, but critical, estimates of the total resources required to achieve particular objectives, the rate at which they will have to be committed, and the likelihood that they will be available. The most common errors are either to fail to make these estimates at all or to be excessively optimistic about them.

---

[10] See "The Tisches Eye Their Next $65 Million," *Fortune,* January 1960, p. 140.

One example of the unfortunate results of being wrong on these estimates is the case of Royal McBee and the computer market:

In January 1956 Royal McBee and the General Precision Equipment Corporation formed a jointly owned company—the Royal Precision Corporation—to enter the market for electronic data-processing equipment. This joint operation was a logical pooling of complementary talents. General Precision had a great deal of experience in developing and producing computers. Its Librascope Division had been selling them to the government for years. However, it lacked a commercial distribution system. Royal McBee, on the other hand, had a great deal of experience in marketing data-processing equipment, but lacked the technical competence to develop and produce a computer.

The joint venture was eminently successful, and within a short time the Royal Precision LPG-30 was the leader in the small-computer field. However, the very success of the computer venture caused Royal McBee some serious problems. The success of the Royal Precision subsidiary demanded that the partners put more and more money into it. This was no problem for General Precision, but it became an ever more serious problem for Royal McBee, which found itself in an increasingly critical cash bind. In March 1962 it sold its interest in Royal Precision to General Precision for $5 million—a price which represented a reported $6.9 million loss on the investment. Concluding that it simply did not have sufficient resources to stay with the new venture, it decided to return to its traditional strengths: typewriters and simple data-processing systems.

Another place where optimistic estimates of resources frequently cause problems is in small businesses. Surveys of the causes of small-business failure reveal that a most frequent cause of bankruptcy is inadequate resources to weather either the early period of establishment or unforeseen downturns in business conditions.

It is apparent from the preceding discussion that a critical strategic decision involves deciding: (1) how much of the company's resources to commit to opportunities currently perceived, and (2) how much to keep uncommitted as a reserve against the appearance of unanticipated demands. This decision is closely related to two other criteria for the evaluation of strategy: risk and timing. I shall now discuss these.

4. DOES THE STRATEGY INVOLVE AN ACCEPTABLE DEGREE OF RISK?

Strategy and resources, taken together, determine the degree of risk which the company is undertaking. This is a critical managerial choice. For example, when the old Underwood Corporation decided to enter the computer field, it was making what might have been an extremely astute strategic choice. However, the fact that it ran out of money before it could accomplish anything in that field turned its pursuit of opportunity into the prelude to disaster. This is not to say that the strategy was "bad."

However, the course of action pursued *was* a high-risk strategy. Had it been successful, the payoff would have been lush. The fact that it was a stupendous failure instead does not mean that it was senseless to take the gamble.

Each company must decide for itself how much risk it wants to live with. In attempting to assess the degree of risk associated with a particular strategy, management may use a variety of techniques. For example, mathematicians have developed an elegant set of techniques for choosing among a variety of strategies where you are willing to estimate the payoffs and the probabilities associated with them. However, our concern here is not with these quantitative aspects but with the identification of some qualitative factors which may serve as a rough basis for evaluating the degree of risk inherent in a strategy. These factors are:

1. The amount of resources (on which the strategy is based) whose continued existence or value is not assured.
2. The length of the time periods to which resources are committed.
3. The proportion of resources committed to a single venture.

The greater these quantities, the greater the degree of risk that is involved.

Uncertain Term of Existence.   Since a strategy is based on resources, any resource which may disappear before the payoff has been obtained may constitute a danger to the organization. Resources may disappear for various reasons. For example, they may lose their value. This frequently happens to such resources as physical facilities and product features. Again, they may be accidentally destroyed. The most vulnerable resource here is competence. The possible crash of the company plane or the blip on the president's electrocardiogram are what make many organizations essentially speculative ventures. In fact, one of the critical attributes of highly centralized organizations is that the more centralized they are, the more speculative they are. The disappearance of the top executive, or the disruption of communication with him, may wreak havoc at subordinate levels.

However, for many companies, the possibility that critical resources may lose their value stems not so much from internal developments as from shifts in the environment. Take specialized production know-how, for example. It has value only because of demand for the product by customers—and customers may change their minds. This is cause for acute concern among the increasing number of companies whose futures depend so heavily on their ability to participate in defense contracts. A familiar case is the plight of the airframe industry following World War II. Some of the companies succeeded in making the shift from aircraft to missiles, but this has only resulted in their being faced with the same problem on a larger scale.

Duration of Commitment. Financial analysts often look at the ratio of fixed assets to current assets in order to assess the extent to which resources are committed to long-term programs. This may or may not give a satisfactory answer. How important are the assets? When will they be paid for?

The reasons for the risk increasing as the time for payoff increases is, of course, the inherent uncertainty in any venture. Resources committed over long time spans make the company vulnerable to changes in the environment. Since the difficulty of predicting such changes increases as the time span increases, long-term projects are basically more risky than are short ones. This is especially true of companies whose environments are unstable. And today, either because of technological, political, or economic shifts, most companies are decidedly in the category of those that face major upheaval in their corporate environments. The company building its future around technological equipment, the company selling primarily to the government, the company investing in underdeveloped nations, the company selling to the Common Market, the company with a plant in the South—all these have this prospect in common.

The harsh dilemma of modern management is that the time span of decision is increasing at the same time as the corporate environment is becoming increasingly unstable. It is this dilemma which places such a premium on the manager's sensitivity to external trends today. Much has been written about his role as a commander and administrator. But it is no less important that he be a *strategist.*

Size of the Stakes. The more of its resources a company commits to a particular strategy, the more pronounced the consequences. If the strategy is successful, the payoff will be great—both to managers and investors. If the strategy fails, the consequences will be dire—both to managers and investors. Thus, a critical decision for the executive group is: What proportion of available resources should be committed to a particular course of action?

This decision may be handled in a variety of ways. For example, faced with a project that requires more of its resources than it is willing to commit, a company either may choose to refrain from undertaking the project or, alternatively, may seek to reduce the total resources required by undertaking a joint venture or by going the route of merger or acquisition in order to broaden the resource base.

The amount of resources management stands ready to commit is of particular significance where there is some likelihood that larger competitors, having greater resources, may choose to enter the company's field.

Thus, those companies which entered the small-computer field in the past few years are now faced with the penetration into this area of the data-processing giants. (Both IBM and Remington Rand have recently introduced new small computers.)

I do not mean to imply that the "best" strategy is the one with the least risk. High payoffs are frequently associated with high-risk strategies. Moreover, it is a frequent but dangerous assumption to think that inaction, or lack of change, is a low-risk strategy. Failure to exploit its resources to the fullest may well be the riskiest strategy of all that an organization may pursue, as Montgomery Ward and other companies have amply demonstrated.

5. DOES THE STRATEGY HAVE AN APPROPRIATE TIME HORIZON?

A significant part of every strategy is the time horizon on which it is based. A viable strategy not only reveals what goals are to be accomplished; it says something about *when* the aims are to be achieved.

Goals, like resources, have time-based utility. A new product developed, a plant put on steam, a degree of market penetration, become significant strategic objectives only if accomplished by a certain time. Delay may deprive them of all strategic significance. A perfect example of this in the military sphere is the Sinai campaign of 1956. The strategic objective of the Israelis was not only to conquer the entire Sinai peninsula; it also was to do it in seven days. By contrast, the lethargic movement of the British troops made the operation a futile one for both England and France.

In choosing an appropriate time horizon, we must pay careful attention to the goals being pursued, and to the particular organization involved. Goals must be established far enough in advance to allow the organization to adjust to them. Organizations, like ships, cannot be "spun on a dime." Consequently, the larger the organization, the further its strategic time horizon must extend, since its adjustment time is longer. It is no mere managerial whim that the major contributions to long-range planning have emerged from the larger organizations—especially those large organizations such as Lockheed, North American Aviation, and RCA that traditionally have had to deal with highly unstable environments.

The observation that large corporations plan far ahead while small ones can get away without doing so has frequently been made. However, the significance of planning for the small but growing company has frequently been overlooked. As a company gets bigger, it must not only change the way it operates; it must also steadily push ahead its time horizon—and this is a difficult thing to do. The manager who has built a successful enterprise by his skill at "putting out fires" or the wheeler-dealer whose firm has grown by a quick succession of financial coups is seldom able to make the transition to the long look ahead.

In many cases, even if the executive were inclined to take a longer range view of events, the formal reward system seriously militates against doing so. In most companies the system of management rewards is closely related to currently reported profits. Where this is the case, executives may understandably be so preoccupied with reporting a profit year by year that they fail to spend as much time as they should in managing the company's long-term future. But if we seriously accept the thesis that the essence of managerial responsibility is the extended time lapse between decision and result, currently reported profits are hardly a reasonable basis on which to compensate top executives. Such a basis simply serves to shorten the time horizon with which the executive is concerned.

The importance of an extended time horizon derives not only from the fact that an organization changes slowly and needs time to work through basic modifications in its strategy; it derives also from the fact that there is a considerable advantage in a certain consistency of strategy maintained over long periods of time. The great danger to companies which do not carefully formulate strategies well in advance is that they are prone to fling themselves toward chaos by drastic changes in policy—and in personnel—at frequent intervals. A parade of presidents is a clear indication of a board that has not really decided what its strategy should be. It is a common harbinger of serious corporate difficulty as well.

The time horizon is also important because of its impact on the selection of policies. The greater the time horizon, the greater the range in choice of tactics. If, for instance, the goals desired must be achieved in a relatively short time, steps like acquisition and merger may become virtually mandatory. An interesting illustration is the decision of National Cash Register to enter the market for electronic data-processing equipment. As reported in *Forbes:*

> "Once committed to EDP, NCR wasted no time. To buy talent and experience in 1953 it acquired Computer Research Corp. of Hawthorne, California. . . . For speed's sake, the manufacture of the 304's central units was turned over to GE. . . . NCR's research and development outlays also began curving steeply upwards."[11]

6. IS THE STRATEGY WORKABLE?

At first glance, it would seem that the simplest way to evaluate a corporate strategy is the completely pragmatic one of asking: Does it work? However, further reflection should reveal that if we try to answer

---

[11] "NCR and the Computer Sweepstakes," *Forbes,* October 15, 1962, p. 21.

that question, we are immediately faced with a quest for criteria. What is the evidence of a strategy "working"?

Quantitative indices of performance are a good start, but they really measure the influence of two critical factors combined: the strategy selected and the skill with which it is being executed. Faced with the failure to achieve anticipated results, both of these influences must be critically examined. One interesting illustration of this is a recent survey of the Chrysler Corporation after it suffered a period of serious loss:

> "In 1959, during one of the frequent reorganizations at Chrysler Corp., aimed at halting the company's slide, a management consultant concluded: 'The only thing wrong with Chrysler is people. The corporation needs some good top executives.' "[12]

By contrast, when Olivetti acquired the Underwood Corporation, it was able to reduce the cost of producing typewriters by one-third. And it did it without changing any of the top people in the production group. However, it did introduce a drastically revised set of policies.

If a strategy cannot be evaluated by results alone, there are some other indications that may be used to assess its contribution to corporate progress:

> The degree of consensus which exists among executives concerning corporate goals and policies.

> The extent to which major areas of managerial choice are identified in advance, while there is still time to explore a variety of alternatives.

> The extent to which resource requirements are discovered well before the last minute, necessitating neither crash programs of cost reduction nor the elimination of planned programs. The widespread popularity of the meat-axe approach to cost reduction is a clear indication of the frequent failure of corporate strategic planning.

Conclusion

The modern organization must deploy expensive and complex resources in the pursuit of transitory opportunities. The time required to develop resources is so extended, and the time-scale of opportunities is so brief and fleeting, that a company which has not carefully delineated and appraised its strategy is adrift in white water.

In short, while a set of goals and major policies that meets the criteria listed above does not guarantee success, it can be of considerable value in giving management both the time and the room to maneuver.

---

[12] "How Chrysler Hopes to Rebound," *Business Week,* October 6, 1962, p. 45.

C. ORGANIZATIONAL PLANNING AND POLICY

1. ORGANIZATION THEORY: AN OVERVIEW AND AN APPRAISAL*

William G. Scott

MAN IS INTENT ON DRAWING himself into a web of collectivized patterns. "Modern man has learned to accommodate himself to a world increasingly organized. The trend toward ever more explicit and consciously drawn relationships is profound and sweeping; it is marked by depth no less than by extension."[1] This comment by Seidenberg nicely summarizes the pervasive influence of organization in many forms of human activity.

Some of the reasons for intense organizational activity are found in the fundamental transitions which revolutionized our society, changing it from a rural culture, to a culture based on technology, industry, and the city. From these changes, a way of life emerged characterized by the *proximity* and *dependency* of people on each other. Proximity and dependency, as conditions of social life, harbor the threats of human conflict, capricious antisocial behavior, instability of human relationships, and uncertainty about the nature of the social structure with its concomitant roles.

Of course, these threats to social integrity are present to some degree in all societies, ranging from the primitive to the modern. But, these threats

---

* From the *Journal of the Academy of Management*, Vol. 4, No. 1, April, 1961, pp. 7–26. Reprinted with permission from the publisher.

[1] Roderick Seidenberg, *Post-Historic Man* (Boston: Beacon Press, 1951), p. 1.

become dangerous when the harmonious functioning of a society rests on the maintenance of a highly intricate, delicately balanced form of human collaboration. The civilization we have created depends on the preservation of a precarious balance. Hence, disrupting forces impinging on this shaky form of collaboration must be eliminated or minimized.

Traditionally, organization is viewed as a vehicle for accomplishing goals and objectives. While this approach is useful, it tends to obscure the inner workings and internal purposes of organization itself. Another fruitful way of treating organization is as a mechanism having the ultimate purpose of offsetting those forces which undermine human collaboration. In this sense, organization tends to minimize conflict, and to lessen the significance of individual behavior which deviates from values that the organization has established as worthwhile. Further, organization increases stability in human relationships by reducing uncertainty regarding the nature of the system's structure and the human roles which are inherent to it. Corollary to this point, organization enhances the predictability of human action, because it limits the number of behavioral alternatives available to an individual. As Presthus points out:

> Organization is defined as a system of structural interpersonal relations . . . individuals are differentiated in terms of authority, status, and role with the result that personal interaction is prescribed. . . . Anticipated reactions tend to occur, while ambiguity and spontaneity are decreased.[2]

In addition to all of this, organization has built-in safeguards. Besides prescribing acceptable forms of behavior for those who elect to submit to it, organization is also able to counterbalance the influence of human action which transcends its established patterns.[3]

Few segments of society have engaged in organizing more intensively than business.[4] The reason is clear. Business depends on what organization offers. Business needs a system of relationships among functions; it needs stability, continuity, and predictability in its internal activities and external contacts. Business also appears to need harmonious relationships

---

[2] Robert V. Presthus, "Toward a Theory of Organizational Behavior," *Administrative Science Quarterly*, June, 1958, p. 50.

[3] Regulation and predictability of human behavior are matters of degree varying with different organizations on something of a continuum. At one extreme are bureaucratic type organizations with tight bonds of regulation. At the other extreme are voluntary associations, and informal organizations with relatively loose bonds of regulation.
This point has an interesting sidelight. A bureaucracy with tight controls and a high degree of predictability of human action appears to be unable to distinguish between destructive and creative deviations from established values. Thus the only thing which is safeguarded is the *status quo*.

[4] The monolithic institutions of the military and government are other cases of organizational preoccupation.

among the people and processes which make it up. Put another way, a
business organization has to be free, relatively, from destructive tendencies
which may be caused by divergent interests.

As a foundation for meeting these needs rests administrative science.
A major element of this science is organization theory, which provides the
grounds for management activities in a number of significant areas of
business endeavor. Organization theory, however, is not a homogeneous
science based on generally accepted principles. Various theories of organization have been, and are being evolved. For example, something called
"modern organization theory" has recently emerged, raising the wrath of
some traditionalists, but also capturing the imagination of a rather elite
avant-garde.

The thesis of this paper is that modern organization theory, when
stripped of its irrelevancies, redundancies, and "speech defects," is a logical
and vital evolution in management thought. In order for this thesis to be
supported, the reader must endure a review and appraisal of more traditional forms of organization theory which may seem elementary to him.

In any event, three theories of organization are having considerable
influence on management thought and practice. They are arbitrarily
labeled in this paper as the classical, the neo-classical, and the modern.
Each of these is fairly distinct; but they are not unrelated. Also, these
theories are on-going, being actively supported by several schools of management thought.

The Classical Doctrine

For lack of a better method of identification, it will be said that the
classical doctrine deals almost exclusively with the *anatomy of formal
organization*. This doctrine can be traced back to Frederick W. Taylor's
interest in functional foremanship and planning staffs. But most students
of management thought would agree that in the United States, the first
systematic approach to organization, and the first comprehensive attempt
to find organizational universals, is dated 1931 when Mooney and Reiley
published *Onward Industry*.[5] Subsequently, numerous books, following
the classical vein, have appeared. Two of the more recent are Brech's,
Organization[6] and Allen's, *Management and Organization*.[7]

Classical organization theory is built around four key pillars. They are

---

[5] James D. Mooney and Alan C. Reiley, *Onward Industry* (New York: Harper
and Brothers, 1931). Later published by James D. Mooney under the title *Principles
of Organization*.

[6] E. F. L. Brech, *Organization* (London: Longmans, Green and Company, 1957).

[7] Louis A. Allen, *Management and Organization* (New York: McGraw-Hill Book
Company, 1958).

the division of labor, the scalar and functional processes, structure, and span of control. Given these major elements just about all of classical organization theory can be derived.

1. *The division of labor* is without doubt the cornerstone among the four elements.[8] From it the other elements flow as corollaries. For example, *scalar* and *functional* growth requires specialization and departmentalization of functions. Organization *structure* is naturally dependent upon the direction which specialization of activities travels in company development. Finally, *span of control* problems result from the number of specialized functions under the jurisdiction of a manager.

2. *The scalar and functional processes* deal with the vertical and horizontal growth of the organization, respectively.[9] The scalar process refers to the growth of the chain of command, the delegation of authority and responsibility, unity of command, and the obligation to report.

   The division of the organization into specialized parts and the regrouping of the parts into compatible units are matters pertaining to the functional process. This process focuses on the horizontal evolution of the line and staff in a formal organization.

3. *Structure* is the logical relationships of functions in an organization, arranged to accomplish the objectives of the company efficiently. Structure implies system and pattern. Classical organization theory usually works with two basic structures, the line and the staff. However, such activities as committee and liaison functions fall quite readily into the purview of structural considerations. Again, structure is the vehicle for introducing logical and consistent relationships among the diverse functions which comprise the organization.[10]

4. *The span of control* concept relates to the number of subordinates a manager can effectively supervise. Graicunas has been credited with first elaborating the point that there are numerical limitations to the subordinates one man can control.[11] In a recent statement on the subject, Brech points out, "span" refers to ". . . the number of persons, themselves carrying managerial and supervisory responsibilities, for whom the senior manager retains his over-embracing

---

[8] Usually the division of labor is treated under a topical heading of departmentation, see for example: Harold Koontz and Cyril O'Donnell, *Principles of Management* (New York: McGraw-Hill Book Company, 1959), Chapter 7.

[9] These processes are discussed at length in Ralph Currier Davis, *The Fundamentals of Top Management* (New York: Harper and Brothers, 1951), Chapter 7.

[10] For a discussion of structure see: William H. Newman, *Administrative Action* (Englewood Cliffs: Prentice-Hall, Incorporated, 1951), Chapter 16.

[11] V. A. Graicunas, "Relationships in Organization," *Papers on the Science of Administration* (New York: Columbia University, 1937).

responsibility of direction and planning, co-ordination, motivation, and control."[12] Regardless of interpretation, span of control has significance, in part, for the shape of the organization which evolves through growth. Wide span yields a flat structure; short span results in a tall structure. Further, the span concept directs attention to the complexity of human and functional interrelationships in an organization.

It would not be fair to say that the classical school is unaware of the day-to-day administrative problems of the organization. Paramount among these problems are those stemming from human interactions. But the interplay of individual personality, informal groups, intraorganizational conflict, and the decision-making processes in the formal structure appears largely to be neglected by classical organization theory. Additionally, the classical theory overlooks the contributions of the behavioral sciences by failing to incorporate them in its doctrine in any systematic way. In summary, classical organization theory has relevant insights into the nature of organization, but the value of this theory is limited by its narrow concentration on the formal anatomy of organization.

Neoclassical Theory of Organization

The neoclassical theory of organization embarked on the task of compensating for some of the deficiencies in classical doctrine. The neoclassical school is commonly identified with the human relations movement. Generally, the neoclassical approach takes the postulates of the classical school, regarding the pillars of organization as given. But these postulates are regarded as modified by people, acting independently or within the context of the informal organization.

One of the main contributions of the neoclassical school is the introduction of behavioral sciences in an integrated fashion into the theory of organization. Through the use of these sciences, the human relationists demonstrate how the pillars of the classical doctrine are affected by the impact of human actions. Further, the neoclassical approach includes a systematic treatment of the informal organization, showing its influence on the formal structure.

Thus, the neoclassical approach to organization theory gives evidence of accepting classical doctrine, but superimposing on it modifications resulting from individual behavior, and the influence of the informal group. The inspiration of the neoclassical school were the Hawthorne studies.[13]

---

[12] Brech, *op. cit.*, p. 78.
[13] See: F. J. Roethlisberger and William J. Dickson, *Management and the Worker* (Cambridge: Harvard University Press, 1939).

Current examples of the neoclassical approach are found in human relations books like Gardner and Moore, *Human Relations in Industry*,[14] and Davis, *Human Relations in Business*.[15] To a more limited extent, work in industrial sociology also reflects a neoclassical point of view.[16]

It would be useful to look briefly at some of the contributions made to organization theory by the neoclassicists. First to be considered are modifications of the pillars of classical doctrine; second is the informal organization.

EXAMPLES OF THE NEOCLASSICAL APPROACH TO THE PILLARS OF FORMAL ORGANIZATION THEORY

1. The *division of labor* has been a long standing subject of comment in the field of human relations. Very early in the history of industrial psychology study was made of industrial fatigue and monotony caused by the specialization of the work.[17] Later, attention shifted to the isolation of the worker, and his feeling of anonymity resulting from insignificant jobs which contributed negligibly to the final product.[18]

   Also, specialization influences the work of management. As an organization expands, the need concomitantly arises for managerial motivation and coordination of the activities of others. Both motivation and coordination in turn relate to executive leadership. Thus, in part, stemming from the growth of industrial specialization, the neoclassical school has developed a large body of theory relating to motivation, coordination, and leadership. Much of this theory is derived from the social sciences.

2. Two aspects of the *scalar and functional* processes which have been treated with some degree of intensity by the neoclassical school are the delegation of authority and responsibility, and gaps in or overlapping of functional jurisdictions. The classical theory assumes something of perfection in the delegation and functionalization processes. The neoclassical school points out that human problems are caused by imperfections in the way these processes are handled.

   For example, too much or insufficient delegation may render an executive incapable of action. The failure to delegate authority

---

[14] Burleigh B. Gardner and David G. Moore, *Human Relations in Industry* (Homewood: Richard D. Irwin, 1955).

[15] Keith Davis, *Human Relations in Business* (New York: McGraw-Hill Book Company, 1957).

[16] For example see: Delbert C. Miller and William H. Form, *Industrial Sociology* (New York: Harper and Brothers, 1951).

[17] See: Hugo Munsterberg, *Psychology and Industrial Efficiency* (Boston: Houghton Mifflin Company, 1913).

[18] Probably the classic work is: Elton Mayo, *The Human Problems of an Industrial Civilization* (Cambridge: Harvard University, 1946, first printed 1933).

and responsibility equally may result in frustration for the delegatee. Overlapping of authorities often causes clashes in personality. Gaps in authority cause failures in getting jobs done, with one party blaming the other for shortcomings in performance.[19]

The neoclassical school says that the scalar and functional processes are theoretically valid, but tend to deteriorate in practice. The ways in which they break down are described, and some of the human causes are pointed out. In addition the neoclassicists make recommendations, suggesting various "human tools" which will facilitate the operation of these processes.

3. *Structure* provides endless avenues of analysis for the neoclassical theory of organization. The theme is that human behavior disrupts the best laid organizational plans, and thwarts the cleanness of the logical relationships founded in the structure. The neoclassical critique of structure centers on frictions which appear internally among people performing different functions.

Line and staff relations is a problem area, much discussed, in this respect. Many companies seem to have difficulty keeping the line and staff working together harmoniously. Both Dalton[20] and Juran[21] have engaged in research to discover the causes of friction, and to suggest remedies.

Of course, line-staff relations represent only one of the many problems of structural frictions described by the neoclassicists. As often as not, the neoclassicists will offer prescriptions for the elimination of conflict in structure. Among the more important harmony-rendering formulae are participation, junior boards, bottom-up management, joint committees, recognition of human dignity, and "better" communication.

4. An executive's *span of control* is a function of human determinants, and the reduction of span to a precise, universally applicable ratio is silly, according to the neoclassicists. Some of the determinants of span are individual differences in managerial abilities, the type of people and functions supervised, and the extent of communication effectiveness.

Coupled with the span of control question are the human implications of the type of structure which emerges. That is, is a tall structure with a short span or a flat structure with a wide span more conducive to good human relations and high morale? The answer is situational. Short span results in tight supervision; wide span requires a good deal of delegation with looser controls. Be-

---

[19] For further discussion of the human relations implications of the scalar and functional processes see: Keith Davis, *op. cit.*, pp. 60–66.

[20] Melville Dalton, "Conflicts between Staff and Line Managerial Officers," *American Sociological Review*, June, 1950, pp. 342–351.

[21] J. M. Juran, "Improving the Relationship between Staff and Line," *Personnel*, May, 1956, pp. 515–524.

cause of individual and organizational differences, sometimes one is better than the other. There is a tendency to favor the looser form of organization, however, for the reason that tall structures breed autocratic leadership, which is often pointed out as a cause of low morale.[22]

THE NEOCLASSICAL VIEW OF THE INFORMAL ORGANIZATION

Nothing more than the barest mention of the informal organization is given even in the most recent classical treatises on organization theory.[23] Systematic discussion of this form of organization has been left to the neoclassicists. The informal organization refers to people in group associations at work, but these associations are not specified in the "blueprint" of the formal organization. The informal organization means natural groupings of people in the work situation.

In a general way, the informal organization appears in response to the social need—the need of people to associate with others. However, for analytical purposes, this explanation is not particularly satisfying. Research has produced the following, more specific determinants underlying the appearance of informal organizations.

1. The *location* determinant simply states that in order to form into groups of any lasting nature, people have to have frequent face-to-face contact. Thus, the geography of physical location in a plant or office is an important factor in predicting who will be in what group.[24]

2. *Occupation* is key factor determining the rise and composition of informal groups. There is a tendency for people performing similar jobs to group together.[25]

3. *Interests* are another determinant for informal group formation. Even though people might be in the same location, performing similar jobs, differences of interests among them explain why several small, instead of one large, informal organizations emerge.

4. *Special issues* often result in the formation of informal groups, but this determinant is set apart from the three previously mentioned. In this case, people who do not necessarily have similar interests, occupations, or locations may join together for a common cause. Once the issue is resolved, then the tendency is to revert to the

---

[22] Gardner and Moore, *op. cit.*, pp. 237–243.

[23] For example: Brech, *op. cit.*, pp. 27–29; and Allen, *op. cit.*, pp. 61–62.

[24] See: Leon Festinger, Stanley Schachter, and Kurt Back, *Social Pressures in Informal Groups* (New York: Harper and Brothers, 1950), pp. 153–163.

[25] For example see: W. Fred Cottrell, *The Railroader* (Palo Alto: The Stanford University Press, 1940), Chapter 3.

more "natural" group forms.[26] Thus, special issues give rise to a rather impermanent informal association; groups based on the other three determinants tend to be more lasting.

When informal organizations come into being they assume certain characteristics. Since understanding these characteristics is important for management practice, they are noted below:

1. Informal organizations act as agencies of *social control*. They generate a culture based on certain norms of conduct which, in turn, demands conformity from group members. These standards may be at odds with the values set by the formal organization. So an individual may very well find himself in a situation of conflicting demands.

2. The form of human interrelationships in the informal organization requires *techniques of analysis* different from those used to plot the relationships of people in a formal organization. The method used for determining the structure of the informal group is called sociometric analysis. Sociometry reveals the complex structure of interpersonal relations which is based on premises fundamentally unlike the logic of the formal organization.

3. Informal organizations have *status and communication* systems peculiar to themselves, not necessarily derived from the formal systems. For example, the grapevine is the subject of much neoclassical study.

4. Survival of the informal organization requires stable continuing relationships among the people in them. Thus, it has been observed that the informal organization *resists change*.[27] Considerable attention is given by the neoclassicists to overcoming informal resistance to change.

5. The last aspect of analysis which appears to be central to the neoclassical view of the informal organization is the study of the *informal leader*. Discussion revolves around who the informal leader is, how he assumes this role, what characteristics are peculiar to him, and how he can help the manager accomplish his objectives in the formal organization.[28]

---

[26] Except in cases where the existence of an organization is necessary for the continued maintenance of employee interest. Under these conditions the previously informal association may emerge as a formal group, such as a union.

[27] Probably the classic study of resistance to change is: Lester Coch and John R. P. French, Jr., "Overcoming Resistance to Change," in Schuyler Dean Hoslett (editor), *Human Factors in Management* (New York: Harper and Brothers, 1951), pp. 242–268.

[28] For example see: Robert Saltonstall, *Human Relations in Administration* (New York: McGraw-Hill Book Company, 1959), pp. 330–331; and Keith Davis, *op. cit.*, pp. 99–101.

This brief sketch of some of the major facets of informal organization theory has neglected, so far, one important topic treated by the neoclassical school. It is the way in which the formal and informal organizations interact.

A conventional way of looking at the interaction of the two is the "live and let live" point of view. Management should recognize that the informal organization exists, nothing can destroy it, and so the executive might just as well work with it. Working with the informal organization involves not threatening its existence unnecessarily, listening to opinions expressed for the group by the leader, allowing group participation in decision-making situations, and controlling the grapevine by prompt release of accurate information.[29]

While this approach is management centered, it is not unreasonable to expect that informal group standards and norms could make themselves felt on formal organizational policy. An honestly conceived effort by managers to establish a working relationship with the informal organization could result in an association where both formal and informal views would be reciprocally modified. The danger which at all costs should be avoided is that "working with the informal organization" does not degenerate into a shallow disguise for human manipulation.

Some neoclassical writing in organization theory, especially that coming from the management-oriented segment of this school, gives the impression that the formal and informal organizations are distinct, and at times, quite irreconcilable factors in a company. The interaction which takes place between the two is something akin to the interaction between the company and a labor union, or a government agency, or another company.

The concept of the social system is another approach to the interactional climate. While this concept can be properly classified as neoclassical, it borders on the modern theories of organization. The phrase "social system" means that an organization is a complex of mutually interdependent, but variable, factors.

These factors include individuals and their attitudes and motives, jobs, the physical work setting, the formal organization, and the informal organizations. These factors, and many others, are woven into an overall pattern of interdependency. From this point of view, the formal and informal organizations lose their distinctiveness, but find real meaning, in terms of human behavior, in the operation of the system as a whole. Thus, the study of organization turns away from descriptions of its component parts, and is refocused on the system of interrelationships among the parts.

One of the major contributions of the Hawthorne studies was the

---

[29] For an example of this approach see: John T. Doutt, "Management Must Manage the Informal Group, Too," *Advanced Management*, May, 1959, pp. 26–28.

integration of Pareto's idea of the social system into a meaningful method of analysis for the study of behavior in human organizations.[30] This concept is still vitally important. But unfortunately some work in the field of human relations undertaken by the neoclassicists has overlooked, or perhaps discounted, the significance of this consideration.[31]

The fundamental insight regarding the social system, developed and applied to the industrial scene by the Hawthorne researchers, did not find much extension in subsequent work in the neoclassical vein. Indeed, the neoclassical school after the Hawthorne studies generally seemed content to engage in descriptive generalizations, or particularized empirical research studies which did not have much meaning outside their own context.

The neoclassical school of organization theory has been called bankrupt. Criticisms range from, "human relations is a tool for cynical puppeteering of people," to "human relations is nothing more than a trifling body of empirical and descriptive information." There is a good deal of truth in both criticisms, but another appraisal of the neoclassical school of organization theory is offered here. The neoclassical approach has provided valuable contributions to lore of organization. But, like the classical theory, the neoclassical doctrine suffers from incompleteness, a shortsighted perspective, and lack of integration among the many facets of human behavior studied by it. Modern organization theory has made a move to cover the shortcomings of the current body of theoretical knowledge.

Modern Organization Theory

The distinctive qualities of modern organization theory are its conceptual-analytical base, its reliance on empirical research data and, above all, its integrating nature. These qualities are framed in a philosophy which accepts the premise that the only meaningful way to study organization is to study it as a system. As Henderson put it, the study of a system must rely on a method of analysis, ". . . involving the simultaneous variations of mutually dependent variables."[32] Human systems, of course, contain a huge number of dependent variables which defy the most complex simultaneous equations to solve.

Nevertheless, system analysis has its own peculiar point of view which

---

[30] See: Roethlisberger and Dickson, op. cit., Chapter 24.

[31] A check of management human relations texts, the organization and human relations chapters of principles of management texts, and texts on conventional organization theory for management courses reveals little or no treatment of the concept of the social system.

[32] Lawrence J. Henderson, Pareto's General Sociology (Cambridge: Harvard University Press, 1935), p. 13.

aims to study organization in the way Henderson suggests. It treats organization as a system of mutually dependent variables. As a result, modern organization theory, which accepts system analysis, shifts the conceptual level of organization study above the classical and neoclassical theories. Modern organization theory asks a range of interrelated questions which are not seriously considered by the two other theories.

Key among these questions are: (1) What are the strategic parts of the system? (2) What is the nature of their mutual dependency? (3) What are the main processes in the system which link the parts together, and facilitate their adjustment to each other? (4) What are the goals sought by systems?[33]

Modern organization theory is in no way a unified body of thought. Each writer and researcher has his special emphasis when he considers the system. Perhaps the most evident unifying thread in the study of systems is the effort to look at the organization in its totality. Representative books in this field are March and Simon, *Organizations*,[34] and Haire's anthology, *Modern Organization Theory*.[35]

Instead of attempting a review of different writers' contributions to modern organization theory, it will be more useful to discuss the various ingredients involved in system analysis. They are the parts, the interactions, the processes, and the goals of systems.

THE PARTS OF THE SYSTEM AND THEIR INTERDEPENDENCY

The first basic part of the system is the *individual*, and the personality structure he brings to the organization. Elementary to an individual's personality are motives and attitudes which condition the range of expectancies he hopes to satisfy by participating in the system.

The second part of the system is the formal arrangement of functions, usually called the *formal organization*. The formal organization is the interrelated pattern of jobs which make up the structure of a system. Certain writers, like Argyris, see a fundamental conflict resulting from the demands made by the system, and the structure of the mature, normal personality. In any event, the individual has expectancies regarding the job he is to perform; and, conversely, the job makes demands on, or has expectancies relating to, the performance of the individual. Considerable attention has been given by writers in modern organization theory to

---

[33] There is another question which cannot be treated in the scope of this paper. It asks, what research tools should be used for the study of the system?

[34] James G. March and Herbert A. Simon, *Organizations* (New York: John Wiley and Sons, 1958).

[35] Mason Haire (editor), *Modern Organization Theory* (New York: John Wiley and Sons, 1959).

incongruencies resulting from the interaction of organizational and individual demands.[36]

The third part in the organization system is the *informal organization*. Enough has been said already about the nature of this organization. But it must be noted that an interactional pattern exists between the individual and the informal group. This interactional arrangement can be conveniently discussed as the mutual modification of expectancies. The informal organization has demands which it makes on members in terms of anticipated forms of behavior, and the individual has expectancies of satisfaction he hopes to derive from association with people on the job. Both these sets of expectancies interact, resulting in the individual modifying his behavior to accord with the demands of the group, and the group, perhaps, modifying what it expects from an individual because of the impact of his personality on group norms.[37]

Much of what has been said about the various expectancy systems in an organization can also be treated using status and role concepts. Part of modern organization theory rests on research findings in social-psychology relative to reciprocal patterns of behavior stemming from role demands generated by both the formal and informal organizations, and role perceptions peculiar to the individual. Bakke's *fusion process* is largely concerned with the modification of role expectancies. The fusion process is a force, according to Bakke, which acts to weld divergent elements together for the preservation of organizational integrity.[38]

The fifth part of system analysis is the *physical setting* in which the job is performed. Although this element of the system may be implicit in what has been said already about the formal organization and its functions, it is well to separate it. In the physical surroundings of work, interactions are present in complex man-machine systems. The human "engineer" cannot approach the problems posed by such interrelationships in a purely technical, engineering fashion. As Haire says, these problems lie in the domain of the social theorist.[39] Attention must be centered on responses demanded from a logically ordered production function, often with the view of minimizing the error in the system. From this standpoint, work cannot be effectively organized unless the psychological, social, and

---

[36] See Chris Argyris, *Personality and Organization* (New York: Harper and Brothers, 1957), esp. Chapters 2, 3, 7.

[37] For a larger treatment of this subject see: George C. Homans, *The Human Group* (New York: Harcourt, Brace and Company, 1950), Chapter 5.

[38] E. Wight Bakke, "Concept of the Social Organization," in *Modern Organization Theory*, Mason Haire (editor) (New York: John Wiley and Sons, 1959), pp. 60–61.

[39] Mason Haire, "Psychology and the Study of Business: Joint Behavioral Sciences," in *Social Science Research on Business: Product and Potential* (New York: Columbia University Press, 1959), pp. 53–59.

physiological characteristics of people participating in the work environment are considered. Machines and processes should be designed to fit
certain generally observed psychological and physiological properties of
men, rather than hiring men to fit machines.

In summary, the parts of the system which appear to be of strategic
importance are the individual, the formal structure, the informal organization, status and role patterns, and the physical environment of work.
Again, these parts are woven into a configuration called the organizational
system. The processes which link the parts are taken up next.

THE LINKING PROCESSES

One can say, with a good deal of glibness, that all the parts mentioned
above are interrelated. Although this observation is quite correct, it does
not mean too much in terms of system theory unless some attempt is made
to analyze the processes by which the interaction is achieved. Role theory
is devoted to certain types of interactional processes. In addition, modern
organization theorists point to three other linking activities which appear
to be universal to human systems of organized behavior. These processes
are communication, balance, and decision making.

(1) Communication is mentioned often in neoclassical theory, but
the emphasis is on description of forms of communication activity, i.e.,
formal-informal, vertical-horizontal, line-staff. Communication, as a mechanism which links the segments of the system together, is overlooked by
way of much considered analysis.

One aspect of modern organization theory is study of the communication network in the system. Communication is viewed as the method by
which action is evoked from the parts of the system. Communication acts
not only as stimuli resulting in action, but also as a control and coordination mechanism linking the decision centers in the system into a synchro-
nized pattern. Deutsch points out that organizations are composed of parts
which communicate with each other, receive messages from the outside
world, and store information. Taken together, these communication functions of the parts comprise a configuration representing the total system.[40]
More is to be said about communication later in the discussion of the
cybernetic model.

(2) The concept of *balance* as a linking process involves a series of
some rather complex ideas. Balance refers to an equilibrating mechanism
whereby the various parts of the system are maintained in a harmoniously
structured relationship to each other.

The necessity for the balance concept logically flows from the nature

---

[40] Karl W. Deutsch, "On Communication Models in the Social Sciences," *Public
Opinion Quarterly*, 16 (1952), pp. 356–380.

of systems themselves. It is impossible to conceive of an ordered relationship among the parts of a system without also introducing the idea of a stabilizing or an adapting mechanism.

Balance appears in two varieties—quasi-automatic and innovative. Both forms of balance act to insure system integrity in face of changing conditions, either internal or external to the system. The first form of balance, quasi-automatic, refers to what some think are "homeostatic" properties of systems. That is, systems seem to exhibit built-in propensities to maintain steady states.

If human organizations are open, self-maintaining systems, then control and regulatory processes are necessary. The issue hinges on the degree to which stabilizing processes in systems, when adapting to change, are automatic. March and Simon have an interesting answer to this problem, which in part is based on the type of change and the adjustment necessary to adapt to the change. Systems have programs of action which are put into effect when a change is perceived. If the change is relatively minor, and if the change comes within the purview of established programs of action, then it might be fairly confidently predicted that the adaptation made by the system will be quasi-automatic.[41]

The role of innovative, creative balancing efforts now needs to be examined. The need for innovation arises when adaptation to a change is outside the scope of existing programs designed for the purpose of keeping the system in balance. New programs have to be evolved in order for the system to maintain internal harmony.

New programs are created by trial and error search for feasible action alternatives to cope with a given change. But innovation is subject to the limitations and possibilities inherent in the quantity and variety of information present in a system at a particular time. New combinations of alternatives for innovative purposes depend on:

a.   the possible range of output of the system, or the capacity of the system to supply information.
b.   the range of available information in the memory of the system.
c.   the operating rules (program) governing the analysis and flow of information within the system.
d.   the ability of the system to "forget" previously learned solutions to change problems.[42] A system with too good a memory might narrow its behavioral choices to such an extent as to stifle innovation. In simpler language, old learned programs might be used to adapt to change, when newly innovated programs are necessary.[43]

---

[41] March and Simon, *op. cit.*, pp. 139–140.

[42] Mervyn L. Cadwallader, "The Cybernetic Analysis of Change in Complex Social Organization," *The American Journal of Sociology*, September, 1959, p. 156.

[43] It is conceivable for innovative behavior to be programmed into the system.

Much of what has been said about communication and balance brings to mind a cybernetic model in which both these processes have vital roles. Cybernetics has to do with feedback and control in all kinds of systems. Its purpose is to maintain system stability in the face of change. Cybernetics cannot be studied without considering communication networks, information flow, and some kind of balancing process aimed at preserving the integrity of the system.

Cybernetics directs attention to key questions regarding the system. These questions are: How are communication centers connected, and how are they maintained? Corollary to this question: what is the structure of the feedback system? Next, what information is stored in the organization, and at what points? And as a corollary: how accessible is this information to decision-making centers? Third, how conscious is the organization of the operation of its own parts? That is, to what extent do the policy centers receive control information with sufficient frequency and relevancy to create a real awareness of the operation of the segments of the system? Finally, what are the learning (innovating) capabilities of the system?[44]

Answers to the questions posed by cybernetics are crucial to understanding both the balancing and communication processes in systems.[45] Although cybernetics has been applied largely to technical engineering problems of automation, the model of feedback, control, and regulation in all systems has a good deal of generality. Cybernetics is a fruitful area which can be used to synthesize the processes of communication and balance.

(3) A wide spectrum of topics dealing with types of decisions in human systems makes up the core of analysis of another important process in organizations. Decision analysis is one of the major contributions of March and Simon in their book *Organizations*. The two major classes of decisions they discuss are decisions to produce and decisions to participate in the system.[46]

Decisions to produce are largely a result of an interaction between individual attitudes and the demands of organization. Motivation analysis becomes central to studying the nature and results of the interaction. Individual decisions to participate in the organization reflect on such issues as the relationship between organizational rewards versus the demands made by the organization. Participation decisions also focus attention on the reasons why individuals remain in or leave organizations.

March and Simon treat decisions as internal variables in an organiza-

---

[44] These are questions adapted from Deutsch, *op. cit.*, 368–370.

[45] Answers to these questions would require a comprehensive volume. One of the best approaches currently available is Stafford Beer, *Cybernetics and Management* (New York: John Wiley and Sons, 1959).

[46] March and Simon, *op. cit.*, Chapters 3 and 4.

tion which depend on jobs, individual expectations and motivations, and organizational structure. Marschak[47] looks on the decision process as an independent variable upon which the survival of the organization is based. In this case, the organization is viewed as having, inherent to its structure, the ability to maximize survival requisites through its established decision processes.

THE GOALS OF ORGANIZATION

Organization has three goals which may be either intermeshed or independent ends in themselves. They are growth, stability, and interaction. The last goal refers to organizations which exist primarily to provide a medium for association of its members with others. Interestingly enough these goals seem to apply to different forms of organization at varying levels of complexity, ranging from simple clockwork mechanisms to social systems.

These similarities in organizational purposes have been observed by a number of people, and a field of thought and research called general system theory has developed, dedicated to the task of discovering organizational universals. The dream of general system theory is to create a science of organizational universals, or if you will, a universal science using common organizational elements found in all systems as a starting point.

Modern organization theory is on the periphery of general system theory. Both general system theory and modern organization theory studies:

1. the parts (individuals) in aggregates, and the movement of individuals into and out of the system.
2. the interaction of individuals with the environment found in the system.
3. the interactions among individuals in the system.
4. general growth and stability problems of systems.[48]

Modern organization theory and general system theory are similar in that they look at organization as an integrated whole. They differ, however, in terms of their generality. General system theory is concerned with every level of system, whereas modern organizational theory focuses primarily on human organization.

The question might be asked, what can the science of administration gain by the study of system levels other than human? Before attempting

---

[47] Jacob Marschak, "Efficient and Viable Organizational Forms" in *Modern Organization Theory*, Mason Haire, editor (New York: John Wiley and Sons, 1959), pp. 307–320.

[48] Kenneth E. Boulding, "General System Theory—The Skeleton of a Science," *Management Science*, April, 1956, pp. 200–202.

an answer, note should be made of what these other levels are. Boulding presents a convenient method of classification:

1. The static structure—a level of framework, the anatomy of a system; for example, the structure of the universe.
2. The simple dynamic system—the level of clockworks, predetermined necessary motions.
3. The cybernetic system—the level of the thermostat, the system moves to maintain a given equilibrium through a process of self-regulation.
4. The open system—level of self-maintaining systems, moves toward and includes living organisms.
5. The genetic-societal system—level of cell society, characterized by a division of labor among cells.
6. Animal systems—level of mobility, evidence of goal-directed behavior.
7. Human systems—level of symbol interpretation and idea communication.
8. Social system—level of human organization.
9. Transcendental systems—level of ultimates and absolutes which exhibit systematic structure but are unknowable in essence.[49]

This approach to the study of systems by finding universals common at all levels of organization offers intriguing possibilities for administrative organization theory. A good deal of light could be thrown on social systems if structurally analogous elements could be found in the simpler types of systems. For example, cybernetic systems have characteristics which seem to be similar to feedback, regulation, and control phenomena in human organizations. Thus, certain facets of cybernetic models could be generalized to human organization. Considerable danger, however, lies in poorly founded analogies. Superficial similarities between simpler system forms and social systems are apparent everywhere. Instinctually based ant societies, for example, do not yield particularly instructive lessons for understanding rationally conceived human organizations. Thus, care should be taken that analogies used to bridge system levels are not mere devices for literary enrichment. For analogies to have usefulness and validity, they must exhibit inherent structural similarities or implicitly identical operational principles.[50]

---

[49] *Ibid.*, pp. 202–205.

[50] Seidenberg, *op. cit.*, p. 136. The fruitful use of the type of analogies spoken of by Seidenberg is evident in the application of thermodynamic principles, particularly the entropy concept, to communication theory. See: Claude E. Shannon and Warren Weaver, *The Mathematical Theory of Communication* (Urbana: The University of Illinois Press, 1949). Further, the existence of a complete analogy between the operational behavior of thermodynamic systems, electrical communication systems,

Modern organization theory leads, as it has been shown, almost inevitably into a discussion of general system theory. A science of organization universals has some strong advocates, particularly among biologists.[51] Organization theorists in administrative science cannot afford to overlook the contributions of general system theory. Indeed, modern organization concepts could offer a great deal to those working with general system theory. But the ideas dealt with in the general theory are exceedingly elusive.

Speaking of the concept of equilibrium as a unifying element in all systems, Easton says, "It (equilibrium) leaves the impression that we have a useful general theory when in fact, lacking measurability, it is a mere pretence for knowledge."[52] The inability to quantify and measure universal organization elements undermines the success of pragmatic tests to which general system theory might be put.

ORGANIZATION THEORY: QUO VADIS?

Most sciences have a vision of the universe to which they are applied, and administrative science is not an exception. This universe is composed of parts. One purpose of science is to synthesize the parts into an organized conception of its field of study. As a science matures, its theorems about the configuration of its universe change. The direction of change in three sciences, physics, economics, and sociology, are noted briefly for comparison with the development of an administrative view of human organization.

The first comprehensive and empirically verifiable outlook of the physical universe was presented by Newton in his *Principia*. Classical physics, founded on Newton's work, constitutes a grand scheme in which a wide range of physical phenomena could be organized and predicted. Newtonian physics may rightfully be regarded as "macro" in nature, because its system of organization was concerned largely with gross events of which the movement of celestial bodies, waves, energy forms, and strain are examples. For years classical physics was supreme, being applied continuously to smaller and smaller classes of phenomena in the physical universe. Physicists at one time adopted the view that everything in their realm could be discovered by simply subdividing problems. Physics thus moved into the "micro" order.

---

and biological systems has been noted by: Y. S. Touloukian, *The Concept of Entropy in Communication, Living Organisms, and Thermodynamics,* Research Bulletin 130, Purdue Engineering Experiment Station.

[51] For example see: Ludwig von Bertalonffy, *Problem of Life* (London: Watts and Company, 1952).

[52] David Easton, "Limits of the Equilibrium Model in Social Research," in *Profits and Problems of Homeostatic Models in the Behavioral Sciences,* Publication 1, Chicago Behavioral Sciences, 1953, p. 39.

But in the nineteenth century a revolution took place motivated largely because events were being noted which could not be explained adequately by the conceptual framework supplied by the classical school. The consequences of this revolution are brilliantly described by Eddington:

> From the point of view of philosophy of science the conception associated with entropy must I think be ranked as the great contribution of the nineteenth century to scientific thought. It marked a reaction from the view that everything to which science need pay attention is discovered by microscopic dissection of objects. It provided an alternative standpoint in which the centre of interest is shifted from the entities reached by the customary analysis (atoms, electric potentials, etc.) to qualities possessed by the system as a whole, which cannot be split up and located—a little bit here, and a little bit there. . . .
>
> We often think that when we have completed our study of *one* we know all about *two*, because "two" is "one and one." We forget that we have still to make a study of "and." Secondary physics is the study of "and"—that is to say, of organization.[53]

Although modern physics often deals in minute quantities and oscillations, the conception of the physicist is on the "macro" scale. He is concerned with the "and," or the organization of the world in which the events occur. These developments did not invalidate classical physics as to its usefulness for explaining a certain range of phenomena. But classical physics is no longer the undisputed law of the universe. It is a special case.

Early economic theory, and Adam Smith's *Wealth of Nations* comes to mind, examined economic problems in the macro order. The *Wealth of Nations* is mainly concerned with matters of national income and welfare. Later, the economics of the firm, micro-economics, dominated the theoretical scene in this science. And, finally, with Keynes' *The General Theory of Employment Interest and Money*, a systematic approach to the economic universe was re-introduced on the macro level.

The first era of the developing science of sociology was occupied by the great social "system builders." Comte, the so-called father of sociology, had a macro view of society in that his chief works are devoted to social reorganization. Comte was concerned with the interrelationships among social, political, religious, and educational institutions. As sociology progressed, the science of society compressed. Emphasis shifted from the macro approach of the pioneers to detailed, empirical study of small social units. The compression of sociological analysis was accompanied by study of social pathology or disorganization.

In general, physics, economics, and sociology appear to have two things in common. First, they offered a macro point of view as their

---

[53] Sir Arthur Eddington, *The Nature of the Physical World* (Ann Arbor: The University of Michigan Press, 1958), pp. 103–104.

initial systematic comprehension of their area of study. Second, as the science developed, attention fragmented into analysis of the parts of the organization, rather than attending to the system as a whole. This is the micro phase.

In physics and economics, discontent was evidenced by some scientists at the continual atomization of the universe. The reaction to the micro approach was a new theory or theories dealing with the total system, on the macro level again. This third phase of scientific development seems to be more evident in physics and economics than in sociology.

The reason for the "macro-micro-macro" order of scientific progress lies, perhaps, in the hypothesis that usually the things which strike man first are of great magnitude. The scientist attempts to discover order in the vastness. But after macro laws or models of systems are postulated, variations appear which demand analysis, not so much in terms of the entire system, but more in terms of the specific parts which make it up. Then, intense study of microcosm may result in new general laws, replacing the old models of organization. Or, the old and the new models may stand together, each explaining a different class of phenomenon. Or, the old and the new concepts of organization may be welded to produce a single creative synthesis.

Now, what does all this have to do with the problem of organization in administrative science? Organization concepts seem to have gone through the same order of development in this field as in the three just mentioned. It is evident that the classical theory of organization, particularly as in the work of Mooney and Reiley, is concerned with principles common to all organizations. It is a macro-organizational view. The classical approach to organization, however, dealt with the gross anatomical parts and processes of the formal organization. Like classical physics, the classical theory of organization is a special case. Neither are especially well equipped to account for variation from their established framework.

Many variations in the classical administrative model result from human behavior. The only way these variations could be understood was by a microscopic examination of particularized, situational aspects of human behavior. The mission of the neoclassical school thus is "microanalysis."

It was observed earlier, that somewhere along the line the concept of the social system, which is the key to understanding the Hawthorne studies, faded into the background. Maybe the idea is so obvious that it was lost to the view of researchers and writers in human relations. In any event, the press of research in the microcosmic universes of the informal organization, morale and productivity, leadership, participation, and the like forced the notion of the social system into limbo. Now, with the advent of modern organization theory, the social system has been resurrected.

Modern organization theory appears to be concerned with Eddington's "and." This school claims that its operational hypothesis is based on a macro point of view; that is, the study of organization as a whole. This nobility of purpose should not obscure, however, certain difficulties faced by this field as it is presently constituted. Modern organization theory raises two questions which should be explored further. First, would it not be more accurate to speak of modern organization theor*ies?* Second, just how much of modern organization theory is modern?

The first question can be answered with a quick affirmative. Aside from the notion of the system, there are few, if any, other ideas of a unifying nature. Except for several important exceptions,[54] modern organization theorists tend to pursue their pet points of view,[55] suggesting they are part of system theory, but not troubling to show by what mystical means they arrive at this conclusion.

The irony of it all is that a field dealing with systems has, indeed, little system. Modern organization theory needs a framework, and it needs an integration of issues into a common conception of organization. Admittedly, this is a large order. But it is curious not to find serious analytical treatment of subjects like cybernetics or general system theory in Haire's, *Modern Organizational Theory* which claims to be a representative example of work in this field. Beer has ample evidence in his book *Cybernetics and Management* that cybernetics, if imaginatively approached, provides a valuable conceptual base for the study of systems.

The second question suggests an ambiguous answer. Modern organization theory is in part a product of the past; system analysis is not a new idea. Further, modern organization theory relies for supporting data on microcosmic research studies, generally drawn from the journals of the last ten years. The newness of modern organization theory, perhaps, is its effort to synthesize recent research contributions of many fields into a system theory characterized by a reoriented conception of organization.

One might ask, but what is the modern theorist reorienting? A clue is found in the almost snobbish disdain assumed by some authors of the neo-classical human relations school, and particularly, the classical school. Re-evaluation of the classical school of organization is overdue. However, this does not mean that its contributions to organization theory are irrelevant and should be overlooked in the rush to get on the "behavioral science bandwagon."

Haire announces that the papers appearing in *Modern Organization Theory* constitute, "the ragged leading edge of a wave of theoretical devel-

---

[54] For example: E. Wight Bakke, *op. cit.*, pp. 18–75.

[55] There is a large selection including decision theory, individual-organization interaction, motivation, vitality, stability, growth, and graph theory, to mention a few.

opment."[56] Ragged, yes; but leading, no! The papers appearing in this book do not represent a theoretical breakthrough in the concept of organization. Haire's collection is an interesting potpourri with several contributions of considerable significance. But readers should beware that they will not find vastly new insights into organizational behavior in this book, if they have kept up with the literature of the social sciences, and have dabbled to some extent in the esoteria of biological theories of growth, information theory, and mathematical model building. For those who have not maintained the pace, *Modern Organization Theory* serves the admirable purpose of bringing them up-to-date on a rather diversified number of subjects.

Some work in modern organization theory is pioneering, making its appraisal difficult and future uncertain. While the direction of this endeavor is unclear, one thing is patently true. Human behavior in organizations, and indeed, organization itself, cannot be adequately understood within the ground rules of classical and neo-classical doctrines. Appreciation of human organization requires a *creative* synthesis of massive amounts of empirical data, a high order of deductive reasoning, imaginative research studies, and a taste for individual and social values. Accomplishment of all these objectives, and the inclusion of them into a framework of the concept of the system, appears to be the goal of modern organization theory. The vitality of administrative science rests on the advances modern theorists make along this line.

Modern organization theory, 1960 style, is an amorphous aggregation of synthesizers and restaters, with a few extending leadership on the frontier. For the sake of these few, it is well to admonish that pouring old wine into new bottles may make the spirits cloudy. Unfortunately, modern organization theory has almost succeeded in achieving the status of a fad. Popularization and exploitation contributed to the disrepute into which human relations has fallen. It would be a great waste if modern organization theory yields to the same fate, particularly since both modern organization theory and human relations draw from the same promising source of inspiration—system analysis.

Modern organization theory needs tools of analysis and a conceptual framework uniquely its own, but it must also allow for the incorporation of relevant contributions of many fields. It may be that the framework will come from general system theory. New areas of research such as decision theory, information theory, and cybernetics also offer reasonable expectations of analytical and conceptual tools. Modern organization theory represents a frontier of research which has great significance for manage-

---

[56] Mason Haire, "General Issues," in Mason Haire (editor), *Modern Organization Theory* (New York: John Wiley and Sons, 1959), p. 2.

ment. The potential is great, because it offers the opportunity for uniting what is valuable in classical theory with the social and natural sciences into a systematic and integrated conception of human organization.

---

2. PATTERNS IN ORGANIZATION STRUCTURING*

Harold Stieglitz

CHANGE IS THE ONLY CONSTANT in company organization structuring. The truth of this cliche, which is both a refuge and a vested interest of the organization planner, becomes evident when one attempts to examine the structure of a large number of companies. In gathering material for this particular report, THE CONFERENCE BOARD was frequently told: "Our latest organization chart is no longer current," or "We are just in the process of reorganizing," or "A new chart reflecting recent changes will be sent as soon as possible."

Many of the organization changes these companies refer to are minor in that they reflect a shift in one or two functions, or a change in several reporting relationships, or merely a change in the personnel occupying given positions. On the other hand, a sizable portion of the changes are major in that they reflect large-scale regroupings of activities or basic changes in the authority structure of the company.

Even some seemingly minor changes may be major. For example, the insertion of an executive vice-president in an organization where none has existed before, may be represented by a relatively small change in the chart, but it may well be a major redistribution of authority. And in some companies, a series of small, seemingly unrelated organization changes takes on a pattern after a while and begins to add up to a major change.

At such a point even a detached observer, not privy to the inside working of the company, begins to realize that a company's chart, at any one time, represents merely one stage in an ever-evolving organization plan. Similarly, the charts of a variety of organizations, taken at any one time, may depict an evolving pattern of business in general adapting its

---

* From N.I.C.B. *Studies in Personnel Policy*, No. 183, 1961, pp. 12–15. Reprinted with permission from the publisher.

organization structure to change. For conceivably, instead of looking at the separate charts of three or four different companies, one might be looking at the chart of one company at four different stages of its development.

Among the sixty-one different companies whose charts make up the bulk of this report, such a pattern is discernible. The pattern reflects the attempts of companies to build organization structures consonant with the requirements of larger and—more importantly—far more complex business. The increase in size and complexity which has confronted many companies has come about through the new markets they are serving, the new products they are producing, and the resulting changed legal and economic climate they are operating in. In some companies the increased complexity has resulted from self-generated expansion; in others it has come about through mergers and acquisitions.

How to manage a large, highly complex business is a problem a relatively few giant companies faced many years ago.[1] The solutions that they reached at the time were viewed as pioneering. But it is becoming more evident that as more companies reach a certain size and complexity, they reach for organizational solutions that are somewhat similar. For some companies this similarity results from emulation of what seems to have been successful for another company with similar problems. But more often today it seems to result from the application of the principles of organization to a given set of circumstances.

The observable pattern among the sixty-one companies has four major elements to it, some more evident than others:

1. A more concerted move to divisionalized organization structures accompanied by greater decentralization.
2. The elaboration and changed role of corporate staff.
3. The emergence of another level of general executives, most often labeled "group executives."
4. The elaboration of the chief executive's office.

The elements of this pattern are by no means unrelated. All stem from the same root problem. All might be viewed as part of the answer to the same question: "How can one man—the chief executive—manage to manage a larger and more complex enterprise?"

Greater Divisionalization Accompanied by Decentralization

As companies move into new fields of operations occasioned by expanded product lines or wider sales regions, they are confronted by new problems of competition, new technological problems, and new marketing

---

[1] For one recent investigation of this point, see "The Great Organizers," by Ernest Dale, McGraw-Hill Publishing Company.

problems. For example, a company historically identified with the production and sale of glass containers meets a whole new field of competitors when it expands its product line to include metal and paper containers. A service company operating in one region meets a new field of competitors when it expands its services to new regions.

The functional-type organization so well fitted to the single-product company or the company operating in one socio-economic region has difficulties in adequately coping with the new problems. For example, it is difficult for a single head of manufacturing to deal with all the different manufacturing problems associated with a variety of different products; or for a single head of sales to give adequate attention to the sale of different products to different customers in different regions. More importantly, it is hazardous to leave the overall coordination of the production, engineering and sale of a variety of products serving a variety of regions and customers to one man. But that is the case in a strictly functional type of organization: one man, the chief executive or his deputy, coordinates all line elements.

For several reasons—adequate emphasis on different product lines, easier identification of profitability, greater flexibility of operations, and increased ability to compete in a variety of markets—more companies have grouped functions on a product basis and delegated responsibility for their coordination to the head of a product division. This divisionalization, almost by definition, has brought with it a greater degree of decentralization. For, in a divisionalized organization, the authority to make decisions involving the coordination of the activities relating to one product and accountablity for profits occurs at a level lower in the organization than the president or the executive vice-president.

Of course, divisionalization may proceed from two different directions. Most often it occurs in a company previously organized along functional lines. But it may also proceed from a totally different direction: for example, where wholly-owned subsidiaries are more closely integrated into the operations of the parent company; or where merged or acquired companies operate as divisions of the overall company. In the process of becoming a division, the subsidiary, merged, or acquired unit loses some of its autonomy.

It has been argued that this loss of autonomy amounts to recentralization rather than decentralization. But from the point of view of the parent or overall company, it is still decentralization. (Because there are other aspects to this point, it will be touched on later.)

Among the companies participating in this report, the tendency to divisionalize operations is noticeable. For some, the move began after World War II and has continued; for many others, it is more recent. It is more noticeable, naturally, among those diversified manufacturing companies whose operations lend themselves readily to grouping of activities on the basis of product. But even companies engaged in businesses whose production processes historically have lent themselves to a functional organization (steel, for example), or those who have a common market for a variety of products (foods, for example), have adopted divisionalized organizational structures.

The move to divisionalize has not been without its problems. One is that as more specialized product groupings are attempted, it becomes increasingly difficult to meet the three basic criteria for optimum divisionalization along product lines: differing production technology, differing markets, and sufficient demands for the product. As a result, some companies have regrouped production (but more often sales) of previously established product units. Instead of having ten different product units, for example, they may regroup to eight, with one unit handling sales of the products that have the same customers.

A second problem arises, in establishing product or regional divisions, over the allocation of staff or service units to the product divisions. Need a division have a full staff complement in accounting, personnel, public relations, and research? Judging from the charts and manuals of the participating companies, economics, tempered by considerations of decentralization, seems to provide the answer. If the requirements of the division are such as to require a full-time staff component in any of the mentioned fields of specialization, the unit is set up. But if the services can be more economically provided by a central unit or a unit serving several divisions or a group of divisions, the staff service is not placed within the division.

However, as mentioned above, this purely economic consideration is tempered by the nature of delegated authority. If the division head or other unit head is held accountable for results, he may require or feel that he requires certain staff units at his elbow.

The companies participating in this report show a variety of staff arrangements so far as their divisions are concerned. In companies whose divisions are virtually major operations, or whose divisions are geographically dispersed, a full staff complement often exists within the division and/or units of the division. More often, when the company is smaller or not so widely dispersed, the product divisions may have less staff or none at all. The head of the product division in such a situation can avail himself of central staff services or, depending upon the degree of decentralization, hire outside consultants to furnish his requirements.

Elaboration and Changing Role of Corporate Staff

As a company grows, staff also grows. Part of this growth in staff is a natural consequence of the need for more services of the same type: it takes a larger accounting department to service a company with $1 million in sales and 1,000 employees than to service one with $500,000 in sales and 400 employees. Part results from companies setting up units to carry on activities previously bought on a contract basis: the company may have grown to the point where it needs a full-time staff department to provide services that were formerly provided by an outside public relations firm or legal counsel on a part-time basis.

Another reason for the growth of corporate staff is evident in the charts of participating companies: many of them are finding a need for types of service that had not been of concern previously. Thus, in some companies certain staff components are now appearing at the corporate level for the first time. Some examples of the "newer" staff functions are: community relations, government relations, stockholder relations, computer technology or electronic data processing, research, product development, marketing and market research, manufacturing, executive development, organization planning, long-range planning, organization development, management services, and control.

Some of these functions arise from the changed competitive environment the business operates in; research, product development, and market research are prime examples, and government and community relations might also come under this heading. Some are more directly attributable to the move to divisionalized operations; for example, organization planning, executive development, and the emergence of marketing and manufacturing as corporate staff activities. And some are consequences of both; for example, electronic data processing, long-range planning, organization development, and management services.

Although the types of staff activity at the corporate level have been increasing, it is not accurate to say that the number of personnel engaged in corporate staff work has also increased. For much of the service-type work with which staff is identified is carried on by staff personnel within the divisions, leaving a smaller but more specialized, versatile, and highly skilled staff at corporate headquarters.

This fact points up another aspect of the elaboration of corporate staff: the general shift of emphasis from its role as a primarily service agency to its role as an agency assisting in planning and control. This change in emphasis is partly apparent in the titles of the emerging corporate staff units. But it is far more apparent in the organization manuals and position guides that detail the responsibilities of corporate staff. The shift is especially common in companies that have moved to divisionalized organization. For in a divisionalized company that practices decentralization, corporate staff takes on the major job of assisting in the formulation of overall corporate objectives and policies. And it acts as the agent of the chief executive in measuring and appraising performance within functional specialties relative to the established objectives and policies.

Possibly the change in the role of corporate staff in a divisionalized and decentralized company might be more easily viewed from the perspective of the chief executive. In a functional type of organization he (or his deputy, the executive vice-president) has responsibility for coordinating the line elements—production and sales.

But, in a divisionalized organization, the chief executive delegates responsibility for coordination of what amounts to separate businesses to two, five, or more division heads. However, if his aim is decentralization rather than fragmentation, he attempts to set up objectives and policies that act as a cohesive and unifying force. Thus, the chief executive concentrates on those responsibilities that affect the organization and its future as a total entity: determination of objectives and long-range plans, policy formulation, surveillance, and control. As the business becomes more complex, the exercise of these reserved responsibilities calls for more and better information. Corporate staff has been characterized as the lobes of the brain that make it possible for the chief executive to carry out these essential responsibilities.

The emergence of corporate staff as a major force in the planning and control of corporate objectives and policies has been characterized as "recentralization"—as a reaction to too much decentralization.[2] Upon analysis, it can be seen that this claim contains some truth. But it can also be seen that other factors may contribute to what has been loosely termed recentralization.

First, some companies attempted to set up "divisionalized, decentralized" operations without first establishing overall corporate objectives, objectives for each of their divisions, and corporate policies. After the effects of such disorganization became evident, the companies sought to establish those unifying elements that had been lacking. In such situations, organization analysts argue, the company was not decentralized in the first instance; it was atomized.

Second, some companies that have decentralized find that over a period of time there are changes in the three factors affecting the degree of decentralization.

1. *Competence.* The demonstrated competence of a position incumbent may fall short of the requirements of the job, or a new replacement may lack the competence required. In either case, the position may be redefined with less authority.

2. *Information.* The information required at a given level of decision making may not be available at that level. Authority is moved up to the level at which it is available.

3. *Scope of impact.* Because of a change in circumstances, certain

---

[2] See, for example, "Top Management Tightens Control," *Dun's Review and Modern Industry*, July, 1959.

decisions made by lower level heads may be found to have a widening scope of impact. Authority to make such decisions is moved up to the level at which all affected units are coordinated. Or where the company decides that a uniform course of action is necessary, the authority to make separate decisions is withdrawn.

In all three of the situations above, there is less decentralization than before; "recentralization" has occurred.

The use of these terms serves to emphasize a basic point: decentralization is a matter of degree. It varies from one company to another; it varies within a given company when, for example, certain organizational units may exercise a higher degree of delegated authority than others.

Other problems confront companies as a result of the elaboration and changing role of corporate staff. One is determining the types of controls the company can use and still maintain a decentralized organization. It is possible for central staff, in the name of control, to set up detailed audits and reporting procedures that amount to a constant check on the division heads. The alternative stressed by organization planners is control or appraisal of performance on the basis of established objectives and accountability for results.

Another problem arises from the fact that, in a divisionalized organization, corporate staff heads tend to be less involved in servicing operations than under a functional type of organization. Also, former heads of such traditionally line functions as manufacturing and sales may now find themselves heading a corporate staff manufacturing or marketing unit. In both cases, changes in relationships and methods of operation are called for. Reports from companies indicate that not all executives find it easy to make this adjustment.

Emergence of Group Executives

As divisionalized companies increase the number of product divisions, effective coordination of the separate divisions becomes a greater problem. A fairly common organizational device many companies have used, and still use, is the setting up of an executive vice-president to ease the load of the president. In some companies, the executive vice-president coordinates staff activities. Far more often he coordinates the operating units or divisions, and the president retains direct supervision of the corporate staff units vital to his overall planning and control responsibilities.

However, with the proliferation of product divisions and corporate staff units, some companies are finding that even an executive vice-president cannot adequately provide the required direction. So they have added general executives accountable for the performance of two or more product divisions that are somewhat related in terms of production technology or markets served. Most often, these executives carry the title of group vice-president or group executive. In some companies, they constitute an additional level between an executive vice-president and product divisions; in others, they are apparently in lieu of the executive vice-president.

The emergence of group executives is not confined to the giants among the companies in this report.

In a few companies, a position somewhat similar to that of group executives also appears at the corporate staff level. Two, three, or more corporate staff units may be grouped together under a senior vice-president or a position titled vice-president, administration.

Cutting down on the chief executive's span of control is the reason most often given for the increased number of group executives. The factors that seem most relevant to the determination to set up a group executive are:

1. Increased demand on the chief executive's time: when the extent of the chief executive's external relations and overall responsibilities rises so that the time remaining for him to furnish personal contact with major unit heads is inadequate, the new level is created to act in lieu of the chief executive.
2. Increased interaction between divisions: when the objectives or plans of several divisions begin to have greater effect on each other, possibly by virtue of overlapping markets, closer coordination is provided by means of a group executive.

For many practical purposes the group executive, like the executive vice-president, may be likened to an assistant president (rather than assistant to the president) as far as the divisions reporting to him are concerned. And as is often the case with assistants, the responsibilities and authority of the group executive, and their impact on the degree of responsibility and authority of those reporting to him, are not always clearly defined. It certainly cannot be found in the charts of companies where this position exists. But judging from position guides and organization analyses, some companies attempt to have it clearly understood that the division heads' accountability for profitable performance, and his attendant authority, are in no way diminished by the insertion of a group executive; the group executive in these companies exercises some of the authority formerly reserved to the president relative to divisional operations. However, it is recognized that in such cases, although there is no lessening of the formal authority of the division head, he may feel he has less "authority" (in a prestige sense) because he is one level removed, or one level further removed, from the president.

Elaboration of the Chief Executive's Office

The elements so far discussed can be viewed as means used by the chief executive to manage a growing and far more complex business; all three allow him to devote more of his time to those responsibilities uniquely reserved to him.

Some of the unique responsibilities of the chief executive have already been mentioned, or at least implied, in the preceding discussion. Analyses of organization indicate that the following are the hard core of the chief executive's reserved responsibilities:[3]

External relations—The chief executive is the company as far as external relations with the public, stockholders, government, and business associates are concerned.

Objectives and long-range planning—The chief executive determines the appropriate long-range and short-range objectives and plans for their accomplishment.

Overall policy formulation—The chief executive sets the code of ethical conduct that the company will adhere to in pursuit of its objectives.

Surveillance and control—The chief executive sees to it that all components of the organization are moving in the direction of established objectives and are conforming with corporate policies.

Development of a successor—The chief executive assures the continued survival and perpetuation of a company by developing the next chief executive.

There seems to be little question that the nature of these reserved responsibilities is the same for a chief executive of a small company, a medium-sized company, or a large or very large company. But as the company grows in size and complexity, the scope of these reserved responsibilities grows to such an extent that they are beyond the capabilities of one man. External relations alone may so preoccupy the chief executive of a giant enterprise as to leave inadequate time for proper attention to the other responsibilities. Or, at different stages of development, the other responsibilities may demand the full attention of the chief executive.

Not only does the scope of the reserved responsibilities grow beyond the capabilities of one man; but also, the abilities required for their performance become so increasingly varied that one individual cannot supply them.

---

[3] For a fuller discussion of these reserved responsibilities and some of the organizational device structures used by the chief executive, see "Organization of the Chief Executive's Job," *Management Record*, February, 1961.

It is evident from the organization structures in this study that companies—or more particularly, chief executives—are using several methods to cope with the expansion of the reserved responsibilities of the chief executive. All the methods elaborate the office of the chief executive so that these reserved responsibilities—the "chief executive function"—are being performed by more than one man. Accountability still rests with the chief executive officer alone, but the function, it might be said, is "decentralized."

One fairly widespread method, by no means new, is the use of personal staff assistants. In some companies, their responsibilities are rather general. They carry out whatever jobs of a temporary or a continuing nature the chief executive may assign to them. In others, the assistants specialize in fields of interest that the chief executive has chosen to reserve to himself; possibly, organization planning, technical development, and market development.

The distinction between these more specialized staff assistants and corporate staff units is not always sharp. Often they provide functional assistance to other units of the organization. Their major emphasis, however, appears to be on studies or plans, sometimes of a confidential nature, that fall within the reserved responsibilities of the chief executive.

Another method that appears quite frequently among the participating companies amounts to an upgrading of the president—executive vice-president relationship. An increasing number of companies are allocating the chief executive function to a chairman of the board designated "chief executive officer." The president in these companies is sometimes designated "chief operating officer," or sometimes "chief administrative officer." In some companies there is a definite split in responsibility of the two men, but quite often they "share the same box" and share responsibilities.

In a very few of the participating companies, not just two but three (a chairman, president, and an executive vice-president) and even four men (a chairman, president, and two executive vice-presidents) share this top box and the duties of the chief executive.

Still another method of coping with the increased complexity of the chief executive function calls for the creation of a council of top executives to carry out this chief executive function. The concept involved here cannot be adequately depicted on any chart. But a few companies use a special charting device to emphasize the idea. One box labeled "executive office" or "executive management" or "office of the president" appears at the top of the chart. It includes not only the chief executive and the executive vice-president(s) but also those group executives and general staff executives accountable for coordinating the operating and corporate staff components of the business.

In effect, the group executives and general staff executives making up this top council wear two hats. As group or general staff executives they are accountable for the performance of the units reporting to them. But, as members of the executive office, they lose their identies as line or staff men and become, to quote one company:

"A group of executives free of detailed administrative and operating matters to assist the president in policy development and the overall leadership and coordination of the company's business and management."

Having men with specified areas of functional and business responsibilities and with complementary abilities in this "office of the president" is viewed as assuring more adequate consideration of all factors that bear on any overall decision. And, the chief executive function, instead of being the sole responsibility of the chief exectuive officer, becomes the responsibility of a composite personality, the chief executive office. The chief executive officer under this concept has the job of coordinating the component parts of his office and gives direction and purpose to their work so the company can reach the objective for which he is accountable.

-----

3. A HEALTHY ORGANIZATION*

James V. Clark

WHAT CONSTITUTES A "GOOD" ORGANIZATION remains a matter of much debate. In this paper, I shall spell out my own current concept of organizational health and illustrate it by describing an organization I call healthy.

I consider an organization to be healthy if its members observe certain unstated but quite uniform codes of behavior which they accept as normal things to do, provided these codes produce behavior which allows all levels of the organization to meet two basic but diverse requirements—maintenance of the status quo, and growth.

Since man is a social being and business a group activity, the healthy organization must afford groups as well as individuals chances to fulfill

* From the *California Management Review*, Summer, 1962, Vol. IV, No. 4, pp. 16–30. Reprinted with permission from the publisher.

AUTHOR'S NOTE: An earlier version of this paper was originally presented at a UCLA Graduate School of Business Administration faculty seminar. Discussants were Professor Richard Barthol, Psychology, and Professor Melvin Seeman, Sociology, for whose commentary the author is grateful. J.V.C.

their tendencies and capacities for equilibrium and growth. It must do this for the individual, for small groups, for inter-group relationships and for the total organization.

It goes without saying that each and all of these tendencies and capacities can never be completely and simultaneously maximized. That's not in the nature of things.[1] But on balance and over time the healthy organization is one in which its component parts—group and individual—somehow manage to achieve an optimal resolution of their tendencies toward equilibrium (maintenance, homeostasis, status quo or call it what you will) and their capacities for growth (elaboration, complication, differentiation, negative entropy, or what not).

Before we go into particulars about the healthy organization, as I have just defined it, we must lay some groundwork. Let us, therefore, take a quick look at some of the different aspects of human behavior and some of the divergent ways in which these aspects have been studied. Then I shall illustrate these different aspects with common examples from business and everyday life. We will need, also, to examine what I mean by a norm which governs social behavior. After we have done all this, I will return to the subject of a healthy organization and try to show one in action.

Aspects of Behavioral Systems

For some time behavioral scientists have described individuals, small groups, intergroup complexes, total organizations and societies as systems, that is, "wholes," composed of interrelated, interdependent parts. Investigators have tended to concentrate on what could be called the "reactive" side of a system, which means that behavior which is analogous to a balloon returning to its original state after a finger has been inserted and withdrawn from its side.

More or less, these various investigators have played on some variation of Freud's "pleasure principle," that the primordial or initial principle of life is to reduce tension. Tension is said to be regarded as pain and absence of tension as pleasure. Individuals, small groups and bureaucracies have all been seen, in this light, as equilibrium-seeking, homeostatic, reacting, defensive, "closed" systems.

Recently, however, interest in so-called "open-ended" systems has intensified. Students regarding systems in such a light stress what might be called the "proactive" side of systems, that behavior which is forward-pushing, growing, striving, learning, becoming. Such writers emphasize

---

[1] Paul R. Lawrence, *The Changing of Organizational Behavior Patterns: A Case Study of Decentralization* (Boston: Division of Research, Harvard Business School, 1958). See Chapter X.

what are often called the "transactional" aspects of behavior—that as a system matures it enters into a more and more complex set of give-and-take relations with its environment, what Gordon Allport has described as "extensive transactional commerce."[2] Growth for a behavioral system, then, involves a greater complexity of relations with its environment, hence "open-ended" is an appropriate term.

While those who emphasize the "reactive" side of behavior often deny the "proactive" side and vice versa, many careful observers maintain that any system requires both aspects. A human being grows, but it also has a capacity to restore itself to health after an invasion of germs or injuries. A small group tends to perpetuate itself, but it also elaborates a complicated structure of power, interaction, beliefs, communication, and so on.

To me, any piece of organizational behavior tends to exhibit both aspects—reaction and proaction, maintenance and growth, even if one capacity is present only by virtue of its frustration. Hence, I will try to show that a healthy organization must somehow take account of both these tendencies. I have discussed briefly the attachment different students have had to these different tendencies so the reader may be on guard against any such parochial leanings in himself.[3]

Levels of Behavioral Systems

In addition to studying one or the other of these tendencies, investigators of behavior in formal organizations have often tended to concentrate on only one or two levels of investigation. This has usually been out of necessity, for one can't study everything. Nevertheless, the impression has sometimes been created that organizational well-being is arrived at only through satisfying individual needs, or small group needs, or by developing inter-group harmony, or by dealing rationally with only the formal organizational structure, or in some other partial manner.

As Koontz has illustrated, the "management theory jungle"[4] is peopled with schools of investigators which often center on aspects of administration and organizational behavior as if these aspects were the totality. It seems to me, however, that the different levels of organizational behavior are all in operation at any one time, and, in some sense, must all be taken into consideration. I cannot visualize a successful formal organization as one which attends only to individual needs for growth, or to small

[2] Gordon Allport, "The Open System in Personality Theory," *Personality and Social Encounter* (Boston: Beacon Press, 1960).

[3] For a fuller treatment, see James V. Clark, "Businessmen vs. Behavioral Scientists: The Dynamics of Misunderstanding," unpublished paper.

[4] Harold Koontz, "The Management Theory Jungle," *Journal of the Academy of Management*, Vol. 4, No. 3, December, 1961, pp. 174–188.

group needs for perpetuity, continuation and elaboration, or to the total firm's needs for accomplishing its purpose to the exclusion of all else.

In summary, it can be said that, notwithstanding the historical preferences of different investigators, behavioral systems in formal organization can be seen on the different levels of individual, small group, inter-group and total organization, and exhibit both reactive and proactive tendencies and capacities at each level.

Behavioral Systems Illustrated

The different aspects and levels of organizational behavior are illustrated in Figure I. In it I show a dotted line weaving back and forth

FIGURE I

ORGANIZATIONAL BEHAVIOR

Level of System	Aspect of System	
	Reactive	Proactive
Total Organization		
Inter-group		
Small Group		
Individual		

between the two aspects of each different level, because it is almost always impossible to identify an instance of purely reactive or purely proactive behavior. As we shall show in succeeding paragraphs, what is apparently proactive behavior often has a hidden reactive meaning. I don't wish to claim or imply here, therefore, that a researcher or an administrator in an organization can categorically state what *the* meaning of a piece of behavior is. In fact that's my point, one can't. Any piece of behavior always has a variety of meanings, and my thesis is that any organization to be healthy must recognize that variety.

To make these points clearer, I shall illustrate aspects of behavior that fit into the different boxes. Hidden meanings will not be alluded to in most instances since psychology and sociology have made us all generally familiar with them. I will, however, discuss such problems in relation to some of the boxes on our diagram, for these are places where we are not so accustomed to look for hidden meanings as we may be in individual behavior. Each of the areas in Figure I will be illustrated one at a time.

Individual Behavior

Instances of reactive behavior on the individual level are familiar to all of us. Typical examples are the student who defends his belief that he is an intelligent person by denigrating his professor's capacity to communicate, the professor who avoids examining his own capacity to teach by bemoaning the decline in student motivation over the past generation, the mother who maintains her self-concept as a loving person by decrying her inconsiderate children, etc. Such individuals are fending off new information which, if allowed to penetrate, would call for too radical a reorganization of the way in which they see themselves.[5]

Proactive behavior on the part of an individual covers the whole range of human behavior designed to reorganize something in the self-world relationship. The ten-year-old boy struggling night and day to build something, the mother testing new ways of behaving with her children, the researcher trying to discover a new uniformity, the contemplative searching for a deeper understanding of man, nature, or God, the industrial worker designing a new tool bit for his lathe—all these show evidence of growthful, proactive behavior.

Of course, as any sensitive participant in human affairs knows, what looks like proactive behavior often turns out, on closer analysis, to have a strong reactive component, but such are the challenges and pitfalls confronted by those who choose to develop a science of human behavior—they simply cannot avoid the study of meaning. We will encounter this problem when I illustrate behavior at the total organizational level.

Small Group Behavior

On the level of the small group, an instance of reactive behavior is seen in the strengthening of shared beliefs and codes which occurs in a group when an outsider attempts to change it. Such behavior has been seen when industrial work groups face a methods man who has new ideas about how they should be organized, or when a branch plant management team receives new directions or a reorganization plan from headquarters, or when a group of high ranking military officers are visted by a critical congressman.

Outside of organizations, such behavior is encountered, for example,

---

[5] P. R. Lawrence *et al.*, *Organizational Behavior and Administration: Cases, Concepts and Research Findings* (Homewood: Irwin-Dorsey Press, 1961), Century Company (A) (B) (C), pp. 126–167.

when an insensitive Easterner wears a suit and tie to a Los Angeles poolside party, or indeed when any representative of one culture encounters a group from another, and so on. Any group finds it difficult to assimilate such deviant people and behaviors and has an almost instantaneous reaction designed to restore its equilibrium roughly to where it was. At least the group members strive to establish equilibrium.

Proaction on the group level is seen in certain aspects of the behavior of a group of smelter workers recently observed by the author. One night this group sweated for an hour over 2000° molten metal to pull out a tool bit which would have left a trace impurity in the metal and for which they could not possibly have been held accountable nor received any credit for correcting. This behavior was not called for either by their formal job requirements (technically, they were supposed to work alone) or their group norms to help one another with their work assignments, but represented a new pattern of behavior and beliefs not seen earlier in the structure of the group.

Something similar occurred in a freezing room group Louis B. Barnes and I studied in 1957.[6] This group of 5 or 6 workers in an ice cream plant spent nearly a year meeting at each other's homes to design and eventually execute a whole new methods handling system in their department. Their work went on unknown to management for months and involved new behavior patterns in the group and new effects on the group environment.

Such developmental behavior was also seen by Trist and his colleagues[7] among longwall method coal workers in Britain, when they were offered the chance to organize their own socio-technological relationships. Similar development was charted by Barnes[8] in an engineering group which was given comparatively high freedom to influence its own job structure.

Of course, groups, like other behavioral systems, will always tend to increase the differentiation of their parts through time. The rich rubric of social interaction which develops around betting, eating, coffee drinking, joking, and gaming rituals among so many white-and-blue-collar work groups in American organizations illustrates this. So one cannot say that group development always helps achieve management goals. In fact, it is only when certain specific variables are present that such activity will tend

---

[6] Louis B. Barnes and James V. Clark, "Lakeview Diary," Harvard University, Unpublished Cases, 1957.

[7] E. L. Trist, G. Murray, G. W. Higgin and A. B. Pollock, "Work Organization at the Coal Face" (London: Tavistock Institute of Human Relations, Doc. No. 506, 1959).

[8] Louis B. Barnes, *Organizational Systems and Engineering Groups: A Comparative Study of Two Technical Systems in Industry* (Boston: Division of Research, Harvard Business School, 1960).

to become conscious and result in a group increasing its transactions with its environment.[9]

Intergroup Behavior

Reactive behavior on the intergroup level is seen when two groups increase their internal solidarity by facing each other, the "us" vs. "them" pattern. An individual member of one of these groups feels good to the extent he feels more securely identified with his group and as it is different from the other group. As an example when a senator says to a large gathering of fearful and angry people in Los Angeles as he did, "Make no mistake about it, the Communists are black and all black. There are no greys among them," he is behaving in such a way as to facilitate the clearcut identification of one group against another. The bewildered and frightened people in his audience feel that they *are* something, and that something is "us" vs. "them." Much of what is called "bickering" between different departments of an organization—the classic disputes between sales and production, for example—can be viewed as serving this same function.

Professor Robert Blake of the University of Texas has illustrated reactive intergroup behavior dramatically in his laboratory simulations of intergroup conflict. Among other things, he has shown conclusively that groups in problem-solving competition situations inevitably pick their own solution as rationally superior to others, even in the absence of any rational criteria for making the judgment. Such phenomena are also encountered at the United Nations or around any labor-management negotiation table.

Proactive behavior between groups occurs when members break through their group boundaries and set up give-and-take relations between their group and another. Thus new patterns of behavior and beliefs emerge which change the relation between the groups. This was seen in R. L. Katz and J. A. Seiler's study[10] of the management organization in a 500-man firm, when individuals clearly emerged as linkers between groups. Of course, as expected, these linkers were almost never the people with the formal authority for relating the activities of the two groups. They emerged as the system matured, and they helped hold the total system together by relating its clearly differentiated subparts; and thus we are brought to the total organization.

---

[9] James V. Clark, "Motivation in Work Groups: A Tentative View," *Human Organization*, Vol. XIX, No. 4, Winter 1960–61, pp. 199–208. Also see the Barnes study, note 8.

[10] R. L. Katz and J. A. Seiler, *Management Behavior: The Physiology of Organization* (Boston: Division of Research, Harvard Business School, 1962).

Total Organizational Behavior

At the level of the total organization great complexity enters the picture. Reactive behavior of a certain kind is easy to identify. For instance, the famous old Boston restaurant Durgin Park, will not serve its renowned Indian Pudding without ice cream, regardless of any customer's pleas to the contrary. The representatives of this organization feel rewarded when they perpetuate its age-old traditions, even in the face of customer derision, irritation, or withdrawal. The belief system of the organization thus reinforces itself against change from the outside.

The problem of analysis becomes complicated here, however, because much of what superficially looks like proactive behavior has a strong reactive component. That is, members of many organizations sense acceptance from their peers if they *talk* in terms of changing things through the use of stronger authority, firmer plans, clearer organization, an active anti-union program, or what not. On the face of it one can't tell whether such talk serves primarily the function of re-establishing cherished belief around which the organization is held together, or of describing actual proactive behavior.

Such questions often require careful research to answer. So much talk about "inner directedness," for example, or "rugged individualism" takes on a different cast when one realizes the extent to which certain individuals get social satisfaction from others by conforming to certain accepted codes. That is, an individual often gains membership in a management group or club to the extent he professes to value rugged individualism.

Here are some instances of behavior which have had the function of re-establishing and underscoring shared beliefs and values held by the powerful figures in an organization, but which were ostensibly proactive.

THE CASE OF THE TOO PRODUCTIVE CREW

In one electronics company recently investigated by Melvin Steckler at Harvard,[11] a small group of production girls was found to be contributing about 120 percent toward the profit of the firm. Because of an explicit action experiment by their foreman, these girls—most of whom had little formal education in general and none at all in electronics—were solving production and design problems which university professors and members of the company's engineering department couldn't cope with. Also productivity was constantly increasing in the group, some 300 percent in two years, and they were not on an incentive system.

---

[11] See note 5, American Radiatronics Corporation (A), pp. 266–302.

As might be expected, these girls had considerable freedom in their jobs. They designed and operated their own testing equipment, their maintenance man made and supervised their expense and supplies budget which constantly showed a lower and lower percentage in relation to volume, they moved around a lot, traded jobs and so forth.

After this had been going on for over a year, higher-ups could stand it no longer, and instituted proceedings to break up the activity. The foreman was promoted away from the group, a new engineer was imported from Europe to "straighten up the confusion in the department," etc. What an engineering executive said to the researcher shortly before these proceedings were launched is instructive. As we listen to him talk, we are hearing strong reactive sentiments, sentiments so strong they even overlook making money—another variable sometimes seen as rewarding by organizational members. Said the engineer:

> Dollarwise they're doing a pretty good job in here, as far as it goes, but they've got one overriding weakness in the way they are presently set up. Do you realize the girls do all their own testing in here? The same girls that make the tubes test them. It just isn't logical. Human nature isn't that way. You can't trust the same people who make something to also test it. It's not healthy.
>
> . . . We've got plans in the works for taking on this place and really making it over. And when we do we'll see to it that the testing operations are carried on in a separate department. We'll really whip this operation into shape. . . . I'd like to make this a model showplace for the company. Right now it's the worst in the company.
>
> This place has never been under engineering control. That's the trouble with it. . . . Most of the product design changes that have been made have been developed and put into practice by the production people themselves. That's not good. . . . They design their own products, they alter and maintain their own production equipment and processes, and they are free to go off in all different directions at once. The first thing we would do if we could get hold of this room would be to put every operation under close engineering surveillance.

This engineer sounds proactive, but it is clear that the main underlying meaning of his behavior is to push back into shape a disequilibrium about which he feels deeply upset. Moreover, it is possible this disequilibrium is felt by him in many ways: as a threat to his knowledge and status, as a threat to the position of the engineering group in the company, as a violation of the status system in the company as a whole, and as a violation of the Western European culture's assumption about authority as appropriately flowing from "up" towards "down" through the vehicles of role incumbents.[12]

---

[12] Walter B. Miller, "Two Concepts of Authority," *American Anthropologist*, Vol. LVII, No. 2 (April, 1955), pp. 271–289. (Condensed and reprinted in Lawrence, *et al., Organizational Behavior and Administration*, pp. 777–786.)

THE CASE OF THE SPEEDING ASSEMBLY LINE

Something similar was observed by Alex Bavelas in a toy factory on a paint line conveyor.[13] There, a group of girls were allowed to control the speed of the conveyor on which they were working. They sped it up when they felt like working, and they slowed it down when they didn't. Productivity and earnings soared, and soared higher by far than that which the engineers had believed to be normal output.

Consequently, the engineers took the control of the line's speed away from the workers, and restored it to a steady predictable pace. The girls, apparently, had established an equilibrium of their own, for they all quit in protest. So did their foreman. As with the engineer in the electronics company, the belief of the management group that control of technological process ought to move from the top down was reinforced, again to the exclusion of other beliefs such as the goodness of high productivity.

These are instances of one of the most commonly encountered findings of organizational research. Time and time again, management groups in business and elsewhere enforce procedures designed to keep behavior in line with beliefs about what "ought to be" under the guise that they are usefully effecting task accomplishment. In the instances above, for example, actual task efficiency was sacrificed for order and congruence with management beliefs.

In summary, it is no accident that the conditions under which groups achieve high job involvement, high productivity, high creativity, high satisfaction, low absenteeism and low turnover are among the best known findings in organizational behavior research and are perhaps those most ignored by managements. Of course this shouldn't surprise us, since the need of any behavioral system—individual, group, organizational or what not—to maintain itself through time is almost always stronger than mere new knowledge. Anyone knows this who has tried to change another's mind through what he believes is logic.

Having underscored in this way the extreme difficulty of assessing the meaning of behavior from the point of view of the total organization, we must realize that classifying behavior as proactive is just as difficult as pegging reactive tendencies.

However, consciously conceived and executed expansion is certainly an instance. Reorganization which introduces new differentiation into the system is another. Other examples can be seen in the increasing variety of special interests of the modern, large corporations. They are relating themselves to their community and wider cultural context in an array of ways hardly considered a few decades ago.

---

[13] William F. Whyte, et al., Money and Motivation (New York: Harper & Bros., 1955, Chapter X).

Art exhibits, gifts to colleges, community relations programs, educational aids and the like are all examples of the variety of transactions being sought and achieved by corporations. It is true that most of these activities are spoken of as having an economic base in good public relations, but the fact that the environment puts such pressure on growing organizations may indicate that the wider social context expects such increasing transactions from a growing sub-unit. Be that as it may, many activities of these kinds have only the vaguest connection to the often allegedly superordinate goal of profit. Indeed, as Robert N. Anthony[14] has pointed out, most corporations today have ceased maximizing profit, and have done so because of their other transactional relations with the wider society.

What Is a Norm?

Having thus illustrated the different aspects of organizational behavior, let us now examine what is meant by a norm.

What is meant by a norm, is a belief which a group of people act as if they hold, so that, if any person exhibits behavior which differs from the norm, the group will act to make the deviant person conform. By way of illustration, we might cite the situation of the Easterner who shows up at a Los Angeles swimming pool party dressed in a suit and tie. An elaboration of this event is instructive. Shortly after the Easterner's arrival the native members of this poolside group, both female and male, began to interact quite heavily with the deviant new member, making jokes about Easterners, expressing desires to someday see the new member in a sport shirt, making overtures of affection and welcome toward the new member, and even presenting him with the local costume, a sport shirt hastily borrowed from the oldest son of the host. The natives said that they wished to make the new member more comfortable this way.

The Easterner, remaining insensitive to the social meaning of the offering—to produce cohesion in the group—refused it, saying he was already comfortable, which was physically true. Thereafter, interaction dropped off sharply with the new member, an outcome predicted by S. Schacter's research on deviation.[15] (Subsequent research, by the way, indicates that in the future the Easterner and his mate are considering clothing themselves in native garments.)

The illustration chosen is perhaps trivial, but groups cannot exist without norms; human beings require affiliation for life, just as they require oxygen and water, and norm-breaking can be a serious thing. Any-

---

[14] Robert N. Anthony, "The Trouble with Profit Maximization," *Harvard Business Review*, Vol. 38, No. 6, November–December 1960, pp. 126–134.

[15] S. Schacter, "Deviation, Rejection and Communication," *Journal of Social and Abnormal Psychology*, Vol. 46 (1951), pp. 190–207.

one who doubts it might, to continue the illustration just cited, try going to an Eastern cocktail party dressed comfortably in a sport shirt.

One Healthy Organization

With this brief description of a norm and its function of maintaining a group, let us turn to some behavior in the Marshall Company, an organization studied by a group of field investigators from Harvard.[16] It is one which illustrates my definition of a healthy organization where members share norms such that they explicitly recognize the validity of the aspects of behavior in each of the areas shown in Figure I. They also work to resolve the inevitable conflicts that arise between these different aspects.

As I state the Marshall Company norms and then illustrate them with behavior, we shall see the extent to which the different aspects of behavioral systems seen in our diagram are legitimatized by the norms we encounter.

The norms surrounding training, development, promotion and transfer in the Marshall Company were most interesting. Members of the organization behaved as if they believed that "Training occurs on the job and occurs when an individual asks questions and otherwise demonstrates a desire to know more about his work. Anyone in a superior position, including higher ranking production crew personnel, should give subordinates a chance to express their views on tasks and problems and allow them to help in areas of interest to them. A subordinate is not required to take initiative and to be eager to learn, though. It is acceptable in the Marshall Company for someone to stay on his present job until he decides he wants to retire."

A number of events were recorded by the field researchers which indicated the existence of such norms. For example, researchers observed the superintendent of the paper machines both training and being trained as he went about his business. Once, a new and very complicated paper machine was starting up, a process which took several hours. During this time, the superintendent's superior, the production manager, stood in the background and watched, along with a crowd of workers from other parts of the plant, as well as several men who had come in on an off day to observe. During the start-up period, the superintendent said to the researcher: "He [the production manager] doesn't often say much to me when I'm starting up a machine. Later on, he will tell me things he thought might have been improved—even some of the little things. But now, he won't bother me."

---

[16] See note 5, Marshall Company (A)–(1), pp. 634–692.

The next day the men attempted to run paper through the machine. The superintendent observed a crew member—the "second hand"—climb up on the machine and try several times to thread new, wet paper into the press rolls. This was a difficult procedure and all gathered to watch. The man tried and failed a half dozen times, after which the superintendent placed his hand on the crewman's leg. The "second hand" immediately got down and the "first hand," who had been watching from a position near his own job, came over and climbed up. On his second try, he was successful. However, the paper started several times, but each time it broke within a few minutes. Once the superintendent himself fed the paper into the driers. Concerning the event with the "second hand," the superintendent said, "He's o.k. He just got a little nervous."

A few days after the machine had been operating, the researchers talked with a young foreman who was having a great deal of trouble with one part of the machine, although production was moving along steadily. The foreman could not solve the problem, and was often observed sitting by himself, staring at the floor. At one point he said, "I wish we had the old machinery back."

The researchers knew that the young foreman's progress in the company was well known to the production superintendent, who felt he had "brought him along" to be foreman. When the researcher, some days later, asked the superintendent about this particular technical problem, he learned that the superintendent had solved the problem mentally but hadn't yet told the young foreman about it. Grinning broadly, the superintendent said, "He's got enough to think about now, and there's no use trying to look too far ahead."

Why Training Really Worked

There were other instances of training practices among the men on the machines. For example, researchers observed a "second hand" on one of the paper machines helping a third hand temporarily perform the "second hand's" work. When asked about this, the "second hand" talked about how crewmen advanced at Marshall, saying, "You really just learn by doing. You master your own job, and then you watch the next fellow working, and do as much as you can. . . . A good man will keep you busy answering his questions; and when he does that, you bring him along. Of course, you've gotta keep learning so you know more than the other guys. . . . There's one fellow, he's no good. He came over from the other side [of the river dividing our plant here] during the war and worked up to be second hand. Now, guys are coming back from the service who know more than he does. Men under him are better than he is, but he gives orders and pretends to know more than anyone else. No one likes him."

In terms of my thesis, what are some of the significances of these various events? First of all, the ways in which individuals grow and learn are not violated by the norms that exist among the members of the Marshall Company. Men are rewarded by learning new tasks, but they are not pushed into such new behavior, except when the organization's pro-action requires it, as it would in the case of the necessity for a faster or better machine, for example. Moreover, a man can choose not to learn any new tasks at all, and he will not be punished for it, so long as he doesn't prevent others from satisfying their proactive needs. Thus an individual's needs for reactive behavior are legitimate in the Marshall Company system.

Notice, too, that the behavior which must surround an individual's proaction becomes the content for group norms in the Marshall Company. That is, behavior which does not support individual proaction is reacted against by the group. These were the instances of deviation observed in our examples: the crew member reporting the social ostracism of the man who gives orders to and doesn't help the people under him, for example, or the superintendent's punishing the young foreman by withholding help and assistance, because the foreman had given up on the problem and not asked for help.

The company-wide codes support requesting and giving help after an individual has tried on his own. Notice that such codes foster reciprocity between groups (superior-subordinate groups, for example), thus encouraging inter-group proactive behavior, and also are functional at the level of the total organization, which needs both to have problems solved and to have problem-solvers developed.

There is another manner in which these codes make legitimate the different aspects of organizational behavior. Notice that an individual must always ask for help, which places him in a subordinate position socially. But one of the basic aspects of elementary social behavior which holds groups together is the exchange of regard for help. At Marshall, the codes demand that not only should one ask for help from others whose knowledge is greater, but also one must give help to those who ask for it. Thus, this kind of social reciprocity, so vital to the continuation of social groups (as such authors as Alvin Gouldner[17] and George C. Homans[18] have pointed out) is institutionalized in such a way as to meet both the proactive and reactive needs of individuals, groups, and the total organization. A truly remarkable social invention.

---

[17] Alvin Gouldner, "The Norm of Reciprocity: A Preliminary Statement," *American Sociological Review,* Vol. XXV, No. 2, April, 1960, pp. 161–178.

[18] George Caspar Homans, *Social Behavior: Its Elementary Forms* (New York: Harcourt, Brace & World, Inc., 1961), Chapters 3 and 4.

Work Groups Cooperate

There are other instances of such multi-dimensionally useful behavior in Marshall, and all of them are not built around training. For example, the researchers noticed how any emergency was met by everyone in the area with the relevant skills jumping in to help. As those familiar with paper making know, the machines are rarely stopped. If a break occurs, a mountain of waste forms almost immediately.

The norm here was stated when a researcher said to a crew member, "I'm interested in the way you fellows jump to the breaks. . . . The first fellow on the spot goes ahead." "Oh, sure, you have to," the crew member replied. "The thing is, you all have to work together. You can't just do your own job, you have to pull with the crew."

Here we see an instance of a group norm which is clearly useful to the group because technological failure is so obviously the responsibility of a given crew at a given time. The Marshall Company technology is such that social relationships are congruent with an identifiable task and form the basis for what E. L. Trist has called an effective "socio-technical system."[19]

Although we cannot examine this extremely important point further here, there is evidence to suggest that when an organization designs a given technological task in such a way as to require an effective, separate social group for its performance, then the group responds by maintaining a high level of contribution to the organizational task.[20] For example, at Marshall, the crews rarely used a fancy resting room facility the company had built since it would take them away from their constant surveillance of their machines. Also, recall how several members of the crews came in on a holiday to watch the start up of the new machine.

Departments Work Together

Although we could continue examining instances of Marshall Company norms and behavior for some time, we shall conclude with one more type. As is well known, the typical company is plagued with conflicts between groups within it. The way the Marshall Company social practices

---

[19] E. L. Trist, "Socio-Technical Systems" (London: Tavistock Institute of Human Relations, Doc. No. 572, 1960).

[20] A. K. Rice, "Productivity and Social Organization in an Indian Weaving Shed," *Human Relations*, Vol. VI, No. 4, 1953. See also Eric J. Miller, "Technology, Territory, and Time," *Human Relations*, Vol. XII, No. 3 (1959), pp. 243–272. See also note 7.

deal with this is extremely interesting. First of all, a person develops his own area of competence in the company. No organization chart exists. The real organization of the company is an on-going creation of the members themselves.

People know who in the company is the person in charge of a given interest, for example, the quality of special coated papers, or the purchase of pulp, or customer relations with the printing industry. People grow into these positions as their interests and their developing competence allow, and no two "generations" of management personnel define these positions in quite the same way. That is, a person takes on a bundle of tasks in which he has interest and demonstrates competence.

There are several such people who interact frequently with the paper making crews and the norm of the organization is "When there are no conflicts between values or points of view, then an individual can contact a paper crew directly." No foreman, therefore, is offended when the quality control man lets his presence be known by his familiar red circle around some item on the "spec sheet" which is posted near a machine during any particular run. He knows that a visit has been made and that one or more of his men has likely been spoken to.

When there are interest conflicts in the company, the code is something like this: "Each of us has our special interest in one or another phase of our operation. We all know and respect the legitimacy of these special interests. We cannot force others to relinquish their interests to solve our problems. We must discuss and resolve conflicts with our peers."

An instance of this norm in operation occurred during the research when a machine was making paper too thick for a book publishing customer's specifications. Since paper was scarce, the customer was reluctantly continuing to accept it, but some people at the plant were worried. Two executives—both concerned with aspects of quality—were discussing the problem. They first discussed running the paper on other machines, which could produce it correctly, but discovered that it would create almost insoluble problems for the scheduling office. They then thought of slowing the machine down, but rejected that since it would cut into the bonus of the production people and also because the tonnage for the month for the whole plant was a little behind projections. Next they considered changing the kind of pulp, but rejected that because other customers had already been promised paper requiring that sort of pulp. A decision was reached to let the situation alone for the time being—it was the lesser of several evils.

Notice the extent to which participants in this conversation considered the different legitimate interests in the organization. Is worker morale more important than total customer satisfaction? Is one customer's satisfaction more important than another's? Is better paper on one run worth slowing down production and consequent delivery of other orders, as would happen if machines were changed? These interests are all legitimate, of course, and somehow must be dealt with in any decision. Notice how this particular form of institutionally supported decision making explicitly dealt with intergroup reciprocity, as they discussed the consequences for the different groups of each possible decision.

Is It Good Business?

Because the Marshall Company sounds so unusual, it may well be asked whether such an organization of people also meets the reactive needs of the organization to make money and satisfy stockholders as well as the proactive needs of the organization to change and advance. Concerning the first of these questions, the Marshall Company, some 14 years after the investigation discussed here, had a production growth rate 33 percent higher than the industry, a sales growth rate 30 percent higher, and a net profit to sales ratio 30 percent above the industry average. Return on invested capital compared even more favorably with the rest of the industry. And market value of common stock was up 900 percent a share. Concerning the second question, Marshall was regarded by the foremost supplier of instruments and electronic control devices for paper making as "one of the most progressive firms in the paper industry."

Summary

Thus we can see that the Marshall Company has norms which make legitimate the behavior of its members addressed toward the satisfaction of needs at all levels of affiliation—individual, group, intergroup and total organizational, and not simply needs for proaction, but maintaining, equilibrium seeking, reactive needs as well.

Although space does not permit us to illustrate this further, it can be seen that I would not call any organization healthy which denied the legitimacy of any of these needs; which denied, for example, the needs of individuals to grow at their own pace, or the needs of small group social systems to develop and maintain themselves around tasks. I say around tasks, for without this important socio-technical qualification, such social systems could develop no transactions with their environment, and they would develop only the internal differentiations seen so much in industrial research, betting, restriction of output, gaming, joking, excessive coffee breaks, etc.

Moreover, any organization which was set up only to meet the needs of individuals to grow, or to participate, or to be creative, or what not, and which did not consider the needs of people to form into groups, or of the total organization to engage in satisfactory transactions with outside groups such as stockholders or customers, cannot be considered healthy.

So many scientifically or humanistically oriented critics of large organizations make an unfortunate mistake in regard to this last point which hinders the progress they so earnestly seek. Such critics make the double observation that (1) an organization is different from other social groupings in that it has a formal purpose, and in that its members seek to guide their own behavior rationally to accomplish that purpose and (2) that many organizations plan without knowledge of the needs of their various components. As a result, the critics maintain, we see the much deplored stunted creativity of individuals, the alienation or senseless social behavior of group members, inefficient intergroup competition and so forth.

But these are not necessary outcomes of planful activity. As Gilbert David[21] and Paul R. Lawrence[22] have pointed out, there is nothing humanistically wrong with planning per se. It is planning without awareness of the individual, small group and intergroup reactive and proactive needs that is scientifically and humanistically wrong, to say nothing of inefficient.

As I hope I have been able to demonstrate, one achieves the values of neither humanism nor efficiency if one maintains either value exclusively. It is my personal opinion that our capacity to understand and produce organizational health will develop only to the extent that we bring to it some kind of a multi-dimensional approach. Whether or not the present conception of the multi-dimensionality which is in the world appears fruitful is not important. What is important is that organizational investigators, management theorists, and administrators adopt some point of view large enough to include the other points of view which exist in any situation and which inevitably conflict with each other.

---

4. MOTIVATION AND THE MANAGER

Michael H. Mescon

SINCE THE BEGINNING OF TIME, management and motivation have been inextricably bound together in a complex yet apparently direct relationship. Management, itself, is defined as a process of accomplishing

---

[21] Gilbert David, "Your Organization . . . In Sickness and in Health," Leader's Digest No. 2 (Chicago: Adult Education Association, 1955).

[22] See note 1, Chapter X.

predetermined objectives through the efforts of others and this definition most certainly indicates the necessity of moving people to action. It follows, then, that an objective of today's manager is one of understanding not only his particular role but also of developing those particular skills which will enable him to successfully direct and control the behavior of others. Once more, the emphasis is placed upon moving others to action through meaningful understanding of self and one's employees.

With these comments serving as a point of departure, an attempt will be made to discuss motivation in the realistic and practical setting of organization, recognizing that motivation, to be understood and utilized, must be interpreted in the light of what is, rather than what ought to be.

Motivation and the Efficient Organization

The basic function or objective of the business organization is the realization of a profit. Profit is as important to the business organization as food and water is to the individual. Without food, water, or oxygen the individual cannot survive. Without profit, the business enterprise is doomed. While there is nothing new about this concept, too many in recent years have apparently overlooked its basic logic. F. W. Taylor, the father of scientific management, put it this way: "The basic object of management is to secure maximum prosperity for the employer coupled with maximum prosperity for the employee." In contemporary behavioral science terms, Keith Davis refers to this as the double plus concept, a situation that is mutually beneficial to both the organization and the needs of the individual when successful.

A Word About Individual Differences

To properly motivate employees, positive recognition must be given to the fact that people are different. For example, imagine the shape, the configuration of your organization. Undoubtedly, it is triangular with the rank and file at the bottom or base, and management at the upper levels with ultimate authority *and* responsibility residing with the president at the apex. This functional hierarchy should, and does, in fact, indicate that while all men are created equal, some tend to be more equal than others. (A triusm more eloquently expressed by George Orwell in his "Animal Farm.") For the manager, or whatever you prefer to call those who must move others to action, this implies that a basic requisite to motivating others is the recognition that these individual differences do exist and that people, unlike machine parts, are usually *not* interchangeable.

If employees were all the same, the problems of motivation would be extremely simple since a universal stimulus could be applied to all people in all situations leading to uniform results. Fortunately, this is not the case. It would be a dull existence if it were. Our first step, then, in increasing our motivating skills, is recognizing that people are different and that there is no such thing as a total or complete solution to the manager's job of accomplishing predetermined objectives through the efforts of others.

Motivation: An Early Approach

Robert Owens, a highly successful Scotch textile manufacturer, gave much thought to the matter of motivation. Interestingly enough, Owen's concepts were expressed and implemented 150 years ago with the kind of success that would make many a plant superintendent turn green with envy. Owen was one of the first to recognize that man is more than another factor of production and that his behavior and output are influenced by his psychological and social being and not merely his physical working surroundings. Owen, advocating the importance of profit, also believed strongly that his "living machinery" (or people), should receive as much attention as his "lifeless machines" since such attention to employees might very well bring a "100 percent" return on investment. Putting his scheme of motivation into action, Owen commented that "Never, perhaps, in the history of the human race has so simple a device created in so short a period so much order, virtue, goodness, and happiness, out of so much ignorance, error, and misery." Owen's "miraculous" solution was a simple four-sided piece of wood, with each side colored and suspended near the work place of the employee. Each color represented worker behavior, i.e., black—bad, indifferent—blue, good—yellow, and white—excellent. Recognizing the importance of peer recognition and management recognition, Owen's "silent monitor" motivated employees to do better work which, in turn, helped both Owen and his employees to prosper. While the silent monitor might be completely out of place in contemporary organization, management recognition as a motivating factor is more important than ever.[1]

The Causal Sequence: Key to Understanding Motivation

Norman R. F. Maier explains behavior by using the causal sequence:[2]

Stimulus ⟷ Organism → Behavior → Accomplishment

---

[1] "The Silent Monitor," *The World of Business*, 1962, pp. 1350–1352.

[2] Maier, Norman R. F., "Psychology in Industry," Boston, Houghton Mifflin Company, 1955, p. 21.

The *stimulus* includes light, sound, work routines, supervision, or any aspect of the environment to which an employee is sensitive.

The *organism* or employee represents a composite of hereditary and environmental factors.

The *behavior* would include bodily movements, talking, thinking, emotional responses, etc.

The *accomplishment* indicates actual changes, for example, higher production, fewer errors, etc.

Therefore, in motivating the employee it is essential that a stimulus perceived meaningful *by the employee* be provided if he is to respond in a desired manner. In other words, additional pay for overtime work may not be perceived as a meaningful stimulus to the employee who wants time off to pursue a hobby. Too often, management does not understand that the relationship between the employee and the stimulus is the trigger mechanism that can be the difference between the efficient and the inefficient operation. *Recognizing this, the effective manager makes a concerted attempt to understand what it is that makes his people tick.*

Empathy and Effective Communication

To employ and motivate the "whole" man, it is necessary that the manager develop the ability to empathize with his subordinates, i.e., to put himself in their shoes. While most managers are capable of sympathizing with employees, with expressing sorrow and compassion for them, very few are capable of actually *understanding* them. This understanding is requisite to motivation for without it, the proper stimulus remains an unknown quantity. Further, since motivation takes place through effective or goal attaining communication, and since this communication is dependent upon a proper understanding of individual needs, a very basic relationship becomes apparent.

Motivation: A Case Study

LITHONIA'S INTERVIEWING PROGRAM*

The mammoth business corporation of today often provides little opportunity for individual need satisfaction. The size of these structures when coupled with the application of our galloping technology has all but emasculated the formal work role of the operative employee. Caught in the web of bureaucracy, the average worker often has little opportunity

---

* Mescon, Michael H., "The Lithonia Story," *Atlanta Economic Review*, March, 1959.

to attain from his sterile work role the status, recognition, and security traditionally associated with work. Because of this bureaucratic blocking of worker needs, the informal organization and the union are often turned to as effective vehicles for enhancing both the individual's bargaining position and his feeling of importance.

It can hardly be questioned that the ideal situation in the business organization would be one in which no informal organization existed, assuming that the informal organization arises because worker needs cannot be satisfied within the framework of formal organization. In other words, it is quite possible that employer misunderstanding of employee needs might very well result in the employee's turning to the informal organization or the union for that type of satisfaction which management is unable to provide. It follows, then, that the goals of the formal and informal organization might very well be diametrically opposed—with the result that segmentation, departmental cleavages, and employee unrest become a normal part of the work environment.

Operating from the above hypothesis, the management of Lithonia Lighting became interested in a mass depth-interviewing program structured about the relationship between employee needs and management's understanding of the needs. The role of the author, then, was to structure and conduct interviews with employees from all levels of the organization structure. Included in these interviews were questions pertaining to the employee's understanding of his work role along with ample opportunity to comment, both favorably and unfavorably, about the company, work environment, management, co-workers, etc. The interviewees were told that all of this information would be confidential to the extent that no names would be used by the interviewer in apprising management of the results of this program. The interviews were conducted in the company conference room which is away from any external disturbances. Every attempt was made to keep the interviews as relaxed and unstructured as possible, providing the interviewee with as much opportunity as possible to talk in an unrestricted manner.

The Operative Employee

What is it that the "average" employee wants from work? Common sense tells us that money is the important thing and that, in effect, money and motivation are virtually synonymous. As far as Lithonia Lighting is concerned, this hypothesis appears to be completely out of touch with reality. Of the 114 operative employees who were interviewed, only eleven, less than ten percent, placed financial compensation in the number one position. Far more important, in terms of frequency, were such factors as:

1. Job security
2. Recognition by co-workers
3. Interesting work
4. Fringe benefits
5. Opportunity for advancement

Wages, in terms of total frequency, did not appear in the top five. Neither job security nor opportunity for advancement should necessarily be thought of as indicative of the worker's desire for higher wages. Job security in some instances appeared to be related to the employee's understanding of what was going on in the company rather than any type of guaranteed annual employment.

Of special interest is the fact that recognition by co-workers was of basic concern to the interviewees, more important even than recognition by management. This might very well be indicative of the existence of a rather strong informal organization whose growth could be nurtured by management's misinterpretation of the true nature of worker needs.

The Office Worker

The office worker, who traditionally is more management-oriented than the factory, or "blue collar" worker, placed job security in the number five position and company teamwork in the number one. In all, twenty office workers were interviewed. In the opinion of this segment of the work force, the following factors were of major concern:

1. Company teamwork
2. Interesting work
3. Recognition by co-workers
4. Opportunity for advancement
5. Job security

For office workers, also, the economic aspects of work appear to be relegated to an inferior position. The phenomenon may, in part, be the result of a preponderance of woman office workers who often view work as a transitional period between school and marriage or simply as a means of supplementing the earnings of the family's chief breadwinner. However, even if the above statement were completely valid, it would not explain why wages appear to be of relatively little significance, in terms of frequency, to the male factory workers who were interviewed.

Management's Views

The interview pattern used in connection with members of management was somewhat different from the pattern utilized with office and factory workers. Office and factory workers were asked to rank factors according to their own needs. The thirty management interviewees were asked to rank factors according to the way they thought these factors would be ranked by the people they supervised. Here, financial compensation is ranked one. The complete ranking is as follows:

1. Financial compensation
2. Opportunity for advancement
3. Job security
4. Working conditions
5. Recognition by management

Perhaps one of the basic causes of friction between management and the worker is the gap between worker needs and management's interpretation of these needs. Such a misunderstanding of the nature of what makes the average worker "tick" would quite naturally increase the social distance between these two groups, thereby strengthening feelings of ethnocentrism within each group, with the end result that empathy and understanding are replaced by suspicion and conflict. In this regard, notice that management makes no mention of the importance of recognition by co-workers, while the workers, both factory and office, are much concerned with peer recognition. Working conditions, while ranked number four by management, do not even appear as a factor of importance in terms of factory and office worker needs.

The critical significance of this attitudinal hiatus is well illustrated by the following statement:

> Supervisors who have a great deal of influence within their organizations are usually regarded very favorably by their workers. That's what two University of Michigan researchers found in a study of supervision in a large electronics firm.

> Their explanation for the findings: Supervisors who are influential and who understand what workers need may be in a better position to do something about these needs than those who don't pull much weight in the organization.[3]

It appears quite possible that the popularity of certain supervisors might very well be the result of concerted attempts to find out what it is that their workers desire in terms of job satisfaction.

Understanding of Work Role

One of the major catastrophes that appear to accompany mass production seems to be a lack of pride in work accomplished. With the atomization of labor, the work role of the operative has been debauched in

---

[3] *The Foreman's Letter*, November 17, 1958, published by the National Foreman's Institute, 635 Madison Avenue, New York, N.Y.

the name of technology. People no longer perform whole jobs, but rather segments or atoms of jobs. Certainly, in this type of work environment, which is perhaps inevitable in a society like ours, it is quite difficult to apply the psychologist Allport's concept of the functional autonomy of motives which describes that situation in which a thing that was formerly a means to an end might eventually become an end in itself. Certainly, if work were to become an end in itself, much of the ambivalence in terms of employees' feelings to work in general and their work roles in particular would be replaced by a more positive attitude toward the whole work process.

The lack of real identification with the formal work role was apparent in the employees' rather nebulous notions of what their jobs entailed. Many were not quite certain what they were supposed to do. Some were insecure about their formal work relationships in the organization. Many of those who occupied supervisory positions were almost notorious in their omission of the human element from their work roles. This is especially paradoxical since the process of management is generally conceived of as a process of goal attainment through the efforts of others.

Employee Comments: A Cross-Section

The overwhelming proportion of worker comments, both positive and negative, were structured about the human element, e.g., getting along with others, the quality of supervision, fair treatment, etc. Only a fraction of the total number of comments pertained to working conditions, work load, work hours, or other areas in this "physical working environment" category that management often stresses as being the most important aspect of employer-employee relationships. The following comments should indicate the general tenor of employee attitudes toward the total work environment.

One supervisor who was favorably impressed with top management at Lithonia commented that there was a general lack of teamwork in the organization. Another supervisor remarked: "From my way of thinking . . . it's the best place I ever worked." This same individual also commented that "most everybody is interested in his wage." The interviewee making this comment indicated that this was not necessarily the way he felt, but he was relatively certain that this was the general feeling of those he supervised. One office worker who felt that top management was very considerate also stated, "One person will tell you something to do, and then another person will tell you something to do." Another office worker voiced the same complaint when she complained about the general lack of organization in work routines. Still another member of the office staff remarked that there is a "lack of job security," and that it is "not fair to keep us hanging on a limb." In terms of employee attitudes toward the mass-interviewing program, one male office worker said, "the interview helps me to feel that the company wants to know how I feel." One factory worker who felt that Lithonia Lighting offered him good opportunities for growth and development felt that relations between the company and the union could be better. Another factory worker stated, "The supervisor tried to be good but doesn't want you to take the responsibility."

In reference to his relationships with his supervisor, one man commented, "The boss is good to you, ain't always hollering at you." Another employee felt that there are "too many men telling us what to do." A tool and die maker indicated that he felt that good teamwork existed in the organization. One high school graduate who was not completely certain what his job was felt that duties and responsibilities should be fixed. One welder who liked the friendly work atmosphere indicated that the supervisors could do a better job of handling employee mistakes. A woman, who liked her job otherwise, remarked that her supervisor "shows partiality between girls." Another woman, who worked in the same department as the above-quoted interviewee, commented, "I really don't enjoy my work." She also remarked that too much partiality was shown by her supervisor. One painter felt that the foreman should be friendlier and more understanding. One supervisor who particularly liked her work felt that there was a lack of teamwork within the organization.

In providing a general overall summary of employee comments, the following observations appear valid:

1. The majority of employees feel that Lithonia Lighting has a bright future and that it is a good place to work.
2. Much employee criticism centered about what was considered to be poor supervision at the lowest level of the supervisory hierarchy.
3. There were relatively few complaints about physical working conditions.

Comments on Employee Comments

An analysis of the result of the mass-interviewing program seems to indicate a need for a thorough reappraisal of some of management's pet stereotypes. These stereotypes are certainly not indigenous to Lithonia, but appear to be native to many business organizations. Unfortunately, many companies are not as interested as is Lithonia Lighting in the problem of how to create a truly positive work climate; and as a partial consequence of this apathy, many stereotypes tend to be nurtured and perpetuated. For example, management, in many instances, thinks of employee satisfaction in terms of high wages and good working conditions. Certainly the significance of wages is recognized as being a vehicle for the satisfaction of certain basic human needs. Good physical working conditions are also helpful, but not necessarily essential in the creation of a positive working climate. This opinion is fairly commonly recognized by those who have been performing research in the area of worker motivation. Yet, management, in many instances, does not appear to want to be confused by the fact. Facts, it seems, tend to disturb the status quo, which, in turn, would probably lead to necessary revisions in attitudes and behavior, but more especially in behavior. One thing appears evident. The quality of employer-employee relationships is contingent upon management's understanding of the personality of the various segments of its work force. Generalizations, spurious principles of management, and judgments based on an "I know what the workers want" framework lead to chaos and conflict.

In Summary

While motivating the operative worker is essential to efficient organization, it poses no problems that are truly peculiar to this group. The real key to motivation rests with a management firmly convinced that it will have first-class, highly-trained supervisors who will put aside hunches, stereotypes, experience, and intuition when these prove fruitless, and will substitute for these a desire and ability to develop deep insights into the nature of human nature.

D. FURTHER POLICY ASPECTS

1. THE IMPACT OF CORPORATE POLICY ON CASH FLOW*

Arthur B. Toan, Jr.

MOST CORPORATE FINANCIAL OFFICERS OF our generation have been forced to live so long with the never-ending appetites for cash which inflation, growth and the changing pattern of buyer-seller relations have forced upon their companies that they have come to regard cash problems as the normal state of affairs.

Financial officers, with a strong assist from banks and other financial institutions, have learned a lot about how to make the most of what cash they do have—through better cash planning and through utilizing devices for more rapidly mobilizing funds. They have learned to raise money from old and new sources of funds, to use both old and new (often ingenious) financing techniques and, by and large, to walk that tightrope which balances safety and realism with urgent corporate needs.

They have, with significant exceptions, not done quite so well in recognizing the enormous potential for cash generation and conservation which lies in an examination of corporate policies themselves—an examination which aims (1) to see how policies affect demands for cash, and (2) to see how policies can, if need be, be altered to make the best use of what cash we have, and (3) to convince other corporate executives that this is an important thing to do.

Corporate policies, it is agreed, should not rise or fall solely or even primarily on the basis of their impact on cash. The purpose of corporate

* From *The Financial Executive,* Vol. 31, No. 11, November, 1963, pp. 13–15, 19. Reprinted with permission of the publisher.

policy is to make the corporation a vital, viable enterprise—not to facilitate the management of bank accounts. This does not mean that the implications of corporate policy in terms of cash flow should be or even can be ignored. There are too many ways to accomplish substantially similar results to have this make sense. More important, however, is the fact that available cash is, in many enterprises, a major factor limiting what the corporation can actually do. Most important of all, imprudent corporate policies leading to imprudent cash management can damage or destroy the company itself.

Take these few corporate policies—by no means all and perhaps not even the most important ones—and see how they influence the flow and supply of cash. As you think about them—and others of equal or greater importance in your own company—you will see:

1. That the relationship between corporate policy and cash is direct and strong—perhaps even stronger and more direct than you have suspected in the past, and
2. That many a corporate policy, which admittedly has as its primary purpose establishing the nature and operational effectiveness of the company itself, also has such important secondary implications in terms of cash that they must be taken into account; and
3. That the financial officer's voice should constantly be heard, raising a question, establishing a cash philosophy, striking a balance and above all not just saying "no" but giving a choice.

Now, let us look at some examples and see what they reveal.

Use of Cash as an Aid to Sales

We can accept the fact that, in the modern business world, most business transactions do not take place for cash. It is inevitable, therefore, that some portion of a corporation's cash resources will be committed to sales which have been made but not yet paid for in full. While some minimum commitment of cash (we call it "extension of credit") is inevitable, the actual level of credit extended by most companies quite definitely is not preordained. It is in large part the result of a conscious choice made as to the extent to which the company can or wishes to use its cash as an aid to sales.

Credit terms, as those of you who have had experience in foreign trade will readily attest, often have as much as price to do with who makes the sale abroad. Credit is often a major factor in deciding who gets the sale at home too, whether a business customer or an individual is involved. The increase in credit (with all its varieties and types) is in fact one of the main characteristics of the changing buyer/seller relationship.

The extension of credit takes money, involves expense, involves risk and may require that higher prices be charged, but also under the proper circumstances favorable credit terms will provide an important competitive advantage to those who have goods to sell.

A corporation's credit policy (at the same time that it is an aid or deterrent to sales) quite clearly also affects its flow of cash. A company can shift to credit, sales formerly made for cash. It can choose to extend credit in varying degrees for varying amounts of time. It can so conduct its business as to grant credit in minimum, moderate or maximum amounts. It can itself extend the credit and thus itself advance the cash. It can arrange with other financial institutions to carry the paper, with or without recourse. It can go into the financing business with a separate financing subsidiary, supply the funds and earn for itself the financing results. It can decide to lease rather than sell. It can provide no financial help at all, and expect its customer to take necessary steps to acquire the funds. It may sell for cash and cut the price.

Each of these approaches sets up a different flow of cash—a flow which can differ from days to weeks to months to years. Obviously, corporate policy with regard to credit cannot even in a cash-short company be made on the basis of the wishes of the finance department alone, since the sales results of the company are so heavily involved. Neither, however, should sales hopes and expectancies alone be able to set financial policy where such important sums and risks are at stake. The financial officer should try to make his influence felt to ensure that a sound and proper balance does exist.

Inventories

Another aspect of the buyer/seller relationship whose impact is clearly visible to the cash-short financial executive involves the questions—"Do I carry your inventory? Do you carry mine?" Buyers, trying to minimize their requirements for cash yet making sure they keep the plant supplied with materials and parts or their store supplied with goods, have one point of view. Sellers, caught between keeping customers happy and optimizing the flow of cash, to a large extent have the opposite. Since most companies both buy and sell, the same company will often unconcernedly express both points of view—each in its proper place.

Even within the same company, these points of view are given unequal weight. Purchasing agents and plant managers are more concerned about the adequacy of inventories to run their plants than upon the effect on cash; sellers worry more about customer desires and needs. If the financial man, stressing cash and the viewpoint of finance, does not raise his voice, to expect that inventory policies will properly balance needs, risks and cash will probably be too much to ask.

Product Line

Credit and inventories are rather obvious illustrations of corporate policies which affect the flow of cash. For our next example let us move somewhat farther afield and consider the range of the product line itself. Should the range of products which a company makes and sells be wide or narrow, in terms of its customers' needs? Should it restrict the product line to a relatively few fast-moving items, expand it to include those which move with moderate speed or provide a full and complete line? Since companies in the same or similar industries or in essentially similar situations have reached conclusions which bear no similarity to each other, it is obvious that questions of corporate policy, not just the facts of business life, must be deeply involved.

While product line might be viewed almost entirely as a marketing problem, it has important implications for cash as well. It has been found, for example, on a large number of occasions when a wide range of products is provided, that very close to 20 percent of the items represent very close to 80 percent of the business. The converse of this—that some 80 percent of the products provide only 20 percent of the business—means almost certainly a slowing down in the utilization of cash when the product line is full. For the 80 percent of the items, turnover of inventory will be lower; the commitment in fixed assets, higher; cash generation will be slowed.

A corporate policy giving little or no weight to the cash implications of a broad product line could easily conclude that, for its marketing value alone, breadth was a highly desirable thing for which to strive. A financial man, thinking of the impact on investment return, can influence this policy to at least some degree. He can show that the slower-moving items, which make up the greater portion of the broad product line, should either bear a price commensurate with the slowness with which cash resources are used, or that the faster-moving items should bear a share of the cost of the fuller line which they require for support, or that a mixture of both approaches should be used. The influence of the financial man may, on the other hand, lead the marketing and general corporate executives to conclude, as they have on many occasions, that the full range of products is not so important after all.

Standardization of Design

A corporate policy or lack thereof with respect to the standardization of product design might seem to be of little or no moment as far as the financial officer's cash requirements are concerned. Such is quite definitely not the case. When product designers, as in some companies I have seen, seem to design every product, model and submodel as though they had just invented it and it were the first of its kind which had ever been produced, the impact on cash is direct and felt for many years to come. Just as the full range of end products involves inventories and fixed assets to support limited volumes of sales, so does the use of the full range of materials and parts involve higher commitments in inventories, more space in which these materials must be stored, more engineering drawings and blueprints galore, additional tools, molds, jigs and dies, and larger inventories of spare parts for a long time ahead.

The commitments made in the design stage, when the freedom to innovate is complete, not only produce immediate problems but leave a residue for years ahead. These effects are felt not just in the plant in the form of operating problems but in the cash balance which is available for general corporate use. Many of these commitments can, as has been demonstrated time and time again, be avoided by a corporate policy which emphasizes standardization and provides lists of preferred or standard parts.

I have yet to meet the engineering department in which standardization has been intelligently administered, which has successfully claimed that its design capabilities were on balance hampered in any significant respect. As a matter of fact, most will state that the use of standard materials has probably saved them from making so many mistakes that they are certain they are ahead.

The commitment of cash, and the variations which can result, should therefore give the financial officer a real interest in corporate policy in the field of product design.

Make or Buy

"Make or buy" has come to serve as an apt handle for a whole set of decisions or policies involving both profits and the use of cash. Fundamentally, it has come to describe the series of situations in which a corporation decides (1) whether to manufacture or buy a part or (2) whether to rent or purchase or itself to provide a service, a facility, a capability. Secondarily, it has come to describe a series of situations involving how to use the company's cash.

"To make" quite obviously requires more in the way of cash than "to buy" in almost every case. Profitability determinations, using the return-on-investment technique, are quite often employed to influence the choice. So, too, do such factors as continuity of need, available capacity, technical know-how and the choice of the kind of business we want to be in. So do additional matters of corporate policy and choice such as are indicated by questions like these:

1. Would the purchase of the part of the service require that corporate secrets or capabilities be revealed?
2. Is quality so important that manufacture should not be entrusted to others?
3. Would manufacture of the part or provision of the service have important implications for research or for future products, which the company wishes to retain for itself?
4. Can others meet the corporate demands for speed and availability?

Or, to take the opposite point of view, are all the foregoing—corporate secrets, quality requirements, research implications, availability on demand —merely figments of the imagination or signs of vanity which should take second place to the corporate need for cash?

The financial officer has an important role to play in determining when to make or when to buy—in making other executives aware of the nature of the choice, of the many times when a choice can be made, and of the commitment of cash for a period of time which the to-make choice normally entails.

There is a second face to make-or-buy situations which for some reason many do not see without the financial officer's prodding, too. This face has essentially to do with time. Let me illustrate:

Should we, in order to diversify or expand, buy what someone else has developed, full blown and ready to yield a return, or should we invest the funds and energy needed for the period of time required to develop new products for ourselves?

The implications of these two approaches in terms of risk of failure or success are quite clear. For some reason, the implications in terms of cash often seem not to be. The process of developing a product often re-quires a period of years in which we must spend cash on R & D, on initial production runs, on test marketing, on plant, on inventories, on advertising before we can expect the flow of cash to reverse.

This is an entirely different situation from that which exists when we obtain a product, new or old, proven and ready to market, by corporate merger or purchase, by royalty or license or by some other means. Differ-ences in risk and potential profit can obviously exist. Differences in the flow of substantial amounts of cash almost surely will vary by a period of years.

Corporate policy, looked at from the standpoint of both product line and cash, should reflect not only the need for products but also the total requirements for funds and the amounts and kinds of financing which are appropriate in terms of the timespan, potential profits and risk involved.

Scope of Business

Let us now move even further afield and consider corporate policy as it defines the scope of activities of the company itself. A financial officer can probably make or "lose" more cash from a redetermination of scope than from any other single type of policy change.

Let me use the gasoline business to illustrate. Supplying gasoline to the ultimate consumer is a long, complex and costly process in which exploration, drilling, production, refining, transportation, wholesale and retail marketing and substantial sums of money are involved. Each of these processes involves different risks and skills, has different rewards—and requires different kinds and amounts of money.

There are companies in this business which perform every one of these functions and some which perform one or two or three. There are large companies which perform all functions and large companies which perform only one; there are small companies which perform more of the functions than you would suspect and companies, considered in the oil business to be of intermediate size, which are integrated from beginning to end. Perhaps, more interesting still, there are companies which at various times in their corporate lives have performed both wider and narrower ranges of work.

There are many reasons why oil companies choose different scopes of activities for themselves—the interests and capabilities of the managing and owning groups, marketing strategies, control of adequate supplies of crude, even historical accidents—are only a few.

Cash is also highly significant, for policy determinations of this type obviously change the need for cash. The outgo and intake from an investment in retailing and wholesaling gasoline bears about as little relation to the ebb and flow of cash in oil production as it does to an investment in an oil refinery. If there is or can be enough cash for all—fine; if there is not, and there usually will not be, the financial officer has a real job to do in helping to establish not only an appropriate scope but also the timing by which corporate plans are to be carried out.

What is true about the oil industry is, of course, true about many other businesses as well. Extraction, manufacture, wholesaling, retailing and service all have their own cash patterns and the decision as to whether or how to participate in them is a major determinant of the flow of cash. In setting or resetting "scope of business" policies, the financial officer's voice should clearly be heard. It is surprising how often this is not the case.

Corporate Personality

To conclude this series of examples, I should like to lump together a number of corporate policies which in some ways are the most "far out" of all for they are concerned essentially with shaping the basic character and personality of the company itself. Taken together, they do have an enormous impact on the flow of cash. Let me cite a few:

1. Do we wish to be an innovator, to spend heavily for the rich gains of an occasional success, or do we wish to be more conservative, satisfied with a margin that is relatively smaller but safe and sure?
2. Do we wish to sell only at home or to venture abroad?
3. Do we wish to promote and advertise heavily, or sell relatively anonymously based on price?
4. Do we wish to emphasize human relations, to restrict or invest heavily in automation, to adopt inventory policies leading to a stabilization of the working force?
5. Are we in business mostly for money, or for excitement, professional attainment, social purposes, patriotic ends?
6. Do we wish to set the size and shape of the company in terms of the abilities of ourselves, our relatives and our friends to manage the enterprise? Do we wish to merge with partners whom we may supplant or who may supplant us in our jobs?
7. Do we wish to limit sources of capital to those which the present owners can supply? To what extent do we wish to permit new owners (and what kind of owners) into the group? How much and what kinds of debt, leases, guarantees are we as owners willing to have the company assume in order to meet the enterprise's needs? Or stated in reverse, is it corporate policy to shape the enterprise to fit the flow of cash, to shape the cash to meet a full-blown view of corporate needs, or is it corporate policy to fall some place in between?

In dealing with these questions, and others which they suggest, the financial officer is dealing in large part with the personalities of the owners and managers themselves. This direct contact which is both significant and frequent when companies are small, does not really cease as companies grow in size. If individual or corporate personalities came already matched with the size of corporate bank accounts, life would be simpler than it is. In the world of reality, the financial officer has a major contribution to make in bringing this match of personality and cash about—in suggesting alternative means, in timing significant change and in getting the cash which the company requires.

Summary

By now, I imagine, it is abundantly clear that one could conduct a veritable filibuster just giving examples of corporate policies which affect the flow of cash. That this is so is due to one fundamental truth—corporate policies and cash flow have the classical relationship of cause and effect. It is not a simple relationship, or a direct one always; certainly it is not one in which "cash" is always the most important factor—either as a cause or as an effect. Nevertheless, the all-pervasive influence is there.

The 6" x 12" signs which proclaim "There's no reason; it's just company policy" will be in no jeopardy of being inappropriate as long as humans exist. As financial executives, with an important voice in corporate affairs, we can make these signs seem a little out of place when it comes to cash.

This is worth doing!

---

2. MAKING MARKETING RESEARCH MORE EFFECTIVE BY USING THE ADMINISTRATIVE PROCESS*

Harper W. Boyd, Jr. and Steuart Henderson Britt

TOO OFTEN MARKETING RESEARCH DEALS only with fragments of a problem; but this may be due to a tendency by both management executives and research executives to view the decision-making process too narrowly.

Decision-making in business is a continuing process, and only well-designed and executed research can help decision-makers in solving problems. While the marketing researcher can and should be creative in designing studies, usually it is not his function also to be creative in the formulation of the goals and strategies of the enterprise.

It is, however, his function to be well versed in new and important concepts pertaining to decision theory, which are coming from the be-

---

* From the *Journal of Marketing Research*, Vol. II, No. 1, February, 1965, pp. 13–19. Reprinted with permission from the publisher.

havioral sciences, as well as from higher mathematics. These interdisciplinary movements are gaining momentum in the "new age of 'intellectronics' which features the combined use of the intellect of man and the 'intellect' of the computer [14]."

Since the primary role of the researcher is one of providing valid information which management can and should use in its decision-making activities, how can the research function be performed most effectively? It is too easy to say that improvement will come only when management specifies what kinds of information are needed. This is not the answer.

Instead, the answer is that researchers *and* decision-makers must strive to interact in such a way as to make explicit the use to which research information will be put. This interacting can best be accomplished through the use of the *administrative process* which consists of (1) *setting objectives;* (2) *developing the plans to achieve these objectives;* (3) *organizing to put these plans into action;* and (4) *controlling and reappraising the program that has been carried out,* in order to determine whether or not the objectives, the plans, and the organization are functioning properly.

Decision-Making and the Administrative Process

The researcher must participate in the formulation of problems, as well as contribute to effective action. Research which divorces itself from action "dies within its own solid covers, too remote or detached to influence the rapidly moving stream of events. Research which disavows any responsibility except that of being objective and nonutilitarian will qualify as 'pure.' But it is a kind of purity which a society—particularly a society in an age of change—can overvalue [2]."

Perhaps if we look closely at the anatomy of a decision we can see how the researcher can not only aid in the formulation of a problem but can also gain valuable insights into the extent to which a solution will contribute to the firm's welfare. Determining the worth of a solution is critical because it indicates to the researcher how he should proceed to build his research design.

ANATOMY OF A DECISION

Decisions are made *only* because decision-makers want to achieve something and have certain goals or objectives. Without understanding these goals, both the researcher and the decision-maker cannot proceed. The problem, however formulated, is not solvable.

Too rarely, however, does the researcher receive a clearcut statement of the objectives. The decision-maker seldom formulates his objectives accurately. He is likely to state his objectives in the form of platitudes which have no operational significance. Consequently, objectives usually have to be extracted by the researcher. In so doing, the researcher may well be performing his most useful service to the decision-maker [2]. Frequently, the researcher will find that the goal reveals the problem to be quite different than initially conceived. Given an understanding of the goal, the decision-maker and the researcher can then evaluate the environment within which the decision-maker operates. Such a procedure will reveal a great deal about the resources commanded by the decision-maker. Knowledge of these resources facilitates the establishment of realistic courses of action. If resources are not available to implement a given course of action, it makes little sense to consider it seriously. Moreover, the researcher may well find out that the implementation of the various courses of action involves other higher executives who need to be consulted before research can be undertaken.

Many marketing problems are more than mere marketing problems. It may not be possible to confine them to just the marketing department. As Peter Drucker has said, marketing

> . . . is the whole business seen from the point of view of its final result, that is, from the consumer's point of view. Concern and responsibility for marketing must therefore permeate all areas of the enterprise [6].

Most problems of any consequence tend to cut across functional lines; any attempt to solve them on a piecemeal basis will often prove unsuccessful or even disastrous. In fact, the solution of a problem in one area may cause a new but related problem to spring up elsewhere. For example: A large manufacturer of consumer goods recently altered its distribution system. The change to franchise dealers and direct selling was accompanied by the decision that the company would absorb more of the stock-carrying function. This decision was made only after considerable marketing research was done on the subject. Six months later this old, well-financed company suffered a severe cash-flow problem. A detailed investigation of this situation indicated that the change in distribution was responsible. Furthermore, and more important, the conclusion was reached that this shift was ill-advised and destined to fail because it was incompatible with the long-run objectives of the company, which were ultimately to produce a variety of related items appealing to different market segments.

In the above illustration, there were two difficulties: First, the decision to effect a change in the functional area was made without considering its impact on another area; second, and equally important, the decision was made with reference to a higher-order prior decision, which was designed to guide the activities of *all* parts of the firm. The decision was made out of context.

Had the research director probed deeply enough and long enough with the various decision-makers involved, he might have been successful in understanding the totality of the problem and thereby helped the other executives to avoid the costly mistake which was made.

THE ADMINISTRATIVE PROCESS

One possible way to ensure that a problem is properly dissected is to focus on the *administrative process* in some detail. In this process, which consists of a series of interlocking steps, no one step can be considered independently. The four steps flow together to form a totality, an overall program [19].

The process is not only useful in visualizing and understanding the activities of management but also in diagnosing problems through the establishment of a basic framework. This framework, which might at first appear to be relatively simple, is complicated by the division of each of the four major steps into a number of parts.

Moreover, the framework typically features several layers, namely, processes within processes. Top management, for example, will set major policies having to do with each step; in turn, each department will operate within these policies by establishing its own *objectives, plans, organizations,* and *control-and-reappraisal systems.*

Research conducted on problems having to do with "the plan" runs the risk of being ineffective unless both the researcher and the decision-maker agree that the problem is not one having to do with the objectives of the firm. If the objectives present difficulties, research in the plan's area usually will not be very helpful. Likewise, it will do little good to focus attention on the organization if the plan is in error.

An illustration of how the use of the administrative process assisted a researcher and a decision-maker to avoid inappropriate research is given below:

> One of the authors was consulted by a company about a problem having to do with its field force. As initially conceived, the problem centered on the declining productivity of the average salesman. Intensive study finally revealed, however, that the fault was not with the sales force but with that part of the plan which specified what dealers should be contacted, how frequently contacts were to be made, and what the salesman was to do on each call. This, in turn, hinged on the company's objectives relative to market segments and the use of certain kinds of dealers (typically small volume) to reach *all* segments.

The value of the administrative process in this respect, as well as in diagnosing problems, can best be demonstrated by discussing each of the steps in the process and the kinds of marketing information needed to implement each.

Setting Objectives

The essential objective of a business firm is to make profits. A company also has basic responsibilities to its stockholders, the community or communities in which it lives, its employees, and its customers. Although management may think of the firm's primary objectives in terms of specific products or services, a more useful approach is to think of the firm's objectives as being rooted in the market.

More precisely, the objectives must be articulated in terms of how certain wants and needs of a segment of consumers can be satisfied. Unless objectives of this sort are set forth in specific terms, it is difficult to devise a meaningful plan of action. Too frequently, however, because of lack of specificity in its customer orientation, management is involved in vague, over-generalized definitions of consumer groups. This results in poor coordination of the plans for research and development, products and product lines, pricing, advertising, physical distribution points, personal selling, and channels of distribution.

In an effort to locate specific marketing-oriented objectives, one of the authors contacted over 100 large American corporations. Only three of the 60 replies contained well-defined statements dealing with corporate objectives. Instead, such high-sounding statements as "to be the best in the industry," "to serve the common good," "to serve in the best interests of our stockholders," and "to exercise integrity in our dealings" were common.

It seems clear that too few firms have used research to help them to specify their objectives on the wants and needs of the parts of the market they wish to satisfy. Without such a statement how can the researcher and the decision-maker understand problems associated with the basic strategy mix of the firm? Lack of objectives makes it all too easy for executives to disagree over the existence of a problem, as well as the alternative courses of action. The reason for this disagreement may not even be understood. In such an environment, it is literally impossible for the researcher to operate effectively, since his research findings and recommendations although valid to one executive, may be deemed worthless and even irresponsible to another.

Failure to set objectives makes it impossible to change objectives in a rational way. There is no base point which can be monitored through research to detect the need for change. If the research executive and the officers of the firm undertook research of a specific nature to obtain data upon which decisions relating to objectives could be made, the first step in the administrative process would then have a real chance of being completed successfully. If this could be done, the chances of accomplishing the second step in the process—the plan of action—would be enhanced substantially. Given an opportunity to participate in the continuous process of setting objectives, the value of the research executive would be increased tremendously, because both he and the decision-maker would have a point of reference in their discussion of problems.

The setting of objectives cannot be accomplished with any high probability of success, unless the researcher can furnish data on the following:

1. What "generic uses" the firm wishes to satisfy.
2. What other products or services are likely to be substituted for the firm's products or services, or are used with those of the firm to satisfy these end uses.
3. What market segments exist and their relative importance, both present and future.
4. The ability of the firm to meet the wants and needs of the individual segments relative to the abilities of present and potential competitors.
5. A selection of the segments to be served.
6. An estimate of the share of sales the firm probably can capture over a given period of time.

Unless the research executive and the other executives perceive the interlocking nature of the above listed specifics and interact in such a way as to undertake the necessary research, it is not likely that the firm will operate at peak efficiency.

GENERIC USE

Generic use relates to the satisfaction of relatively general wants whose gratification is not too critical for most American consumers. It is a truism that basic needs do not change, but that ways of satisfying these needs do. Thus, it is essential for the firm to use marketing research in studying the relationships between basic needs and wants and generic use; it is also important to plot the changing cultural, social, and psychological situations and what these changes imply for strategies of advertising, selling, pricing, and channels of distribution. Because our society is one of change, research into the social and cultural scene should be a continuing process.

This means that the researcher should help the other executives to perceive objectives in terms of consumer satisfactions, rather than simply hold to the more traditional point of view of emphasis on products. Companies do sell products, but even more important they sell the *functions* that these products perform. This point of view, as conceptualized by one researcher, helped his company to improve its understanding of its basic mission. He pointed out that the company's product—a ball-point pen—should be perceived as a writing instrument which relates to an intimate form of personal expression. While the product was a physical object with specific attributes, it had to be manufactured and sold on the basis of how it facilitated or helped to accomplish certain forms of expression.

CONSUMPTION SYSTEMS

The next step in the process of setting objectives is to determine what other products and services are likely to be substituted for those of the firm, or are used along with those of the firm to satisfy end uses [3]. The researcher can make a contribution at this stage in the setting of objectives. Few executives think in terms of such systems and consequently have a framework for evaluating new product ideas, product changes, and advertising copy. Awareness of the existence of such systems should enable the researcher to query the decision-maker, when they are discussing product and advertising copy problems, regarding his assumptions about the system into which the product fits.

A consumption system is a series of steps which incorporate the use of one or more products plus various actions by one or more consumers relative to solving a given problem. Thus, bed-making, bill-paying, food preparation, window-washing, car operation, floor-cleaning, vacation trips, excursions, shopping, and recreational activities are examples of consumption systems common to most households.

The idea of problem-solving or goal-directedness is essential. An understanding of the goals and standards set by consumers, and the degree to which these goals and standards are satisfactorily achieved, is essential to an understanding of the consumption system. Consumers are likely to think of a product in terms of functions or benefits, for example, the suds generated by a detergent, the lightness of a cake mix, the ease of closing an automobile door. Manufacturers, on the other hand, are likely to think in terms of ingredients, design, and manufacturing processes [15].

Frequently more than one goal is involved. For example, ownership of a car involves not just the goal of transportation but, typically, security and status as well. Housewives cook meals to provide their families with nourishment, but also to demonstrate love and approval. Knowledge of the steps involved enables a seller more readily to assess his opportunities for innovation. After all, most innovations are, in reality, achieved by re-arranging and integrating the steps in a given system. Only rarely is the system replaced [13].

Examples of such innovations include self-polishing wax, contour sheets, remote-control television sets, completely automatic cameras (built-in light meters and range-finders), electric windows, push-button window washers in cars, butane lighters, cartridge refills for fountain pens, drip-dry clothing, detergents with bluing and softeners added, and timers on electrical appliances.

There are additional steps involved in setting objectives. More specifically, determination of segments; evaluation of the ability of the firm to meet the needs and wants of the alternative segments; and a selection of the target segments require marketing information in considerable amounts and on a continuing basis. Certainly, further elaboration is not needed here [5, 8, 12].

Development of Plans to Achieve Objectives

Once the executives of a firm have articulated their objectives, preferably *in writing,* they are in a position to develop a plan of action, but not before this. Any plan must of necessity deal primarily with marketing strategies, including: product, product line, packaging, pricing, discounts and dealer margins, channels of distribution, and sales and promotion activities. Essentially, a plan is a specification of the ways by which the firm intends to attain its objectives for a stated time period.

Every plan depends upon a thorough understanding of where the company is at the present, that is, an assessment of its present market position. To know where the company is requires not only an audit of present resources but, more explicitly, an evaluation of the worth of these resources in action, or what they have accomplished as seen through the eyes of consumers. Too frequently, market share is used as an indication of managerial performance in lieu of a detailed assessment of all resources of the firm.

If the researcher and the decision-maker do not have an up-to-date picture of the company's position in the marketplace, it will be difficult to assess the magnitude of a problem, but also to devise corrective action. An analogy would be a military commander who had to develop basic strategy without knowing precisely where his troops were and what the enemy was doing.

A PAY-OFF MATRIX

In developing a plan, management is faced with the problem of fitting together certain strategies that are compatible with one another. Management must consider various ways of accomplishing the objectives, and this requires an evaluation of the inputs and outputs. Increasing use should be made of a "pay-off matrix," which requires decision-makers to state the possible consequences that might be derived from the acceptance of a proposed course of action. Possible results can be made meaningful by assigning values to their possible occurrence. And these values, coupled with the probability of the reactions occurring, can provide meaningful guides for making useful decisions.

Decision theory is a powerful tool which the researcher may use to force a formalization of the intuitive process of choosing among various possibilities. "While this may not improve the judgment of the individual decision-maker, it improves his communication with others and facilitates the collection and analysis of further information [4]." Thus, the pay-off matrix provides a way for the researcher and the decision-maker to assess risks and to determine what marketing information would be most helpful.

It is of particular value in structuring the need for research, because it shows in relatively precise form what assumptions are critical. Too frequently, research is carried out which has little effect on the key assumptions. A matrix can target the research effort by showing what information is needed to reduce the probability of making the wrong decision, or to increase the probability of adopting the right decision.

An example will illustrate how research can help the management decision-maker. A manufacturer of small appliances was faced with the problem of deciding what to do as a result of a competitor's reduction of the price of a $30 retail list item by $10 when a trade-in was made. Initially, the company considered the following alternative courses of action: (1) wait and see whether other competitors would take action; (2) cut the retail price of its item by $10 with no trade-in required; (3) cut the retail price of its item by $10 with a trade-in; (4) cut the retail price of its item by $12 with no trade-in; and (5) effect a trade-loading deal which would increase retail margins by one-third, assuming no reduction in retail price.

The marketing researcher suggested an investigation among leading dealers and, as a result of this study, the company learned that the action taken by the competitor had reduced company sales by better than 50 percent. It was also found that dealers were already overstocked with the item as a result of loading up to take advantage of the special deal. Because of this information, the company reduced its alternative courses of action to numbers (2), (3), and (4).

The possible consequences of matching the competitor's deal were then stated as follows:

POSSIBLE CONSEQUENCES	PROBABILITY OF OCCURRING	WORTH IN TERMS OF COMPANY PRE-TAX PROFITS
1. Competitor continues, and no other companies follow	.50	$275,000
2. One major competitor follows price cutter	.30	275,000
3. All major manufacturers follow	.20	425,000

The probabilities assigned to consequences 2 and 3 above were based on assumptions regarding the dealers' and distributors' inventory of the item in question, as well as the inventory at the manufacturer's level. Research revealed that, while retailer and distributor stocks were unusually high, the competitor had recently refused to accept orders at the old price. This information changed the probabilities assigned to the possible consequences. Ultimately, the above inventory research data were instrumental in leading to the decision in favor of a temporary matching offer.

EXPERIMENTATION

The administrative process should facilitate experimentation in marketing, because it draws together the researcher and the decision-maker and, in the process of their interaction, makes explicit how little is known regarding the relation between certain inputs and outputs. This lack of knowledge is most in evidence when a plan of action is being constructed. If a set of strategies is conceptualized as a product which can take many different forms, it makes special sense for the researcher and the decision-maker to think of marketing research in terms of a Research and Development function. The amount of money involved in implementing marketing plans, as well as the implied risks, should warrant the expenditure of sizeable amounts of money for marketing R & D; to be effective, such work should be carried out on a continuing basis.

However, "marketing seldom receives the active and continuous experimental support that all other corporate functions are so abundantly getting. All it gets is money for more advertising and 'sales push' [11]." It is difficult to name specific firms with the marketing equivalents of their R & D departments, yet:

> Almost 50 cents of each dollar the American consumer spends for goods goes for activities that occur after the goods are made, that is, after they have come in finished form off 'the dry end of the machine,' to use the papermaker's graphic term. This is distribution, one of the most sadly neglected, most promising areas of American business [7].

The idea of experimentation has always been an important one to business executives, *except* in marketing. Yet the techniques and advantages of experimentation are well known to more sophisticated marketing research practitioners, many of whom have been trained in the social sciences.

Marketing offers abundant opportunities for the use of various experimental designs, for example, in the area of advertising. There is a great need to know more about the number of times a given message should be communicated over a given period of time to gain maximum effectiveness; the degree to which mass media serve to reinforce existing conditions; the effects of the status of the communicator on the acceptance and retention of the message; the desirable conditions for presenting both sides of an argument for use of a product; and the degree to which "scare" advertising really works. These are but a few examples dealing with areas of decision-making in advertising about which little is known [10].

In personal selling, there is the question of how frequently a salesman should call, as well as whether the same salesman can service old accounts and also open new accounts, and the impact of different compensation plans on productivity [9, 18]. With regard to price elasticity, little is known about either the short-run or long-run effects of various promotional price offers. As to channels of distribution, there is a real need to learn more about programs for different types of accounts, including what special functions to perform.

The trends toward giant retailing, the growth of leased departments, the diminishing role of the salesman, the possible era of store brands, and the factory-financed inventory should be studied and evaluated by the seller of consumer goods [20]. It is difficult to believe that management can do an effective job of planning without extensive use of the marketing research function. Certainly, experimentation should be an essential part of the research program which feeds into the planning process.

Organization for Putting Plan into Action

Little is known about the ways in which an organization reacts to marketing intelligence, or about the specific ways in which the organization and operation of a department, such as marketing or R & D, tends to function in the presence of an adequate flow of information.

Traditionally, marketing research has had its greatest usefulness in connection with the organization of the sales function. This includes the development of information as to the number and size of sales territories; establishment of quotas by individual items in the product line; setting of quotas by key accounts; and analysis of the duties of salesmen, including what outlets to call on, frequency of call, services to perform, and what sales appeals to use.

Of course, marketing research has contributed directly to the efficiency of other parts of the firm. For example, it is difficult to conceive of an effective R & D function without some "targeting" by marketing research, as well as a continuing check on whether seeming progress is *really* effective in the eyes of customers. Yet surprisingly large numbers of R & D departments do not even know the strengths and weaknesses of present company products [16].

Controlling and Reappraising the Program

Control and reappraisal represent two steps that form the bridge between completing the administrative process and starting the process anew. In other words, controlling and reappraising the program apply to all the previous steps in the administrative process, namely, *setting objectives, developing plans to achieve these objectives,* and *organizing to put these plans into action.*

Marketing research has long functioned as a means of measuring changes in the administrative process. In essence, it has attempted to provide the firm's management with quality-control information. The discovery of change may provide a warning that the administrative process needs to be investigated, in order to see what has happened and why. It is the why aspect that is so important, for it enables management to take remedial action. In this way, marketing research may turn up new ideas which can be programmed into the appropriate step, or steps, in the administrative process [17].

Probably most marketing research is of the control type, although it usually is not so labeled. But control of what? Without some base or criterion, the researcher can do little to develop adequate control data. By pointing out the nature of the control step in the administrative process, he may force the decision-maker to recognize that one cannot control unless one has already accomplished the earlier steps in the administrative process.

Control information should not be obtained on a piecemeal basis. Rather, control systems should be specially constructed to meet the needs of a company at a given point in time. Control systems will vary among companies and also within the same company over a period of time. For example, when a consumer-goods company launches a new product, it may be decided that what is needed initially is rather extensive control information, such as a stock movement, effective distribution, repeat consumer purchases, and market-share data at frequent intervals throughout the year.

An understanding of the control function will bring appreciation of the fact that a control system will be efficient only if it brings together a variety of data from many sources. Too frequently, control systems are geared around accounting and finance data with little information about the marketplace.

Since the administrative process cuts between departments the decision-maker, with the help of the researcher, may better perceive the need for a single control system, which includes reappraisal data relative to certain expenditure inputs, such as advertising, personal selling, and channel relations. The excuse usually given for failing to undertake evaluative action is that it is too expensive to measure the effectiveness of certain strategies. Admittedly, such data are difficult to obtain, but the researcher, given enough time and money, can usually make a contribution, especially if he can undertake experimentation.

Implications

Many problems encountered by business in making marketing research more efficient indicate the need for a clearer understanding of the decision-making process by both marketing research executives and management executives. The authors believe that an understanding of the administrative process will facilitate the solving of business problems and hence improve the research operation.

Marketing research executives cannot make decisions for management executives. But marketing research executives can provide management executives with information which will help them in solving and diagnosing problems. As more and more companies adopt the marketing concept in the operation of their businesses, the marketing researcher may be called upon to play an increasingly important role in aiding the decision-maker to set objectives, develop plans, organize to carry out these plans, and control and reappraise the activities of the firm.

References

1. Russell L. Ackoff, *Scientific Methods*, New York: John Wiley & Sons, Inc., 1962, 71.
2. *Annual Report for 1959*, New York: The Twentieth Century Fund, 1960, 11.
3. Harper W. Boyd, Jr., and Sidney J. Levy, "New Dimensions in Consumer Analysis," *Harvard Business Review*, 41 (November–December 1963), 129–140.
4. Robert D. Buzzell and Charles C. Slater, "Decision Theory and Marketing Management," *Journal of Marketing*, 26 (July 1962), 7–16.
5. Lincoln H. Clark, ed., *Consumer Behavior: The Life Cycle and Consumer Behavior*, Vol. 2 (New York: New York University Press, 1955), 28–35.
6. Peter F. Drucker, *The Practice of Management*, New York: Harper & Brothers Publishers, 1954, 39.
7. ———, "The Economy's Dark Continent," *Fortune*, 65 (April 1962), 103, 265–270.
8. Morris J. Gottlieb, "Segmentation by Personality Types," in Lynn H. Stockman, ed., *Advancing Marketing Efficiency*, Chicago, Ill.: American Marketing Association, 1958, 148–158.
9. George N. Kahn and Abraham S. Bushman, "Specialize Your Salesmen," *Harvard Business Review*, 39 (January–February 1961), 90–98.
10. Joseph T. Klapper, "What We Know About the Effects of Mass Communication: The Brink of Hope," *The Public Opinion Quarterly*, 22 (Winter 1958), 453–466.

11. Theodore Levitt, *Innovation in Marketing*, New York: McGraw-Hill Book Co., Inc., 1962, 100.
12. Pierre Martineau, "Social Classes and Spending Behavior," *Journal of Marketing*, 22 (October 1958), 121–130.
13. Elting E. Morrison, "A Case Study of Innovation," *Engineering and Science Monthly*, 13 (April 1950).
14. Joseph W. Newman, "Put Research into Marketing Decisions," *Harvard Business Review*, 40 (March–April 1962), 105–112.
15. *Product Evaluation: An Evaluation of Research Procedures*, Chicago, Ill.: Market Facts, Inc., 1962.
16. C. Wilson Randle, "Problems of R & D Management," *Harvard Business Review*, 37 (January–February 1959), 128–136.
17. Harry V. Roberts, "The Role of Research in Marketing Management," *Journal of Marketing*, 21 (July 1957), 21–32.
18. Samuel N. Stevens, "The Application of Social Science Findings to Selling and the Salesman," *Aspects of Modern Marketing*, AMA Management Report No. 15, New York: American Management Association, Inc., 1958, 85–94.
19. Edward T. P. Watson, "Diagnosis of Management Problems," *Harvard Business Review*, 36 (January–February, 1958), 69–76.
20. E. B. Weiss, *Merchandising For Tomorrow*, New York: McGraw-Hill Book Co., Inc., 1961.

---

3. LEVERAGE IN THE PRODUCT LIFE CYCLE*

Donald K. Clifford, Jr.

NOT LONG AGO, A LEADING packaged goods maker was promoting a brand of toilet soap. Growth had been fair but not spectacular. Finally, product and market tests suggested that an increase in spot television advertising, backed by a change in copy, could help the product to reach the "escape velocity" it needed to become a sales leader. But management, feeling that the funds would be better spent in launching a new product, vetoed the proposal.

The new product was, to be sure, a moderate success. But the promising soap brand went into a gradual sales decline from which it never recovered. Management had pulled the props out from under the product at a critical point in its growth period.

Again, a product manager at a firm making light industrial equipment

* From *Dun's Review*, May, 1965, pp. 62–70. Reprinted with permission from the publisher.

felt that his principal product was not getting the sales support it deserved. Unconvinced by the salesmen's claims that the product was "hard to sell," he developed new presentations and sales kits and persuaded sales management to run special campaigns. At year-end, however, volume had shown no improvement. With the power of hindsight, management recognized that this product had long since passed its zenith and that no amount of additional sales support could have profitably extended its growth. Yet the expensive promotion drive had cut into the marketing budgets of several promising new products. In short, management had 'failed to consider each product's position in its life cycle.

As these two cases suggest, the concept of the product life cycle—familiar as it is to most business executives—is frequently forgotten in marketing planning. Yet there is conclusive evidence that if properly used it can transform a company's profit-and-loss statement. The concept is based on the fact that a product's sales volume follows a typical pattern that can be charted as a four-phase cycle (*see chart, page 556*). After its birth, the product passes through a low-volume introduction phase. During the following growth phase, volume and profit both rise. Volume stabilizes during the period of maturity, although unit profits start to fall off. Eventually, in the obsolescence stage of the product, sales volume declines.

The length of the life cycle, the duration of each phase and the shape of the curve vary widely for different products. But in every case, obsolescence eventually occurs either because the need disappears (as when frozen orange juice hit sales of orange juice squeezers), because a better or cheaper product may be developed to fill the same need (oil-based paint is losing its position in the home to water-based paint, and plastics are replacing wood, metal and paper in products ranging from dry-cleaning bags to aircraft parts) or because a competitive product suddenly gains a decisive advantage through superior marketing strategy (as happened to competing products when Arthur Godfrey promoted Lipton Tea and again when the American Dental Association publicly endorsed Procter & Gamble's decay-prevention claims for Crest toothpaste).

The profit cycle of a product is quite different from its sales cycle. During introduction, a product may not earn any profit because of high initial advertising and promotion costs. In the growth period, before competition catches up, unit profits typically attain their peak. Then they start declining, although total profits may continue to climb for a time on rising sales volume. (In the chemical industry, for example, rapid increases in volume often more than offset the effect of price reductions early in the growth phase.)

During late growth and early maturity, increasing competition cuts deeply into profit margins and ultimately into total profits. For instance, as a result of drastic price-cutting, general-purpose semiconductors, once highly profitable, now return so little unit profit that major companies such as the Columbia Broadcasting System and Clevite Corp. have left the business entirely. Finally, in the obsolescence phase, declining volume eventually pushes costs up to a level that eliminates profits entirely.

What does this mean for the marketing manager? At the very least, he should always bear in mind that the factors behind a product's profitability change with each phase of its life cycle, and plot his sales strategy accordingly. Typically, product development and design are crucial in the introduction phase. For industrial products, where customers are slow to change from a proven product, technical superiority or demonstrable cost savings are often needed to open the door. For consumer products, heavy marketing spending may be critical in building volume.

During the growth period, reliability is vital to the success of most industrial products and technically complex consumer products. A well-grounded reputation for quality can win a manufacturer the leading position in the market, as it did for Zenith Radio Corp. in black-and-white television sets. For consumer packaged goods and other nontechnical products, on the other hand, effective distribution and advertising are crucial.

The key requirement during maturity, though harder to define, can be described as "overall marketing effectiveness." Marketing skill may pay off in a variety of ways; for example, by cutting price so as to reach new consumers, by promoting new uses for the product, or by upgrading distribution. During obsolescence, cost control is the key factor in generating profits. The product of the low-cost producer and distributor often enjoys a profitable "old age" long after its rivals have disappeared from the scene.

But although they are valid within their limits, these generalizations about the product life cycle do not really go far enough. For they fail to take into account a key fact: life cycles can be managed.

Life-cycle management, which adds a vital new dimension to the traditional life-cycle concept, has two basic aspects: 1) Controlling individual product life cycles to generate new profits. 2) Controlling the mix of product life cycles in the product line by carefully planned new-product introduction, product-line pruning and allocation of money and manpower among existing products according to their profit potential.

A product's introduction phase can often be shortened by increasing marketing expenditures or securing national distribution more quickly. In the next phase, growth can be speeded and sales and profits ultimately pushed to higher levels by exploiting additional markets, by pricing the product to encourage wider usage, and by more productive advertising or sales efforts; in short, by more effectively planned and implemented marketing strategy.

PROFILE OF A PRODUCT

The wise marketer is aware of the critical factors underlying the course of his product's sales volume and profits. More importantly, he knows how to manipulate those factors to swell earnings. The chart below shows the typical shape of a product's sales volume and profit. The table shows a life-cycle "audit" of a product in early maturity.

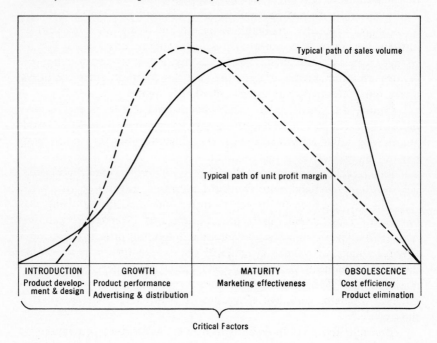

Critical Factors

PRODUCT XYZ, MARCH 1965	CHANGE IN PAST YEAR	AVERAGE ANNUAL CHANGE OVER PAST FIVE YEARS
Annual sales volume ..... $28.6 million	+2.5%	+11.8%
Gross margin 31.0%	−5.0%	−17.0%
Profit contribution 9.0%	−5.0%	−12.0%
Return on invested capital 14.0%	−4.0%	−12.0%
Price .... $.85/lb.	−$.04	−$.11/lb.
Market share 16.0%	−	+ 8.0%

Cheating Old Age

But it is in maturity that the shape and duration of a product's life cycle can be changed most radically. Is the product really approaching obsolescence? Or does it merely seem to be because consumers' needs are not being truly filled or because a competitor has done a superior marketing job? The question is crucial, since often the real challenge of "maturity" is not to adapt to it but to change it by revitalizing the product—through repackaging, for example, or by product modifications, repricing, appealing to new users or adding new distribution channels. And often a successfully revitalized product offers a higher return on management time and funds invested than does a new product.

Take, for example, the case of E. I. du Pont, which as a major force in packaging materials has been strongest in cellophane, a product so well-known it has become almost a synonym for transparent packaging. After World War II, flexible packaging, and cellophane in particular, entered a period of rapid growth. By the 1950s, however, new products began to meet certain packaging needs better. Polyethylene film, for example, was not so easily ruptured in cold weather, and in time it also became lower in price. As a result, cellophane began losing its share of the flexible-packaging market, and it was clear that sales would soon begin falling unless strong corrective action was taken.

Faced with this threat, du Pont launched a series of product modifications. These included special coatings to reduce winter breakage and increase protection, new types of cellophane for different products and lighter grades of cellophane more competitive in price with the newer packaging materials. All in all, the customers' choice of cellophane types mushroomed from a handful to well over 100.

The results have been impressive. In the face of widespread predictions of rapid decline, cellophane as a whole has maintained its sales volume—of which the traditional grades now represent a relatively small fraction.

Further testimony to du Pont's effectiveness in life-cycle management is its control of the life-cycle mix of its flexible packaging products. Recognizing the maturity of cellophane, du Pont has developed a strong position in polyethylene and in other new packaging materials. So while maintaining its position by reshaping the life cycle of cellophane, the company has also provided for growth by adding new products to strengthen its product mix.

Another success in life-cycle manipulation was scored in the cake-mix market, where P & G introduced a large number of new cake types. This built sales in three ways. First, by broadening its line, P & G appealed to a wider market. Second, by increasing the variety of cakes, it persuaded women to make them more often. Third, by vastly increasing the number of cake mixes to be stocked in supermarkets, P & G achieved a billboard of cake mixes on shelves that inevitably drew the shopper's eye. In brief, Procter & Gamble increased the demand for cake mix and then filled that demand through the strength of its distribution.

Not all products, of course, can be revitalized in maturity. Maturity is forced upon some products by a basic change in consumer habits or a radically superior new competitor. In such cases it is important to recognize the fact promptly, and to cut back on the time and money invested in the product. In obsolescence, finally, marketing effectiveness is a matter of knowing when to cut short the life of a product that is demanding more than the small share of management attention it deserves.

Not long ago, a small candy company drastically changed its life-cycle mix by eliminating no fewer than 796 of the 800 items in its product line. By putting its muscle behind a single strong growth brand, and maintaining just three other products to offset swings in production, the company shifted its life-cycle balance from early obsolescence to growth. From a marginal producer, it has become one of the most profitable small companies in the confectionery business.

This type of successful product and product-line strategy is clearly the result of imagination, courage and sound judgment. It took imagination and initiative for P & G to expand its cake-mix line rather than modify its prices or advertising approach. It took marketing courage as well as judgment for the small candy company to cut its line by 99.5% rather than seek new brokers or start a fresh promotion program.

These companies, and others like them, were able to manipulate the life cycle of their products by making disciplined, periodic reviews of their progress. Such reviews should include not only a formal audit of each product's progress and outlook that pinpoints its position in its life cycle, but a profile of the life-cycle mix of the product line as a whole.

Tracing a Life Story

Although the steps involved in the first part of a life-cycle analysis often vary, the following are typical:

• Developing historical "trend" information for a period of three to five years, using such data as unit and dollar sales, profit margins, total profit contribution, return on invested capital, market share and price.

• Tracing trends in the number and nature of competitors, the number and market-share rankings of competing products and their quality and performance, shifts in distribution channels and the relative advantages of competitive products in each channel.

• Analyzing developments in short-term competitive strategy, such as competitors' announcements of new products or plans for expanding capacity.

• Developing (or updating) historical information on the life cycles of similar or related products, to help suggest the shape and duration of the life cycle for the product under study.

• Projecting sales for the product over the next three to five years and estimating an incremental profit ratio for the product during each of these years. The incremental profit ratio is the ratio of total direct costs to pretax profits. Expressed as a ratio—for example, 4.8 to 1 or 6.3 to 1—it measures the number of dollars required to generate each additional dollar of profit. The ratio typically improves (that is, falls) as the product enters its growth period, then begins to rise as the product approaches maturity, and climbs even more sharply as it reaches obsolescence.

Estimating the number of profitable years remaining in the product's life cycle and—based on all the information at hand—assigning the product to one of seven positions on its life-cycle curve: introduction, early or late growth, early or late maturity, early or late obsolescence.

Once the life-cycle positions of all the company's major products have been determined, a life-cycle profile of the company's entire product line can be drawn up. It works this way: Management first determines what percentages of sales and profits fall within each of the seven stages of this product life cycle, thus creating a "life-cycle profile" in terms of both sales and profits; it then calculates the change in the life-cycle and profit profiles over the past five years, and projects these profiles over the next five years; and finally it develops a *target* life-cycle profile for the company as a whole.

The target profile shows the desirable share of company sales that should fall within each phase of the product life cycle. It is determined on the basis of obsolescence trends in the industry, the pace of new-product introduction in the industry, the average length of product life cycles in the company's line, and management's objectives for growth and profitability. As a rule, the target profile for companies whose life cycles tend to be short, and for companies aiming for ambitious growth, will call for a high proportion of sales in the introductory and growth phases.

By comparing the company's target profile and its present life-cycle profile, management is now in a position to assign priorities to such functions as new-product development, acquisitions and product-line pruning. And once corporate effort has been broadly allocated in this way among products at various stages of their life cycles, marketing plans should be developed for individual product lines. Since each product's life-cycle position and outlook has been calculated, marketing executives, from the product managers up to the marketing vice president, have a far sounder basis for setting up individual product plans.

Time for an Audit

To illustrate the use of life-cycle analysis, consider a well-diversified company in the packaging business—a field where new materials and new forms of packaging are being introduced every year and where mature and obsolescent products still account for the bulk of sales volume. As a basis for planning individual product and product-line strategies, this company carried out a life-cycle audit, developing sales and profit information for each of its products.

For product XYZ, a packaging film (*see table, page 556*), sales growth slackened last year. Gross margins, profit contribution and return on investment, which had all been declining since 1959, fell more sharply last year. Prices were largely to blame, but increased costs were also significant. Market share, meanwhile, had doubled in the previous five years, but showed no gain in 1964.

Two new competitors and four new competitive products had appeared, eliminating a former quality advantage of product XYZ. Sales analysis indicated that the top fifty accounts did 82% of product XYZ's volume in 1964, as against 68% five years earlier. In the same period, the total number of customers somewhat decreased. Finally, the incremental profit ratio appeared about to deteriorate from 11–1 to 12–1 in the coming year, rising to 15–1 by 1969.

On the basis of this analysis, marketing executives determined that product XYZ was in early maturity, with at least ten more years of profitable life in prospect. They decided, however, that a further increase in maturity could be offset, and additional growth achieved, if the film's tensile and tear strength could be improved by 25% at no increase in cost —an objective that appeared technically feasible. This then became a major element of their marketing strategy.

In similar fashion, the company developed life-cycle and profit profiles of its entire line. Only 6% of its current sales were represented by products in the introduction and growth stages, a far cry from the target profile of 25% called for (based on the expected length of life cycles in the business and growth and profit objectives). Management therefore decided to step up its acquisition program and new-product development sharply and to eliminate two obsolescent products. These steps cut the share of total volume represented by obsolescent products from 15% to 11%—close to the target profile of 10%.

The depth of life-cycle analysis, and the factors it must consider, vary almost as widely as do company needs, objectives and product lines. There is, then, no reliable formula for weighting the various factors that determine the life-cycle position of a product. But a management that makes good use of life-cycle analysis knows that it is this very flexibility that makes life-cycle analysis such an effective and widely applicable route to profits.

4. THE SOCIAL RESPONSIBILITY OF THE CORPORATION*

Joseph W. McGuire

FOR THE PAST TWENTY YEARS a fresh breeze known as social responsibilities has riffled the pages of the corporate literature. Whether it has also passed through the air conditioned halls of the modern corporate enterprise, or, in fact, whether the windows *should* be opened to permit the breeze to enter, is the subject of considerable debate.

Our friends from quantitative areas inform us that the concept of social responsibilities is "soft." Since I find the notion of a soft breeze more appealing than that of a harsh wind, this charge does not bother me at all.

What does concern me deeply is the opinion that, despite all that has been said and written about the subject of social responsibilities, it still remains at best a vague and fuzzy concept. In this paper I hope to dispel some of this vagueness, and to cut away a few of the tattered ends that remain. To accomplish this objective we shall focus directly upon two unsettled issues that appear to be significant. First, what precisely is the concept of social responsibilities? And, second, what are the relationships between the economic theory of resource allocation (the maximization of efficiency) and the theory of social responsibilities?

Corporate Choice and Social Responsibilities

Is it possible for corporations in our complex modern society to act in a manner that is truly socially responsible? How can the decision-making unit in a corporation know consistently that the alternative which will tend to maximize the social welfare is being selected? How can an objective observer ascertain the extent to which corporate behavior is responsible?

Obviously, the social content of a corporate decision cannot be evaluated expost by an examination of the social benefits stemming from its outcome, for in a business world dominated by uncertainty this outcome

* From *Evolving Concepts in Management, Proceedings of the 24th Annual Meeting,* Academy of Management, December, 1964, pp. 21–28. Reprinted with permission from the publisher.

is often unintended. Any decision process, therefore, must be appraised for its social content prior to or at the decision point. A corporate decision is socially responsible when that alternative the decision-maker believes will result in the highest social benefit is elected.

There are, of course, degrees of social responsibility. A corporation may choose alternatives that it feels may advance the social welfare only slightly, and by-pass (because of a set of variables that it considers and balances) that alternative which it believes to be more responsible. A corporation is not socially responsible when it selects that alternative which it believes will not further the public cause.

It is essential to our argument, then, that we recognize that social responsibility is a factor that is imbedded in the decision-making process, and must therefore be valuated at that point. The extent of social responsibilities cannot be appraised properly in terms of results, for it is possible for socially desirable outcomes to stem (through chance) from socially neutral (or even anti-social) decisions; just as socially responsible decisions may have unfortunate social consequences.

Given the point that social responsibility enters into the *a priori* considerations of the decision-maker, it is also evident that this concept can be expressed as a scaler or ordinal function. It would seem to follow that decisions made without any consideration of social costs or social benefits would be devoid of responsibility. From this point it would be possible to describe degrees of negative responsibility (criminal and irresponsible elements) and positive responsibility. However, it should be emphasized that we are not here measuring the propriety of these social elements, but only the influence which they have in decision-making. Whether, in fact, these convictions are indeed "better" for society than others must remain for our subsequent discussion herein.

The extent to which responsibility factors enter into corporate decisions is, as a minimum, a function of the pressures of both industry and society, and the effectiveness of the mechanism for transferring these pressures to the decision-maker. Today societal forces constitute a *minimal* responsibility constraint that is probably above that behavioral level imposed by our legal system. Thus, the law, and very likely certain ethical factors, establish a certain minimum level of responsible corporate behavior. Typically set above this constraint is a level established by the individual industry. In most industries there are amorphous rules of behavior that tend to guide the conduct of its corporate members. These rules are not often codified as in the medical or accounting professions, but nevertheless they do exist with varying degrees of influence.[1]

---

[1] I suppose that at times these industry influences may be negative or below the minimum set by society, e.g., perhaps the electrical industry in the period preceding the conspiratorial indictments.

Superimposed upon these two constraints are: (1) The expected profitability of the corporation and, (2) the moral character and social perceptions of the decision-making mechanism. Minimal societal and industry influences for responsible decisions are exogenous forces over which the corporation typically has little control, at least in the short-run. These influences must be considered by the corporation. Failure to (at least) consider them is irrational and failure to operate above these minima may result in losses. The corporate decision character and perceptions, on the other hand, are internal; but by their very nature cannot be overlooked in the decision process. Nor can these internal variables be discarded without loss.

Social responsibility, then, may be examined as a complex element in the corporate decision process. Every decision in business involves some corporate or personal cost. If it may be assumed that this cost is a function of the number of variables that enter the decision and of their nature (e.g., uncertainty, complexity, vagueness, etc.), *ceteris paribus*, in the short-run corporate decision costs are inversely related to profit and have a direct relationship to degree of social responsibility possessed by the decision-maker. We could, then, relate corporate decision-making costs to profit and social character, pointing out that these costs are especially high when profits are low (because of the probable conflict of interest within the decision-making mechanism), and that they fall as profits increase.

The analysis set forth above does not, however, directly attack the crux of the problem of social responsibilities. The responsible nature of corporate decisions hinges upon the basic premise that what the decision-maker *believes* will forward the public welfare *does*, in fact, do so. This premise in turn rests upon two fundamental assumptions: (1) That there is, indeed, some system of values which a society holds dear and a set of goals toward which it strives. (2) That these values and goals are typically reflected in the corporate decision character and its perceptions. If these assumptions are valid it should be possible to evaluate corporate decisions on the basis of their responsible content, and not only on the premise that such content must be based upon belief rather than fact.

The value system of a society is never obvious. A society is not a group, a coalition, a team or a foundation. A society lacks the cohesiveness and coherence of even the most loosely formed organization. Yet, to assume that there is no value or goal consensus in a viable, on-going society is absurd. Without such a consensus a society ceases to exist. In every society a set of values and goals is maintained and recharged. Like a weather front, there is turbulence and stress and movement at the margin of this system.

Social values and goals permeate societal institutions, and both society and its institutions are mutually reinforced and sustained, and possibly altered. Institutions that are completely disparate with societal values and goals fail to exist. Vital institutions that differ fundamentally with one another on basic goals and values produce anomie. The very fact that institutions coexist with each other in the same society over time is indicative of a fundamental institutional and societal compatibility of values and goals.

Each society also scales values and goals in a broad and general manner. An individual is "socialized" and oriented—with varying degrees of completeness—by his social environment. He learns, through societal interactions, a certain pattern of role behavior, and becomes aware of the roles of his fellowman. Loose as these words are, he knows in a general way what is "good" and "bad" (i.e., what is socially acceptable behavior), and there is often a consensus of opinion what is "better." Each person, so cognitive psychologists inform us, carries in his mind a "model of the universe." The factors that determine this model include cultural or environmental forces as well as the individual's motivations, fears, and needs. These establish that pattern, out of all the possible patterns that the person will *perceive* in reality. This pattern is consistent, so that individuals are able to insert new data into their new models, and make sense of them. These models, of course, may be of infinite variety, but I suspect that the curve that encompasses them within a particular society is not too far removed from normal. (There are, naturally, many "extremists," but in any society the number of these relative to the population must be small.) In other words, most members of a society have basic behavioral patterns, perceptions and cultural beliefs that are marked more by their similarities than by their differences. As Rothenberg has pointed out in his excellent analysis of welfare economics:

> "The individual . . . is always faced by 'established procedure.' He exists within a social system and already has developed basic preconceptions which are not independent of his social context. He is never in this sense free and without chains. So his appraisal of any decision process, whether established or hypothetical, is grounded on his saturation in community values."[2]

In every society there is a hard core of rules and opinions, myths and beliefs, to which rational citizens subscribe. This base is widely known and held and persons cannot plead, for example, that they are ignorant of the fact that murder or burglary is against societal codes. Above this fundamental societal block, however, the social prescriptions are distressingly vague. For example, are there criteria for resolving the real or apparent societal dichotomy between freedom and security; between economic progress and non-economic values; between individual and social welfare; between the groups that compete for larger shares in the corporate largess?

---

[2] Jerome Rothenberg, *The Measurement of Social Welfare* (Englewood Cliffs, N.J.: Prentice-Hall, Inc., 1961), p. 333.

To assert that these sorts of difficulties destroy the centrality of social beliefs, or to assume that basic beliefs also are obscure and are not transmitted effectively to the corporate decision-maker is to advocate that there can be no unresolved problems in society, i.e., that society must be a static rather than a dynamic concept. There are always, and always will be, in any on-going society, issues and problems that produce conflict. These issues, like snow on a mountain peak, attract attention and seem predominant, but underlying them is a vast mass of social belief that is both accepted and acceptable.

Where, then, has our argument led us? We began with the point that social responsibility was an element in the corporate decision process which could be measured on an ordinal "desire" or "belief" scale. Thus, the decision-maker, faced with a range of alternatives, might deliberately select that one alternative which he believes will conform most satisfactorily to the public interest, or he might select others which he believes might produce less desirable outcomes for the public good. To the extent that he tries to maximize the public welfare we say that he is socially responsible.

We then raised the question of responsibility in fact and responsibility in belief. Is it valid to assume that what the corporate decision-maker feels or believes is in the public interest is indeed in the public interest? Here the evidence is perhaps not conclusive, but our argument was that there are a vast number of signals from society to the decision-maker that are well-known to him and that reflect ethical principles, traditions, mores, and moral sentiments. The responsibility elements in most corporate decisions fall within this realm of accepted and acceptable societal values, and as such may be appraised by an observer. In these instances it is probable that most persons would agree that the selection of alternative B would be more in the public interest than alternative A. Thus, there exists a wide range of decisions in which the ordering of alternatives by the social content could be generally agreed upon, and which would reflect in fact, as well as in belief, the societal value system.

Nevertheless, because of the dynamic nature of an on-going society there are corporate decision areas where the societal prescriptions are obscure, and where there would be little agreement as to that alternative which is most suitable for the public welfare. In these cases belief does not necessarily coincide with fact. However, it is precisely in these situations that the societal value system is dynamic . . . where the corporate decision-maker, caught up in his social matrix, is at the same time acting to affect, and possibly to change or establish values. It is at this periphery that a clear-cut social mandate is not to be found. At this fringe social policy is largely a matter of belief that has not been widely accepted and that, in fact, is in the process of being shaped. It may not, therefore, be possible at these extremes to match corporate decision beliefs with societal values as it is in more normal situations. Thus, at the extremes legitimate efforts to further the public cause through corporate decision-making cannot be so matched, and must be the subject of thoughtful discussion and debate. And this, of course, is what occurs. And it is in this area, also, that corporate decisions are most instrumental in defining the public interest.

Resource Allocation and Social Responsibilities

One of the most appealing features of the classical theory of resource allocation is its maximization of the economic welfare function without fuss or bother. The true believer in the efficacy of the traditional model scoffs at the ridiculous postures of the devotee of social responsibilities. He *knows* that the lack of wage and price flexibility and the failure of businessmen to maximize are the only factors that can seriously interfere with the optimization of economic welfare.

Of course, the traditional economist also *knows* (to paraphrase Gertrude Stein) that "a firm is a firm is a firm." A corporation is solely and simply an economic transformation unit, and has its only social objective public service through economic efficiency. The firm, so defined, cannot hope to attain noneconomic goals, for these are external to the system and therefore are irrelevant. Furthermore, the attempt of the corporation to strive for noneconomic goals—justice, security, or equity, for example— results only in economic chaos and a failure to benefit society in any meaningful fashion.

But, indeed, this traditional argument is much too simple a description of the modern corporation and its function. There are a number of institutional barriers to the efficient allocation of resources in today's economy—government, labor unions, and large size corporate units. Then too, the evidence would seem to indicate that the corporation is not only an economic organization. To be sure, the efforts to increase profits and reduce costs form a central feature of corporate life: but to assume that the corporate entrepreneur is *only* an economic man and that the corporation is *only* an economic unit is patently incorrect. Further, there is some question about the relationships between the general welfare and its "components." History would seem to illustrate that concerted efforts to "maximize" any one aspect of the public welfare may have undesirable side-effects. Indeed, a great deal of criticism has been directed toward the materialism, the harshness, and the cultural sterility that results from the emphasis upon profits and the business way of life. Finally, the efficiency of resource allocation does not—and I think that this could be illustrated also by history in a general way—constitute a super-goal for society, alone and inviolate above all other societal objectives. The furtherance of economic ends is certainly desirable but not at the expense of other goals. The ranking of societal objectives is a product of society, and not of one group or segment therein.

These sorts of pros and cons on the efficacy of the goal of efficient resource allocation are somewhat irrelevant, perhaps, to the mechanics that we want to examine. Let us concede, with some reservations, that efficiency is a desirable societal and business goal. What effect will socially responsible corporate decision behavior have upon the allocation of resources?

The efficient allocation of resources within the enterprise is contingent upon the assumption that entrepreneurs have a strong drive (1) to maximize profits and, as necessary corollary, (2) to reduce costs to a bare minimum.

There are several alternative ways of reviewing the insertion of social responsibilities into this simple model. First, it is far from clear what the profit maximization prescription really means. Obviously this entrepreneurial propensity must be confined within certain societal parameters, i.e., there are many factors that restrict the range of alternatives available to the corporate decision-maker who wants to maximize profits. Some of these factors condition the entrepreneur so that he simply does not perceive certain alternatives. Other alternatives have to be discarded, even though perceived because they obviously do not conform to societal values and goals. In a passive sense, then, some minimum level of responsible behavior may be taken as one of the parameters within which profit maximizing activities occur. This interpretation of the relationship between profit maximization and social responsibilities is not, however, in full accord with the concept developed in the earlier section of this paper, unless it can be assumed that, within the societal parameters established, the decision to maximize profits is in fact the most responsible decision that can be made.

A second view relates more emphatically and actively the maximization of profits with social responsibilities. It is evident, for strictly economic reasons, that the profits to be maximized are long-run. Yet, in the long-run the profit-maximizing motive becomes fuzzy—if not meaningless. Corporate entrepreneurs may decide on alternatives which enhance the corporate image. These may not pay off immediately in increased profits, but the decision-maker may conclude that institutional advertising or corporate giving, for example, will increase profits in the long-run. Whether such ventures are actually worth their expense in dollar terms is typically difficult to determine, but it is evident that they are common among modern corporations. Now, it might be argued, and has been so argued, that corporate efforts to behave in a socially responsible manner will result in the highest long-run profits. Thus, social responsibility is simply long-run profit maximization. This fortunate coincidence between the two has always seemed to me to be much too happy and pat, and to fail to account for some forms of corporate behavior which seem directly to conflict with even the long-run maximization of profits (e.g., anonymous gifts by the corporation).

Third, suppose that, as would seem sometimes to be the case, that alternative which the decision-maker believes will result in the highest social benefit does not coincide with that alternative which he believes will maximize profits. Assume that, in this corporation, the decision-maker always selects only socially responsible alternatives, some of which maximize profits; and the overall effect of this behavior produces "satisfactory" profits. Resources obviously will not be allocated most efficiently in this case, economic welfare will not be maximized; but we cannot conclude that societal welfare is automatically reduced as a result. We would have to make inter-welfare comparisons (probably as impossible as interpersonal utility comparisons) to show that society's gain as a result of the decision-maker's, let us say, "kind and humane" acts was greater or less or equal to society's loss from inefficiency.

Let us now turn to the element of cost. Economic theory demands that costs at each level of output be a minimum in order to maximize profits and to allocate resources most efficiently. However, the elements of cost are not specified. Thus, whatever costs within the enterprise are, we know only that (a) they must be minimal, and (b) that, if in this minimum cost mix there are certain elements that raise this minimum in firm A above that in firm B, then, under perfect competition, firm A will fail.

A corporation that is socially responsible will undoubtedly be able to minimize its costs at all levels of output. Unfortunately, it is likely that the elements in the cost mix of a socially responsible corporation will cause costs to be larger than for a competitor which is oriented in traditional economic fashion, i.e., the total costs at each level of output will be larger for the former. The latter, assuming that per unit prices are identical for both concerns, will be more profitable.[3] The socially responsible corporation will probably be less efficient and more costly to operate.

Yet, given the present population of business corporations it seems probable that some percentage of this total number is socially responsible. Furthermore, many of these responsible corporations are not only viable,

---

[3] We have to assume here, unrealistically perhaps, that long-run profits are unaffected by image or demand effects, and are simply the difference between total revenues based upon constant prices for the commodities produced by both concerns and total costs that differ between both firms by the "social responsibility" increment of one.

but are actually prosperous. This result may be ascribed to institutional rigidities and monopolistic behavior, or, and this seems equally reasonable, it may occur because the corporate "families" (present and potential suppliers, employees, managers, owners, and customers) prefer these corporations because they conduct their affairs in socially responsible fashions. That is, viability and positive profits of these corporations (or of at least some of them) may actually depend upon the fact that these corporations are socially responsible rather than economically efficient. It may be that the public involved with these corporations is so involved because of the non-economic rewards that it perceives or obtains.

Finally, if we consider costs to encompass other than economic variables we have to relax the assumption that socially responsible corporations have higher per unit costs. For example, it is possible that employees may accept a lower money wage from such corporations because of the reputation that these units possess for justice, honest employee relations, and the "taking-care of their own," or customers may pay higher prices because of the corporate reputations for reliability and integrity. Once the assumption that only conventional economic costs may be considered is relaxed, and long-run profits are permitted, the analysis becomes too complicated, at least to cover within the space of this paper. Suffice it to say that such analysis could illustrate that one possibility would be that socially responsible corporate behavior is traditional economic behavior in the sense that resources are efficiently allocated at minimum costs.

Summary

In this paper I have tried to explore, in more rigorous terms than have customarily been employed, the concept of social responsibilities and the relationship that this concept may bear to the economic theory of resource allocation. As I look back upon what I have written I think that the first subject has been fairly stated. Social responsibilities emerge as an effort by the corporate decision-maker to further the public cause in his decision process. The factors affecting this effort, and its relations to societal values and goals are treated. However, there is much more that remains to the discussion of responsibilities and resource allocation. The incompleteness of this latter section stems from an ambition to resolve the questions involved and a lack of time and space to develop the argument fully. Nevertheless, some of the possible relationships have been treated and the subject introduced. It is evident that more thought and discussion on this relationship is needed. The matter is of vital importance if we are to come to grips with the social nature of corporate activities, and to appraise them for their welfare content, in our modern society.

INDEX